LAW
AND
ECONOMICS

The Addison-Wesley Series in Economics

Abel/Bernanke
Macroeconomics

Allen
Managerial Economics

Berndt
The Practice of Econometrics

Bierman/Fernandez
Game Theory

Binger/Hoffman
Microeconomics with Calculus

Bowles/Edwards
Understanding Capitalism

Branson
Macroeconomic Theory and Policy

Brown/Hogendorn
International Economics

Browning/Zupan
*Microeconomic Theory and
    Applications*

Burgess
*The Economics of Regulation and
    Antitrust*

Byrns/Stone
Economics

Canterbery
The Literate Economist

Carlton/Perloff
Modern Industrial Organization

Caves/Frankel/Jones
World Trade and Payments

Cooter/Ulen
Law and Economics

Ehrenberg/Smith
Modern Labor Economics

Ekelund/Tollison
*Economics: Private Markets and
    Public Choice*

Filer/Hamermesh/Rees
The Economics of Work and Pay

Fusfeld
The Age of the Economist

Gibson
*International Finance: Exchange
    Rates and Financial Flows*

Gordon
Macroeconomics

Gregory
Essentials of Economics

Gregory/Ruffin
Basic Economics

Gregory/Stuart
*Soviet and Post Soviet Economic
    Structure and Performance*

Griffiths/Wall
Intermediate Microeconomics

Gros/Steinherr
*Winds of Change: Economic Transition
    in Central and Eastern Europe*

Hartwick/Olewiler
*The Economics of Natural
    Resource Use*

Hogendorn
Economic Development

**Hoy/Livernois/McKenna/
Rees/Stengos**
Mathematics For Economics

Hubbard
*Money, the Financial System, and the
    Economy*

Hughes/Cain
American Economic History

Husted/Melvin
International Economics

Invisible Hand
*Economics in Action, Interactive
    Software*

Krugman/Obstfeld
*International Economics: Theory
    and Policy*

Kwoka/White
The Antitrust Revolution

Laidler
The Demand for Money

Lesser/Dodds/Zerbe
*Environmental Economics and
    Policy*

Lipsey/Courant
Economics

McCarty
Dollars and Sense

Melvin
International Money and Finance

Miller
Economics Today

Miller/Benjamin/North
The Economics of Public Issues

Miller/Fishe
*Microeconomics: Price Theory in
    Practice*

Miller/Van Hoose
*Essentials of Money, Banking, and
    Financial Markets*

Mills/Hamilton
Urban Economics

Mishkin
*The Economics of Money, Banking,
    and Financial Markets*

Parkin
Economics

Petersen
Business and Government

Phelps
Health Economics

Riddell/Shackelford/Stamos
Economics

Ritter/Silber/Udell
*Principles of Money, Banking, and
    Financial Markets*

Rohlf
Introduction to Economic Reasoning

Ruffin/Gregory
Principles of Economics

Salvatore
*Microeconomics: Theory and
    Applications*

Sargent
Rational Expectations and Inflation

Scherer
*Industry Structure, Strategy, and
    Public Policy*

Schotter
Microeconomics: A Modern Approach

Sherman/Kolk
Business Cycles and Forecasting

Smith
Case Studies in Economic Development

Studenmund
Using Econometrics

Su
Economic Fluctuations and Forecasting

Tietenberg
*Environmental and Natural Resource
    Economics*

Tietenberg
Environmental Economics and Policy

Todaro
Economic Development

Zerbe/Dively
Benefit-Cost Analysis

LAW
AND
ECONOMICS

SECOND EDITION

Robert Cooter
University of California, Berkeley

Thomas Ulen
University of Illinois, Urbana–Champaign

 **ADDISON-WESLEY**

An imprint of Addison Wesley Longman, Inc.

Reading, Massachusetts • Menlo Park, California • New York • Harlow, England
Don Mills, Ontario • Sydney • Mexico City • Madrid • Amsterdam

Acquisitions Editor: Bruce Kaplan
Text and Cover Design and Project Coordination: Interactive Composition Corporation
Cover Photo: Abrams/Lacagnina 1995 © The Image Bank
Art Studio: Interactive Composition Corporation
Electronic Production Manager: Eric Jorgensen
Manufacturing Manager: Hilda Koparanian
Electronic Page Makeup: Interactive Composition Corporation
Printer and Binder: RR Donnelley & Sons Company
Cover Printer: Phoenix Color Corp.

Library of Congress Cataloging-in-Publication Data

Cooter, Robert.
    Law and economics / Robert Cooter, Thomas Ulen, — 2nd ed.
        p.   cm.
    Includes bibliographical references and index.
    ISBN 0-673-46332-X
    1. Law and economics. I. Ulen, Thomas. II. Title.
K487.E3C665   1996
343'.07—dc20
[342.37]   96-15012
                                                                          CIP

ISBN 0-673-46332-X

34578910—DOC—999897

CONTENTS

9

Topics in the Economics of Tort Liability 295

10

An Economic Theory of the Legal Process 334

11

An Economic Theory of Crime and Punishment 383

12

Topics in the Economics of Crime and Punishment 408

PREFACE

The second edition of *Law and Economics* continues an intellectual collaboration that began when we met as students in the Legal Institute for Economists organized by Dean Henry Manne in Key Biscayne in 1980. During many long runs and conversations, beginning in Key Biscayne and continuing in California and the Midwest, we planned a textbook on law and economics. To distinguish that book from the very good texts already available, we felt that we had to combine the very different modes of teaching economics and law. The teaching of economics proceeds from general theory to particular instances, whereas the teaching of law in the United States begins with actual cases and never arrives at a general theory. Like economics, we wanted our book unified by a general theory. Like law, we wanted our book to explain actual cases. Existing law-and-economics texts provided an economic *commentary* on the law; we wanted to provide an economic *explanation* of the law.

Economics is an apt discipline for explaining law. Critics might complain that economic theory sacrifices reality to formality (hence the joke, "The economist's prediction was correct, but the economy was mistaken") and is, therefore, inappropriate for explaining law. But, like physicians studying a virus, economists race to stay ahead of a changing society. Although important problems continue to elude solutions (physicians cannot cure AIDS, and economists cannot eliminate unemployment), economists understand society better each year, just as physicians understand viruses better each year.

We believe that economics is "catching up with law," by which we mean that economics now explains much of the law that previously was inexplicable. To demonstrate this fact, we needed to synthesize a large corpus of research published in specialized journals and technical books and to state the results in language accessible to both law students and economics students. Accessibility posed a difficult problem because of the differences between legal and economic methodologies. Traditional legal theory often proceeds by identifying key concepts and exploring their definition. ("What is a promise?" "When is it legally enforceable?" "What is law?") An ideal definition states the essence of something—the necessary and sufficient conditions to be the thing in question. Thus, the ideal definition of a contract states the necessary and sufficient conditions for a promise to be legally enforceable. However, economics, like other sciences, concerns causes and effects, not definitions. Finding causes and effects requires a radically different methodology from finding definitions. Economists use mathematical theories and quantitative proofs to establish causes and effects. These are tools that law student and lawyers view with alarm.

To reconcile these methodologies, we hit upon a didactic approach that combines cases, definitions, and causes. We introduce a legal rule or institution by describing simplified examples and discussing their essence as identified in traditional legal theory.

After this introduction, we proceed to model the legal rule or institution in economic terms. Not surprisingly, we find that our economic models supply a coherency that was missing.

Given the novelty of our enterprise, we inevitably made mistakes in the first edition of the book. The second edition gives us a chance to correct these mistakes—and to make some fresh ones. Readers familiar with the first edition will find that the second edition retains the original form. We improve on the first edition in three ways. First, we have clarified the exposition. Clearer thinking on our part has led to better writing. Second, we have used more game theory. Many legal situations are strategic (i.e., what each person does depends on what he or she thinks others will do). Lawyers and law students seem to find game theory more congenial than marginal analysis or models of perfect competition. Thus, game theory can make the economic analysis of law more accessible to an important audience. Third, we have incorporated many new developments found in the deluge of research in law and economics since we wrote the first edition. We are especially pleased by the increase in the amount of empirical research, which we, like others, have found lamentably scarce relative to theory in law and economics.

What remains to be done? First, we hope to include more examples from other legal systems. Microeconomics is the same whether taught in Tokyo, Helsinki, or New York, but the law is different in each country. Economic analysis can help to unify the world by unifying the theory of law. We take pride in the widespread use of our book in international legal education. The first edition was translated into several foreign languages, and the second edition will be translated into several more. Unfortunately, all the examples in the first edition came from the United States and the United Kingdom. Some examples in this edition come from other countries. We hope to internationalize subsequent editions. In the meantime, three distinguished Italian professors of comparative law and economics, Ugo Mattei, P. G. Monateri, and Roberto Pardolesi, will produce a European edition of this book that develops the material with special reference to the continental legal systems. Second, we shall soon issue a teacher's manual to accompany this text. That manual will include additional questions, examples, references to the professional literature, excerpts from cases, newspaper articles, and more.

Finally, we want to acknowledge the considerable help we have had in completing this work. We want to thank our own students and colleagues who have read earlier versions and discussed this material with us, contributing much to its improvement. We have also had suggestions from many students and professors who used the first edition. We are very grateful to them for taking the time to send us their thoughtful comments. The reviewers of this edition made many helpful suggestions. Earl Clay Ulen Jr. read the entire manuscript several times and made invaluable stylistic and substantive suggestions and corrections. Bruce Kaplan at HarperCollins and Pat McCutcheon at ICC both supervised the production with a light and always helpful hand. Finally, both of our families—Blair, Bo, John, and Joe Cooter, and Julia, Ted, and Tim Ulen–provided unfailing, cheerful, and loving support.

— Robert Cooter, Berkeley, CA
— Thomas Ulen, Champaign, IL

1

AN INTRODUCTION TO LAW AND ECONOMICS

"For the rational study of the law the black-letter man may be the man of the present, but the man of the future is the man of statistics and the master of economics. . . . We learn that for everything we have to give up something else, and we are taught to set the advantage we gain against the other advantage we lose, and to know what we are doing when we elect."

—

Oliver Wendell Holmes, The Path of the Law,
10 HARVARD LAW REVIEW 457, 469, 474 (1897)[1]

"To me the most interesting aspect of the law and economics movement has been its aspiration to place the study of law on a scientific basis, with coherent theory, precise hypotheses deduced from the theory, and empirical tests of the hypotheses. Law is a social institution of enormous antiquity and importance, and I can see no reason why it should not be amenable to scientific study. Economics is the most advanced of the social sciences, and the legal system contains many parallels to and overlaps with the systems that economists have studied successfully."

—

Judge Richard A. Posner, in Michael Faure and Roger Van den Bergh, eds.,
ESSAYS IN LAW AND ECONOMICS (1989)

Until recently, law confined the use of economics to the areas of antitrust law, regulated industries, tax, and the determination of monetary damages. Law needed economics in these areas to answer such questions as "What is the defendant's share of the market?",

---

[1] Our citation style is a variant of the legal citation style most commonly used in the U.S. Here is what the citation means: the author of the article from which the quotation was taken is Oliver Wendell Holmes; the title of the article is "The Path of the Law"; and the article may be found in volume 10 of the *Harvard Law Review*, which was published in 1897, beginning on page 457. The quoted material comes from pages 469 and 474 of that article.

"Will price controls on automobile insurance reduce its availability?", "Who really bears the burden of the capital gains tax?", and "How much future income did the children lose because of their mother's death?"

This limited interaction changed dramatically in the early 1960s when the economic analysis of law expanded into the more traditional areas of the law, such as property, contracts, torts, criminal law and procedure, and constitutional law.[2] This new use of economics in the law asked such questions as, "Will private ownership of the electromagnetic spectrum encourage its efficient use?", "What remedy for breach of contract will cause efficient reliance upon promises?", "Do businesses take the right amount of precaution because the law holds them strictly liable for injuries to consumers?", "Will harsher punishments deter violent crime?", and "How does bicameralism affect the discretionary power of courts?"

Economics has changed the nature of legal scholarship, the common understanding of legal rules and institutions, and even the practice of law. As proof, consider these indicators of the impact of economics on law. By 1990 at least one economist was on the faculty of each of the top law schools in North America and some in Western Europe. Joint degree programs (a Ph.D. in economics and a J.D. in law) exist at many prominent universities. Law reviews publish many articles using the economic approach, and there are several journals devoted exclusively to the field.[3] Recently, an exhaustive study found that articles using the economic approach are cited in the major American law journals more than articles using any other approach.[4] Most law school courses in America now include at least a brief summary of the economic analysis of law. By the early 1990s, there were professional organizations in law and economics in Europe, Canada, America, and Latin America. The field received the highest level of recognition in 1991 and 1992 when consecutive Nobel Memorial Prizes in Economic Science were awarded to economists who helped to found the economic analysis of law—Ronald Coase and Gary Becker. Summing this up, Professor Bruce Ackerman of the Yale Law School described the economic approach to law as "the most important development in legal scholarship of the twentieth century."

The new field's impact extends beyond the universities to the practice of law and the implementation of public policy. Economics provided the intellectual foundations for the deregulation movement in the 1980s, which resulted in such dramatic changes in America as the dissolution of regulatory bodies that set prices and routes for airlines, trucks, and railroads. In another policy area, a commission created by Congress in 1984 to reform criminal sentencing in the federal courts explicitly used the findings of law and economics to reach some of its results. Furthermore, several prominent law-and-economics scholars have become federal judges and use economic analysis in their opinions—Justice Stephen Breyer of the U.S. Supreme Court,

---

[2] The modern field is said to have begun with the publication of two landmark articles—Ronald H. Coase, *The Problem of Social Cost*, 3 JOURNAL OF LAW AND ECONOMICS 1 (1960) and Guido Calabresi, *Some Thoughts on Risk Distribution and the Law of Torts*, 70 YALE LAW JOURNAL 499 (1961).

[3] For example, the JOURNAL OF LAW AND ECONOMICS began in 1958; the JOURNAL OF LEGAL STUDIES in 1972; and RESEARCH IN LAW AND ECONOMICS, the INTERNATIONAL REVIEW OF LAW AND ECONOMICS, and the JOURNAL OF LAW, ECONOMICS, AND ORGANIZATION in the 1980s.

[4] William M. Landes and Richard A. Posner, *The Influence of Economics on Law: A Quantitative Study*, 36 J. LAW & ECONOMICS 385 (1993).

Judges Richard A. Posner and Frank Easterbrook of the U.S. Court of Appeals for the Seventh Circuit, Judge Guido Calabresi of the U.S. Court of Appeals for the Second Circuit, Judge Douglas Ginsburg and former Judge Robert Bork of the U.S. Court of Appeals for the D.C. Circuit; and Judge Alex Kozinski of the U.S. Court of Appeals for the Ninth Circuit.

I. WHAT IS THE ECONOMIC ANALYSIS OF LAW?

Why has the economic analysis of law succeeded? Like the rabbit in Australia, economics found a vacant niche in the "intellectual ecology" of the law and rapidly filled it. To explain the niche, consider this classical definition of the law: "A law is an obligation backed by a state sanction."

Lawmakers and adjudicators often ask, "How will a sanction affect behavior?" For example, if punitive damages are imposed upon the maker of a defective product, what will happen to the safety and price of the product in the future? Or, will the amount of violent crime decrease if third-time offenders are automatically imprisoned? Lawyers answered such questions in 1960 in much the same way as they had in 60 B.C.—by consulting intuition and any available facts.

Economics provided a scientific theory to predict the effects of legal sanctions on behavior. To economists, sanctions look like prices, and presumably, people respond to these sanctions much as they respond to prices. People respond to higher prices by consuming less of the more expensive good, so presumably people respond to heavier legal sanctions by doing less of the sanctioned activity. Economics has mathematically precise theories (price theory and game theory) and empirically sound methods (statistics and econometrics) of analyzing the effects of prices on behavior.

Consider an example. Suppose that a manufacturer knows that his product will sometimes injure consumers. How safe will he make the product? The answer depends upon two costs: first, the actual cost of safety, which depends in turn upon facts about design and manufacture; and the "implicit price" of injuries to consumers imposed through the manufacturer's legal liability. Liability is a sanction for injuring others. The producer will need the help of lawyers to estimate this implicit price. After obtaining the needed information, the producer will compare the cost of safety and the implicit price of accidents. To maximize profits, the producer will adjust safety until the actual cost of additional safety equals the implicit price of additional accidents.

Generalizing, we can say that economics provides a behavioral theory to predict how people respond to changes in laws. This theory surpasses intuition, just as science surpasses common sense.

In addition to a scientific theory of behavior, economics provides a useful normative standard for evaluating law and policy. Laws are not just arcane technical arguments; they are instruments for achieving important social goals. In order to know the effects of laws on those goals, judges and other lawmakers must have a method of evaluating laws' effects on important social values. Economics predicts the effects of policies on efficiency. Efficiency is always relevant to policy making, because it is always better to achieve any given policy at lower cost than at higher cost. Public officials never advocate wasting money.

Besides efficiency, economics predicts the effects of policies on another important value: *distribution*. Among the earliest applications of economics to public policy was its use to predict who really bears the burden of alternative taxes. More than other social scientists, economists understand how laws affect the distribution of income and wealth across classes and groups. While economists often recommend changes that increase efficiency, they try to avoid taking sides in disputes about distribution, usually leaving recommendations about distribution to policy-makers or voters.

II. SOME EXAMPLES

To give you a better idea of what law and economics is about, we turn to some examples based upon classics in the economic analysis of law. First, we try to identify the implicit price created by the legal rule in each example. Second, we predict the consequences of variations in that implicit price. Finally, we evaluate the effects in terms of efficiency and, where possible, distribution.

> **EXAMPLE 1:** A commission has been appointed to consider some reforms of the criminal law. The commission has identified certain white-collar crimes (such as embezzling money from one's employer) that are committed after rational computation of the potential gain and the risk of getting caught and punished. Currently, those convicted of committing these crimes are sentenced to a term in prison. After taking extensive testimony, much of it from economists, the commission decides that a monetary fine, rather than incarceration, is the appropriate punishment for these offenses. The commission ranks each offense by seriousness and determines that the fine should increase with the seriousness of the offense, but by how much?

The economists who testified before the commission persuaded the members that certain white-collar crimes occur only if the expected gain to the criminal exceeds the expected cost. The expected cost depends upon two factors: the probability of being caught and convicted and the magnitude of the punishment. We can define the expected cost of crime to the criminal as the product of the probability and the magnitude of the punishment.

Suppose that the probability of punishment decreases by 5% and the magnitude of punishment increases by 5%. In that case, the expected cost of crime to the criminal remains the same. Because of this, the criminal will presumably respond by committing the same amount of crime. (Later we shall explain the exact conditions for this conclusion to be true.)

So far, we have described the implicit price of a criminal sanction and predicted its effect on behavior. Now we evaluate the effect with respect to economic efficiency. When a decrease in the probability of punishment offsets an increase in the magnitude of punishment, then the expected cost of crime remains the same for criminals. But the costs of crime to the criminal justice system may change. The probability of being caught and convicted depends in large part on the resources devoted to apprehending and prosecuting white-collar criminals—for example, on the number and quality of auditors, tax and bank examiners, police, prosecuting attorneys, and the like. These resources are costly. By contrast, administering fines is relatively cheap. These facts imply a prescription for holding crime down to any specified level at least cost to the state: invest little in apprehending and prosecuting offenders, and fine severely those who are apprehended. Indeed, it can be shown that the most serious offense should be punished by the maximum monetary fine that the offender can bear. (Professor Gary Becker derived this result in a famous paper cited by the Nobel Prize Committee in its award to him.) Furthermore, it can be shown that incarcerating any criminal—not just white-collar criminals—is inefficient unless the ability to pay fines has been completely exhausted. Thus, the commission might recommend very high monetary fines in its schedule of punishments for white-collar offenses. We shall discuss these findings in much more detail in Chapter 12.

> **EXAMPLE 2:** An oil company signs a contract to deliver oil by a certain date from the Middle East to a European manufacturer. Before the oil is delivered, war breaks out in the exporting country, so that the oil company cannot perform the contract as promised. The lack of oil causes the European manufacturer to reduce production and lose profits. The manufacturer brings an action (*i.e.*, files a lawsuit) against the oil company for breach of contract and asks the court to award it a sum of money, called "damages," that is equal to the amount of profits the manufacturer would have realized if the oil had been delivered as promised. Unfortunately, the contract is silent about the risk of nonperformance in the event of war, so that the court cannot simply read the contract and resolve the dispute on the contract's own terms. In resolving the suit, the court must decide whether to excuse the oil company from performance on the ground that the war made the performance "impossible" or to find the oil company in breach of contract and to require the oil company to compensate the manufacturer for lost profits.[5]

For an economist analyzing this case, the crucial point is that the parties failed to allocate between themselves the risk of a contingency—in this instance, war—that has arisen to frustrate performance of the contract. War is a risk of doing business in the Middle East, a risk that must be borne by one of the parties to the contract. Because the contract is silent about the allocation of this risk, the court must allocate it, and, depending on how the court decides the case, one party or the other will have to bear the costs of that risk.

What are the consequences of different court rulings on how to allocate the loss? If the court excuses the oil company from responsibility for performing the contract, then the manufacturer is going to bear the losses that arise from the nondelivery of oil. On the other hand, if the court holds the oil company responsible for compensating the European manufacturer for the profits lost because of the failure to deliver the oil, then the oil company bears the losses that arise from nondelivery of the oil. Therefore, the way the court decides the case accomplishes an apportionment of losses between the two parties.

Can economics provide a method for the court to decide which apportionment is better? From the standpoint of economic efficiency, the court should assign the loss from nondelivery so as to make future contractual behavior more efficient. A rule for

---

[5] For a full discussion of the cases on which this example is based, see Richard Posner and Andrew Rosenfield, *Impossibility and Related Doctrines in Contract Law*, 6 JOURNAL OF LEGAL STUDIES 88 (1977).

doing this assigns the losses to the party that could have borne the risk at less cost.[6] One way to make risk more bearable is to take precaution against it. The company doing business in the Middle East is in a better position than a European manufacturer to assess the risk of war in that region and to take precaution against it. For example, the oil company could have arranged for alternative shipping routes that might not have been blocked by a Middle Eastern war. The oil company also could have arranged to purchase oil elsewhere in the event of war in the Middle East.

Because the oil company is better able to bear the risk of war, economic efficiency requires the court to hold the oil company liable for breach of contract and, therefore, make it responsible for paying for the European manufacturer's lost profits due to non-performance. This conclusion is consistent with the outcome of some actual cases that arose as a consequence of the 1967 war in the Middle East. Notice that these beneficial effects of the court's general rule extend beyond the market for oil to include all contracts where performance might be impossible. We shall consider the principles underlying this example in detail in Chapters 6 and 7.

> **EXAMPLE 3:** *Eddie's Electric Company* emits smoke, which dirties the wash hanging at nearby *Lucille's Laundry*. *Eddie's* can abate the pollution by installing scrubbers on its stacks, and *Lucille's* can reduce the damage by installing filters on its ventilation system. The installation of scrubbers by *Eddie's* or filters by *Lucille's* completely eliminates pollution or the damage from it. Installing filters is cheaper than installing scrubbers. No one else is affected by pollution because *Eddie's* and *Lucille's* are near to each other and far from anyone else. *Lucille's* initiates court proceedings to have *Eddie's* declared to be a "nuisance." If the action succeeds, the court will order *Eddie's* to abate its pollution. Otherwise, the court will not intervene in the dispute.

First, assume that *Eddie's* and *Lucille's* cannot bargain together or cooperate. If *Lucille's* wins the action and *Eddie's* is ordered by the court to abate the pollution, *Eddie's* will have to install scrubbers, thus reducing its profits and eliminating the pollution. However, if *Lucille's* loses the action, then *Lucille's* will have to install filters, thus reducing its profits and eliminating the harm from the pollution. We assume that installing filters is the cheaper of the two ways to eliminate the damage from pollution. Consequently, it is efficient for *Lucille's* to lose the action.

Now, consider how the analysis changes if *Eddie's* and *Lucille's* can bargain together and cooperate. Their joint profits (the sum of the profits of *Eddie's* and *Lucille's*) will be higher if they choose the cheaper means of eliminating the harm from pollution. When their joint profits are higher, they can divide the gain between them in order to make both of them better off. The cheaper means is also the efficient means. As a result, efficiency is achieved in this example when *Lucille's* and *Eddie's* bargain together and cooperate, regardless of the rule of law. (Ronald Coase derived this result in a famous paper cited by the Nobel Prize Committee when he received the award.)

---

[6] We assume in this example that the entire loss from nonperformance must be allocated by the court to one of the parties. Alternatively, the court might divide the loss between the parties.

III. WHY SHOULD LAWYERS STUDY ECONOMICS?
WHY SHOULD ECONOMISTS STUDY LAW?

The economic analysis of law is an interdisciplinary subject that brings together two great fields of study and facilitates a greater understanding of both. Economics helps us to perceive law in a new way, one that is extremely useful to lawyers and to anyone interested in issues of public policy. You probably are already accustomed to thinking of rules of law as tools for justice. Indeed, many people view the law *only* in its role as a provider of justice. This book will teach you to view laws as incentives for changing behavior (implicit prices) and as instruments for policy objectives (efficiency and distribution).

While our main focus will be on what economics can bring to the law, we shall also find that law brings something to economics. Economic analysis often takes for granted such legal institutions as property and contract, which dramatically affect the economy. For example, the absence of secure property and reliable contracts paralyzes the economies of some nations in Eastern Europe and the third world. As another illustration, differences in laws cause capital markets to be organized very differently in Japan, Germany, and the United States, and these differences can contribute to differences in those countries' economic performance.

Besides substance, economists can learn techniques from lawyers. Lawyers spend much of their time trying to resolve practical problems, and the techniques of legal analysis have been shaped by this devotion to practice. The outcome of a case often turns upon the labels used to describe the facts, so law students learn sensitivity to verbal distinctions. These verbal distinctions, which sometimes strike nonlawyers as sophistry, are based on subtle but important facts that economists have ignored. To illustrate, economists frequently extol the virtues of voluntary exchange, but economics does not have a detailed account of what it means for exchange to be voluntary. As we shall see, contract law has a complex, well-articulated theory of volition. If economists will listen to what the law has to teach them, they will find their models being drawn closer to reality.

IV. THE PLAN OF THIS BOOK

The benefits of interdisciplinary study can be had only at a cost: lawyers must learn some economics, and economists must learn something about the law. We ask the reader to incur this cost in the next two chapters. Chapter 2 is a brief review of microeconomic theory. If you are familiar with that theory, then you can read the material quickly as a review or skim the headings for topics that you may not have covered in your study of microeconomic theory. As a check on whether you need to spend some more time in Chapter 2, you might try the problems at the end of the chapter.

Chapter 3 is an introduction to the law and the legal process. This material will be essential reading for those who have had no formal legal training. We try to show in that chapter how the legal system works, how the U.S. legal system is different from those in the rest of the world, and what counts as "law."

Chapter 4 begins the substantive treatment of the law from an economic viewpoint. The chapters on substantive legal issues are arranged in pairs (with the exception of Chapter 10 on the legal process). Chapters 4 and 5 will focus on property law; Chapters 6 and 7, on contract law; Chapters 8 and 9, on tort law; and Chapter 10, on the rules of civil procedure. The first chapter of the pair begins with a brief summary of the elements of that area of the law and the remainder of that chapter develops the economic analysis of it. The second chapter of each pair then extends the core economic theory to a series of topics. To illustrate, Chapter 8 develops an economic theory of tort liability, and Chapter 9 extends the theory and applies it to special problems that arise in connection with automobiles, medical practice, and accidents caused by commercial products. Chapters 4 through 10 deal with areas that are sometimes referred to as *private law*, because the plaintiff and defendant are typically private persons.

Beginning with Chapters 11 and 12, we shall turn to criminal law, where the state is the plaintiff or prosecutor.

SUGGESTED READINGS

At the end of every chapter we shall list some of the most important writings on the subject of that chapter. This list is not exhaustive; the field of law and economics is growing so rapidly that significant additions to the literature occur every month. The *Legal Periodicals Index* and the *Journal of Economic Literature* contain indexes of all articles published in law reviews and economics journals; both contain headings for "Economics" and "Law and Economics."

Barnes, David, and Lynn Stout, CASEBOOK ON LAW AND ECONOMICS (1992).

Dau-Schmidt, Ken, and Thomas S. Ulen, eds., A LAW AND ECONOMICS ANTHOLOGY (1997).

Easterbrook, Frank, *Foreword: The Court and the Economic System*, 98 HARVARD LAW REVIEW 4 (1984). See also Laurence Tribe, *Constitutional Calculus: Equal Justice or Economic Efficiency?* 98 HARVARD LAW REVIEW 592 (1984) and Easterbrook, *Method, Result, and Authority: A Reply,"* 98 HARVARD LAW REVIEW 622 (1984).

Goetz, Charles, LAW AND ECONOMICS (1984).

Hirsch, Werner Z., LAW AND ECONOMICS: AN INTRODUCTORY ANALYSIS (2d ed., 1989).

Leff, Arthur, *Economic Analysis of Law: Some Realism about Nominalism*, 60 VIRGINIA LAW REVIEW 451 (1974). [A book review of the first edition of Posner, ECONOMIC ANALYSIS OF LAW (1974).]

Malloy, Robin, LAW AND ECONOMICS: A COMPARATIVE APPROACH TO THEORY AND PRACTICE (1990).

Polinsky, A. Mitchell, AN INTRODUCTION TO LAW AND ECONOMICS (2d ed., 1989).

Posner, Richard A., *The Decline of Law as an Autonomous Discipline: 1962–1987*, 100 HARV. L. REV. 761 (1987).

Posner, Richard A., ECONOMIC ANALYSIS OF LAW (4th ed., 1992).

2

A REVIEW OF MICROECONOMIC THEORY

"Practical men, who believe themselves to be quite exempt from any intellectual influences, are usually the slaves of some defunct economist. . . . It is ideas, not vested interests, which are dangerous for good or evil."

—

John Maynard Keynes, THE GENERAL THEORY OF EMPLOYMENT, INTEREST, AND MONEY (1936)

"Economics is the science which studies human behavior as a relationship between ends and scarce means which have alternative uses."

—

Lionel Charles Robbins, Lord Robbins, AN ESSAY ON THE NATURE AND SIGNIFICANCE OF ECONOMIC SCIENCE (1932)

The economic analysis of law draws upon the principles of microeconomic theory, which we review in this chapter. For those of you who have not studied that branch of economics, reading this chapter will prove challenging but essential for understanding the remainder of the book. For those who have already mastered microeconomic theory, reading this chapter is unnecessary. For those readers who are somewhere in between these extremes, we suggest that you begin reading this chapter, skimming what is familiar and studying carefully what is unfamiliar. If you're not sure where you lie on this spectrum of knowledge, turn to the questions at the end of the chapter. If you have difficulty answering them, perhaps you should study this chapter carefully before going on.

I. OVERVIEW: THE STRUCTURE OF MICROECONOMIC THEORY

Microeconomics concerns decision-making by small groups, such as individuals, families, clubs, firms, and governmental agencies. In this chapter we shall develop the basic tools of microeconomics that we use in subsequent chapters to analyze legal rules and institutions.

Microeconomics is frequently defined as the study of how scarce resources are allocated among competing ends. Should you buy that digital audio tape player you'd like, or should you buy a dapper interview suit for your job interview? Should you take a trip with some friends this weekend or study at home? Because you have limited income and time, you have to make choices. Microeconomic theory offers a general theory about how people make such decisions.

We divide our study of microeconomics into five sections. The first is the theory of consumer choice and demand. This theory describes how the typical consumer, constrained by a limited income, chooses among the many goods and services offered for sale.

The second section deals with the choices made by business organizations or firms. We shall develop a model of the firm that helps us to see how the firm decides what goods and services to produce, how much to produce, and at what price to sell its output.

In the third section, we shall consider how consumers and firms interact. By combining the theory of the consumer and the firm, we shall explain how the decisions of consumers and firms are coordinated through movements in market price. Eventually, the decisions of consumers and firms must be made consistent in the sense that somehow the two sides agree about the quantity and price of the good or service that will be produced and consumed. When these consumption and production decisions are consistent in this sense, we say that the market is in equilibrium. We shall see that powerful forces propel markets toward equilibrium, so that attempts to divert the market from its path are frequently ineffectual or harmful.

The fourth section of microeconomic theory describes the supply and demand for inputs into the productive process. These inputs include labor, capital, land, and managerial talent; more generally, inputs are all the things that firms must acquire in order to produce the goods and services that consumers or other firms wish to purchase.

The final section of microeconomics deals with the area known as *welfare economics*. There we shall discuss the organization of markets and how they achieve efficiency.

These topics constitute the core of our review of microeconomic theory. There are two additional topics that do not fit neatly into the sections noted above, but we think you should know about them in order to understand the economic analysis of legal rules and institutions. These are game theory and the economic theory of decision-making under uncertainty. We shall cover these two topics in the final sections of this chapter.

II. SOME FUNDAMENTAL CONCEPTS: MAXIMIZATION, EQUILIBRIUM, AND EFFICIENCY

Economists usually assume that each economic actor *maximizes* something: consumers maximize utility (*i.e.*, happiness or satisfaction); firms maximize profits, politicians maximize votes, bureaucracies maximize revenues, charities maximize social welfare, and so forth. Economists often say that models assuming maximizing behavior work because most people are rational, and rationality requires maximization. Different people want different things, such as wealth, power, fame, love, happiness, and so on. The alternatives faced by an economic decision-maker give her different amounts of what she wants. One conception of rationality holds that a rational actor can rank alternatives according to the extent that they give her what she wants. In practice, the alternatives available to the actor are constrained. For example, a rational consumer can rank alternative bundles of consumer goods, and the consumer's budget constrains her choice among them. A rational consumer should choose the best alternative that the constraints allow.

Choosing the best alternative that the constraints allow can be described mathematically as *maximizing*. To see why, consider that the real numbers can be ranked from small to large, just as the rational consumer ranks alternatives according to the extent that they give her what she wants. Consequently, better alternatives can be associated with larger numbers. Economists call this association a "utility function." Furthermore, the constraint on choice can usually be expressed mathematically as a "feasibility constraint." Choosing the best alternative that the constraints allow corresponds to maximizing the utility function subject to the feasibility constraint. To illustrate, the consumer who goes shopping is said to maximize utility subject to her budget constraint.

Maximizing suggests that an agent tries to do the very best that she can, not merely making do. But isn't much of what we do irrational and uncalculated, and aren't our goals often ill-defined? Scholars now debate vigorously how to model diminished rationality, as opposed to the full rationality assumed in traditional economics. To model diminished rationality, some scholars modify the assumptions in the traditional economic model, whereas others abandon it in favor of novel alternatives from psychology. In this chapter, however, we review the traditional core of microeconomics, not critique it.

Turning to the second fundamental concept, there is no habit of thought so deeply ingrained among economists as the urge to characterize each social phenomenon as an *equilibrium* in the interaction of maximizing actors. An equilibrium is a pattern of interaction that persists unless disturbed by outside forces. Economists usually assume that interactions tend towards an equilibrium, regardless of whether they occur in markets, elections, clubs, games, teams, corporations, or marriages.

There is a vital connection between maximization and equilibrium in microeconomic theory. We characterize the behavior of every individual or group as maximizing something. Maximizing behavior tends to push these individuals and groups towards a point of rest, an equilibrium. They certainly do not intend for an equilibrium to result; instead, they simply try to maximize whatever it is that is of interest to them. Nonetheless, the interaction of maximizing agents usually results in an equilibrium.

A *stable* equilibrium is one that will not change unless outside forces intervene. To illustrate, the snowpack in a mountain valley is in stable equilibrium, whereas the snowpack on the mountain's peak may be in unstable equilibrium. An interaction headed towards a stable equilibrium actually reaches this destination unless outside forces divert it. In social life, outside forces often intervene before an interaction reaches equilibrium. Nevertheless, an equilibrium analysis makes sense. The simplest interaction to analyze is one that does not change. Tracing out the entire path of change is far more difficult. Advanced microeconomic theories of growth, cycles, and disequilibria exist, but we shall not need them in this book. The comparison of equilibria, called *comparative statics*, will be our basic approach.

Turning to the third fundamental concept, economists have several distinct definitions of *efficiency*. A production process is said to be productively efficient if either of two conditions holds:

1. it is not possible to produce the *same* amount of output using a lower-cost combination of inputs, or
2. it is not possible to produce *more* output using the same combination of inputs.

Consider a firm that uses labor and machinery to produce a consumer good called a "widget." Suppose that the firm currently produces 100 widgets per week using 10 workers and 15 machines. The firm is productively efficient if

1. it is not possible to produce 100 widgets per week by using 10 workers and fewer than 15 machines, or by using 15 machines and fewer than 10 workers, or
2. it is not possible to produce more than 100 widgets per week from the combination of 10 workers and 15 machines.

The other kind of efficiency, called *Pareto efficiency* after its inventor,[1] concerns the satisfaction of individual preferences. A particular situation is said to be *Pareto efficient* if it is impossible to change it so as to make at least one person better off (in his own estimation) without making another person worse off (again, in his own estimation). For simplicity's sake, assume that there are only two consumers, Smith and Jones, and two goods, umbrellas and bread. Initially, the goods are distributed between them. Is the allocation Pareto efficient? Yes, if it is impossible to reallocate the bread and umbrellas so as to make either Smith or Jones better off without making the other person worse off.

These three basic concepts—maximization, equilibrium, and efficiency—are fundamental to explaining economic behavior, especially in decentralized institutions, like markets that involve the coordinated interaction of many different people. Nonetheless, some lawyers who are critical of the economic analysis of law are doubtful that these concepts are really useful in explaining important social phenomena. They ask, "Why stress equilibria instead of change? Isn't it better to base predictions upon the psychology of choice rather than to prescribe rationality?" While these criticisms sometimes have merit, the fact remains that the three basic economic concepts have wide application to law.

III. MATHEMATICAL TOOLS

You may have been anxious about the amount of mathematics that you will find in this book. There is not much. We use simple algebra and graphs.

A. Functions

Economics is rife with functions: production functions, utility functions, cost functions, social welfare functions, and others. A *function* is a relationship between two sets of numbers such that for each number in one set, there corresponds exactly one number in

---

[1] Vilfredo Pareto was an Italian political scientist and economist who wrote at the turn of the twentieth century.

the other set. To illustrate, the columns below correspond to a functional relationship between the numbers in the left-hand column and those in the right-hand column. Thus, the number 4 in the x-column below corresponds to the number 10 in the y-column.

In fact, notice that each number in the x-column corresponds to exactly one number in the y-column. Thus, we can say that the variable y is a function of the variable x, or in the most common form of notation

$$y = f(x)$$

This is read as "y is a function of x" or "y equals some f of x."

y-column	x-column
2	3
3	0
10	4
10	6
12	9
7	12

Note that the number 4 is not the only number in the x-column that corresponds to the number 10 in the y-column; the number 6 also corresponds to the number 10. In this table, for a given value of x, there corresponds one value of y, but for some values of y, there corresponds more than one value of x. A value of x determines an exact value of y, whereas a value of y does not determine an exact value of x. Thus, in $y = f(x)$, y is called the *dependent variable*, because it depends on the value of x, and x is called the *independent variable*. Because y depends upon x in this table, y is a function of x, but because x does not (to our knowledge) depend for its values on y, x is not a function of y.

Now suppose that there is another dependent variable, named z, that also depends upon x. The function relating z to x might be named g:

$$z = g(x).$$

When there are two functions, $g(x)$ and $f(x)$, with different dependent variables, z and y, remembering which function goes with which variable can be hard. To avoid this difficulty, the same name is often given to a function and the variable determined by it. Following this strategy, the preceding functions would be renamed as follows:

$$y = f(x) \Rightarrow y = y(x)$$

$$z = g(x) \Rightarrow z = z(x)$$

Sometimes an abstract function will be discussed without ever specifying the exact numbers that belong to it. For example, the reader might be told that y is a function of x, and never be told exactly which values of y correspond to which values of x. The point then is simply to make the general statement that y depends upon x but in an as-yet unspecified way. If exact numbers are given, they may be listed in a table, as we have seen. Another way of showing the relationship between a dependent and an independent variable is to give an exact equation. For example, a function $z = z(x)$ might be given the exact form

$$z = z(x) = 5 + x/2,$$

which states that the function z matches values of x with values of z equal to five plus one-half of whatever value x takes. The table below gives the values of z associated with several different values of x:

z-column	x-column
6.5	3
12.5	15
8.0	6
6.0	2
9.5	9

A function can relate a dependent variable (there is always just one of them to a function) to more than one independent variable. If we write $y = h(x,z)$, we are saying that the function h matches one value of the dependent variable y to every pair of values of the independent variables x and z. This function might have the specific form

$$y = h(x,z) = -3x + z,$$

according to which y decreases by 3 units when x increases by 1 unit, and y increases by 1 unit when z increases by 1 unit.

B. Graphs

We can improve the intuitive understanding of a functional relationship by graphing it so that it can be visualized. In a graph, values of the independent variable are usually read off the horizontal axis, and values of the dependent variable are usually read off the vertical axis. Each point in the grid of lines corresponds to a pair of values for the variables. For an example, see Figure 2.1. The upward-sloping line on the graph represents all of the pairs of values that satisfy the function $y = 5 + x/2$. You can check this by

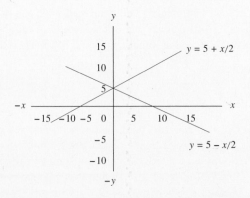

FIGURE 2.1 Graphs of the linear relationships $y = 5 + x/2$ (with a positive slope) and $y = 5 - x/2$ (with a negative slope).

finding a couple of points that *ought* to be on the line that corresponds to that function. For example, what if $y = 0$? What value should x have? If $y = 0$, then a little arithmetic will reveal that x should equal -10. Thus, the pair $(0, -10)$ is a point on the line defined by the function. What if $x = 0$? What value will y have? In that case, the second term in the right-hand side of the equation disappears, so that $y = 5$. Thus, the pair of values $(5, 0)$ is a point on the line defined by the function.

The graph of $y = 5 + x/2$ reveals some things about the relationship between y and x that we otherwise might not so easily discover. For example, notice that the line representing the equation slopes upward, or from southwest to northeast. The *positive slope*, as it is called, reveals that the relationship between x and y is a *direct* one. Thus, as x increases, so does y. And as x decreases, y decreases. Put more generally, when the independent and dependent variables move in the same direction, the slope of the graph of their relationship will be positive.

The graph also reveals the strength of this direct relationship by showing whether small changes in x lead to small or large changes in y. Notice that if x increases by 2 units, y increases by 1 unit. Another way of putting this is to say that in order to get a 10-unit increase in y, there must be a 20-unit increase in x.[2]

The opposite of a direct relationship is an *inverse* relationship. In that sort of relationship, the dependent and independent variables move in opposite directions. Thus, if x and y are inversely related, an *increase* in x (the independent variable) will lead to a *decrease* in y. Also, a *decrease* in x will lead to an *increase* in y. An example of an inverse relationship between an independent and a dependent variable is $y = 5 - x/2$. The graph of this line is also shown in Figure 2.1. Note that the line is downward-sloping, that is, the line runs from northwest to southeast.

> **QUESTION 2A:** Suppose that the equation were $y = 5 + x$. Show in a graph like the one in Figure 2.1 what the graph of that equation would look like. Is the relationship between x and y direct or inverse? Is the slope of the new equation greater or less than the slope shown in Figure 2.1?
>
> Now suppose that the equation were $y = 5 - x$. Show in a graph like the one in Figure 2.1 what the graph of that equation would look like. Is the relationship between x and y direct or inverse? Is the slope of the new equation positive or negative? Would the slope of the equation $y = 5 - x/2$ be steeper or shallower than that of the one in $y = 5 - x$?

The graph of $y = 5 + x/2$ in Figure 2.1 also reveals that the relationship between the variables is *linear*. This means that when we graph the values of the independent and dependent variables, the resulting relationship is a straight line. One of the implications of linearity is that changes in the independent variable cause a constant rate of change in the dependent variable is constant. In terms of Figure 2.1, if we would like to know the effect on y of doubling the amount of x, it doesn't matter whether we investigate that effect when x equals 2 or 3147. The effect on y of doubling the value of x is proportionally the same, regardless of the value of x.

The alternative to a linear relationship is, of course, a *nonlinear* relationship. In general, nonlinear relationships are trickier to deal with than are linear relationships. They

---

[2] The slope of the equation we have been dealing with in Figure 2.1 is $\frac{1}{2}$, which is the coefficient of x in the equation. In fact, in any linear relationship the coefficient of the independent variable gives the slope of the equation.

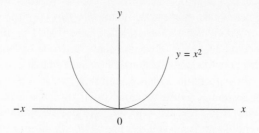

FIGURE 2.2 The graph of a nonlinear relationship, given by the equation $y = x^2$.

frequently, although not always, are characterized by the independent variable's being raised to a power by an exponent. Examples are $y = x^2$ and $y = 5/x^{1/2}$. Figure 2.2 shows a graph of $y = x^2$. Another common nonlinear relationship in economics is given by the example $A = xy$, where A is a constant. A graph of that function is given in Figure 2.3.

IV. THE THEORY OF CONSUMER CHOICE AND DEMAND

The economist's general theory of how people make choices is referred to as the *theory of rational choice*. What it means to make a rational choice will emerge in the course of this section of the chapter. In this section we show how that theory has been elaborated to explain the consumer's choice of what goods and services to purchase and in what amounts.

A. Consumer Preference Orderings

The construction of the economic model of consumer choice begins with an account of the preferences of consumers. Consumers are assumed to know the things they like and dislike and to be able to rank the available alternative combinations of goods and services according to their ability to satisfy the consumer's preferences. This involves no

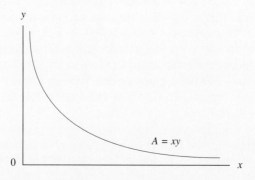

FIGURE 2.3 The graph of a nonlinear relationship, $A = xy$.

more than ranking the alternatives as better than, worse than, or equally as good as one another. Indeed, some economists believe that the conditions they impose on the ordering or ranking of consumer preferences constitute what an economist means by the term "rational." What are those conditions? They are that a consumer's preference ordering or ranking be *complete, transitive,* and *reflexive.* For an ordering to be *complete* simply means that the consumer be able to tell us how she ranks all the possible combinations of goods and services. Suppose that *A* represents a bundle of certain goods and services and *B* represents another bundle of the same goods and services but in different amounts. Completeness requires that the consumer be able to tell us that she prefers *A* to *B*, or that she prefers *B* to *A*, or that *A* and *B* are equally good (*i.e.*, that the consumer is indifferent between having *A* and having *B*). The consumer is *not* allowed to say, "I can't compare them."

Reflexivity is an arcane condition on consumer preferences. It means that any bundle of goods, *A*, is at least as good as itself. That condition is so trivially true that it is difficult to give a justification for its inclusion.

Transitivity means that the preference ordering obeys the following condition: if bundle *A* is preferred to bundle *B* and bundle *B* is preferred to bundle *C*, then it must be the case that *A* is preferred to *C*. This also applies to indifference: if the consumer is indifferent between (*i.e.*, equally prefers) *A* and *B* and between *B* and *C*, then she is also indifferent between *A* and *C*. Transitivity precludes the circularity of individual preferences. That is, transitivity means that it is impossible for *A* to be preferred to *B*, *B* to be preferred to *C*, and *C* to be preferred to *A*. Most of us would probably feel that someone who had circular preferences was extremely young or childish or crazy.

> **QUESTION 2B:** Suppose that you have asked James whether he would like a hamburger or a hot dog for lunch, and he said that he wanted a hot dog. Five hours later you ask him what he would like for dinner, a hamburger or a hot dog. James answers, "A hamburger." Do James' preferences for hot dogs *versus* hamburgers obey the conditions above? Why or why not?

It is important to remember that the preferences of the consumer are *subjective.* Different people have different tastes, and these will be reflected in the fact that they may have very different preference orderings over the same goods and services. Economists leave to other disciplines, such as psychology and sociology, the study of the source of these preferences. We take consumer tastes or preferences as given, or, as we sometimes say, as *exogenous,* which means that they are determined outside the economic system.[3]

An important consequence of the subjectivity of individual preferences is that economists have no accepted method for comparing the strength of peoples' preferences. Suppose that Stan tells us that he prefers bundle *A* to bundle *B*, and Jill tells us that she feels the same way: she also prefers *A* to *B*. Is there any way to tell who would prefer

---

[3] This statement inevitably raises the hackles of those who think that economists ignore one of the most fundamental aspects of the modern economy, the molding of consumer tastes through advertising. We do not at all ignore this; we quite readily acknowledge the size and importance of advertising and other industries devoted to altering consumer tastes. But we hold to the view that economics per se has nothing to say about how that alteration takes place.

having *A* more? In the abstract, the answer is, "No, there is not." All we have from each consumer is the *order* of preference, not the *strength* of those preferences. The inability to make *interpersonal comparisons of well-being* has some important implications for the design and implementation of public policy, as we shall see in the section on welfare economics.

B. Utility Functions and Indifference Curves

Once a consumer describes what his or her preference ordering is, we may derive a *utility function* for that consumer. The utility function identifies higher preferences with larger numbers. Suppose that there are only two commodities or services, *x* and *y*, available to a given consumer. If we let *u* stand for the consumer's utility, then the function $u = u(x,y)$ describes the utility that the consumer gets from different combinations of *x* and *y*.

A very helpful way of visualizing the consumer's utility function is by means of a graph called an *indifference map*. An example is shown in Figure 2.4. There we have drawn several *indifference curves*. Each curve represents all the combinations of *x* and *y* that give the consumer the same amount of utility or well-being. Alternatively, we might say that the consumer's tastes are such that he is indifferent among all the combinations of *x* and *y* that lie along a given curve—hence the name *indifference curve*. Thus, all those combinations of *x* and *y* lying along the indifference curve marked u_0 give the consumer the same utility. Those combinations lying on the higher indifference curve marked u_1 give this consumer similar utility, but this level of utility is *higher* than that of all those combinations of *x* and *y* lying along indifference curve u_0.

The problem of consumer choice arises from the collision of the consumer's preferences with obstacles to his or her satisfaction. The obstacles are the constraints that force decision-makers to choose among alternatives. There are many constraints, including time, energy, knowledge, and one's culture, but foremost among these is limited income. We can represent the consumer's *income constraint* or *budget line* by the line so labeled in Figure 2.5. The area below the line and the line itself represent all the

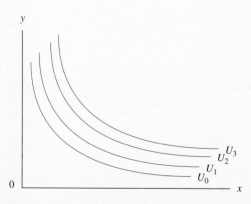

FIGURE 2.4 The consumer's indifference map.

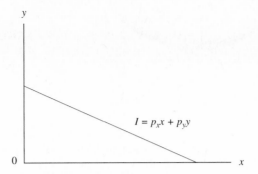

FIGURE 2.5 The consumer's income constraint or budget line.

combinations of x and y that are affordable, given the consumer's income, I.[4] Presumably, the consumer intends to spend all of her income on purchases of these two goods and services, so that the combinations upon which we shall focus are those that are on the budget line itself.

QUESTION 2C: In a figure like the one in Figure 2.5 and beginning with a budget line like the one in Figure 2.5, show how you would draw the new income constraint to reflect the following changes:

1. an increase in the consumer's income, prices held constant;
2. a decrease in the consumer's income, prices held constant;
3. a decrease in the price of x, income and the price of y held constant;
4. an increase in the price of y, income and the price of x held constant.

C. The Consumer's Optimum

We may now combine the information about the consumer's tastes given by the indifference map and the information about the income constraint given by the budget line in order to show what combination of x and y maximizes the consumer's utility, subject

---

[4] The equation for the budget line is $I = p_x x + p_y y$, where p_x is the price per unit of x and p_y is the price per unit of y. As an exercise, you might try to rearrange this equation, with y as the dependent variable, in order to show that the slope of the line is negative. When you do so, you will find that the coefficient of the x-term is equal to $- p_x/p_y$. This ratio is referred to by economists as *relative price*.

You might further want to see if you can show how you would represent the new budget line that would result from:

1. an increase in income to I', the prices of x and y remaining constant; and
2. a lowering of the price per unit of x, I and the price of y held constant.

Finally, see if you can show that the y-intercept of the budget line is equal to I/p_y and the x-intercept is equal to I/p_x.

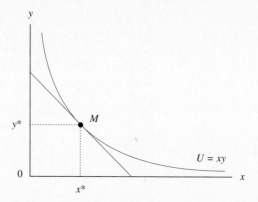

FIGURE 2.6 The consumer's optimum.

to the constraint imposed by her income. See Figure 2.6. There the consumer's optimum bundle is shown as point M, which contains x^* and y^*. Of all the feasible combinations of x and y, that combination gives this consumer the greatest utility.[5]

D. A Generalization: The Economic Optimum as Marginal Cost = Marginal Benefit

Because of the central importance of constrained maximization in microeconomic theory, let us take a moment to examine a more general way of characterizing such a maximum:

> A constrained maximum, or any other economic optimum, can be described as a point where *marginal cost* equals *marginal benefit*.

Let's see how this rule characterizes maximizing decisions.[6] Begin by assuming that the decision-maker chooses some initial level of whatever it is he is interested in maximizing. He then attempts to determine whether that initial level is his maximum; is that level as good as he can do, given his constraints? He can answer the question by making very small, what an economist calls *marginal*, changes away from that initial level. Suppose that the decision-maker proposes to *increase* slightly above his initial level whatever it is he is doing. There will be a cost associated with this small increase called *marginal cost*. But there will also be a benefit of having or doing more of whatever it is that he is attempting to maximize. The benefit of this small increase is called *marginal benefit*. The decision-maker will perceive himself as doing better at this new level, by

---

[5] Because we have assumed that the normal indifference curves are convex to the origin, there is a *unique* bundle of x and y that maximizes the consumer's utility. For other shapes of the indifference curves it is possible that there is more than one bundle that maximizes utility.

[6] This rule could describe equally well an economic optimum where the goal of the decision-maker is to *minimize* something. In that case, the optimum would still be the point at which $MC = MB$, but the demonstration of the stylized decision-making that got one to that point would be different from that given in the text.

comparison to his initial level, so long as the *marginal benefit* of the small increase is greater than the *marginal cost* of the change. He will continue to make these small, or marginal, adjustments so long as the marginal benefit exceeds the marginal cost, and he will stop making changes when the marginal cost of the last change made equals (or is greater than) the marginal benefit. That level is the decision-maker's maximum.

> **QUESTION 2D:** Suppose that, instead of *increasing* his level above the initial choice, the decision-maker first tries *decreasing* the amount of whatever it is he is attempting to maximize. Explain how the comparison of marginal cost and marginal benefit for these decreases is made and leads the decision-maker to the optimum. (Assume that the initial level is *greater than* what will ultimately prove to be the optimum.)

We can characterize the consumer's income-constrained maximum, *M* in Figure 2.6, in terms of the equality of marginal cost and benefit. Small changes in either direction along the budget line, *I*, represent a situation in which the consumer spends a dollar less on one good and a dollar more on the other. To measure the cost and benefit of these marginal changes along the budget line, we use the notion of small or marginal changes in utility. For example, a dollar less of *y* can be purchased, so that this shift causes a loss in utility that we may call the marginal cost of the budget reallocation. But the dollar previously spent on *y* can now be spent on *x*. More units of *x* mean greater utility, so that we may call this increase the marginal benefit of the budget reallocation. Suppose that the consumer is contemplating spending a dollar less on good *y* and a dollar more on *x*. Should she do so? Only if the marginal cost (the decrease in utility from one dollar less of *y*) is less than the marginal benefit (the increase in utility from having one dollar more of *x*). The consumer will continue to reallocate dollars away from the purchase of *y* and toward the purchase of *x* so long as the process will stop and the consumer's income-constrained maximum will be attained when the marginal benefit of the last change made is equal to the marginal cost. This occurs at the point *M* in Figure 2.6.

Figure 2.7 applies constrained maximization to reduce the amount of pollution. Along the vertical axis are dollar amounts. Along the horizontal axis are units of pollution reduction. At the origin there is no effort to reduce pollution. At the vertical line labeled "100%," pollution has been completely eliminated.

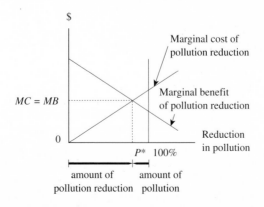

FIGURE 2.7 The socially optimal amount of pollution-reduction effort.

The curve labeled *MB* shows the marginal benefit to society of reducing pollution. We assume that this has been correctly measured to take into account health, aesthetic, and all other benefits that accrue to members of society from reducing pollution at various levels. This line starts off high and then declines. This downward slope captures the fact that the very first efforts at pollution reduction confer large benefits on society. The next effort at reducing pollution also confers a societal benefit, but not in quite as great an amount as the initial efforts. Finally, as we approach the vertical line labeled "100%" and all vestiges of pollution are being eliminated, the benefit to society of achieving those last steps is positive, but not nearly as great as the benefit of the early stages of pollution reduction.

The curve labeled *MC* represents the societal cost of achieving given levels of pollution reduction. The individuals and firms that pollute must incur costs of complying with the societal directive to reduce pollution: they may have to adopt cleaner and safer production processes that are also more expensive; they may have to install monitoring devices that check the levels of pollution they generate; and they may have to defend themselves in court when they are accused of violating the pollution-reduction guidelines. We have drawn the *MC* curve to be upward-sloping to indicate that the costs of achieving any given level of pollution-reduction increase. This means that the cost of reducing the very worst pollution may not be very high, but that successive levels of reduction will be ever more expensive.

Given this declining marginal benefit and rising marginal cost, the question then arises, "What is the optimal amount of pollution-reduction effort for society?" An examination of Figure 2.7 shows that *P** is the socially optimal amount of pollution-reduction effort. (Note that (100%−*P**) is the optimal amount of pollution.) Any more effort will cost more than it is worth. Any less would cause a reduction in benefits that would be greater than the savings in costs.

Note that there is a potentially controversial conclusion in the figure—namely, that it would not be optimal for society to try to eliminate pollution entirely. Put somewhat differently, according to the figure, it might be socially optimal to tolerate *some* pollution.

This does not strike most economists as a startling conclusion. The reason, which may be obvious, is that economists try to take account of costs as well as benefits. Nothing is free. Much of the wisdom of economics comes from the recognition of this fact and of the derivation of techniques for computing the costs of things and then balancing these costs against benefits.

QUESTION 2E: Suppose that society's goal with regard to pollution were to *maximize the total benefits* to society of pollution reduction, regardless of the costs. What level of pollution-reduction effort in Figure 2.7 would correspond to this goal?

QUESTION 2F: Suppose that we were to characterize society's decision-making with regard to pollution-reduction efforts as an attempt to maximize the *net benefit* of pollution-reduction efforts. Let us define *net benefit* as the difference between marginal benefit and marginal cost. What level of pollution-reduction effort corresponds to this goal?

QUESTION 2G: Using a graph like Figure 2.7, show the effect on the determination of the socially optimal amount of pollution-reduction effort of the following:

1. a technological change that *lowers* the marginal cost of achieving any level of pollution reduction;

2. a discovery that there are greater health risks associated with every given level of pollution than were previously thought to be the case;

3. the discovery that the intersection of the *MB* and *MC* lines occurred to the right of the vertical line labeled "100%".

If you understand that for economists, *the optimum for nearly all decisions occurs at the point at which marginal benefit equals marginal cost*, then you have gone a long way toward mastering the microeconomic tools necessary to answer most questions where a choice must be made.

E. Individual Demand

We have described the behavior of a rational consumer in sufficient detail to suggest the axiomatic foundation of modern microeconomic theory. In this section we look at one of the most famous implications of the theory of consumer choice.

We may use the model of consumer choice of the previous sections to derive a relationship between the price of a good and the amount of that good in a consumer's optimum bundle. We will leave the precise derivation of this relationship to another day. Let's describe here the method of derivation and the result.

Starting from point M in Figure 2.6, note that when the price of x is that given by the budget line, the optimal amount of x to consume is x^*. But what amount of x will this consumer want to purchase so as to maximize utility when the price of x is lower than that given by the budget line in Figure 2.6? We can answer that question by holding P_y and I constant, letting P_x fall, and writing down the amount of x in the succeeding optimal bundles. Not surprisingly, the result of this exercise will be that the price of x and the amount of x in the optimum bundles are inversely related. That is, when the price of x goes up, the amount of x that the consumer will purchase goes down, and *vice versa*. This result is the famous *law of demand*.

We may graph this relationship between P_x and the quantity of x demanded to get the individual demand curve, D, shown in Figure 2.8.

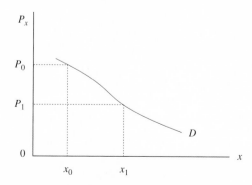

FIGURE 2.8 An individual's demand curve, showing the inverse relationship between price and quantity demanded.

F. Price Elasticity of Demand

The demand curve we have drawn in Figure 2.8 could have had a different slope than that shown; it might have been either flatter or steeper. The steepness of the demand curve is related to an important concept called the *price elasticity of demand*, or simply *elasticity of demand*.

Elasticity of demand measures the response of the quantity of a good to changes in its price. The elasticity is calculated as the percentage change in quantity demanded divided by the percentage change in price. The measure is frequently denoted by the letter e, and the ranges of elasticity are called "inelastic" ($e < 1$), "elastic" ($e > 1$), and "unitary elastic" ($e = 1$).[7] For an inelastically demanded good, the percentage change in price exceeds the percentage change in quantity demanded. Thus, a good that has $e = 0.5$ is one for which a 50% decline in price will cause a 25% increase in the quantity demanded, or for which a 15% increase in price will cause a 7.5% decrease in quantity demanded. For an elastically demanded good, the percentage change in price is less than the percentage change in quantity demanded. As a result, a good that has $e = 1.5$ is one for which a 50% decline in price will cause a 75% increase in quantity demanded, or for which a 20% increase in price will cause a 30% decline in quantity demanded.

The most important determinant of the price elasticity of demand is the presence of substitutes for the good. The more substitutes for the good, the greater the elasticity of demand; the fewer the substitutes, the lower the elasticity. Thus, one would expect a relatively large price elasticity of demand for individual kinds of food such as beef, pork, chicken, or white bread, and a relatively small price elasticity for a more encompassing category of goods such as meat. One might also expect a relatively low elasticity of demand for addictive commodities such as cigarettes and heroin.

Economists have measured price elasticities of demand for numerous goods and services. Table 2.1 shows some of these measurements. We have included both short-run (up to one year) and long-run (more than one year) elasticities. The longer the period of time during which consumers can make an adjustment to a price change, the more elastic one would expect their demand to be. Consider the case of gasoline. Suppose that there is a sudden increase in the price of gasoline. In the very short run, say, the next several months, there will be few substitutes for gasoline, and consumers will be able to make only limited adjustments in their gasoline consumption habits. As a result, one would expect a relatively low elasticity of demand for gasoline in the short run. In fact, the reported figure in Table 2.1 is 0.14, which indicates that if the price of gas doubles, there will only be a 14% decline in the quantity of gasoline demanded. But over a longer period of time, consumers can make more extensive adjustments to the increase in the price of gas by, for example, walking more, car pooling, and bicycling.

---

[7] By convention, e, the price elasticity of demand, is a positive (or absolute) number, even though the calculation we suggested will lead to a negative number.

Table 2.1[8]

LONG-RUN AND SHORT-RUN PRICE ELASTICITIES

	ELASTICITY	
Good	*Short-run*	*Long-run*
Gasoline, oil	0.14	0.48
China, glassware	1.34	8.80
Alcohol	0.90	3.63
Movies	0.87	3.67
Bus travel (local)	0.77	3.54
Bus travel (intercity)	0.20	2.17
Air travel (foreign)	0.70	4.00
Rail travel (commuter)	0.54	1.70
Natural gas (residential)	0.15	10.70
Electricity (residential)	0.13	1.90
Newspapers, magazines	0.10	0.52

[8] The table is taken, in part, from Heinz Kohler, *INTERMEDIATE MICROECONOMICS: THEORY AND APPLICATIONS* (3d ed. 1990).

V. THE THEORY OF SUPPLY

We now turn to a review of the other side of the market: the supply side. The key institution in supplying goods and services for sale to consumers is the business firm. In this section we shall see what goal the firm seeks and how it decides what to supply. In the following section, we merge our models of supply and demand to see how the independent maximizing activities of consumers and firms achieve a market equilibrium.

A. The Profit-Maximizing Firm

The firm is the institution in which output (products and services) is fabricated from inputs (capital, labor, land, etc.). Just as we assume that consumers rationally maximize utility subject to their income constraint, we assume that firms *maximize profits subject to the constraints imposed on them by consumer demand and the technology of production.*

In microeconomics, *profits* are defined as the difference between *total revenue* and the *total costs* of production. Total revenue for the firm equals the number of units of output sold multiplied by the price of each unit. Total costs equal the costs of each of the inputs times the number of units of input used, summed over all inputs. The profit-maximizing firm produces that amount of output that leads to the greatest positive difference between the firm's revenue and its costs. Microeconomic theory demonstrates that the firm will maximize its profits if it produces that *amount of output whose marginal cost equals its marginal revenue*. (In fact, this is simply an application of a general rule: To achieve an optimum, equate marginal cost and marginal benefit.)

There are some new terms here, and we must define and explain them. *Marginal cost* is defined as the increase in total costs that results from producing the last (marginal) unit of output. Similarly, *marginal revenue* is defined as the increase in total revenue that results from the sale of one more unit of output. Suppose that a firm is attempting to maximize its profits and is producing some level of output, q_1. Further suppose that in producing q_1 the firm's accountants report that the addition to total revenues from the sale of the q_1th unit was greater than the addition to total costs from producing that unit. What can be concluded? Clearly, the production of the q_1th unit of output increased the firm's profits because total revenues increased more than total costs.

Now suppose that the firm is contemplating the production of the q_2th unit of output. The accountants report that for that unit of output the marginal cost will exceed the marginal revenue; that is, the production of q_2 will add more to total costs than it will add to total revenue. Clearly then, production of q_2 will decrease profits.

These considerations suggest that when marginal revenue exceeds marginal cost, the firm should expand production, and that when marginal cost exceeds marginal revenue, it should reduce the amount of output produced. It follows that profits will be maximized for that output for which marginal cost and marginal revenue are equal. Note the economy of this rule: To maximize profits, the firm need not concern itself with its total cost or total revenues; instead, it can simply experiment unit-by-unit of production in order to discover the output level that maximizes its profits.

In Figure 2.9 the profit-maximizing output of the firm is shown at the point at which the marginal cost curve and marginal revenue curve of the firm are equal. The profit-maximizing output level is denoted q^*. Total profits at this level of production, denoted by the shaded area in the figure, equal the difference between the total revenues of the firm (p times q^*) and the total costs of the firm (the average cost of producing q^* times q^*).

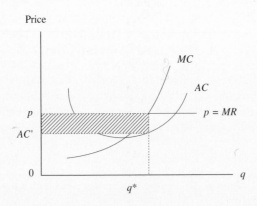

FIGURE 2.9 The profit-maximizing output for a firm.

There are several things you should note about the curves in the graph. We have drawn the marginal revenue curve as horizontal and equal to the prevailing price. This implies that the firm can sell as much as it likes at that prevailing price. Doubling its sales will have no effect on the market price of the good or service. This sort of behavior is referred to as *price-taking* behavior. It characterizes industries in which there are so many firms, most of them small, that the actions of no single firm can affect the market price of the good or service. An example might be farming. There are so many suppliers of wheat that the decision of one farmer to double or triple output or cut it in half will have no impact on its market price. (Of course, if *all* farms decide to double output, there will be a substantial impact on market price.)

B. The Short Run and the Long Run

In microeconomics the firm is said to operate in two different time frames: the short run and the long run. These time periods do not correspond to calendar time. Instead they are defined in terms of the firm's inputs. In the short run at least one input is fixed, and the usual factor of production that is fixed is capital (the firm's buildings, machines, and other durable inputs). Because capital is fixed in the short run, all the costs associated with capital are called *fixed costs*. In the short run the firm can, in essence, ignore those costs: they will be incurred regardless of whether the firm produces nothing at all or 10 million units of output. The long run is distinguished by the fact that all factors of production become variable. There are no longer any fixed costs. Established firms may expand their productive capacity or leave the industry entirely, and new firms may enter the business.

Another important distinction between the long and the short run has to do with the equilibrium level of profit-maximizing output for each firm. At any point in time there is an average rate of return earned by capital in the economy as a whole. When profits being earned in a particular industry, exceed the average profit rate for industry as a whole, firms will enter the industry, assuming there are no barriers to entry. As entry occurs, the price of the output in the industry goes down, causing each firm's revenue to decrease. Also, the increased competition for the factors of production causes input prices to rise, pushing up each firm's costs. The combination of these two forces causes each firm's profits to decline. Entry ceases when profits fall to the average rate.

Economists have a special way of describing these facts. The average return on capital is treated as part of the costs that are subtracted from revenues to get "economic profits." Thus, when the rate of return on invested capital in this industry equals the average for the economy as a whole, it is said that "economic profits are zero."[9]

---

[9] When profits in a given industry are less than the average in the economy as a whole, economic profits are said to be negative. When that is the case, firms exit this industry for other industries where the profits are at least equal to the average for the economy. As an exercise, see if you can demonstrate the process by which profits go to zero when negative economic profits in an industry cause exit to take place.

A DIGRESSION: OPPORTUNITY COST AND COMPARATIVE ADVANTAGE

We have been implicitly using one of the most fundamental concepts in microeconomics: opportunity cost. This term refers to the economic cost of an alternative that has been foregone. When you decided to attend a college, graduate school, or law school, you gave up certain other valuable alternatives, such as taking a job, training for the Olympics, or traveling around the world on a tramp steamer. In reckoning the cost of going to college, graduate school, or law school, the true economic cost was that of the next best alternative. This point is true of the decisions of all economic actors: when maximizing utility, the consumer must consider the opportunities given up by choosing one bundle of consumer goods rather than another; when maximizing profits, the firm must consider the opportunities foregone by committing its resources to the production of widgets rather than to something else.

In general, the economic notion of opportunity cost is more expansive than the more common notion of accounting cost. An example will make this point.[10] Suppose that a rich relative gives you a car whose market value is $15,000. She says that if you sell the car, you may keep the proceeds, but that if you use the car yourself, she'll pay for the gas, oil, maintenance, repairs, and insurance. In short she says, "The use of the car is FREE!" But is it? Suppose that the $15,000 for which the car could be sold would earn 12% interest per year in a savings account, giving $1,800 per year in interest income. If you use the car for one year, its resale value will fall to $11,000—a cost to you of $4,000. Therefore, the opportunity cost to you of using the car for one year is $4,000 plus the foregone interest of $1,800—a total of $5,800. This is far from being free. The accounting cost of using the car is zero, but the opportunity cost is positive.

Comparative advantage is another useful economic concept related to the notion of opportunity cost. The law of comparative advantage asserts that people should engage in those pursuits where their opportunity costs are lower than others. For example, someone who is seven feet tall has a comparative advantage in pursuing a career in professional basketball. But what about someone whose skills are such that she can do many things well? Suppose, for example, that a skilled attorney is also an extremely skilled typist. Should she do her own typing or hire someone else to do it while she specializes in the practice of law? The notion of comparative advantage argues for specialization: the attorney can make so much more money by specializing in the practice of law than by trying to do both jobs that she could easily afford to hire someone else who is less efficient at typing to do her typing for her.

[10] The example is taken from Roy Ruffin and Paul Gregory, PRINCIPLES OF MICROECONOMICS 156 (2d ed. 1986).

This leads to the conclusion that economic profits are zero in an industry that is in long-run equilibrium. Because this condition can occur only at the minimum point of the firm's average cost curve, where the average costs of production are as low as they can possibly be, inputs will be most efficiently used in long-run equilibrium. Thus, the condition of zero economic profits, far from being a nightmare, is really a desirable state.

VI. MARKET EQUILIBRIUM

Having described the behavior of utility-maximizing consumers and profit-maximizing producers, our next task is to bring them together to explain how they interact. We shall first demonstrate how a unique price and quantity are determined by the interaction of supply and demand in a perfectly competitive market and then show what happens to price and quantity when the market structure changes to one of monopoly. We conclude this section with an example of equilibrium analysis of an important public policy issue.

A. Equilibrium in a Perfectly Competitive Industry

An industry in which there are so many firms that no one of them can influence the market price by its individual decisions and in which there are so many consumers that the individual utility-maximizing decisions of no one consumer can affect the market price is called a *perfectly competitive industry*. For such an industry the aggregate demand for and aggregate supply of output can be represented by the downward-sloping demand curve, $d = d(p)$, and the upward-sloping supply curve, $s = s(p)$, shown in Figure 2.10. The *market-clearing* or *equilibrium* price and quantity occur at the point of intersection of the aggregate supply and demand curves. At that combination of price and quantity, the decisions of consumers and suppliers are consistent.

One way to see why the combination P_c, q_c in Figure 2.10 is an equilibrium is to see what would happen if a different price-quantity combination obtained. Suppose that the initial market price was P_1. At that price, producers would maximize their profits by supplying q_{s1} of output, and utility-maximizing consumers would be prepared to purchase q_{d1} units of output. These supply and demand decisions are inconsistent: at P_1, the amount that suppliers would like to sell exceeds the amount that consumers would like to buy. How will the market deal with this excess supply? Clearly, the market price must fall. As the price falls, consumers will demand more and producers will supply less, so the gap between supply and demand will diminish. Eventually the price may

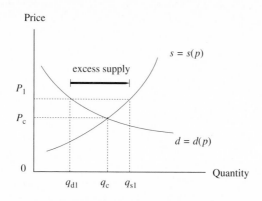

FIGURE 2.10 Market equilibrium in a perfectly competitive market.

reach P_c. And at that price, as we have seen, the amount that suppliers wish to sell and the amount that consumers wish to purchase are equal.

B. Equilibrium in a Monopolistic Market

Monopoly is at the other extreme of market structure. In a monopoly there is only one supplier, so that firm and industry are identical. A monopoly can arise and persist only where there are barriers to entry that make it impossible for competing firms to appear. In general, such barriers can arise from two sources: first, from statutory and other legal restrictions on entry; and second, from technological conditions of production known as *economies of scale*. An example of a statutory restriction on entry was the Civil Aeronautics Board's refusal from the 1930s until the mid-1970s to permit entry of new airlines into the market for passenger traffic on such major routes as Los Angeles-New York and Chicago-Miami.

The second barrier to entry is technological. Economies of scale are a condition of production in which the greater the level of output, the lower the average cost of production. Where such conditions exist, one firm can produce any level of output at less cost than multiple firms. A monopolist that owes its existence to economies of scale is sometimes called a *natural monopoly*. Public utilities, such as local water, telecommunications, cable, and power companies, are often natural monopolies. The technological advantages of a natural monopoly would be partially lost if the single firm is allowed to restrict its output and to charge a monopoly price. For that reason, natural monopolies are typically regulated by the government.

The monopolist, like the competitive firm, maximizes profit by producing that output for which marginal cost equals marginal revenue. Marginal cost of the monopolist, as for the competitive firm, is the cost of producing one more unit of output. This cost curve is represented in Figure 2.11 by the curve labeled *MC*. But marginal revenue for the monopolist is different from what it was for the competitive firm. Recall that marginal revenue describes the change in a firm's total revenues for a small, or marginal,

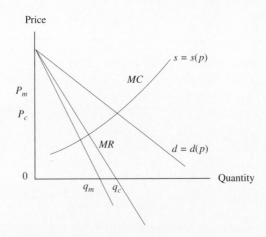

FIGURE 2.11 Profit-maximizing output and price for a monopolist.

change in the number of units of output sold. For the competitive firm marginal revenue is equal to the price of output. Because the competitive firm can sell as much as it likes at the prevailing price, each additional unit of output sold adds exactly the sale price to the firm's total revenues. But for the monopolist marginal revenue declines as the number of units sold increases. This is indicated in Figure 2.11 by the downward-sloping curve labeled *MR*. Notice that the *MR* curve lies below the demand curve. This indicates that the marginal revenue from any unit sold by a monopolist is always less than the price. *MR* is positive but declining for units of output between 0 and q_c; thus, the sale of each of those units increases the firm's total revenues but at a decreasing rate. The unit q_c actually adds nothing to the firm's total revenues ($MR = 0$), and for each unit of output beyond q_c, *MR* is less than zero, which means that each of those units actually reduces the monopolist's total revenues.

The reason for this complex relationship between marginal revenue and units sold by the monopolist is the downward-sloping demand curve. The downward-sloping demand curve implies that the monopolist must lower the price; but in order to sell an additional unit of output he or she must lower the price not just on the last or marginal unit but on all the units sold.[11] From this fact it can be shown, using calculus, that the addition to total revenues from an additional unit of output sold will always be less than the price charged for that unit. Thus, because *MR* is always less than the price for all units of output and because price declines along the demand curve, the *MR* curve must also be downward-sloping and lie below the demand curve.

The monopolist maximizes his profit by choosing that output level for which marginal revenue and marginal cost are equal. This output level, q_m, is shown in Figure 2.11. The demand curve indicates that consumers are willing to pay P_m for that amount of output. Notice that if this industry were competitive instead of monopolized, the profit-maximizing actions of the firms would have resulted in an equilibrium price and quantity at the intersection of the aggregate supply curve, *S*, and the industry demand curve, *D*. The competitive price, P_c, is lower than the monopolistic price, and the quantity of output produced and consumed under competition, q_c, is greater than under monopoly.

Economists distinguish additional market structures that are intermediate between the extremes of perfect competition and monopoly. The most important among these are *oligopoly* and *imperfect competition*. An oligopolistic market is one containing a few firms that recognize that their individual profit-maximizing decisions are interdependent. That means that what is optimal for firm *A* depends not only on its marginal costs and the demand for its output but also on what firms *B*, *C*, and *D* have decided to produce and the prices they are charging. The economic analysis of this interdependence requires a knowledge of game theory, which we discuss below. An imperfectly competitive market is one that shares most of the characteristics of a perfectly competitive market—for example, free entry and exit of firms and the presence of many firms—but has one important monopolistic element: firms produce differentiable output rather than the homogeneous output produced by perfectly competitive firms. Thus, imperfectly competitive firms distinguish their output by brand names, colors, sizes, quality, durability, and so on.

---

[11] Assuming the monopolist cannot price-discriminate (*i.e.*, charge different prices to different consumers for the same product).

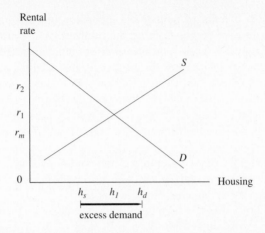

FIGURE 2.12 The consequences of a rent-control ordinance where rents are constrained to be below the market-clearing rental rate.

C. An Example of Equilibrium Analysis

It is useful to have an example applying this theory to a real problem. Let us imagine a market for rental housing like the one shown in Figure 2.12. The demand for rental housing is given by the curve D, and the supply of rental housing is given by the upward-sloping supply curve S. Assuming that the rental housing market is competitive, then the independent actions of consumers and of profit-maximizing housing owners will lead to a rental rate of r_1 being charged and of h_1 units of rental housing being supplied and demanded. Note that this is an equilibrium in the sense we discussed above: the decisions of those demanding the product and of those supplying it are consistent at the price r_1. Unless something causes the demand curve or the supply curve to shift, this price and output combination will remain in force.

But now suppose that the city government determines that r_1 is too high. It passes an ordinance that specifies a maximum rental rate for housing of r_m, considerably below the equilibrium market rate. The hope of the government is that at least the same amount of housing will be consumed by renters but at a lower rental rate. A look at Figure 2.12, however, leads one to doubt that result. At r_m, consumers demand h_d units of rental housing, an increase over the quantity demanded at the higher rate, r_1. But at this lower rate suppliers are only prepared to supply h_s units of rental housing. Apparently it does not pay them to devote as much of their housing units to renters at that lower rate; perhaps if r_m is all one can get from renting housing units, suppliers prefer to switch some of their units to other uses, such as occupancy by the owner's family or their sale as condominiums. The result of the rate ceiling imposed by the government is a shortage of, or excess demand for, rental units equal to $(h_d - h_s)$.

If the rate ceiling is strictly enforced, the shortage will persist. Some non-price methods of determining who gets the h_s units of rental housing must be found, such as queuing. Eventually, the shortage may be eased if either the demand curve shifts inward or the supply curve shifts outward. It is also possible that landlords will let their property deteriorate by withholding routine maintenance and repairs, so that the quality of their property falls to such an extent that r_m provides a competitive rate of return to them.

If, however, the rate ceiling is *not* strictly enforced, then consumers and suppliers will find a way to erase the shortage. For example, renters could offer free services or secret payments (sometimes called *side payments*) to landlords in order to get the effective rental rate above r_m and induce the landlord to rent to them rather than to those willing to pay only r_m. Those services and side payments could amount to $(r_2 - r_m)$ per housing unit.

VII. GAME THEORY

In a previous section we noted the need for a new analytical tool called the *theory of games* to analyze the market structure known as oligolopy. This section gives you a brief overview of that tool.

The law frequently confronts situations in which there are few decision-makers and in which the optimal action for one person to take depends on what another actor chooses. These situations are like games in that people must decide upon a strategy. A strategy is a plan for acting that responds to the reactions of others. Game theory deals with any situation in which strategy is important. Game theory will, consequently, enhance our understanding of some legal rules and institutions. For those who would like to pursue this topic in more detail, there are now several excellent introductory books on game theory.[12]

To characterize a game, we must specify three things:

1. the *players*,
2. the *strategies* of each player, and
3. the *payoffs* to each player for each strategy.

Let's consider a famous example—the prisoner's dilemma. Two people, *Suspect 1* and *Suspect 2*, conspire to commit a crime. They are apprehended by the police outside the place where the crime was committed, taken to the police station, and placed in separate rooms so that they cannot communicate. The authorities question them individually and try to play one suspect against the other. The evidence against them is circumstantial—they were simply in the wrong place at the wrong time. If the prosecutor must go to trial with only this evidence, then the suspects will have to be charged with a minor offense and given a relatively light punishment—say, one year in prison. The prosecutor would very much prefer that one or both of the suspects confesses to the more serious crime that they are thought to have committed. Specifically, if either suspect confesses (and thereby implicates the other) and the other does not, the non-confessor will receive 7 years in prison, and as a reward for assisting the state, the confessor will only receive

---

[12]For those who would like to pursue game theory in more detail, there are now several excellent introductory texts: Eric Rasmusen, GAMES AND INFORMATION: AN INTRODUCTION TO GAME THEORY (2nd ed. 1995); David Kreps, GAME THEORY AND ECONOMIC MODELLING (1990); and Avinash Dixit and Barry Nalebuff, THINKING STRATEGICALLY: THE COMPETITIVE EDGE IN BUSINESS, POLITICS, AND EVERYDAY LIFE (1991). More advanced treatments may be found in Roger Myerson, GAME THEORY (1991) and Drew Fudenberg and Jean Tirole, GAME THEORY (1991). With special reference to law, see Douglas Baird, Robert Gertner, and Randal Picker, GAME THEORY AND THE LAW (1995).

one-half of a year in prison. If both suspects can be induced to confess, each will spend 5 years in jail. What should each suspect do—confess or keep quiet?

The strategies available to the suspects can be shown in a *payoff matrix* like that in Figure 2.13. Each suspect has two strategies: confess or keep quiet. The payoffs to each player from following a given strategy are shown by the entries in the four cells of the box, with the payoff to *Suspect 2* given first, and the payoff to *Suspect 1* given second.

Here is how to read the entries in the payoff matrix. If *Suspect 1* confesses and *Suspect 2* also confesses, each will receive 5 years in prison. (This is the cell with entry (−5, −5).) If *Suspect 1* confesses and *Suspect 2* keeps quiet, *Suspect 1* will spend half a year in prison, and *Suspect 2* will spend 7 years in prison. (This is the cell with entry (−7, −0.5).) If *Suspect 1* keeps quiet and *Suspect 2* confesses, then *Suspect 2* will spend half a year in prison, and *Suspect 1* will spend 7 years in prison. (This is the cell with entry (−0.5, −7).) Finally, if both suspects keep quiet, each will spend 1 year in prison. (This is the cell with entry (−1, −1).)

There is another way to look at *Suspect 1*'s options. The payoff matrix is sometimes referred to as the *strategic form* of the game. An alternative is the *extensive form*. This puts one player's options in the form of a decision tree, which is shown in Figure 2.14.

We now wish to explore what the optimal strategy—confess or keep quiet—is for each player, given the options in the payoff matrix and given some choice made by the other player. Let's consider how *Suspect 1* will select her optimal strategy. Remember that the players are being kept in separate rooms and cannot communicate with one another. (Because the game is symmetrical, this is exactly the same way in which *Suspect 2* will select his optimal strategy.)

First, what should *Suspect 1* do if *Suspect 2* confesses? If she keeps quiet when *Suspect 2* confesses, she will spend 7 years in prison. If she confesses when *Suspect 2* confesses, she will spend 5 years. So, if *Suspect 2* confesses, clearly the best thing for *Suspect 1* to do is to confess.

But what if *Suspect 2* adopts the alternative strategy of keeping quiet? What is the best thing for *Suspect 1* to do then? If *Suspect 2* keeps quiet and *Suspect 1* confesses, she will spend only half a year in prison. If she keeps quiet when *Suspect 2* keeps quiet, she will spend 1 year in prison. Again, the best thing for *Suspect 1* to do if the other suspect keeps quiet is to confess.

Thus, *Suspect 1* will always confess. Regardless of what the other player does, confessing will always mean less time in prison for her. In the jargon of game theory this

	Suspect 1	
	Confess	Keep quiet
Suspect 2 Confess	−5, −5	−0.5, −7
Suspect 2 Keep quiet	−7, −0.5	−1, −1

FIGURE 2.13 The strategic form of a game, also known as a payoff matrix.

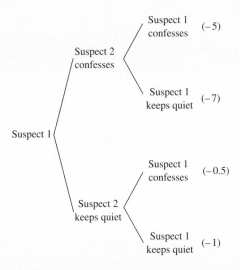

FIGURE 2.14 The extensive form of the prisoner's dilemma.

means that confessing is a *dominant strategy*—the optimal move for a player to make is the same, regardless of what the other player does.

Because the other suspect will go through precisely the same calculations, he will also confess. Confessing is the dominant strategy for each player. The result is that the suspects are *both* going to confess, and, therefore, each will spend 5 years in prison.

The solution to this game, that both suspects confess, is an equilibrium: there is no reason for either player to change his or her strategy. There is a famous concept in game theory that characterizes this equilibrium—a *Nash equilibrium*. In such an equilibrium, no individual player can do any better by changing his or her behavior so long as the other players do not change theirs. (Notice that the competitive equilibrium that we discussed in previous sections is an example of a Nash equilibrium when there are many players in the game.)

The notion of a Nash equilibrium is fundamental in game theory, but it has shortcomings. For instance, there are some games that have no Nash equilibrium. There are some games that have several Nash equilibria. And finally, there is not necessarily a correspondence between the Nash equilibrium and Pareto efficiency, the criterion that economists use to evaluate many equilibria. To see why, return to the prisoner's dilemma above. We have seen that it is a Nash equilibrium for both suspects to confess. But you should note that this is *not* a Pareto-efficient solution to the game. When both suspects confess, they will each spend 5 years in prison. It is possible for *both* players to be better off. That would happen if they would both keep quiet. Thus, cell 4 (where each receives a year in prison) is a Pareto-efficient outcome. Clearly, that solution is impossible because the suspects cannot make binding commitments not to confess.[13]

We may use the prisoner's dilemma to discuss another important fundamental concept of game theory—*repeated games*. Suppose that the prisoner's dilemma were to be

---

[13] Can you think of a workable way in which the suspects might have agreed never to confess before they perpetrated the crime? Put in the language of game theory, can a participant in a game like the prisoner's dilemma make a *credible commitment* not to confess if she and her partner are caught?

played not just once but a number of times by the same players. Would that change our analysis of the game? If the same players play the same game according to the same rules repeatedly, then it is possible that cooperation can arise and that players have an incentive to establish a reputation—in this case, for trustworthiness.

An important thing to know about a repeated game is whether the game will be repeated a *fixed* number of times or an *indefinite* number. To see the difference, suppose that the prisoner's dilemma above is to be repeated exactly ten times. Each player's optimal strategy must now be considered across games, not just for one game at a time. Imagine *Suspect 2* thinking through, before the first game is played, what strategy he ought to follow for each game. He might imagine that he and his partner, if caught after each crime, will learn (or agree) to keep quiet rather than to confess. But then *Suspect 2* thinks forward to the final game, the tenth. Even if the players had learned (or agreed) to keep quiet through Game 9, things will be different in Game 10. Because this is the last time the game is to be played, *Suspect 1* has a strong incentive to confess. If she confesses on the last game and *Suspect 2* sticks to the agreement not to confess, he will spend 7 years in prison to her half year. Knowing that she has this incentive to cheat on an agreement not to confess in the last game, the best strategy for *Suspect 2* is also to confess in the final game. But now Game 9 becomes, in a sense, the final game. And in deciding on the optimal strategy for that game, exactly the same logic applies as it did for Game 10—both players will confess in Game 9, too. *Suspect 1* can work all this out, too, and she will realize that the best thing to do is to confess in Game 8, and so on. In the terminology of game theory, the game *unravels* so that confession takes place by each player every time the game is played, *if it is to be played a fixed number of times*.

Things may be different if the game is to be repeated an indefinite number of times. In those circumstances there may be an inducement to cooperation. Robert Axelrod has shown that in a game like the prisoner's dilemma repeated an indefinite number of times the optimal strategy is *tit-for-tat*—if the other player cooperated on the last play, you cooperate on this play; if she didn't cooperate on the last play, you don't on this play.[14]

These considerations of a fixed *versus* an indefinite number of plays of a game may seem removed from the concerns of the law, but they really are not. Consider, for example, the relations between a creditor and a debtor. When the debtor's affairs are going well, the credit relations between the creditor and the debtor may be analogized to a game played an indefinite number of times. But if the debtor is likely to become insolvent soon, the relations between debtor and creditor become much more like a game to be played a fixed (and, perhaps, few) number of times.

We shall see that these concepts from game theory will play an important role in our understanding of legal rules and institutions.

VIII. THE THEORY OF ASSET PRICING

The area of microeconomic theory that deals with capital and labor markets is beyond the scope of the material in this book. There is, however, one tool from this area that we shall use: the theory of asset pricing.

---

[14] See Robert Axelrod, THE EVOLUTION OF COOPERATION (1984).

Assets are resources that generate a stream of income. For instance, an apartment building can generate a stream of rental payments; a patent can generate a stream of royalty payments; an annuity can generate a fixed amount per year. There is a technique for converting these various streams of future income (or future expenses or, still more generally, net receipts) into a lump sum today. The general question that is being asked is, "How much would you be prepared today to pay for an asset that generated a given future flow of net receipts in the future?"

We can answer that question by computing the *present discounted value* of the future flow of net receipts. Suppose that ownership of a particular asset will generate F_1 in net receipts at the end of the first year; F_2 in net receipts at the end of the second year; F_3 in net receipts at the end of the third year; and F_N at the end of the nth year. The present discounted value of that asset is equal to

$$V = F_1 + \frac{F_2}{(1 + r)} + \frac{F_3}{(1 + r)^3} + \ldots + \frac{F_N}{(1 + r)^N}.$$

This result has many applications to law. For instance, suppose that a court is seeking to compensate someone whose property was destroyed. One method of valuing the loss is to compute the present discounted value of the future flow of net receipts to which the owner was entitled.

IX. GENERAL EQUILIBRIUM AND WELFARE ECONOMICS

The microeconomic theory we have been reviewing to this point has focused on the fundamental concepts of maximization, equilibrium, and efficiency in describing the decisions of consumers and firms. The part of microeconomic theory called *welfare economics* explores how the decisions of many individuals and firms interact to affect the well-being of individuals. Welfare economics is much more philosophical than other topics in microeconomic theory. Here the great policy issues are raised. For example, is there an inherent conflict between efficiency and fairness? To what extent can unregulated markets maximize individual well-being? When and how should the government intervene in the marketplace? Can economics identify a just distribution of goods and services? In this brief introduction, we can only hint at how microeconomic theory approaches these questions. Nonetheless, this material is fundamental to the economic analysis of legal rules.

A. General Equilibrium and Efficiency Theorems

One of the great accomplishments of modern microeconomics is the specification of the conditions under which the independent decisions of utility-maximizing consumers and profit-maximizing firms will lead to the inevitable, spontaneous establishment of equilibrium in all markets simultaneously. Such a condition is known as *general equilibrium*. General equilibrium will be achieved only when competitive forces have led to the equality of marginal benefit and marginal cost in the market for every single commodity and service. As you can well imagine, this condition is unlikely to be realized in the real world. However, there are two practical reasons for knowing what conditions must hold for general equilibrium to obtain. First, while *all* real-world markets may not obey those conditions, many of them will. Second, the specification of the conditions that lead to general equilibrium provides a benchmark for evaluating various markets and making recommendations for public policy.

Modern microeconomics has demonstrated that general equilibrium has characteristics that economists describe as socially optimal—that is, the general equilibrium is both productively and allocatively efficient.

B. Market Failure

General equilibrium is such a desirable outcome that it would be helpful to know the conditions under which it will hold. Stripped of detail, the essential condition is that all markets are perfectly competitive. We can characterize the things that can go wrong to prevent this essential condition from being attained in a market. In this section we shall describe the four sources of *market failure*, as it is called, and describe the public policies that can, in theory, correct those failures.

1. Monopoly and Market Power   The first source of market failure is monopoly in its various forms: monopoly in the output market, collusion among otherwise competitive firms or suppliers of inputs, and monopsony (only one buyer) in the input market. If the industry were competitive, marginal benefit and marginal cost would be equal. But as illustrated in Figure 2.11, the monopolist's profit-maximizing output and price combination occurs at a point where the price exceeds the marginal cost of production. The price is too high and the quantity supplied is too low from the viewpoint of efficiency.

The public policies for correcting the shortcomings of monopoly are to replace monopoly with competition where possible, or to regulate the price charged by the monopolist. The first policy is the rationale for the antitrust laws. But sometimes it is not possible or even desirable to replace a monopoly. Natural monopolies, such as public utilities, are an example; those monopolies are allowed to continue in existence but government regulates their prices. Another example of a monopoly that is encouraged but regulated is the patent system: inventors are allowed a 17-year monopoly as an inducement to invest in the inventive process. (We shall investigate the efficiency of the patent system in Chapter 5.)

2. Externalities   The second source of market failure is the presence of what economists call *externalities*. Exchange inside a market is voluntary and mutually beneficial. Typically, the parties to the exchange capture all the benefits and bear all the costs. But sometimes the benefits of an exchange may spill over onto other parties than those explicitly engaged in the exchange. Moreover, the costs of the exchange may also spill over onto other parties. The first instance is an example of an *external benefit*; the second, an *external cost*. An example of an external benefit is the pollination that a beekeeper provides to his neighbor who runs an apple orchard. An example of an external cost is air or water pollution.

Let's explore the idea of an external cost (frequently called simply an *externality*) to see how it can lead to market failure and what public policies can correct this failing.

Suppose that a factory located upstream from a populous city dumps toxic materials into the river as a by-product of its production process. This action by the factory imposes an unbargained-for cost on the townspeople downstream: they must incur some additional costs to clean up the water or to bring in safe water from elsewhere. In what way has the market failed in this example? The reason the market fails in the presence of external costs is that the generator of the externality does not have to pay for harming others, and so exercises too little self-restraint. He or she acts as if the cost of disposing of waste as zero, when, in fact, there are real costs involved, as the people downstream can testify. In a technical sense, the externality-generator produces too much output and the associated harm because there is a difference between *private* marginal cost and *social* marginal cost.

Private marginal cost, in our example, is the marginal cost of production for the factory. Social marginal cost is the sum of private marginal cost and the additional marginal costs involuntarily imposed on third parties by each unit of production. The difference is shown in Figure 2.15, which depicts the private and the social marginal cost curves. Because the former lies below the latter, social marginal cost is greater than private marginal cost at every level of output. The vertical difference between the two curves equals the amount of the external marginal cost at any level of output. Note that if production is zero, there is no externality, but that as production increases, the amount of external cost per unit of output increases.

The profit-maximizing firm operates along its private marginal cost curve and maximizes profits by choosing that output level for which $P_C = PMC$—namely, q_p. But from society's point of view, this output is too large. Society's resources will be most efficiently used if the firm chooses its output level by equating P_C and SMC at q_S. At that level the firm has taken into account not only its own costs of production but also any costs it imposes on others involuntarily.

What public policies will induce the externality-generator to take external costs into account? That is one of the central questions that this book will seek to answer. The key to achieving the social optimum where there are externalities is to induce private profit-maximizers to restrict their output to the socially optimal, not privately optimal, point. This is done by policies that cause the firm to operate along the social marginal cost curve rather than along the private marginal cost curve. When this is accomplished, the

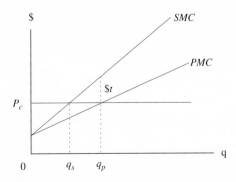

FIGURE 2.15 The difference between private and social marginal cost.

externality is said to have been *internalized* in the sense that the private firm now takes it into consideration.

> **QUESTION 2H:** In Figure 2.15, if the firm is producing q_S output, is there any external cost being generated? If so, why is this output level called a social optimum? Would it not be optimal to have *no* external cost? At what level of output would that occur? Does our earlier discussion that characterized any social optimum as the point at which (social) marginal cost equals (social) marginal benefit provide any guidance? Is the point at which social marginal cost and social marginal benefit are equal consistent with the existence of *some* external cost? Why or why not?

3. Public Goods   The third source of market failure is the presence of a commodity called a *public good*. A public good is a commodity with two very closely related characteristics:

1. *nonrivalrous consumption*: consumption of a public good by one person does not leave less for any other consumer, and
2. *nonexcludability*: the costs of excluding nonpaying beneficiaries who consume the good are so high that no private profit-maximizing firm is willing to supply the good.

Consider national defense. Suppose, for the purposes of illustration, that national defense were provided by competing private companies. For an annual fee a company would sell protection to its customers against loss from foreign invasion by air, land, or sea. Only those customers who purchase some company's services would be protected against foreign invasion. Perhaps these customers could be identified by special garments, and their property denoted by a large white X painted on the roof of their homes.

Who will purchase the services of these private national defense companies? Some will but many will not. Many of the nonpurchasers will reason that if their neighbor will purchase a protection policy from a private national defense company, then they, too, will be protected: it will prove virtually impossible for the private company to protect the property and person of the neighbor without also providing security to the nearby nonpurchaser. Thus the consumption of national defense is nonrivalrous: consumption by one person does not leave less for any other consumer. For that reason, there is a strong inducement for consumers of the privately provided public good to try to be *free riders*: they hope to benefit at no cost to themselves from the payment of others.

The related problem for the private supplier of a public good is the difficulty of excluding nonpaying beneficiaries. The attempt to distinguish those who have from those who have not subscribed to the private defense companies is almost certain to fail: for example, the identifying clothes and property markings can easily be counterfeited.

As a result of the presence of free riders and the high cost of distinguishing nonpaying from paying beneficiaries, it is not likely that the private company will be able to induce many people to purchase defense services. If private profit-maximizing firms are the only providers of national defense, too little of that good will be provided.

How can public policy correct the market failure in the provision of public goods? There are two general correctives. First, the government may undertake to *subsidize* the private provision of the public good, either directly or indirectly through the tax system. An example might be research on basic science. Second, the government may undertake to provide the public good itself and to pay the costs of providing the service through the revenues raised by compulsory taxation. This is, in fact, how national defense is supplied.

4. Severe Informational Asymmetries   The fourth source of market failure is an imbalance of information between parties to an exchange, one so severe that exchange is impeded.

To illustrate, it is often the case that sellers know more about the quality of goods than do buyers. For example, a person who offers his car for sale knows far more about its quirks than does a potential buyer. Similarly, when a bank presents a depository agreement for the signature of a person opening a checking account, the bank knows far more than the customer about the legal consequences of the agreement.

When sellers know more about a product than do buyers, or vice versa, information is said to be distributed asymmetrically in the market. Under some circumstances, these asymmetries can be corrected by the mechanism of voluntary exchange, for example, by the seller's willingness to provide a warranty to guarantee the quality of a product. But severe asymmetries can disrupt markets so much that a social optimum cannot be achieved by voluntary exchange. When that happens, government intervention in the market can ideally correct for the informational asymmetries and induce more nearly optimal exchange. For example, the purchasers of a home are often at a disadvantage *vis-à-vis* the current owners in learning of latent defects, such as the presence of termites or a cracked foundation, in the home. As a result, the market for the sale of homes may not function efficiently; purchasers may be paying too much for homes or may inefficiently refrain from purchases because of a fear of latent defects. Many states have responded by requiring sellers to disclose knowledge of any latent defects to prospective purchasers of houses. If the sellers do not make this disclosure, then they may be responsible for correcting those defects.

C. Potential Pareto Improvements or Kaldor-Hicks Efficiency

Dissatisfied with the Pareto criterion, economists developed the notion of a potential Pareto improvement (sometimes called Kaldor-Hicks efficiency). This is an attempt to surmount the restriction of the Pareto criterion that only those changes are recommended in which at least one person is made better off and no one is made worse off. That criterion requires that gainers explicitly compensate losers in any change. If there is not explicit payment, losers can veto any change. This has clear disadvantages as a guide to public policy.

By contrast, a potential Pareto improvement allows changes in which there are both gainers and losers but requires that the gainers gain more than the losers lose. If this condition is satisfied, the gainers can, in principle, compensate the losers and still have a surplus left for themselves. For a potential Pareto improvement, compensation does not actually have to be made, but it must be possible in principle. In essence, this is the technique of cost-benefit analysis. In cost-benefit analysis, a project is undertaken when its benefits exceed its costs, which implies that the gainers could compensate the losers. There are both theoretical and empirical problems with this standard, but it is indispensable to applied welfare economics.

Consider how these two criteria—the Pareto criterion and the Kaldor-Hicks criterion—would help us to analyze the efficiency and distributive justice of a manufacturing plant's decision to relocate. Suppose that the plant announces that it is going to move from town A to town B. There will be gainers—those in town B who will be employed by the new plant, the retail merchants and home builders in B, the shareholders of the corporation, and so on. But there will also be losers—those in town A who are now unemployed, the retail merchants in A, the customers of the plant who are now located further away from the plant, and so on. If we were to apply the Pareto criterion to this decision, the gainers would have to pay the losers whatever it would take for them to be indifferent between the plant's staying in A and moving to B. If we were to apply the potential Pareto criterion to this decision, the gainers would have to gain more than the losers lose.

X. DECISION-MAKING UNDER UNCERTAINTY: RISK AND INSURANCE

In nearly all of the economic models we have examined so far, we have implicitly assumed that uncertainty did not cloud the decision. This is clearly a simplifying assumption. It is time to expand our basic economic model by explicitly allowing for the presence of uncertainty.

A. Primary and Market Uncertainty

Economists distinguish between two different kinds of uncertainty. The first, called *primary* uncertainty, exists because future events that are crucial to economic decisions taken today are unknown. For example, a farmer's decisions about what to plant and how much of it to plant this spring depend in large part on the future prices of various farm outputs, on the weather during the growing season, on whether there will be an embargo on the export of various commodities, and so on, all of which lie in the future. Clearly, a decision-maker like the farmer has (or could have) *some* information on the various possibilities for these future events, such as the history of weather patterns in the area.

A second form of uncertainty, called *secondary* uncertainty, arises because information about certain future or present events is known to some economic actors but, not to all. (We have already mentioned this condition as an informational asymmetry and have noted that it may be a source of market failure.) This asymmetry may arise because there is uncertainty about what prices are being charged by different retailers, about the quality of various products (*e.g.*, their durability and service record), and about what may and may not be legally done in the future to correct a problem. In what follows here, we concentrate on primary uncertainty.

B. Expected Monetary Value

Suppose that an entrepreneur is considering two possible projects in which to invest. The first, D_1, involves the production of an output whose market is familiar and stable. There is no uncertainty about the outcome of project D_1; the entrepreneur can be confident of earning a profit of $200 if he takes D_1. The second course of action, D_2, involves a novel product whose reception by the consuming public is uncertain. If consumers like the new product, the entrepreneur can earn profits of $400. However, if they do not like it, he stands to lose $50.

How is the entrepreneur supposed to compare these two projects? One possibility is to compare their *expected* monetary values. An *expected value* is the sum of the probabilities of each possible outcome times the value of each of those outcomes. For example, suppose that there are four possible numerical outcomes, labeled O_1 through O_4, to a decision. Suppose also that there are four separate probability estimates, labeled p_1 through p_4, associated with each of the four outcomes. If these are the only possible outcomes, then these probabilities must sum to 1. The expected value (*EV*) of this decision is then:

$$EV = p_1 O_1 + p_2 O_2 + p_3 O_3 + p_4 O_4.$$

If the outcomes are monetary, then the expected value is also monetary. To return to our entrepreneur, he may compute the expected monetary value (*EMV*) of D_1 as the product of the probability of that event (here, because we have assumed the outcome is certain, the probability is 1) and the expected monetary value of the outcome (here, profits of $200):

$$EMV(D_1) = 1\,(200) = 200.$$

The computation of the expected monetary value of decision D_2 is harder. There are two possible outcomes, and in order to perform the calculation the entrepreneur needs to know the probabilities of the two outcomes. Let p denote the probability of the new product's succeeding. Thus, $(1 - p)$ is the probability that it fails. Then, the expected monetary value of D_2 is given by the expression:

$$EMV(D_2) = 400p + (-50)(1 - p)$$

$$= 450p - 50, \text{ for any } p.$$

Thus, if the probability of success for the new product equals 0.3, the expected monetary value of the decision to introduce that new product equals $85.

Where does the decision-maker get information about the probabilities of the various outcomes? Perhaps the seasoned entrepreneur has some intuition about p or perhaps marketing surveys have provided a scientific basis for assessing p. Still another possibility might be that he calculates the level of p that will make the expected monetary value of D_2 equal to that of the certain event, D_1. A strong reason for doing that would be that, although he might not know for sure what p is, it would be valuable to know how high p must be in order for it to give the same expected profits as the safe course of action, D_1. For example, even if there was no way to know p for sure, suppose that one could calculate that in order for the uncertain course of action to have a higher expected value than the safe course of action the probability of success of the new product would have to be 0.95, a near certainty. That would be valuable information.

It is a simple matter to calculate the level of p that equates the expected monetary value of D_1 and D_2. That is the p that solves the following equation:

$$450p - 50 = 200, \text{ or}$$

$$p = 5/9 = 0.556.$$

The implication, of course, is that if the probability of the new product's success is 0.556 or greater, then D_2 has a higher expected monetary value than does D_1, and the entrepreneur will choose D_2. The economic analysis typically assumes that decision-makers can form probabilities one way or another so that expectations can be computed.

C. Maximization of Expected Utility: Attitudes Toward Risk

Do people deal with uncertainty by maximizing expected monetary values? Suppose that the two decisions of the previous section, D_1 and D_2, have the same expected monetary value. Would you be indifferent between the two courses of action? Probably not. D_1 is a sure thing. D_2 is not. Upon reflection, many would hesitate to take D_2 unless the expected monetary value of D_2 was greater than that of D_1. The reason for this hesitation may lie in the fact that many of us are reluctant to gamble, and D_2 certainly is a gamble. We are generally much more comfortable with a sure thing like D_1. Can we formalize our theory of decision-making under uncertainty to take account of this attitude?

The formal explanation for this phenomenon of avoiding gambles was first offered in the 18th century by the Swiss mathematician and cleric Daniel Bernoulli. Bernoulli often noticed that people who make decisions under uncertainty do not attempt to maximize

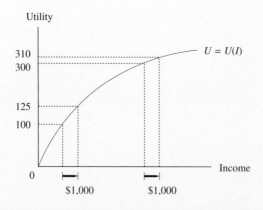

FIGURE 2.16 Risk aversion as a diminishing marginal utility of income.

expected *monetary* values. Rather they *maximize expected utility*. The introduction of utility allows us to introduce the notion of decision-makers' attitudes toward risk.

1. Risk Aversion Assume that utility is a function of, among other things, money income:

$$U = U(I).$$

Bernoulli suggested that a common relationship between money income and utility was that as income increased, utility also increased, but at a decreasing rate. Such a utility function exhibits *diminishing marginal utility of income*. For example, if one's income level is $10,000, an additional $100 in income will add more to one's total utility than will $100 added to that same person's income of $40,000. A utility function like that shown in Figure 2.16 has this property. When this person's income is increased by $1,000 at a low level of income, her utility increases from 100 to 125 units, an increase of 25 units. But when her income is increased by $1,000 at a higher level of income, her utility increases from 300 to 310 units, an increase of only 10 units.

A person whose utility function in money income exhibits diminishing marginal utility is said to be *risk-averse*. Here is a more formal definition of risk aversion:

> A person is said to be risk-averse if she considers the utility of a certain prospect of money income to be higher than the expected utility of an uncertain prospect of equal expected monetary value.

For example, recall the entrepreneur's project:

$$EMV(D_2) = (\$400)(.3) + (-\$50)(1 - .3)$$

$$= \$85$$

A risk-averse decision-maker would rather have the certain $85 than undertake a project whose *EMV* equals $85.

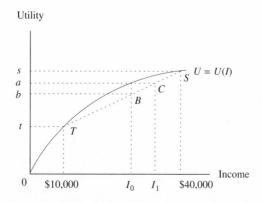

FIGURE 2.17 The formal demonstration of risk aversion.

We can illustrate this definition with the help of Figure 2.17. Suppose that the person whose utility function is shown must choose between two courses of action. The first, A_1, will result in income I_0 with certainty. The expected monetary value of this course of action is $EMV(A_1) = I_0$. The expected utility of this amount of income, $U = U(I_0)$, is read from the utility curve in Figure 2.17 to be the vertical distance $0a$.

The second course of action, A_2, has two possible outcomes, \$10,000 and \$40,000. In order to calculate the expected monetary value of A_2, let the probability of the out-come's being \$10,000 equal p; the probability of an outcome of \$40,000 is then $(1 - p)$. Thus,

$$EMV(A_2) = 10{,}000p + 40{,}000(1 - p).$$

Suppose, for example, that we somehow learned that the \$10,000 outcome was certain. Thus, $p = 1$, and $EMV(A_2) = 10{,}000\,(1) + 40{,}000\,(0) = 10{,}000$. In that case, the utility of a *certain* prospect of 10,000 would be given by the vertical distance $0t$.

At the other extreme, if achieving \$40,000 became a certainty, that is, $p = 0$, then $EMV(A_2) = 10{,}000\,(0) + 40{,}000\,(1) = 40{,}000$. The utility of a *certain* prospect of \$40,000 is then the vertical distance $0s$.

When p takes on values between 0 and 1, the EMV of A_2 and the expected utility of that EMV must be read from the dotted-line segment TS in Figure 2.17. Suppose that we let p be such that $EMV(A_2) = I_0$, the same as $EMV(A_1)$. This occurs at point B on the line segment TS. But notice that the expected *utility* of this *uncertain* prospect of an income of I_0 is the vertical distance $0b$. Clearly $0b$ is less than $0a$. Thus, the utility of a certain prospect of income I_0 is greater than the expected utility of an uncertain prospect of income I_0.

The question arises whether a risk-averse person will ever take a gamble like A_2. The answer is yes, but only if the probability of an uncertain outcome of \$40,000 increases substantially. To be specific, only if the probability of an uncertain outcome places the expected monetary value of A_2 above point C on line segment TS will this

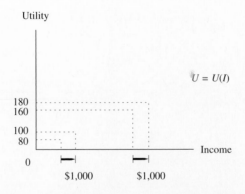

FIGURE 2.18 Risk neutrality as the constant marginal utility of income.

risk-averse person get greater expected utility from the uncertain prospect of income I_1 than from the certain prospect of income I_0.

2. Risk Neutrality Economists presume that most people are averse toward risk, but some people are either neutral toward risk or, like gamblers, rock climbers, and race car drivers, prefer risk. Like aversion, these attitudes toward risk may also be defined in terms of the individual's utility function in money income and the marginal utility of income.

Someone who is risk neutral has a *constant marginal utility of income* and is, therefore, indifferent between a certain prospect of income and an uncertain prospect of equal expected monetary value. A risk-neutral decision-maker is indifferent between receiving \$85 or the project $EMV(D_0)$ = \$85. Figure 2.18 gives the utility function for a risk-neutral person. It is a straight line because the marginal utility of income to a risk-neutral person is constant.

The figure compares the change in utility when the risk-neutral person's income is increased by \$1,000 at two different levels of income. When this person's income is increased by \$1,000 at a low level of income, his utility increases from 80 to 100 units, an increase of 20 units. And when his income is increased by \$1,000 at a high level of income, his utility increases by exactly the same amount, 20 units, from 160 to 180 units. Thus, for the risk-neutral person the marginal utility of income is constant.

Economists and finance specialists very rarely attribute an attitude of risk-neutrality to individuals. However, they quite commonly assume that business organizations are risk-neutral.

3. Risk-Seeking or Risk-Preferring Someone who is risk-seeking or risk-preferring has an increasing marginal utility of income and, therefore, prefers an uncertain prospect of income to a certain prospect of equal expected monetary value. A risk-preferring decision-maker prefers the project $EMV(D_2)$ = \$85 to receiving \$85 for certain. Figure 2.19 gives the utility function of a risk-preferring individual. The figure

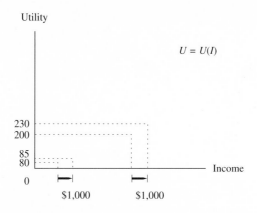

FIGURE 2.19 Risk-preferring as an increasing marginal utility of income.

allows us to compare the change in utility when the risk-preferring person's income is increased by $1,000 at two different levels of income. When this person's income is increased by $1,000 at a low level of income, her utility increases from 80 to 85 units, an increase of 5 units. However, when her income is increased by $1,000 at a high level of income, her utility increases from 200 to 230 units, an increase of 30 units. Thus, for the risk-preferring person the marginal utility of income increases.

QUESTION 2I: Using the utility function of Figure 2.19 and an analysis like that accompanying Figure 2.17, show graphically that for a risk-preferring person the expected utility of A_2 is *greater than* the utility of A_1 when $EMV(A_1) = EMV(A_2)$.

D. The Demand for Insurance

One of the most important behavioral implications of risk aversion is that people will pay money to avoid having to face uncertain outcomes. That is, a risk-averse person would rather have a lower certain income than a higher uncertain income.

There are three ways in which a risk-averse person may convert an uncertain into a certain outcome. First, he may purchase insurance from someone else. Second, he may self-insure. This may involve incurring expenses to minimize the probability of an uncertain event's occurring or to minimize the monetary loss in the event of a particular contingency. An example is the installation of smoke detectors in a home. Another form of self-insurance is the setting aside of a sum of money to cover possible losses. Third, a risk-averse person who is considering the purchase of some risky asset may reduce the price he is willing to pay for that asset.

For the purposes of illustrating the market insurance option, consider Figure 2.20, which depicts the function for a risk-averse person. Suppose that this person faces an uncertain prospect, say, the loss of earnings due to catastrophic illness in the coming year. He is self-employed and is currently not covered by a medical insurance plan. If he does not get ill, he is certain to earn $25,000 over the course of the year. A money

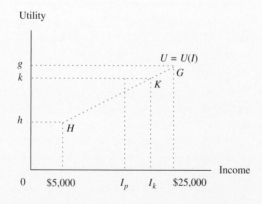

FIGURE 2.20 The demand for insurance by a risk-averse individual.

income of \$25,000 gives him a utility of O*g*, corresponding to the vertical distance from \$25,000 on the income axis to the point *G* on the utility function. If he falls catastrophically ill, this person will be unable to work, and his income will decrease to \$5,000. An income of \$5,000 will give him a utility of O*h*.

To see if he should purchase insurance against catastrophic illness, the individual needs to estimate the probability that he will get ill, compute the expected monetary value of that outcome, and compare that expectation with the cost of an insurance policy (the premium). The probability of catastrophic illness determines a point along the line segment *GH* from which the expected monetary value of the uncertain event can be computed Assume that the probability of illness is given by point *K* on *GH*. The expected monetary value of that uncertain outcome is I_K, and the expected utility is O*k*. Notice that a certain income of I_P would give this person a utility of O*k*, exactly equal to that of the uncertain income I_K. It follows that this risk-averse person would be willing to surrender up to, but slightly less than, (\$25,000 − I_P) of his certain income in exchange for not having to bear the risk of catastrophic illness, and that he would consider himself better off with a lower but certain income of slightly more than I_P than with an uncertain income of I_K.

This is precisely what an insurance contract will provide the risk-averse person: in exchange for giving up a certain amount of income (the insurance premium), the insurance company will bear the risk of the uncertain event. The risk-averse person considers himself better off with the lower certain income than facing the uncertain higher income.

E. The Supply of Insurance

The material of the previous section concerns the *demand* for insurance by risk-averse individuals. Let us now turn to a brief consideration of the supply of insurance by profit-maximizing insurance companies. Insurance companies are presumed to be profit-maximizing firms. They offer insurance contracts not because they prefer gambles to certainties but because of a mathematical theorem known as the *law of large numbers*. This law holds that unpredictable events for individuals become predictable among large groups of individuals. For example, none of us knows whether our house will burn down next year. But the occurrence of fire in a city, state or nation is regular enough so that an insurance company can easily determine the objective probabilities. By insuring a large number of people, an insurance company can predict the total amount of claims.

1. Moral Hazard   Any insurer faces two well-known problems called *moral hazard* and *adverse selection*. Moral hazard arises when the behavior of the insuree changes after the purchase of insurance so that the probability of loss or the size of the loss increases. An extreme example is the insured's incentive to burn his home when he has been allowed to insure it for more than its market value. A more realistic example comes from loss due to theft. Suppose that you have just purchased a new stereo tape deck for your car but that you do not have insurance to cover your loss from theft. Under these circumstances you are likely to lock your car whenever you leave it, to park it in well-lighted places at night, to patronize only well-patrolled parking garages, and so on.

Now suppose that you purchase an insurance policy. With the policy in force you now may be less assiduous about locking your car or parking in well-lighted places. In short, the very fact that your loss is insured may cause you to act so as to increase the probability of a loss.

Insurance companies attempt to set their premiums so that, roughly, the premium modestly exceeds the expected monetary value of the loss. Therefore, a premium that has been set without regard for the increased probability of loss due to moral hazard will be too low and thus threaten the continued profitability of the firm. Every insurer is aware of this problem and has developed methods to minimize it. Among the most common are *coinsurance* and *deductibles*. Under coinsurance the insuree shoulders a fixed percentage of his loss; under a deductible plan, the insuree shoulders a fixed dollar amount of the loss, with the insurance company paying for all losses above that amount. In addition, some insurance companies offer reductions in premiums for certain easily established acts that reduce claims. For example, life insurance premiums are less for non-smokers; auto insurance premiums are less for non-drinkers; and fire insurance rates are lower for those who install smoke detectors.

2. Adverse Selection   The other major problem faced by insurance companies is called *adverse selection*. This arises because of the high cost to insurers of accurately distinguishing between high- and low-risk insurees. Although the law of large numbers helps the company in assessing probabilities, what it calculates from the large sample are average probabilities. The insurance premium must be set using this average probability of a particular loss. For example, insurance companies have determined that unmarried males between the ages of 16 and, say, 25, have a much higher likelihood of being in an automobile accident than do other identifiable groups of drivers. As a result, the insurance premium charged to members of this group is higher than that charged to other groups whose likelihood of accident is much lower.

But even though unmarried males between the ages of 16 and 25 are, on average, much more likely to be involved in an accident, there are some young men within that group who are even more reckless than average and some who are much less reckless than the group's average. If it is difficult for the insurer to distinguish these groups from the larger group of unmarried males aged 16 to 25, then the premium that is set equal to the average likelihood of harm within the group will seem like a bargain to those who know they are reckless and too high to those who know that they are safer than their peers.

Let us assume, as seems reasonable, that in many cases the individuals know better than the insurance company what their true risks are. For example, the insured alone may know that he drinks heavily and smokes in bed or that he is intending to murder his spouse, in whose insurance policy he has just been named principal beneficiary. If so, then this asymmetrical information may induce only high-risk people to purchase insurance and low risk people to purchase none.

The same devices that insurance companies employ to minimize risks of moral hazards also may serve to minimize the adverse selection problem. Coinsurance and deductible provisions are much less attractive to high-risk than to low-risk insurees so that an insuree's willingness to accept those provisions may indicate to the insurance company to which risk class the applicant belongs. Exclusion of benefits for loss arising from pre-existing conditions is another method of trying to distinguish high- and low-risk people. The insurer can also attempt, over a longer time horizon, to reduce the adverse selection bias by developing better methods of discriminating among the insured, such as medical and psychological testing, so as to place insurees in more accurate risk classes.

REVIEW QUESTIONS

2.1. Define the role of the mathematical concepts of maximization and equilibrium in microeconomic theory.

2.2. Define and distinguish between productive efficiency and allocative efficiency.

2.3. What are consumers assumed to maximize? What are some constraints under which this maximization takes place? Describe the individual consumer's constrained maximum. Can you characterize this constrained maximum as a point where marginal cost and marginal benefit are equal?

2.4. A married couple with children is considering divorce. They are negotiating about two elements of the divorce: the level of child support that will be paid to the partner who keeps the children, and the amount of time that the children will spend with each partner. Whoever has the children would prefer more child support from the other partner and more time with the children. Furthermore, the partner who keeps the children believes that as the amount of child support increases, the value of more time with the children declines relative to the value of child support.

a. Draw a typical indifference curve for the partner who keeps the children with the level of child support on the horizontal axis and the amount of time that the children spend with this partner on the vertical axis. Is this indifference curve convex to the origin? Why or why not?

b. Suppose that the partner who keeps the children has this utility function: $u = cv$, where $c =$ the weekly level of child support and $v =$ the number of days per week that the children spend with this partner. Suppose that initially the weekly support level is $100, and the number of days per week spent with this partner is 4. What is the utility to this partner from that arrangement? If the other partner wishes to reduce the weekly support to $80, how many more days with the children must the child-keeping partner have in order to maintain utility at the previous level?

2.5. Define price elasticity of demand and explain what ranges of value it may take.

2.6. Use the notion of opportunity cost to explain why "There's no such thing as a free lunch."

2.7. *True* or *False*. The cost of a week of vacation is simply the money cost of the plane, food, and so forth. (Explain your answer.)

2.8. What are firms assumed to maximize? Under what constraints do firms perform this maximization? Describe how the individual firm determines the output level that achieves that maximum. Can you characterize the firm's constrained maximum as one for which marginal cost equals marginal benefit?

2.9. Characterize these different market structures in which a firm may operate: perfect competition, monopoly, oligopoly, and imperfect competition. Compare the industry output and price in a perfectly competitive industry with the output and price of a monopolist.

2.10. What conditions must hold for a monopoly to exist?

2.11. Suppose that the local government determines that the price of food is too high and imposes a ceiling on the market price of food that is below the equilibrium price in that locality. Predict some of the consequences of this ceiling.

2.12. The minimum wage is typically set above the market-clearing wage in the market for labor. Using a graph with an upward-sloping supply of labor, a downward-sloping demand for labor, with the quantity of labor measured on the horizontal axis and the wage rate measured on the vertical axis, show the effect on the labor market of a minimum wage set above the equilibrium wage rate.

2.13. *True* or *False*: In Japan, workers cannot be fired once they have been hired; therefore, in Japan a minimum wage law (where the minimum would be set above the wage that would cause the market for labor to clear) would not cause unemployment.

2.14. In the last decade, no-fault divorce laws have become the norm. Ignoring for the sake of this problem all the other factors that influence the marriage decision and that have changed during the same time period, what does the move to no-fault divorce do to the implicit (legal) price of divorce? What would be your prediction about the effect of this change in the implicit price of divorce on the quality and quantity of marriages and divorces? If in the next decade, the states were to repudiate the experiment in no-fault divorce and return to the old regime, would you predict a change in the quality and quantity of marriages and divorces?

2.15. The Truth-in-Lending Act (15 U.S.C. §§1601–1604 (1982)) requires the uniform disclosure of the interest rate to borrowers in a readily intelligible form. Assume that before the Act, there was uncertainty among borrowers about the true level of the interest rate, but that after the Act, that uncertainty is reduced. What effect on the amount of borrowing would you predict from passage of the Act? Would there be disproportionate effects on the poor and the rich? Why? Does the Act increase the marginal cost of lenders? Does it reduce the profits of lenders?

2.16. What is general equilibrium and under what conditions will it be achieved? What are the welfare consequences of general equilibrium?

2.17. What are the four sources of market failure? Explain how each of them causes individual profit- and utility-maximizers to make decisions that may be privately optimal but are socially suboptimal. What general policies might correct each of the instances of market failure?

2.18. Which of the following are private goods and might, therefore, be provided in socially optimal amounts by private profit-maximizers? Which are public goods and should, therefore, be provided by the public sector or by the private sector with public subsidies?

a. A swimming pool large enough to accommodate hundreds of people.

b. A fireworks display.

c. A heart transplant.

d. Vaccination against a highly contagious disease.

e. A wilderness area.

f. Vocational education.

g. On-the-job training.

h. Secondary education.

2.19. What is meant by Pareto efficiency or Pareto optimality? What is the importance of the initial distribution of resources in determining what the distribution of resources will be after all Pareto improvements have been made?

2.20. A valuable resource in which we typically forbid voluntary exchange is votes. This may be inefficient in that, as we have seen, given any initial endowment of resources, voluntary exchange *always* makes both parties better off (absent any clear sources of market failure). Show that it would be a *Pareto improvement* (*i.e.*, that at least some people would be better off and no one would be worse off) if we were to allow a legal market for votes. Are there any clear sources of market failure in the market for votes? If so, what regulatory correctives would you apply to that market? Is it bothersome that there is a wide variance in income and wealth among the participants in this market, and if so, why is that variance more troubling in this market than in others, and what would you do about it in the market for votes?

2.21. Distinguish between the Pareto criterion for evaluating a social change in which there are gainers and losers and the Kaldor-Hicks (or potential Pareto) criterion.

2.22. What is a *dominant strategy* in a game? Where both players in a two-person game have a dominant strategy, is there an equilibrium solution for the game? What is a *Nash equilibrium*? Is a dominant-strategy equilibrium a Nash equilibrium? What are the possible shortcomings of a Nash equilibrium in a game?

SUGGESTED READINGS

We have divided the books below into elementary, intermediate, and advanced references on microeconomic theory.

Introductory

Baxter, William A., PEOPLE OR PENGUINS: THE CASE FOR OPTIMAL POLLUTION (1974).

Levi, Maurice, THINKING ECONOMICALLY (1985).

Miller, Roger L., and Douglass C. North, THE ECONOMICS OF PUBLIC POLICY ISSUES (4th ed. 1984).

Thomas, Robert Paul, ECONOMICS: PRINCIPLES AND APPLICATIONS (1991).

Intermediate

Frank, Robert, MICROECONOMICS AND BEHAVIOR (1990).

Katz, Michael, and Sherwin Rosen, MICROECONOMICS (1990).

Pindyk, Robert, and Daniel Rubinfeld, MICROECONOMICS (2d ed. 1991).

Varian, Hal, INTERMEDIATE MICROECONOMICS: A MODERN APPROACH (3d ed. 1992).

Advanced

Hirshleifer, Jack, PRICE THEORY AND APPLICATIONS (3d ed. 1984).

Kreps, David, A COURSE IN MICROECONOMIC THEORY (1990).

General Reference

Eatwell, John, Murray Milgate, and Peter Newman, eds., THE NEW PALGRAVE: A DICTIONARY OF ECONOMICS, 4 vols. (1991).

3

AN INTRODUCTION TO LAW AND LEGAL INSTITUTIONS

"You are old," said the youth, "and your jaws are too weak
For anything tougher than suet.
Yet you finished the goose, with the bones and the beak.
Pray, how do you manage to do it?"
"In my youth," said his father, "I took to the law,
And argued each case with my wife.
And the muscular strength, which it gave to my jaw,
Has lasted the rest of my life."

—

From "Father William" in Lewis Carroll, ALICE'S ADVENTURES IN
WONDERLAND

"The life of the law has not been logic: it has been experience. The felt
necessities of the time, the prevalent moral and political theories, institutions
of public policy, avowed or unconscious, even the prejudices which judges
share with their fellow-men, have had a good deal more to do than the
syllogism in determining the rules by which men should be governed."

—

Oliver Wendell Holmes, THE COMMON LAW 1 (1881)

An economist who picks up a law journal will understand much more of it than a lawyer who picks up an economics journal. For this reason, it is not hard to convince a lawyer that he does not know economics. (Convincing him that he *should* learn economics is harder!) On the other hand, economists are sometimes hard to convince that any aspect of social life is not, at its root, really economics. With respect to the law, economists sometimes wonder what lawyers really study: Is the law a branch of philosophy? Is it a list of famous cases? Is it a collection of rules? Perhaps economists imagine that knowledge must have a mathematical form and that is why they are unappreciative of lawyers.

In any case, economists cannot contribute significantly to law without studying it. This chapter, therefore, provides an introduction to the law for nonlawyers. We shall explain, first, differences and similarities between the two great legal traditions that spread from Europe to much of the world; second, the structure of the United States' federal and state court systems; third, how a legal dispute gets raised and resolved in systems like that of the United States; and finally, how the legal rules made by judges evolve.

I. THE CIVIL LAW AND THE COMMON LAW TRADITIONS

Legislatures make laws by enacting bills, which judges must interpret and apply. If legislation is deliberately vague or inadvertently ambiguous, judges can choose among several different interpretations. Sometimes the choice of an interpretation overshadows the enactment of the bill, in which case the judge makes the law more than the legislature. Judges make law by interpreting legislation in all legal systems with independent courts.

Judges make law in other ways as well. In medieval Europe, the king in most countries could issue pronouncements that were law, and the king's courts possessed similar powers. However, the king's courts were not free to pronounce as law any rule that they wished. According to one tradition in legal theory, the courts of the English king were to examine community life and "find" law as it already existed. The courts of the English king were to select among social norms and enforce some of them. These enforceable social norms were supposedly the "laws of nature," which reason and necessity prescribed.

The finding of a rule of law by a court of the English king created a *precedent* that future courts were expected to follow. Precedent was followed flexibly, not slavishly, so the law changed gradually. Over many years, the king's courts "found" many important laws, especially in the areas of crimes, property, contracts, and accidents ("torts"). These findings are called "the common law" because they are allegedly rooted in the common practices of people. Common law is still applied in the English-language countries, except where superseded by legislation.

The history is different in France. When France revolted at the end of the eighteenth century, the revolutionaries thought that the judges were as corrupt and worthless as the king, so they killed the king and extinguished his laws, thus abolishing the common law of France. A comprehensive set of statutes was required to fill the void, so people would know what counts as property, how a valid contract is formed, and who is to bear the cost of accidents. Napoleon supplied them by commissioning legal scholars to draft the rules called the *Code Napoleon*, which was promulgated in 1804. The scholars who drafted it took as their model the *Corpus Juris Civilis* ("The Body of the Civil Law"), which was compiled and edited in AD 528–534 at the behest of the Roman Emperor Justinian. Thus, the French revolutionaries looked to ancient sources and pure reason for law, rather than to the more immediate heritage derived from medieval times.

Napoleon's armies spread the *Code Napoleon* through much of Europe, where it remained long after his troops withdrew. Similarly, the armies of Europe spread its law throughout the world, and this influence persisted long after the colonial empires collapsed. The civil law tradition predominates in most of Western Europe, Central and South America, the parts of Asia colonized by European countries other than Britain, and even in pockets of the common law world such as Louisiana, Quebec, and Puerto Rico. The common law tradition, which originated in England, prevails not only in Great Britain, but also in Ireland, the United States, Canada, Australia, New Zealand, and the parts of Africa and Asia that Britain colonized, including India.

Besides these two great traditions, the unique history of each country puts its own stamp on the law. For example, Japan, which was never colonized, voluntarily adopted a code that draws heavily on the German civil code while yet remaining distinctively Japanese. In much of the Middle East, Islamic law blended with, or displaced, the law of the European colonialists. In eastern Europe, communism bent the civil law tradition to its own purposes, and now the post-communist regimes are trying to straighten it.

The common law and civil law traditions differ significantly with respect to how judge-made law is justified. Common law judges traditionally justify their findings of law by reference to precedent and social norms, or by broad requirements of rationality presupposed by public policy. Civil law judges traditionally justify their interpretation of a code directly by reference to its meaning, which scholars tease out in lengthy commentaries. The difference in the pattern of justification affects the training of lawyers. The common law method is taught by reading cases and arguing directly from them, whereas the civil law method is taught by reading the code and arguing from commentaries on it.

All such generalizations about the difference between the two traditions, however, seem simplistic relative to the subtlety and complexity of reality. For example, although the United States is ostensibly a common law country, the American states have tried to obtain greater uniformity in commercial law by enacting the *Uniform Commercial Code*. Deciding disputes that fall under the *Uniform Commercial Code* in America has many similarities to deciding disputes that fall under the French civil code. Additionally, the American Law Institute, an organization founded in the 1920s, meets periodically to restate the law as it is emerging in the various states. These restatements, such as the *Restatement (Second) of Contract Law* and the *Restatement (Second) of Tort Law*, serve a similar function to the codes that are thought to be characteristic of the civil law countries. Comparative law scholars vigorously debate whether the differences between civil and common law are more apparent than real.

Besides the difference in history between common and civil law, the laws are applied differently in the two traditions. In the common law countries, the arguments for the two sides in a dispute are made exclusively by their lawyers, and the judge is not supposed to direct a line of questioning or develop an argument. In this *adversarial process*, the judge acts more or less as a neutral referee who makes the lawyers follow the rules of procedure and evidence. The principle underlying the adversarial system is that the truth will emerge from a vigorous debate by the two sides.

In contrast, the civil law judge takes an active role in directing questions and developing arguments. In this *inquisitorial process*, the judge is supposed to ferret out the truth. The lawyers often have to respond to the judge, rather than develop the case themselves. The principle underlying the inquisitorial system is that the court has a direct interest in finding the truth regarding private disputes or crimes.

Another difference between the two systems concerns the use of juries. In the common law system, the judge was originally supposed to decide questions of law, whereas the jury was supposed to decide questions of fact. In America, either party to a dispute usually has the right to a jury trial, although both parties sometimes waive this right and allow the judge to decide matters of fact, as well as matters of law. In England the jury has since 1966 been abolished in almost all civil trials,[1] but it is often used in criminal trials. (Notice the different use of "civil" in the preceding sentence.[2]) In France, however, the jury has been abolished for all trials except the most serious crimes, like murder. In general, the abolition of juries is more advanced in continental Europe than in some common law countries.

In every legal system, laws form a hierarchy. The constitution takes precedence over statutes, and statutes usually take precedence over rules issued by the executive or government agencies. In countries with common law, statutes take precedence over it. "Taking precedence" means that the higher law prevails in the event of conflict. The courts, as the main interpreters of law, must decide whether laws conflict. We have explained that judges make law indirectly by interpreting statutes or codes. Another way that judges make law is by finding a conflict between laws and setting aside the lower-level law. Finally, judges make common law directly in those countries that maintain the common law system.

Constitutions are necessarily general and vague, so their interpretation is especially problematic. The power to review legislation for its constitutionality gives courts the power, in principle, to set aside laws enacted by the legislature. This power is potentially dangerous because it brings judges into conflict with the elected representatives of the nation. The extent to which this power is exercised varies greatly from one country to another. In the United States, the federal courts have few limits on their ability to strike down laws which, in the courts' opinion, contradict the constitution. Some of the most profound laws in America have been made by courts interpreting the constitution, as in *Brown v. Board of Education* in 1954, which eventually ended laws mandating racial segregation of schools. In other countries, such as Great Britain, the courts do not have the power to review statutes for their constitutionality, and the courts never strike down legislation as unconstitutional. The scope of constitutional review, which is fundamental to the power and prestige of courts, has no necessary connection with whether the country's legal tradition is common or civil law.

---

[1] Defamation is the exception.

[2] "Civil law" has two meanings. It may refer to the system of law in most of continental Europe that rejects common law. In addition, "civil law" refers to laws controlling disagreements between two private parties, which might arise, say, from a broken contract or an automobile accident. In this latter sense, the opposite of "civil law" is criminal law, in which actions are initiated by the state's prosecutor against someone accused of violating a criminal statute, such as forgery or murder. Thus the common law of, say, contracts can be described as "civil law," meaning "private law" or "not criminal law."

II. THE INSTITUTIONS OF THE FEDERAL AND THE STATE COURT SYSTEMS IN THE UNITED STATES

In the United States, whether at the state or the federal level, the court systems are organized in three tiers. These tiers constitute a hierarchical pyramid, with a very broad base of many courts, an intermediate level with a smaller number of courts, and a single court at the top of the pyramid. At the lowest level are the *trial courts of general jurisdiction*. These are the "entry level" courts where a wide array of civil and criminal disputes are first heard. The trial courts of general jurisdiction are "courts of record"; that is, the proceedings are written down and saved by the government. In the state systems these courts are usually organized along county lines. For example, in the State of Illinois there are 102 counties, and each has a circuit court that serves as the trial court of general jurisdiction within the county. These trial courts have different names in different states: in California they are called superior courts; in New York State, supreme courts. The nearly universal practice is for each civil and criminal case to be tried to a single judge and possibly to a jury.

In the federal system the entire country is divided into 93 judicial districts, each of which contains a federal district court, which is the trial court of general jurisdiction for the federal judiciary. Every state in the Union has at least one federal district court, and about half have *only* one. The District of Columbia has its own district court. The larger states, where larger numbers of disputes involving federal questions arise, have up to four district courts, usually organized along geographical divisions of the state. New York has four districts: the Southern, the Northern, the Eastern, and the Western. Illinois has three federal districts: the Northern, the Eastern, and the Southern. The number of federal judicial districts has remained fixed at 93 for a long time. As the volume of federal litigation has grown, Congress has responded not by creating more districts but by appointing more judges within each district. One of the busiest districts is the Southern District of New York, which contains most of New York City, and there are 25 judges on that district's bench. Another busy district, the Northern District of Illinois, has 12. Wisconsin's Eastern District (Milwaukee) has three, while the Western District (Madison) has only one. The usual procedure in the federal districts is for a single judge to hear each case, but a three-judge panel sometimes hears a case.

In addition, the federal court system includes several specialized tribunals. For example, there are special tax courts, and the federal administrative agencies, such as the Interstate Commerce Commission and the Federal Communications Commission, have administrative law judges who hear arguments about matters before those agencies.

Above the trial courts in the state and federal systems are *appellate courts* or *courts of appeal*. In most state court systems, there is only one court of appeal. But about one-third of the states and all of the federal districts have *intermediate appellate courts* that stand between the trial courts of general jurisdiction and the highest court or *court of last resort*. For example, in Illinois there are twenty intermediate appellate courts. Where these courts exist, parties from the trial court may appeal that lower decision "as of right." That means that, so long as they are willing to pay the costs involved, parties may always seek appellate review of a lower court's judgment. Appeal is also a right in the federal system, at least from the district courts to the intermediate courts of appeal.

While there may be a right for either party to appeal the judgment of the trial courts of general jurisdiction, matters may be different if either party wishes to appeal the judgment of an intermediate appellate court. In both the state and the federal judiciary, the highest appellate court typically has a *discretionary* right to review. This means that the Supreme Court of Illinois, the Supreme Court of the United States, and all other courts of last resort may select which cases they will review, within certain limits. Some cases—for example, disputes between two states—come to the United States Supreme Court directly and without the discretion of the justices. And in many states the highest court is obligated to review death sentences. Thus the United States Supreme Court and the highest courts in the states control most but not all of their docket.

An intermediate court of appeal in the federal judiciary is called the "Court of Appeals for the ___ Circuit." There are twelve of these circuits, as Figure 3.1 indicates. Eleven of these courts of appeal are numbered; for example, the First Circuit is in New England; the Seventh Circuit covers Indiana, Illinois, and Wisconsin; and the Ninth Circuit covers the West Coast, some of the mountain states, and Alaska and Hawaii. The District of Columbia constitutes its own circuit and also has its own district court. All the other circuits include several states. An unsuccessful litigant from the federal district court can take an appeal, as a matter of right, to the court of appeals. Those courts usually sit in a panel of three judges. Sometimes, for a particularly significant case, all of the circuit judges will sit together to decide the case. In that case the court is said to be sitting *en banc* or "in bank." Where more than one judge hears a case, the matter is decided by majority vote.

The Supreme Court of the United States is the highest court in the federal judiciary. That court has nine members, consisting of the Chief Justice of the United States and eight associate justices. All of the justices, rather than a panel, decide each case. The Court begins its work on the first Monday in October and concludes its term some time in June of the following year. The workload of the Supreme Court has increased signif-

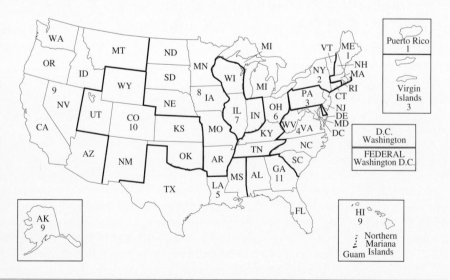

FIGURE 3.1 United States Courts of Appeal and United States District Courts

icantly over the last quarter of a century. Typically, the justices decide less than 10% of the cases submitted to them for review. There is lively dispute about whether this figure is too large or too small. In the recent past some commentators have urged Congress to establish a national court of appeals between the courts of appeals and the Supreme Court. The argument is that this National Court would handle the more routine appeals arising from the twelve circuits (*e.g.*, those in which there is a split among the circuits, which means that some circuits say the law is one way and other circuits say the opposite.) Proponents say this would free up the Supreme Court to devote more of its energies to truly important cases.

Finally, there are rules that specify whether a dispute should be heard in the state or the federal court system. This is often a matter of great strategic significance in an attorney's handling of a case. The rules for resolving who should hear a case are complex and themselves constitute a special course in law school called "Conflict of Laws." The general rules for deciding jurisdiction are relatively straightforward. State courts have jurisdiction in disputes involving state statutes or in civil actions between residents of that state or in cases arising under federal law when Congress has not given exclusive jurisdiction to the federal courts.

The jurisdiction of the federal courts is defined by Congress, through the powers assigned in the Constitution. That jurisdiction is limited to three principal areas:

1. Federal questions, that is, those matters arising under the United States Constitution or federal laws or treaties.[3]

2. Cases to which the United States is a party. Typically, these are criminal cases under federal statute law.

3. Diversity cases—any civil dispute, involving more than $50,000, between citizens of different states. In the late 18th century, Congress allowed these disputes to be removed from state to federal courts because it felt that state loyalties were so strong that the citizen of another state might lose in a state court, regardless of the merits of his or her case, simply because he or she was a "foreigner."[4]

In the event that a federal district court hears a diversity dispute *not* involving a federal question, the Court will generally apply the law of the state in which it sits. Today diversity of citizenship is no longer as compelling a reason for the federal courts to assume jurisdiction as it was 200 years ago. Indeed, former Chief Justice Burger has urged Congress to ease the caseload of the federal judiciary by entirely removing the diversity cases from federal jurisdiction.[5]

---

[3] There used to be a minimum dollar amount in controversy ($10,000), even in a federal question, before parties were allowed access to the federal courts. That minimum no longer applies.

[4] Congress has varied the minimum amount in controversy in diversity cases in order to alter the caseload in the federal judiciary. Clearly, the greater the minimum amount, the fewer the number of diversity cases that will be eligible for resolution by the federal courts.

[5] But there is still an argument for maintaining federal jurisdiction in diversity cases where the benefits of a decision accrue to the people of one state and the costs fall on the people of another state.

As to the selection and tenure of judges, there are two broad practices. For the federal bench the rule is appointment by the President with the advice and consent of the Senate for life tenure. For state judges in a majority of the states the rule is election to the bench and limited tenure. For the remainder of the states, the state judiciary is nominated by the executive and approved by the legislature for varying, but fixed, terms.

III. THE NATURE OF A LEGAL DISPUTE

In this section we shall consider how a legal dispute develops between private persons.

A legal dispute arises when someone claims to have been harmed at the hands of another. It is possible that the victim and the injurer can resolve their dispute themselves, but sometimes they cannot. The person who feels injured may believe that he has a *cause of action*, that is, a valid legal claim against another person or organization. To assert that action, he files a *complaint* and is, therefore, referred to as the *plaintiff*. The complaint must state what has happened, why the plaintiff feels that he has been injured, what area of law is involved, what statute or other law is relevant, what relief he wishes the court to give him, and other matters of that sort. The service of a lawyer is required to draft the complaint.

The person who is alleged to have injured the victim or plaintiff is called the *defendant* and must *answer* the complaint. The answer does not go into detail about the matters at hand; rather, it is a short statement of what the defendant intends to argue in detail if the matter goes to trial. Thus, the answer may say that the facts as alleged are true but that even so, the defendant is not legally responsible for the plaintiff's misfortune. Figuratively, this form of answer says, "So what?" Or the answer may say that the facts as alleged in the complaint are incorrect and that when the true facts are known, the defendant will be seen to be innocent of any wrongdoing.

The dispute may well stop at this point. A judge must make a determination, based on the complaint and the answer, whether there is sufficient reason to proceed to trial. The judge may determine that the plaintiff has failed to state a valid cause of action or that the defendant has made a complete and convincing answer to the complaint. If so, she might dismiss the complaint or enter *summary judgmen*t for the defendant. Usually, she will allow the parties to proceed to trial. Parties may appeal from a summary judgment or a dismissal.

If the dispute proceeds to trial, a jury may be empaneled to determine the facts, or else the case will be tried to a judge without a jury. Evidence and testimony will be developed by each side, and then the jury or judge will retire to determine who wins. The standard that the jury or judge will use to make this determination is by a *preponderance-of-the-evidence*. That means, simply, that if the plaintiff's arguments are more believable than the defendant's, then the plaintiff wins; if the defendant's are more believable, the defendant wins. Some people say that the preponderance-of-the-evidence standard means that if the plaintiff's story is 51% believable, she wins. Notice that this standard, which is the routine standard in cases involving private parties as litigants, is different from the one that is used in criminal proceedings. There the prosecution must convince the jury that the defendant is guilty *beyond a reasonable doubt*, a much more exacting standard than is preponderance-of-the-evidence. The courts can and have established other standards for prevailing in court. For example, *clear and convincing* evidence is an easier standard to meet than beyond a reasonable doubt.

The jury returns with a *verdict*, which says, simply, which party wins. But the verdict is not the end of the matter. The judge must *enter judgment on the verdict*. It is the *judgment*, not the verdict, that is the controlling action of the court. Most of the time the judge issues a judgment that follows exactly the jury verdict. But in a few rare cases the judge decides that the jury got the matter entirely wrong and enters a *judgment non obstante verdicto* or j.n.o.v. (judgment notwithstanding the verdict), holding the exact opposite of what the jury decided.

Either party, winner or loser, may appeal the court's holding. The winner may appeal because he feels that he has not received everything to which he is entitled; the loser may appeal for the obvious reason that he thinks that he ought to have won. Interestingly, the ground for the appeal must be that the court below made a mistake about the relevant *law*, including the relevant general principle that was applied and the procedures that were used in court, but not about the *facts*. For instance, the appellant (the party filing the appeal) may allege that the judge gave the jury improper instructions about what the relevant law was or about what facts they could and could not consider or that the judge improperly excluded some evidence or testimony from the jury's consideration.

At the appellate level there will be no new evidence or facts introduced. The appellate court takes the facts as developed in the trial court as given. The only people to appear before the appellate panel will be the attorneys for the appellant and appellee. The attorneys will submit written briefs to the appellate panel and then appear before the panel for oral argument, during which they may receive very close questioning on the matters at hand. There may be additional briefs submitted by parties who are called *amici curiae* (friends of the court); these parties are not directly involved in the legal dispute but feel that the legal issue involved touches their interests sufficiently that they would like the court to consider their arguments in addition to those of the appellant and appellee.

The appellate panel retires to consider the matter and at some later time issues its opinion. The judges may be in unanimous agreement and issue only one opinion. However, there may be a split in the panel, and that split may result in multiple opinions: a majority and a minority or dissenting opinions.

IV. HOW LEGAL RULES EVOLVE

We consider a sequence of cases in order to apply the preceding ideas and show how law evolves. The three cases come from England and concern *tort law*, which covers accidents.

Butterfield v. Forrester
11 East 60 (K.B., 1809)[6]

This was an action on the case for obstructing a highway, by means of which obstruction the plaintiff [Butterfield], who was riding along the road, was thrown down with his horse, and injured, etc. At the trial before BAYLEY, J.[7] at Derby, it

---

[6] Our selection and discussion of these cases owes a great debt to the stimulating lectures given by Professor Bob Summers to the Fifth Legal Institute for Economists.

[7] "J." means judge, and by tradition opinions are headed by the last name of the justice who wrote the majority opinion, followed by "J." or, as below, "C.J." for chief judge or chief justice.

appeared that the defendant [Forrester], for the purpose of making some repairs to his house, which was close by the roadside at one end of the town, had put up a pole across part of the road, a free passage being left by another branch or street in the same direction. That the plaintiff left a public house [a tavern] not far distant from the place in question at 8 o'clock in the evening in August, when they were just beginning to light candles, but while there was light enough left to discern the obstruction at one hundred yards distance; and the witness who proved this, said that if the plaintiff had not been riding very hard, he might have observed and avoided it; the plaintiff, however, who was riding violently, did not observe it, but rode against it, and fell with his horse and was much hurt in consequence of the accident; and there was no evidence of his being intoxicated at the time. On this evidence, BAYLEY, J., directed the jury, that if a person riding with reasonable and ordinary care could have seen and avoided the obstruction; and if they were satisfied that the plaintiff was riding along the street extremely hard, and without ordinary care, they should find a verdict for the defendant, which they accordingly did.

QUESTION 3.1:

    a. Who is the plaintiff? What is he asking the court to do?

    b. Is there a statute involved in this dispute?

    c. Who won?

    d. Was the jury asked to determine fact or law? How was the law stated?

When this case was tried, English law accepted the settled principle that a defendant whose negligence caused the plaintiff's injury would be held liable. Consequently, the judge instructed the jury that the defendant should be held liable if he could have avoided the accident by taking "reasonable" care. This case presented a novel issue: suppose that the defendant was negligent, *but* further suppose that the *victim* was also negligent. Should the defendant be held liable for the victim's losses? This novel issued caused an appeal of the case. An excerpt from the opinion of the judge in this appeal follows.

    LORD ELLENBOROUGH, C.J. A party is not to cast himself upon an obstruction which had been made by the fault of another, and avail himself of it, if he does not himself use common and ordinary caution to be in the right. In case of persons riding upon what is considered to be the wrong side of the road, that would not authorize another purposely to ride up against them. One person being in fault will not dispense with another's using ordinary care for himself. Two things must concur to support this action: an obstruction in the road by the fault of the defendant, and no want of ordinary care to avoid it on the part of the plaintiff. . . . [C]ontributory negligence is a complete bar to recovery.

QUESTION 3.2:

    a. Who appealed the judgment?

    b. Who won the appeal?

    c. What is the judge's holding?

When precedent does not provide a clear rule for resolving a dispute, the judges must *create* one. *Novel disputes* are the occasion for altering the law made by judges. Lord Ellenborough created a new precedent in this case. How broad is the new precedent? The case is unclear. Under a narrow interpretation, the judge held that riders of horses cannot recover money damages for their injuries from a negligent defendant if they do not ride with ordinary care, and this lack of care contributes to the accident. This narrow interpretation says that the rule applies only to accidents like this one. Indeed, Lord Ellenborough's example of a horseman riding on the wrong side of the road into another horseman riding on the correct side would seem to support this narrow interpretation. But a broader interpretation of the court's holding is possible, and did, in fact, come to be the common interpretation. Under a broad interpretation of the holding, Lord Ellenborough held that no plaintiffs can recover when their own negligence contributes to their injury (even if the defendant was negligent). This was new law.

Subsequently, another novel case arose involving similar facts.

Davies v. Mann
10 M. & W. 545 (Ex., 1842)[8]

At the trial, before ERSKINE, J., it appeared that the plaintiff, having fettered the fore-feet of an ass belonging to him, turned it into a public highway, and at the same time in question the ass was grazing on the off side of a road about eight yards wide, when the defendant's wagon, with a team of three horses, coming down a slight descent, at what the witness termed a smartish pace, ran against the ass,

---

[8] The traditional English court system that took shape in the late 12th century and prevailed until the late 19th century consisted of three common law courts and a court of equity. The first of the common law courts was the Court of Common Pleas. The members of that court were called "justices" and were presided over by the chief justice. The court originally concentrated on civil disputes concerning land but came to consider a wide range of civil disputes. The Court of King's Bench, the second common law court, was originally a criminal court but in time became a court of review over the civil issues appealed from the Court of Common Pleas. The third common law court was the Court of Exchequer of Pleas or, simply, the Court of Exchequer. The Exchequer was the King's treasury, and this court originally heard disputes arising from tax liability and other matters concerning the King's revenue. By the late 16th century the Court of Exchequer had extended its jurisdiction to cover nearly all civil disputes. Members of that court, in which the appeal in *Davies v. Mann* was heard, were called "baron," abbreviated "B.," and were presided over by the chief baron, abbreviated "C.B."

The equity court was the Court of Chancery, so called because it was presided over by the chancellor, the most important member of the king's council. By the late 15th century, Chancery was established as a separate court that dispensed a more flexible justice, especially in regard to remedies, than did the common law courts. There is a great historical difference between the courts of law and the courts of equity. One of the most important of those differences has to do with the types of remedies available to a successful plaintiff. Roughly speaking, a court of law will award only compensatory money damages. A court of equity will do more than that if the plaintiff can demonstrate that the loss is such that money damages are not adequate compensation. In Chapter 4 we shall distinguish more clearly between equitable and legal remedies.

In the Judicature Act of 1873 and the Supreme Court of Judicature (Consolidation) Act of 1925 the British Parliament replaced all of these courts with a greatly simplified structure that drew no distinction between common law and equity. Today Britain has a court of appeals with separate civil and criminal divisions.

knocked it down, and the wheels passing over it, it died soon after . . . The learned judge told the jury, that . . . if they thought that the accident might have been avoided by the exercise of ordinary care on the part of the driver, to find for the plaintiff. The jury found their verdict for the plaintiff. . . .

Godson now moved for a new trial, on the ground of misdirection. [That is, the defendant's lawyer appealed the judgment on the ground that the judge in the trial court had incorrectly instructed the jury on the law to be applied to the facts in this case.] The act of the plaintiff in turning the donkey into the public highway was an illegal one, and, as the injury arose principally from that act, the plaintiff was not entitled to compensation for that injury which, but for his own unlawful act would never have occurred. . . . The principle of law, as deducible from the cases is, that where an accident is the result of faults on both sides neither party can maintain an action. Thus, in *Butterfield v. Forrester*, 11 East 60, it was held that one who is injured by an obstruction on a highway, against which he fell, cannot maintain an action, if it appear that he was riding with great violence and want of ordinary care, without which he might have seen and avoided the obstruction.

LORD ABINGER, C.B.

[A]s the defendant might, by proper care, have avoided injuring the animal, and did not, he is liable for the consequences of his negligence, though the animal may have been improperly there.

PARKE, B. . . . [T]he negligence which is to preclude a plaintiff from recovering in an action of this nature, must be such as that he could, by ordinary care, have avoided the consequences of the defendant's negligence. . . . [A]lthough the ass may have been wrongfully there, still the defendant was bound to go along the road at such a pace as would be likely to prevent mischief. Were this not so, a man might justify the driving over goods left on a public highway, or even over a man lying asleep there, or the purposely running against a carriage going on the wrong side of the road . . .

[New trial denied.]

QUESTION 3.3:

    a. Who appealed the judgment?

    b. Who won the appeal?

    c. What is the judge's holding?

A plaintiff has suffered a loss: his donkey was killed, allegedly because the defendant was driving a wagon too quickly for the conditions on the road. However, the plaintiff himself was negligent for having left his donkey unattended, although fettered, beside a public road. Strictly following the rule in *Butterfield*, the plaintiff's fault or negligence contributed to his losses and thus should bar his recovery. That is precisely what Mann's lawyer argued in appealing the judgment for the plaintiff in the lower court. But at the trial the jury believed that the facts in *Davies v. Mann* were distinguishable from those in earlier cases in which a contributorily negligent plaintiff was not allowed to recover from a negligent defendant. There appears to be two reasons for excusing the plaintiff's negligence in Lord Abinger's and Baron Parke's opinions. First, there is the element of time. Although the plaintiff was negligent in leaving his donkey unattended on the public highway, the defendant's negligence came afterward. And, if the defendant had not been driving recklessly, he would have had time to avoid the donkey by stopping or swerving. Apparently, the defendant's negligence came afterward and controlled the outcome. This doctrine has come to be known as the "last clear chance" rule: if both parties to an accident are negligent, the party who had the last clear chance to avoid the accident will be held responsible for losses arising from the accident.

The second argument for excusing the plaintiff's negligence is to encourage precautions in the future by people situated like the defendant. Again, Baron Parke puts the point nicely, "[A]though the ass may have been wrongfully there, still the defendant was bound to go along the road at such a pace as would be likely to prevent mischief. Were this not so, a man might justify the driving over goods left on a public highway, or even over a man lying asleep there, or the purposely running against a carriage going on the wrong side of the road." This interpretation of the law suggests that rules should create incentives for avoiding accidents.

Notice that *Davies v. Mann* changes the law handed down in *Butterfield v. Forrester*. The blanket rule from the earlier case—contributory negligence is a complete bar to recovery—was amended by judges who faced a new situation. We may say that after *Davies v. Mann* the legal rule became:

> contributory negligence is a complete bar to recovery *unless the defendant had the last clear chance to avoid the accident and did not take that chance*.

The "last clear chance" doctrine was quickly adopted throughout the common law world.[9]

CONCLUSION

To summarize, we compared the two great legal traditions—the civil law and the common law. We examined the hierarchical structure of U.S. courts. We saw some of the general characteristics of a legal dispute: a plaintiff who alleges that he or she has been wronged by a defendant and seeks the courts' help in getting relief. We learned some methods that judges use to resolve novel issues. Finally, we looked at the evolution of the doctrine of contributory negligence as developed by courts. This chapter provides a brief, selective introduction to some of the basic facts about law, which we analyze using economics in the rest of the book.

SUGGESTED READINGS

Berman, Harold J., and William R. Greiner, THE NATURE AND FUNCTIONS OF LAW (4th ed. 1980).

Cardozo, Benjamin, THE NATURE OF THE JUDICIAL PROCESS (1921).

Eisenberg, Melvin A., THE NATURE OF THE COMMON LAW (1989).

---

[9] But that is not the end of the story. For the next episode, see *British Columbia Electric Rail Co., Ltd. v. Loach*, [1916] 1 A.C. 719.

Franklin, Marc A., THE BIOGRAPHY OF A LEGAL DISPUTE: AN INTRODUCTION TO AMERICAN CIVIL PROCEDURE (1968).

Holmes, Oliver W., THE COMMON LAW (1881).

Levi, Edward H., AN INTRODUCTION TO LEGAL REASONING (1949).

Merryman, John H., THE CIVIL LAW TRADITION: AN INTRODUCTION TO THE LEGAL SYSTEMS OF WESTERN EUROPE AND LATIN AMERICA (2nd ed. 1985).

4

AN ECONOMIC THEORY OF PROPERTY

"There is nothing which so generally strikes the imagination and engages the affections of mankind, as the right of property; or that sole and despotic dominion which one man claims and exercises over the external things of the world, in total exclusion of the right of any other individual in the universe. And yet there are very few, that will give themselves the trouble to consider the origin and foundation of this right."

—

William Blackstone, COMMENTARIES ON THE
LAWS OF ENGLAND, Bk. II, Ch. 1, p.2 (1765–69)

In the African tribe called the Barotse, "property law defines not so much the rights of persons over things as the obligations owed between persons in respect of things."

—

Max Gluckman, IDEAS IN BAROTSE JURISPRUDENCE 171 (1965)

The law of property supplies the legal framework for allocating resources and distributing wealth. As the contrasting quotes above indicate, people and societies disagree sharply about how to allocate resources and distribute wealth. Blackstone viewed property as providing its owner with complete control over resources, and he regarded this freedom to control material things as "the guardian of every other right." Gluckman found that property in the Barotse tribe conveyed to its owner responsibility, not freedom. For example, the Barotse hold rich persons responsible for contributing to the prosperity of their kin. Finally, Marx and Engels regarded property as the institution by which the few enslaved the many.

We cannot here resolve these deep disputes over social organization. Instead, we shall use economic theory to analyze legal rules about property. We shall examine what things, both material and immaterial, may be legally protected as property and what it means to have property rights; what things owners may do with their property; and what duties owners owe to others. Here are some examples of the sorts of questions with which property law deals:

EXAMPLE 1: "This morning in a remote meadow in Wyoming, a mule was born. To whom does that mule belong?"[1] Does the mule belong to (1) the owner of the mule's mother, (2) the owner of the property on which she was born, (3) the lumber company that has leased the land, or (4) the federal government because the property is a national park?

EXAMPLE 2: Orbitcom, Inc., spent $125 million designing, launching, and maintaining a satellite for the transmission of business data between Europe and the United States. The satellite is positioned in a geosynchronous orbit 25 miles above the Atlantic Ocean.[2] Recently a natural resource-monitoring satellite belonging to the Windsong Corporation has strayed so close to Orbitcom's satellite that the company's transmissions between Europe and the United States have become unreliable. As a result, Orbitcom has lost customers and has sued Windsong for trespassing upon Orbitcom's right to its geosynchronous satellite orbit.

EXAMPLE 3: Foster inspects a house under construction in a new subdivision on the north side of town and decides to buy it. The day after she moves in, the wind shifts and begins to blow from the north. She smells a powerful stench. Upon inquiring, she learns that a large cattle feedlot is located north of the subdivision, just over the ridge, and, to make matters worse, the owner of this old business plans to expand it. Foster joins other property owners in an action to shut down the feedlot.

EXAMPLE 4: Bloggs inherits the remnant of a farm from his father, most of which has already been sold for a housing development. The remaining acreage, which his father called "The Swamp," is currently used for fishing and duck hunting, but Bloggs decides to drain and develop it as a residential area. However, scientists at the local community college have determined that Bloggs' property is part of the wetlands that nourish local streams, as well as the fish in the town's river. The town council, hearing of Bloggs' plans, passes an ordinance forbidding the draining of wetlands. Bloggs sues for the right to develop his property, or, failing that, for an order compelling the town to buy the property from him at the price that would prevail if development were allowed.

EXAMPLE 5: A county ordinance requires houses to be set back five feet from the property line. Joe Potatoes buys some heavily wooded land in an undeveloped area and builds a house on it. Ten years later Fred Parsley, who owns the adjoining lot, has his land surveyed and discovers that Potatoes' house extends two feet over the property line onto Parsley's property. Potatoes offers to compensate Parsley for the trespass, but Parsley rejects the offer and sues to have Potatoes relocate the house in conformity with the ordinance.

These five examples capture some of the most fundamental questions that any system of property law must answer. The first and second examples ask how property rights are initially assigned. Orbitcom apparently bases its ownership claim on having placed a satellite in the orbit in dispute before anyone else. This claim appeals to a legal principle called the *rule of first possession*, according to which the first party to

---

[1] This remarkable question is how Professor John Cribbet, one of the leading scholars of property law, opens his first lecture on property to first-year law students at the University of Illinois College of Law.

[2] A geosynchronous orbit means that the satellite is traveling around the Earth at exactly the same speed at which the Earth is turning so that the satellite appears to remain stationary above a point on the Earth's surface.

use an unowned resource acquires a claim to it. (How might this rule apply to the mule born on the remote Wyoming meadow?) The general issue raised here is, "How does a person acquire ownership of something?"

The second example also asks what kinds of things may be privately owned. Orbitcom asserts that a satellite orbit may be privately owned like land or a musical composition, whereas Windsong feels, perhaps, that orbits should be *publicly* owned and open to all on the same terms, like the high seas or a fashion style. Economics has a lot to say about the consequences of resources' being privately owned, publicly owned, or unowned.

The third example concerns a problem sometimes known as "incompatible uses." May one property owner create a stench on his own property that offends his neighbors? In general, the law tries to prevent property owners from interfering with each other, but in this example, as in many other cases, there is a tradeoff between competing activities. Is the cattle feedlot interfering with the homeowner by creating the stench, or is the homeowner interfering with the feedlot by seeking to shut it down? The legal outcome turns in part upon whether the stench constitutes a "nuisance" as defined by law. Economics has a lot to say about this determination.

The fourth example, like the third, raises the question, "What may owners legitimately do with their property?" The difference is that Example 3 concerns a dispute between private owners and Example 4 concerns a dispute between a private owner and a government. The specific question in Example 4 is whether a property owner can develop his land according to his own wishes or must conform to severe restrictions upon development imposed by a local government. The general question concerns the extent to which government may constrain a private owner's use of her property. We will show that economics has a lot to say about government's regulating and taking private property.

In the last example, one property owner has encroached upon the land of another, but that encroachment has gone undetected and without apparent harm for many years. The question raised by this example concerns the remedy for trespass. Should the owner be denied a remedy because the trespass has persisted for so long? Alternatively, should the court award compensatory damages to the owner? Or should the court enjoin the trespasser and force him to move his house? As we shall see, economics predicts the effects of various remedies and thus provides a powerful tool for choosing the best one.

The examples raise these four fundamental questions of property law:

1. How are ownership rights established?
2. What can be privately owned?
3. What may owners do with their property?
4. What are the remedies for the violation of property rights?

In the next two chapters we shall be using economics to answer these questions. Traditional legal scholarship on property law is notoriously weak in its use of theory, at least in comparison to contracts and torts.[3] This fact contributes to the feeling of many

---

[3] In contracts and torts there was a classical theory that dominated American law at the beginning of the twentieth century. The introductory chapters on contracts and torts describe these classical theories. There was, however, no classical theory of property of comparable coherence, detail, or stature. Instead there is a long philosophical tradition of analyzing the institution of property at a very abstract level. Some of these philosophical theories of property are described in the appendix to this chapter.

students that the common law of property is diffuse and unorganized. Through economics it is possible to give the subject more coherence and order. In this chapter we concentrate upon developing fundamental tools for the economic analysis of property: bargaining theory, public goods theory, and the theory of externalities. In the next chapter we apply these tools to a large number of property laws and institutions.

I. THE LEGAL CONCEPT OF PROPERTY

From a legal viewpoint, property is a *bundle of rights*. These rights describe what people may and may not do with the resources they own: the extent to which they may possess, use, transform, transfer, or exclude others from their property. These rights are not immutable; they may, for example, change from one generation to another. But at any point in time, they constitute the detailed answer of the law to the four fundamental questions of property law listed above.

Two facts about the bundle of legal rights constituting ownership are fundamental to our later understanding of property. First, the owner is free to exercise the rights over his or her property, by which we mean that no law forbids or requires the owner to exercise those rights. In our example at the beginning of the chapter, Parsley can farm his land or leave it fallow, and the law is indifferent as to which he chooses to do. Second, others are forbidden to interfere with the owner's exercise of his rights. Thus, if Parsley decides to farm his land, Potatoes cannot put stones in the way of the plow. This protection is needed against two types of interlopers—private persons and the government.

The legal conception of property is, then, that of a bundle of rights over resources that the owner is free to exercise and whose exercise is protected from interference by others. Thus, property creates a zone of privacy in which owners can exercise their will over things without being answerable to others, as stressed in the preceding quote from Blackstone. These facts are sometimes summarized by saying that property gives owners liberty over things.

This general definition of property is compatible with many different theories of what particular rights are to be included in the protected bundle and of how to protect those rights. It is also consistent with different accounts of the responsibilities that a person assumes by becoming an owner. The law has tended to look beyond itself to philosophy for help in deciding which rights to include in the bundle of property rights. In the appendix to this chapter we discuss some of these philosophical approaches.

II. BARGAINING THEORY[4]

To develop an economic theory of property, we must first develop the economic theory of bargaining games. At first you may not see the relevance of this theory to property law, but later you will recognize that it is the very foundation of the economic theory of property. The elements of bargaining theory can be developed through an example of a familiar exchange—selling a used car. Consider these facts:

> Adam, who lives in a small town, has a 1957 Chevy convertible in good repair. The pleasure
> of owning and driving the car is worth $3000 to Adam. Blair, who has been coveting the car

---

[4] Bargaining theory is a form of game theory. See the section on game theory in Chapter 2 for some useful background information.

for years, inherits $5000 and decides to try to buy the car from Adam. After inspecting the car, Blair decides that the pleasure of owning and driving it is worth $4000 to her.

According to these facts, an agreement to sell will enable the car to pass from Adam, who values it at $3000, to Blair, who values it at $4000. The potential seller values the car less than the potential buyer, so there is scope for a bargain. Assuming that exchanges are voluntary, Adam will not accept less than $3000 for the car, and Blair will not pay more than $4000, so the sale price will have to be somewhere in between. A reasonable sale price would be $3,500, which splits the difference.

The logic of the situation can be clarified by restating the facts in the language of game theory. The parties to the kind of game represented by this example can *both* benefit from cooperating with each other. To be specific, they can move a resource (the car) from someone who values it less (Adam) to someone who values it more (Blair). Moving the resource in this case from Adam, who values it at $3000, to Blair, who values it at $4000, will create $1000 in value. The *cooperative surplus* is the name for the value created by moving the resource to a more valuable use. Of course, the share of this surplus that each receives depends on the price at which the car is sold. If the price is set at $3500, each will enjoy an equal share of the value created by the exchange, or $500. If the price is set at $3800, the value will be divided unequally, with Adam enjoying $4/5$ or $800, and Blair enjoying $1/5$ or $200. Or if the price is set at $3200, Adam will enjoy $200 or $1/5$ of the value created, whereas Blair will enjoy $800 or $4/5$.

The parties typically bargain with each other over the price. In the course of negotiating, the parties may assert facts ("The motor is mechanically perfect . . . "), appeal to norms ("$3700 is an unfair price . . . "), threaten ("I won't take less than $3500 . . . "), and so forth. These are the tools used in the art of bargaining. The fact that the parties can negotiate is an advantage of bargaining or cooperative games relative to other games (called *noncooperative* games), such as the famous Prisoner's Dilemma, which we examined in Chapter 2. Even when negotiation is possible, however, there is no guarantee that it will succeed. If the negotiations break down and the parties fail to cooperate, their attempt to shift resources to a more valuable use will fail, and they will not create value. Thus, the obstacle to creating value in a bargaining game is that the parties must agree on how to divide it. Value will be divided between them at a rate determined by the price at which the car is sold. Agreement about the car's price marks successful negotiations, whereas disagreement marks a failure in the bargaining process.

To apply game theory to this example, let us characterize the possible outcomes as a cooperative solution and a noncooperative solution. The cooperative solution is the one in which Adam and Blair reach agreement over a price and succeed in exchanging the car for money. The noncooperative solution is the one in which they fail to agree upon a price and they fail to exchange the car for money. To analyze the logic of bargaining, we must first consider the consequences of noncooperation. If the parties fail to cooperate, they will each achieve some level of well-being on their own. Adam will keep the car and use it, which is worth $3000 to him. Blair will keep her money—$5000—or spend it on something other than the car. For simplicity, assume that the value she places on this use of her money is its face value, specifically, $5000. Thus, the payoffs to the parties in the noncooperative solution, called their *threat values*, are $3000 for Adam (the value to him of keeping the car) and $5000 to Blair (the amount of her cash). The total value of the noncooperative solution is $3000 + $5000 = $8000.

In contrast, the cooperative solution is for Adam to sell the car to Blair. Through cooperation, Blair will own the car, which is worth $4000 to her, and in addition the two parties will each end up with a share of Blair's $5000. For example, Adam might accept $3500 in exchange for the convertible. Blair then has the car, worth $4000 to her, and $1500 of her $5000. Thus, the value of the cooperative solution is $4000 (the value of the car to Blair) + $1500 (the amount that Blair retains of her original $5000) + $3500 (the amount received by Adam for the car) = $9000. The surplus from cooperation is the difference in value between cooperation and noncooperation: $9000 − $8000 = $1000.

In any voluntary agreement, each player must receive at least the threat value or there is no advantage to cooperating. A reasonable solution to the bargaining problem is for each player to receive the threat value plus an equal share of the cooperative surplus: specifically, $3500 for Adam and $5500 for Blair.[5] To accomplish the division, Blair should pay Adam $3500 for the car. This leaves Adam with $3500 in cash and no car, and leaves Blair with a car worth $4000 to her and $1500 in cash.

QUESTION 4.1: Suppose Adam receives a bid of $3200 from a third party named Clair. How does Clair's bid change the threat values, the surplus from cooperation, and the reasonable solution?

We have explained that the process of bargaining can be divided into three steps: establishing the threat values, determining the cooperative surplus, and agreeing upon terms for distributing the surplus from cooperation. These steps will be used in the next section to understand the origins of the institution of property.

III. THE ORIGINS OF THE INSTITUTION OF PROPERTY: A THOUGHT EXPERIMENT

The bargaining model shows how cooperation can create a surplus that benefits everyone. This type of reasoning can be used to perform a thought experiment that is helpful in understanding the origins of property.

Let us imagine a simplified world in which there are people, land, farm tools, and weapons but no courts and no police. In this imaginary world, government does not vindicate and protect the rights to property asserted by the people who live on the land.

---

[5] Economists have long struggled with the fact that self-interested rationality alone does not seem sufficient to determine the distribution of the cooperative surplus. That is why we use the term "reasonable solution," which invokes social norms, rather than "rational solution." To see the difference, consider this *rational* account of the division of the cooperative surplus. Suppose that somehow Adam knows that the cooperative surplus resulting from an agreement between Blair and him is $1000. Being perfectly rational, he says to Blair that he will sell the car to her for $3995. And, further, he explains to her why she should accept that price, even though it gives Adam $995 of the cooperative surplus and Blair, $5: "If you do not accept that price, I will not do business with you, in which case you will realize $0 worth of cooperative surplus. At the $3995 price, you get $5 of the cooperative surplus and that surely is better than nothing." Leaving aside all the strategic reasons that Blair might balk at this (will Adam *really* walk away if she refuses?), this division of the cooperative surplus is perfectly rational, but it may not be reasonable. In fact, carefully controlled experiments have demonstrated that most people would *not* accept Adam's offer, rational though it be.

A CIVIL DISPUTE AS A BARGAINING GAME

Because trials are costly, both parties can usually gain by settling out of court. That is why so few disputes ever come to trial. As we will see in Chapter 10, the best current estimate is that approximately 5% of all disputes that reach the stage of filing a legal complaint in the United States actually result in litigation. Here is a problem in which you must apply bargaining theory to a civil dispute:

FACTS: Arthur alleges that Betty borrowed a valuable kettle and broke it, so he sues to recover its value, which is $300. The facts are very confusing. Betty contends that she did not borrow a kettle from Arthur; even if it is proved that she borrowed a kettle from Arthur, she contends it is not broken; even if it is proved that she borrowed a kettle from Arthur and that it is broken, she contends that she did not break it.

Assume that because the facts in the case are so unclear, Arthur and Betty independently believe that the chances of either side's winning in court are an even 50%. Further assume that litigation in small claims court will cost each party $50 and that the costs of settling out of court are nil. So, cooperation in this case is a matter of settling out of court and saving the cost of a trial. Noncooperation in this case means trying the dispute.

QUESTION 4.2:

a. What is Arthur's threat value?

b. What is Betty's threat value?

c. If Arthur and Betty cooperate together in settling their disagreement, what is the net cost of resolving the dispute?

d. What is the cooperative surplus?

e. A reasonable settlement would be for Betty to pay Arthur_____.

f. Suppose that instead of both sides' believing that there is an even chance of winning, both sides are optimistic. Specifically, Arthur thinks that he will win with probability 2/3, and Betty thinks that she will win with probability 2/3.

   1. What is Arthur's putative threat value (what he believes he can secure on his own without Betty's cooperation)?

   2. What is Betty's putative threat value (what she believes she can secure on her own without Arthur's cooperation)?

   3. The putative cooperative surplus equals_____.

   4. Describe the obstacle to settlement in a few words.

Individuals, families, or alliances of families enforce property rights to the extent that they defend their land holdings. People must decide how many resources to devote to defending their property claims. Rational people allocate their limited resources so that, as we saw in Chapter 2, the marginal cost of defending land is just equal to the marginal benefit. This means that at the margin, the value of the resources used for military ends (the marginal benefit) equals their value when used for productive ends, such as raising crops and livestock (marginal [opportunity] cost). For example, the occupants are rational if allocating a little more time to patrolling the perimeter of the property preserves as much additional wealth for the defenders as they would enjoy by allocating a little more time to raising crops. The same statement could be made about allocating land between crops and fortifications, or about beating metal into swords or plowshares.

These facts describe a world in which farming and fighting are individually rational. But are they socially efficient? In Chapter 2 we offered the following definition of inefficient production: the same (or fewer) inputs could be used to produce a greater total output. Can some mechanism be found that uses fewer resources to achieve the same level of protection for property claims? One possible mechanism is law. Suppose that the costs of operating this system of property rights are less than the sum of all individual costs of private defense. Such a mechanism would allow the transfer of resources from fighting to farming. For example, the landowners might create a government to protect their property rights at lower cost in taxes than each individual spends on fighting. The savings might come from economies of scale in having one large army in the society to defend everyone, rather than many small, privately owned armies.[6] In other words, there may be a natural monopoly on force.

We could imagine the parties bargaining together over the terms for establishing a government to recognize and enforce their property rights. They are motivated by the realization that there are economies of scale in protecting property. By reaching an agreement to have one government backed by one army, everyone can enjoy greater wealth and security. The bargain eventually reached by such negotiations is called the *social contract* by philosophers because it establishes the basic terms for social life.[7] It would be rational for the parties negotiating the social contract to take account of other rights of owners besides the right to exclude. Many of the rights that are currently in the bundle called property could be considered, such as the right to use, transfer, and transform. Indeed, many rights other than property rights could be a part of the social contract, such as freedom of speech and freedom of religion, but they do not concern us in this chapter.

The same bargaining model used to explain the sale of a secondhand car can be applied to this thought experiment, in which a primitive society develops a system of property rights. First, a description is given of what people would do in the absence of civil government, when military strength alone established ownership claims. That situation—called the *state of nature*—corresponds to the threat values of the noncooperative solution, which prevails if the parties cannot agree. Second, a description is given of the advantages of creating a government to recognize and enforce property rights. Civil society, in which such a government exists, corresponds to the game's

---

[6] Recall that economies of scale occur when the cost per unit (or average cost of production) declines as the total amount of output increases. A production technology for which the unit costs are falling at every level of production, even very large levels, is called a *natural monopoly* because a larger producer can sell at a lower price than any smaller producer.

[7] The social contract has usually been thought of as a logical construct, but some theorists have used it to explain history. For example, it has been argued that feudalism in the Middle Ages corresponds roughly to the conditions of our imaginary world. The economic factors that caused this system to be replaced in some parts of Western Europe by a system of private property rights enforced by a central government are discussed in Douglass C. North and Robert Paul Thomas, THE RISE OF THE WESTERN WORLD (1973).

cooperative solution, which prevails if the parties can agree. The social surplus, defined as the difference between the total amount spent defending land in the state of nature and the total cost of operating a property rights system in civil society, corresponds to the cooperative surplus in the game. Third, an agreement is described for distributing the advantages from cooperation. In the car example, this agreement arises from the price that the buyer offers and the seller accepts. In the thought experiment, this agreement arises from the social contract that includes the fundamental laws of property.

To see the parallel more clearly, imagine that our world consists of only two people, A and B. In a state of nature, each one grows some corn, steals corn from the other party, and defends against theft. Each of the parties has different levels of skill at farming, stealing, and defending. Their payoffs in a state of nature are summarized in Table 4.1. Taken together, A and B produce 200 units of corn, but it gets reallocated by theft. For example, A steals 40 units of corn from B and loses 10 units of corn to B through theft. Notice that A ultimately enjoys 80 units of corn, and B enjoys 120 units, after taking into account the gains and losses from theft.

Instead of persisting in a state of nature, A and B may decide to enter into a cooperative agreement, recognize each other's property rights, and adopt an enforcement mechanism that puts an end to theft. Let us assume that cooperation will enable them to devote more resources to farming and fewer resources to fighting, so that total production will rise from 200 units to 300 units. 100 units thus constitutes the social or cooperative surplus. In civil society there will be a mechanism for distributing the surplus from cooperation, such as government taxes and subsidies. The parties must decide through bargaining how this is to be done. A reasonable division of that surplus gives each party an equal share. So, in civil society, each party receives half the cooperative surplus plus the individual net consumption in the state of nature, which is each party's threat value. These facts are summarized in Table 4.2.

What is the meaning of this "thought experiment" concerning the origins of property? Read literally, you might conclude that tribes acquire government by meeting together and agreeing to create a system of law, including property rights. This literal reading is bad history and bad anthropology. In reality, the thought experiment is about processes that go on all the time. In a changing society, new forms of property arise continually. To illustrate, property law for underground gas and the electromagnetic spectrum (radio and television broadcasting) developed in the United States during the last century, and property law for computer software and genetically engineered forms of life developed in the last decade. The need for a new form of property law arises in

Table 4.1

THE STATE OF NATURE

Farmer	Corn grown	Corn gained by theft	Corn lost through theft	Net corn consumption
A	50	40	−10	80
B	150	10	−40	120
Totals	200	50	−50	200

Table 4.2

CIVIL SOCIETY

Farmer	Threat value	Share of surplus	Net corn consumption
A	80	50	130
B	120	50	170
Totals	200	100	300

situations corresponding to our thought experiment. For example, like corn, computer software can be stolen. Without effective property law, people invest a lot of resources in stealing software or trying to prevent its theft. These efforts redistribute software, rather than invent or manufacture it. Now the United States has property law that prevents the stealing of computer software by large organizations (but not so clearly by individuals). The imposition of these laws has greatly stimulated the invention and manufacture of software. So, our thought experiment is really a parable about the incentive structure that motivates societies to continually create property law.

The first question that we posed about property law is, "How are property rights established?" This is a question about how an owner acquires the legal right to property. Our thought experiment answers the question, "Why are ownership rights established?" This is a question about why a society creates property as a legal right. The two questions are closely connected. Societies create property as a legal right to encourage production, discourage theft, and reduce the costs of protecting goods. Law prescribes various ways that someone can acquire a property right, such as by finding and purchasing land with natural gas beneath it, inventing a computer program, or discovering sunken treasure.

We now turn to the elaboration of how bargaining theory can help the law prescribe ways for the acquisition of property that also encourage production, or discourage theft, and reduce the costs of protecting goods.

QUESTION 4.3:

    a. Is the cooperative solution *fair*? Can the resulting inequality in civil society be justified?

    b. Suppose that the bargaining process did not allow destructive threats, such as the threat to steal. How might this restriction affect the distribution of the surplus?

    c. What is the difference between the principle, "To each according to his threat value," and this principle, "To each according to his productivity"?

IV. AN ECONOMIC THEORY OF PROPERTY

The fact that the same theory of bargaining can be applied to selling a used car or creating a civil society is proof of that theory's generality and power. Indeed, bargaining theory is so powerful that, as this section will show, it serves as the basis for an economic theory of property and of property law. Let us briefly summarize where we are going.

By bargaining together, people frequently agree upon the terms for interacting and cooperating. But sometimes the terms for interacting and cooperating are imposed on people from the outside—for example, by law. The terms are often more efficient when people agree upon them than when a lawmaker imposes them. It follows that law is unnecessary and undesirable where bargaining succeeds, and that law is necessary and desirable where bargaining fails.

These propositions apply to the four questions about property. In certain circumstances we do not need property law to answer the four questions that we posed at the beginning of this chapter. Rather, in those special circumstances, private bargaining will establish what things are property, who has claims to that property, what things an owner may and may not do with the property, and who may interfere with an owner's property. The special circumstances that define the limits of law are specified in a remarkable proposition called the *Coase theorem*. This theorem, to which we now turn, helped to found the economic analysis of law and won its inventor the Nobel Prize in economics.

A. The Coase Theorem[8]

Different commentators formulate the Coase theorem differently. We will expound a simple version of the theorem and then acquaint you with some of the commentary.

Consider this example. A cattle rancher lives beside a farmer. The farmer grows corn on some of his land and leaves some of it uncultivated. The rancher runs cattle over all of her land. The boundary between the ranch and the farm is clear, but there is no fence. Thus, from time to time the cattle wander onto the farmer's property and damage the corn. The damage could be reduced by building a fence, keeping fewer cattle, or growing less corn—each of which is costly. The rancher and the farmer could bargain with each other to decide who should bear the cost of the damage. Alternatively, the law could intervene and assign liability for the damages.

There are two specific rules the law could adopt:

1. The farmer is responsible for keeping the cattle off his property, and he must pay for the damages when they get in (a regime we could call "ranchers' rights" or "open range"), or

2. the rancher is responsible for keeping the cattle on her property, and she must pay for the damage when they get out ("farmers' rights" or "closed range").

Under the first rule, the farmer would have no legal recourse against the damage done by his neighbor's cattle. To reduce the damage, the farmer would have to grow less corn or fence his corn fields. Under the second rule, the rancher must build a fence to keep the cattle on her property. If the cattle escape, the law could ascertain the facts, determine the monetary value of the damage, and make the rancher pay the farmer.

---

[8] The theorem is discussed in Professor Ronald H. Coase's *The Problem of Social Cost* 3 J. LAW & ECON. 1 (1960). The article has been reprinted in numerous legal and economic anthologies, notably R. Berring ed., GREAT AMERICAN LAW REVIEWS (1984) (a compendium of the 22 "greatest" articles published in the United States' law reviews before 1965).

Which law is better? Perhaps you think that fairness requires injurers to pay for the damage they cause. If so, you will approach the question as traditional lawyers do, by thinking about causes and fairness. Professor Coase answered in terms of *efficiency*. All other things equal, we would like the legal rule to encourage efficiency in both ranching and farming. This approach yielded a counterintuitive conclusion, which can be explained using some numbers. Suppose that, without any fence, the invasion by the cattle costs the farmer $100 per year in lost profits from growing corn. The cost of installing and maintaining a fence around the farmer's corn fields is $50 per year, and the cost of installing a fence around the ranch is $75 per year. Thus, we are assuming that damage of $100 can be avoided at an annual cost of $50 by the farmer and $75 by the rancher. Obviously, efficiency requires the farmer to build a fence around his corn fields, rather than the rancher building a fence around her ranch.

Now, consider what will happen under either legal rule. Under the first legal rule (ranchers' rights), the farmer will bear damage of $100 each year from the wandering cattle. He can eliminate this damage at a cost of $50 per year, for a net savings of $50 per year. Therefore, the first rule will cause the farmer to build a fence around his corn fields. Under the second rule (farmers' rights), the rancher can escape liability for $100 at a cost of $75. Consequently, the second rule will cause the rancher to build a fence around her ranch, thus saving $25. Apparently, the first rule, which saves $50, is more efficient than the second rule, which saves $25. But this efficiency is only apparent; it is not real.

We may begin our understanding of this apparent puzzle by first imagining how the rancher and the farmer could have resolved their problem by cooperative bargaining and then comparing that outcome with the apparent outcomes under the different legal rules. Suppose that the farmer and the rancher had fallen in love, married, and combined their business interests. They would then maximize the combined profits from farming and ranching, and these joint profits will be highest when they build a fence around the corn fields, not around the ranch. Consequently, the married couple will build a fence around the corn fields, regardless of whether the law is the first rule or the second rule. In other words, they will cooperate to maximize their joint profits, regardless of the rule of law.

We have seen that the first rule is more efficient than the second if the farmer and the rancher follow the law without cooperating, but that the law makes no difference to efficiency when they cooperate. The farmer and the rancher do not need to get married in order to cooperate. Rational businesspeople can often bargain together and agree upon terms of cooperation. By bargaining to an agreement, rather than following the law noncooperatively, the rancher and the farmer can save $25. That is, if the parties can bargain successfully with each other, the efficient outcome will be achieved, regardless of the rule of law.

Recall that the most efficient outcome is for the farmer to build a fence around his corn fields, and that when the parties simply follow the law without cooperating, the second rule (farmers' rights) leads to the apparent inefficiency of the *rancher* building a fence around her ranch. But consider how bargaining might proceed under the second rule:

RANCHER: "The law makes me responsible for building the fence. I can fence my ranch for $75 per year, whereas you can fence your corn fields for $50 per year. Let's make a deal. I'll pay you $50 per year to fence your corn field."

FARMER: "If I agree, and you pay me $50 per year to fence my corn fields, I won't be any better off than if I did nothing and you had to fence your ranch. However, you'll save $25. You shouldn't receive all of the gains from cooperation. You should give me a share of the gains by paying me *more* than $50 per year for fencing my corn fields."

RANCHER: "OK. Let's split the savings from cooperation. I'll pay you $62.50 per year, and you build the fence. That way we'll each receive half of the $25 gained by cooperating."

FARMER: "Agreed."

Note the important implication: cooperation leads to the fence's being built around the *farmer's* corn fields, despite the fact that the second legal rule (farmers' rights) was controlling. The efficiency of the first legal rule is apparent, not real. Note, also, the parallel between bargaining over the right of ownership of a used car from earlier in the chapter and the rights of ownership of land. Adam owns the car, and Blair values it more than Adam. By bargaining to an agreement, they can create a surplus and divide it between them. Similarly, the second legal rule imposes an obligation on the rancher to constrain her cattle, but the farmer can constrain them at less cost than the rancher. By bargaining to an agreement, both parties can save costs and divide the savings between them.[9]

Let's generalize what we have learned from this exercise. When one activity interferes with another, the law must decide whether one party has the right to interfere or whether the other party has the right to be free from interference. Efficiency requires allocating the right to the party who values it the most. When the parties follow the law noncooperatively, the legal allocation of rights matters to efficiency. When the parties bargain successfully, the legal allocation of rights does not matter to efficiency. Given successful bargaining, the use of resources (the placement of a fence, the number of cattle run, the extent of land planted in corn fields, and so forth) is efficient, regardless of the legal rule.

We have discussed "successful bargaining," but we have not discussed why bargains sometimes succeed and sometimes fail. Bargaining occurs through communication between the parties. Communication has various costs, such as renting a conference room, hiring a stenographer, and spending time in discussion. Coase used the term "transaction costs" to refer to the costs of communicating, as well as to a variety of other costs that we will discuss later. In fact, he used "transaction costs" to encompass *all* of the impediments to bargaining. Given this definition, bargaining *necessarily* succeeds when transaction costs are zero. We can summarize this result by stating this version of the Coase theorem:

---

[9] The bargaining situation is quite different if the law adopts the first rule (ranchers' rights), rather than the second rule (farmers' rights). Under the first rule, the farmer is responsible for building a fence to keep the cattle out of his corn fields. In these circumstances, cooperation between the farmer and the rancher does not save costs relative to following the law noncooperatively. Consequently, under the first rule, the farmer will go ahead and build the fence, without any bargaining. The first rule has an analogy in the used-car example. Recall that Blair values the car more than does Adam, which is why a surplus can be created by Adam's selling the car to Blair. If Blair initially owns the car, there is nothing to be gained by bargaining with Adam or cooperating with him. Thus, Blair's owning the car is analogous to ranchers' rights. In the car example, there is no scope for a bargain because the party who values the car the most already owns it; in the cattle-corn example, there is no scope for a bargain because the party who can fence the cattle at least cost already has the duty to build the fence.

When transaction costs are zero, an efficient use of resources results from private bargaining, regardless of the legal assignment of property rights.

Now we must relate the Coase theorem to our larger project of developing an economic theory of property. The theorem states abstractly what our example showed concretely: if transaction costs are zero, then we do not need to worry about specifying legal rules regarding property in order to achieve efficiency. Private bargaining will take care of such issues as which things may be owned, what owners may and may not do with their property, and so on. By specifying the circumstances under which property law is unimportant to efficient resource use, the Coase theorem specifies implicitly when property law *is* important. To make the point more explicit, we posit this corollary to the Coase theorem:

When transaction costs are high enough to prevent bargaining, the efficient use of resources will depend upon how property rights are assigned.

To appreciate the corollary, let us return to the rancher and the farmer. Bargaining to an agreement requires communication. Assume that communication is costly. Specifically, assume that the transaction costs of bargaining are $35. Transaction costs must be subtracted from the surplus in order to compute the net value of cooperating. Suppose that the first legal rule (farmers' rights) prevails, so that a surplus of $25 can be achieved by an agreement that the rancher will pay the farmer to fence the corn fields. The net value of the bargain is the cooperative surplus minus the transaction costs—$25 − $35 = −$10. Recognizing that the net value of the bargain is negative, the parties will not bargain. If the parties do not bargain, they will follow the law noncooperatively. Specifically, the farmer will assert his right to be free from invasions of cattle, and the rancher will fence the ranch, which is inefficient. In order to avoid this inefficiency, the law would have to adopt the second rule (ranchers' rights), in which case the parties will not bargain and they will achieve efficiency by following the law noncooperatively.

QUESTION 4.4: Suppose that a railroad runs beside a field in which commercial crops are grown. The railroad is powered by a steam locomotive that spews hot cinders out of its smokestack. From time to time those cinders land on the crops nearest to the track and burn them to the ground. Assume that each year, the farmer whose crops are burned loses $3000 in profits, and that the annual cost to the railroad of installing and maintaining a spark-arrester that would prevent any damage to the crops is $1750. Does it matter to the efficient use of the farmer's land or to the efficient operation of the railroad whether the law protects the farmer from invasion by sparks or allows the railroad to emit sparks without liability? Why or why not?

The Coase theorem is so remarkable that many people have questioned it. Although we cannot discuss this rich literature here, we have embodied some of the most important points in the following questions:

QUESTION 4.5: The long run. Some commentators thought that the Coase theorem might be true in the short run but not in the long run. In the example of the farmer and the rancher, changing the use of fields takes time. For example, to convert a field from grazing land to farmland, the farmer must fence and plough the land. The efficiency of the Coase theorem in the long run depends on the ability of private bargaining to accommodate any additional costs of altering resource use over long time periods as relative prices and opportunity costs change. Discuss some ways that a contract for long-run cooperation between the rancher and the farmer would differ from a contract for short-run cooperation.

QUESTION 4.6: Invariance. With zero transaction costs, the farmer fences the corn field rather than the rancher fencing the ranch—regardless of the rule of law. Notice that in this example, the use of the fields for cattle-ranching and corn-growing is the same, regardless of the initial assignment of property rights. This version of the Coase theorem is called the *invariance* version (because the use of resources is *invariant* to the assignment of property rights). This version turns out to be a special case. The more general case is one in which the resource allocation will be *efficient* (but not necessarily identical), regardless of the assignment of property rights. There will be a Pareto-efficient allocation of goods and services, but it may be different from the Pareto-efficient allocation that would have resulted from assigning that same entitlement to someone else.

To illustrate, assume that farmers like to eat more corn and less beef, whereas ranchers like to eat more beef and less corn. Assume that farmers and ranchers own their own land, that transaction costs are zero, and that fence is costly relative to their incomes. The change from "ranchers' rights" to "farmers' rights" will increase the income of farmers and decrease the income of ranchers. Consequently, the demand for corn will increase, and the demand for beef will decrease. Greater demand for corn requires the planting and fencing of more corn fields. Thus, the change in law causes the building of more fences. Remember the distinction between "price effects" and "income effects" in demand theory? Can you use these concepts to explain this example?[10]

QUESTION 4.7: Endowment effects. Surveys and experiments reveal that people sometimes demand much more to give up something that they have than they would be willing to pay to acquire it. To illustrate, contrast a situation in which people have an opportunity to "sell" the clean air that they currently enjoy to a polluter to one in which people currently enjoying clean air have an opportunity to "buy" clean air from a polluter. Evidence suggests that people may demand a higher price to "sell" a right to clean air than they would pay to "buy" the same right. An "endowment" is an initial assignment of ownership rights. The divergence between buying and selling price is called an "endowment effect" because the price varies depending upon the initial assignment of ownership.

Why might farmers place a different value upon the right to be free from straying cattle depending upon whether they were selling or buying that right? Is it rational to place different values on those rights? How do these flip-flops in the relative valuation complicate an efficiency analysis of the assignment of property rights?

QUESTION 4.8: Social norms. Social norms often evolve to cope with external costs, without bargaining or law. For example, a social norm in a county in northern California requires that ranchers assume responsibility for controlling their cattle, even though parts of the county are "open range" (*i.e.*, areas in which legal responsibility rests with farmers). Furthermore, the ranchers and farmers in this county apparently do not engage in the kind

---

[10] On the various versions of the Coase theorem, see Robert D. Cooter, *The Coase Theorem,* THE NEW PALGRAVE: A DICTIONARY OF ECONOMICS (1987). On the special assumptions underlying the invariance version of the Coase theorem, see the graphical treatment in Thomas S. Ulen, *Flogging a Dead Pig: Professor Posin on the Coase Theorem,* 38 WAYNE L. REV. 91 (1991).

of bargaining envisioned by the Coase theorem. How damaging are these facts to Coase's analysis? Why would you expect neighbors in long-run relationships to adopt efficient norms to control externalities?[11]

B. The Elements of Transaction Costs

What are transaction costs? Are they ever really negligible? We cannot use the Coase theorem to understand law without answering these questions. Transaction costs are the costs of exchange. An exchange has three steps. First, an exchange partner has to be located. This involves finding someone who wants to buy what you are selling or sell what you are buying. Second, a bargain must be struck between the exchange partners. A bargain is reached by successful negotiation, which may include the drafting of an agreement. Third, after a bargain has been reached, it must be enforced. Enforcement involves monitoring performance of the parties and punishing violations of the agreement. We may call the three forms of transaction costs corresponding to these three steps of an exchange: (1) search costs, (2) bargaining costs, and (3) enforcement costs.

QUESTION 4.9: Classify each of the following examples as a cost of searching, bargaining, or enforcing an agreement to purchase a 1957 Chevrolet:

a. Haggling over the price.

b. Collecting the monthly payments for the purchase of he car.

c. Taking time off from work for the buyer and seller to meet.

d. Purchasing an advertisement in the "classified" section of the newspaper.

e. Purchasing a newspaper to obtain the "classified" section.

f. The buyer asking the seller questions about its ignition system.

When are transaction costs high, and when are they low? Consider this question by looking at the three elements of the costs of exchange. Search costs tend to be high for unique goods or services, and low for standardized goods or services. To illustrate, finding someone to sell a 1957 Chevrolet is harder than finding someone to sell a soft drink.

Turning from search costs to bargaining costs, note that our examples of bargaining assumed that both parties *know* each other's threat values and the cooperative solution. Game theorists say that information is "public" in negotiations when each party knows these values. Conversely, information is "private" when one party knows some of these values and the other does not. If the parties know the threat values and the cooperative solution, they can compute reasonable terms for cooperation. In general, public information facilitates agreement by enabling the parties to compute reasonable terms for cooperation. Consequently, negotiations tend to be simple and easy when information about the threat values and the cooperative solution is public. To illustrate, negotiations for the sale of a watermelon are simple because there is not much to know about it.

Conversely, negotiations tend to be complicated and difficult when information about threat values and the cooperative solution is private. Private information impedes bargaining because much of it must be converted into public information before computing

---

[11] See Robert Ellickson, ORDER WITHOUT LAW (1991).

reasonable terms for cooperation. In general, bargaining is costly when it requires converting a lot of private information into public information. To illustrate, negotiations for the sale of a house involve many issues of finance, timing, quality, and price. The seller of a house knows a lot more about its hidden defects than the buyer knows, and the buyer knows a lot more about his or her ability to obtain financing than the seller knows. Each attempts to extract these facts from the other over the course of negotiations. To a degree, the parties may want to divulge some information. But they may be reluctant to divulge all. Each party's share of the cooperative surplus depends, in part, on keeping some information private. But concluding the bargain requires making some information public. Balancing these conflicting pulls is difficult and potentially costly.

There is an extensive literature on bargaining games, including a large number of carefully constructed experiments testing the Coase theorem.[12] One of the most robust conclusions of these experiments is that bargainers are more likely to cooperate when their rights are clear and less likely to agree when their rights are ambiguous. Put in more formal terms, bargaining games are easier to solve when the threat values are public knowledge. The rights of the parties define their threat values in legal disputes. One implication of this finding is that property law ought to favor criteria for determining ownership that are clear and simple. For example, a system for the public registration of ownership claims to land avoids many disputes and makes settlement easier for those that arise. Similarly, the fact that someone possesses or uses an item of property is easy to confirm. In view of this fact, the law gives weight to possession and use when determining ownership.

Most of our bargaining examples concern two parties. Communication between two parties is usually cheap, especially when they are near each other. However, many bargains involve three or more parties. Bargaining becomes more costly and difficult as it involves more parties, especially if they are dispersed from one another. This fact may explain why treaties involving many nations are so difficult to conclude.

Finally, the parties may want to draft an agreement, and this may be costly because it must anticipate many contingencies that can arise to change the value of the bargain.

Another obstacle to bargaining is hostility. The parties to the dispute may have emotional concerns that interfere with rational agreement, as when a divorce is bitterly contested. People who hate each other often disagree about the division of the cooperative surplus, even though all the relevant facts are public knowledge. To illustrate, many jurisdictions have rules for dividing property on divorce that are simple and predictable for most childless marriages. However, a significant proportion of these divorces are litigated in court rather than settled by negotiation. In these circumstances, lawyers can facilitate negotiations by interposing themselves between hostile parties.

Even without hostility, however, bargaining can be costly because negotiators may behave unreasonably—for example, by pressing their own advantage too hard (what lawyers refer to as "overreaching"). An essential aspect of bargaining is forming a strategy. In forming a bargaining strategy, each party tries to anticipate how much the opponent will concede. If the parties miscalculate the other party's resolve, each will be

---

[12] See J. Keith Murnighan, BARGAINING GAMES (1992), for a highly readable summary of this literature. For specific experiments on the Coase theorem, see Elizabeth Hoffman and Matthew Spitzer, *The Coase Theorem: Some Experimental Tests*, 25 J. LAW & ECON. 73 (1982), and Hoffman and Spitzer, *Experimental Tests of the Coase Theorem with Large Bargaining Groups,* 15 J. LEGAL STUD. 149 (1986).

surprised to find that the other does not concede, and as a result, negotiations may fail. Miscalculations are likely when the parties do not know each other, when cultural differences obscure communication, or when the parties are committed to conflicting moral positions about fairness.

Enforcement costs, the third and final element of transaction costs, arise when an agreement takes time to fulfill. An agreement that takes no time to fulfill has no enforcement costs. An example is simultaneous exchange, in which I give you a dollar and you give me a watermelon. For complex transactions, monitoring behavior and punishing violations of the agreement can be costly. To illustrate, consider the example from the beginning of this chapter of Bloggs' desire to drain a wetlands on his property in order to develop it as a residential area. Suppose that the city permits him to build on a small part of the wetlands, provided that he does not harm the rest. Officials must watch him to be sure that he keeps his promise. Furthermore, officials may require Bloggs to post bond, which will be confiscated if he harms the rest of the wetlands and returned to him if he completes construction without doing harm. In general, enforcement costs are low when violations of the agreement are easy to observe and punishment is cheap to administer.

Let us summarize what we have learned about transaction costs. Transactions have three stages, each of which has a special type of cost—search costs, bargaining costs, and enforcement costs. These costs vary along a spectrum from zero to indefinitely large, depending upon the transaction. Characteristics of transactions that affect their costs are summarized in Table 4.3.

QUESTION 4.10: Rank the following six transactions from lowest to highest transaction costs. Explain your ranking by reference to the costs of search, bargaining, and enforcement. (There is no uniquely correct answer.)

Table 4.3

FACTORS AFFECTING TRANSACTION COSTS

Lower Transaction Costs	*Higher Transaction Costs*
1. Standardized good or service	1. Unique good or service
2. Clear, simple rights	2. Uncertain, complex rights
3. Few parties	3. Many parties
4. Friendly parties	4. Hostile parties
5. Familiar parties	5. Unfamiliar parties
6. Reasonable behavior	6. Unreasonable behavior
7. Instantaneous exchange	7. Delayed exchange
8. No contingencies	8. Numerous contingencies
9. Low costs of monitoring	9. High costs of monitoring
10. Cheap punishments	10. Costly punishments

a. getting married

b. buying an artichoke

c. acquiring an easement to run a gas line across your neighbor's property

d. selling a Burger King franchise

e. going to college

f. purchasing a warranty for a new car

C. The Level of Transaction Costs and the Appropriate Legal Rule

The Coase theorem holds that the efficient use of resources does not depend on the assignment of property rights in situations of zero transaction costs. This implies that the assignment of property rights might be crucial to the efficient use of resources when transaction costs are *not* zero (an issue to which we shall turn in the next section). And in the previous section we said that transaction costs lie along a spectrum between zero and indefinitely large. We must now try to bring this issue to some practical conclusion by being more specific about the relationship between the level of transaction costs and the appropriate legal rule.

Suppose that we first put in graphical form the argument of the previous section that transaction costs lie on a spectrum from zero to infinity—like that shown in Figure 4.1. We may assign any potential transaction to some point on the spectrum, depending on our assessment of the level of transaction costs (as suggested by the factors in Table 4.3). Then we must ask if these costs are low enough for us to let bargaining determine the efficient use of the resources involved or so high that bargaining will fail—so that some alternative to bargaining is required.

There will be a threshold level of transaction costs on the spectrum that divides the spectrum into a region in which bargaining will work and one in which it will not. Figure 4.1 gives an example of where such a threshold line might be drawn.

Reasonable people may have very different ideas about where that threshold lies. What happens when people have different views about when bargaining will work and when it will fail? Figure 4.2 examines this question. The person whose views are

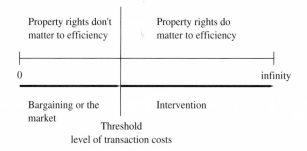

FIGURE 4.1 A threshold level of transaction costs that distinguishes the areas in which the Coase theorem applies and does not apply.

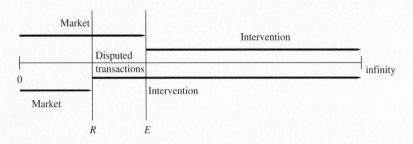

FIGURE 4.2 Different threshold levels of transaction costs, with different views about the appropriate legal rule in property issues.

shown above the spectrum places the threshold at a relatively high level of transaction costs, indicated by line *E*. She believes that bargaining can succeed even at a relatively high level of transaction costs. The person whose views are shown below the spectrum places the threshold at a lower level of transaction costs, indicated by line *R*. He believes that bargaining will succeed in a smaller number of situations. He is, therefore, willing to intervene legally in more situations than the person whose beliefs are shown above the spectrum. We might characterize these two views as one arguing for a (relatively) expansive role for unimpeded bargaining and one arguing for a (relatively) restrictive role for bargaining in deciding issues of efficient resource allocation.

Note that these two people agree that legal intervention improves efficiency for all situations in which transaction costs are above line *E*, and that unimpeded bargaining succeeds for all situations in which transaction costs are below line *R*. They have a disagreement about whether bargaining or legal intervention is the more appropriate means of dealing with those transactions that lie between the two vertical lines.

Consider an example. Suppose that the issue arises as to the appropriate legal rule for dealing with cigarette, cigar, or pipe smoking in restaurants. Should restaurants decide for themselves whether to permit smoking and how much, or should there be legal regulation of the amount and kind of smoking in restaurants? The person who believes that bargaining can succeed in a wider range of situations may be content to let private bargaining between smokers, nonsmokers, and restaurant owners handle the matter. Smokers can pay nonsmokers to allow them to smoke in restaurants. Or nonsmokers can pay smokers not to smoke in restaurants. Either way, the more valuable activity will prevail. Alternatively, restaurant owners have an incentive (profit maximization) to efficiently distribute their restaurant space between smokers and nonsmokers.

Someone else might believe that the transaction costs between smokers and nonsmokers in restaurants are so high as to preclude a bargaining solution to their conflicting interests. He fears that unpleasant and antisocial behavior will take place between smokers and nonsmokers. The government should not delegate the task of separating these potentially warring parties to bargaining, nor to restaurant owners. Rather, the government must intervene and structure a solution. For instance, the government could require restaurants to set aside nonsmoking areas.

This stylized description of the practical application of the Coase theorem points out a common source of disagreement among analysts about matters of public policy.

QUESTION 4.11 Will the people whose threshold values for transaction costs differ as shown in Figure 4.2 agree or disagree about the appropriate method of assigning property rights to smoke or to be free from smoke in the following situations?

   a. smoking in a private residence.

   b. smoking in a public area such as a shopping mall, an indoor arena or concert hall, or an outdoor stadium.

   c. smoking in hotel rooms.

   d. commercial airline flights.

What sorts of arguments will the two people make for and against a bargaining or more interventionist means of dealing with each issue?

D. The Normative Hobbes and Coase Theorems

We have been speaking thus far as if the Coase theorem's only lesson for property law is that the law should determine the level of transaction costs and react accordingly. But we can go further.

Thus far, we have spoken of transaction costs as if they are exogenous to the legal system—that is, as if they are determined solely by objective characteristics of bargaining situations outside the domain of the law. This is not always the case. Some transaction costs are *endogenous* to the legal system in the sense that legal rules can lower obstacles to private bargaining. The Coase Theorem suggests that the law can encourage bargaining by lowering transaction costs.

Lowering transaction costs "lubricates" bargaining. One important way for the law to do this is by defining simple and clear property rights. It is easier to bargain when legal rights are simple and clear than when they are complicated and uncertain. To illustrate, the rule "first in time, first in right" is a simple and clear way to determine ownership claims. Similarly, requiring public recording of property claims makes determining ownership easier. You will encounter many examples throughout this book of other ways that law lubricates bargaining. By lubricating bargaining, the law enables the private parties to exchange legal rights, thus relieving lawmakers of the difficult task of allocating legal rights efficiently.

We can formalize this principle as the *normative Coase theorem*:

Structure the law so as to remove the impediments to private agreements.

The principle is "normative" because it offers guidance to lawmakers. The principle is inspired by the Coase theorem because it assumes that private exchange can allocate legal rights efficiently.

Besides encouraging bargaining, a legal system tries to minimize disagreements and failures to cooperate, which are costly to society. The importance of minimizing the losses from disagreements was especially appreciated by the seventeenth-century English philosopher Thomas Hobbes. Hobbes thought that people would seldom be rational enough to agree upon a division of the cooperative surplus, even when there were no serious impediments to bargaining.[13] Their natural cupidity would lead them to quarrel unless a third, stronger party forced them to agree. These considerations suggest the following principle of property law, which can be called the *normative Hobbes theorem*:

> Structure the law so as to minimize the harm caused by failures in private agreements.[14]

According to this principle, the law should be designed to prevent coercive threats and to eliminate the destructiveness of disagreement.

When the parties fail to reach a private agreement, they lose the surplus from exchange. To minimize the resulting harm, the law should *allocate property rights to the party who values them the most*. By allocating property rights to the party who values them the most, the law makes exchange of rights unnecessary and thus saves the cost of a transaction. To illustrate, the normative Hobbes theorem requires the law to create "open range" (ranchers' rights), rather than "closed range" (farmers' rights) in situations corresponding to our previous example.

These two normative principles of property law—minimize the harm caused by private disagreements over resource allocation (the normative Hobbes theorem), and minimize the obstacles to private agreements over resource allocation (the normative Coase theorem)—have wide application in law. In combination with the Coase theorem discussed earlier and its corollary, these principles will form the heart of our economic analysis of property law in the remainder of this and in the following chapter.

F. Graphing Coase and Hobbes

We can depict these two theorems graphically. The vertical axis in Figure 4.3 depicts the surplus from transferring a legal right from the party who currently holds it to another party. To illustrate, return to our example of the farmer and the rancher, in which transferring the obligation to fence from the rancher (farmers' rights) to the farmer (ranchers' rights) creates a surplus of $25. Thus, "$25" on the vertical axis indicates the surplus from trade when the rule is "farmers' rights." Now reverse the example. Instead of assuming that the rancher has the obligation to fence (farmers' rights), assume that the farmer has the obligation to fence (ranchers' rights). Transferring the obligation to fence from the farmer (ranchers' rights) to the rancher (farmers' rights) creates a surplus of −$25. Thus, −$25 on the vertical axis indicates the surplus from trade when the rule is "ranchers' rights."

A positive surplus from transferring a legal right exists because the lawmaker initially allocates it to the wrong party. The "initial" allocation refers to the allocation before private parties reallocate rights by trading them. The "wrong" party refers to someone who values the right less than someone else. When the law allocates a right to someone who values it less than someone else, the parties can obtain a surplus from trading the right. Such a trade corrects the initial misallocation of rights by the law.

The horizontal axis in Figure 4.3 depicts transaction costs of private exchange of a legal right. In the ideal world of the Coase theorem, transaction costs are zero. In

---

[13] Because Hobbes wrote in the seventeenth century, he did not express himself in quite these terms, but this kind of argument is pervasive in his classic work, LEVIATHAN (1651).

[14] This idea is developed at length in Cooter, *The Cost of Coase*, 11 J. LEGAL STUD. 1 (1982).

Figure 4.3, transaction costs are zero along the vertical axis. In reality, transaction costs are positive, not zero, for the private exchange of legal rights. When transaction costs are positive, they must be subtracted from the surplus to compute the net benefit of private exchange. Thus, if the surplus from exchange is $25, and the transaction costs of private exchange are $10, then the net benefit of private exchange of the legal right is $15. These facts are represented in Figure 4.3 by point (25,10), which is labeled A.

Alternatively, let the surplus continue to be $25, but let the transaction costs be $30. Now the parties would obtain a net benefit of $25 − $30 = −$5 from a private agreement. These facts are represented in the figure by point (25,30), which is labeled B.

Efficiency requires the private exchange of the legal right whenever the surplus exceeds the transaction costs. At every point above the 45° line, the surplus exceeds the transaction costs. So, efficiency requires private exchange of the legal right for all points above the 45° line. Conversely, efficiency requires no exchange of the legal right whenever the transaction costs exceed the surplus. So, efficiency requires no private exchange of the legal right for all points below the 45° line.

When will private exchange occur in fact? If transaction costs exceed the surplus, the net benefit from private exchange is negative. In other words, at least one of the parties will lose from private exchange. A rational person will not voluntarily trade at a loss. So private exchange will not occur among rational people when the net benefit is negative. This fact is indicated in Figure 4.3 by the label "no trade" for points below the 45° line. For example, private exchange of legal rights will not occur at point B.

Conversely, if the surplus exceeds transaction costs, the net benefit from private exchange is positive. In other words, both parties can gain from private exchange. Rational people will usually trade when both can benefit. So private exchange will ordinarily occur among rational people when the net benefit is positive. This fact is indicated in the figure by the label "trade" for points above the 45° line. For example, private exchange of legal rights will occur at point A. Notice that for all points above the 45° line, the parties will trade until the legal right is held by the party who values it the most, even though the law initially allocated the right to the party who valued it less.

We can use Figure 4.3 to illustrate two ways in which law can increase efficiency when transaction costs are positive. First, law can lubricate private exchange by lowering transaction costs. To illustrate using our example of the farmer and the rancher, assume that law assigns the obligation to fence to the rancher (farmers' rights), so a

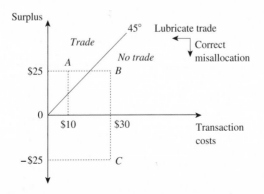

FIGURE 4.3 A graphical representation of the normative Coase and Hobbes theorems.

surplus of $25 could be achieved by transferring the obligation to fence from the rancher to the farmer (ranchers' rights). Assume, however, that transaction costs of private exchange equal $35, so the transfer is blocked. If law can lower the transaction costs of exchange from $35 to $10, transaction costs will no longer block private exchange. When private exchange is not blocked, the obligation of the rancher to build the fence (farmers' rights) can be transferred to the farmer (ranchers' rights), thus creating a net benefit of $15. In terms of the graph, we assume that the initial situation corresponds to B, but law lubricates exchange and changes the situation into A. In general, lubricating the law corresponds to moving from right to left in Figure 4.3. When law lubricates private exchange sufficiently to cross the 45° line from below, the law enables an exchange of legal rights to occur that would not otherwise occur.

Second, law can allocate rights to the party who values them the most. To illustrate using our example of the farmer and the rancher, assume, as before, that law assigns the obligation to fence to the rancher (farmers' rights), so that a surplus of $25 could be achieved by transferring the obligation to fence from the rancher to the farmer (ranchers' rights). Assume, also as before, that transaction costs of private exchange equal $35, so that the transfer is blocked. Finally, assume that law cannot lower the transaction costs of exchange. The other possible remedy is to change the law and assign the obligation to fence to the farmer (ranchers' rights), not the rancher (farmers' rights). If the farmer has the obligation to fence, the legal rights are allocated efficiently. When the right is already allocated efficiently, exchange of the right would produce a negative surplus. In our example, the negative surplus equals −$25, which corresponds to point C in Figure 4.3. Consequently, changing the law from farmers' rights to ranchers' rights corresponds to a move from B to C in the figure. In general, changing the law to reallocate legal rights from the party who values them less to the party who values them more corresponds to moving down in Figure 4.3. When law reallocates legal rights sufficiently to cross the horizontal axis from above, the law makes private exchange unnecessary.

Figure 4.3 illustrates that, by allocating rights initially to the party who values them the most, lawmakers save society the transaction cost of trading the rights. However, lawmakers often do not know who values rights the most, and finding out can be very difficult. To illustrate, consider the problem of finding out the cost of fencing the farmer's crops. When testifying in court, the farmer has an incentive to exaggerate these costs. Knowing this fact, the judge and the jury are not sure whether to believe the farmer. As another example, assume that the courts need to compensate the owners of Blackacre, which has been the estate of the Gascoyne-Stubbs family for 15 generations. Blackacre has a market value of $1 million. Its present owner, Brewster Gascoyne–Stubbs, must value it at more than $1 million or else he would have sold it. But how much more? Courts and legislators cannot tell, especially because, when asked, Mr. Gascoyne-Stubbs has incentives to exaggerate.

Efficient lawmakers apparently face a trade-off between transaction costs and information costs. By strictly following precedent, courts avoid the information costs of determining who values a right the most and leave to the parties whatever transaction costs of trading legal rights there may be. By determining who values a legal right the most, courts relieve the parties of the transaction costs of trading legal rights but incur the information costs of determining who values a right the most. Efficiency requires the courts to do whichever is cheaper. To formalize this claim, let *IC* denote the information cost to a court of determining who values a legal right the most. Let TC indicate the transaction cost of trading legal rights. Efficient courts would follow this rule:

$IC < TC \quad \Rightarrow \quad$ allocate the legal right initially to the person who values it the most;

$TC < IC \quad \Rightarrow \quad$ strictly follow precedent.

QUESTION 4.12:

a. When transaction costs are low enough, efficient resource allocation will follow regardless of the particular assignment of property rights. When transaction costs are high enough, efficient resource allocation requires assigning property rights to the party who values them the most. How is this threshold indicated in Figure 4.3?

b. To achieve efficiency when transaction costs are high, the courts must allocate the legal right to the party who values it the most. Use Figure 4.3 to explain this proposition.

c. Can you use the normative Hobbes theorem to justify legislation regulating the collective bargaining process between employers and employee unions?

d. When people strongly disagree, they may try to harm each other, or they may walk away from a potentially profitable exchange. What does the normative Hobbes theorem suggests the response of the law should be to these two possibilities?

V. HOW ARE PROPERTY RIGHTS PROTECTED?

Now we have the tools to answer one of the four fundamental questions of property law that we posed at the beginning of this chapter: "What are the remedies for the violation of property rights?" This question concerns how a court should respond when a private person or the government interferes with someone's property rights. Our discussion in this chapter will focus on interference by a private person. We consider government interference in the next chapter.

A. Damages and Injunctions

First, we need some background. The remedies available to a common law court are either *legal* or *equitable*. The principal *legal* remedy is the payment of *compensatory money damages* by the defendant to the plaintiff. These damages are a sum of money that compensates the plaintiff for the wrongs inflicted upon her by the defendant. The court determines the appropriate amount of money that will, as the saying goes, "make the plaintiff whole." The measurement of this sum is a complex subject itself, which we discuss later.[15] *Equitable* relief consists of an order by the court directing the defendant to perform an act or to refrain from acting in a particular manner. This order is

---

[15] There are two more things you should be aware of. First, if a defendant fails to pay a judgment that a court has awarded against him or her, the defendant's property may be seized and sold in order to raise the judgment amount. Second, compensatory damages are to be distinguished from *punitive damages*, which are money damages over and above compensatory damages assessed against the defendant. The purpose of punitive damages is to punish the defendant, not to compensate the plaintiff. We discuss punitive damages in Chapter 9.

frequently in the form of an *injunction*, which is said to "enjoin" the defendant to do or to refrain from doing a specific act.[16]

Notice that legal relief is "backward-looking" in the sense that it compensates a plaintiff for a harm already suffered, whereas equitable relief is "forward-looking" in the sense that it prevents a defendant from inflicting a harm on the plaintiff in the future. Thus, a court may combine the two forms of relief, awarding money damages for past harms and enjoining acts that could cause future harm.

Damages are the usual remedy for broken promises and accidents, whereas injunction is the usual remedy for appropriating, trespassing, or interfering with another's property. In other words, damages are the usual remedy in the law of contracts and torts, whereas injunction is the usual remedy in the law of property. To illustrate, the farmer will have to pay damages to the rancher for breach of a contract to deliver hay or for accidentally shooting the rancher's cow while hunting. But if the cattle trespass on the farmer's crops (and if farmers have a right to be free from the depredations of stray cattle), then the court will probably award damages for past harm and enjoin the rancher to constrain her cattle in the future.

B. Laundry and Electric Company: An Example

An injunction may appear to be an absolute proscription on an act. For example, if the court were to enjoin the future invasion of the farmer's corn fields by the rancher's cattle, one might interpret that as meaning that the rancher will have to erect a fence. This is a mistake. The injunctive remedy does not prevent the invasion of the farmer's property by the rancher's cattle from ever occurring, only from its occurring without the consent of the farmer. The farmer is free to make a contract promising *not* to enforce the injunction. To illustrate, the farmer might agree not to enforce the injunction in exchange for payment of a sum of money by the rancher.

Given these facts, the right to an injunction should be regarded as a clear assignment of a property right. Once the property right is clearly assigned, its owner may strike a bargain to sell it. Thus, if the court enjoined the rancher from allowing future invasion by her cattle, this could be viewed as a declaration that the farmer has the legally enforceable right to be free from invasion by cattle. If the rancher's value on being allowed to invade the farmer's property is greater than the farmer's value on being free from invasion, there is scope for a bargain in which the rancher buys the right from the farmer.

Most legal disputes are settled by bargaining between the parties without going to trial, but the terms of the bargain are affected by the remedy that would be available at trial.[17] Specifically, the terms of the bargain are different depending upon whether the remedy is damages or injunction. An example from Chapter 1 will help you to understand the relationship between remedies and bargains.

---

[16] The consequences to a defendant of violating an equitable decree are far more serious than the consequences of failing to pay a monetary judgment. A defendant's failure to abide by an injunction not only leaves the plaintiff at a loss, but it also constitutes an insult to the authority of the court. A defendant who ignores an equitable order may be held in contempt of court and imprisoned until she agrees to abide by the order.

[17] This is referred to as "bargaining in the shadow of the law."

FACTS: The E Electric Company emits smoke, which dirties the wash at the L Laundry. No one else is affected because E and L are near each other and far from anyone else. E can abate this external cost by installing scrubbers on its stacks, and L can reduce the damage by installing filters on its ventilation system. The installation of scrubbers by E or filters by L completely eliminates the damage from pollution. Table 4.4 shows the profits of each company, depending upon what action is taken to reduce the pollution. (The profits that are shown in the matrix exclude any compensation that might be paid or received as a consequence of a legal dispute.)

The numbers in Table 4.4 can be explained as follows. When E does not install scrubbers, its profits are 1000 (regardless of what the laundry does). When L does not install filters and does not suffer pollution damages (because E has installed scrubbers), L's profits are 300. Pollution destroys 200 of L's profits. L can avoid this by installing filters at a cost of 100, or E can avoid it by installing scrubbers at a cost of 500. Check to see that you can use these facts to explain the numbers in the table.

The most efficient outcome is, by definition, a situation in which the total profits for the two parties, called the "joint profits," are greatest. The joint profits are found by adding the two numbers in each cell of the table. Joint profits are maximized in the northeast cell, where 1200 is attained when E does not install scrubbers and L installs filters.

The harm caused by pollution represents a source of contention between E and L. They may be able to settle their disagreement and cooperate with each other, or they may fail to cooperate and litigate their dispute. What we are interested in determining here is how the remedy available from a court may induce the parties to achieve the efficient solution and thus to minimize the harm of pollution.

Suppose that E and L litigate their disagreement. Three alternative rules of law could be applied in the event of a trial:

1. E is free to pollute.
2. L is entitled to compensatory damages from E. (Compensatory damages are a sum of money that E pays to L to make up for L's reduced profits due to E's pollution.)
3. L is entitled to an injunction forbidding E to pollute. (An injunction is a court order requiring E to stop polluting.)

Let us determine the value of the noncooperative solution under each of these rules.

Table 4.4

PROFITS BEFORE LEGAL ACTION

		Laundry	
		No filter	*Filter*
Electric Company	No Scrubbers	100; 1000	200; 1000
	Scrubbers	300; 500	200; 500

‡ The laundry's profits are given first in each cell; the electric company's profits are given second in each cell.

Beginning with rule 1, if E is free to pollute, the most profitable action for E is not to install scrubbers and to enjoy profits of 1000. The most profitable response for L is to install filters and enjoy profits of 200. Thus, the noncooperative value of the rule of free pollution is 1200. This is the efficient solution, which is in the northeast cell of the table.

Turning to rule 2, if E must pay damages to L for polluting, then L will not bother to install filters. E will have to pay damages to L equal to the difference between the profits L enjoys when there is no pollution, 300, and the profits L enjoys with pollution, 100. E has a choice between installing the scrubbers and paying damages of 200 to L. The more profitable alternative is for E *not* to install the scrubbers: it initially realizes 1000 in profits, from which 200 must be subtracted to pay damages, leaving E with net profits of 800. L enjoys net profits of 300 (100 from its operations plus 200 from E). The noncooperative value under rule 2 (a rule of liability for compensatory damages) is then $1100 = 300 + 800$. This is the value in the northwest cell in the table.

Turning to rule 3, if E is enjoined from polluting and responds by installing scrubbers, E's profits equal 500. When E installs scrubbers, L will not bother to install filters, so L's profits will be 300. Thus, the noncooperative value under the rule of enjoining pollution is $800 = 500 + 300$, which corresponds to the southwest cell of the table.

Under the pessimistic assumption that E and L cannot cooperate, only one of the legal rules produces an efficient outcome—namely, rule 1. Instead of making the pessimistic assumption that the parties will be unable to cooperate, suppose we make the optimistic assumption that the parties can settle their disagreement cooperatively. (We are assuming that transaction costs are very low.) When E and L cooperate, their best strategy is to maximize the joint profits of the two enterprises. The profits are maximized when they take the efficient course of action, which, in this case, is for L to install filters and E not to install scrubbers, yielding joint profits of 1200. This is the efficient solution in the northeast cell.

There are, thus, two ways to achieve the efficient solution. One way is for the law to adopt the rule for which the noncooperative solution is efficient. This solution is commended by the normative Hobbes theorem. In our example (but not necessarily other pollution examples), the noncooperative solution is efficient under rule 1, which gives E the freedom to pollute. The other way to achieve efficiency is for the parties to cooperate. The cooperative solution is efficient under all three of the possible laws. According to the Coase theorem, inefficient allocations of legal rights by laws such as rules 2 and 3 will be cured by private agreements, provided that bargaining is successful.

If transaction costs equal zero and successful bargaining can cure inefficient laws, what difference does the law make? One answer is that the law affects the distribution of the cooperative product, which affects bargaining. To illustrate this point about distribution, recall how the structure of the law—such as rules 1, 2, and 3—affects the threat values of the parties. A reasonable bargaining solution is for each party to receive his or her threat value plus an equal share of the cooperative surplus. Each party to a bargain would prefer the rule of law that provides him or her with the largest threat value. Specifically, the threat value of the plaintiff in a property dispute is at least as great when the remedy for future harm is injunctive relief as when the remedy is damages. The plaintiff, consequently, prefers the remedy of injunctive relief for future harm, or, better yet, injunctive relief for future harm and damages for past harm. In contrast, the defendant prefers the damage remedy for future harm or, better yet, no remedy.

The effect of the rule of law on the distribution of the cooperative product can be computed precisely for E and L. Imagine that E and L enter into negotiations, and, to keep the arithmetic simple, assume that negotiating a settlement or going to trial is costless for the parties (swallow hard!). The noncooperative payoffs—that is, the profits the parties can get on their own if negotiations fail—are shown in Table 4.5 under each of the three rules. The cooperative surplus, which equals the difference between the joint profits from cooperation and the threat values, is shown in the middle column. A reasonable bargaining solution is for each party to receive his or her threat value plus half the surplus from cooperation. The payoffs to the two parties from cooperation are given in the two columns on the right side of the table. Notice that in each case the cooperative payoffs sum to 1200, but that L receives the largest share under the injunctive rule (rule 3), an intermediate share under damages (rule 2), and the smallest share when E is free to pollute (rule 1).

QUESTION 4.13: Why is the cost to the defendant of implementing an injunction to end future interference at least as great as paying damages for future interference? Is this fact generally true or just a special feature of this example?

C. Efficient Remedies

We mentioned that injunction is the usual remedy for breach of a property right. We would like to explain this generalization, as well as exceptions to it, in terms of efficiency. The preceding example showed that damages and injunctions are equally efficient remedies when transaction costs equal zero. Consequently, differences in their efficiency must depend upon transaction costs. To explain why injunction is an efficient remedy for breach of a property right, we must discuss the connection between property rights and transaction costs.

Earlier we noted that bargaining is more successful when the legal rights of the parties are clear and simple. Injunction is often clearer and simpler than damages. Injunction is clearer and simpler because the determination of damages by courts can be unpredictable. To illustrate, it is difficult for a court to assign monetary value to the damage caused by the Windsong satellite's straying into the orbit of Orbitcom's satellite in Example 2. Similarly, it is difficult for a court to assign monetary value to the damage caused by the intrusion of Potatoes' house onto two meters of Parsley's land in Example 5. In contrast,

Table 4.5

PROFITS FROM BARGAINING UNDER THREE LEGAL RULES

	Noncooperation		Surplus	Cooperation	
	E	*L*		*E*	*L*
rule 1	1000	200	0	1000	200
rule 2	800	300	100	850	350
rule 3	500	300	400	700	500

the right to an injunction gives the parties a clear position from which to bargain. In the course of bargaining, they may establish the value of the damage themselves.

These facts suggest that the injunctive remedy may be more efficient than damages when the parties can bargain with each other. In other words, the best policy for the law is to lubricate bargaining by defining clear and simple rights when transaction costs are already low.

If, however, transaction costs are so high as to preclude bargaining, defining clear and simple rights contributes little to efficiency. To illustrate, suppose that each of the homeowners affected by the stench from the feedlot in Example 3 at the beginning of the chapter had the legal right to enjoin the feedlot from emitting the stench. In order to continue operating, the feedlot would have to negotiate an agreement not to enforce the injunction with each of the homeowners. Transaction costs preclude negotiating so many agreements. On the other hand, if each of the affected homeowners were entitled to money damages, the court might order compensation according to a simple, "wholesale" formula, so that the feedlot could pay damages and continue operating. These facts suggest that damages may be a more efficient remedy when transaction costs are high.

We have reached the conclusion of a famous article by Professor (now Judge) Guido Calabresi and A. Douglas Melamed,[18] who proposed the following rules for determining the best remedy for violating a legal right:

> Where there are obstacles to cooperation (*i.e.*, high transaction costs), the more efficient remedy is the award of compensatory money damages.

> Where there are few obstacles to cooperation (*i.e.*, low transaction costs), the more efficient remedy is the award of an injunction against the defendant's interference with the plaintiff's property.

These two propositions have a simple interpretation in terms of Figure 4.3. In the "no-trade" zone, which consists of points *below* the 45° line, the more efficient remedy is damages. In the "trade" zone, which consists of points *above* the 45° line, the more efficient remedy is an injunction.

To illustrate these rules, consider a modification of the example of the laundry and the electric company. Instead of assuming that bargaining costs are zero, let us assume that these costs are so high as to preclude bargaining. Consequently, the outcome that will prevail is the "noncooperative" solution in Table 4.5. The noncooperative solution under the damage rule yields joint profits of 1100, whereas the noncooperative solution under the injunction rule yields joint profits of 800. Thus, the example illustrates the fact that the damage remedy is at least as efficient as the injunctive remedy when transaction costs preclude bargaining.

The reason that damages are more efficient than injunctions when transaction costs preclude bargaining is easy to see from this example. If damages perfectly compensate the laundry, its profits remain the same (specifically, 300) regardless of whether or not

---

[18] Calabresi and Melamed, *Property Rules, Liability Rules, and Inalienability: One View of the Cathedral*, 85 HARV. L. REV. 1089 (1972). As the title indicates, the authors consider a third method of encouraging the efficient use of property—inalienability, the forbidding of a bargaining solution to the use of a property right. We discuss the efficiency of that method briefly in the next chapter.

the electric company pollutes. So, the laundry is indifferent between the damage and injunction remedies (assuming no bargaining). Under the damages remedy, the electric company can pollute and pay damages, or it can abate and not pay damages. Its profits increase from 500 to 800 when it pollutes and pays damages, rather than abating. In contrast, an injunction (with no bargaining) removes this choice. Specifically, the injunction forces the electric company to abate, in which case its profits are 500. In general, when transaction costs preclude bargaining, a switch in remedy from injunction to compensatory damages makes the victim no worse off, whereas the injurer may be better off and cannot be worse off.

We have illustrated the superiority of the damages remedy when transaction costs are high. Now we modify the example to illustrate the superiority of the injunctive remedy when transaction costs are low. Assume that bargaining (or transaction) costs are positive but that, because an injunction is so simple and clear, these bargaining costs are less under the injunctive remedy than under the damages remedy. Specifically, assume that transaction costs equal 150 under the damages rule and 50 under the injunction rule. As indicated in Table 4.5, the surplus from cooperation under the damages rule equals 100, so the net benefit from cooperation equals -50 ($= 100 - 150$). Given negative net benefits from cooperating, the parties have no scope to bargain under the damages rule. Instead of bargaining, the electric company will pollute and pay damages, yielding net profits of 800 to E and 300 to L, and joint profits of 1100 ($= 800 + 300$).

In contrast, the surplus from cooperation under the injunction rule equals 400, and bargaining costs equal 50, so the net benefit from cooperation equals 350 ($= 400 - 50$). Given positive net benefits from cooperating, the parties have scope to bargain. A reasonable agreement would give each company its threat value plus half of the net benefits from cooperating. Specifically, a reasonable agreement yields net profits equaling 675 to E and 475 to L, and joint profits of 1150. In this example, the injunctive remedy is more efficient because it lubricates private bargaining sufficiently to induce cooperation.

When these two rules are applied in practice, the preferred legal remedy depends in large part upon how many parties must participate in a settlement. Most of our bargaining examples concern two parties. Communication between two parties is usually cheap, especially when they are near each other. Similarly, many property disputes frequently involve small numbers of contiguous land owners. The obstacles to cooperation are usually few in disputes involving a small number of geographically concentrated people who know each other well. In those circumstances, communication costs are obviously low; the parties can monitor the agreement at low cost because each person can observe what happens on her own land; and, finally, the strategic costs are low if land ownership is stable and contiguous owners know each other well. Bargaining is likely to be successful in these circumstances and, therefore, the most efficient remedy for resolving most property disputes is injunctive relief.[19]

However, many bargains involve three or more parties. The greater the number of people involved and the more dispersed they are, the greater the costs of communicating among them. Private bargaining is unlikely to succeed in disputes involving a large number of geographically dispersed strangers because communication costs are high,

---

[19] This explains Calabresi and Melamed's characterization of equitable remedies as "property rules."

monitoring is costly, and strategic behavior is likely to occur. Large numbers of land owners are typically affected by nuisances, such as air pollution or the stench from the feedlot in Example 3. In these cases, damages are the preferred remedy.

QUESTION 4.14: Use the theory of transaction costs to explain whether the following rights should be protected by injunction or damages:

    a. a land owner's right to exclude from his property a neighbor's gas line.

    b. a new car owner's right to have her car's defective transmission replaced by the seller.

    c. a homeowner's right to be free from air pollution by a nearby factory.

    d. a spouse's right to half the house upon divorce.

QUESTION 4.15: Suppose that two people choose to litigate a dispute. Should the law presume that if two parties are prepared to litigate, transaction costs must be high, and therefore the court should choose damages as the remedy, not an injunction?

VI. WHAT CAN BE PRIVATELY OWNED?

In this section we turn to another fundamental question of property law: should property rights be privately or collectively held? First, we use the economic distinction between public and private goods (developed in Chapter 2) to differentiate those resources that will be most efficiently used if privately owned from those that will be most efficiently used if publicly owned. Second, we look at property rights in information as an example of the distinction between the efficiency of private and public ownership.

A. Public and Private Goods[20]

Most examples of property that we have discussed thus far in this book are what economists call "private goods." Goods that economists describe as purely private have the characteristic that one person's use precludes another's: for example, when one person eats an apple, others cannot eat it; a pair of pants can be worn only by one person at a time; a car cannot go two different directions simultaneously; and so forth. These facts are sometimes summarized by saying that there is rivalry in the consumption of private goods.

The polar opposite is a purely public good, for which there is no rivalry in consumption. A conventional example of a public good is military security in the nuclear age. Supplying one citizen with protection from nuclear attack does not diminish the amount of protection supplied to other citizens. For a purely public good, there is no rivalry in consumption.

There is also another attribute that distinguishes private and public goods. Once property rights are defined over private goods, they are (relatively) cheap to enforce. Specifically, the owner can exclude others from using them at low cost. For example, a farm can be fenced at relatively low cost to exclude trespassing cattle. With public

---

[20] Before reading this section, you may find it helpful to review the material on public goods in Chapter 2.

goods, however, it is costly to exclude anyone from enjoying them. To illustrate, it is virtually impossible to supply different amounts of protection against nuclear attack to different citizens.

Having explained the private-public distinction in economics and law, we can now relate them to each other. The relationship is very simple: efficiency requires that private goods should be privately owned and public goods should be publicly owned. In other words, efficiency requires that rivalrous and excludable goods should be controlled by individuals or small groups of people, whereas nonrivalrous and nonexcludable goods should be controlled by a large group of people such as the state. Thus, the distinction between private and public goods should guide the development of property rules to answer the question, "What can be privately owned?"

We can explain the central idea, not the details, for this prescription. Being rivalrous, private goods must be used and consumed by individuals, not enjoyed equally by everyone. Efficiency requires the use and consumption of each private good by the party who values it the most. In a free market, exchanges occur until each good is held by the party who values it the most. Thus, the law can achieve the efficient allocation of private goods by, for example, lowering bargaining costs by assigning clear and simple ownership rights. Once the state recognizes private property rights, the owner of a private good can exclude others from using or consuming that right, except by the owner's consent. The owner's power to exclude channels the use or consumption of private goods into voluntary exchange, which fosters the efficient use of those goods. This is an example of "lubricating bargaining."

In contrast, the technical character of public goods obstructs the use of bargaining to achieve efficiency. To illustrate, suppose that a particular city block is plagued by crime, so some residents propose hiring a private guard. Many residents will voluntarily contribute to the guard's salary, but suppose that some refuse. The paying residents may instruct the guard not to aid nonpayers in the event of a mugging. Even so, the presence of the guard on the street will make it safer for everyone, because muggers are unlikely to know who has and who has not paid for the guard's services. Given these facts, there is not much that the payers can do to compel nonpayers to contribute.

Those people who do not pay for their consumption of a public good are called "free riders." To appreciate this concept, imagine that a street car has an electric meter in it and, in order to make the street car move, the riders must put money into the meter. The riders will realize that anyone who pays provides a free ride for everyone else. Perhaps some riders will, nonetheless, put their full fare into the meter; some will put some money in but not their full fare; and some will not put anything in at all. Because of "free riders," not enough money will be put in the meter, so the street car company will provide fewer street cars than efficiency requires. In general, markets supply too little of a public good because the private supplier cannot exclude users of it who do not pay their share of the costs.

We have explained that private goods, which exhibit rivalry and exclusion, ought to be privately owned, and that public goods, which exhibit nonrivalry and nonexclusion, ought to be publicly owned. We illustrate this proposition as applied to land. Some efficient uses of land involve a small area and affect a small group of people, such as building a house or growing corn. "Housing" and "corn" are rivalrous goods with low exclusion costs, so markets easily form for housing and corn. Other efficient uses of land involve a large area and affect a large group of people. For example, the use of an uncongested airspace by airplanes or the use of the high seas for shipping are not rivalrous and exclusion is costly.

Thus, airspace and the high seas are public goods. As congestion increases from more planes and ships, governments impose rules on the use of the air and seas.

These are examples in which private goods are privately owned and public goods are publicly owned, as required for efficiency. There are, however, many examples of private goods that are publicly owned. Public ownership of a private good typically results in its misallocation, by which we mean that it is used or consumed by someone other than the person who values it the most. For example, leases for grazing cattle on public lands may be granted to the friends of politicians. Similarly, the officials who administer the leases may not monitor compliance to prevent overgrazing, the ranchers who overgraze the land may cause it to erode. Much of the impetus for "deregulation" has come from the realization that much government activity concerns private goods where markets should be lubricated, rather than government intruding directly in the process of allocation. For example, the realization that transportation by railroad, airplane, and barge are private services that should be supplied by free markets has lead to the dismantling of the Interstate Commerce Commission, the Civil Aeronautics Board, and other regulatory agencies in the United States.

One way to contrast private and public ownership is in terms of transaction costs. Private ownership imposes various transaction costs of private enforcement and exchange. Public ownership imposes transaction costs in terms of public administration and collective decision-making. To illustrate the difference, consider two possible ways to control air pollution from a factory. The private property approach is to grant each property owner the right to clean air, protected by the remedy of compensatory damages. This method will result in many landowners suing for damages or bargaining to settle out of court. Alternatively, the public property approach would declare that clean air is a public good, and assign the task of air quality control to a government agency. This method will result in political bargaining and regulations, as well as the misallocation of resources. From this perspective, the choice between private and public ownership should depend upon whether the costs of private enforcement and exchange are more or less than the costs of public administration, political bargaining, and resource misallocation.

In the next chapter we will continue developing these themes by discussing two important questions: for what specific resources is private ownership more efficient than public or communal ownership and vice versa? And under what circumstances should government be allowed to take private property from citizens?[21]

QUESTION 4.16: If everyone has free access to a public beach, who, if anyone, has the power to control the use of this resource?

B. An Example of a Public Good: Property Rights in Information

An example of a public good that is increasingly important in modern society is information. What special problems exist in defining property rights in information? On the

---

[21] We are not, of course, suggesting that the current division of responsibility between public and private providers of goods and services necessarily follows the rules we have just set down. That is, there are current instances of the government provision or subsidization of private goods and of the private (under-) provision of public goods. The extent to which these anomalies exist and why they persist are two of the central concerns of the branch of microeconomic theory called "public choice theory."

demand side, consumers are uncertain about the utility of information because it is difficult to determine its value until one has it. But consumers cannot have information until they have paid for it. Yet they cannot know how much to pay for information until they have determined its utility by having it. There is no easy way into this circle. The problems on the supply side are just as formidable. Information is costly to produce, and yet it costs relatively little to transmit. Thus, it is extremely hard for anyone who has devoted resources to the production of information to appropriate its value through the sale of that information. This is because the instant the producer sells the information to one consumer, that consumer becomes a potential competitor of the original producer, owing to the low cost of transmitting information.[22] Consumers desire to become "free riders" for information, paying no more than the cost of transmission for the commodity. (Have you ever copied for free a computer program or taped a friend's record or a televised concert?)

These considerations suggest that the unregulated market will produce suboptimal amounts of information, such as in inventive ideas and in creative works like books, paintings, and music. And this, in turn, suggests the need for governmental intervention in the market for information. This governmental intervention can take one of two general forms: (1) governmental supply of information or (2) governmental subsidization of the private provision of information (either directly from general governmental revenues or indirectly through the tax system). In fact, the government does both of these things. An example of the governmental production and dissemination of information is the weather forecasting services offered by federal and state governments. Examples of the governmental subsidization of the private provision of information are the governmental funding of basic research in the sciences, humanities, and the arts, and the awarding of monopoly rights to the creators of information through the patent, copyright, and trademark systems. In the next chapter we shall explore the economics of intellectual property.

VII. WHAT MAY OWNERS DO WITH THEIR PROPERTY?

We used the theory of private and public goods to answer the question, "What can be privately owned?" Closely related to the theory of public goods is the theory of externalities, which we discussed in Chapter 2. Now we return to that theory in order to answer the question, "What may owners do with their property?"

Legislation imposes many restrictions upon what a person may do with his or her property. But at common law there are relatively few restrictions, with the general rule being that any use is allowed that does not interfere with other people's property or other rights. Indeed, we could say that common law approximates a legal system of *maximum liberty*, which allows owners to do anything with their property that does not interfere with other peoples' property or other rights. The restriction of noninterference finds justification in the economic concept of *external cost*. Recall that external costs are those costs involuntarily imposed upon one person by another. Because market transactions are voluntary, externalities are outside the market system of exchange—hence their name. For example, a factory that emits

---

[22] In the literature on the economics of information this problem is frequently referred to as the problem of *nonappropriability*.

thick, cloying smoke into a residential neighborhood is generating an externality. In Example 3 at the beginning of this chapter, the stench from the cattle feedlot is an externality that interferes with Foster's enjoyment of her house. In Example 4, the development of Bloggs' wetlands will interfere with the town's enjoyment of its rivers and streams. Notice that these types of interference are like a public good in that they affect many property owners. There is, as it were, no rivalry or exclusion from smelling the feedlot's stench among Foster and her neighbors. These forms of interference are thus like a public good, except they are bad rather than good.

We have already explained why markets cannot arise to supply public goods efficiently. The same set of considerations explains why private bargaining cannot solve the problem of externalities, or, as we called them in a previous section, public bads. To illustrate, suppose that Foster had enough money to pay the feedlot to stop emitting its stench. If she made this private deal with the feedlot, all of her neighbors would also benefit but without having to pay for that benefit. This fact suggests that Foster will not pay the feedlot to stop its malodorous activities. More generally, the free-rider problem prevents private bargaining solutions to the problem of externalities or public bads. Some form of legal intervention is called for. One possibility is a rule forbidding involuntary invasion, supported by provisions for remedies if that invasion takes place. We have already noted how bargaining theory can help to design the form that remedy should take, namely, the payment of compensatory money damages. An alternative remedy that we will consider in the following chapter is regulation of the public bad or external-cost-generating activity by an administrative agency.

By contrast, *private* bads may be self-correcting through private agreements (recall the rancher-farmer example), so that there may be no need for an intrusive legal solution. Instead, the courts can stand prepared to issue an injunction in the confident expectation that they will seldom be required to do so.

VIII. ON DISTRIBUTION

We have developed an economic theory of property based upon efficient ownership. However, some critics of economics believe that property law should be based upon distribution, not efficiency. To illustrate using our example of the farmer and the rancher, we saw that the alternative legal rules are equally efficient when transaction costs are zero but that they distribute costs differently. The farmer prefers for the rancher to pay the costs of fencing, whereas the rancher prefers for the farmer to pay. Like the farmer and rancher, everyone *is* concerned about the distribution of wealth. Indeed, many people consider the distribution of wealth to be more important to public policy than the efficient allocation of resources. In general, a property right is valuable and the person to whom it is assigned becomes richer.

When transaction costs are zero, the assignment of legal rights affects distribution but not efficiency. So why shouldn't the law assign property rights explicitly on wealth-distribution grounds?

Some people think that government should redistribute wealth from rich to poor for the sake of social justice, whereas other people think that government should avoid redistributing wealth. Like the rest of the population, economists disagree among themselves about redistributive *ends* or *goals*. However, economists generally agree about redistributive *means*. Many economists believe that redistributive goals can be accomplished better in modern states by progressive taxation than by reshuffling property rights. If economists are right, people who believe that government should redistribute wealth for the sake of social justice should not advocate using property law for this purpose.

There are many reasons why taxation is superior to property law as a means of redistribution. First, the income tax precisely targets inequality, whereas property law relies upon crude averages. To illustrate, suppose that the rule of law in a particular county in Montana is "ranchers' rights." If ranchers are richer than farmers on average in this county, then changing the rule to "farmers' rights" would redistribute wealth towards greater equality. However, while ranchers are richer than farmers *on average*, some farmers are undoubtedly richer than some ranchers. Changing the property rights to favor farmers over ranchers will aggravate the inequality between the rich farmers and poor ranchers. In contrast, progressive taxation will ameliorate unequal incomes.

A second objection is that reshuffling property rights may not really have the distributive effects anticipated. To illustrate, suppose that both farmers and ranchers rent their land from absentee owners. If property law shifts the cost of fencing from farmers to ranchers, competition among landlords may cause them to adjust rents to offset the change in costs. Specifically, the landlords who own farm land will increase the rent charged to farmers, and the landlords who own ranch land will decrease the rent charged to ranchers. Consequently, the reshuffling of property rights will not affect the distribution of wealth between farmers and ranchers. Instead, the landlords who own farms will gain and the landlords who own ranches will lose. In general, any change in the value of land gets "capitalized" into rent. Consequently, the wealth effects of reshuffling property rights in a world with zero transaction costs tend to fall upon the owners of land, not its users.[23]

So far we have discussed the case against redistribution through property rights in a world of zero transaction costs. In such a world, property rights can be reshuffled to pursue distributive goals without any efficiency costs. In reality, transaction costs are positive, and reshuffling property rights for the sake of redistribution has efficiency costs. For each dollar of value transferred from one group to another, a fraction of a dollar is typically used up in accomplishing the transfer.

A vivid example will help you to appreciate the costs of redistribution.[24] Suppose that there are two oases in the desert, one of which has ice cream and the other has none. The state declares that fairness requires the first oasis to share its ice cream with the second oasis. A large bowl is filled with ice cream in the first oasis, and a youth begins running across the desert carrying the bowl to the second oasis. The hot sun

---

[23] Professor Coase make this argument in *Notes on the Problem of Social Cost* in THE FIRM, THE MARKET, AND THE LAW (1988). In general, taxes and other government impositions finally fall upon factors in relatively fixed supply, such as land.

[24] Professor George Stigler of the University of Chicago, a Nobel Laureate in economics, developed this example.

melts some of the ice cream, so the first oasis gives up more ice cream than the second oasis receives. The melted ice cream represents the cost of redistribution. The faster the runner, the less the ice cream melts. Efficient redistribution requires choosing the fastest runner to transport the ice cream.

When a dollar is transferred from one group to another, the fraction of a dollar used up is much larger for transfers through property law than through income taxation. Redistribution through property law, rather than progressive income taxation, is like choosing one of the slowest youths to run with the ice cream. The enforcement of legal rights requires attorneys. A plaintiff's attorney in the United States routinely charges one third of the judgment. In contrast, the fee paid to an accountant who prepares someone's income tax return is a small fraction of the person's tax liability.

In addition, there is another reason for the relative inefficiency of redistribution by property law. Redistribution by property law distorts the economy more than progressive taxation in the long run. For example, if property law favors farmers over ranchers, some rich ranchers may switch to farming to gain valuable legal rights. In contrast, a comprehensive income tax precludes people from reducing their tax liability by changing the source of their income.[25] For these reasons and more, economists who favor redistribution and economists who oppose it can agree that property law is usually the wrong way to pursue distributive justice. Unfortunately, these facts are not appreciated by many lawyers who have not studied economics.

CONCLUSION

We viewed property law as a device to facilitate private bargaining and minimize the harm that results from failures to reach private agreements. Property law creates, protects, and enhances the transactional structure of voluntary exchanges. Voluntary exchange transfers property rights from one person to another. We developed the distinction between private goods and public goods to answer the question, "What can be privately owned?" We concluded that private ownership is appropriate when there is rivalry and exclusion in the use of goods. Next, we developed the economic concept of an externality to answer the question, "What can owners do with their property?" We showed a close fit between economic analysis and the common law principle that allows owners to do anything with their property that does not interfere with others. Finally, we asked how property rights are protected. We concluded that owners should be protected by injunction when doing so results in low transaction costs for private bargaining, whereas owners should be protected by damages when high transaction costs preclude private bargaining. Specifically, we concluded that owners should be protected against externalities of the private-bad type by the injunctive remedy and that they should be protected against externalities of the public-bad type by receiving compensatory damages.

---

[25] A fundamental principle in public finance is that taxes distort less when applied to a broad base rather than to a narrow base. Distortion decreases with the breadth of the base because demand becomes less elastic. To illustrate, the demand for food is less elastic than the demand for vegetables, and the demand for vegetables is less elastic than the demand for carrots. Income is a very broad base.

SUGGESTED READINGS

Ackerman, Bruce, ed., THE ECONOMIC FOUNDATIONS OF PROPERTY LAW (1976).

Barzel, Yoram, THE ECONOMICS OF PROPERTY RIGHTS (1988).

Becker, Lawrence, PROPERTY RIGHTS: PHILOSOPHICAL FOUNDATIONS (1977).

Cribbet, John, PRINCIPLES OF THE LAW OF PROPERTY (2d. ed. 1975).

Dukeminier, Jesse, and James Krier, PROPERTY (1981).

Epstein, Richard, *Possession as the Root of Title,* 13 GA. L. REV. 1221 (1979).

Furubotn, E., and S. Pejovich, eds., THE ECONOMICS OF PROPERTY RIGHTS (1974).

Manne, Henry, ed., THE ECONOMICS OF LEGAL RELATIONS: READINGS IN THE THEORY OF PROPERTY RIGHTS (1975).

Munzer, Stephen R., A THEORY OF PROPERTY (1990).

Polinsky, A. Mitchell, *Resolving Nuisance Disputes: The Simple Economics of Injunctive and Damage Remedies,* 32 STAN. L. REV. 1075 (1980).

Rose, Carol M., *Possession as the Origin of Property,* 52 U. CHI. L. REV. 73 (1985).

The Coase Theorem

There is a vast literature on the Coase theorem, some of which has been cited in the text. Here are some others:

Calabresi, Guido, *The Pointlessness of Pareto: Carrying Coase Further*, 100 YALE L. J. 1043 (1991).

Coursey, Dan, Elizabeth Hoffman, and Matthew Spitzer, *Fear and Loathing in the Coase Theorem: Experimental Tests Involving Physical Discomfort*, 16 J. LEGAL STUD. 217 (1987).

Donohue, John J., III, *Diverting the Coasean River: Incentive Schemes to Reduce Unemployment Spells*, 99 YALE L. J. 549 (1989).

Ellickson, Robert, *The Case for Coase and Against 'Coaseanism,'* 99 YALE L. J. 611 (1989).

Ellickson, Robert, ORDER WITHOUT LAW: HOW NEIGHBORS SETTLE DISPUTES (1991).

Hovenkamp, Herbert, *Marginal Utility and the Coase Theorem,* 75 CORNELL L. REV. 783 (1990).

Schlag, Pierre, *An Appreciative Comment on Coase's The Problem of Social Cost: A View from the Left,* 1986 WISC. L. REV. 919.

Schlag, Pierre, *The Problem of Transaction Costs,* 62 SO. CAL. L. REV. 1661 (1989).

APPENDIX

The Philosophical Concept of Property

Philosophers generally perceive property to be an instrument for achieving fundamental values. Some philosophers of property have concentrated on its ability to advance values such as utility, justice, self-expression, and social evolution. These traditions of thought have influenced the law. This appendix introduces the reader to four of these traditions and relates them to the economic analysis of property.

1. Utilitarianism

Utilitarians measure the value of a good or an act by the net pleasure or satisfaction that it creates. For utilitarians, the purpose of the institution of property is to maximize the total pleasure or satisfaction obtained from material and other resources. Bentham thus defines property as an expectation of utility: "Property is nothing but a basis of expectation; the expectation of deriving advantages from a thing, which we are said to possess, in consequence of the relation in which we stand towards it."[26] The objective of maximizing total utility constitutes a standard against which property rules can be evaluated. In our examples at the beginning of the chapter, each of the disputes could be resolved on utilitarian grounds by establishing a legal rule that seeks to maximize the sum of utilities or pleasure of society as a whole.

The utilitarian approach makes a person's claim to property tentative. It can be taken from him in principle if the beneficiaries of the expropriation gain more in utility than the owner loses. Suppose, for example, that a young son is living with his aged parents in their home. On utilitarian grounds, the young son may be excused for throwing the parents out of the home if their loss in utility from being dispossessed is less than his gain in utility from having them out of the house. Critics of utilitarianism have often wondered whether the theory makes ownership too tentative. Isn't ownership more than an expectation? Do we really think that a person could be rightfully deprived of his property just because the loss is more than offset by the gain to others?

This objection to the utilitarian theory of property applies with equal force to the conventional economic theory that holds that the purpose of property is to maximize wealth. Isn't ownership more than a right to a stream of income? Do we really think that a person could be rightfully deprived of her property just because the loss of wealth is more than offset by the gain in wealth to others?

2. Distributive Justice

Another philosophical approach to property law emphasizes property law's ability to achieve distributive justice, rather than pleasure or satisfaction. Aristotle, for example, held that a conception of distributive justice is implicit in various forms of social organization. For Aristotle, the principle of justice is different for different societies, but it is appropriate for each type of society to promote its own conception of distributive justice through its constitution and laws, including its notion of property rights. He argued that a democracy will favor an equal distribution of wealth, whereas an aristocracy (the form preferred by Aristotle) will favor the distribution of wealth according to the virtues of various classes. In Aristotle's conception, it is just that aristocrats receive an unequal share of wealth because they use it for more worthy ends than do others.

From the Aristotelian conception of democratic equality we might infer a policy of redistributive justice whereby the valuable assets of society are periodically redistributed so as to achieve a roughly equal distribution of that property. In general, this sort of redistribution would favor the poor and penalize the wealthy. On the other hand, from the Aristotelian justification of aristocratic inequality we might infer the polar-opposite policy of redistributive justice whereby the assets of society would be periodically redistributed to

---

[26] Jeremy Bentham, Theory of Legislation: Principles of the Code 111–113 (Hildreth ed. 1931).

the aristocrats. To the extent that the aristocracy and the wealthy are the same group, this redistribution of property would favor the rich and penalize the poor. In either case, these notions of distributive justice make property claims as tentative as they were under utilitarianism and, therefore, open to the same criticisms.

There is another school of philosophical thought relating to distributive justice and property that emphasizes a just *process* for defining and enforcing property rights rather than a just *outcome* or end result in the distribution of wealth from property.[27] According to one version of this theory, any distribution of wealth is just provided that it starts from a just initial distribution of resources and achieves the final distribution by voluntary exchange. In practice this means that the process of voluntary market exchange is just and that ownership claims are most justly established and enforced in an unfettered market in which there is free and perfect competition. In Nozick's memorable rephrasing of Marx, "From each as he chooses; to each as he is chosen." Whatever distribution of wealth results from this just process is also just. Thus, according to this theory, redistributing property to dilute the effects of competition is unjust.

Several criticisms have been made of this notion of distributive justice. The most telling criticism is that the competitive process can lead to a multitude of distributive outcomes, from one in which each individual has an equal share to one in which one individual has 99% of the property and everyone else divides up the remaining 1%. All of the outcomes are efficient. But clearly not all of them are equitable or just. The notion of the competitive process as distributive justice is not a sufficient guide to designing rules of property law. At a minimum, there must be an additional, independent standard by which to appraise various initial endowments of property.

3. LIBERTY AND SELF-EXPRESSION

Besides utility and distributive justice, another value that may underlie property law is liberty. Private property is a precondition for markets, and markets are a decentralized mechanism for allocating resources. Most markets can, and do, operate without extensive government interference or supervision. The practical alternative to markets in the modern economy is some form of government planning. Government planning involves centralizing power over economic matters in the hands of state officials. Control over economic life provides officials with leverage that can be used to control other aspects of life, whereas private property creates a zone of discretion within which individuals are not accountable to government officials. Private property has thus been viewed by some philosophers as a bulwark against the dictatorial authority of governments.[28] It has been argued, for example, that capitalism was deliberately invented to thwart absolutism by depriving the king of economic power. The U.S. Constitution was probably drafted with this idea in mind.

Another connection between property and liberty focuses on individual self-expression. Hegel stressed the idea that people, through their works, transform nature into an expression of personality, and, by doing so, perfect the natural world. A painter takes materials in

---

[27] The most forceful modern statement of this view is in R. Nozick, ANARCHY, STATE, AND UTOPIA (1974).

[28] This is a theme in THE FEDERALIST PAPERS (1786) and in the work of the late Friedrich Hayek (see, for example, THE CONSTITUTION OF LIBERTY (1972)).

no particular order and rearranges them into a work of art. By investing personality in work, the artist transforms natural objects and makes them the artist's own. It is difficult to imagine a system of property law that did not recognize this fact. Thus, to encourage self-expression, the state needs to recognize the creators' rights of ownership over their creations. Notice that this proposition extends beyond art to most of the works of humans.

4. CONSERVATISM AND THE ORIGINS OF PROPERTY

The philosophical theories discussed so far tend to regard the institution of property as serving ultimate values, such as utility, distributive justice, or liberty. Another philosophical tradition focuses not upon the purposes of property but upon its origins. To illustrate, in medieval times there were many encumbrances and restrictions on the use and sale of real estate. The common law of private property emerged from feudalism and acquired its modern character by chipping away at these encumbrances upon the marketability of real property. Political conservatives like Burke and Hayek idealize forms of social order that, like the common law of property, evolve over time in much the same manner as the myriad species of life. Like organisms, social forms are, in this view, subject to the rules of natural selection. The conservative philosophers condemn institutions imposed upon us by planners, engineers, politicians, and other social-decision-makers for much the same reasons that environmentalists condemn actions that interfere with an area's environment.

5

TOPICS IN THE ECONOMICS OF PROPERTY LAW

In the preceding chapter, we developed an economic theory of property rights and remedies. We saw that property law creates a bundle of rights that the owners of property are free to exercise as they see fit, without interference by the state or private persons. Consistent with this freedom is a system of allocation by voluntary exchange. Property law fosters voluntary exchange by removing the obstacles to bargaining. When the obstacles to bargaining are low, resources will be allocated efficiently. We used this framework and economic theory to answer the following four questions that must be addressed by a theory of property law:

1. What can be privately owned?
2. How are ownership rights established?
3. What may owners do with their property?
4. What are the remedies for the violation of property rights?

To answer the first question, we distinguished between private and public goods, and we claimed that the former should be privately owned. To answer the second question, we presented a thought experiment to illustrate how property law encourages production, discourages theft, and reduces the cost of protecting goods. We noted that the rules of acquisition are shaped to achieve these ends. We answered the third question by developing the theory of externalities, especially the connection between public bads in economics and nuisances in law. We noted that common law approximates a system of maximum liberty, which allows any use of property by its owner that does not interfere with other peoples' property. In answering the fourth question, we used bargaining theory to conclude that the injunctive remedy is preferred for private bads and the damage remedy is preferred for public bads.

These answers given in the previous chapter are very general. In this chapter, we reexamine these questions in detail, with concrete applications. The topics are organized roughly according to the four fundamental questions of property law.

I. WHAT RESOURCES SHOULD BE PROTECTED BY PROPERTY RIGHTS?

As explained in the preceding chapter, the clear delineation of property rights facilitates bargaining and voluntary exchange. However, delineation and enforcement of property rights is costly, especially for intangible resources such as ideas. It is necessary, consequently, to balance the benefit from delineating property rights against the costs. In this section we consider how the law strikes such a balance.

A. Fugitive Property and the Rule of First Possession

The problem of defining property rights seems straightforward for objects like land and houses, which have definite boundaries and stay put. But what about objects that move around or have indefinite boundaries, like natural gas or wild animals? "Fugitive property," as such things are called, creates a legal problem as illustrated by the case of *Hammonds v. Central Kentucky Natural Gas Co.*, 255 Ky. 685, 75 S.W.2d 204 (Court of Appeal of Kentucky, 1934). The Central Kentucky Natural Gas Company leased tracts of land above large deposits of natural gas. Some of the leased tracts were separated from one another by land that the company did not own or lease. The geological dome of natural gas from which the company drew its supply lay partially under the leased land and partially under unleased land. Hammonds owned 54 acres of land that lay above the geological dome tapped by the Central Kentucky Natural Gas Company, but she had not let the subsurface rights in her land to the company. When the Central Kentucky Natural Gas Company extracted natural gas and oil from the dome, she sued the company on the theory that some of the natural gas that was under her land had been wrongfully appropriated by the defendant.

It is difficult in this case, if not impossible, to identify which natural gas came from under unleased land and which came from under leased land. The problem of establishing ownership can be ameliorated by adopting either of two legal rules:

1. oil and gas are not the property of anyone until reduced to actual possession by extraction, or

2. the owner of the surface has the exclusive right to subsurface deposits.

Under the first rule, the Central Kentucky Natural Gas Company was entitled to extract all the natural gas from the dome, regardless of whether it held the surface rights. But under the second rule the Central Kentucky Natural Gas Company was only entitled to extract the natural gas under the ground that it owned or leased.

The consequences of these two rules for the efficient exploration and extraction of natural gas are very different. According to the first rule, fugitive oil or gas is not owned by anyone until someone possesses it, and the first person to possess it thereby becomes the owner. This rule can, consequently, be called the *rule of first possession.* The rule of first possession applies the legal maxim "first in time, first in right." This rule has been used to establish ownership rights for centuries. To illustrate, in the arid American Southwest, state law allowed a person to obtain a right to water in a stream by being the first to tap it for use in mining or irrigation. (See the box entitled "Owning the Ocean.") By now, there are few opportunities to claim unpossessed land or water, but the rule of first possession applies to important forms of intangible property, such as inventions.

A great advantage of the rule of first possession is that it focuses on a few simple facts, so it is relatively easy and cheap to apply. In the event of a dispute about ownership, determination of who first possessed the property in question is usually straightforward. For example, material evidence usually proves who tapped a water supply first. There is, however, an economic disadvantage of the rule of first possession: it creates an incentive for some people to preempt others by making uneconomic investments to obtain ownership of property. The reason why the rule of first possession creates an incentive to invest too much too early is easily explained. According to the rule of first possession, an appropriate investment transfers the ownership of a resource to the investor. The owner of a scarce resource can rent it to others. Rent increases as a resource becomes more scarce. Indeed, rent is the scarcity value of the resource. Under the rule of first possession, an investment thus yields two types of benefits to the investor: (1) production (more is produced from existing resources), and (2) future rent (scarcity value of the resource in the future).

To illustrate, assume that the law allows a person to acquire ownership of "waste" land by fencing it. Fencing land increases its productivity from, say, grazing cattle on it. By assumption, fencing the land also transfers ownership of it to the person who built the fence. Assume that fencing waste land costs more than the profit from grazing cattle on it at current prices, but everyone expects the use value of the land to increase as population grows in the future. Investors may build useless fences to "preempt" others and secure title to the land.

Preemptive investment illustrates a general economic principle applicable to the rule of first possession. When the state awards property rights, people contest vigorously to obtain title. In a contest for title, persons try to get ownership rights transferred to themselves. Economic efficiency is concerned with the *production* of wealth, not the *transfer* of it. Investments for the sake of transferring wealth, not producing it, are socially inefficient.

In technical terms, social efficiency requires investors to improve property until the marginal cost equals the marginal increase in productive value. The rule of first possession causes investors to improve property until the marginal cost equals the marginal value of the sum of increased production *plus* transferred ownership. The transfer effect under the rule of first possession thus causes over-investment in the activities that the law defines as necessary to obtain legal possession. It is in the self-interest of investors, but not in the interests of social efficiency, to improve property in order to transfer ownership.

To illustrate, consider the Homestead Act of 1862 in the United States, which established rules allowing private citizens to acquire up to 160 acres of public lands in the west. The act required claimants to fulfill certain requirements before they acquired title. For example, the claimant had to file an affidavit swearing that he or she was either the head of a family or 21 years old, and that the claim was "for the purpose of actual settlement and cultivation, and not, either directly or indirectly, for the use of benefit of any other person or persons whomsoever." Moreover, before full title was acquired for $1.25 per acre, the claimant had to reside on the claim for six months and make "suitable" improvements on the land. These requirements were meant to minimize transfer effects and to encourage production. In practice, however, the requirements were fleetingly enforced (as was usually the case with the residence requirement) and easily evaded (as when "suitable" improvements consisted of placing miniature houses—really large doll houses—on the claim). The occupation and development of the American frontier occurred at a faster pace than competitive markets or a strictly enforced Homestead Act would have produced.

The rule of first possession also applies to sea creatures, which can be owned by whoever catches them. Consequently, sea mammals such as whales, seals, and otters have been hunted to the point that some species risk extinction. Similarly, most of the world's fisheries are depleted far beyond the level appropriate to economics or ecology.

In contrast to the rule of first possession, there is no gap in ownership under the second rule for fugitive gas, according to which all the gas under the ground already belongs to the people who own the surface. By extension, the second rule suggests that wild animals belong to the owners of some piece of land, such as the land where the wild animal was born. Ownership of fish and other marine resources should perhaps be tied to ownership of the ocean floor. In general, the second rule, called the *rule of tied ownership*, ties ownership of fugitive property to settled property.

Tying ownership of fugitive property to settled property avoids preemptive investment *so long as the ownership claims in the resource to which the fugitive property is tied are already established.* To illustrate, all the gas is already owned under the second rule because all the surface rights are already owned, so the rule does not provide an incentive to acquire ownership by extracting too much gas too soon. Similarly, if salmon were the property of the people who own the streams where they spawn, the owners would not deplete the salmon by catching too many of them.

The problem with the second rule, as illustrated by the facts in Hammonds, is the difficulty of establishing and verifying ownership rights. The homogeneity of natural gas and its dispersion in caverns makes proving its original underground location difficult and costly.

Our analysis of fugitive resources reveals a common trade-off in property law:

> Rules that tie ownership to possession have the advantage of being easy to administer and the disadvantage of providing incentives for uneconomic investment in possessory acts, whereas rules that allow ownership without possession have the advantage of avoiding preemptive investment and the disadvantage of being costly to administer.

Choosing the more efficient rule in a case such as *Hammonds* requires balancing the incentive to overinvest under the rule of first possession against the cost of administering and enforcing ownership without possession.

QUESTION 5.1: The case of Pierson v. Post,[1] which is a staple in introductory courses on property law in American universities, concerns which hunter owns a fox. Explain the costs and benefits to weigh in an efficiency analysis of this case.

". . . Post, being in possession of certain dogs and hounds under his command, did, 'upon a certain wild and uninhabited, unpossessed and waste land, called the beach, find and start one of those noxious beasts called a fox,' and whilst there hunting, chasing and pursuing the same with his dogs and hounds, and when in view thereof, Pierson, well

---

[1] 3 Cal. R. 175, 2 Am. Dec. 264 (Supreme Court of New York, 1805).

knowing the fox was so hunted and pursued, did, in the sight of Post, to prevent his catching the same, kill and carry it off. A verdict having been rendered for [Post, who was] the plaintiff below, [Pierson appealed] . . . However uncourteous or unkind the conduct of Pierson towards Post, in this instance, may have been, yet his act was productive of no injury or damage for which a legal remedy can be applied. We are of opinion the judgment below was erroneous, and ought to be reversed.

QUESTION 5.2: Can you make any sense of the proposition that the rule of first possession is a principle of "natural justice"?

B. When to Privatize Open-Access Resources

We have discussed various examples from history of unowned resources that become private property. *When* do unowned resources become owned? Economics suggests an answer.

The rule of first possession often applies when there is "open access" to a resource, which means that many people compete to possess it. For example, many people could homestead land, hunt whales, and fish in the sea. In contrast, a private owner can exclude others from using his or her resource. Granting private property rights over land, whales, or fish would close access by limiting it to the owner. Consequently, we can restate the trade-off between the two property rules discussed above: a rule of open access causes overuse of a resource, whereas private property rights require costly exclusion of nonowners.

This formulation suggests when an economically rational society will change the rule of law for a resource from open access to private ownership. When the resource is uncongested and boundary maintenance is cheap, open access is cheaper than private ownership. As time passes, however, congestion may increase and the technology of boundary maintenance may improve. Eventually, a point may be reached where private ownership is cheaper than open access. An economically rational society will privatize a resource at the point in time where boundary maintenance costs less than overuse of the resource.[2]

This theory makes definite predictions about privatization. For example, it predicts that the invention of barbed wire, which lowered the cost of boundary maintenance, would promote the privatization of the public domain. As another example, it predicts that property rights will be created in the electromagnetic spectrum when broadcasters begin to interfere with each other. The predictions of this theory are confirmed by some facts and disconfirmed by others. Apparently, societies are often rational, as the theory

---

[2] This is the central point made by Harold Demsetz in *Toward a Theory of Property Rights,* 57 AM. ECON. REV. 347 (1967). He argues, for example, that American Indians did not establish property rights in land when the costs of administering the rules exceeded the benefits from private ownership. Proceeding along these lines, he tries to explain why certain North American Indian tribes, such as those in the Northeast, whose principal economic activity was trapping animals for their fur, developed a notion of property rights and others, such as the Plains Indians, whose principal resource was the migratory buffalo, did not. The extent to which his arguments can be squared with history or anthropology is still open to question.

OWNING THE OCEAN

Water covers 70% of the Earth's surface in the form of oceans, yet almost all of that vast amount of water is unaffected by well-defined property rights. In the late sixteenth and early seventeenth centuries, the great voyages of discovery and the resulting sea-borne empires in Europe necessitated internationally accepted rules on rights to use the ocean. These rights were first catalogued in the famous *Mare Liberum* of Hugo Grotius of Holland. He noted that the "sea, since it is as incapable of being seized as the air, cannot have been attached to the possessions of any particular nation." In the system that Grotius suggested and that prevailed in international law for nearly 300 years, each nation was to have exclusive rights to the use of the ocean within 3 miles of its shoreline, with that area to be called the "territorial seas." (The 3-mile distance was not picked at random; it was the distance that an early seventeenth-century cannonball could carry.) Beyond the 3-mile limit, Grotius urged that the "high seas" should be a common resource from which none, save pirates, could legitimately be excluded.

Increasing use of the high seas in the early and mid–nineteenth century led to the replacement of the doctrine of "free use" with that of "reasonable use." After World War II, the increasing importance of shipping, fishing, offshore oil and gas deposits, and seabed mining caused the legal system of ocean rights to crumble. In 1945 President Truman announced that the United States' exclusive rights to subaqueous organic resources—such as oil and natural gas—extended to the edge of the continental shelf or margin, an area that stretched 200 miles from the Atlantic coast of the United States. Other nations quickly made similar claims. Unlike these unilateral actions, attempts at international cooperation have achieved mixed results. To illustrate, when the third United Nations Conference on the Law of the Sea (UNCLOS) convened in 1974, there was widespread agreement that the territorial

continued . . .

assumes, but not perfectly rational. Politics leads to bargains and compromises that violate the requirements of economic efficiency. For examples of these compromises, read the box entitled "Owning the Ocean".

QUESTION 5.3: Read the following account of the history of water law and discuss whether or not the law appears to have evolved towards economic efficiency.

Water has always been one of the most valuable natural resources, but because it tends to run away, there have always been problems in defining and assigning property rights in water. Centuries ago in England, the general rule was that rights were vested in the "riparian owner," that is, in the person who owned the land on the bank of the river. The riparian owner's principal right was to a flow of water past his land. It would be a violation of someone else's rights for an upstream user to use the water that passed by his property in such a way as to reduce the flow to downstream users. The upstream user could not, therefore, divert so much of the water to his own use that the flow was

Owning the Ocean Continued . . .

sea would be established at the 12-mile limit and that there should be an "economic zone," largely but not completely controlled by the coastal state, stretching to 200 miles beyond the shoreline, the general extent of the continental shelf.

There was not general agreement on what to do with property rights to the areas beyond this 200-mile limit, and it was the disposition of these areas that raised the really hard issues. The developed countries urged a private-property-rights-based system of development, whereas the developing countries offered a common-property-rights system. In the end a compromise, called the *parallel system*, was agreed upon. There would be both private development and a UN-funded and UN-operated company, called the "Enterprise." In order to give the Enterprise the ability to compete with the more advanced countries of the developed world, an International Seabed Authority (ISA) would be created to allocate rights to mine the oceans. The conference specified an ingenious variant of the "I cut, you choose" method of cake-cutting in order to allocate mining rights. Before it could begin operation, a private or state organization had to submit to the ISA two prospective sites of operations. The Authority would then choose one of those sites for later development by the Enterprise and allow the applicant to proceed with the mining of the other.

The United States refused to sign the final treaty, although 117 countries eventually signed it in December 1982.

QUESTION 5.4: In what ways do these historical developments respond to efficiency, and to what extent do they respond to political power and distribution?

significantly diminished for those downstream. A riparian was restricted in his ability to sell water to nonriparians (*i.e.*, people who do not own land along the water).

However, in the nineteenth century this legal arrangement had to be altered because industrial demand on the natural flow of a river frequently exceeded the supply. In the eastern United States, these issues were resolved by elaborating the natural-flow theory of water rights that had been adopted from the English common law. An alternative theory of water rights appeared in the western United States. Under the reasonable-use theory, the riparian owner is entitled to use the water flow in any reasonable way. It was deemed reasonable for one owner to use all of the water in a stream or lake when others are making no use of it. Under the reasonable-use theory, a riparian owner does not have a right to the natural water flow. Furthermore, a riparian owner may transfer rights to nonriparians.

C. Information Economics

Everyone with a television or computer buys information like other commodities, but the supply of information differs from that of oranges or razor blades. Producing information costs a lot, but transmitting it costs relatively little. When the producer sells information, the buyer can resell it at the cost of transmission. Thus, producers who bear the cost of production and transmission are undercut by resellers who bear only the cost of transmission.

Consequently, producers have difficulty selling information for a fraction of its value to the people who use it. This problem is called *nonappropriability*. According to the original economics of information, the producers of information undersupply it because they cannot appropriate its value to society. That is why economists originally concluded that a private market would provide less than the efficient amount of information.

Consider the connection between nonappropriability and public goods. Information contains ideas. One person's use of an idea does not diminish its availability for others to use. Thus, information is *nonrivalrous*. Excluding some people from learning about a new idea can be expensive, because the transmission of ideas is so cheap. Thus, information is *nonexcludable*. These are the two characteristics of public goods identified in Chapter 4. As we have already explained, the private market often undersupplies public goods because the producer cannot appropriate their value. So the problem of nonappropriability is essentially the same for information and public goods.

These theoretical considerations suggest that an unregulated market will undersupply creative works that embody ideas, such as inventions, books, and paintings. This fact, in turn, suggests the need for state intervention in the market for information. State intervention can take one of three general forms: (1) state supply of information, (2) public subsidies for the private provision of information, or (3) the creation and protection of property rights in information. In fact, the state intervenes in all three ways. To illustrate, the state supplies weather forecasts, funds scientific research by private universities, and grants patents to inventors.

In this chapter, we focus on the third form of intervention—creating and protecting property rights in information. Before turning to property rights, however, we need to explain a recent development in information economics. As explained, the original economics of information concluded that an unregulated market will undersupply information. While this view still dominates most policy discussions, situations can occur in which no regulation results in too much information or just the right amount.[3] To see why, consider the invention of a superior means of forecasting the weather. The original theory argued that the inventor cannot appropriate the value of the invention because people who buy her forecasts can resell them to others. However, there are alternative means for inventors to earn profits. The inventor of the weather forecast, for example, can profit by speculating on agricultural prices. To see how, let's suppose that the inventor forecasts a rainy autumn that will reduce harvests and cause the price of corn to rise. She can keep this information secret and buy corn in the summer for delivery in the autumn. When the harvest arrives in the fall, farmers will fulfill their contracts by delivering corn to the inventor at the low, summer price. Subsequently, the inventor can resell the corn on the spot market at the high price caused by a rainy autumn.

In general, the producers of information can obtain profits from speculative investments. Following this line of thought, some scholars have argued that some markets produce too much investment in information. For example, consider the stock market. An investor who finds out sooner than others that one corporation is buying another

---

[3] See J. Hirschleifer, *The Private and Social Value of Information and the Reward to Innovative Activity,* 61 AMERICAN ECONOMIC REVIEW 561 (1971). See also R. Posner, *The Social Costs of Monopoly and Regulations,* 83 J. POLITICAL ECONOMY 807 (1975), and E. Rice and T. Ulen, *Rent-Seeking and Welfare Loss,* 3 RESEARCH IN LAW & ECON. 53 (1981).

can make large profits by purchasing the target company's stock. The gains to society from faster price movements in the target company's stocks are modest compared to the vast wealth redistributed from uninformed stockholders to the informed investor. Consequently, critics argue that stock markets encourage overinvestment in obtaining information with large private value and little social value. Similarly, critics argue that private companies that are searching for a cure for cancer perform duplicative and wasteful experiments and that social efficiency would be served by merging their efforts. We do not comment on the merits of these criticisms of stock markets and cancer research, but we accept the general point that free markets can supply too little or too much information.

> **QUESTION 5.5:** Suppose that the inventor of a weather-forecasting technique determines that the weather during the growing season will be perfect, causing a bumper harvest. Explain how the inventor could use this information to make profitable investments.

> **QUESTION 5.6:** The directors of a corporation are often the first people to know about facts that affect its stock price. American law forbids directors and other "insiders" from using "inside information" to speculate on the value of the company's stocks. Use the theory of first appropriation and the economics of information to makes arguments for and against the efficiency of this prohibition.

D. Intellectual Property: Patents, Copyrights, and Trademarks

Now we turn to laws creating property rights for ideas. As noted, the creator of an idea has difficulty appropriating its social value. Granting exclusive property rights to the creator of an idea allows him or her to appropriate much of its social value. Consequently, the incentive to create ideas aligns closely with their social value, as required for efficient innovation. However, this clear social benefit may also entail social costs. The owner of an idea has the right to exclude others from using it. Excluding others from using an idea impedes their dissemination and application. In general, the broader the scope and the longer the duration of the creator's property rights, the stronger the incentive for creating ideas and the weaker the incentive for disseminating and applying them.

An analogy between monopolies and patents clarifies this point. A valuable invention creates a new product or a cheaper way to produce an old product. Since a valuable invention has no close substitutes, granting a patent creates a monopoly. And as we know, monopolists earn profits that exceed the ordinary rate of return on an investment. These monopoly profits are the inventor's reward supplied by the patent system. However, monopolies impose social costs in that too little of the monopolized good is produced and the price is too high. Specifically, a patented good typically sells at a higher price and in lower quantities as long as the patent lasts; the price falls and the quantity increases as soon as the patent expires. So patents are a temporary monopoly that reward invention and impede dissemination.

Intellectual-property law confronts this tradeoff and resolves it somewhat differently in each of its three principal areas. The patent system establishes ownership rights to inventions and other technical improvements. The copyright system grants ownership rights to authors, artists, and composers. The trademark system establishes property in distinctive commercial marks or symbols. In each of these three areas of law, the scope and duration of property rights is somewhat different, and the differences generally respond to economic efficiency, as we will explain.

1. Patents   Most countries require an inventor to register the invention in order to obtain a patent. After the invention is registered and the patent is granted, no one can use the invention except by its owner's consent. Thus, patents create an exclusive property right in an invention. The exclusive property right has two dimensions: duration and breadth. "Duration" refers to the number of years between a patent's registration and its expiration. For example, most U.S. patents last for 17 years. "Breadth" refers to how similar another invention can be without infringing upon the patent for the original invention. To illustrate, the "Rubik's Cube" is a popular puzzle in which each of the six sides of the cube are divided into a 3×3 grid, and each of the cells in the grid is colored. The object of the game is to manipulate the cube in order to align rows of same-colored cells. An American court ruled that the Rubik's Cube did not infringe an earlier patent by Moleculon for a similar game using a 2×2 grid.[4]

To appreciate the history of patent law, consider the evolution of the U.S. system. European patents for inventions began in the Republic of Venice in 1474 and were formalized in England in the Statute of Monopolies in 1623. Article I, Section 8 of the U.S. Constitution gives Congress the power to protect both copyright and patent: "to promote the progress of science and useful arts, by securing for limited time to authors and inventors the exclusive right to their respective writings and discoveries." To put this power into action with respect to patents, the U.S. Congress passed America's first patent law in 1790, which was revised in 1793, 1836, and 1952. To secure an exclusive right to an invention, the inventor must submit an application to the U.S. Patent Office establishing that the invention is for a "new and useful process, machine, manufacture, or composition of matter, or [a] new and useful improvement thereof." (35 U.S. Code 101.) The invention must be "non-obvious," must have "practical utility" (a characteristic that is more or less presumed for all applicants), and must not have been commercialized or known to the public for more than a year before the date of application. Approximately three-fourths of all applications are granted by the Patent Office. Throughout the 1970s, between 70,000 and 80,000 patents were granted per year.[5] The successful applicant receives a 17-year monopoly on the use of the invention. Others who wish to use the invention must purchase the right to do so from the patent-holder. The holder may, at his or her discretion, *license* the use of the patent in exchange for the licensee's payment of a fee known as a *royalty*.[6]

1a. Breadth   An important policy question concerns the efficient breadth and duration of a patent. To understand the difference in incentive effects between narrow and broad

---

[4] *Moleculon Research Corp. v. CBS., Inc.*, 872 F.2d 407, 409 (Fed. Cir. 1989).

[5] Of those issued between 1971 and 1975, 51% were granted to domestic corporations, 23% to foreign corporations and governments, 2% to the U.S. federal government, and 23% to individual inventors. This distribution represents a trend in the century toward corporate ownership and away from individual ownership of new patents. Frederick Scherer, INDUSTRIAL MARKET STRUCTURE AND ECONOMIC PERFORMANCE (2d ed. 1980).

[6] Over 95% of the patents granted in the United States go to men. If society determined that women ought to receive a greater share of the patents granted, would it be wise to encourage women inventors by giving their inventions a longer patent life (say, 25 years) than that given to the inventions of men?

patents, contrast two inventors, two inventions, and two rules. Assume that two inventors are contemplating investing in research on two inventions. The first invention would improve oil-cracking processes and the second invention would provide a substitute for lead in gasoline. The inventors expect the two inventions to be similar but not identical. Under a broad rule, a single patent would encompass both inventions. Since the party who makes the first invention receives exclusive rights to both inventions, the party who makes the first discovery gets all of the profits and the other party gets nothing. Thus, the broad rule encourages fast, duplicative research. In contrast, under a narrow rule, a separate patent would be required for each invention. The party who makes the first invention would receive exclusive rights to it, and the party who makes the second invention would have exclusive property rights to it. Thus the narrow rule encourages slower, complementary research.

To appreciate this contrast between broad and narrow patents, consider a typical relationship between research and development (R&D). Research sometimes yields a pioneering discovery with no immediate commercial value, but with large commercial potential. To realize its potential, a pioneering discovery must be developed and "brought to market." Development involves a series of small improvements. Thus, a pioneering invention is followed by a series of applications. The legal question is whether a patent for the pioneering discovery extends to the applications. Broad patents encourage fundamental research, and narrow patents encourage development.

To illustrate, suppose that an investment of $100,000 in research yields a pioneering invention that has no commercial value. Subsequently, an investment of $50,000 in development yields an improvement that has commercial value of $1 million. If the law grants broad patents, a patent for the pioneering invention would also cover the application, but if the law grants narrow patents, separate patents would be required for the pioneering invention and the application.

What breadth of patents is most efficient? If the social value of investment on fundamental research exceeds the social value of investment on developing applications, then patents should be broadened. Conversely, if the social value of investment on developing applications exceeds the social value of investment on fundamental research, then patents should be narrowed.

In reality, questions of breadth are decided in law according to the "doctrine of equivalents," which refers to a series of court findings about how nearly equivalent two inventions must be before finding patent infringement. This doctrine is obscure and unpredictable. Courts have sometimes reasoned that an improvement with great commercial value should not be interpreted as infringing upon a pioneering invention with little stand-alone value.[7] After all, the improvement, not the pioneering invention, is what people really value.

Howard Chang, an economist-lawyer, has recently shown that this argument is flawed for purposes of maximizing the social value of inventive activity.[8] If the people who do fundamental research receive the sale value of the pioneering invention, but they do not receive any of the sale value of the commercial applications, there will not

---

[7] See W*estinghouse v. Boyden Power Brake Co*, 170 U.S. 537, 572 (1898).

[8] See Robert P. Merges and Richard R. Nelson, *On the Complex Economics of Patent Scope*, 90 COLUM. L. REV. 839 (1990). See also Howard F. Chang, *Patent Scope, Antitrust Policy, and Cumulative Innovation, Harvard Law School Program in Law and Economics, Discussion Paper Number 96* (1991).

be enough fundamental research. To see why, consider an analogy between pioneering inventions and raising sheep. Sheep are sold for mutton and wool. Assume that the mutton from a sheep is worth much more than the wool. If shepherds are paid the value of the wool, but not the value of the mutton, then shepherds will not be paid enough, and they will raise too few sheep. Mutton and wool are *joint products* of rearing sheep. Efficient incentives require that shepherds receive the sale value of their product (sheep), which is the sum of the sale value of mutton and wool.

Similarly, commercial applications and pioneering inventions are joint products of fundamental research. Commercial applications require pioneering inventions, and pioneering inventions require fundamental research. A joint product will be undersupplied if the supplier's compensation equals the commercial value of only one of the joint products. Ideally, the fundamental research and commerical development would be joined together in a single firm. If the activities are joined under a single producer, then the producer will receive the sum of the value of the fundamental research and commercial application, just like paying the shepherd the sum of the value of the mutton and wool.

Even if one firm conducted fundamental research and another firm developed commercial applications, the incentive problem could be solved if transactions costs were zero. If transaction costs were zero, then the Coase theorem would apply. Applied to inventions, the Coase theorem asserts that breadth of patent does not matter to economic efficiency so long as inventors can bargain with each other costlessly and make efficient contracts.

Problems arise under the realistic assumption that transaction costs impede bargaining between suppliers of fundamental research and commercial development. Two legal remedies are available: lubricate bargaining (normative Coase theorem) or allocate rights to the party who values them the most (normative Hobbes theorem). Instead of pursing these two remedies, U.S. law has been perverse in both respects.

Bargaining among inventors sometimes leads to joint research ventures, in which competing manufacturers share an R&D facility and compete with each other in production and sales. In America, antitrust laws have inhibited joint ventures for research and development. Thus, the application of antitrust law to R&D obstructed a solution to the problem of the joint production of inventions. Fortunately, American officials have recognized this failure in policy and taken steps to correct it.

When separate producers make joint inventions, officials face a difficult problem in determining the breadth of the patents. If the pioneering invention has little stand-alone value, then some of the improvement's value must be paid to the pioneer in order to provide an adequate incentive for pioneering inventions. On the other hand, if the pioneering invention has large stand-alone value, then its inventor often will be rewarded adequately already, even if he or she receives no share of the value of the improvement. Thus, patent protection for pioneering inventions should be *broader* for those with *little* stand-alone value, and the patent protection for pioneering inventions should be *narrower* for those with *large* stand-alone value. This is just the opposite of the result sometimes reached when courts apply the doctrine of equivalents.

QUESTION 5.7: When the patent expired on a drug named "Librium" (a sedative that was the forerunner of Valium), its price dropped from \$15 to \$1.10.[9] Explain why this drop in

---

[9] "'When Librium, Hoffmann-LaRoche's forerunner to Valium, came off patent, prices dropped from \$15 to \$1,' said William Haddad, president of the Generic Pharmaceutical Industry Association." See "The Shift to Generic Drugs," *New York Times*, July 23, 1984, p. 19.

price occurred. Relate your explanation to the problem of efficient incentives for creating and transmitting an idea.

QUESTION 5.8: Recall our example of an investment of $100,000 in research that yields a pioneering invention that has no commercial value, and a subsequent investment of $50,000 in development that yields an improvement that has commercial value of $1 million. Assume that Firm *A* is uniquely situated to do the pioneering research, and Firm *B* is uniquely situated to develop the application. Predict the difference in investment resulting from a broad patent law and a narrow patent law. In making your prediction, distinguish between a situation in which transaction costs prevent Firm *A* and Firm *B* from bargaining with each other and a situation in which transaction costs of bargaining are zero.

QUESTION 5.9: When inventions take the form of discovery and application, the authorities may issue a "dominant patent" to the pioneering discovery and a "subservient patent" to the improvement. The subservient invention cannot be manufactured legally without the agreement of the holders of the dominant patent and the subservient patent. Thus, the two parties are compelled to bargain, each having veto power, and agree on the division of future profits before manufacturing the improvement. Absent such an agreement, only the pioneering invention can be manufactured. Answer Question 5.8 under the assumption that, instead of prescribing broad or narrow patents, the law grants a dominant patent and a subservient patent.

1b. Duration As noted, the rights to a patent last for a fixed time period. What is the *optimal patent life*? We provide an economic framework for answering this question. Recall that patents create a temporary monopoly on the use of an invention. Monopoly profits reward the inventor and encourage creativity, whereas monopoly prices overcharge buyers and discourage the dissemination of new ideas. The optimal life of a patent is modeled in Figure 5.1 as a tradeoff between encouraging creativity and discouraging dissemination. The horizontal axis in Figure 5.1 indicates the life of a patent in years. The vertical axis indicates the dollar costs and benefits of inventions. The cost is the loss from monopoly pricing, which results in buyers' purchasing too little of the good. The marginal social cost of the patent is indicated by the MSC_P curve, which slopes upward to indicate that, in the absence of substitutes, the longer the patent monopoly persists, the greater the social cost. The benefit is the increase in creative

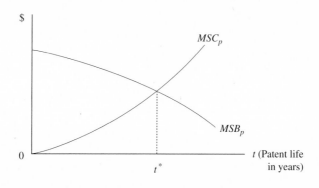

FIGURE 5.1 The social costs and benefits of patent life.

activity stimulated by the patent. The marginal social benefit of a patent is indicated by the MSB_P curve, which slopes downward to indicate that extending the life of patents increases the amount of investment activity, but at a diminishing rate.

Following the usual principle for optimality developed in Chapter 2, the intersection of the two curves indicates the optimal patent life, denoted t^* in the figure. At t^*, the marginal social cost of extending the patent's life for that period equals the marginal social benefit of having a patent life of that duration. Put somewhat differently but equivalently, the net social benefit from the patent in question is maximized by granting a patent for a term of t^* years.

Figure 5.1 describes the optimal patent life in abstract terms. But what particular life is optimal? As we have seen, in the United States an invention that meets certain conditions is given a 17-year patent. Can we use economics to demonstrate that t^* in Figure 5.1 equals 17? No. In general, the shape of the curves varies from one invention to anther. For example, the shape of the curve is typically different for a pioneering invention and an application. Ideally, there would be a different patent life for each invention.

Such a scheme of individualized patent terms is impractical, but practical alternatives exist to granting a 17-year patent for every invention. Germany, for example, has established a two-tiered patent system. Major inventions in Germany receive full-term patents, while minor inventions and improvements receive *petty patents* for a term of three years. In addition, Germany requires patent holders to pay an annual fee to continue the patent. The annual fee is relatively modest for the first several years of a patent's life, but thereafter escalates at regular intervals until the patent period is exhausted. Consequently, fewer than 5% of German patents remain in force for their entire term, the average patent life being a little less than eight years. This fact is not surprising when you consider that, given an interest rate of 10%, a promise to pay $1 in eight years is worth less than $.50, and a promise to pay $1 in 17 years is worth less than $.20.

QUESTION 5.10:

a. If the *total* social benefit of granting patent life of t years is equal to the area under the MSB_P curve up to point t and the *total* social cost of that patent life is equal to the area under the MSC_P curve up to point t, show the area that represents the net social benefit of granting a patent life of t^* years.

b. Demonstrate that, given the curves in Figure 5.1, a patent life of $(t^* + 1)$ years would give less net social benefit than a life of t^* years.

c. Make the same demonstration for a patent life of $(t^* - 1)$ years.

Comment on Figure 5.1. Note that the ownership right persists unimpaired for the life of the patent and then abruptly dissolves, whereas the value of a typical patent depreciates gradually with time.

QUESTION 5.11: One possible pitfall of the renewal-fee system for determination of optimal patent life is that, ideally, we want the patent-holder to compare the renewal fee with the *social* benefit of continuing the patent for another year, not just the *private* benefit. Can you suggest how, in setting the annual renewal fee, we might induce patent-holders to make the appropriate social calculation?

QUESTION 5.12: A third means of reducing the social costs of granting a patent life that is too long is a policy of *compulsory licensing*. This policy, which forms part of the patent systems of most West European countries, allows frustrated licensees to ask courts to compel patentees to license them if they can show that patent-holders have failed to use their patents in the domestic market within a specified time period, have failed to license when that is essential to bringing a complementary invention into use, or have abused their positions by, for example, excessively restricting the supply of their inventions. If the court is persuaded by the licensee to compel licensing, then it also determines a *reasonable* royalty. Give an economic evaluation of the policy of compulsory licensing.

2. Copyright and Trademark   In our analysis of patents, we applied the economics of information to answer the two fundamental questions about breadth and duration. This same framework applies to other topics in intellectual property, notably copyright and trademark, which we discuss briefly. Copyright grants writers, composers, and other artists a property right in her creation upon demonstration that her work is an *original expression*.[10] Unlike the patent system, the U.S. copyright system does not require creators to register their work in order to receive the protection of copyright. But very much like the patent law, copyright protection is limited in breadth and duration.

The breadth of a copyright concerns the uses to which copyrighted material can be put without authorization. A broad copyright forbids any unauthorized use, whereas a narrow copyright permits some unauthorized uses. For example, books are quoted in reviews and satires, or photocopied for educational purposes. The law handles these uses through so-called *fair-use* exclusions. For example, in *Sony Corporation of America v. Universal City Studios, Inc.*, 464 U.S. 417 (1984), the *Betamax* case, the U.S. Supreme Court held that recording over-the-air copyrighted television programs on a videocassette recorder is fair use when done for "time-shifting" purposes, but not necessarily for purposes of "archiving." A vague line, frequently litigated, divides fair and unfair unauthorized copying.

Since its eighteenth-century beginning, the United States has lengthened the duration of a copyright until it now stands as the creator's life plus 50 years. The optimal duration of a copyright involves a different problem from patents—specifically, *tracing costs*.[11] Before using copyrighted material, the user must trace the owner and obtain permission. Tracing can be difficult when a creative work is old and the owner signed many contracts for its use. However, tracing is unnecessary when the user knows that the material is so old that the copyright expired. So the limited duration of copyright ameliorates the tracing problem.

Now we turn from copyright to trademarks. Many modern businesses and service organizations invest vast sums of money to establish easily recognizable symbols for their products. For example, children in many countries recognize the golden arches

---

[10] As Lord Macaulay put it, copyright is "a tax on readers for the purpose of giving a bounty to writers." Thomas B. Macaulay, SPEECHES ON COPYRIGHT 25 (C. Gaston ed. 1914).

[11] William Landes and Richard A. Posner, *An Economic Analysis of Copyright Law,* 18 J. LEGAL STUD. 325 (1989). See also Wendy Gordon, *On Owning Information: Intellectual Property and the Restitutionary Impulse,* 78 VA. L. REV. 149 (1992).

signaling the location of a McDonald's hamburger franchise. Such symbols are *trade-marks* or *servicemarks*. The common law and statutes protected trademarks from as early as the thirteenth century in England. Modern trademark law in the United States stems from the Federal Trademark Act of 1946, commonly called the *Lanham Act*. The act provides a method for obtaining federal registration for trademarks or servicemarks.[12] As in the case of patents, the successful applicant must establish that the mark passes certain criteria, the most important of which is distinctiveness. Registration with the U.S. Trademark Office entitles the holder to certain protections and rights, among which is the privilege of placing beside one's trademark a sign, ®, that indicates a registered trademark.[13]

Trademarks help to solve the problem of consumer ignorance about the quality of a product. When quality is opaque, the consumer can use the trademark as a signal of quality. As an example of this point, consider that when the former Soviet Union abolished marks that could be used to identify the plant that produced various consumer goods in the 1950s, the average quality of those goods fell.[14] Furthermore, trademarks reduce the cost to consumers of searching for a product with specific qualities. The principal economic justification for granting property rights to trademarks is that they lower consumer search costs and create an incentive for producers to supply goods of high quality.

Can we make the same economic argument for limiting the duration of the property rights in trademarks as we did in the case of patents and copyrights? The answer is no. Limits on the duration of patents and copyrights were justified as attempts to minimize the social costs of monopoly and tracing. However, trademarks encourage competition and do not impose tracing costs.[15] Perhaps this is why trademarks last forever, until abandoned. In this respect, trademarks are like property rights in land and unlike other forms of intellectual property.

The question of breadth in trademarks has an interesting twist. Nothing is more settled in the law of trademarks than the proposition that generic product names cannot be trademarks. For example, no producer of cameras may register the word "camera" as a trademark. To allow such a trademark would enable its owner to sue every camera manufacturer that advertised its product by use of the word "camera." If generic product names could be trademarks, then the law of trademarks would create monopoly power, rather than facilitating competition. Sometimes, however, a competitive product succeeds so far that its trademark becomes a generic name. For instance, people today speak of "xeroxing" when they mean "photocopying," or they speak of "Scotch tape" when they mean cellophane tape, or they speak of a

---

[12] Note, however, that one does not have to register a mark in order to receive a property right in that mark.

[13] Some producers place the symbol TM or SM (for servicemark) on their products, but those symbols have no legal status.

[14] See Goldman, *Product Differentiation and Advertising: Some Lessons from Soviet Experience,* 68 J. POL. ECON. 346 (1960) and Scherer, INDUSTRIAL MARKET STRUCTURE AND ECONOMIC PERFORMANCE 379, n. 14 (2d ed. 1980).

[15] See, for general information, William Landes and Richard A. Posner, *Trademark Law: An Economic Perspective,* 30 J. LAW & ECON. 265 (1987).

"COKE" IS IT!

One of the best-known trademarks in the world is the word "Coke" to describe the Coca-Cola Company's cola soft drink. Precisely because it is so well known, there is the danger to the Coca-Cola Company that consumers might use the designation "Coke" to refer to any cola soft drink and not just the one the Coca-Cola Company produces. If that should happen, then "Coke" will have become a generic product name that any producer may use. The Coca-Cola trade research department, which has an annual budget of about $2 million, employs a team of about 25 investigators whose job it is to roam the United States asking at restaurants and soda fountains for "Coke" and "Coca-Cola." The investigators then send samples of what they are served to the corporate headquarters in Atlanta for chemical analysis. If the company determines that a restaurateur has served them something other than Coca-Cola, then that business is advised of its wrongdoing.

Since 1945, Coca-Cola has sued approximately 40–60 retailers per year. Retailers claim that what lies behind the company's vigorous campaign is not a fear of trademark infringement but an insidious and anticompetitive attempt to browbeat retailers into dealing only with the Coca-Cola Company. They note that it is frequently too costly for them—as on a busy night—to tell each customer who asks for a rum and Coke that they are really going to get a rum and Pepsi. Rather than face a lawsuit for trademark infringement, many of the retailers simply signed up with Coca-Cola as their exclusive supplier, saying that to do so was less costly to them. The retailers point to the fact that Coke has an 80% market share in the fountain-soda market but a much smaller share of the supermarket sales as evidence that the trade research department's work is part of an anticompetitive marketing operation.

(See "Mixing with Coke Over Trademarks Is Always a Fizzle: Coca-Cola Adds a Little Life in Court to Those Failing to Serve the Real Thing," *Wall Street Journal,* March 9, 1978, p. 1, col. 4.)

"Hoover" when they mean a vacuum cleaner. When this situation happens, the trademark-owner must protect the trademark by suing rivals who use the generic name to describe their products. Otherwise, the producer loses its property right in the generic name.

This sort of thing happened to the Sterling Drug Company in 1921. In that year a U.S. federal district court determined that Sterling's trademarked name for acetyl salicylic acid, "Aspirin," had become the common word for any brand of that drug, not just Sterling's. After this ruling, all producers of acetyl salicylic acid could use the term "aspirin" to describe their product. Bayer has managed to prevent this erosion of its trade name Aspirin in Mexico and Canada, where no company but Bayer may describe its acetyl salicylic acid as "aspirin." To learn how manufacturers of very successful products protect their trademarks, read the box on "Coke."

QUESTION 5.13: The duration of copyright increased under U.S. law in several steps since the eighteenth century until it reached the life of the author plus 50 years. Suppose that a writer completes a novel at age 40. If the writer lives to be 75, then the copyright will last for 85 years. At an interest rate of 10%, the present value of $1 paid after 85 years equals much less than a penny. What does this fact suggest about whether the efficient duration of copyright is longer or shorter than currently provided by law?

QUESTION 5.14: Explain the market conditions under which a patent on an oil-cracking process and a copyright on a new musical drama would lead to monopoly power.

QUESTION 5.15: Use economic theory to distinguish "fair use" from "unfair use" of copyrighted material.

QUESTION 5.16: Why is it efficient to limit the duration of patents and copyrights, whereas real property rights endure almost forever?

QUESTION 5.17: Trademark law does not allow a holder to sell a trademark independent of the good to which it is attached. Thus, Coca-Cola cannot sell its use of the trademark "Coke" to another producer of cola syrup; that mark may be sold only with the syrup produced by or under the supervision of the Coca-Cola Company. Can you provide an economic rationale for this restriction?

II. HOW ARE PROPERTY RIGHTS ESTABLISHED AND VERIFIED?

Branding cattle, stamping a serial number on an automobile engine, stenciling a social security number on a TV—these are some ways that private persons try to prove their ownership of valuable goods. In addition to these private remedies, the state sometimes provides registries of ownership. In spite of these devices, people sometimes "buy" goods that were not the seller's to sell. This section concerns verifying ownership and remedies when a good is "sold" without the owner's permission.

A. Recording and Transferring Title

Suppose you decide to fulfill a lifelong dream and buy a farm. You find a parcel in the country that you like and approach the farmer who is living there. After discussing the parcel's boundaries, fertility, and drainage, the farmer offers to sell the land at an attractive price. You shake hands to seal the agreement. The next week you return with a check, hand it over to the farmer, and shortly thereafter move onto the property. Two weeks later, a man knocks at the cottage door, announces that he is the owner of the property, and explains that he has come to evict the nefarious tenant who rented the cottage in which you are living. At this point you recall the joke that begins: "Hey buddy, how would you like to buy the Brooklyn Bridge?"

When you buy property, you should ascertain the rightful owner and deal with him or her. A reliable and inexpensive method for determining ownership prevents fraudulent conveyances, such as tenants' representing themselves as owners. There are various ways to create a record of ownership. Consider the story—presumably apocryphal—of "recording" title in England in the Middle Ages, when few people could read. It is said that the seller handed the buyer a clod of turf and a twig from the property in a ceremony before witnesses known as *livery of seisin*. Then, the adults thrashed a child who had witnessed the passing of turf and twig severely enough so that the child would remember that day as long as he or she lived, thus creating a living record of the transfer.

Fortunately, we now have better methods of recording title in land. In the United States, there is no uniform method of land registration,[16] but each of the fifty states has some system for the public recording of title to land. A change in ownership of real property must be recorded in an official registry of deeds, such as the county recorder's officer. Recording is a formal process and the records are open to the public. The record of ownership on file usually contains a formal description of the property's location, a list of restrictions that apply to the property, and an account of who has owned the property at each point in time.

While a system of recording title is maintained for land and a few other valuable items, like automobiles, there is no such system for most goods. In most exchanges the buyer does not devote resources to determining whether the seller truly owns what he or she is selling. For example, you rarely question whether the books you purchase at the bookstore were rightly the bookstore's to sell. Your presumption is that whoever possesses a book rightfully owns it. Further proof of ownership is in the memory of witnesses to the sale, like the child in the medieval example, or perhaps in a written sales contract. A system of recording the ownership of books would burden commerce and impede the efficient movement of goods.

We have, thus, encountered another trade-off in property law. On the one hand, verifying title by formal means, such as recording the transfer of a deed, reduces uncertainties that burden commerce. On the other hand, the verification of title through formal means is costly. Property law thus has to develop rules that *balance the impediments to commerce created by uncertain ownership against the cost of maintaining a system of verification*. For costly items like houses and cars, the law reduces the uncertainties that burden commerce by providing a system for recording title, and the law typically forces all sales through the recording process by refusing to protect unrecorded transactions in these items. For small transactions, however, the cost of maintaining a system of verification would exceed the benefit from reduced risk.

B. Can a Thief Give Good Title?

Let us consider how people respond to laws allocating the responsibility to verify ownership. Imagine that you have made a shrewd deal for the purchase of a television from

---

[16]There is an alternative land registration system, known as the *Torrens system*, after Sir Richard Torrens, who introduced this simplified mechanism into South Australia in 1858, and that system or something like it is in use in many parts of the world. In the Torrens system, the state operates a registry and a title insurance fund. Defects in title caused by the state record-keeper are compensated from the insurance fund. Several of the United States tried the Torrens system, but everyone of them has abandoned the system, because incompetent bookkeeping caused such a drain on the state-operated title insurance funds that the funds went bankrupt. (See Sheldon Kurtz and Herbert Hovenkamp, AMERICAN PROPERTY LAW 1151–1244 (1987).)

a person whom you met in the parking lot outside a local bar. The seller told you a tale about his urgent need to raise cash by selling his TV and handed it over from the trunk of his car. One evening while you are enjoying your new television, the police arrive at your apartment with the person from whom the TV was stolen. Should the law allow you to keep the TV or require you to return it?

This question is answered differently in different jurisdictions. According to the rule in America, transferors can usually convey only those property rights that they legitimately have. Thus a person without title cannot convey title to a purchaser.[17] In this example, the thief did not have good title to the television, so he could not give you good title to it. Instead, title rests with the person from whom the TV was stolen. According to the American rule, you must return the television set to its owner. You are entitled to recover your money from the thief (technically, the thief breached his warranty of title), but this legal nicety does you no good unless he is caught and has money.

A different rule prevails in much of Europe, where the buyer acquires title by purchasing the good "in good faith." The good-faith requirement means that the buyer must genuinely believe that the seller owns the good. The good-faith requirement prevents a "fence" of stolen goods from hiding behind the law. The law may also require the buyer to make reasonable efforts to verify ownership, such as checking that the serial number was not filed off the television. Applied to this example, the European law presumably permits you to keep the television. The original owner may recover your money from the thief, but this legal nicety does her no good unless the thief is caught and has money.

In general, law must allocate the risk that stolen goods will be bought in good faith. The American rule places the entire risk on the *buyer*, whereas the European rule places that risk on the original owner. The American rule gives buyers an extra incentive to verify that the seller is truly the owner. The European rule gives owners an extra incentive to protect their property against theft. One of these rules is more efficient in the sense of imposing a lower burden upon commerce and promoting the voluntary exchange of property.

Which rule is it? Here is a method for finding out. Let C_O indicate the lowest cost to the original owner of protecting against theft by, say, engraving his or her Social Security number on the object. Let C_P indicate the lowest cost to the purchaser of verifying that the seller is the owner by, say, confirming this fact with the party from whom the seller originally obtained the good. For the sake of efficient incentives, liability should fall on the party who can verify ownership at least cost. Thus, the efficiency of the competing rules may be determined as follows:

1. If it is generally true that $C_O < C_P$, then it is more efficient for the good-faith purchaser to acquire good title against the original owner.

---

[17] This is true as a generalization, but there are important exceptions. For example, if a thief steals money and uses it to buy goods from a merchant, the original owner of the money cannot recover the money from the merchant. A thief can convey good title to money. Moreover, the Uniform Commercial Code allows regular dealers in goods sometimes to give *better* title than they got. Thus, if a television store happens to have taken possession of and sold a stolen television, the buyer is entitled to presume that the dealer had good title to the television. Any liability to the true owner of the television lies with the dealer. Can you suggest an economic reason why this is a sensible rule?

2. If it is generally true that $C_O > C_P$, then it is more efficient for the original owner to retain title against the good-faith purchaser.

Unfortunately, the absence of empirical evidence about the values of C_O and C_P prevents us from answering this question. Indeed, the lack of evidence also prevents different countries from identifying the more efficient rule and adopting it.

C. Breaks in the Chain of Title

Uncertain ownership burdens commerce and causes deep discounting of the value of an asset by prospective purchasers. Consequently, economic efficiency requires clearing away uncertainties from the title to property, or *clouds* as they are called. This section briefly examines how property law removes the clouds that accumulate over titles.

1. Adverse Possession   In the preceding chapter we discussed an example in which Joe Potatoes built his house so that two feet of it extended over the property line onto Fred Parsley's lot. Recall that Parsley did not discover the trespass and sue until ten years had passed. Has Potatoes acquired any right to the part of Parsley's property that he has occupied? According to Anglo-American law, he may have. If the owner "sleeps on his rights," allowing trespass to age, the trespasser may acquire ownership of the property.

The relevant legal doctrine is *adverse possession*. The phrase refers to the fact that a trespasser's possession of the land is adverse to the owner's interest.[18] Someone can acquire ownership of another's property by occupying it for a period of time specified in a statute, provided the occupation is adverse to the owner's interests and the original owner does not protest or take legal action.[19]

---

[18] It is also possible to acquire an easement by adverse use of another's property. For example, someone who habitually cuts across someone's property without protest by the owner may acquire the right to continue cutting across the property.

[19] To be precise, traditional scholarship distinguishes four conditions that adverse possession must satisfy:

1. The adverse possessor must have actually entered the contested property and have assumed exclusive possession.

2. That possession must be "open and notorious." This phrase means that the trespass must not be done in secret; an alert owner should be able to detect it.

3. The trespasser's possession must be adverse or hostile and under a "claim of right." This condition requires the trespass to be inconsistent with the owner's use rights and against the owner's interests.

4. Finally, the trespass must be continuous for a statutorily specified period.

Some states in the American West also require the adverse possessor to pay property taxes for a statutorily specified period before acquiring title. See Lawrence Friedman, A HISTORY OF AMERICAN LAW 360–361 (2d ed. 1985). Note that these conditions do not inquire into the intentions of the adverse possessor. Despite this, there is evidence that courts are more likely to apply the adverse-possession rule when the trespass is accidental. See Richard Helmholz, *Adverse Possession and Subjective Intent,* 61 WASH. U. L. Q. 331 (1983).

The economic advantage of adverse possession is that it clears the clouds from title. To illustrate, assume that you want to buy a house that was built in 1910 and sold in the years 1925, 1937, and 1963. Your search of title reveals a confusion in the legal records about whether the sale in 1937 was legal. However, the current owner has resided on the property since 1963 without a legal challenge. The law for this jurisdiction stipulates that adverse possession for 25 years transfers ownership to the trespasser. The adverse-possession statute and the current owner's unchallenged occupancy since 1963 have thus removed the cloud from the title dating to 1937. In general, a rule for acquiring title by adverse possession lowers the cost of establishing rightful ownership claims by removing the risk that ownership will be disputed on the basis of the distant past.

Another efficiency justification for adverse possession was emphasized in the past: adverse possession prevents valuable resources from being left idle for long periods of time by specifying procedures for a productive user to take title from an unproductive user. Under such a rule, persons who neglect to monitor their property boundaries run the risk of losing idle parts of them to someone who makes use of them. In this respect the rule tends to move property from idleness to productive use. Sometimes squatters have acquired land from absentee owners through adverse possession. In the American West, settlers historically acquired much Indian land through adverse possession. The settlers viewed themselves as putting the land to a higher use, whereas the Indians viewed the settlers as thieves.

Besides the two types of economic benefit, adverse possession has a cost. The cost is that owners must actively monitor their land to eject trespassers who might otherwise become owners through adverse possession. Without adverse-possession statutes, owners might reduce monitoring costs and more trespassers would enjoy using other peoples' land.

QUESTION 5.18: Apply the concept of adverse possession to the electromagnetic spectrum.

QUESTION 5.19: Why do you think that the statutory time period for adverse possession tends to be short in states like Oklahoma where Indians owned a lot of land?

QUESTION 5.20: Suppose the statute of limitations for adverse possession is 10 years. After 9.9 years of trespass owners retains full rights, but after 10.0 years of trespass owners lose all of their rights. Instead of owners losing their rights abruptly at the end of 10 years, the statute could be written so that the rights depreciate gradually over time. For example, the trespasser could be granted a 10% interest in the property for each year of adverse possession, so that after one year the trespasser would own 10% of it and after 10 years the trespasser would own all of it. Compare the efficiency of the "discontinuous rule" and the "continuous rule."

2. Estray Statutes   Suppose that while strolling down an alley in Manhattan you stumble over a brown paper bag. Opening the bag, you find that it contains a diamond brooch. Naturally, you would like to claim it for your own. But clearly someone has lost it. Are you entitled to keep it if the owner does not demand it back after a reasonable period of time? Are you obligated to make efforts to locate the owner, say, by advertising in the paper? Who owns property that has been abandoned, lost, or mislaid? *Estray statutes* answer these questions.

A typical estray statute in the United States stipulates a procedure for the finder to acquire ownership of lost or abandoned property. If the property exceeds a stipulated value, the finder may have to appear before a court official and sign a document concerning the facts about the property found. The court official then places an advertisement concerning the found item. If the owner does not appear to claim it within a stipulated time period (*e.g.*, one year), the finder becomes the owner. A finder who keeps the item without complying with the statute is subject to a fine.

Like registering title, estray statutes discourage the theft of property. Given an estray statute, a thief who is caught with another's property cannot avoid liability by claiming that he or she found it. ("Where did you get that watch?" Sherlock asked the suspect. "It fell off the back of a truck," he replied.) Thus an estray statute helps to distinguish a good-faith finder from a thief. Like adverse-possession rules, estray statutes tend to clear the clouds from title and transfer property to productive users. Like adverse-possession rules, estray statutes also provide an incentive for owners to monitor their property. Finally, estray statutes induce the dissemination of information by finders and thus reduce the search costs of owners who lose or mislay their property.

> **QUESTION 5.21:** If the value of a lost object is low enough, the estray statutes do not apply. Consequently, the finder has no legal obligation to advertise. Discuss the costs that need to be balanced to the most efficient lower bound in the value of a lost object for purposes of the estray statutes.

> **QUESTION 5.22:** In admiralty law, there have to be rules for allocating ownership rights to property lost at sea. In the United States, the finder of an abandoned ship is generally awarded ownership, but in some cases the government takes possession of abandoned ships in its waters. Where that latter condition holds, a salvor (*i.e.*, one who salvages an abandoned ship) is usually entitled to a salvage award determined by the court.
>
> Does this practice of making awards to salvors encourage dishonesty, or does it attract an efficient number of resources into the business of searching for lost ships? Is the system of awarding complete ownership rights to the finder more or less efficient than the award-to-salvors system?

III. LEGAL RESTRAINTS ON PROPERTY RIGHTS

What may owners do with their property? In this section we analyze some traditional restrictions on property rights, and we postpone discussing modern government regulations such as zoning ordinances.

A. Bequests and Inheritances

In a feudal or tribal world, law typically stipulates the heirs to land, rather than the owner choosing heirs. To illustrate, the eldest son inherited all of his father's land in medieval England,[20] and in matrilineal tribes the land is often inherited by the niece from her aunt. Furthermore, feudal and tribal societies typically restrict the sale of land. As law modernizes, owners increase their power to stipulate the terms of inheritance and sales. The law in Western countries has evolved over centuries toward more free-dom for the owner to specify who may have the property after his or her death and what they may do with it. We discuss briefly the economic analysis of this trend.

Any restriction upon the owner's choices creates an incentive to circumvent it. To illus-trate, imagine an owner who wants to bequeath her land to a particular friend, and imagine that the law will award the property to someone else. The owner can circumvent the law, say, by transferring title to the friend today and leasing it back for $1 per year until her death. Circumventing the law usually requires the assistance of a good lawyer. In general, owners use costly legal resources to circumvent restrictions on the use of property.

Now change the example and imagine that tight laws and costly lawyers prevent the owner from circumventing restrictions on bequests. Because her desire to designate her heir was frustrated, the owner may deplete her property before she dies. For example, she might cut timber prematurely, or exhaust the soil's fertility by intensive farming, or postpone needed improvements to buildings. In general, rules that restrict transfer undermine the owner's incentive to maximize the value of the property.

Circumvention costs and depletion costs provide two reasons for allowing an owner freedom in transferring property. However, these same reasons justify restricting the freedom of an owner in special circumstances. Most property rights live forever, but all owners die. Sometimes one generation of owners wants to limit the discretionary power of subsequent owners. To illustrate, suppose that I own my family's ancestral home, Blackacre, and I stipulate in my will that no one will ever use Blackacre for pur-poses other than a residence. Subsequently, I die and my heir wants to develop Blackacre into a golf course. Should the law enforce the restrictions in my will or set it aside and allow my heir to build a golf course? If the law sets aside such restrictions, then I have an incentive to deplete the resource or circumvent the law. If the law enforces such restriction, then my heir has an incentive to deplete the resource or cir-cumvent the law.

In the preceding example, the owner apparently wants to restrict future uses of Blackacre for aesthetic reasons. In other examples, an owner creates a trust to protect someone from his or her own bad judgment,[21] or a bequest attempts to keep property in the family forever,[22] or a restrictive covenant attempts to channel future sales to certain classes of buyers.[23] In general, the principle that the current owner should be free to structure transactions as he or she wishes runs up against a difficulty when the owner wants to restrict future owners. In these cases, a conflict exists between the freedom of

---

[20] In most of England from 1066 (the date of the Norman conquest) until 1925, the general rule for disposing of real estate upon one's death was that it passed intact to the decedent's eldest son, a system called *primogeniture*. Testators were not free to alter this rule except under very narrow circumstances.

[21] For example, a trust is created in which the beneficiary receives the interest income from the trust property but cannot touch the capital until she is middle-aged.

[22] For example, the owner leaves instructions that, at his death, his land is to be given to his oldest son, at whose death the land is to be given to *his* oldest son, and so on.

[23] In the past in America, covenents sometimes blocked future sales to buyers belonging to certain races.

sequential owners of the same property. Any reduction in the freedom of any owner in the sequence causes economic waste, regardless of whether the reduction in freedom comes from law or a private transaction.

English common law responded to these facts by a complicated law called the *rule against perpetuities*. The rule imposes a time limit on property restrictions imposed by the terms of a gift, sale, bequest, or other transaction. Instead of lasting in perpetuity, restrictions automatically lapse when a legal time limit expires. The legal time limit has the curious formulation "lives-in-being plus 21 years." To illustrate its meaning, assume that my only child is an unmarried daughter and I stipulate in my will that she will inherit Blackacre on the condition that it never be used except as a residence. According to the rule, the restriction must ordinarily lapse 21 years after my daughter's death.

Notice that the rule against perpetuities is a "generation-skipping rule." By this phrase we mean that it allows an owner to skip over the living generation by restricting their use of the property, but the property passes unrestricted to the unborn when they reach the age of 21 and become legal adults. A generation-skipping rule has an economic rationale. Assume that you must choose a principle concerning the power of one generation to impose restrictions on the use of property by subsequent generations. The principle that you choose will apply to every generation. You know that the world changes in unpredictable ways, so no restriction is good forever. You also know that most owners are prudent and benevolent towards their heirs, and a few are foolish and venal. In effect, you want a principle to protect against an occasional fool in an unending sequence of owners, given a constantly changing world.

A prudent owner will not restrict a prudent heir, and a prudent owner will restrict a foolish heir. Given these facts, an attractive principle for you to choose allows each generation to restrict the next generation, but not subsequent generations. When prudent owners apply this principle, only foolish heirs will be restricted. Furthermore, the restrictions that prudent owners impose on foolish heirs may prevent the foolish heirs from imposing restrictions on the next generation. So the rule against perpetuities appears to maximize the value of property across generations.

> **QUESTION 5.23:** Instead of "lives-in-being plus 21 years," the rule might be "lives-in-being plus 10 years," or "lives-in-being plus 35 years." Compare these rules as means for "generation-skipping."

> **QUESTION 5.24:** Suppose that a testator imposes a condition that cannot be met. For example, the decedent gives her property to be used for a medical school in Lebanon, Indiana, but after the testator's death, the State of Indiana abandons its plans to build a medical school there. In this situation American courts apply the doctrine of *cy pres* (pronounced "see pray" and meaning, in law French, "so nearly"). Under that doctrine the court will find an alternative condition that is as close as possible to the decedent's intentions. For example, the proceeds from the sale of the decedent's property in Lebanon, Indiana, might be given to a medical school located somewhere else. Use the concepts of circumvention costs and depletion costs to provide an economic rationale for this rule.

> **QUESTION 5.25:** We suggested above that an annually increasing renewal fee would be an efficient means of setting optimal patent life. Similarly, suppose that owners who wanted to restrict future use of their property had to pay a fee for each year that the restriction

runs. For example, if my will stipulates that Blackacre should be used exclusively as a residence for 100 years, then I would have to make provision in my will to pay the state for each year that the restriction runs. In effect, the state deducts an annual fee from a bequest for a testator who desires to impose posthumous restrictions on property for a specified number of years. At what level would you set such a fee? Would it be the same for all types of conditions and all types of property? Is such a fee more efficient than the rule against perpetuities?

B. Rights to Use Someone Else's Property

In general, no one may use another's property without the permission of the owner. Use of another's property without the owner's permission is an illegal trespass. As we saw in Chapter 4, this rule and moderate transaction costs induce those who want to use another's property to bargain with the owner. Bargaining leads to the use of property by the party who values it the most, as required for allocative efficiency.

Can someone ever use another's property lawfully without the owner's permission? This issue arose in the famous case of *Ploof v. Putnam*.[24] Putnam was the owner of a small island in Lake Champlain, a large body of water in northern Vermont. In November, 1904, Ploof was sailing on that lake in a sloop with his wife and two children when a violent storm arose very suddenly. Ploof needed a safe harbor quickly and the nearest one was Putnam's island. Ploof moored his sloop to a pier on that island, hoping that his ship and family would be able to ride out the storm in safety. However, an employee of Putnam's, fearing that the sloop would damage his employer's property by being cast repeatedly against it during the storm, untied the ship from the pier. The sloop and its passengers were then at the mercy of the storm. The ship was ultimately driven by the storm onto the shore and wrecked.

Ploof sued Putnam, alleging that the losses to his ship and the injuries to himself and his family were the result of wrongful action by the defendant, through his employee. Ploof argued that the storm caused an emergency that justified his trespassing on the defendant's property. He asked for compensatory damages for his losses. Putnam replied that every property owner has a right to exclude trespassers. This principle is so firmly settled, he asserted, that the court should award him summary judgment without proceeding to trial. The trial judge denied the defendant's motion for summary judgment, and the defendant appealed. The Supreme Court of Vermont affirmed the decision and held that *private necessity* like that of Ploof was an exception to the general rule against trespass.

In an emergency, one person can use another's property without permission. However, the user must compensate the owner for the costs of use. To illustrate, a hiker who gets lost in a remote wilderness may break into an uninhabited cabin in order to obtain food and shelter, but the hiker must compensate the owner for damage to the

---

[24] 81 Vt. 471, 71 A. 188 (Supreme Court of Vermont, 1908).

cabin and food consumed. In brief, the private-necessity doctrine allows compensated trespass in an emergency.

Bargaining theory rationalizes the *private-necessity* exception to the general rule against trespass. In an emergency, transaction costs may preclude bargaining. For example, the suddenness with which the storm arose precluded Ploof from finding Putnam and bargaining with him. When bargaining is precluded, voluntary transactions do not necessarily cause goods to be used by the party who values them the most. A rule allowing compensated trespass assures that trespass occurs only when its value to the trespasser exceeds the cost to the owner.

Suppose that Ploof found Putnam on the dock and bargained with him. The emergency has conveyed monopoly power on Putnam, who has the *only* nearby dock. Given Putnam's monopoly and Ploof's desperation, Putnam might demand an exorbitant amount of money for use of the dock. Ploof might promise to pay it, and then refuse to do so after the emergency passes. Litigation of such "bad-Samaritan contracts" is discussed later, when we come to the "necessity doctrine" in contract law.

> **QUESTION 5.26:** An interesting variation on the facts in *Ploof* occurred in *Vincent v. Lake Erie Transport Co.*, 109 Minn. 456, 124 N.W. 221 (Supreme Court of Minnesota, 1910). In late November, 1905, the steamship *Reynolds*, owned by the defendant, was moored to the plaintiff's dock in Duluth and discharging cargo. A storm suddenly arose on Lake Erie. The *Reynolds* signaled for a tug to take her away from the dock, but because of the storm, none could be found. The ship remained moored to the dock during the storm. The violence of the storm threw the steamship repeatedly against the plaintiff's dock, causing damage in the amount of $300. The plaintiff asked for that amount. The Lake Erie Transport Co. contended that its steamship was an involuntary trespasser. The *Reynolds* had tried to leave the plaintiff's property but had not been able to do so *through no fault of its own*. The court held that the plaintiff was entitled to damages. Argue that this holding is efficient.

C. Inalienability

The law forbids the sale of some valuable things, such as body organs, sex, heroin, children, votes, atomic weapons, or human rights. You cannot even *give away* some of these things, such as heroin or your vote in a national election. You cannot lose some of these things by *any* legal means, such as your human rights. One meaning of "alienation" is losing something, especially an intimate part of yourself. In law, the term *"inalienable"* refers to something of yours that you cannot lose by specified means. Thus, body organs, sex, and children are inalienable by sale, your vote is inalienable by sale or gift, and your human rights are inalienable by any means.

The sale of sex or children is prohibited by conventional morality, as well as law. Many forms of inalienability express conventional morality. Other forms of inalienability, such as the enactment of human rights, express the aspirations of eminent political theorists. What about economic theorists? Occasionally a regulation increases the efficiency of a transfer. This fact provides an economic rationale for regulation. However, inalienability goes far beyond regulation. Whereas regulations restrict transfers, inalienability prohibits them. The efficiency of a transfer cannot increase by prohibiting it. In general, prohibitions on transfers are inefficient because they prevent people from getting what they want. Following this line of thought, some economic writers have attacked laws that make certain goods inalienable.[25] Is there *any* economic rationale for inalienability?[26]

Some theorists argue that the sale of certain commodities undermines their transfer by superior means. For example, consider the supply of blood to hospitals. Two complementary means are used to insure that blood is free from infection: a medical history is taken from the individuals who supply blood, and the blood is tested in laboratories. The individual suppliers are more likely to provide an accurate medical history when they give their blood away than when they sell it. Consequently, donated blood is freer from infection. This fact provide an economic rationale for obtaining blood by donations rather than purchases, but not a reason for prohibiting the sale of blood. [27] For example, in the United States most blood is obtained by donations, but some blood is purchased.[28]

However, assume that the sale of blood undermines voluntary donations. For example, people might feel that giving blood away for free is stupid so long as it can be sold. If these facts were true, then prohibiting the sale of blood might be necessary in order to divert transfers into the superior channel of gifts. Similarly, anthropologists have argued that markets destroy gift economies among tribal people. Although plausible, the factual support for this theory is not strong enough to provide a convincing defense of inalienability. It seems, then, that inalienability rests upon conventional morality and political philosophies that stress values other than Pareto efficiency.

QUESTION 5.27: Assume that every adult in a particular jurisdiction is eligible to serve as a juror. Panels of potential jurors are drawn by rotation from the qualified population. Currently, no jurisdiction allows someone called for jury service to hire a qualified replacement. Would society be better off if people were allowed to engage in a market for jurors?

IV. CONFLICTING PROPERTY RIGHTS: THE PROBLEM OF SEPARABILITY

As noted in Chapter 4, common law approximates a legal system of *maximum liberty*, which allows owners to do anything with their property that does not interfere with other peoples' property. When applying this principle, the amount of liberty afforded to

---

[25] For example, see Elizabeth Landes and Richard A. Posner, *The Economics of the Baby Shortage,* 7 J. LEGAL STUD. 323 (1978) and J. Robert Pritchard, *A Market for Babies?* 34 U. TORONTO L. J. 341 (1984).

[26] See Susan Rose-Ackerman, *Inalienability and the Theory of Property Rights,* 85 COLUM. L. REV. 931 (1985), Margaret Jane Radin, *Market-Inalienability,* 100 HARV. L. REV. 1849 (1987), and Richard Epstein, *Why Restrain Alienation?* 85 COLUM. L. REV. 970 (1985).

[27] See Richard Titmuss, THE GIFT RELATIONSHIP: FROM HUMAN BLOOD TO SOCIAL POLICY (1971), in which the author argues that inalienability is an efficient method of assuring quality control. See also Kenneth Arrow, *Gifts and Exchanges,* 1 PHILOSOPHY & PUBLIC AFFAIRS 343 (1972) and Reuben Kessel, *Transfused Blood, Serum Hepatitis, and the Coase Theorem,* 17 J. LAW & ECON. 265 (1974).

[28] Blood can be purchased in the U.S., but the federal Food and Drug Administration requires labels to distinguish whether the source is a "paid donor" or "volunteer donor." Note that nonprofit institutions that collect blood from "volunteer donors" usually sell it to hospitals.

owners depends upon disentangling one owner's use of property from another's. When uses are separate, the effect of one owner upon another occurs through voluntary agreements, such as market exchange. When uses join, one owner affects another involuntarily, as when my smoke blows over your property. In this section we discuss the special legal and economic problems caused by entangled uses.

A. Externalities and Public Bads

When people agree to impose costs and benefits on each other, they make a contract. Contracts exemplify the working of markets. In contrast, when the utility or production functions of different people are interdependent, they impose benefits or costs upon each other, regardless of whether or not they have agreed. Such interdependence is called an "externality," because the costs or benefits are conveyed outside of a market. To illustrate the difference, if I buy so many watermelons at my local fruit store that the seller raises the price, my action affects other buyers, but bidding up a price exemplifies the ordinary working of markets, not an externality. In contrast, if my rooster's crowing annoys my neighbors, my action affects them independent from market transactions, so the noise is an externality

Costs or benefits conveyed outside of the market are not priced. Whenever costs or benefits are not priced, the supplier lacks incentives to supply the efficient quantity. Overcoming this incentive problem requires pricing the externality. When an externality gets priced, its supply is channeled through a market, which is called "internalizing the externality." Thus, the solution to interdependent uses of property is to channel them through the market, or to internalize the externality.

The efficient solution to the problem of internalization depends upon the number of affected people. If interdependence affects a small number of people, the externality is "private." For example, the crowing of my rooster affects a few neighbors, so the noise is a private externality. If the interdependence affects a large number of people, the externality is "public." For example, the smoke from a factory affects many households, so it is a public externality. Similarly, when one additional car enters a congested freeway, all the other drivers slow down a little, so congestion is a public externality. The private-public distinction in economics rests on a continuum describing the number of people who are affected by someone's actions. As the number of people affected by someone's action increases, a vague boundary is crossed separating "private" from "public."

In Chapter 4 we explained that one person's consumption of a public good does not diminish the amount available to others, and that excluding some people from enjoying a public good is difficult. Public externalities typically have these characteristics of nonrivalry and nonexcludability. For example, when one person breathes dirty air, just as much dirty air remains for others to breathe, and preventing some people in a given air-quality region from breathing the air is difficult. Consequently, harmful public externalities are also called "public bads."

We summarize these points by using some notation. Imagine a small economy with two people, denoted a and b, and three private goods, denoted x_1, x_2, x_3. Consumption of the first two goods involves no externalities, but consumption of the third good imposes external costs. For example, the first two goods might be apples and pears, and the third good might be cigarettes. We attach a superscript on a good to indicate who consumes. Thus, the utility of person a can be written as a function of the three goods that she consumes: $u^a = u^a(x_1{}^a, x_2{}^a, x_3{}^a)$. Assume that person b consumes the first two goods, but not the third good; that is, person b does not smoke cigarettes. Furthermore, assume that person b dislikes breathing the smoke from person a's cigarettes. Thus, the utility of person b can be written $u^b = u^b(x_1{}^b, x_2{}^b; x_3{}^a)$. The utility functions of a and b are interdependent because a's consumption of the third good is an argument in b's utility function. In other words, the presence of a variable in b's utility function bearing the superscript a indicates an externality.

Let us add additional notation to indicate incomplete markets. Suppose that the three goods (x_1, x_2, x_3) are purchased in a store at prices (p_1, p_2, p_3). The price that person a must pay for x_3 presumably reflects the cost at which the store purchases the good. This price does not include the cost of the harm that a's consumption of x_3 imposes on b. Consequently, there is no price associated with the variable $x_3{}^a$ in b's utility function. In order to attach such a price, persons a and b would have to bargain with each other. Through such bargaining, the externality might be internalized.

Our two-person example is a private externality. Alternatively, assume that there are $1, 2, 3, \ldots, n$ people just like person b. Choose any one of these n people and call this person j. Person j's utility function has the form $u^j = u^j(x_1{}^j, x_2{}^j; x_3{}^a)$, for $j = 1, 2, 3, \ldots, n$. Now the harmful externality from a's consumption of x_3 affects so many people that it is a public bad. The transaction cost of bargaining with n people is presumably prohibitive, so the externality cannot be internalized by a private bargain. Instead, an alternative means of pricing the externality must be found.

QUESTION 5.28: Classify the items in the following list as markets, private externalities, or public externalities.

  a. a lighthouse warns ships about rocks

  b. my building blocks your sunlight

  c. you outbid me at the auction

  d. my bees pollinate your apple trees

  e. airport noise lowers the sale value of my house

QUESTION 5.29: Assume that the third good, x_3, represents miles driven in cars by persons $1, 2, 3 \ldots, n$, and assume that cars are polluting. Rewrite the utility function of the person j in the preceding formulation to represent these facts.

B. Remedies for Externalities

In property law, a harmful externality is called a *nuisance*. Remember that our discussion of remedies for nuisance in Chapter 4 distinguished between injunctions and damages, and that the relative efficiency of these remedies has a lot to do with the public-private distinction. If the nuisance is private, few parties are affected by it, and, as a result, the costs of bargaining together are low. When bargaining costs are low, the parties will ordinarily reach a cooperative agreement and do what is efficient. Consequently, in those circumstances the choice of remedies makes little difference to the efficiency of the bargaining outcome. The traditional property law remedy—injunctive relief—is attractive under these circumstances, because the court need not undertake the difficult job of computing damages. If one views an injunction as always and forever prohibiting the offensive activity, then its inflexibility is costly. However, if one views an injunction as an instruction to the parties to resolve their dispute through voluntary exchange, then it is an attractive remedy for private nuisances.

In contrast, trying to correct a harmful externality of the public-bad type by bargaining would involve the cooperation of all the affected parties. Bargaining fails in these circumstances because it requires the cooperation of too many people. The law refers to a harmful externality of the public type as a *public nuisance*. Our analysis suggests that damages will be a more efficient remedy for a public nuisance than an injunction would be.

To apply this prescription for choosing between injunctions and damages, the court has to examine the number of people affected by the externality. However, the court does not have to perform a cost-benefit analysis comparing injunctions and damages. Cost-benefit analysis requires more information than courts typically possess, so legal rules whose application requires a cost-benefit analysis should be avoided.

When compensatory damages are perfect, they restore the victim to the same utility curve as he or she would have enjoyed without the harm. Compensatory damages can be *temporary* or *permanent*. With temporary damages, the plaintiff receives compensation for the harms the defendant has inflicted upon him or her in the past. If harms continue in the future, the plaintiff must return to court in order to receive additional damages. Thus, temporary damages impose high transaction costs for dispute resolution. With temporary damages, reductions in future harms translate directly into reductions in liability. Consequently, temporary damages create incentives for injurers to continually adopt technical improvements that reduce external costs.

With permanent damages, the plaintiff receives compensation for past harms plus the present discounted value of all reasonably anticipated future harms.[29] To illustrate, let D_1 through D_{10} represent the damages that will occur in years one through ten. Let the rate of interest be r. The present discounted value, V, of this stream of future damages is equal to

$$V = D_1 / (1 + r) + D_2 / (1 + r)^2 + D_3 / (1 + r)^3 + \ldots + D_{10} / (1 + r)^{10}.$$

With permanent damages, one lump-sum payment extinguishes claims for past and future harms at the level specified in the judgment. Unfortunately, future changes in technology and prices are difficult to predict, so the estimation of future harms suffers from error. Thus, permanent damages impose high error costs. Furthermore, by paying permanent damages the injurer "purchases" the right to external harm up to the amount stipulated in the judgment. Consequently, permanent damages create no incentive for injurers to adopt technical improvements that reduce external costs below the level stipulated in the judgment.[30]

As explained, temporary damages impose high transaction costs, whereas permanent damages impose high error costs and undermine incentives for reducing future harms. Transaction costs of resolving disputes, whether by trial or settlement, are low when liability is certain and damages are easily measured. Error costs are high when

---

[29] See Chapter 2 for more on discounting.

[30] In his dissent in *Boomer v. Atlantic Cement Co.,* which we discuss below, Justice Jasen recognized this point in his criticism of the majority's award of permanent damages. He wrote, "Furthermore, once permanent damages are assessed and paid, the incentive to alleviate the wrong would be eliminated, thereby continuing air pollution in an area without abatement."

innovation improves abatement technology and changes the understanding of the harms caused by externalities. Thus, temporary damages tend to be more efficient given easily measured damages and rapid innovation. Conversely, permanent damages tend to be more efficient given costly measurement of damages and slow innovation.

We commend damages as the remedy for a public nuisance. However, common law has not traditionally followed this prescription. When the public is harmed by a nuisance, courts traditionally allow the affected parties to enjoin it. The following case suggests that the common law has become more receptive to damage remedies for public nuisances. Read the case and test your knowledge of externality theory by answering the questions.

Boomer v. Atlantic Cement Co., Inc.
309 N.Y.S.2d 312, 257 N.E.2d 87 (Court of Appeals of New York, 1970)

BERGAN, J. Defendant operates a large cement plant near Albany. These are actions for injunction and damages by neighboring land owners alleging injury to property from dirt, smoke and vibration emanating from the plant.

[At the trial court and on appeal, the defendant's cement-making operations were found to be a nuisance to the plaintiff neighbors. Temporary damages were awarded, but an injunction against future dirt, smoke, and vibration from the plant causing the same or greater harms was denied. Plaintiffs have brought this appeal in order to receive the traditional remedy against a nuisance—an injunction.]

The ground for denial of injunction . . . is the large disparity in economic consequences of the nuisance and of the injunction. This theory cannot, however, be sustained without overruling a doctrine which has been consistently reaffirmed in several leading cases in this court and which has never been disavowed here, namely, that where a nuisance has been found and where there has been any substantial damage shown by the party complaining, an injunction will be granted.

The rule in New York has been that such a nuisance will be enjoined although marked disparity be shown in economic consequences between the effect of the injunction and the effect of the nuisance . . .

The court at Special Term [the trial court] also found the amount of permanent damage attributable to each plaintiff, for the guidance of the parties in the event both sides stipulated to the payment and acceptance of such permanent damage as a settlement of all the controversies among the parties. The total of permanent damages to all plaintiffs thus found was $185,000 . . .

This result . . . is a departure from a rule that has become settled; but to follow the rule literally in these cases would be to close down the plant at once. This court is fully agreed to avoid that immediately drastic remedy; the difference in view is how best to avoid it. [Footnote by Court: Atlantic Cement Co.'s investment in the plant is in excess of $45,000,000. There are over 300 people employed there.]

If the injunction were to be granted unless within a short period—e.g., 18 months—the nuisance be abated by improved techniques found, there would inevitably be applications to the court at Special Term for extensions of time to perform on showing of good faith efforts to find such techniques. The parties could settle this private litigation at any time if defendant paid enough money and the imminent threat of closing the plant would build up the pressure on defendant . . .

Moreover, techniques to eliminate dust and other annoying by-products of cement making are unlikely to be developed by any research the defendant can undertake within any short period, but will depend on the total resources of the cement industry nationwide and throughout the world. The problem is universal wherever cement is made.

For obvious reasons the rate of the research is beyond control of defendant. If at the end of 18 months the whole industry has not found a technical solution, a court would be hard put to close down this one cement plant if due regard be given to equitable principles.

On the other hand, to grant the injunction unless defendant pays plaintiffs such permanent damages as may be fixed by the court seems to do justice between the contending parties. All of the attributions of economic loss to the properties on which plaintiffs' complaints are based will have been redressed . . .

It seems reasonable to think that the risk of being required to pay permanent damages to injured property owners by cement plant owners would itself be a reasonably effective spur to research for improved techniques to minimize nuisance . . . Thus it seems fair to both sides to grant permanent damages to plaintiffs which will terminate this private litigation . . . The judgment, by allowance of permanent damages imposing a servitude on land, which is the basis of the actions, would preclude future recovery by plaintiffs or their grantees.

This should be placed beyond debate by a provision of the judgment that the payment by defendant and the acceptance by plaintiffs of permanent damages found by the court shall be in compensation for a servitude on the land.[31]

The orders should be reversed, without costs, and the cases remitted to Supreme Court, Albany County, to grant an injunction which shall be vacated upon payment by defendant of such amounts of permanent damage to the respective plaintiffs as shall for this purpose be determined by the court.

JASEN, J., dissenting. I agree with the majority that a reversal is required here, but I do not subscribe to the newly enunciated doctrine of assessment of permanent damages, in lieu of an injunction, where substantial property rights have been impaired by the creation of a nuisance . . .

I see grave dangers in overruling our long-established rule of granting an injunction where a nuisance results in substantial continuing damage. *In permitting the injunction to become inoperative upon the payment of permanent damages, the majority is, in effect, licensing a continuing wrong. It is the same as saying to the cement company, you may continue to do harm to your neighbors so long as you pay a fee for it.* [Authors' emphasis.] Furthermore, once such permanent damages

---

[31] A *servitude on the land* is a restriction or burden on a piece of real property. The servitude typically "runs with the land," which means that it becomes permanently attached to the particular piece of land and is not, therefore, dependent on the identity of the owner. In our discussion of the case, we will see why the court wishes to make the obligation to pay permanent damages for the nuisance a servitude on the land rather than being a mere obligation to pay particular individuals.

are assessed and paid, the incentive to alleviate the wrong would be eliminated, thereby continuing air pollution of an area without abatement.

It is true that some courts have sanctioned the remedy here proposed by the majority in a number of cases, but none of the authorities relied upon by the majority are analogous to the situation before us. In those cases, the courts, in denying an injunction and awarding money damages, grounded their decision on a showing that the use to which the property was intended to be put was primarily for the public benefit. Here, on the other hand, it is clearly established that the cement company is creating a continuing air pollution nuisance primarily for its own private interest with no public benefit . . . The promotion of the interests of the polluting cement company, has, in my opinion, no public use or benefit. . . .

I would enjoin the defendant cement company from continuing the discharge of dust particles upon its neighbors' properties unless, within 18 months, the cement company abated this nuisance...

QUESTION 5.30: Is the externality in *Boomer* private or public?

QUESTION 5.31: Are the transaction costs of bargaining among the parties low or high?

QUESTION 5.32: Suppose the households had a right to enjoin the cement company to stop polluting. What obstacles would the cement company face if it tried to purchase the right to pollute from the households?

QUESTION 5.33: Explain the remedy given by the court. Suppose that at some time in the future the cement company doubles its rate of output, thus increasing the noise, smoke, dust, and vibration inflicted on the neighbors. Do the homeowners have a remedy?

QUESTION 5.34: Contrast the difference between temporary and permanent damages on the incentives of people to build new houses near the cement factory.

QUESTION 5.35: To what extent can the private law of property solve the problem of pollution?

C. Graphing Externalities

Let us graph how the award of damages can internalize an externality and restore efficiency. We assume that a firm like Atlantic Cement is held liable for the external costs it inflicts upon others. The situation facing the firm is shown in Figure 5.2. The company's marginal private-cost curve, *MPC*, indicates the private cost to the firm of producing different quantities of cement. Private costs include the capital, labor, land, and materials, but not the external harm caused by pollution. The external costs of pollution are added to the private costs to yield the social costs of producing cement. Figure 5.2 depicts two marginal social-cost curves representing two different technologies. Under the old technology, the addition of external costs of pollution to the private costs of production yields the marginal social-cost curve *MSC*. This curve depicts the true cost to society of each level of production under the old technology. There is, however, a new technology that pollutes less. Its marginal social costs are shown along line *MSC′*. The superiority of the new technology lies in the fact that it causes half as much pollution at any given level of output as the old technology. For example, the old technology

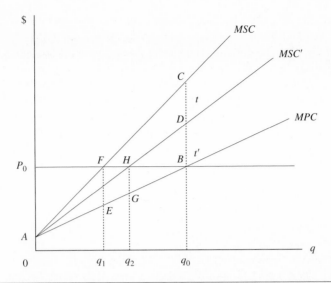

FIGURE 5.2 The incentives to adopt a new, superior technology under a rule of temporary damages.

might use filters in the smoke stack, and the new technology might use scrubbers in the smoke stack.

Under either technology and in the absence of any court or regulatory action, the company's profit-maximizing rate of output, q_0, is determined at the intersection of the private marginal-cost curve and the prevailing output price, P_0. Under the old technology the total amount of external cost inflicted by the output rate q_0 is the area ABC. Under the new technology the total amount of external cost inflicted by the output rate q_0 is the area ABD. The social cost inflicted by the last unit of output is t under the old technology and t' under the new technology. Note that it is easy to see here that, even if there is no legal compulsion for the firm to take external costs into account, society is better off if the firm is producing q_0 under the new technology rather than under the old technology. However, if the firm is not required to internalize these external costs, it has no incentive to adopt the new technology.

However, matters change if the firm can be made to internalize the social cost of its production of cement. Under the old technology and with the firm held responsible for its external costs, the profit-maximizing rate of output is determined by the intersection of P_0 and MSC at q_1. But under the new technology and with the firm held responsible for its external costs, the profit-maximizing rate of output is determined by the intersection of P_0 and MSC' at q_2. The total social cost inflicted by those two rates of output is, under our assumptions, the same; that is, the area AEF is equal to the area AGH. But because $q_2 > q_1$, society prefers that the firm adopt the new technology and operate along MSC'.

But what about the firm? Is it still indifferent between the two technologies? No. Assuming that the firm pays pollution costs, its maximum profits under the old technology are the area AP_0F, whereas maximum profits under the new technology are AP_0H. It is obvious that $AP_0H > AP_0F$.

How do these considerations relate to the question we asked above about the incentives for adopting superior technologies of production under the alternative damage measures? The intuitively plausible answer is that the cement company will adopt the cleaner technology more quickly under temporary damages than under permanent damages, and that intuition is borne out by our formal analysis. However, these economic advantages to temporary damages over permanent damages must be balanced against the potentially higher administrative costs of temporary awards.

QUESTION 5.36: The price line P_0 is horizontal in Figure 5.2 What does this fact indicate about competition?

QUESTION 5.37: Assume that science reveals a new health hazard caused by breathing pollution from cement factories. How would such a discovery modify the graph and change the efficient level of production of cement?

V. PUBLIC AND PRIVATE PROPERTY

The first part of this chapter concerned delineating the rights of property owners, and we discussed the content of these rights at length. But we did not discuss who the owners should be. Should ownership of valuable resources be assigned only to individuals? Or should it be given to families, communities, organizations, or to all of society? In this section, we turn from discussing the content of the bundle of rights called "property" to a discussion of the types of owners—individuals, organizations, and the community.

We distinguished between private and public externalities by the number of affected people. Similarly, private and public ownership can be distinguished by the number of owners. A resource owned by a single individual is private. Corporations owned by a small group of stockholders ("closely held corporations") are "private companies." Corporations owned by many shareholders are "public companies." The state belongs to all of the citizens, so the state is the "public sector."

What difference does the number of owners make? In discussing the Coase theorem, we described bargaining among the owners of separate properties, such as the rancher and the farmer. Bargaining also occurs when several people own the same property. For example, the partners in a business bargain over the allocation of tasks. The difference between private and public ownership can be described as a difference in the structure of bargaining.

Among private owners, bargaining occurs over the exchange of resources in markets. Bargaining in markets usually has no prescribed form or fixed procedures, although social norms are relevant. The decisions to exchange resources are made by individual owners. The conclusion of a bargain requires the agreement of each of the parties. In contrast, public owners must participate in the government of their institution. Among public owners, bargaining occurs in governing the institution. Governance follows prescribed forms and fixed procedures as stipulated in the constitution of the organization and its other rules. The decisions are made collectively, and making a decision does not usually require the agreement of everyone. For example, citizens elect a president by majority rule, and directors of a corporation elect a chairman of the board by majority rule.

Private ownership divides people into small groups. So long as externalities are private, private owners can advance their interests by cooperating with a small number of people. Bargaining among small groups of people tends to result in cooperation and achieve efficiency. Consequently, the case for private ownership is easy to make when production and utility functions are separable, or when externalities are private. In these circumstances, public ownership is a costly mistake.

An illustration comes from a study of oyster beds along the Atlantic and Gulf coasts of the United States.[32] At an early stage in their lives oysters attach themselves permanently to some subaqueous material, such as rock. This attachment makes it possible to imagine defining private property rights in oysters for commercial fishing operators. However, the states along the Atlantic and Gulf coasts that have commercial oyster industries have not settled on a single system of property rights for oysters. Some states have determined that the subaqueous areas where oysters tend to congregate are to be *common* property for oyster harvesters; any of them may take oysters from those areas, and none may exclude another. Other states have held that these areas are to be available for private leasing from the state and that the lessee will have the usual rights to exclude and transfer (with some limitations). This difference allowed Professors Agnello and Donnelly to compare the relative efficiency of the private and communal property-rights systems. The measure of efficiency they used was labor productivity (output per person-hour in oyster-fishing). Their finding was that labor was much more productively employed in the privately leased oyster beds than in the communal oyster beds. Put dramatically, the authors of this study concluded that if all oyster beds had been privately leased in 1969, the average oyster harvester's income would have been 50% higher than it was. That implies a sizable welfare loss due to public ownership.

The public oyster beds are an example of the depletion of an open-access resource by overuse. The depletion of an open-access resource by overuse is called "the tragedy of the commons."[33] Open access to a congested natural resource has a remorseless logic with a terrible ending, like a Greek tragedy.

We have discussed the easy case in which private ownership can separate utility and production functions and in which externalities are private. A more difficult case for choosing between public and private ownership arises when production and utility functions of many owners are interdependent and externalities are public. To address this problem through private ownership, the affected parties must bargain with each other, and the transaction costs are prohibitive. Public ownership is a possible solution. Instead of unstructured bargaining and a requirement that everyone agree, the switch

---

[32] See R.J. Agnello and L.P. Donnelly, *Property Rights and Efficiency in the Oyster Industry,* 18 J. LAW & ECON. 521 (1975). See also G. Power, *More About Oysters Than You Wanted to Know,* 30 MD. L. REV. 199 (1970).

[33] Classical articles are Garret Hardin, *The Tragedy of the Commons,* in ECONOMICS FOUNDATIONS OF PROPERTY LAW 2 (Bruce A. Ackerman ed., 1975) and H. Scott Gordon, *The Economic Theory of a Common Property Resource: The Fishery,* 62 J. POL. ECON. 124 (1954).

from private to public ownership substitutes structured bargaining and a collective-choice principle, such as majority rule.

To illustrate, consider pasture land in the mountains of Iceland.[34] Dividing the mountain pasture among individual owners would require fencing it, which is prohibitively expensive. Instead, the highland pasture is held in common, with each village owning different pastures that are separated by natural features such as lakes and mountain peaks. If each person in the village could place as many sheep as he or she wanted in the common pasture, the meadows might be destroyed and eroded by overuse. In fact, the common pastures in the mountains of Iceland have not been overused and destroyed because the villages have effective systems of governance. They have adopted rules to protect and preserve the common pasture. The sheep are grazed in common pasture in the mountains during the summer and then returned to individual farms in the valleys during the winter. The total number of sheep allowed in the mountain pasture during the summer is adjusted to its carrying capacity. Each member of the village receives a share of the total in proportion to the amount of farmland where he or she raises hay to feed the sheep in the winter.

Some discussions of the superiority of private ownership over public ownership equate public ownership with open-access. This equation is too simple. In fact, the general public does not have free access to most public property. To illustrate, the national parks in the United States are publicly owned, but a fee is charged to enter; many activities require reservations in advance (a form of rationing by time), and no one can graze animals or cut wood. The tragedy of the commons, in its fully disastrous form, requires a political paralysis that prevents government from stopping the destruction of a resource. This paralysis seems to have reached an advanced stage for some resources, such as fisheries. For other resources, there are symptoms of paralysis, but not the full disaster. For example, the federal government owns vast lands in the American west and sells permits for grazing, forestry, and mining on these lands. There is evidence that much of this federal domain is inefficiently managed. As a result, the environment is deteriorating, in part because the communal interest provides much less incentive for efficient use of that resource than would private ownership.[35]

It would be surprising if a small, homogenous village in Iceland were paralyzed politically to the point of being unable to manage public resources. However, a large, heterogeneous country such as the United States faces far more difficult problems in managing public resources. One solution is to reduce public ownership by selling federally owned land. The market value of the products yielded by lands in the American west would surely be higher if the land currently under public control were transferred to private control.

This argument, however, is unlikely to persuade those who *want* to see the wilderness underutilized. Most ecologists believe that public land should *not* be managed with the aim of maximizing the market value that it yields. Everyone tends to think

---

[34] See the discussion of common mountain pastures in Iceland in Thrainn Eggertsson, ECONOMIC BEHAVIOR AND INSTITUTIONS (1990).

[35] For an introduction to federal ownership of American land, see Marion Clawson, THE FEDERAL LANDS REVISITED (1983).

that some things are more valuable than wealth (at least at the margin), such as liberty or truth; for some people, wilderness is such a value. Just as people who love liberty would never decide whether persons have the right to speak by asking whether people would pay more to hear them or to shut them up, so those who love the wilderness would never decide whether to build condominiums on the nesting site of the California condors by asking whether developers would pay more for the land than would the ecologists. Ecologists usually oppose the sale of public lands to private interests because their aim is to limit development rather than to increase yield. Given the scope of disagreement between ecologists and developers, it seems certain that vast resources will be used up in political disputes over the governance of public lands in the western United States.

> **QUESTION 5.38:** Cooperative enterprises are collectively owned, and their affairs are directed through shared governance. Use the preceding theory to discuss the management of some cooperative enterprises with which you are familiar, such as a cooperative diary, a cooperative apartment building, an Israeli kibbutz, a Hutterite farm, a commune, etc.

VI. THE PUBLIC USE OF PRIVATE PROPERTY: TAKINGS AND REGULATION

The theory of property developed in Chapter 4 stresses that clear and certain property rights facilitate bargaining, which creates a surplus from cooperation and exchange. Conversely, unclear and uncertain property rights impede bargaining, which destroys the social surplus. The power of the state to take property and regulate its use reduces the clarity and certainty of property rights. The resulting destruction in social surplus represents the economic cost of the state's power to take property and regulate its use. Offsetting the economic cost is the benefit of providing public goods at lower cost. In this section we develop these ideas into an economic theory of the taking and regulatory powers.

A. Takings

In many countries, the constitution circumscribes the state's power to take private property. For example, the takings clause of the Fifth Amendment to the U. S. Constitution reads, "nor shall private property be taken for public use, without just compensation." Thus, the Fifth Amendment prohibits the state from taking private property except under two conditions: (1) the private property is taken for a public use, and (2) the owner is compensated. We will explain the economic rationale for these two conditions.

1. Compensation To understand the compensation requirement, contrast takings and taxes. Taxes are assessed on a broad base, such as income, property, sales, or bequests. Everyone subject to the tax faces the same schedule of rates. In contrast, a taking involves a particular piece of property owned by a particular person. Tyrannies sometimes finance government and enrich officials by taking property from individuals. To finance the state by takings, the private owner whose property is appropriated must not receive compensation. If the private property owner received compensation equal to the market value for his or her property, the state could not profit from taking it. So the requirement of compensation can be viewed as a device to channel government finance into taxes and away from takings.

Economics provides strong reasons for financing the state by taxes rather than takings. Any kind of expropriation distorts people's incentives and causes economic efficiency, but taxes distort far less than uncompensated takings. To see why, consider the basic principle in public finance that focused taxes distort more than broad taxes. Applying this principle, a given amount of revenues can be raised with less distortion by a tax on food rather than vegetables, or a tax on vegetables rather than carrots. This principle follows from the fact that avoiding broad taxes is harder than avoiding narrow taxes. For example, avoiding a tax on food requires eating less, whereas avoiding a tax on carrots requires eating another vegetable such as cucumbers. Broad taxes distort behavior less because many people cannot change their behavior to avoid broad taxes. Thus, efficiency requires the state to collect revenues from broad taxes such as income or consumption.[36] In contrast, takings have a very narrow base. Individual owners will go to great expense to prevent the state from taking their property without compensation. Indeed, the possibility of uncompensated takings would divert effort and resources away from production and toward the politics of redistribution.

2. Public Use We explained that requiring the compensation of takings at market prices channels state finance into less distorting taxes. The requirement of compensation does not preclude another political abuse, in which the state takes one person's property and sells it to someone else. To appreciate the problem, consider the difference between a taking and a sale. Sales are motivated by mutual gain, which is created by moving property from lower-valued to higher-valued uses. To illustrate, Blair's purchase of Adam's 1957 Chevrolet creates a surplus because Blair values it more than Adam. The fact that both parties must consent to the sale guarantees mutual gain. In contrast, a taking does not require the consent of the property owner, so unilateral gain can motivate a taking. A property owner may value his or her property more than whoever takes it.

For example, assume that Samson owns his family's estate, the market value of which equals $30,000, but Samson does not want to sell it because he values the estate at $100,000 for sentimental reasons. Delilah covets Samson's estate and would be willing to pay up to $40,000 for it. Assume that the state can compel Samson to sell his property at its "fair market value." So Delilah contributes $5,000 to the campaign fund of a prominent government official, who takes Samson's estate, pays him $30,000, and resells the estate to Delilah for $30,000. Thus, Delilah and the government official each gain $5,000, although Samson loses $70,000.

By taking Samson's property and giving it to Delilah, the state transfers property from one private person to another, so that Delilah does not have to pay Samson's subjective price for the estate. The requirement of compensation at market prices does not prevent this abuse, which occurs because the owner's subjective value exceeds the

---

[36] The precise proposition is that goods should be taxed at a rate inversely proportional to their elasticity of demand and supply. Broad taxes fall on aggregates that are inelastically demanded and supplied.

market price paid as compensation. To eliminate the abuse, the state could compensate the owner's subjective price rather than the market price. However, no one but the owner knows the subjective price. In a voluntary sale, the owner receives at least the subjective price or does not sell. If the state wanted to compensate at least the owner's subjective price, the state would have to buy the property, not take it.

The "public-use" requirement avoids the abuse in this example. Delilah's use of Samson's estate is private, not public. Consequently, the taking in this example violates the public-use requirement. The public-use requirement forbids the use of takings to bypass markets and transfer private property from one private person to another. Instead, property must be taken for a public use. For example, Samson's estate could be taken for a park, school, or highway.

The public-use requirement does not solve the problem of inefficiency in involuntary transfers. To illustrate, suppose that motorists would be willing to pay $40,000 to use a highway through Samson's estate, the market value of which is $30,000. By taking the land, paying Samson $30,000, and building a highway, the government anticipates a surplus of $10,000. In reality, Samson values his estate at $100,000, so the net social loss will equal $60,000, and Samson will lose $70,000.

This example suggests that the state should not take property with compensation merely to produce a public good. In reality, the state buys most of the resources that it uses to supply public goods. For example, the state buys cement, pencils, trucks, light bulbs, and labor. In fact, takings are circumscribed more than the requirements of compensation and public use suggest.

3. Holdouts   The government must purchase large tracts of land from many owners in order to provide some public goods, such as military bases, airports, highways, and wilderness areas. These projects often demand "contiguity," which means that the parcels of land must touch each other. To illustrate, the segments of a highway do not connect unless they are on contiguous parcels of land. Contiguity disrupts bargaining by creating opportunities for owners to hold out.

To illustrate, assume that the state proposes to construct a road across three parcels of land owned by three different people. The state determines that motorists would pay $200,000 more than the construction costs for such a road. Consequently, efficiency requires undertaking the project provided that the land's value is less than $200,000. The three owners value the land at $30,000 per parcel, so construction of the road would create a social surplus of $110,000. Assume that the state acquires an option to buy one of the parcels for $30,000. The state could pay up to $160,000 for the other two parcels and still come out ahead. Knowing this, each of the owners demands $100,000 for her parcel of land. If the state must buy the land, not take it, the project fails.

The last owner frequently "holds out" when the state acquires contiguous parcels of land needed for a public project. In a real-life example, the developers of a new baseball stadium in Denver purchased all the land except for the property of one "holdout," whom the newspaper called "the guy who owns first base." Even when owners do not hold out, the possibility of doing so can dramatically increase the transaction costs of purchasing contiguous property. The taking power eliminates this problem. The government should resort to compulsory sale only when there are many sellers, each of whom controls resources that are necessary to the project. Thus, takings should be guided by this principle:

In general, the government should only take private property with compensation to provide a public good when transaction costs preclude purchasing the necessary property.

QUESTION 5.39: What if the government needs to purchase a single, large piece of property in order to provide a public good, say, a satellite-tracking station? There is only one private owner with whom to deal. And his property is the only one that is suitable for the station. Should the government be allowed to compel this individual, a monopolist for the contemplated public use, to sell at fair market value?

QUESTION 5.40: The State of Michigan condemned many properties in a residential neighborhood on the border of Detroit known as "Poletown," assembled a large parcel of land, and sold it to General Motors to construct an automobile factory. The courts upheld the taking of private property for this project. Use the economic analysis to argue for or against the legality of these takings.

QUESTION 5.41: Compare the efficiency of the following two methods of amending the just-compensation constraint:

a. Define just compensation to be fair market value (including relocation costs) plus, say, 20%.

b. Allow private property owners to make their own assessments of the value of their property. Property owners agree to pay property taxes on that self-assessed value. If the government ever takes the property, it agrees to pay the self-assessed property value as just compensation.

4. Insurance People typically purchase insurance on assets whose value constitutes a significant proportion of their wealth, such as a house. Most homeowners purchase fire insurance. Similarly, people want insurance against takings. Private companies provide fire insurance, whereas the state provides insurance against takings by compensating property owners. Why does the private sector provide insurance against fires, and the state sector provide insurance against takings?

This question challenges you to relate takings to the economics of insurance. Insurance spreads risk among policy holders. In general, spreading risk more broadly reduces the amount that anyone must bear. The state can spread the risk of takings through the base of all taxpayers, which is broader than the base of all policy holders in any insurance company. So risk-spreading argues for public insurance.

Administrative efficiency argues for private insurance. The discipline of competition causes a higher level of administrative efficiency in private insurance funds than in state insurance funds. Many state insurance funds, such as depository insurance in American savings banks, have a dismal history.

Risk-spreading and administrative costs are not decisive. The decisive case for public insurance against takings rests upon incentive effects for the state. Decisions about takings are made by the state. If the state did not have to pay compensation, it might take property to finance itself, or it might take property for redistribution to the friends of politicians, or it might purchase too many public goods.[37]

---

[37] For more on takings as insurance, see Larry Blume and Dan Rubinfeld, *Compensation for Takings: An Economic Analysis,* 72 CAL. L. REV. 569 (1984).

5. Regulations Earlier in this chapter we discussed how interdependent utility or production functions can cause the externalization of social costs. Nuisance suits provide a
remedy. State regulations provide another remedy. Regulations restrict the use of the
property without taking title from the owner. Enacting regulations involves a political
fight between the beneficiaries and victims. Since the outcome depends upon politics,
not cost-benefit analysis, the total costs of regulations often exceed the total benefits.
However, a chapter on property is not the place to develop a full critique of regulations.
In this section, we focus upon a narrower issue related to takings.

Regulations typically cause a fall in the value of some target property, which may
prompt a suit for compensation. To illustrate, an industrialist who acquires land to build
a factory may be blocked when the local government "downzones" and forbids industrial uses. The industrialist may sue, alleging that the state took the value of the property but not the title. When courts find for the plaintiff in such cases, they say there was
a "taking." When courts find for the defendant in such cases, they say there was a "regulation." The difference is that a taking requires compensation and a regulation requires
no compensation.

We want to discuss the incentive effects of this classification into compensated
restrictions (takings) and uncompensated restrictions (regulations). If the state need not
compensate for restrictions, then it will impose too many of them. If there are too many
restrictions, then resources will not be put to their highest-valued use. Thus, uncompensated restrictions result in inefficient uses. Conversely, if the state must compensate
fully for restrictions, then property owners will be indifferent about whether or not the
state restricts them. If property owners are indifferent about whether or not the state
restricts them, they will improve their property as if there were no risk that restrictions
will prevent the use of the improvements. If restrictions subsequently prevent the use of
the improvements, the investment will be wasted. Thus, compensated restrictions result
in wasteful improvements.

We illustrate this argument by an example.[38]

> **FACTS:** Xavier is a government official whose wall contains a map with a thick blue line
> across it. Currently, the land-use planning laws allow the area to the south of the blue line
> to be used for any commercial, industrial, or residential purpose. The government
> proposes to change the law and forbid industrial uses, although commercial uses would
> still be allowed.
>
> Yvonne owns a building that is located on the blue line. She currently uses the building
> as a retail outlet, but she is contemplating expanding and improving the building for use as
> a factory. Yvonne must decide how much to invest in improving her building. If she
> abandons the idea of using her building as a factory, she will make a smaller investment in
> improving it for use as retail space, and the government's land-use regulation decision will
> not affect her. But if she proceeds with the idea of using her building as a factory, she will
> make a large investment, and the government's decision *will* affect her. Should the
> government carry out its proposed change, she will lose money on the large investment,
> and a court will then have to decide whether she is entitled to compensation for the loss.
> The decision will turn upon whether the court declares the change in the governmental

---

[38] See Cooter, *Unity in Tort, Contract, and Property: The Model of Precaution,* 73 CAL. L. REV. 1 (1985).

land-use plan to be a regulation, in which case no compensation is due, or a taking, in which case compensation is due.

Consider the incentive effects of the court's decision on Yvonne. If she is confident that downzoning is a taking and she will receive compensation, she bears no risk from making a large investment, so she will invest as if there were no risk of loss from governmental action. On the other hand, if she is confident that downzoning is a regulation and she will not receive compensation, she bears the risk that the value of her investment would be destroyed by the governmental action, and she will restrain her investment.

Figure 5.3 illustrates these facts. The vertical axis indicates dollars and the horizontal axis measures the size of Yvonne's renovated building. The straight line labeled "Total Cost" indicates the amount that she spends on enlarging the building. Two curves, labeled R_{nr} and R_r, indicate possible revenues yielded by the building as a function of its size. The higher revenue curve, labeled R_{nr}, indicates the revenues obtainable when there is no regulation, so that the building can be used as a factory. The lower revenue curve, labeled R_r, indicates the revenues obtainable when there is regulation, so that the building cannot be used as a factory.

Applying the usual economic logic, Yvonne will maximize profits by choosing the size of building for which the marginal cost equals the marginal revenues. Marginal values are given by the slopes of total value curves in the graph. Y_0 is the point at which the slope of the lower revenue curve equals the slope of the total cost curve, so Y_0 is the profit-maximizing investment level when industrial use is forbidden. If Yvonne were certain that the courts would hold that down-zoning is a regulation, then she would maximize profits by investing at the low level Y_0.

Y_1 is the point at which the slope of the higher revenue curve equals the slope of the total cost curve, so Y_1 is the profit-maximizing investment level when industrial use is

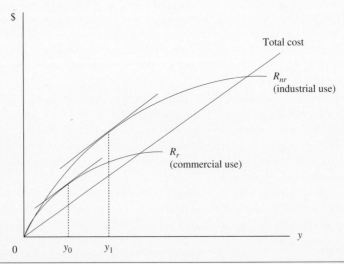

FIGURE 5.3 The incentive effects on private investors of a difference between compensable takings and noncompensable regulations.

allowed. If Yvonne were certain that down-zoning would be deemed a taking by the courts, then she would maximize profits (including compensation) by investing at the high level.

Now consider the efficient level of investment. Social efficiency requires Yvonne to take account of real risks, including the risk that the value of her contemplated investment will be destroyed by governmental action. If it were certain that government would *not* alter the land-use regulations in this area, then efficiency would require Yvonne to invest at the high level Y_1. One the other hand, if it were certain that government would alter the rules, then efficiency would require Yvonne to invest at the low level Y_0. In reality, it is uncertain whether government will make the alteration, so efficiency requires Yvonne to invest at a level in between Y_1 and Y_0.[39]

No compensation causes Yvonne to internalize the risk. When she internalizes the risk, she invests efficiently, at a level above Y_0 and below Y_1. We conclude that *no compensation for the loss of value in investments caused by uncertain governmental action provides incentives for efficient private investment.* However, compensation causes her to invest at Y_1, as if the risk were zero. We conclude that *full compensation for the loss of value in investments caused by uncertain governmental action provides incentives for excessive private investment.*

This argument concerns incentives for private persons, not the state. The effect of the two legal institutions—regulations and takings—is quite different when we turn from private persons to government officials. If the court decides that the alteration in the allowable uses of land in the relevant area is a mere regulation, so that compensation need not be paid, then the alteration costs government nothing. On the other hand, if the court decides that this particular action is a taking so that compensation must be paid, then this type of action is very costly to the government. Obviously, *the noncompensability of regulations gives government officials an incentive to overregulate, whereas the compensability of takings makes government officials internalize the full cost of expropriating private property.* When government action is likely to be judged a taking, the government internalizes the cost of its actions and thus restrains its taking of private property. On the other hand, when government action is likely to be judged a mere regulation, the government lacks material incentives to conserve its use of valuable private property rights.

If the state compensates property owners for governmental takings, property owners have an incentive toward excessive improvements, whereas if the state does not compensate, the government has an incentive to overregulate private property. This is the *paradox of compensation*, which we shall meet it again in our study of contracts and torts.

B. Zoning and the Regulation of Development

Some goods, called *complements*, are better consumed together, such as hot dogs and sauerkraut, and other goods, called *substitutes*, are better consumed separately, such as ice cream and sauerkraut. A similar categorization may be made regarding the spatial

---

[39] To be precise, efficiency requires her to make additional improvements until the resulting increase in her profits when there is no government action, multiplied by the probability of no governmental action, equals the loss in profits when there is government action, multiplied by the probability of governmental action.

separation of economic activities: it is best to locate restaurants near offices, and it is best to separate smokestack industries from residences. There is, however, an important difference between culinary and spatial separation: no law prohibits eating ice cream with sauerkraut, but zoning ordinances in most localities *do* prohibit locating industry in residential neighborhoods.

It is the element of compulsion in the segregation of economic activities by zoning laws that we here seek to explain. It is possible to make a case for zoning as a response to an important kind of market failure. When demand for a good increases, the price rises and producers respond by supplying more of it. The rise in price is a signal for producers to devote more resources to producing the good. This signal is usually appropriate in the sense that society is better off when resources are shifted to producing goods whose price is rising. There are, however, special circumstances in which the signals get crossed. In these special circumstances, it would be better for society if producers of a certain good responded to a rise in the price of that good by supplying *less* of it; but in a free market, they will respond to the rise in price by supplying more of it.

To illustrate by an historical example, suppose that in 1900 industry locates on the shore of an undeveloped bay in California. The original purpose for locating industry on the shore was that of obtaining easy access to boats, but by 1960 the manufacturers were supplied by truck rather than by boat. Moreover, the harbor now has great aesthetic and recreational appeal. Given the change in circumstances, efficiency requires gradually relocating industry into the interior and constructing residences or recreational parks on the harbor.

To cause factories to move out and residences to move in, residential developers should bid up the price of harbor land relative to land in the interior. There is, however, an obstacle to the unregulated market's accomplishing this end. The problem is that no one wants to live next door to a factory, so that residential developers are unwilling to pay much for harbor land as long as industry is present. Instead of factories' moving away from the harbor, the opposite may happen: as industry expands, residences may be driven farther away from the water. If the relative price of land near the water is falling as residents flee to the interior to escape industry, the unregulated market in this situation is giving the wrong signals.

The technical explanation for the false signal given by the market, and the resulting justification for compulsory zoning, is the existence of what economists call a *nonconvexity* in the production technology. We can see this in an example. Suppose that an electrical company burns coal and that the soot soils a nearby commercial laundry. There is, then, a trade-off between the amount of electricity that can be generated and the amount of clean laundry that can be produced using a given amount of resources. This tradeoff is depicted by the production frontier in Figure 5.4. Along the vertical axis we measure the amount of clean laundry that can be produced in a given time period; if all local resources are devoted to clean-laundry production, then the maximum amount of clean-laundry output that can be produced is L^*. Along the horizontal axis we measure the amount of electricity that can be generated in a given time period; if all local resources are devoted to the production of electricity and none to the cleaning of laundry, then E^* electricity can be produced. The production frontier (sometimes called the *production-possibilities frontier*) is the curve that runs between L^* and E^* and thus represents the combinations of laundry and electricity that are feasible when a given amount of productive resources is allocated between the two uses (and each

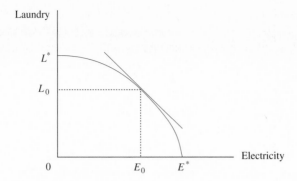

FIGURE 5.4 A production-possibilities frontier showing the normal convex production set.

enterprise uses its resources efficiently). The production frontier has the standard shape assumed in microeconomic theory; the frontier bows out in a direction that carries it away from the origin of the graph. We shall indicate in a moment how the market signals to the producers how those productive resources are to be allocated.

Suppose that Figure 5.4 depicts the production frontier when the laundry is 10 miles away from the electrical company. Figure 5.5 includes new production frontiers that depict the consequences of moving the laundry closer to the electrical company. The main effect of moving the industries closer together is that the interference with the laundry from soot is greater. Thus, when the distance is, say, 6 miles, the amount of clean laundry that can be produced, for any given level of electrical production, is lower than at 10 miles, so the interior points on the production frontier shift towards the origin. The end points, however, do not shift, because they represent a situation in which one of the plants shuts down, so there is no problem of soot interfering with laundry. Moving the two industries from 6 miles to 3 miles apart causes another shift to occur. At a distance of 3 miles the production frontier has shifted so that it bows *in* toward the origin of the graph rather than out from it. At 10 miles, where the production-possibilities frontier bows out, the production possibilities form a convex set. That is, the area bounded by the frontier and the axes (the production set) is convex. But at 3 miles, where the production frontier bows in, the production possibilities form a nonconvex set.[40] The point of this example is that spatial externalities can produce nonconvex production sets.

But what is so bad about a nonconvex production set? The difficulty is that when a production set is nonconvex, the unregulated market sends the wrong price signals to producers regarding the efficient allocation of resources between competing productive ends. To see the problem, start at the top of the production frontier (at L^*) in Figure 5.4 and begin drawing lines tangent to the production frontier as you move down it. The slope of these lines represents the relative price of laundry and electricity at different levels of production in a free market. Notice that as you move down the production set, the tangent lines become steeper, which indicates that the production of clean laundry becomes more valuable as it becomes more scarce.

---

[40] A set is convex if, for any pair of points in it, a straight line connecting the two points is entirely contained in the set. Circles and rectangles form convex sets; a quarter-moon forms a nonconvex set.

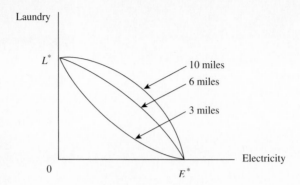

FIGURE 5.5 The production set becomes nonconvex as externalities increase.

For the nonconvex production set in Figure 5.7 (the production frontier when the laundry and the electrical plant are 3 miles apart), the opposite is true: as you move down the production set from L^* to E^*, the tangent lines become flatter, indicating that the laundry's output becomes less valuable relative to electricity as it becomes more scarce. The result of their being a nonconvex production set is that, in formal economic terms, the optimal solution is a *corner solution*, in which all resources are used by one or the other enterprise. That is, either L^* or E^* will be produced, but not both.

In contrast, when the production set is convex, there is an *interior solution* in which both clean laundry and electricity are produced. (In Figure 5.4, L_0 and E_0 represent the optimal combination of laundry and electricity for a convex production set for an arbitrary relative price of the two outputs.)

This analysis can be applied to the example of industrial and residential use of a harbor. This is done in Figures 5.6 and 5.7. The vertical axis in the figures indicates the level of industrial production in the harbor area, and the horizontal axis indicates the level of residential use in the harbor area. The curved line is the production frontier, which shows the feasible combinations of industry and housing. The production frontier in Figure 5.6 is a convex set, whereas the production frontier in Figure 5.7 forms a nonconvex set. Our example (stated at the beginning of this section, and hypothesizing an increase in industry in the harbor area) assumes that the production set is nonconvex. When that is the case, the unregulated market will generate a harbor area given over entirely to industrial use or to residential use (a corner solution) but not some of each (an interior solution). Because there is a strong suspicion that the more valuable use of the harbor area is now as a residential area, some corrective action is required to prevent the wrong price signals from generating the inefficient outcome, namely, the outcome in which all residential uses are driven away from the harbor area.

Although zoning can be justified in this way as a device to correct a market failure and produce an efficient spatial allocation of resources, in reality zoning is a highly political institution that bears little resemblance to the cool, technocratic balancing of benefits and costs implied by our model. A change in zoning, or the granting of an exemption (called a *variance*) to a particular property owner can often result in increasing the value of the land by multiples of 2, 3, or even 100. With these multiples at stake, zoning boards are bound to be subjected to pressures from the self-interested and to be highly politically charged, and there is the possibility that they will be corrupt.

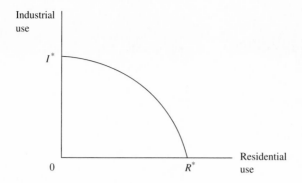

FIGURE 5.6 The normal convex production set between industrial and residential uses of property.

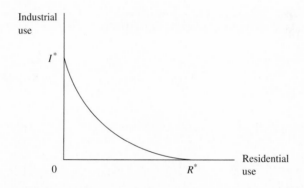

FIGURE 5.7 A nonconvex production set between competing uses of contiguous property.

Several investigators have attempted to discover the objectives that zoning boards actually follow. One plausible idea is that zoning boards tend to impose restrictions upon new developments that maximize the value of the property of the people who elect the board. To illustrate, the zoning board of a wealthy suburb might require a residential developer to donate land for a new park for the town and a new school as the price of its granting to her the variances required for her construction of new homes. The zoning board may reason that the new park and school will cause the property values of existing voters to rise. Another plausible idea is that zoning makes little difference to the spatial allocation of economic activities because much the same ends can be accomplished through the insertion, by private parties, of restrictive covenants in deeds. To illustrate, in Houston, where until recently there has been virtually no zoning, the developer of a housing estate often inserts in the deeds to the lots in the estate restrictions against industrial or commercial uses of the property.[41]

---

[41] There is no better place to begin an investigation of the law and economics of zoning than Robert Ellickson, *Alternatives to Zoning: Covenants, Nuisance Rules, and Fines as Land Use Controls*, 40 U. CHI. L. REV. 681 (1973).

CONCLUSION

In Chapters 4 and 5 we developed an economic theory of property and applied it to a wide-ranging set of legal problems. Our theory views property as the institution that gives people freedom over resources; property law can encourage the efficient use of resources by creating rules that facilitate bargaining and exchange and that minimize the losses when bargaining fails. We organized our theoretical discussion of property rules around four questions that a system of property law must answer. In answering these questions, we revealed the economic logic underlying much of property law.

SUGGESTED READINGS

Baxter, William and Lillian R. Altree, *Legal Aspects of Airport Noise,* 15 J. LAW & ECON. (1972).

Ellickson, Robert, *Suburban Growth Controls: An Economic and Legal Analysis,* 86 YALE L. J. 385 (1977).

Fischel, William, THE ECONOMICS OF ZONING LAW: A PROPERTY RIGHTS APPROACH TO AMERICAN LAND USE CONTROLS (1985).

Kaplow, Louis, *An Economic Analysis of Legal Transitions,* 99 HARV. L. REV. 509 (1986).

Rose, Carol M., *Mahon Reconstructed: Why the Takings Issue is Still a Muddle,* 85 COL. L. REV. 931 (1985).

Zerbe, R. and J. Palmer, eds., *The Economics of Patents and Copyrights,* 8 RESEARCH IN LAW & ECON 1.

6

AN ECONOMIC THEORY OF CONTRACT

"[T]he movement of the progressive societies has hitherto been a movement from Status to Contract."

—

Henry Maine, ANCIENT LAW 170 (1861)

"Whoever offers to another a bargain of any kind, proposes to do this: Give me that which I want, and you shall have this which you want, is the meaning of every such offer; and it is in this manner that we obtain from one another the far greater part of those good offices which we stand in need of. It is not from the benevolence of the butcher, the brewer, or the baker, that we expect our dinner, but from their regard to their own interest."

—

Adam Smith, THE WEALTH OF NATIONS 22 (5th ed. 1789)

"A promise invokes trust in my future actions, not merely in my present sincerity."

—

Charles Fried, CONTRACT AS PROMISE 11 (1981)

People continually make promises: sales people promise happiness; lovers promise marriage; generals promise victory; and children promise to behave better. The law becomes involved when someone seeks to have a promise enforced. Here are some examples:

EXAMPLE 1: The Rich Uncle. The rich uncle of a struggling college student learns at the graduation party that his nephew graduated with honors. Swept away by good feeling, the uncle promises the nephew a trip around the world. Later the uncle reneges on his promise. The student sues his uncle, asking the court to compel the uncle to pay for a trip around the world.

EXAMPLE 2: The Rusty Chevy. One neighbor offers to sell a used car to another for $1000. The buyer gives the money to the seller, and the seller gives the car keys to the buyer. To her great surprise, the buyer discovers that the keys fit the rusting Chevrolet in the backyard, not the shiny Cadillac in the driveway. The seller is equally surprised to learn that the buyer expected the Cadillac. The buyer asks the court to order the seller to turn over the Cadillac.

EXAMPLE 3: The Grasshopper Killer. A farmer, in response to a magazine advertisement for "a sure means to kill grasshoppers," mails $25 and receives in the mail two wooden blocks with the instructions, "Place grasshopper on Block A and smash with Block B." The buyer asks the court to require the seller to return the $25 and to pay $500 in punitive damages.

Should the courts enforce the promises in these examples? A promise is enforceable if the courts offer a remedy to the victim of the broken promise. Traditionally, courts have been cautious about enforcing promises that are not given in exchange for something. In Example 1, the promise of a trip around the world is a gift to the nephew. The rich uncle does not receive anything in exchange, so, according to the traditional analysis, the courts should not enforce the uncle's promise. In Example 2, money exchanges for a promise, but the seller thought that he gave a different promise than the buyer thought she received. Courts often refuse to enforce confused promises. In Example 2, the courts would probably require the seller to return the money and the buyer to return the car keys. Example 3 involves deception, not confusion. A "sure method to kill grasshoppers" means something more than what the seller delivered. The courts ordinarily offer a remedy to the victims of deceptive promises.

If an enforceable promise was broken, what should be the remedy? One remedy requires the promise-breaker to keep the promise. For example, if the court decided that the seller in Example 2 broke his promise, then the court might order the seller to deliver the Cadillac to the buyer. This kind of remedy is unavailable in Example 3 because the seller cannot exterminate grasshoppers as promised. Instead, the remedy in Example 3 must involve the payment of money damages as compensation for the failure to provide an effective grasshopper killer.

Our examples illustrate the two fundamental questions in contract law: "What promises should be enforced?" and "What should be the remedy for breaking enforceable promises?" Courts face these questions when deciding contract disputes and legislatures face these questions when debating bills to regulate contracts. A theory of contract law must guide courts and legislatures by answering these two questions.

I. BARGAIN THEORY: AN INTRODUCTION TO CONTRACTS

In the late nineteenth and early twentieth centuries, Anglo-American courts and legal commentators developed the "bargain theory of contracts" to answer the two fundamental questions of contract law. The bargain theory held that the law should enforce promises given in a bargain. To implement this answer, theorists isolated and abstracted the minimal elements of a typical bargain. The minimal elements of a bargain remain fundamental to the way lawyers think about contracts. We will explain the bargain theory in order to isolate the minimal elements of a bargain, and then use these elements as building blocks in an economic theory of contracts.

A. What Promises Should Be Enforceable At Law?

"What promises should be enforceable at law?" The bargain theory has a clear answer to this question, which we call *the bargain principle: a promise is legally enforceable if it is given as part of a bargain; otherwise, a promise is unenforceable.* The bargain theory makes enforcement hinge upon classifying promises as "bargains" or "nonbargains." Consequently, the theory requires an exact specification of the necessary and sufficient conditions for the court to conclude that a bargain occurred.

The bargain theorists distinguished three conditions: offer, acceptance, and consideration. "Offer" and "acceptance" have the same meaning in this theory as they do in ordinary speech: one party must make an offer ("I'll take that rusty Chevy over there for $1000"), and the other must accept it ("Done"). Sometimes business practices and social conventions prescribe the signals for making and accepting offers. For example, a buyer at an auction may signal an offer to buy by raising his or her hand, and the auctioneer may signal acceptance by shouting "Sold!" Sometimes contract law and statutes specify procedures for offer and acceptance. For example, most states require written contracts and registration for sales of land.

The "promisor" refers to the person who gives a promise, and the "promisee" refers to the person who receives a promise. In a bargain, the promisee induces the promisor to give the promise. The inducement may be money, as when the farmer pays $25 for the promise of a device that kills grasshoppers. The inducement may be goods, as when an automobile dealer delivers a car in exchange for the promise of future payment. The inducement may be a service, as when a painter paints a house in exchange for the promise of future payment. Or the inducement may be another promise, as when a farmer promises to deliver wheat to a wholesaler in the fall, and the wholesaler promises to pay a certain price upon delivery. The forms of a bargain thus include money-for-a-promise, goods-for-a-promise, service-for-a-promise, and promise-for-a-promise.

Regardless of form, each bargain involves *reciprocal inducement*: the promisee gives something to induce the promisor to give the promise, and the promisor gives the promise as inducement to the promisee. Law uses the technical term *consideration* to describe what the promisee gives the promisor to induce the promise. Thus, the farmer's payment of $25 is consideration for the promise to supply a device that kills grasshoppers. The delivery of a car, the painting of a house, or a promise to deliver crops may be consideration for a promise of future payment.

According to the bargain theory, the contract remains incomplete until the promisee gives something to the promisor to induce the promise. When completed, the contract becomes enforceable. In other words, *consideration makes the promise enforceable.* The bargain theory holds that promises secured by consideration are enforceable and promises lacking consideration are unenforceable.

Let us illustrate the bargain theory by applying it to the three examples at the beginning of this chapter. In Example 1 the nephew apparently did not give anything as inducement for his rich uncle's promise of a trip around the world. Apparently there was no consideration, so the promise is unenforceable. In general, the promise to give a pure gift, which is not induced by the promise of something in return, is not enforceable under the bargain theory.

In contrast, consideration *was* given in Example 2 in exchange for the promise to supply the used car. The question raised in Example 2 is whether there was offer and acceptance. The seller thought they were discussing the rusty Chevy and the buyer thought they were discussing the immaculate Cadillac. The seller offered to sell one good and the buyer agree to buy another good. There was no "meeting of the minds." Without a meeting of the minds, there is no offer and no acceptance, just a failure to communicate.

In Example 3, the seller offered a sure method for killing grasshoppers in exchange for $25, the buyer accepted the offer, and consideration took the form of the payment of $25. Therefore, the promise is enforceable according to the bargain theory.

We conclude this section by relating bargains to fairness. Most people have beliefs about fair bargains. In a fair bargain, each party gives equivalent value. In the language of law, a contract is fair when the value of the promise is proportional to the value of the consideration. Conversely, in an unfair bargain, the value of the promise is disproportional to the value of the consideration. To illustrate an unfair bargain, the elder brother (Esau) in a famous Bible story promised to give his inheritance rights to a younger brother (Jacob) in exchange for a bowl of soup.

According to bargain theory, a court should enforce promises induced by consideration, regardless of whether the consideration was equivalent in value to the promise. It is enough for enforceability under the bargain theory that the promisor found the consideration adequate to induce the promise. Bargain theory holds that courts should determine whether a bargain occurred, not inquire into whether the bargain was fair. Consequently, the doctrine of consideration requires courts to enforce some unfair promises, such as exchanging one's inheritance for a bowl of soup.[1]

An alternative theory would limit courts to enforcing fair bargains. To apply such a theory, a court would have to ask whether the value of the promise was equivalent to the value of the consideration. People often disagree about the value of goods, and litigants often disguise values from courts. Determining whether equivalents were exchanged requires courts to obtain a lot of information. Supervising all bargains for fairness would burden the courts and inhibit commerce. Consequently, most people want the courts to enforce bargains, not to supervise them. Perhaps this fact explains why courts do not routinely examine bargains for fairness. However, some bargains are so one-sided that most people require little information to condemn them as unfair. Modern U.S. courts sometimes refuse to enforce extremely one-sided bargains. (See the discussion of "unconscionability" in the next chapter.)

QUESTION 6.1: People often change the form of a promise in an attempt to increase their certainty that courts will enforce it according to its terms. For example, suppose the rich uncle in Example 1 wanted to assure his nephew of the enforceability of the promise of a trip around the world. Courts are more certain to enforce bargain-promises than gift-promises. Tradition prescribes how to change the form of a promise from a gift to a

---

[1] If Esau were starving to death when he promised his inheritance for a bowl of soup, the contract might not be enforceable under the bargain doctrine because of an exception, discussed in the next chapter, called the "necessity defense."

HUMPTY-DUMPTY JURISPRUDENCE:
THE LIFE HISTORY OF THE WORD "CONSIDERATION"

"When I use a word, it means just what I choose it to mean—
neither more nor less,"

—Humpty-Dumpty in Lewis Carroll, THROUGH THE LOOKING-GLASS.

In the bargain theory of contracts, "consideration" means something the promisee gives the promisor to induce the promise. According to the bargain theory, consideration makes the promise enforceable. Anglo-American courts accepted the bargain theory in the early years of this century and adopted the legal principle that consideration makes a promise enforceable. Then, as the years passed, exceptions to the principle accumulated. Courts, however, are slow to discard the abstract principles that they adopt. Instead of renouncing the principle of consideration, the courts did something characteristic of them: they changed the meaning of "consideration." Instead of meaning "something the promisee gives the promisor to induce the promise," the word "consideration" as used by the courts came to mean "the thing that makes a promise enforceable."

A tautology is a proposition that is true by definition of the words, such as "All husbands are married." When the courts changed the meaning of "consideration," they reduced the legal principle of consideration to a tautology. If "consideration" means "the thing that makes a promise enforceable," then the principle "consideration makes a promise enforceable" has no bite. When reduced to a tautology, a legal principle merely draws our attention to the meaning of a word, rather than telling us something about the legal consequences of our actions. Having made the principle of consideration into a tautology, the courts could assert its truth without fear of being wrong. Hence, we have an example of Humpty-Dumpty jurisprudence.

---

bargain. According to tradition, the uncle would solemnly offer to give his nephew a trip around the world in exchange for a peppercorn (a piece of pepper), and the nephew would solemnly give the uncle a peppercorn. More recently, people disguise a gift as a bargain by intoning the phrase "in consideration for which, I give you $1." Will this charade make the uncle's promise enforceable under the bargain theory? Answer this question by using the doctrine that courts inquire into the presence of consideration but not its adequacy. Also answer this question using the doctrine that courts should refuse to enforce extremely unfair bargains.

QUESTION 6.2: Roman law enforced certain kinds of promises and withheld enforcement of other kinds of promises. Enforcement of a promise in Roman law usually required offer and acceptance, but enforcement did not generally require consideration. Roman law lacked the doctrine of consideration because it was not based upon bargain theory. Relate these facts about Roman law to the enforceability of a promise to give a gift.

B. What Should Be the Remedy for the Breach of Enforceable Promises?

The bargain theory also had an answer to the second fundamental question of contract theory: "What should be the remedy for the breach of enforceable promises?" According to the bargain theory, the promisee is entitled to the "benefit of the bargain"—that is, to the benefit her or she would have obtained from performance of the promise. Computing compensation under this formula involves answering the counterfactual question "How well-off would the promisee have been if the promise had been kept?" The counterfactual question concerns the benefit that the promisee could reasonably expect from performance. Consequently, the damage measure under the bargain theory is called *expectation damages*.

Note the connection between the answers to the questions "What promises should be enforced?" and "What should be the remedy for breach of enforceable promises?" Promises should be enforced, according to the bargain theory, if they are part of a bargain, and the remedy for the breach of an enforceable promise is an award of the value expected of the bargain. The fact of a bargain establishes enforceability, and the expected value of a bargain measures damages.

Assume that the promises are enforceable in the three examples at the beginning of the chapter. What measures expectation damages? The student's expectation damage in Example 1 equals the value to him of a trip around the world. The buyer's expectation damage in Example 2 equals the difference in the value that she places on the rusty Chevy and the value that she places on the immaculate Cadillac. In Example 3, the farmer's expectation damage equals the value of the crops destroyed by grasshoppers.

Counterfactual values are difficult to compute. The cost of a trip around the world, as in Example 1, depends on the route taken and whether the traveler goes first class or economy class. The value of a unique, old Cadillac, as in Example 2, depends upon the buyer's subjective preferences. The value of killing the grasshoppers in Example 3 depends upon the value of the crops that would have been harvested if they had not been destroyed by insects.

C. A Criticism of the Bargain Theory

The answer that the bargain theory gives to the first question of contract law is clear. Unfortunately, the answer is also wrong. Sometimes the person who makes a promise wants it enforced and so does the person who receives it. Contract law should enforce such a promise in order to help the people get what they want. However, the bargain theory denies enforcement when the promise did not arise from a bargain.

For example, assume that a buyer begins her search for a car by taking a new Chevrolet for a test drive. After the test drive, the buyer plans to continue her search by visiting other car dealers. The seller wants to induce the buyer to consider carefully the purchase of the new Chevrolet. Consequently, the seller promises to sell the new

Chevrolet to the buyer for a stated price, provided that the buyer accepts within one week. In other words, the seller makes a "firm offer" and promises to "keep it open" for one week. The buyer does not want to waste her time by considering the offer carefully and then finding that the seller has reneged. Consequently, the buyer wants the promise to be enforceable. The seller knows that the buyer is more likely to consider the offer carefully if the promise is enforceable, so the seller wants the promise to be enforceable. Thus, the promisor and the promisee want the promise to be enforceable. Despite the wishes of both parties, the bargain theory withholds enforcement of the promise because the buyer gave nothing to the seller in exchange for the seller's promise to keep the offer open ("no consideration").

As another example, assume that a prominent alumna promises to give Old Siwash University the funds to construct a new building. The university wants to begin construction immediately. The alumna also wants the university to begin construction immediately. To obtain cash for the donation, the alumna must liquidate assets, which will take some time. The university dare not begin construction without an enforceable promise. In this example, both parties want the promise to be enforceable, but the bargain theory withholds enforcement of this promise. The bargain theory withholds enforcement because the promise "lacks consideration." Gift-promises are not induced by the prospect of gain, so they always lack consideration.

In the two preceding examples, both parties to the promise want it to be enforceable, yet the bargain theory withholds enforcement. A legal theory that frustrates the desires of the people affected by the law can be called *dogmatic*. In contrast, a legal theory that satisfies the desires of the people affected by the law can be called *responsive*. Contemporary courts in America prefer to be responsive rather than dogmatic. Consequently, contemporary courts in America often enforce firm offers and gift-promises.[2] As a result of such facts, the bargain theory is typically regarded as wrong.[3]

II. AN ECONOMIC THEORY OF CONTRACT

We want to replace the bargain theory with a less dogmatic, more responsive theory of contracts. In the two preceding examples, enforceability of the contract apparently makes two people better off, as measured by their own desires, without making anyone worse off. Whenever a change in the law makes someone better off without making anyone worse off, "Pareto efficiency" requires changing the law. "Pareto-efficient law" is a technical name for responsive law. A theory of law based upon Pareto efficiency is responsive, not dogmatic.

In general, *economic efficiency requires enforcing a promise if the promisor and promisee both wanted enforceability when it was made.* We will develop this central

---

[2] The *Uniform Commercial Code* § 2–205 allows for certain, but not all, firm offers to be enforceable for a period not exceeding three months. (The *UCC* is described in a box at the beginning of Chapter 7.) American courts generally enforce gift-promises to the extent of reasonable reliance. Where the promisee is a non-profit organization like a university, American courts sometimes enforce gift-promises to the full extent of the promise.

[3] One famous commentator on the history of contract theory—Grant Gilmore, THE DEATH OF CONTRACT (1974)—believed that the classical or bargain theory was dead almost as soon as it was born.

idea in the economic theory of contracts to answer the first question of contract law, "What promises should be enforced?"

A. Cooperation and Commitment

Many exchanges occur instantly and simultaneously, as when a shopper pays cash for goods in the grocery store. In a simultaneous, instantaneous exchange, there is little reason to promise anything. The making of promises typically concerns *deferred exchanges*—that is, transactions that involve the passage of time for their completion. For example, one party pays now and the other promises to deliver goods later ("payment for a promise"); one party delivers goods now and the other promises to pay later ("goods for a promise"); or one party promises to deliver goods later, and the other promises to pay when the goods are delivered ("promise for a promise").

The passage of time between the exchange of promises and their performance creates uncertainties and risks. Uncertainties and risks present obstacles to exchange and cooperation. To illustrate, consider deferred exchange when promises are *un*enforceable. The seller asks the buyer to pay now for future delivery of goods. This unenforceable promise involves a high risk that the seller will not deliver the goods as promised. A cautious buyer may refuse to pay now for an *un*enforceable promise to deliver goods in the future. The cautious buyer wants something stronger than a moral obligation of the seller to deliver the goods. In addition, the cautious buyer wants a legal obligation of the seller to deliver the goods. The cautious buyer may be willing to pay now for an *enforceable* promise to deliver goods in the future. Thus, the enforceability of promises encourages exchange and cooperation among people.

Notice that both parties in this example want the seller's promise to be enforceable at the time it is made. The cautious buyer wants enforceability to provide an incentive for seller's performance and a remedy for seller's breach. The seller wants enforceability in order to induce the buyer to make the purchase. By enforcing the promise, the court can give both parties what they want. Giving them what they want promotes exchange and encourages cooperation by reducing uncertainty and risk.

To develop this insight, we describe a situation called the "agency game" that often arises in business. In this game, the first player decides whether or not to put a valuable asset under the control of the second player. The first player might be an investor in a corporation, a consumer advancing funds to purchase goods, a depositor at a bank, the buyer of an insurance policy, or a shipper of goods, to list some possibilities. If the first player puts the asset under the second player's control, the second player decides whether to cooperate or appropriate. Cooperation is productive. Productivity could take the form of the profit from investment, the surplus from trade, or the interest from a loan. The parties divide the product of cooperation between them, so both of them benefit. Appropriation is redistributive. Redistribution benefits the second player at the expense of the first player.

We depict these alternatives in Figure 6.1 and attach numbers to them. The numbers indicate the difference in the wealth of the two players before playing the agency game and after playing it. The first player to move in Figure 6.1 decides whether or not to make an investment of 1. If no investment is made, the game ends and the players receive nothing. If an investment is made, the second player decides whether to cooperate or appropriate. Cooperation produces a total payoff of 1. The players divide the total payoff equally: the first player recovers the investment of 1 and also receives a

	Second player	
	Cooperate	Appropriate
First player Invest	.5, .5	1.0, −1.0
Don't invest	0, 0	0, 0

FIGURE 6.1 Agency game without contract.

payoff of .5, and the second player receives a payoff of .5. Thus, the two players benefit equally from playing the agency game. Alternatively, the second player can appropriate. Appropriation enables the second player to acquire the first player's investment, while producing nothing: the first player loses 1, and the second player gains 1.

Consider the best moves for each player to make in Figure 6.1. If the first player invests, then the second player receives more from appropriating than cooperating. Consequently, the second player's best move is to appropriate.[4] The first player may anticipate that the second player will appropriate. Consequently, the first player's best move is "don't invest." We have shown that the solution to the agency game in Figure 6.1 is "don't invest."

The payoffs to the agency game in Figure 6.1 assume that the parties cannot make an enforceable contract. The barrier to an enforceable contract might be dogmatic law or corrupt courts. Now consider how the matrix changes if we assume responsive law and honest courts, so the parties can make an enforceable contract. We assume that the second player offers to cooperate in exchange for an investment by the first player, and the first player accepts the offer by investing. The first player's investment is consideration for the second player's promise. We assume that the law will hold the second player liable for compensatory damages in the event that the player breaks the promise and appropriates.

Figure 6.2 depicts the revised payoffs in the agency game when the first player offers to invest in exchange for an *enforceable* promise by the second player to cooperate. Consider the payoffs to the first player. If the first player invests and the second player performs, the first player recovers his or her investment and receives an additional payoff equal to .5. If the first player invests and the second player breaches, the first player receives compensatory damages. We assume that compensatory damages restore the first player's payoff to the level that he or she would have enjoyed if the second player had performed. If the second player had performed, the first player would have recovered the investment of 1 and received a payoff of .5. Thus, the first player receives a net payoff of .5 from investing, regardless of what the second player does. Alternatively, the first player can receive a payoff of 0 from not investing. Faced with these two alternatives, investing is the first player's best move.

Assume that the first player invests and consider the payoffs to the second player. The second player receives a payoff of .5 from performing as promised (cooperating). In contrast, breaching the contract (appropriating) yields a payoff of 1 to the second

---

[4] Game theorists describe a move that is best against *any* possible move by the other side as a "dominant strategy." In Figure 6.1, the second player has a dominant strategy. The first player does not have a dominant strategy, but the first player has a best reply to the second player's dominant strategy.

		Second player	
		Perform	Breach
First player	Invest (contract)	.5, .5	–.5, .5
	Don't invest (no contract)	0, 0	0, 0

FIGURE 6.2 Agency game with contract.

player, from which the second player must pay compensation to the first player. As compensation, the first player must receive 1 that he or she invested and .5 that was expected in profits. Consequently, liability of 1.5 must be subtracted from the second player's payoff of 1, yielding a net payoff of –.5 for breaching the contract. So the best move for the second player is to cooperate.

Figure 6.1 shows that the first player does not invest when promises are *un*enforceable. Figure 6.2 shows that the first player invests and the second player cooperates when promises are enforceable. Thus, an enforceable contract converts a game with a noncooperative solution into a game with a cooperative solution. *The first purpose of contract law is to enable people to cooperate by converting games with noncooperative solutions into games with cooperative solutions.*

We have shown that the unique solution of the agency game with a contract is "invest" and "perform" (cooperate). So far we have discussed the best move for each player from that player's viewpoint. Now consider the sum of the payoffs to both players. The sum of the payoffs to both players is found by adding the two numbers in each cell in Figure 6.1 or Figure 6.2. Efficiency requires choosing the cell that maximizes the sum of the payoffs.[5] The numbers sum to 1 when the first player invests and the second player cooperates. Otherwise, the numbers sum to zero. Investing and cooperating are productive, whereas "don't invest" changes nothing and "appropriate" merely redistributes money from the first player to the second player. Given these facts, we could restate the preceding conclusion: *The first purpose of contract law is to enable people to convert games with inefficient solutions into games with efficient solutions.*

The language of game theory clarifies how enforceable contracts promote cooperation. In game theory, a *commitment* forecloses an opportunity. To illustrate, Julius Caesar sometimes burned the bridges behind him as his army advanced on the enemy. Burning the bridges committed his army to attack by foreclosing the opportunity to retreat. Similarly, making a contract commits the second player in Figure 6.2 to cooperate. Commitment is achieved by foreclosing the opportunity to appropriate. The opportunity to appropriate is foreclosed by the high cost of liability.

A commitment is *credible* when the other party observes the foreclosing of an opportunity. To illustrate, Caesar's commitment to advance was credible in so far as his enemies observed the burning bridges. Similarly, the second player makes a credible commitment to cooperate in Figure 6.2 provided that the first player knows the second

---

[5] To be precise, cost-benefit efficiency requires choosing the cell that maximizes the sum of the payoffs, and cost-benefit efficiency in this example corresponds to Pareto efficiency.

player's payoffs. If the first player knows the second player's payoffs in Figure 6.2, the first player recognizes that cooperating is in the second player's best interest.

We answered the first question of contract law, "What promises should be enforced?", by asserting that a promise should be enforced if both parties wanted it to be enforceable when it was made. Both parties want a promise to be enforceable so that the promisor can credibly commit to performing. A credible commitment to performing enables the parties to cooperate, and cooperation is efficient.

To illustrate, recall the example of the rich uncle who promised his nephew a trip around the world. The rich uncle may need to liquidate some assets to obtain the money needed for his nephew's trip. In the meantime, the nephew may need to prepare for the trip by making some purchases (plane tickets, luggage, snowshoes for the arctic, etc.). The nephew is reluctant to use his own money to make the purchases unless the law will enforce his uncle's promise. Consequently, the nephew wants the promise to be enforceable when it is made. The uncle wants the nephew to prepare for the trip. Consequently, the uncle also wants the promise to be enforceable when it is made. Enforceability of the promise enables the uncle to make a credible commitment to his nephew, and a credible commitment enables them to cooperate.

In the second example in the beginning of this chapter, the buyer thought that she was buying a shiny Cadillac, and the seller thought that he was selling a rusty Chevrolet. The buyer wanted a promise to be enforceable when made, and so did the seller, but the buyer and seller had different promises in mind. They mistakenly believed that both of them had the same promise in mind. In reality, cooperation between them could not produce a surplus. The case of the rusty Chevy illustrates the *absence* of an agreement to cooperate.

In the third example in the beginning of this chapter, the farmer sent $25 for a promise to supply "a sure means to kill grasshoppers." The seller knew that he made a deceptive offer. A deceptive offer provides no basis for cooperation. We have stated that economic efficiency requires enforcing a promise if the promisor and promisee both wanted enforceability when the promise was made. In the example of the grasshopper killer, the promisee wanted the promise to be enforceable and the promisor wanted the promise to be *un*enforceable. In this example, the law does not enforce the promise to enable the parties to cooperate. Rather, the law enforces the promise to discourage one party from deceiving the other. Enforcing some deceitful promises discourages people from making them. Example 3 illustrates that efficiency sometimes requires enforcing a promise even though one of the parties did not want enforceability when the promise was made. We encounter more examples in the next chapter when we discuss asymmetrical information between promisor and promisee.

QUESTION 6.3: Explain why the economic theory of contracts would enforce the firm offer to sell a Chevrolet and the promise of a gift to old Siwash University.

QUESTION 6.4: Explain why the numbers in Figure 6.2 indicate that the second player is liable for *expectation* damages in the event of breach.

QUESTION 6.5: In Figure 6.2, both parties desire enforceability of the second player's promise when the promise is made, but when the time comes to perform, the promisor may not want enforceability. What do these facts say about the Pareto efficiency of enforcing the second player's promise? (Hint: Distinguish between the Pareto efficiency of enforceability when the promise is made, which can be called *ex ante* Pareto efficiency, and the Pareto efficiency of actually enforcing the promise when the time comes to perform, which can be called *ex post* Pareto efficiency.)

QUESTION 6.6: As an exercise in legal vocabulary, let us modify the facts about the contract in Figure 6.2 and describe it differently. Assume that the first player offers to invest in exchange for the second player's promise to cooperate, and the second player accepts by promising to cooperate. What is the "consideration" in this contract?

QUESTION 6.7: Figure 6.2 describes a game based upon a bargain. Construct a similar matrix to describe a game based upon a firm offer.

B. Performance

Now we turn to the second question of contract law, "What should be the remedy for breaking enforceable promises?" We will answer the second question by using the same analytical framework as we used to answer the first question. Think of the remedy as the "price" paid by the promisor for breaching the contract. The higher the price of breach, the stronger the promisor's commitment to perform. The *second purpose of contract law is to secure optimal commitment to performing*. We will explain this proposition at length.

1. Perfect Expectation Damages   The parties to a contract sometimes take a short-sighted view of their self-interest. For example, traveling carnivals and used-car sales-persons deal sharply with customers. Similarly, homeowners often deal sharply with each other in real-estate transactions. In general, one-time transactions and large stakes cause sharp dealing. In one-time transactions with large stakes, the promisor may show little regard for the loss that breach imposes on the promisee. Indeed, the promisor's concern with breach may not go beyond his or her liability. If liability is the promisor's only concern about breach, he or she will perform when it costs less than the liability for breach and will breach when performing costs more than the liability for breach. The following formula summarizes these facts:

actual performance and breach by self-interested, short-sighted promisor
    [promisor's cost of performing > promisor's liability for breaching] ⇒ breach;
    [promisor's cost of performing < promisor's liability for breaching] ⇒ perform.

We have been discussing the promisor's actual commitment to perform. Now we turn from the actual to the ideal. Efficiency requires maximizing the sum of the payoffs to the promisor and promisee. Performing a promise benefits the promisee and costs the promisor. Thus, efficiency requires the promisor to perform when his or her costs are less than the promisee's benefits, and efficiency requires the promisor to breach when the opposite is true. The following formula summarizes these facts:

optimal performance and breach
    [promisor's cost of performing > promisee's benefit from performing]
                    ⇒ efficient to breach;
    [promisor's cost of performing < promisee's benefit from performing]
                    ⇒ efficient to perform.

Comparing the two preceding formulas reveals the remedy that promotes efficient performance and breach. The promisor faces incentives to behave efficiently when actual performance aligns with efficient performance as indicated by the formulas. Comparing the formulas in the two preceding boxes, we see that they are equivalent when the promisee's benefit from performance equals the promisor's liability for breach. In other words, *the promisor has efficient incentives for performance and breach when the liability for breach equals the benefit foregone by the promisee.*

We can restate this proposition in several different ways. Notice that when the promisor's liability equals the benefit foregone by the promisee, the promisor internalizes the costs of breach. Consequently, the *promisor has efficient incentives to perform when liability internalizes the costs of breach.* This restatement draws attention to an implicit assumption in our discussion. The implicit assumption is that liability encompasses all the costs that the promisor's breach imposes upon others. The next chapter discusses some costs of breach that liability may not encompass.[6]

As mentioned above, the law frequently awards "expectation damages" as compensation for breach. *Perfect* expectation damages restore the promisee to the position that he or she would have enjoyed if the promise had been kept. In other words, perfect expectation damages equal the benefit foregone by the promisee as a result of breach. To illustrate, the first player in Figure 6.2 receives the same payoffs regardless of whether the second player performs or breaches, so Figure 6.2 embodies the assumption that the victim of breach receives perfect expectation damages. Perfect expectation damages cause the promisor to internalize the costs of breach. Consequently, *perfect expectation damages create incentives for efficient performance and breach.*

The promise commits the promisor to perform. The higher the cost of liability, the stronger the commitment to perform created by the promise. When liability is set at the efficient level, the promisor will perform if performance is more efficient than breaching, and the promisor will breach if breaching is more efficient than performing. *Consequently, perfect expectation damages elicit efficient commitment from the promisor to perform.*

2. Optimal Performance: An Example
To illustrate optimal commitment, we construct an example in which performing is sometimes more efficient than breaching, and breaching is sometimes more efficient than performing. Promising precedes performing. The gap in time may create uncertainties over the cost of performing. To illustrate, the second player in the game may not know whether or not urgent business will arise after giving the promise. If urgent business arises, the cost of performing will be high. The cost will be high because performing uses scarce resources required elsewhere. In these circumstances, the high cost of performing may exceed the benefit.

Alternatively, if the second player has no pressing business, the cost of performing may be low. The cost may be low because performing uses surplus resources not required elsewhere. In these circumstances, the benefit of performing may exceed its low cost. In general, variations in the opportunity cost of resources affect the cost of performing.

We modify Figure 6.1 to represent variations in the cost of performing. Figure 6.1 implicitly assumes that cooperating costs the second player zero. If the cost of cooperating equals zero, then the payoff of cooperation equals .5 for the first player and .5 for

---

[6] Liability typically excludes two significant costs: (1) the promisee's litigation costs, and (2) the costs of breach imposed upon third parties (*i.e.*, people other than the promisor and promisee).

the second player, as in Figure 6.1. Now consider the possibility that the cost of cooperating equals 1.5. If the cost of cooperating equals 1.5, then the payoff of cooperation equals .5 for the first player and $.5 - 1.5 = -1.0$ for the second player.

The payoffs are summarized in Figure 6.3 when cooperating sometimes costs the second player zero and sometimes costs 1.5. The first column indicates the payoffs when cooperation costs are zero. This column is identical to the first column in Figure 6.1. The second column indicates payoffs when cooperation costs 1.5. The second column represents an addition to Figure 6.1. The third column indicates the payoffs from appropriation. The third column is identical to the second column of Figure 6.1. Like Figure 6.1, the payoffs in Figure 6.3 assume no enforceable contract between the parties.

In Figures 6.1 and 6.2, performing is always more efficient than breaching. In Figure 6.3, breaching is sometimes more efficient than performing. Efficiency requires the players to choose the actions that maximize the sum of the payoffs to the first player and the second player. The sum of the payoffs is found by adding the two numbers in each cell in Figure 6.3. When the cost of performing equals 1.5, the sum of the payoffs to cooperation equals $.5 - 1.0 = -.5$. Consequently, cooperating is inefficient. In contrast, appropriation always yields the sum of payoffs equal to zero. When cooperating costs 1.5, it would be more efficient to appropriate than to cooperate. Efficiency requires the second player to cooperate when it costs zero, whereas efficiency requires the second player to appropriate when cooperation costs 1.5.

We have explained efficient behavior with the payoff in Figure 6.3. Now consider whether players act efficiently when pursuing their private advantage. If the first player invests, then the second player receives more from appropriating than cooperating. Consequently, the second player's best move is to appropriate. The first player may anticipate that the second player will appropriate. Consequently, the first player's best move is "don't invest." Thus, the solution to the agency game in Figure 6.3 is "don't invest." As in Figure 6.1, the absence of an enforceable contract in Figure 6.3 prevents the parties from cooperating.

Consider the change in Figure 6.3 caused by an enforceable contract. Assume that the second player promises to cooperate and the promise is enforceable. Also assume that the first player receives perfect expectation damages if he or she invests and the second player breaches. Figure 6.4 illustrates the payoffs with an enforceable contract and perfect expectation damages for breach. The first player's payoff from investing equals .5, regardless of whether the second player performs or breaches. In contrast, the first player's payoff equals zero if he or she does not invest. Consequently, the best move for the first player is to invest.

		Second player		
		Cooperating (costs 0)	Cooperating (costs 1.5)	Appropriate
First player	Invest	.5, .5	–1.0, .5	1.0, –1.0
	Don't invest	0, 0	0, 0	0, 0

FIGURE 6.3 Agency game with variable cooperation costs and without contact.

Second player

First player		Performing (costs 0)	Performing (costs 1.5)	Breach
	Invest (contract)	.5, .5	−1.0, .5	−.5, .5
	Don't invest (no contract)	0, 0	0, 0	0, 0

FIGURE 6.4 Agency game with contract and variable cooperation costs.

Now consider the best strategy for the second player as depicted in Figure 6.4. The second player must promise to cooperate in order to induce the first player to invest. Let us consider the second player's payoff when he or she makes an enforceable promise. If the second player performs, the payoffs are the same with an enforceable contract as without one. Consequently, the second player's payoffs are the same in the first two columns of Figure 6.3 and in Figure 6.4. If the cost of performing equals zero, performing yields a net payoff of .5 to the second player. If the cost of performing equals 1.5, performing yields a net payoff of −1.0. Now consider breach. If the second player breaches, his or her payoff is the same as indicated for breach in Figure 6.2, specifically −.5.

We have described the second player's payoffs from performance and breach, assuming that the player makes an enforceable promise whose breach causes liability for perfect expectation damages. Comparing the payoffs reveals that the best strategy for the second player who makes an enforceable promise is to perform when it costs zero and breach when it costs 1.5. We explained previously that efficiency requires the second player to perform when it costs zero and breach when it costs 1.5. Thus, we have demonstrated that perfect expectation damages typically provide incentives for efficient performance and breach.

Expectation damages are the most common remedy for breach of contract in the United States. However, the actual remedy typically differs from the ideal remedy. In other words, expectation damages actually awarded by courts are typically imperfect. The imperfections are caused by practical difficulties, especially the difficulty courts have obtaining accurate information. For example, foregone profits may be difficult to estimate. Sometimes practical difficulties cause courts to abandon expectation damages and give alternative remedies, as we will explain in the next chapter.

Suppose the promisor and the promisee want the contract to specify the remedy for breach. Would they typically prefer the contract to specify perfect expectation damages, or would they typically prefer an alternative remedy? As explained, perfect expectation damages induce efficient commitment to performance and breach. Efficient commitment maximizes the surplus from the contract, which the parties can divide between them. Consequently, both parties to a contract typically benefit from having perfect expectation damages as the remedy for breach, rather than having an alternative remedy. By awarding expectation damages, the courts typically give the parties the remedy that both of them preferred when making the contract.

In general, the best damage measure creates an efficient level of commitment to performance by the promisor, whereas the wrong damage measure creates an inefficient level of commitment. Damages below the best level cause the promisor to breach too often, which makes the promisee reluctant to make a contract. Damages above the best level require the promisor to perform when it is too costly, which makes the promisor reluctant to make a contract. We will demonstrate these facts in a formal model in the next chapter.

QUESTION 6.8: Assume that the high costs of performing cause the promisor to breach a contract and pay perfect expectation damages to the promisee. Would the promisee have preferred that the promisor perform?

QUESTION 6.9: Explain the gain in total payoffs from allowing the promisor to breach and pay expectation damages when performing is efficient.

C. Reliance

We have explained that the enforceability of contracts enables the parties to cooperate, which typically involves two kinds of behavior. First, the promisor invests in performing. To illustrate, recall the rich uncle's promise to give his nephew a trip around the world. The uncle must prepare to perform by liquidating some assets to obtain money for his nephew's trip. Second, the promisee invests in reliance upon the promise. To illustrate using our example, the nephew must prepare for the trip by making some purchases needed for the journey. Perhaps the nephew will buy luggage, snowshoes, a pith helmet, etc. Or consider the example of the farmer who mails money to purchase a "grasshopper killer." The farmer may expand his barn in anticipation of the need to store more crops. In general, the promisor invests in performing and the promisee invests in relying. Investment may take the form of money, time, effort, or foregone opportunities.

Reliance is a change in the promisee's position induced by the promise. The change in the promisee's position increases the value of performance to the promisee. For example, the trip around the world is more valuable to the nephew if he has purchased the items needed for the trip, and a "sure means to kill grasshoppers" is more valuable to the farmer if he has a larger barn to store the additional crops. However, the increase in the value of performance comes at a price. Reliance typically makes breach more costly to the promisee. For example, if the nephew relies on his uncle's promise by purchasing items needed for a trip around the world, and if the uncle breaks his promise, then the nephew will lose money when he tries to resell the items that he bought for the trip. Similarly, the farmer will have expanded his barn unnecessarily if the "sure means to kill grasshoppers" fails. Think of reliance on a promise as a gamble that increases the gain from performance and the loss from breach. The *third purpose of contract law is to secure optimal reliance.*

1. Optimal Reliance   How much reliance is optimal? The expected gain from additional reliance equals the increase in the value of performance to the promisee multiplied by the probability of performance. For example, the expected gain to the nephew from buying a pith helmet for the tropics might equal the probability that his uncle keeps his promise to give him the trip multiplied by the increase in the value he places on traveling to the tropics with a pith helmet. The expected loss from additional reliance equals the increase in the loss from breach to the promisee multiplied by the probability of nonperformance. For example, the expected loss to the nephew from buying a pith helmet equals the probability that his uncle breaches his promise multiplied by the loss when he resells the pith helmet. Efficiency requires more reliance if the expected gain exceeds the expected loss. Conversely, efficiency requires less reliance if the expected loss exceeds the expected gain.

optimal reliance
   (probability of promisor's performing) ×
   (increase in the value of performance caused by additional reliance) >
   (probability of promisor's breaching) ×
   (increase in cost of breach caused by additional reliance)
   ⇒ efficient to rely more.

2. Optimal Reliance: An Example   We return to the agency game to provide a numerical example of optimal reliance. As before, we first describe the payoffs without an enforceable contract, and subsequently we show the change caused by an enforceable contract. Figure 6.5 depicts the payoffs for reliance without an enforceable contract. Assume that the second player promises to perform if the first player will invest. The first player invests and, after investing, the first player subsequently relies. The first player can choose between low reliance and high reliance. The first row of Figure 6.5 depicts the payoffs given low reliance by the first player. The second row of Figure 6.5 depicts the payoffs given high reliance by the first player.

As before, performance costs the second player zero or 1.5. The second player performs when doing so costs zero and breaches when performing costs 1.5. The northwest cell of Figure 6.5 depicts the payoffs given low reliance by the first player and performance by the second player. The northeast cell of Figure 6.5 depicts the payoffs given low reliance by the first player and breach by the second player.

If the first player relies at the high level, he or she invests an additional 1.0. This investment increases the value of performance to the first player from .5 to .6, as indicated in the southwest cell of Figure 6.5. However, the first player loses the investment in reliance if the second player breaches. Consequently, the first player's payoff from breach falls to –2.0, as indicated by the southeast cell in Figure 6.5.

Efficiency requires maximizing the payoffs to both players. The payoff to both players equals the sum of the two numbers in each cell of Figure 6.5. If the second player were certain to perform, then efficiency would require high reliance by the first player. If the second player were certain to breach, then efficiency would require low reliance by the second player. Optimal reliance is high when performance is certain, and optimal reliance is low when performance is uncertain.

As the probability of performance increases, a "tipping point" is reached where optimal reliance changes from low to high. Let us calculate the tipping point. Let p denote the probability of performance. The expected net payoff from low reliance equals

		Second player	
		Perform	Breach
First player	Invest & low reliance	.5, .5	1.0, –1.0
	Invest & high reliance	.5, .6	1.0, –2.0

FIGURE 6.5   Agency game with variable reliance and no enforcable contract.

$$p(.5 + .5) \qquad\qquad + \qquad (1 - p)(-1.0 + 1.0)$$

expected joint   expected joint
gain from performance   loss from breach

The expected net payoff from high reliance equals

$$p(.6 + .5) \qquad\qquad + \qquad (1 - p)(-2.0 + 1.0)$$

expected joint   expected joint
gain from performance   loss from breach

The tipping point, denoted p^*, is the value of p where the expected net payoff from high reliance equals the expected net payoff from low reliance.

$$p^*(.5 + .5) + (1 - p^*)(-1.0 + 1.0) = p^*(.6 + .5) + (1 - p^*)(-2.0 + 1.0)$$

$$\Rightarrow p^* = .91.$$

Thus, high reliance is optimal if the probability of performance exceeds 91%, whereas low reliance is optimal if the probability of breach exceeds 9%.

3. Legal Incentives for Reliance   We have already explained how contract law induces optimal commitment to perform. Now we explain how contract law induces optimal reliance. (The next chapter contains a more detailed explanation.) The law induces optimal reliance by a simple method. As explained, more reliance causes an increase in the promisee's loss from breach. As the promisee's loss from breach increases, the damages that the promisee can recover from the breaching promisor also increase. However, recoverable damages do not increase forever. Instead, recoverable damages have an upper limit. The upper limit on recoverable damages equals the loss arising from breach when reliance is optimal.

Reliance exceeding the optimum can be described as "overreliance." Overreliance causes excessive harm from breach. Excessive harm from breach exceeds the upper limit of recoverable damages. The law does not allow the victim of breach to recover damages caused by overreliance. The law discourages overreliance by compensating the victim of breach for actual losses up to a maximum equal to the loss from optimal reliance and requiring the victim to bear any additional losses caused by overreliance.

As defined earlier, *perfect* expectation damages restore the promisee to the position that he or she would have enjoyed if the promise had been kept. That position depends upon the extent of the promisee's reliance. For the sake of economic efficiency, the promisee's reliance should be optimal. We incorporate this fact into our definition of perfect expectation damages. By definition, *perfect* expectation damages restore the promisee to the position that he or she would have enjoyed if the promise had been kept and if reliance had been optimal. If courts award perfect expectation damages as defined here, the victim of breach receives no compensation for overreliance. Consequently, the promisee has a strong incentive to avoid overrelying.

We revise Figure 6.5 to depict how the law discourages overreliance. Recall that the promisee in Figure 6.5 can rely at a low level or a high level. To keep the example simple, assume that the probability of breach is high enough so that efficiency requires a low level of reliance by the first player.[7] Consequently, high reliance in these circumstances is "over-reliance."

Assume that the second player makes an enforceable promise to perform, and assume that perfect expectation damages are the remedy for breach. Perfect expectation damages restore the victim of breach to the position that he or she would have enjoyed if he or she had relied optimally and the promisor had performed. The first player in Figure 6.6 receives a payoff of .5 when he or she relies optimally and the second player performs. Consequently, the first player receives damages of .5 in the event of breach. In the event that the first player overrelies and the second player breaches, the first player receives .5 in damages and loses 1.0 from investment in overreliance, so the net payoff equals -1.5.

It is easy to see from Figure 6.6 that the first player's best strategy depends upon the probability of breach by the second player. When the probability of breach is high enough that efficiency requires low reliance, the probability of breach is also high enough that the first player's best strategy is to invest and rely at the low level.[8]

Various legal doctrines define *overreliance*. An important doctrine in common law concerns foreseeability. Reliance by the promisee is *foreseeable* by the promisor if it equals the amount that the promisor could reasonably expect under the circumstances. Reliance by the promisee is *un*foreseeable if it exceeds the amount that the promisor could reasonably expect under the circumstances. Anglo-American law defines over-reliance as unforeseeable, and, consequently, noncompensable.[9]

To illustrate the definition of over reliance as unforeseeable reliance, assume that a telegraph company fails to transmit a telegram containing a "sell" order by a stock-broker. With so much at stake, the stockbroker should have relied less on this telegram. For example, the stockbroker should have asked the recipient to immediately acknowledge receipt of the telegram. The telegraph company could not foresee the stockbroker's failure to take reasonable precautions. Consequently, the telegraph company could not foresee several million dollars in losses from failing to transmit this one telegram.

As another example, suppose that the nephew prepares for his world tour by buying a white silk suit for the tropics and a matching diamond belt buckle. When his uncle refuses to pay for the world tour, the nephew resells the silk suit and the matching diamond belt buckle at a loss. The nephew subsequently sues his uncle for the difference between the purchase price and the resale price. The court might find that the uncle

---

[7] Recall our calculation that low reliance is efficient when the probability of breach exceeds 9%. We implicitly assume that the probability of breach exceeds 9% in this example, so that efficiency requires low reliance.

[8] To be precise, the first player's best strategy is to invest at a low level if $.5 > .6p - (1 - p)1.5$, where p denotes the probability that the second player will perform. Solving this inequality indicates that the first player should rely at the low level if the probability of breach exceeds .05. We have already shown that efficiency requires a low level of reliance if the probability of breach exceeds .09, and we assumed that for purposes of our example the probability of breach exceeds .09. We are, therefore, assuming that the probability of breach exceeds the level at which efficiency requires low reliance and perfect expectation damages induce low reliance.

[9] See the discussion of *Hadley v. Baxendale* in the next chapter.

		Second player	
		Perform	Breach
First player	Invest & low reliance	.5, .5	–.5, .5
	Invest & high reliance	.5, .6	–.5, –1.5

FIGURE 6.6 Agency game with variable reliance and enforcable contract.

should have foreseen that his promise would cause his nephew to purchase a silk suit for the tropics. The court might also find that the uncle could not foresee that his promise would cause his nephew to buy a diamond belt buckle. The court might make the uncle compensate the nephew for the difference between the purchase price and the resale price of the silk suit, whereas the court might make the nephew bear the loss from reselling the diamond belt buckle.[10]

QUESTION 6.10: Explain why compensating the victim of breach for expectation damages causes efficient performance and breach, whereas compensating the victim of breach for excessive reliance may cause inefficient performance and breach.

QUESTION 6.11: Suppose that the stockbroker told the telegraph company that failure to transmit the telegram could cause millions of dollars in losses. This is called "giving notice." Are the actual losses now foreseeable by the telegraph company? (The next chapter discusses how giving "giving notice" affects liability for breach in common law.)

D. Transaction Costs

Contracts often involve risks. To illustrate, suppose that the McGuire family signs a contract with the Wabash Construction Company to build a house. Floor plan, construction materials, style of carpets, landscaping, compliance with zoning codes—all of this and more is specified, as well as the price to be paid and the date for completing the house. Now imagine some of the things that can go wrong. A strike by the suppliers of hardwood flooring could delay the whole project. War in a remote country may cause the cost of copper pipe to soar. Zoning officials in the local government might reject the landscaping plans. A suit by an injured employee might bankrupt Wabash. Mr. McGuire might die, in which case the rest of the family might no longer want the house. The McGuires might go bankrupt, in which case they could no longer afford the house.

The contract allocates some of these risks explicitly. For example, the contract may stipulate that the completion date will be deferred in the event of a crippling strike. On the other hand, the contract may remain silent about many risks. For example, the contract may say nothing about who bears the risk that zoning officials reject the landscaping plans. Real contracts suffer from gaps. When a contract remains silent about a risk,

---

[10] In American law, gift promises are usually enforceable to the extent of reasonable reliance.

the contract has a "gap." Gaps are events not explicitly addressed in the contract that affect obligations created by it.

Gaps may be inadvertent. To illustrate, assume that a contract says nothing about the possibility that a hijacking closes an airport and prevents the seller from delivering goods on time. The parties may leave this gap in the contract inadvertently because they do not foresee the possibility of a hijacking. Alternatively, gaps may be deliberate. To illustrate, a contract may say nothing about the possibility that a wildcat strike prevents the manufacturer from producing the promised goods. The parties may leave this gap in the contract deliberately because they believe that the possibility of a wildcat strike is remote. Remote risks do not justify the cost of negotiating and drafting terms to allocate them.

1. Rational Gaps   Let us consider the calculations that might lead the parties to leave gaps deliberately in contracts. Return to our example of a crippling strike that could delay construction of the McGuires' house by the Wabash Construction Company. Negotiating the allocation of this risk imposes transaction costs with certainty when the contract is made. Alternatively, the McGuires and Wabash could leave a gap in their contract and wait to see whether the strike occurs. Leaving a gap in the contract will require the parties to allocate a loss *if* it materializes.

We describe this trade-off abstractly. "*Ex ante* risks" refer to the risk of future losses faced by the parties when they negotiate a contract. "*Ex post* losses" refer to losses that actually materialize after making the contract. In general, the parties to a contract must choose between allocating *ex ante* risks and allocating *ex post* losses.

Consider the difference in transaction costs between allocating risks and losses. If the parties negotiate explicit terms to allocate risks, they will bear transaction costs for certain. If they leave a gap, they will bear transaction costs with positive probability. The *expected* transaction cost of a gap in the contract equals the probability that the loss materializes multiplied by the cost of allocating it. The parties expect to save transaction costs by leaving gaps in contracts whenever the actual cost of negotiating explicit terms exceeds the expected cost of filling a gap. The following rule summarizes these facts:

minimizing transaction costs of contracts
> cost of allocating a risk > cost of allocating a loss × probability of a loss ⇒ leave gap,
> cost of allocating a risk < cost of allocating a loss × probability of a loss ⇒ fill gap.

Parties typically reach agreement on allocating a risk more easily than a loss. To illustrate, return to our example of the risk that a crippling strike will delay construction of the McGuires' house. Negotiating an explicit term in the construction contract to allocate this risk may cost $25. Given an explicit term in the contract, the parties can easily allocate the resulting losses if a crippling strike materializes. Alternatively, the parties can leave a gap in the contract. Given a gap in the contract, the parties will have disagreements and difficulties allocating the losses caused by a crippling strike. Assume that the transaction cost of allocating such losses after they materialize equals $500. The higher cost of allocating losses rather than risks must be discounted by the probability that the loss never materializes. Assume that the probability of a crippling strike equals .04. Thus, the expected transaction cost of leaving a gap in the contract equals $20.[11] In this example, the parties save $5 in expected transaction costs by leaving a gap in the contract.

---

[11] $500 × .04 = $20.

2. Gap-Filling by Courts Courts need rules to fill gaps in contracts. Officials who make the rules need guidance. A theory of contracts should provide guidance by answering the question "How should courts fill gaps in contracts?" We will explain how economic theory answers this question.

Gaps in contracts often cause disputes, and some disputes go to court. To decide such disputes, the court must fill the gap in the contract. Courts sometimes fill gaps by "imputing" a term to the contract, which means acting as if the parties had negotiated a term that they did not actually negotiate. For example, courts may impute a term excusing nondelivery of certain goods during a war. Alternatively, courts may enforce only the explicit terms in the contract. For example, courts may hold the seller liable for nondelivery of certain goods during war on grounds that the contract does not name war as an excuse for nonperformance.

Sometimes explicit terms in a contract conflict with the terms that the law would have supplied to fill a gap. To illustrate, consider the contract between the construction company and the McGuires. Assume that the contract explicitly states that the completion date for construction will be extended by the number of days of a crippling strike. If the contract said nothing about crippling strikes, the court would probably hold Wabash responsible for construction delays caused by crippling strikes. Thus, an explicit term in the contract conflicts with the term that the law would supply to fill a gap.

When legal obligations conflict, the law must decide which one prevails. Faced with the conflict in this example, the court will probably extend the construction deadline by the length of the strike, rather than holding Wabash liable for the delay. Explicit terms in a contract usually prevail over the terms that the court would supply to fill a gap. When explicit terms prevail over implicit terms, the implicit terms fill gaps by *default*, which means "in the absence of explicit terms to the contrary." Gap-filling terms in contract law are mostly "default terms."

We already explained that replacing inefficient contract terms with efficient terms creates a surplus. Similarly, replacing *inefficient default* terms with *efficient default* terms creates a surplus. It is easy to see why. We already explained that the parties to a contract can often save transaction costs by leaving gaps in it. When they leave a gap, the court fills it with a default term. Efficient default terms maximize the surplus to the parties, whereas inefficient default terms reduce the surplus. In general, *both parties to a contract can benefit when lawmakers replace inefficient default terms with efficient default terms.*

To illustrate, recall our example in which the McGuires and Wabash can negotiate the allocation of the risk of a crippling strike at a cost of $25, or they can leave a gap in the contract, which causes expected transaction costs of $20. In this example, leaving a gap in the contract saves the parties $5 in expected transaction costs. However, transaction costs are not the only relevant costs. In addition, the parties must consider the cost of bearing the risk of a crippling strike. Assume that Wabash can bear the risk of a crippling strike at a cost of $60, whereas the McGuires can bear the risk at a cost of $20. Thus, an efficient allocation of the risk of a crippling strike saves $40 relative to an inefficient allocation.

Compare the consequences of an efficient default rule and an inefficient default rule. An efficient default rule allocates the risk of a crippling strike to the McGuires. If the actual default rule is the efficient default rule, then the parties can leave a gap in the contract and save $5 in transaction costs. In general, efficient default rules enable the parties to minimize the transaction costs of negotiating contracts by leaving gaps in them.

Alternatively, an *in*efficient rule allocates the risk of a crippling strike to Wabash. An *in*efficient default rule presents Wabash and the McGuires with a trade-off. Given the *in*efficient default rule, leaving a gap in the contract will waste $40 in the cost of risk-bearing. Alternatively, the two parties can negotiate an efficient allocation of risk. Replacing the inefficient default term with an efficient explicit term will save them $40 in the cost of risk-bearing. However, negotiating a term to fill the gap will cost them an additional $5 in expected transaction costs. In general, inefficient default rules impose a trade-off between transaction costs and risk-bearing.

As explained, both parties prefer efficient terms to the contract rather than inefficient terms. Similarly, both parties prefer efficient default terms rather than inefficient default terms. When law supplies default terms preferred by both parties, they can omit these terms from the contract. By omitting these terms from the contract, the parties can focus their negotiations on other terms. The fewer the terms requiring negotiation, the cheaper is the contracting process. Thus, the law can save money for contracting parties by supplying efficient default terms to fill gaps in contracts. The *fourth purpose of contract law is to minimize transaction costs of negotiating contracts by supplying efficient default terms.*

3. Hypothetical Bargain   Economic analysis offers a simple rule for courts to follow in order to supply efficient default terms for a contract. Consider the terms the parties would have reached if they had filled the gaps by negotiation. *Impute the terms to the contract that the parties would have agreed to if they had bargained over all the relevant risk.* To illustrate, suppose that the contract between the McGuires and Wabash remains silent about the risk that the price of copper pipe will soar. According to the preceding principle, the court should allocate the risk as the parties would have done if they had negotiated with each other.

The actual bargain consists in the terms negotiated by the parties. The hypothetical bargain consists in the terms the parties would have reached if they had filled the gaps in the contract by negotiation. The preceding principle requires courts to fill gaps in contracts according to the hypothetical bargain. When courts fill gaps by imputing terms of the hypothetical bargain, the parties receive their preferred contract from the court. Further negotiations between the parties cannot improve upon the allocation of risk by the courts. Consequently, the parties can minimize transaction costs by leaving gaps or filling them, whichever is cheaper.

Implementing the principle of the hypothetical bargain has two aspects. In developing a model of bargaining in Chapter 4, we concluded that agreements reached under zero transaction costs exhaust the surplus from cooperation, as required for efficiency. First, the court must establish the most efficient form of cooperation. In Chapter 4 we also noted that an equal division of the surplus is reasonable. Second, the court must divide the surplus that cooperation would have achieved. In other words, *the court should respond to gaps in the contract by allocating obligations efficiently and adjusting the price reasonably.*

We illustrate this principle using several variations of our example. Assume that when the McGuires and Wabash sign the contract, Wabash *knows* that the cost of copper pipe in the house may soar by $2000 with probability .5. The increase in costs expected by Wabash is $2000 $\times$ .5 = $1000. Furthermore, assume that Wabash can hedge against this risk for $400. By hedging, Wabash would avoid an expected cost of $1000 at a cost of $400, which yields a surplus of $600.[12] In contrast, assume that the

---

[12] $2000 $\times$ 5 − $400 = $600.

McGuires could *not* foresee changes in the price of copper or hedge against them. Consequently, efficiency requires Wabash, not the McGuires, to hedge.

Unfortunately, Wabash does not hedge and the price of copper soars. Wabash completes constructing the house and sends the McGuires a bill for an additional $2000. The McGuires refuse to pay and Wabash sues them. The actual contract is silent about the risk of soaring copper prices.

Consider how the court could resolve the case by imputing the hypothetical contract that the parties would have reached under zero transaction costs. Creating the hypothetical contract involves two steps. First, the court must establish who could bear the risk of soaring copper prices at least cost. In this example, Wabash is the *more efficient risk-bearer*. Consequently, the court concludes that the ideal contract would allocate the risk of soaring copper prices to Wabash, as required for efficiency.

Second, the court must consider adjusting the price of the contract to reflect the efficient allocation of risk. Constructing houses generally involves many risks that builders routinely foresee and assume as an unstated part of the contract, including the risk of price increases for construction materials. Because Wabash foresaw the risk, Wabash ought to have negotiated a price that included compensation for bearing the risk. Any failure to negotiate such a price is Wabash's fault. The court will conclude that Wabash was responsible for seeing that the contract price *already* included compensation for bearing the risk of soaring copper prices, so the McGuires owe Wabash zero damages.

In general, imputing terms to a contract involves a detailed inquiry into the customs of the trade and the information known to the parties. When the efficient risk-bearer *actually* foresaw the risk, or *ought* to have foreseen the risk, the court should presume that the negotiated price included compensation for bearing the risk. Whether Wabash actually foresaw the risk in this case is a question of fact, and whether Wabash ought to have foreseen the risk is a question of good business practices.

Sometimes, however, neither party to a contract foresees a risk and neither party ought to have foreseen it. To illustrate, assume that subterranean politics in the copper worker's union in a distant country cause a strike that inflates the price of copper. Neither Wabash nor the McGuires ought to foresee such an obscure event. In these circumstances, the law must allocate an unforeseen loss between blameless parties.

Once again, the law can take the ideal contract as a guide. The ideal contract allocates the risk of unforeseeable losses to the more efficient risk-bearer. In this example, Wabash can respond to unforeseeable changes in the price of building materials and minimize the damage. Wabash is apparently the more efficient risk bearer. So the court might find that Wabash must bear this risk. However, the court might also find that the actual contract price did not reflect the risk that Wabash bears. Consequently, the court might adjust the price to reasonably reflect the risk.[13]

---

[13] Assume that if Wabash had foreseen the risk, it would have charged an extra $700 to bear it. Thus, the ideal contract would have allocated the risk of losing $2000 to Wabash at a price of $700 to the McGuires. Following the ideal contract, the court will enter a judgment of $700 in favor of Wabash and against the McGuires. The McGuires lose $700. Wabash gains $700 from the court and loses $2000 in additional costs of copper pipe, for a net loss equal to $1300. Thus, the $2000 loss has been divided between the parties as if the actual contract were ideal.

Consider another variation on this example. Promisors often perform late. Sometimes contracts stipulate damages for later performance, such as $100 per day. However, many contracts remain silent about late performance. When the contract remains silent, the court must determine damages for late performance. To illustrate, assume that Wabash promises to complete the house for occupancy by the McGuires on September 1, but inclement weather in July imposes unavoidable delays. Wabash could continue at the planned pace and finish on October 1, or it could accelerate work during August and complete the construction on September 1 as promised. Accelerating the work in August costs an additional $2000. The McGuires rent a house for $1000 per month during the construction of the new house. The contract is silent about damages for late performance. Wabash decides to proceed at the usual pace, completes construction on October 1, and offers to pay the McGuires $1000 in damages to cover rental costs, plus an addition $500 for settling the dispute.

Unknown to Wabash, the McGuires invited their relatives to a reunion on September 15. The new house would have accommodated the relatives. Instead of accommodating their relatives in the new house, the McGuires spent $1500 on hotel bills. The McGuires ask the court to award compensation of $2500 for rent and the relatives' hotel bills.

How would the ideal contract allocate the risk of late performance? As explained, accelerated work would save $2500 at a cost of $2000, thus creating a net *benefit* of $500. Wabash did not know this. Instead, Wabash believed that accelerated work would save $1500 at a cost of $2000, thus creating a net *cost* of $500. In order to behave efficiently, Wabash needed to know about the unusual losses from delay. The McGuires failed to provide the information to Wabash. Efficient contracts typically allocate losses caused by someone's fault to the party at fault. In this case, the fault of the McGuires caused losses of $500. The efficient default contract would apparently hold Wabash liable for damages of $1500 and the McGuires would bear the additional losses of $1000.

This example illustrates overreliance by the McGuires. Wabash reasonably expected a low level of reliance by the McGuires. In fact, the McGuires relied at a high level. Furthermore, the McGuires failed to give notice of their high level of reliance to Wabash. Consequently, the McGuires must bear the increase in the cost of breach caused by overreliance. This prescription corresponds to an important rule of common law. The rule holds that the promisor must bear the usual costs of breach ("reasonably expected costs of breach"), whereas the promisee must bear the unusual costs of breach ("unforeseeable costs of breach"), unless the promisee notified the promisor about the unusual costs of breach.[14]

QUESTION 6.12: "Default rules save transaction costs in direct proportion to their efficiency." Explain this proposition.

QUESTION 6.13: Suppose that Wabash completes the house one month later than promised. Inclement weather, which was no one's fault, caused the tardiness. Explain how the court might compute efficient damages.

---

[14] This is the rule from *Hadley v. Baxendale*, 9 EXCH. 341 (1854).

QUESTION 6.14: Some gaps in contracts are the fault of one of the parties. To illustrate, assume that one party to a contract has private information about a significant risk. Efficiency may require the party with private information to initiate negotiations to allocate risk. Failing to initiate negotiations leaves a gap in the contract. If the risk materializes, the courts may allocate liability for the loss to the party with private information. In this case, liability can be regarded as a penalty for fault. Consequently, such allocations of liability are called *penalty default rules*.[15] The preceding section discusses an example in which the McGuires failed to disclose their unforeseeable reliance on Wabash's promise to complete construction of the house by September 1. Explain why the common law legal rule applied to this case can be regarded as a penalty default rule.

QUESTION 6.15: Finally, doctors who form a partnership may say nothing in the partnership agreement concerning its future dissolution. The parties may deliberately avoid discussing dissolution for fear of breeding distrust. Provide some other examples of gaps left in contracts for strategic reasons.

E. Perfect Contracts and Market Failures

We have discussed enforcing terms that are not explicitly in a contract (default terms). Now we discuss not enforcing terms that are explicitly in a contract. Besides gaps, real contracts sometimes contain explicit terms that seem inappropriate to events as they actually unfold. Sometimes the court sets aside the explicit terms of a contract. For example, the court may disregard the terms of a contract by which a consumer waives the right to recover for injuries caused by a defective product. Sometimes the court supplies terms to replace the contract's explicit terms. For example, when a child below the age of legal competence signs a contract, the court may replace the actual terms with its own, new terms.

When the law disregards or changes the terms in a contract, we say that law *regulates* the contract. Regulating contracts resembles regulating markets. In both cases, the state deflects a private transaction from its course. Furthermore, the economic rationale for regulating contracts resembles the economic rationale for regulating markets. The economic rationale for regulating markets begins with a description of a perfectly competitive market, which requires no regulation. Next, the theory describes the ways that actual markets depart from this ideal, or the forms of *market failure*. We will adapt this approach to contracts. Underlying this approach is the insight that the *fifth purpose of contract law is to correct market failures by regulating the terms of contracts*.

To develop the theory of market failures, imagine that the parties to a deferred transaction draft a *perfect contract*. A perfect contract is *complete*. Every contingency is anticipated; the associated risk is efficiently allocated between the parties; all relevant information has been communicated; nothing can go wrong. A perfect contract is also *efficient*. Each resource is allocated to the party who values it the most; each risk is allocated to the party who can bear it at least cost; and the terms of the contract exhaust the possibilities for mutual gain by cooperation between the parties.

---

[15] See Ian Ayres and Robert Gertner, *Filling Gaps in Incomplete Contracts: An Economic Theory of Default Rules,* 99 YALE L. J. 87 (1989).

If the parties have negotiated a perfect contract, then the contract has no gaps, so the parties do not need the court to supply default terms. If the parties have negotiated a perfect contract, then the contract has no failures, so the parties do not need the court to regulate its terms. We conclude that the parties to a perfect contract need the state to enforce their agreement according to its terms, but nothing more is required of the state. Specifically, the state need not supply default terms to fill gaps or regulate explicit terms in a perfect contract.

Under what circumstances will parties negotiate a perfect contract? The circumstances are already familiar to you from our discussion of the Coase theorem in Chapter 4. According to the Coase theorem, rational parties will craft a perfect contract when transaction costs are zero. When transaction costs are zero, the contract will be complete, because negotiating additional terms costs nothing. When transaction costs are zero, the contract will be efficient, because each right is allocated to the party who values it the most and each risk is allocated to the party who can bear it at least cost. Given a perfect contract, state regulation that discards or modifies its terms will create inefficiencies. In general, regulation of contract terms negotiated by rational people under zero transaction costs causes inefficiency.

Conversely, contracts are imperfect when the parties are irrational or transaction costs are positive. We will add some more detail to this proposition by developing the theory of market failures. We will then use that theory to classify the regulations of contract according to the market failure that they ideally correct.

1. Individual Rationality   In our review of microeconomics in Chapter 2, we identified three assumptions about rational choice by individuals. First, a rational decision-maker can rank outcomes in order from least preferred to most preferred. In order to rank outcomes, decision-makers must have stable preferences. If the promisor's preferences are sufficiently unstable or disorderly, then he or she is legally *incompetent* and cannot conclude an enforceable contract. For example, children and the insane are legally incompetent.

Second, the rational decision-makers' opportunities are moderately constrained so that they can achieve some, but not all, of their objectives. Dire constraints destroy freedom of action. Two major contract doctrines excuse promise-breaking on the ground that the promisor faced dire constraints: *duress* and *necessity.* If the beneficiary of the promise extracted it by threats, then promise-breaking is excused by reason of duress. For example, in a famous movie the "godfather" of a criminal syndicate makes contract offers that "cannot be refused" because the victim signs the contract with a gun held to his head. No court would enforce such a contract.

Similarly, if a promise is extracted from a desperate promisor, the court may excuse nonperformance on the ground of *necessity.* For example, suppose a surgeon runs out of gas on a lonely desert road where she might perish. A passerby offers to sell her five liters of gas for $50,000. Even if the surgeon accepts the offer, the court will not enforce her promise to pay. The court will not enforce the promise because it was given out of *necessity.*

Notice that *duress* and *necessity* both apply when the promisor is in dire circumstances, but the cause is different. The cause of necessity is usually the promisor's bad judgment, bad luck, or a third person. For example, the surgeon may have run out of gas in the desert because she did not check the gas gauge, a hidden defect caused the gas gauge to fail, or her enemy secretly punctured the gas tank. In contrast, the cause of duress is usually the promisee. For example, the godfather held the gun to the promisor's head. Thus, duress can be regarded as necessity caused by the promisee.

In these examples, the dire constraint *preceded* the promise. Sometimes a dire constraint *follows* the promise. A dire constraint that follows a promise can prevent the promisor from performing. For example, a surgeon may promise to operate and then break her hand before the scheduled operation. If a promise is made in good faith and fate intervenes to make performance impossible, then promise-breaking may be excused by reason of *impossibility*. For example, a manufacturer may be excused from fulfilling his contracts because his factory burned down. In general, the impossibility doctrine applies to unlikely events that prevent performance. In the next chapter we discuss the optimal allocation of the risk of such events.

2. Transaction Costs   Now we turn from rationality to transaction costs. Making a contract involves searching for partners, negotiating terms, drafting the contract, and enforcing it. Searching takes effort; negotiating takes time; drafting takes expertise; and enforcing takes perseverance. In many contracts, these transaction costs are small relative to the surplus from cooperation. In other cases, however, these transaction costs are large relative to the surplus from cooperation. Indeed, sometimes these transaction costs are large enough relative to the surplus to preclude cooperation. We will distinguish three kinds of obstacles to efficiency that arise when transaction costs obstruct bargaining.

a. Spillovers   Sometimes transaction costs prevent people from participating in negotiations that affect them. To illustrate, if an electric utility generates power by a dirty process, such as burning soft coal, then the production of power may affect others adversely. Alternatively, if the utility generates power by a clean process, such as burning natural gas, then the production will not directly affect third parties. Thus, a contract to supply electricity may have third-party effects, depending upon whether the electricity is generated by a clean process or a dirty process.

We already discussed such spillovers under the name *externalities*. External costs cause the individual's self-interest to diverge from social efficiency. The divergence from social efficiency creates scope for corrective legal action. Although contracts often have external effects, the legal remedy seldom involves *contract* law. In most cases, the plaintiff in a suit for breach of contract must be the person to whom the promise was made (the promisee) or the person to whom the promisee's rights were transferred (the transferee).[16] A third party is, by definition, not the promisee or transferee. Third parties who allege that a contract harmed them cannot find relief in contract law except under special circumstances.[17] Contract law proceeds on the

---

[16]Thus, an heir can usually sue for breach of promise made to the deceased. Similarly, when one firm takes over another, the acquiring firm can usually sue for breach of a promise made to the acquired firm by other parties.

[17]Contracts often create relationships out of which duties arise to third parties. For example, the director of a corporation has a fiduciary duty to stockholders that prevents him or her from entering certain kinds of contracts. Sometimes it is unclear whether duties that arise out of contractual relationships should be classed as contractual duties. Furthermore, many countries in Europe impose strict liability for consumer accidents on the basis of implied warranties, whereas the Anglo-American tradition achieves the same result through tort law.

assumption that other branches of law will protect third parties. Instead of suing for relief under contract law, third parties must usually seek relief under the law of torts, property, crimes, or regulations. For example, a contract to purchase goods from a polluting manufacturer causes more pollution, but the victims of pollution cannot sue under contract law. Instead, the victims must sue under nuisance law or under an environmental regulation.

Sometimes contract law protects third parties by refusing to enforce a contract between the first and second party. The courts may refuse to enforce such a contract when it *derogates public policy*. To illustrate, companies often wish to make contracts not to compete with each other. Agreements not to compete enable cartels to exploit buyers by charging monopoly prices. Courts in England and America were reluctant to enforce nineteenth century contracts to create cartels. Such contracts derogated public policy. Subsequent antitrust statutes outlawed cartels. For example, contracts to create a cartel are void in Europe by the law of the European Union (European Union Treaty, Section 85, paragraph 2).

Similarly, courts are reluctant to enforce contracts that "tie the hands" of parties involved in negotiations. To illustrate, assume that Company *A* offers to pay its workers $10 per hour, and the union demands $15 per hour. The union threatens to strike Company *A* and stay on strike until Company *A* concedes. To make the threat credible, the union signs a contract with Company *B* promising to work for $1 per hour for Company *B* *if* the union ever agrees to work for Company *A* for less than $15 per hour. The purpose of the contract with Company *B* is to raise the union's cost of conceding to Company *A*. Raising the cost of conceding to Company *A* precludes the union from making concessions to Company *A*.

U.S. law imposes a statutory obligation upon the union to "bargain in good faith" with Company *A*. The union's contract with Company *B* obstructs bargaining with Company *A*. Consequently, the contract between the union and Company *B* "derogates a statutory duty" that the union owes to Company *A*. Thus, the contract between the union and Company *B* is unenforceable.

b. Information Sometimes one or more of the parties to a contract lacks essential information about it. The lack of information can have several causes. Sometimes people lie or withhold information in order to gain an advantage in bargaining. Sometimes people fail to transmit information to save communication costs. When facts are transmitted, the recipient may not comprehend them.

In general, ignorance is rational when the cost of acquiring information exceeds the expected benefit from being informed. To illustrate, many rational people throw away the finely printed warning on medicine without reading it. Conversely, ignorance is irrational when the expected benefit from being informed exceeds the cost of acquiring information. To illustrate, some people refuse to write a will or purchase life insurance because they do not want to contemplate death.

Psychologists have recently identified systematic irrationalities that occur when people process information. For example, consider the following experiment. The psychologist shows the subject a pack with one-third black cards and two-thirds red cards. The psychologist shuffles the cards and picks one from the deck at random. The subject must guess whether the card is red or black. After the subject guesses, the psychologist turns the card over and reveals its color. Then the psychologist puts the card back in the deck, reshuffles, and repeats the process. A rational person would guess "red" every time. In fact, some people guess "red" two-thirds of the time and "black" one-third of the time, which is irrational.

We have discussed some causes of uninformed contracts. Now we discuss several doctrines in contract law that excuse promise-breaking on the ground that the promise resulted from bad information: *fraud, failure to disclose, frustration of purpose*, and *mutual mistake*.

If the beneficiary of the promise extracted it by lies, then breaking the promise is excused by reason of *fraud*. For example, the seller of the "sure method to kill grasshoppers" defrauded the farmer. Fraud violates the negative duty not to misinform the other party to a contract. Besides this negative duty, parties sometimes have the affirmative duty to disclose information. In the civil law tradition, your contract may be void because you did not supply the information that you should have. Civil law calls this doctrine *culpa in contrahendo*. In most sales contracts, a seller must warn the buyer about hidden dangers associated with the use of the product, even though this information may cause the buyer not to buy it. For example, the manufacturer of a drug must warn the user about side effects. In these circumstances, common law finds a duty to disclose.

Sometimes disguised defects lower the value of a good without making it dangerous or unfit for use. Common law apparently contains no general duty to disclose such disguised defects.[18] For example, common law does not require a used-car dealer to disclose the faults in a car offered for sale (only a duty not to lie about those faults). The law is different for new goods such as new cars, as opposed to used goods such as used cars. For new goods, U.S. law imputes a "warranty of fitness."[19] An "implied warranty" is a guarantee that the court reads into the contract, even though the actual contract did not explicitly contain such a guarantee. According to the implied warranty of fitness, the seller of a new good promises that it is fit to use for its intended purposes. For example, the seller of a new car breaches this warranty and must return the purchase price if a fault in the car's design prevents its use for transportation. However, the implied warranty of fitness does not apply to using a car as a golf cart or a boat.

If people make contracts premised upon misinformation that they gathered for themselves, then there is no legal principle releasing them from their contractual duties. For example, a stock trader who promises to supply 100 shares of Exxon in six months at a predetermined price cannot escape his obligation just because the price of the stock rose when he expected it to fall.

Most of the preceding examples concern contracts in which one party was misinformed and the other party was well-informed. Another possibility is that *both* parties premise the contract upon the same misinformation. This is the basis of a legal excuse for breaking a promise known as *frustration of purpose*. English law provides some famous examples known as the Coronation Cases. In the early years of the twentieth century, rooms in buildings situated along certain London streets were rented in advance for the day on which the new king's coronation parade would pass by. However, the heir to the throne became ill, and the coronation was postponed. Postponing the parade made

---

[18] We say "apparently" because the law is not perfectly clear on this point.

[19] See UCC §§2–314 and 2–315.

the rental agreement worthless to the renter. Some owners of the rented rooms tried to collect the rent anyway. The courts refused to enforce the contracts on the ground that the change in circumstances frustrated the purpose of the contracts.

Yet another possibility is that both parties premise the contract upon different mis-information. If promises are exchanged on the basis of contradictory, but reasonable, conceptions of what is promised, then the contract is said to rest upon what is called a *mutual mistake.* To illustrate using our Example 2, the seller genuinely believed that he was negotiating to sell his rusty Chevrolet in the back yard, and the buyer genuinely believed that she was negotiating to purchase the immaculate Cadillac in the driveway. Like frustration of purpose, mutual mistake justifies the court's setting the contract aside. In our example, the court might order the buyer to return the car keys, and the seller to return the money.

c. Monopoly Competitive markets contain enough buyers and sellers that each person has many alternative trading partners. In contrast, oligopoly limits the available trading partners to a small number, and monopoly limits the available trading partners to a sin-gle seller. When trading partners are limited, bargains can be very one-sided. Under the bargain theory, the courts enforce bargained promises and do not ask if the terms are fair. Consequently, the common law historically contains weak protection against exploitation by monopolies. Most protections against monopolies were supplied by statutes, not by common law.

One of the few historical examples of common law protection against monopoly is the doctrine of necessity, which we discussed above. In recent years, however, a new common law doctrine has evolved that allows judges to scrutinize the substantive terms of contracts. When a contract seems so unfair that its enforcement would violate the conscience of the judge, it may be set aside according to the doctrine of *unconscionability.* For example, assume a consumer signs a contract allowing a furniture seller to repossess all the furniture in her house if she misses one monthly payment on a single item of furniture. The court may find the repossession term "unconscionable" and refuse to enforce it. We discuss this elusive doctrine in the next chapter. The civil law tradition contains a concept similar to unconscionability. "Lesion" refers to a contract that is too unequal to have legal force.

Table 6.1 summarizes the connection between rationality, transaction costs, and the regulation of promises by contract law.

To help you appreciate Table 6.1, we will summarize its use. Given low transaction costs, rational people will make contracts that approach perfection. A perfect contract has no gaps for courts to fill or inefficiencies for regulations to correct. If a contract approaches perfection, the court should simply enforce its terms. As transaction costs increase, however, people leave gaps in contracts. Courts should fill the gaps with effi-cient default terms. Transaction costs can also cause externalities, misinformation, or monopolies. Serious imperfections can cause markets to fail and create a need to regu-late contracts. *The farther the facts depart from the ideal of perfect rationality and zero transaction costs, the stronger the case for judges regulating the terms of the contract by law.* Table 6.1 associates the leading doctrines for regulating contracts with the mar-ket failure that they attempt to correct.

Like contracts, the officials who regulate them are imperfect. The officials who reg-ulate contracts need information and motivation to correct market failures. In reality,

Table 6.1

RATIONALITY, TRANSACTION COSTS, AND REGULATORY DOCTRINES OF CONTRACT LAW

Assumption	*If violated, contract doctrine*
A. *INDIVIDUAL RATIONALITY*	
1. stable, well-ordered preferences	1. incompetency; incapacity
2. constrained choice	2. coercion; duress; necessity; impossibility
B. *TRANSACTION COSTS*	
1. spillovers	1. unenforceability of contracts derogating public policy or statutory duty
2. information	2. fraud; failure to disclose; frustration of purpose; mutual mistake
3. monopoly	3. necessity; unconscionability or lesion.

courts have limited information and some judges lack motivation. Contract law should take the imperfection of officials into account by discouraging them from exceeding their own limitations in attempting to correct imperfect contracts.

QUESTION 6.16: The bargain theory of contract denies enforceability to promises to give a gift, but Anglo-American courts frequently enforce promises to give a gift under the doctrine of *detrimental reliance*.[20] A court might enforce a promise to give a gift if the promisee relied to his or her detriment—for example, by incurring a debt or foregoing some valuable opportunity—on the promisor's fulfilling the promise. The law-and-economics literature recognizes that the enforceability of a promise to give a gift may increase the well-being of both the donor and of the donee. Still, some law-and-economics scholars are reluctant

---

[20] The original *Restatement of Contracts*, when issued in 1932, generally embraced the bargain theory in §75. However, in §90 the *Restatement* established enforceability of gift promises upon which a reasonable person had detrimentally relied without consideration. §90 is entitled "Promise Reasonably Inducing Definite and Substantial Action" and reads as follows:

"A promise which the promisor should reasonably expect to induce action or forbearance of a definite and substantial character on the part of the promisee and which does induce such action or forbearance is binding if injustice can be avoided only by enforcement of the promise."

This principle is generally referred to as "promissory estoppel," although that phrase does not appear in §90. That section of the *Restatement* is used mainly in commercial, rather than gift, settings. For instance, it might be invoked to enforce a subcontractor's bid upon which a contractor has relied. For recent attempts to reexamine the enforceability of gift promises, see Richard A. Posner, *Gratuitous Promises in Economics and Law,* 6 J. LEGAL STUD. 411 (1977); Melvin A. Eisenberg, *Donative Promises,* 47 U. CHI. L. REV. 1 (1979); Charles Goetz and Robert Scott, *Enforcing Promises: An Examination of the Basis of Contract,* 89 YALE L. J. 1261 (1980); Steven A. Shavell, *An Economic Analysis of Altruism and Deferred Gifts,* 20 J. LEGAL STUD. 401 (1991); and Andrew Kull, *Reconsidering Gratuitous Promises,* 21 J. LEGAL STUD. 39 (1992).

to make gift promises generally enforceable because of three problems: (1) evidentiary (*i.e.*, determining whether a gift promise was really made and whether the donor truly meant to be held to it or was masquerading); (2) cautionary (*i.e.*, most gift promises should not be made because the benefits from completion are small); and (3) channeling (*i.e.*, most gift promises are made impulsively so that nonenforceability protects potential donors from their impulsive acts). Discuss each of these problems in terms of the categories of contract failure in Table 6.1.

F. Contractual Relations: The Economics of the Long-Run

Contracts often create relationships and relationships create legal duties that are not part of the contract. For example, when a customer opens a checking account with a U.S. bank, she signs a contract called a "depository agreement," which creates a "fiduciary relationship." This relationship imposes many duties upon the bank that are not stated in the depository agreement. As another illustration, a "franchisee" (local investor) may sign a contract with the "franchiser" (parent corporation) to buy a local fast-food restaurant. The franchise relationship creates many legal duties that the contract does not mention.

Business relationships often endure for years. Conditions change over the life of the relationship. The parties must respond to changing conditions as they pursue their own interests through the relationship. Accommodating the changes requires flexible understandings, not rigid rules. Consequently, formal rules do not tightly control human relationships, whether in business or personal life.

The parties to long-run relations often rely upon informal devices, rather than enforceable rules, to secure cooperation. Thus, an overbearing partner may be brought back into line by a warning rather than a law suit. Or a businessman who oversteps the ethical boundaries of his profession may be chastened by gossip and ostracism.[21] These informal devices usually operate within enduring relationships. Economists have studied how enduring relationships, as opposed to enforceable contracts, affect behavior.[22] We will explain some of the central conclusions by using our example of the agency game.

1. Repeated Game   In the agency game, the first player invests by placing some funds under the control of the second player. Economists call the first player who risks funds the "principal." For example, the depositor is the principal in a fiduciary relationship with a bank, and the franchisee is the principal in a franchise relationship with a fast-food corporation. Economists call the second player, who controls the principal's funds, the "agent." For example, the bank is the agent in the fiduciary relationship, and the franchisor is the agent in the franchise relationship. The economic model of the

---

[21] The role of reputation in inducing compliance with contracts is analyzed by Benjamin Klein and Keith Leffler, *The Role of Market Forces in Assuring Contractual Performance,* 89 J. POL. ECON. 615 (1981).

[22] Among lawyers, a leading representative of this school is Ian Macneil, and among economists, leading representatives are Oliver Williamson, Ben Klein, and Victor Goldberg. See also the classic study by Stewart Macaulay mentioned in the suggested readings at the end of this chapter.

	round	$n-1$	n	$n+1$	$n+2$	$n+3$	$n+4$	$n+5$	$n+6$
Strategy of second player	appropriate	...	1	0	0	1	0	0	...
	cooperate	...	.5	.5	.5	.5	.5	.5	...

FIGURE 6.7 Payoffs to second player (agent) when first player (principal) plays tit-for-tat.

"principal-agent relationship" applies to many legal relationships, including the fiduciary relationship and the franchiser-franchisee relationship.

To depict cooperation in an enduring relationship, assume that the agency game in Figure 6.1 is repeated indefinitely, thus transforming a "one-shot game" into a "repeated game." In any round of the repeated game in which the principal (first player) invests, the agent (second player) enjoys an immediate advantage from appropriating. However, the principal can retaliate in subsequent rounds of the game to punish the agent.

Figure 6.7 illustrates an effective strategy for the principal to deter appropriation by retaliating against it. Assume that the agent appropriates in round n of the game. The agent receives a payoff of 1 in round n. However, the principal retaliates by not investing in rounds $n+1$ and $n+2$. The agent receives a payoff of zero in rounds $n+1$ and $n+2$. Thus, the strategy of appropriation yields a total payoff to the agent equal to 1 in rounds n through $n+2$. These facts are summarized in the first row of Figure 6.7.

Alternatively, assume that the agent could follow the strategy of cooperating in each round of the game. When the agent cooperates, the principal responds by investing. The agent's payoffs in rounds n, $n+1$, and $n+2$ thus equal .5, .5, and .5. The strategy of cooperating yields a total payoff to the agent equal to 1.5 in rounds n through $n+2$.[23] These facts are summarized in the second row of Figure 6.7.

Figure 6.7 shows that the agent's payoff in rounds n through $n+2$ is higher from cooperating than appropriating. This will be true for any three rounds of the game, provided that the principal continues playing the same strategy. For example, the total payoff to the agent who appropriates in rounds $n+3$ through $n+5$ equals 1, whereas the total payoff for cooperating equals 1.5. The agent benefits in the long run from cooperating rather than appropriating. The principal's strategy of retaliation can teach this lesson to the agent. If the agent follows the strategy of appropriating in round n, he or she will probably learn a lesson by receiving zero payoff in rounds $n+1$ and $n+2$. After learning the lesson, the agent will probably switch to the strategy of cooperating in round $n+3$.

We have described a strategy in which the principal repays the agent's cooperation by investing, and the principal retaliates against the agent's appropriation by not investing.

---

[23] Figure 6.7 assumes no discounting for time. Strictly speaking, payoffs should be discounted by the time of receipt. Let r denote the discount rate. Thus, the second player's total payoff is higher from cooperating in round n rather than appropriating provided the following inequality is satisfied:

$$.5 + .5/(1+r) + .5/(1+r)^2 > 1.$$

Rewarding cooperation and punishing appropriation has been called "tit-for-tat."[24] When the principal plays the strategy of tit-for-tat, the agent maximizes payoff by cooperating. What about the principal? Does he or she maximize payoff by playing tit-for-tat? Experimental evidence indicates that tit-for-tat comes very close to maximizing the principal's payoff in a variety of circumstances, and these empirical findings are generally supported by theory.[25] Thus, the strategy of tit-for-tat is an efficient equilibrium to a repeated agency game.[26]

Let us summarize our theoretical conclusions. Figure 6.1 describes a problem of cooperation: the principal will not invest unless the agent has an incentive to cooperate. Figure 6.2 depicts a legal solution to the problem. The legal solution is to make an enforceable contract. An enforceable contract solves the problem by increasing the cost of appropriation to the agent. An enforceable contract presupposes an effective state to enforce contract and property law. In contrast, Figure 6.7 depicts a nonlegal solution to the problem. The nonlegal solution is to form an enduring relationship. An enduring relationship solves the problem by enabling the principal to retaliate when the agent appropriates. An enduring relationship does not necessarily require an effective state.

Long-run relationships require commitment. Traditional forms of commitment include friendship, kinship, ethnicity, and religion. Traditional forms of commitment can facilitate economic cooperation without state protection. Consequently, traditional forms of commitment often dominate economic life in communities with weak state protection. Business communities with weak state protection include

---

[24] R. Axelrod, THE EVOLUTION OF COOPERATION (1984).

[25] Maskin and Fudenberg have proved that in any game (see the discussion of repeated games in Chapter 2) in which (1) players maximize the discounted sum of single period utilities, (2) the discount rate is not too high, and (3) the players can observe the past history of moves in the game, any pair of payoffs which Pareto-dominate the minimax can arise as average equilibrium payoffs of the repeated game. Thus, repetition of the game makes a Pareto improvement possible. This theorem, however, still leaves unexplained why the probability of a Pareto-efficient solution is as high as empirical studies suggest it to be. See Drew Fudenberg and Eric Maskin, *The Folk Theorem in Repeated Games with Discounting, or With Incomplete Information,* 54 ECONOMETRICA 533–554 (1986).

   An element of mystery also surrounds the "end-game" problem. As we saw in Chapter 2, if a game of distribution is repeated an infinite number of times, cooperation is individually rational. If, however, such a game is repeated a finite number of times, "cheating" on the last round is individually rational. But if cheating is individually rational on the last round, it is also individually rational on the next to last round, and so forth. Thus, strict individual rationality causes the game to unwind. If, however, the players are willing to settle for a strategy that is very close to the self-interested maximum, but a little short of it, the end-game problem can be solved and the players will cooperate. In general, see Avinash Dixit and Barry Nalebuff, THINKING STRATEGICALLY: THE COMPETITIVE EDGE IN BUSINESS, POLITICS, AND EVERYDAY LIFE (1991) and Drew Fudenberg and Jean Tirole, GAME THEORY (1991).

[26] As usual, our model has some implicit assumptions. The most important implicit assumptions are that the players can observe each others' moves and they do not discount the future too heavily. The exceptional games without cooperative solutions need not concern us here. See Glenn W. Harrison and Jack Hirshleifer, *An Experimental Evaluation of Weakest Link/Best Shot Models of Public Goods,* 97 J. POLITICAL ECON. 201–225 (1989) and Jack Hirshleifer and Juan Carlos Martinez Coll, *What Strategies Can Support the Evolutionary Emergence of Cooperation?,* 32 J. CONFLICT RESOLUTION 367–398 (1988).

international merchants, businesses in countries with weak or corrupt governments, businesses caught in civil wars, and foraging tribes that remain unsubordinated to states. Our model predicts, correctly, that traditional forms of commitment should flourish in these circumstances. Our model also predicts, correctly, that traditional forms of commitment will decline in these communities if the state brings effective law to them.

Similarly, traditional forms of commitment often dominate economic life in communities that face the state's hostility. Businesses facing state hostility include organized crime and much private business in communist states. Our model predicts, correctly, that traditional forms of commitment should flourish in these circumstances.

Long-run relations can arise from commitments to institutions. For example, Japanese employees show a high level of commitment to the corporation, as evidenced by low rates of labor mobility. Our theory predicts correctly that long-run relationships will cause Japanese corporations to rely less on enforceable contracts as compared to American or European corporations. Long-run relations in the Japanese economy create more order and less law than in other countries.

Businesses have devised clever informal mechanisms to protect themselves against advantage-taking in long-run relationships. For example, David Teece found that large manufacturers like Ford often buy components from smaller companies through long-run contracts. In these contracts, Ford typically owns the specialized equipment needed in the manufacturing process and rents these machines to the contractor. This method of structuring the relationship protects Ford from being held hostage by its suppliers.

To see why, suppose that a small contractor supplied Ford with a vital part for its cars and suppose that the small contractor owned the specialized equipment needed for making the part. Consequently, the small contractor would have the power to hold up Ford's entire manufacturing process by refusing to supply the vital parts. This would disrupt Ford's plans. By retaining ownership of the specialized machinery, Ford protects itself against this possibility. If the contractor refuses to deliver the vital parts, Ford reclaims the specialized equipment, shifts it to another supplier, and obtains the vital parts without undue delay.[27]

As an alternative to this practice, Ford could try to stipulate terms in its contracts with suppliers that preclude them from holding up production. However, formal contracts are often more clumsy and bureaucratic than informal mechanisms. Businesses often resort to long-run relationships to save transaction costs. As explained, enduring relations create repeated games that solve the problem of cooperation with less reliance on enforceable contracts.

A long-run business contract is more like a marriage than a one-shot exchange. Conversely, sharp practices are likely when the contractual partners never expect to deal with each other again.

We have discussed forms of commitment that precede the state and persist without its support. Other long-run relationships arise within a framework of contract and

---

[27] An excellent introduction to the economic theory suggested by Professor Teece's study is Benjamin Klein, Robert Crawford, and Armen Alchian, *Vertical Integration, Appropriable Rents, and the Competitive Contracting Process,* 21 J. LAW & ECON. 297 (1978).

property law. For example, law created the fiduciary relationship and the franchise relationship. We will discuss how law facilitates long-run relationships, but first we must develop our theory further, beginning with a problem that plagues long-run relationships.

2. Endgame Problem Even long-run relationships end eventually. Near their end, business relationships often encounter trouble. To see why, return to our example of tit-for-tat as depicted in Figure 6.7. Recall that when the agent appropriates, the principal retaliates by not investing for several rounds. However, the principal has no power to retaliate on the *last* round of the game. Thus, the final round of the agency game has the same logic as a one-shot agency game.

To illustrate, assume that the repeated game in Figure 6.7 has an end and both parties know it. To be concrete, assume that both parties know the game will end after round $n + 3$. The agent does not fear retaliation for appropriating in round $n + 3$, because the agent knows that there will not be any more rounds. On round $n + 3$, the agent will receive a payoff of 1 from appropriating and a payoff of .5 from cooperating. Consequently, the agent maximizes his or her payoff in round $n + 3$ by appropriating. Knowing this, the principal will refuse to invest in round $n + 3$. Thus, the players cannot cooperate in round $n + 3$.

We have shown that the last round in a repeated agency game has the same logic as a one-shot game. Consequently, the players in the agency game cannot cooperate in the last round without enforceable contracts. Worse still, the players could fail to cooperate in *every* round of the game. To see why, consider the strict logic of the situation. We explained that the principal follows the strategy of tit-for-tat, which rewards cooperation by subsequent investing and punishes appropriation by not investing in subsequent rounds. We also explained that the principal will not invest in the last round, which is round $n + 3$. Consequently, the principal cannot use round $n + 3$ to reward cooperation or punish appropriation by the agent in round $n + 2$. Knowing this fact, the agent can appropriate in round $n + 2$ without fearing retaliation in round $n + 3$. If the fear of retaliation is removed, the agent will maximize his or her payoff by appropriating in round $n + 2$. Knowing this, the principal will refuse to invest in round $n + 2$.

The same logic now applies to round $n + 1$ and so forth back to the first round. In general, the demonstration that the players cannot cooperate in any given round leads to the conclusion that they cannot cooperate in the preceding round. If strictly rational parties know the round in which the repeated agency game ends, then the whole game unwinds and the players fail to cooperate in any round.

The phrase "the endgame problem" describes the unwinding of cooperation as a repeated game approaches its final round. Eastern Europe provided a dramatic example of the endgame problem after 1989, as discussed in the following box.

3. Tentative Commitments So far we have discussed commitment to enduring relationships. However, most business relationships are "open-ended." Open-ended relationships have no predetermined end. They can persist indefinitely or end unexpectedly. Open-ended relationships dissolve and reform easily as circumstances change. Next we want to model open-ended relationships.

Assume as before that the agency game is repeated indefinitely. However, change the assumption that there are only two players. Instead, assume that there is an indefinite

THE ENDGAME PROBLEM OF EASTERN EUROPE IN 1989

The disintegration of communist governments in Eastern Europe accelerated dramatically in 1989. Central planning failed irreparably, and markets rapidly replaced central planning as the organizing economic principle. Unfortunately, production declined throughout Eastern Europe at this time. Why did the shift to markets immediately produce economic decline rather than economic growth?

The "endgame problem" provides the key. Under communism, much production occurred through the "black market" (illegal) or the "gray market" (semilegal). Even the large state enterprises relied upon the black market or the gray market to perform their assigned tasks. The black market and the gray market did not enjoy protection from the state. Our theory predicts that businesses lacking effective legal protection will secure cooperation through long-run relationships. That is how communist economies functioned. For example, a truck driver would haul goods for "free" as a "favor" to his friend who operated a gas station, and the gas-station operator would supply petrol for the trucker when supplies ran short.

The demise of communism massively disrupted political life. The disruptions caused people to doubt the persistence of their long-run economic relationships. With the end of relationships in sight, cooperation failed. For example, the trucker lost confidence that the gas-station operator could continue to supply petrol (the gas-station operator might lose her job), so the trucker stopped hauling the gas-station operator's goods for free.

The failure of cooperation caused production to decline all over Eastern Europe after 1989. This situation could be corrected by effective legal protection for property and contracts. Some Eastern European states have made the correction. In other states, however, entrepreneurs still enjoy higher profits from stealing property (especially state property) than from producing goods.

---

amount of players, who form into pairs to play each round of the game. At the end of each round, some of these relationships continue in the next round and others dissolve. Relationships dissolve in two ways. First, unforeseeable changes cause the parties to abandon the relationship. Second, the principal exits from the relationship after the agent appropriates.

To illustrate, assume that principal P and agent A form a business relationship in round n of the game. In round n, P invests and A responds by cooperating. Each player enjoys a payoff of .5 in round n. At the end of round n, unforeseeable events might cause the relationship to dissolve. If unforeseeable events do not materialize, the parties continue the relationship in round $n + 1$. Assume that P invests in round $n + 1$ and A responds by appropriating. P will not continue in business with a partner who appropriates rather than cooperating. Consequently, P will dissolve the relationship at the end of round $n + 1$ and refuse to continue in business with agent A. Thus, the relationship between P and A may dissolve because of unforeseeable events or because of A's appropriation.

When a relationship dissolves, the players must find new partners for the next round of the game. To illustrate, if the relationship dissolves between P and A in round n, then each one must search for another partner in round $n + 1$. The search does not automatically succeed. Players who look for a partner and fail to find one receive a payoff of zero during the rounds spent searching.

Assume that the principal follows the strategy of exiting whenever an agent appropriates. Thus, the principal punishes a disloyal agent by dissolving the relationship. Exit from a tentative relationship resembles tit-for-tat in an enduring relationship. In both cases, appropriation by the agent causes the principal to retaliate in the next round of the game.

When principals respond to disloyalty by exiting, the agents in the game face a choice between two alternative strategies. The first strategy is to cooperate, in which case the relationship continues until dissolved by an unforeseeable event. This strategy yields a payoff of .5 in each round that the relationship persists. The second strategy is to appropriate, thus provoking the first player to dissolve the relationship. By following the second strategy, the agent receives a payoff of 1.0 in the few rounds when he or she finds a partner, and a payoff of zero in the other rounds when the search for a partner is unsuccessful. In brief, the agent chooses between cooperating and receiving a modest payoff in most rounds of the game, or appropriating and receiving a large payoff in a few rounds of the game.

Notice that these two strategies in the agency game correspond to familiar facts about business. Some businesses try to make modest profits on many transactions. These businesses focus on long-run relationships with repeat customers. Other businesses try to make large profits on few transactions. These businesses focus on attracting new customers for one-time sales.

In a competitive equilibrium, both strategies must earn the same payoff. In other words, the strategy of cooperating in long-run relationships must yield the same payoff as the strategy of appropriating in one-shot relationships.

To illustrate, assume that in a *stable equilibrium* 70% of the agents follow the strategy of cooperating and 30% follow the strategy of appropriating. In other words, assume that the payoff to agents from cooperating equals the payoff from appropriating when 70% of them cooperate and 30% of them appropriate. To see how the system gets to equilibrium, assume that the system is out of equilibrium. Specifically, assume that the *actual* proportion of cooperating agents equals 75%, and the *actual* proportion of appropriating agents equals 25%. We are assuming that cooperating agents exceed the equilibrium by 5%. The excess of actual cooperators over the number required for equilibrium will cause the payoff from cooperating to fall below its equilibrium value. We are assuming that appropriating agents fall short of the equilibrium by 5%. The deficit of actual appropriators over the number required for equilibrium will cause the payoff from appropriating to rise above its equilibrium value. Now the payoff to appropriating exceeds the payoff to cooperating. Some cooperators will respond by switching strategies and appropriating. The switch will continue until the two strategies yield the same payoff. By assumption, the two strategies will yield the same payoff when 70% of the agents cooperate and 30% appropriate.

This account corresponds to the dynamics of real markets. To illustrate, consider the market for trial lawyers. Most trial lawyers realistically assess their clients' prospects at trial and use this assessment as the basis for a settlement out of court. These lawyers correspond to cooperators in the agency game. These lawyers attract repeat customers and maintain long-run relationships with their clients. However, some lawyers provide unrealistically optimistic assessments of their clients' prospects at trial and use these assessments to induce their clients to engage in costly litigation. These lawyers correspond to appropriators in the agency game. These lawyers attract relatively few repeat customers and maintain short-run relationships with most clients. The proportion of lawyers of each type adjusts in response to the profitability of the two strategies.

We have shown that the power of principals to exit from agency relationships makes some cooperation possible even without enforceable contracts. However, more effective laws can increase the amount of cooperation. To illustrate, the equilibrium ratio of cooperators to appropriators among agents in the preceding example was 70% to 30%. This ratio might rise if the state could effectively protect principals from appropriation. For example, effective contract and property law might increase the ratio to 95% to 5%.

The increase in cooperation would increase economic production. To illustrate, recall that the joint payoff from cooperation equals 1, and the joint payoff from appropriation equals zero. If 70% of the agents cooperate in each round, then production equals 70 per round. If 90% of the agents cooperate in each round, then production equals 90 per round. If effective contract law can increase cooperating agents from 70% to 90%, then production rises by 20 units, which is an increase in production of almost 30%.

We can apply this reasoning to the two kinds of trial lawyers. If the bar find ways to reduce the profitability of trials relative to settlements for the lawyers, then more lawyers will try to settle cases and fewer lawyers will provoke trials. The lawyers who try to settle cases out of court resolve more disputes in less time than the lawyers who provoke trials. Consequently, inducing a shift in strategy by lawyers towards settlements and away from trials will increase their productivity in resolving disputes.

4. Law of Long-Run Relations   We have explained that securing cooperation typically requires enforceable promises in one-shot transactions, exit in tentative relationships, and tit-for-tat in enduring relationships. As the time perspective lengthens, contract law becomes less concerned with enforcing promises and more concerned with facilitating relationships. *The sixth purpose of contract law is to foster enduring relationships, which solve the problem of cooperation with less reliance on contracts.*

The courts foster enduring relationships by providing a legal framework that encourages their formation. For example, we have seen that courts impute duties to relationships that arise out of contract, such as the fiduciary relationship and the franchise relationship. The imputation of these duties helps the parties to form the relationships. For example, the depositor knows that the law protects her deposit from appropriation by her fiduciary agent. Similarly, the franchisee knows that the law protects his investment against appropriation by the franchiser.

Disputes often arise in the course of a business relationship that bring the parties into court. When the parties to an enduring relationship become entangled in a legal dispute, the court may try to *repair the relationship.* Repairing the relationship is different from enforcing the rights of the parties. Consequently, the courts sometimes adopt a different style of adjudication for long-run relationships than for one-shot transactions.

To illustrate, compare a divorce involving children and a dispute over the sale of an automobile. The divorcing parents of children need a long-run relationship with each other in order to care of the children. The court should try to promote a working relationship between them. A working relationship between them depends upon compromise.

HOW TO EXCHANGE HOSTAGES

Medieval kings used to guarantee the peace among themselves by exchanging hostages. If the hostage-giver starts a war, then the hostage-taker will refuse to return the hostage. Oliver Williamson has analyzed the logic of the exchange of hostages and applied it to modern contracts, especially in long-run relationships. (See Oliver Williamson, *Credible Commitments: Using Hostages to Support Exchange*, 83 AM. ECON. REV. 519 [1983].) Ask yourself this question: suppose that a king wants to exchange hostages with another monarch to guarantee the peace. Assume that the king likes diamonds as much as he likes his children. That is, he values a diamond ring just as much—neither more nor less than—as he values his own son. Which would make a better hostage: the king's diamond ring or his son?

The better hostage is the one that deters both the hostage-giver and the hostage-taker from starting a war. By assumption, the king values the diamond ring and his son equally; the fear of losing the ring by starting a war equals the fear of losing his son. They are equally good deterrents against the hostage-giver starting a war. However, they are not equally good deterrents against the hostage-*taker* starting a war. The hostage-taker would presumably like to have the diamond ring but presumably places little intrinsic value on having the son of the neighboring king. The hostage-taker, therefore, is more inclined to start a war and keep the hostage if he holds the diamond ring rather than the king's son. That is why the king's son is a better hostage than the diamond ring.

In general, a good hostage is something that the hostage-giver values highly and the hostage-taker values little. Asymmetrical valuation makes a good hostage.

QUESTION 6.17: What sorts of things can corporations give as hostages in long-run contractual relations? Does hostage-giving in long-run relationships serve the same or a different function as consideration in a short-run contract?

Searching for a compromise requires the judge to consider the broad equities of the relationship. Thus, the judge may perform some functions of a mediator.

In contrast, the buyer and seller of an automobile typically engage in a one-shot transaction. They do not need to deal with each other in the future after they resolve their suit. The judge does not need to promote a working relationship between them. Instead of searching for a compromise, the judge may try to find the rights of the parties. The rights of the parties can be decided on narrow facts in dispute, so the judge may ignore the broad equities of the relationship. Deciding the rights of the parties may produce a decision that completely favors one party over the other. A decision that completely favors one party over the other provides a clear definition of rights. A clear definition of rights facilitates bargaining and exchange, whereas a muddy definition of rights promotes future disagreements.

Legal sociologists have argued in recent years that many modern business disputes resemble divorces more closely than disputed automobile sales. These sociologists favor alternatives to traditional means of resolving disputes. The alternative means of resolving disputes focus on repairing relationships. For example, when a franchiser and franchisee come to the court with a contract dispute, the judge may initially refuse to decide the rights of the parties. Instead the judge may hold that each party owes a duty to bargain in good faith with the other party to resolve their dispute. As this example illustrates, alternative dispute resolution focuses on processes rather than outcomes. Much research remains to be done in order to assess whether a focus on process can improve the performance of courts in resolving disputes among people with long-run relationships.[28]

CONCLUSION

Contract law and the courts help people to cooperate by enforcing, interpreting, and regulating promises. By enforcing promises, the courts enable people to make credible commitments to cooperate with each other. By enforcing promises optimally, the courts create incentives for efficient cooperation. Cooperation is efficient when the promisor invests in performing at the efficient level and the promisee relies at the efficient level. By interpreting promises, the courts can reduce the transaction costs of cooperating. Specifically, the courts reduce the costs of negotiating contracts by supplying efficient default terms. By regulating contracts, the courts can correct market failures. By correcting market failures, the law reduces the threat of opportunistic behavior that undermines the willingness of people to make commitments to each other. Finally, contract law helps to solve the problem of cooperation with minimal reliance on the apparatus of the state. The problem of cooperation is solved with minimal reliance upon the state by fostering enduring relationships.

We analyzed these purposes of contract law through a model of the agency game. We evaluated the agency game by the standard of Pareto efficiency. Pareto efficiency requires the law to help private parties achieve their goals as fully as possible. Economic analysis necessarily produces a theory of law that responds to the parties who make contracts, rather than a dogmatic theory of law that elevates ideas above interests.

SUGGESTED READINGS

Eisenberg, Melvin, *The Bargain Principle and Its Limits,* 95 HARV. L. REV. 741 (1982).

Freid, Charles, CONTRACT AS PROMISE (1981).

Goetz, Charles, and Robert Scott, *Enforcing Promises: An Examination of the Basis of Contract,* 89 YALE L. J. 1261 (1980).

Goldberg, Victor, ed., READINGS IN THE ECONOMICS OF CONTRACT LAW (1989).

Gordley, James, THE PHILOSOPHICAL ORIGINS OF MODERN CONTRACT LAW (1991).

Macaulay, Stewart, *Non-Contractual Relations in Business: A Preliminary Study,* 28 AM. SOCIOLOGICAL REV. 55 (1963).

---

[28] Theoretical research has reached negative conclusions about alternative dispute resolution in some settings. See Lisa Bernstein, *Understanding the Limits of Court-Connected ADR: A Critique of Federal Court-Annexed Arbitration Programs,* 141 U. PA. L. REV. 2169 (1993).

7

TOPICS IN THE ECONOMICS
OF CONTRACT LAW

In the preceding chapter, we explained that a theory of contracts must answer two questions: "What promises should be enforced?" and "What should be the remedy for breaking an enforceable promise?" We summarized the economic theory developed to answer these questions. Cooperation is productive. People often make promises to cooperate. Enforcing promises enables people to make their commitments credible. Courts should enforce promises when the parties want enforceability in order to make a credible commitment to cooperate. Enforcement ideally induces optimal performance and reliance at low transaction costs. Optimal performance and reliance maximize the expected value of cooperation to both parties.

This economic theory allowed us to develop a framework for analyzing contracts in the preceding chapter. In this chapter we add texture and detail to the economic framework. In the first part of this chapter we focus upon remedies for breach of contract. The best remedy for breach secures optimal commitment to the contract, which causes efficient performance and reliance.

Explicit terms in a contract require interpretation, gaps require filling, and inefficient or unfair terms require regulation. We developed a general theory in the preceding chapter for optimal interpretation, gap-filling, and regulation of contracts. According to this theory, legal doctrines should perfect contracts by minimizing transaction costs and correcting market failures. We analyze the relevant legal doctrines in detail in the second part of this chapter.

I. REMEDIES AS INCENTIVES

When a party to a contract fails to perform as promised, the victim may ask the court for a remedy. Remedies fall into three general types. First, the contract may *stipulate* a remedy. The contract stipulates a remedy when it contains explicit terms prescribing what to do if someone breaches. For example, a construction contract may stipulate that the builder will pay $200 per day for late completion of a building. Instead of stipulating a specific remedy, the contract may stipulate a remedial process. For example, the contract may specify that disputes between the parties will be arbitrated by the International Chamber of Commerce, which has its own rules about remedies.

Because negotiating and drafting are costly, an efficient contract will not explicitly cover every contingency. In fact, most contracts do not specify remedies for breach. When the contract omits a remedy, the court must supply one. The court may order the breaching party to pay money damages to the victim. Alternatively, the court may order the breaching party to perform.

Damages and specific performance are the two general types of court-designed remedies for breach of contract. Different legal systems in different countries disagree about the preferred remedy. In common law countries and in France, courts say that damages are the preferred remedy, whereas German courts say that specific performance is the preferred remedy. The difference between alternative legal traditions, however, is greater in theory than in practice. In practice, each legal system prescribes damages as the remedy in some circumstances and specific performance as the remedy in other circumstances. Furthermore, the prescriptions largely overlap in many different legal systems. Presumably, the prescriptions overlap because different systems of law respond to the same economic logic. Common law and civil law traditions both tend to specify the efficient remedy for breach of contract.

A. Alternative Remedies

Different remedies create different incentives for the parties to a contract. We will develop models to compare the incentive effects of different remedies on investment in performance and reliance. First, however, we must examine alternative remedies in greater detail.

1. Expectation Damages   Damages for breach of contract compensate the promisee for the injury caused by the promisor. In a contract setting, the term "injury" has several different meanings. First, the promisee is worse off than if the contract had been performed. Performance provides a baseline for computing the injury. Using this baseline, the courts award damages that place the victim of breach in the position he or she would have been in if the other party had performed.

The promisee expects to gain from performance. Consequently, the common law tradition refers to damages based upon the value of expected performance as "expectation damages." The civil law tradition refers to these damages as "positive damages" (*lucrum cessans*), because the damages replace income that would have accrued in the future. If expectation damages or positive damages achieve their purpose, the potential victim of breach is equally well off whether there is performance, on the one hand, or breach and payment of damages, on the other hand. We say that *perfect expectation damages* leave potential victims *indifferent* between performance and breach.

To illustrate, assume the Apex Ticket Agency offers opera tickets at the price p_A. A consumer orders x_k tickets and Apex breaches close to the date of the performance. The consumer cannot get equivalent tickets except by paying the high price p_B to the Bijou Ticket Agency. The promised performance can be replaced at the cost x_k. Replacing the promised performance with a perfect substitute puts the consumer in the same position

THE UNIFORM COMMERCIAL CODE, RESTATEMENTS OF CONTRACTS, AND STATUTE OF FRAUDS

In the civil law countries, which include the nations of continental Europe, committees of scholars have formulated contract law into codes that legislatures enacted. In common law countries, which include the United States, judges have formulated contract law in deciding cases. This contrast, however, can be overstated. Americans have actually codified much of the common law of contracts in three important documents: the *Uniform Commercial Code*, the American Law Institute's *Restatements of Contracts*, and statutes revising the old English *Statute of Frauds*.

The National Conference of Commissioners on Uniform State Laws was founded in the 1890s to unify common law in the American states. The Conference and the American Law Institute (described below) adopted the *Uniform Commercial Code* in 1952 and extensively revised it in 1956. Forty-nine states (all but Louisiana, which has a civil law tradition) have adopted the *Uniform Commercial Code*. It consists of nine articles covering all aspects of commercial transactions. For example, Article 1 sets out the general provisions of the code; Article 2 covers the sale of goods (services are not covered), and Article 9 covers secured transactions.

The *Restatements* of the law are a project of the American Law Institute, a private group of judges, lawyers, and law professors founded in 1923, whose purpose "is to state clearly and precisely in the light of the decisions the principles and rules of the common law." The Institute's first project was the *Restatement of Contracts*, which was published in 1932 and subsequently revised in 1979. The ALI has also sought to restate the common law in property, contracts, torts, and other subjects.

The *Statute of Frauds* ("An Act for Prevention of Frauds and Perjuries") was passed by English Parliament in 1677. The purpose of the act was to prevent fraud in the proof of contracts, deeds to land, trusts, and wills. To guarantee a trustworthy record, the statute required a signed writing in certain contractual transactions, possibly supplemented by witnesses. The requirement of a written record for contracts whose value exceeds a certain minimum has become the most important feature in the modern revisions of the statute, which every American state has adopted.

that he would have been in if the promisor had performed. Accordingly, perfect expectation damages equal $x_k(p_B - p_A)$.[1]

As another illustration, assume that Seller promises Buyer to build a boat with an Alpha compass, which will give the boat a market value of m_A. Instead, he delivers a boat with a Beta Compass, which causes the boat to have a lower market value of m_B. Replacing the

---

[1] This specific formula for damages is called the "substitute-price formula." The substitute-price formula awards the victim of breach the cost of replacing a promised performance with a substitute performance. If a commodity is homogeneous, the substitute performance may be identical to the promised performance. In that case, the substitute-price formula awards perfect expectation damages. However, if the commodity is differentiated rather than homogeneous, the substitution is imperfect.

compass after installation is prohibitively expensive. If Buyer's subjective valuations correspond to market prices, then expectation damages equal the difference between the value of the boat promised and the value of the boat delivered, or $(m_A - m_B)$.[2]

2. Reliance Damages   Now we consider the second meaning of "injury" in a contract setting. The promisee may invest in reliance upon the promise. Reliance increases the loss resulting from breach. Breach usually diminishes or destroys the value of the investment in reliance. Consequently, breach makes promisees who rely worse off than if they had not made contracts. "No contract" provides a baseline for computing injury. Using this baseline, the courts may award damages that place victims of breach in the position that they would have been in if they never contracted with another party.

Damages computed relative to this baseline are called "reliance damages" in the common law tradition. The civil law tradition refers to these damages as "negative damages," because the damages replace income that was actually lost. If reliance damages or negative damages achieve their purpose, the potential victim of breach is equally well off whether there is no contract, on the one hand, or breach of contract and payment of damages, on the other hand. We say that *perfect reliance damages* leave potential victims *indifferent* between no contract and breach.

To illustrate, assume that a consumer promises to buy x_k opera tickets from the Apex Agency at price p_A. In reliance on the contract, Apex purchases x_k tickets at the wholesale price p_W. When the consumer breaches, Apex resells the tickets at the spot price p_S, which has fallen below the original wholesale price of p_W. Perfect reliance damages equal the loss from resale, or $x_k(p_W - p_S)$.[3]

3. Opportunity Cost   Now we consider the third meaning of "injury" in a contract setting. Making a contract often entails the loss of an opportunity to make an alternative contract. The lost opportunity provides a baseline for computing the injury. Using this baseline, the courts award damages that place victims of breach in the position that they would have been in if they had signed the contract that was the best alternative to the one that was breached. In other words, damages replace the value of the lost opportunity.

Damages computed relative to this baseline are called "opportunity-cost" damages. If opportunity-cost damages achieve their purpose, the potential victim of breach is equally well off whether there is breach of contract, on the one hand, or the best alternative contract, on the other hand. We say that *perfect opportunity-cost damages* leave potential victims *indifferent* between breach and performance of the best alternative contract.

Previously we discussed the fact that the promisee may invest in reliance on a contract. Similarly, the promisee may forego an opportunity in reliance on a promise. Consequently, the common law tradition considers opportunity-cost damages to be a form of reliance damages. This form of reliance damages takes into account the opportunity lost from relying on a promise, not merely the promisee's investment in reliance.

---

[2] This is called the "diminished-value formula." When performance of a contract is partial or imperfect, the diminished-value formula awards the victim of breach the difference between (1) the postbreach value of a commodity that was to be received or improved under the contract, and (2) the value the commodity would have had if the contract had been properly performed.

[3] This specific formula is called the "out-of-pocket-cost" formula. The out-of-pocket-cost formula awards the victim of breach the difference between (1) the costs incurred in reliance on the contract prior to breach, and (2) the value produced by those costs that can be realized after breach.

Similarly, the civil law tradition considers opportunity-cost damages a form of negative damages (*damnum emergens*).

To illustrate perfect opportunity-cost damages, assume that a consumer foregoes the opportunity of buying x_k cinema tickets from the Bijou Agency at price p_B, and instead contracts to buy x_k tickets from the Apex Agency at the lower price p_A. If she is then compelled to purchase at the higher price p_s after Apex's breach, the opportunity-cost formula sets damages equal to $x_k(p_s - p_B)$.[4]

Example: Hawkins v. McGee   The famous case of *Hawkins v. McGee*, 84 N.H. 114, 146 A. 641 (N.H., 1929), dramatically illustrates the distinction between the three forms of damages. The plaintiff, George Hawkins, suffered a childhood accident that left a permanent scar on his hand. When Hawkins was 18 years old, his family physician, McGee, persuaded him to submit to an operation that the doctor asserted would restore the hand to perfection. In the operation, skin from the plaintiff's chest was grafted onto his hand. The result was hideous. The formerly small scar was enlarged, covered with hair, and irreversibly worse. (Generations of American law students know *Hawkins v. McGee* as "the case of the hairy hand.") Hawkins prevailed against McGee in a suit alleging that the doctor had broken his contractual promise to make the hand perfect.

The question on appeal was, "What damages should be awarded to Hawkins?" This issue is illustrated in Figure 7.1. The horizontal axis in this figure indicates the range of possible conditions of the hand, which vary from perfection to total disability. The vertical axis indicates the dollar amount of damages. The curved lines on the graph indicate the relationship between the extent of the disability and the amount of money needed to compensate for it.

Courts compute compensatory damages for physical injuries every day. Juries typically make the computation in America, whereas judges typically make the computation in Europe. Doubt remains as to exactly how courts make, or should make, the computation. The idea that money compensates for a serious physical injury perplexes some people. Please set aside your perplexity for the moment and consider an economic theory of compensation.

Assume that welfare or utility remains unchanged while moving along a curve in Figure 7.1. Welfare or utility remains unchanged because a change in compensation exactly offsets a change in the patient's condition when moving from one point to another on the same curve. Therefore, the curves are analogous to indifference curves in the microeconomic theory of consumer choice. We postpone discussing in detail the perplexities of compensating for physical injury until Chapter 9.

Now we can use Figure 7.1 to contrast damages based upon expectation, reliance and opportunity cost. First, consider expectation damages in *Hawkins v. McGee* as represented by the curved line labeled "expectation." The physician promised to make the boy's hand perfect. If the physician had performed, Hawkins would have a 100% perfect hand and no compensation. Assume that after the operation the patient's hand was 25% perfect. Expectation damages are the amount of money needed to compensate for the shortfall between the 100% perfect hand that was promised and the 25% perfect hand

---

[4] In general, if breach causes the injured party to purchase a substitute performance, the opportunity-cost formula equals the difference between the best alternative contract price available at the time of contracting and the price of the substitute performance obtained after the breach.

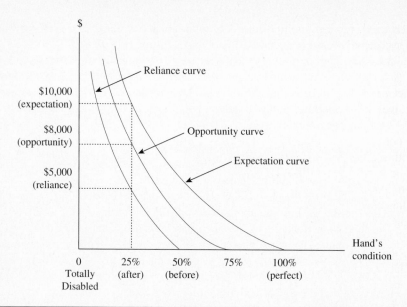

FIGURE 7.1 Expectation, opportunity-cost, and reliance measures of damages in *Hawkins v. McGee*.

that was achieved. To measure these damages, locate the 25% point on the horizontal axis, move vertically up to the curve labeled "expectation," and then move horizontally over to the vertical axis to determine the corresponding dollar amount of damages—$10,000. By assumption, the patient is as well off with $10,000 in damages and a 25% perfect hand as with no damages and a 100% perfect hand.

Now consider reliance damages, which are graphed by the curve labeled "reliance." Under the reliance conception, the uninjured state is the condition in which the patient would have been if he had not made the contract with the breaching party. Assume that if there had never been a contract, the patient would have had a 50% perfect hand, whereas after the operation the hand was 25% perfect. Reliance damages are the amount of money needed to compensate the deterioration of the hand from 50% to 25%. Like the expectation curve, the reliance curve represents the relationship between the extent of the disability and the amount of money needed to compensate for it. The only difference is that the reliance curve touches the horizontal axis at the point where the hand is 50% perfect, rather than 100% perfect. By following the same steps as in expectation damages, we find that the patient is equally well off with $5,000 in damages and a 25% perfect hand as with no damages and a 50% perfect hand. Thus, reliance damages equal $5,000.[5]

Finally, consider the opportunity-cost measure of damages. Perhaps the operation performed by Dr. McGee caused Hawkins to lose the opportunity of having another doctor perform the operation successfully. If such an opportunity were lost, its value provides another baseline for computing damages. The value of the foregone opportunity

---

[5] In fact, Hawkins received $3000 from the original jury; subsequently, after the appellate court ordered a new trial, the plaintiff settled for $1400 plus lawyer's fees.

depends upon how close to perfection the hand would have been after an operation by another doctor. To illustrate, suppose that another doctor would have restored the hand to the 75% level. The injury from relying on Dr. McGee equals the difference between the 75% level that the other doctor would have provided and the 25% level achieved by Dr. McGee.

To measure opportunity-cost damages, consider the "opportunity-cost" curve in Figure 7.1. The opportunity-cost curve touches the horizontal axis at the 75% point, corresponding to condition of the hand after an operation by the best alternative doctor. As with the other two curves, the opportunity-cost curve is constructed so that every point on it represents the same level of welfare. Consequently, a change in the hand's condition represented by a move along the new curve is exactly offset by the corresponding change in damages. The value of the lost opportunity is read off the graph by moving vertically from the 25% point on the horizontal axis up to the "opportunity curve," and then horizontally to the intersection with the vertical axis. Following these steps, the opportunity-cost measure of damages equals $8,000, which is less than expectation damages ($10,000) and more than reliance damages stripped of the opportunity cost ($5,000).

Figure 7.1 shows that expectation, reliance, and opportunity cost damages differ according to the baseline for measuring the injury, where "baseline" refers to the uninjured state. For measuring expectation damages, the uninjured state is the promisee's position if the actual contract had been performed.[6] For measuring reliance damages, the uninjured state is the promisee's position if no contract had been made. For measuring opportunity-cost damages, the uninjured state is the promisee's position if the best alternative contract had been performed.

In general, *perfect compensation* means a sum of money sufficient to make the victim of an injury equally well off with the money and with the injury as he or she would have been without the money and without the injury. The curves in Figure 7.1 depict perfect expectation, opportunity-cost, and reliance damages.[7]

Performance of the actual contract would make the promisee at least as well off as performance of the next best alternative. Consequently, perfect expectation damages are at least as high as perfect opportunity-cost damages. Performance of the next best alternative would make the promisee at least as well off as no contract. Consequently, perfect opportunity-cost damages are at least as high as perfect reliance damages. The following inequalities generally hold:

perfect expectation damages $\geq$
    perfect opportunity cost damages $\geq$
    perfect reliance damages.

Perfectly competitive markets especially interest economic theorists. Many buyers and sellers participate in perfectly competitive markets. Each one substitutes

---

[6] This proposition implicitly assumes that the rate of breach is low. When the rate of breach is high, it can be anticipated to some extent, and so the promisee can plan for breach, just as airlines and hotels plan for "no-shows." The phenomenon of statistically predictable breach creates a special set of problems for expectation damages.

[7] Note that the curves in Figure 7.5 illustrate the logic of compensation, not the actual computation of damages in this case.

perfectly for the other. A person who signs a contract in a perfectly competitive market foregoes the opportunity of signing an identical contract with someone else. Since the actual contract is identical to the best alternative contract, the promisee expects to benefit from the actual contract by the same amount that he or she would have benefitted from performance of the best alternative contract. Consequently, perfect expectation damages equal perfect opportunity-cost damages in perfectly competitive markets.

QUESTION 7.1: Buyer B pays \$10,000 to New Orleans grain dealer D in exchange for D's promise to deliver grain to buyer B's London office on October 1. As a result of signing this contract, B decides not to sign a similar contract with another dealer for \$10,500. D contracts with shipping company S to transport the grain. Buyer B agrees to resell the grain upon arrival in London for \$11,000 to another party. B pays \$100 in advance (nonrefundable) as docking and unloading fees for the ship's projected arrival in London.

The ship begins taking water several days out of New Orleans and returns to port. Inspection reveals that the grain is badly damaged by salt water, and D sells it as cattle fodder for \$500. D conveys the news to B in London, who then purchases the same quantity of grain for delivery on October 1 at a price of \$12,000.

a. How would you measure expectation damages for D's breach of contract with B?

b. How would you measure reliance damages?

c. How would you measure opportunity-cost damages?

QUESTION 7.2: The actual choice of a damage measure often depends upon practical problems, not theory. Give some examples of breached contracts in which opportunity-cost damages are easier to implement than expectation damages. Give some examples of breached contracts in which reliance damages are easier to implement than opportunity-cost damages.

QUESTION 7.3: Perfectly competitive markets contain many buyers and sellers of the same contract, so the best alternative contract is identical to the actual contract signed. What does this fact imply about the relationship between perfect expectation damages and perfect opportunity-cost damages for breach in perfectly competitive contract markets?

QUESTION 7.4: Airlines routinely sell more tickets for flights than the seats on the plane. "Overbooking" seldom causes problems because a statistically predictable number of ticket-holders fail to show up for flights. In contrast, each retailer of hearing aids typically has the capacity to sell many more hearing aids per week than it actually sells. "Excess capacity" is routine for retailers of hearing aids. Contrast the effects of overbooking and excess capacity on profits lost by the seller when the buyer breaches a contract to buy.[8]

4. Restitution   In a deferred exchange, one party often gives something in exchange for the other party's promise to do something later. In these circumstances, a remedy for breach is to require the breaching party to return what was given. For example, the

---

[8] This question concerns what is called the "lost-volume" problem.

buyer of a car often makes a "down payment" before receiving the car. If the seller breaches the contract to deliver the car, the court may order the seller to return the down payment. This remedy is called "restitution," because it requires the injurer to give back what he or she took from the victim. [9] Restitution is a minimal remedy. It does not compensate the victim of breach for expectation, opportunity, or reliance.

5. Disgorgement   Perfect compensation is a sum of money that substitutes for the injury and leaves the victim indifferent about its occurrence. The victim who receives perfect compensation has no basis to complain about the injury. Consequently, the law often does not punish people who compensate perfectly for the injuries that they cause.

We can restate this argument in economic terms. Perfect compensation completely internalizes the external costs of an injury. When costs are completely internalized, efficiency requires freedom of action, not deterrence. Given cost internalization and freedom, a rational person injures others whenever the benefit is large enough to pay perfect compensation and have some left over, as required for efficiency.

Perfect compensation is impossible in principle for some kinds of injuries. For example, vague promises create uncertainty about the value of performance. When the value of performance is uncertain, perfect compensation is impossible. Compensation for breaking vague promises is inevitably imperfect.

Vague promises are often made in long-run relationships. Although vague, the promises can be important to sustaining the relationship. Consequently, the parties may want vague promises to be enforceable, but they may want a different remedy than compensatory damages.

To illustrate, consider the relationship between stockholders and directors of a corporation. Instead of promising the stockholders a definite rate of return on their investment, directors make vague promises to be loyal and do their best. Even if directors make no such promises, the common law tradition requires directors to be loyal to stockholders and to do their best.[10] Sometimes, however, directors behave disloyally and stockholders sue. To illustrate, assume that a corporate director learns about valuable minerals on the company's land. Before anyone else finds out, the director induces the company to sell her the land. The director violates her duty of loyalty by taking valuable minerals for herself that belong to the corporation.

The relationship between directors and stockholders involves trust. Trust would be undermined by allowing a director to take assets that belong to the corporation. The law deters disloyalty by various means, including requiring the injurer to give the profits of wrongdoing to the victim. "Disgorgement damages" are damages paid to the victim to eliminate the injurer's profit from wrongdoing. To illustrate, assume that the director who purchased the corporation's mineral-bearing land resold it to a third party

---

[9] See E. Allan Farnsworth, *Your Loss or My Gain?: The Dilemma of the Disgorgement Principle in Contract Damages*, 94 YALE L. J. 1339 (1985); Robert Cooter and Bradley J. Freedman, *The Fiduciary Relationship: Its Economic Character and Legal Consequences*, 66 NEW YORK UNIVERSITY LAW REVIEW 1045 (1991).

[10] The common law tradition holds directors to a "duty of loyalty" by virtue of the fiduciary relationship. Furthermore, the common law tradition applies the "business-judgment rule" to their decisions. The business-judgment rule holds directors responsible for making their best efforts to gather information and deliberate on decisions affecting the company, but excuses directors whose best efforts result in bad judgments.

at a high price. The director might be required to "disgorge" her profits from the sale by giving them to her corporation.

When disgorgement is perfect, the injurer is indifferent between doing right, on one hand, or doing wrong and paying disgorgement damages, on the other hand. Thus, perfect disgorgement is identical to perfect compensation, with the roles of injurer and victim reversed. The injurer achieves no gain from wrongdoing net of perfect disgorgement damages, just as the victim suffers no harm from the injury net of perfectly compensatory damages.

6. Specific Performance[11] Instead of damages, the court may order the breaching party to perform a specific act as a remedy. "Specific performance" usually requires the promisor to do what he or she promised in the contract.[12] As mentioned, specific performance is the traditional remedy for breach of contract in some civil law countries, and damages are the traditional remedy in common law countries, but in practice most legal systems use similar remedies in similar circumstances.

The typical case in which courts adopt specific performance as the remedy involves the sale of goods for which no close substitute exists. Examples include land, houses, antiques, works of art, and specialized labor contracts. In contrast, when breach involves the sale of goods for which close substitutes exist, courts typically award damages as the remedy. The victim can use the damages to purchase substitute performance. Examples include new cars, wheat, televisions, and stock in public companies.

To understand the role of substitution, consider two contrasting examples. First, the Apex ticket agency breaks its promise to supply a pair of opera tickets, so the customer has to pay more to purchase equivalent tickets from a "scalper" on the night of the performance. The tickets are equivalent, so the difference in their price perfectly measures the expectation damages. Second, assume that a dealer in rare books breaks his promise to sell the only manuscript copy of William Faulkner's *The Sound and the Fury* to a wealthy collector. The value of this unique manuscript is highly subjective. The court cannot determine subjective value accurately. The computation of expectation damages in this case is highly imperfect. Consequently, the court may order the dealer to deliver the manuscript to the collector.

In general, the error in the court's estimation of expectation damages decreases as the ease of substitution increases for the promised performance. The error decreases because the court can award damages at a level enabling the victim to purchase a substitute for the promised performance. When a good has a close substitute that is readily available in the market, no one is likely to value the good at much more than the price of the available substitute.

In contrast, the remedy of specific performance gives the promisee the good itself, rather than its value. By adopting the remedy of specific performance for breach of promise to deliver unique goods, courts avoid the impossible task of determining the

---

[11] This section is based on material in Ulen, *The Efficiency of Specific Performance: Toward a Unified Theory of Contract Remedies*, 83 MICH. L. REV. 358 (1984).

[12] Sometimes the court orders the promisor to do something similar to what was promised, and sometimes the court forbids the promisor from performing with anyone other than the promisee.

promisee's subjective valuation. Later we compare the advantages and disadvantages of damages and specific performance.

7. Party-Designed Remedies: Liquidated Damages

7. Party-Designed Remedies: Liquidated Damages   Contracts often specify the remedy for breaching one of their terms. The contract might stipulate a sum of money that the promise-breaker will pay to the innocent party ("liquidated damages"). Alternatively, the parties may leave valuable assets on deposit with a third party and specify that the assets should be given to the victim in the event of a breach ("performance bonds"). Or the parties may specify a process for resolving disputes between them, such as arbitration by the International Chamber of Commerce.

Courts examine terms specifying remedies more skeptically and critically than other terms in contracts. Instead of enforcing terms specifying remedies, courts sometimes set the terms aside and substitute court-designed remedies. To illustrate, sellers in America frequently present buyers with a form contract stipulating that disputes will be resolved by arbitration in the seller's home city. Thus, a manufacturer in New York City offers a contract to a buyer in Los Angeles specifying that disputes will be resolved by the American Arbitration Association in New York City. If the buyer sues the seller in a California court, the court will be reluctant to concede jurisdiction to the arbitrator in New York City.

The common law and civil law traditions differ with respect to enforcing penalty clauses in contracts. A common law tradition prevents courts from enforcing terms stipulating damages that exceed the actual harm caused by breach. Courts call a term a "penalty" when it stipulates damages exceeding the actual harm caused by breach. Courts call a term "liquidated damages" when it stipulates damages that do not exceed the actual harm caused by breach. (A "liquid asset" is money or easily converted to money.) The common law tradition enforces liquidated damages and withholds enforcement of penalties. In contrast, courts in civil law countries tend not to object to penalties as such. Courts in civil law countries show more willingness to enforce contract penalties or to reduce them without setting them aside.

Some economists now believe that the civil law countries are right to enforce penalty clauses. Stipulation of damages exceeding the requirements for compensation can serve two functions. First, the punitive element may be considered as payment on an insurance contract written in favor of the innocent party by the breaching party.[13] This situation arises when one party to the contract places a high subjective valuation on performance of the contract, and the other party is the best possible insurer against its loss.

To illustrate, consider professors Goetz and Scott's delightful example of the Anxious Alumnus. An alumnus of the University of Virginia charters a bus to carry his friends to the site of an important basketball tournament where his college team will play. The alumnus is anxious about mishaps. Suppose the bus breaks down; suppose inclement weather prevents the bus from proceeding; or suppose traffic is so heavy that the fans do not arrive in time. He values performance of the contract to deliver him to the game at far more than the price he has paid to hire the bus, yet the subjective value

---

[13] See Charles Goetz and Robert Scott, *Liquidated Damages Penalties and the Just Compensation Principle: Some Notes on an Enforcement Model of Efficient Breach*, 77 COLUM. L. REV. 554 (1977).

is too speculative for courts to measure accurately. So the bus company agrees to pay the alumnus a stipulated penalty in the event of the bus company's breach. In exchange, the alumnus agrees to pay the bus company a price for renting the bus that exceeds the usual price. The difference between the contract price and the usual price represents the premium on an insurance policy written by the bus company in favor of the alumnus. The insurance policy compensates the alumnus for his subjective losses in the event that the bus company's fault prevents him from attending the basketball game.

A second reason for enforcing penalty clauses is that they often convey information about the promisor's reliability. To illustrate, consider a contract that specifies the date for completing a construction project. Perhaps the builder is certain of her ability to complete performance by the specified date, but the buyer doubts the builder's ability to meet the deadline. If the builder promises to pay a large penalty for late construction, she signals her certainty about finishing on time. A penalty clause may be the cheapest way for the builder to communicate credibility to the buyer.

> **QUESTION 7.5:** Earlier we explained that specific performance is the usual remedy for breach of a contract to deliver goods for which no close substitutes exist, whereas damages are the usual remedy when close substitutes exist. Use the "closeness of substitutes" to explain why the death of an artist releases his estate from any contracts that he signed to paint portraits, whereas the death of a house painter does not release her estate from contracts that she signed to paint houses.

> **QUESTION 7.6:** Restitution is usually inadequate to compensate the victim. What practical reasons do courts have for using restitution as a remedy?

> **QUESTION 7.7:** Assume that a swindler must disgorge her profits if she gets caught. In order to make swindling unprofitable (expected value of swindling equals zero), how high must the probability of getting caught be?

> **QUESTION 7.8:** Can you describe conditions when specific performance is an impossible remedy? Can you describe conditions when specific performance is an unfair remedy to a third party? (Hint: Suppose the dealer in New York breached his contract and sold Faulkner's manuscript to someone else.)

B. Models of Remedies

Having described the remedies for breach of contract, we now analyze them. An economic analysis of remedies models their effects upon behavior. Remedies affect many kinds of behavior, but we cannot model all of them.[14] Our analysis concentrates upon these three:

---

[14] Here is a partial list of affected behaviors: (1) searching for trading partners; (2) negotiating exchanges; (3) drafting contracts (explicitness); (4) keeping or breaking promises; (5) taking precaution against events causing breach; (6) acting in reliance upon promises; (7) acting to mitigate damages caused by broken promises and; (8) resolving disputes caused by broken promises.

1. the promisor's decision to breach or perform,

2. the promisor's investment in performing, and

3. the promisee's investment in reliance upon the promise.

1. Efficient Breach and Performance   Sometimes breaching a contract is more efficient than performing. Breaching is more efficient than performing when the costs of performing exceed the benefits to all parties. The costs of performing exceed the benefits when a contingency materializes that makes the resources needed for performance more valuable in an alternative use.

Two types of contingencies reorder the value of resources. First, an *unfortunate* contingency increases the cost of performance. For example, a crippling strike imposes prohibitive costs on timely completion of a construction project. Consequently, the resources needed to complete construction on time can be put to more valuable use in another construction project unaffected by the strike. Second, a *fortunate* contingency makes nonperformance even more profitable than performance. For example, the seller who promises to deliver a good to a buyer might discover a third person who values it even more. We will discuss each type of contingency in turn.

a. Unfortunate Contingency   We modeled an unfortunate contingency in the preceding chapter by using the agency game. In the relevant version of the agency game, the agent (second player) promises to cooperate with the principal (first player). When making the promise, the future cost of cooperating remains uncertain. The cost of cooperating might be low or high. Low costs are likely and high costs are unlikely. High costs of performing are an unfortunate contingency that makes breach efficient.

Figure 7.2, which reproduces Figure 6.3 from the preceding chapter, depicts these payoffs in a matrix. Cooperating sometimes costs the agent zero and sometimes costs 1.5. The first column indicates the payoffs when cooperation costs zero, and the second column indicates payoffs when cooperation costs 1.5. The third column indicates the payoffs from appropriation.

Figure 7.2 describes payoffs when the parties do *not* have an enforceable contract. If the principal invests, then the agent receives more from appropriating than cooperating. Consequently, the agent's best move is to appropriate. The principal, who anticipates that the agent will appropriate, has no legal remedy. Consequently, the principal's best move is "don't invest." Thus, absence of an enforceable contract in Figure 7.2 prevents the parties from cooperating.

		Second player (agent)		
		Cooperating (costs 0)	Cooperating (costs 1.5)	Appropriate
First player (principal)	Invest	.5, .5	−1.0, .5	1.0, −1.0
	Don't invest	0, 0	0, 0	0, 0

FIGURE 7.2 Agency game with variable cooperation costs and without contract.

		Second player (agent)		
		Performing (costs 0)	Performing (costs 1.5)	Breach & pay damages
First player (principal)	Invest (contract)	.5, .5	– 1.0, .5	– .5, .5
	Don't invest (no contract)	0, 0	0, 0	0, 0

FIGURE 7.3 Agency game with contract and variable cooperation costs.

The payoffs in the agency game *with* an enforceable contract are shown in Figure 7.3, which reproduces Figure 6.4 from the preceding chapter. If the agent performs, then the principal's net payoff equals .5, as shown in columns one and two of Figure 7.2 and Figure 7.3. The agent may perform voluntarily to satisfy the contract, in which case columns one and two illustrate keeping the contract. Alternatively, the agent may perform involuntarily to satisfy a court order, in which case columns one and two illustrate the remedy of specific performance for breach. The remedy of expectation damages puts the principal in the same position as if the agent had performed. In column three, the principal's net payoff after breach and damages equals .5, so column three depicts expectation damages.

Consider whether the principal in Figure 7.3 maximizes profits by investing or not investing. The first row in the figure indicates that the principal receives .5 from investing, regardless of whether the agent performs or breaches. Alternatively, the second row in the figure indicates that the principal receives a payoff of zero from not investing. The principal maximizes his or her payoff by investing.

Now consider whether the agent in Figure 7.3 maximizes profits by performing or breaching. If the cost of performance is low, the agent's best move is to perform, which pays .5. If the cost of performing is high, the agent's best move depends upon the remedy for breach. Damages and specific performance yield different decisions. First consider the remedy of damages. The remedy of damages gives the agent a choice between performing or breaching and paying damages. The agent's payoff from performing at high cost in Figure 7.3 equals –1.0. Alternatively, the agent's payoff from breaching and paying damages equals – .5. Thus, the agent in Figure 7.3 breaches and pays damages whenever the cost of performance is high.

Now consider the remedy of specific performance. This remedy gives the principal a right to the agent's performance, regardless of its cost. If the principal asserts this right, then the agent will be forced to perform even when the costs of performance are high. If the principal in Figure 7.3 forces the agent to perform at high costs, the agent receives –1.0 and the principal receives .5.

Instead of exercising this right, however, the principal might respond to the unfortunate contingency by renegotiating the contract. If renegotiations succeed, the principal will agree to accept damages in exchange for allowing the agent to breach. When the agent breaches, the joint payoffs equal zero in Figure 7.3. Alternatively, if renegotiations fail, the principal will exercise his or her right to performance. The joint payoffs for performing at high cost equal − 1.0 + .5 in Figure 7.3. The difference in joint payoffs between performing at high cost and breaching equals the surplus from successful renegotiations. The surplus from successful renegotiations in Figure 7.3 thus equals $0 - (-1.0 + .5) = .5$.

Successful renegotiation allows the parties to share the surplus of .5. We discussed the division of a bargaining surplus at length in Chapter 4. Rationality, alone, does not generally prescribe a division of the surplus. Consider a reasonable way to divide the surplus. Without renegotiating the contract, the principal can force the agent to perform, which yields a payoff of .5 to the principal. The principal must receive at least .5 in order to benefit from renegotiating the contract. In addition to .5, the principal will want a share of the surplus. A reasonable division of the surplus gives half of it, or .25, to each player. Consequently, a reasonable renegotiation of the contract gives the principal .5 + .25. The agent pays .75 to the principal in exchange for not exercising his or her right to specific performance. (Can you demonstrate that this solution also gives the agent the payoff that he or she can get independently plus half the surplus from cooperation?[15])

Efficiency requires the players to choose the actions that maximize the sum of the payoffs to the principal and agent. The sum of the payoffs is found by adding the two numbers in each cell in Figure 7.3. It is easy to see that performing at low cost is more efficient than breaching, whereas breaching is more efficient than performing at high cost. We have shown that the remedy of damages causes the agent to perform at low cost and to breach rather than performing at high cost. In contrast, the remedy of specific performance causes the agent to perform at low cost, and the agent sometimes breaches and sometimes performs at high cost. The agent performs at high cost when renegotiations fail. Consequently, the damage remedy is always efficient, whereas specific performance is sometimes inefficient.

The difference in efficiency between the two remedies is easy to understand. The remedy of damages gives the promisor the choice of performing or breaching and paying damages. The promisor can choose the cheaper alternative.[16] In contrast, the remedy of specific performance gives the promisee the right to performance, regardless of its costs. Exercising this right in the wrong circumstances causes the inefficiency. To avoid the inefficient exercise of the right to specific performance, the parties must succeed in renegotiating the contract. Successful renegotiation can restore efficiency to the decision to breach. As long as the principal and agent can renegotiate successfully, the damage remedy affects distribution but not efficiency.

You should already know this conclusion about renegotiations from studying the positive Coase theorem in Chapter 4. According to the positive Coase theorem, private bargaining under zero transaction costs always succeeds in allocating resources efficiently. Given zero transaction costs, the law influences distribution but not efficiency. We have just applied the Coase theorem to contracts. We found that the agent will breach efficiently, regardless of the rule of law, provided that renegotiations succeed. Given costless renegotiations, the legal remedy for breach of contract influences distribution but not efficiency.

---

[15] Without renegotiation, the agent will be forced to perform at high costs, which yields the agent a payoff equal to –1.0. A reasonable renegotiation gives the agent half the surplus, or .25. Therefore, the agent's payoff after renegotiation should equal $-1.0 + .25 = -.75$.

[16] Recall that perfect expectation damages internalize the full cost of breach to the promisor. Consequently, the promisor chooses the cheaper alternative based upon *social costs*, as required for efficiency.

b. Fortunate Contingency Now we apply this line of argument to a *fortunate* contingency. Assume that person *A* values living in his house at $90,000, and person *B* values living in *A*'s house at $110,000. *A* promises to sell the house to *B* for $100,000, which will create a surplus of $20,000. Before completing the sale, however, person *C* appears on the scene and offers to buy the house from *A*. *C* values the house at $126,000. *C* offers to pay $118,000 for the house. *C*'s appearance creates a new, more profitable alternative to the original contract. Transferring the house from *A*, who values it at $90,000, to *C*, who values it at $126,000, creates a surplus of $36,000. Figure 7.4 summarizes these numbers in the first column, which is labeled "Value placed on house."

Assume that the appearance of *C* causes *A* to breach the contract by refusing to sell the house to *B*. *B* sues *A*. Consider the payoffs to the three parties when the law gives *B* no remedy, thus allowing *A* to sell the house to *C*. *A*'s payoff equals the difference between the value of the house to him ($90,000) and the sale price to *C* ($118,000), or $28,000. *B*'s payoff equals zero. *C*'s payoff equals the difference between the purchase price ($118,000) and the value of the house to her ($126,000), or $8,000. Figure 7.4 summarizes these numbers in the second column, which is labeled "Distribution of surplus if no remedy."

Now assume that the courts respond to *B*'s suit against *A*'s breach by the remedy of specific performance. Specific performance is an order from the court for *A* to sell the house to *B* for $100,000 as promised. *A*'s payoff equals the difference between the value of the house to him ($90,000) and the sale price to *B* ($100,000), or $10,000. *B* will presumably resell the house to *C* for $118,000. *B*'s payoff equals the difference between her purchase price ($100,000) and her sale price ($118,000), or $18,000. *C*'s payoff equals the difference between the purchase price ($118,000) and the value of the house to her ($126,000), or $8,000. Figure 7.4 summarizes these numbers in the third column, which is labeled "Distribution of surplus if remedy is specific performance."

Finally, assume that the courts respond to *B*'s suit against *A*'s breach by the remedy of damages. *A* breaches the contract with *B* and sells the house to *C* for $118,000. *A*'s payoff equals the difference between the value of the house to him ($90,000) and the sale price to *B* ($118,000), or $28,000. Having obtained a surplus of $28,000, *A* must now pay damages to compensate *B* for breaching the contract. The extent of the damages will determine the division of the surplus of $28,000 between *A* and *B*. Assume that the damages have been designed by the court to put *B* in the position she expected to be in if *A* had delivered the house and *B* had kept it. *B* expected to get a house that she values at $110,000 for a price of $100,000, yielding an expected surplus of $10,000. By this calculation, *B*'s expectation damages equal $10,000. Expectation damages produce the result that *A* gets $18,000 in surplus, *B* gets $10,000 in cash, and *C* gets a surplus of $8,000 on purchasing the house. Figure 7.4 summarizes these numbers in the fourth column, which is labeled "Distribution of surplus if remedy is expectation damages."

Now let us compare the remedies of specific performance and expectation damages. Economic efficiency requires allocating resources to their highest-valued use. *C* values the use of the house more than *A* or *B*. Thus, an efficient remedy requires that *C* get the house. With specific performance, *C* buys the house from *B*, and *B* gets more of the surplus than *A*. With expectation damages, *C* buys the house from *A*, and *A* gets more

	Value placed on house	Distribution of surplus if no remedy	Distribution of surplus if remedy is specific performance	Distribution of surplus if remedy is expectation damages
Person A	$90,000	$28,000	$10,000	$18,000
Person B	$110,000	$0	$18,000	$10,000
Person C	$126,000	$8,000	$8,000	$8,000
Total		$36,000	$36,000	$36,000

FIGURE 7.4 Remedies.

of the surplus than *B*. Either court-designed remedy creates efficient incentives for allocating the house, but the remedies differ in the pathway of the sale and the distribution of the surplus from exchange.

Recall the positive Coase theorem from Chapter 4. According to the positive Coase theorem, private bargaining under zero transaction costs will allocate resources efficiently regardless of the law. Given zero transaction costs, the law affects distribution but not efficiency. Figure 7.4 expresses this result. As long as *A*, *B*, and *C* can bargain successfully at zero transaction costs, the damage remedy affects distribution but not efficiency.

The remedy of expectation damages gives the promisor a choice between performing or breaching and paying damages. The distribution of the surplus favors the promisor when the remedy for breach is damages. In contrast, the remedy of specific performance gives the promisor no choice but to perform. The distribution of the surplus favors the promisee when the remedy for breach is specific performance.

The Coase theorem implies that court-designed remedies differ with respect to efficiency only when transaction costs are positive. When transaction costs are positive, the most efficient court-designed remedy minimizes the transaction costs of moving the good to its highest-valued use. Applied to our example, the most efficient court-designed remedy minimizes the transaction costs of moving ownership of the house from *A* to *C*. Figure 7.4 assumes the move can be made with zero transaction costs, which implies that both remedies are equally efficient.

Now consider the change caused by positive transaction costs. The two relevant forms of transactions costs are real-estate sales and dispute resolution. In the United States, realtors' fees for the sale of a house conventionally equal 6% of the price.[17] Real-estate transactions in Europe typically do not cost less, although the organization is very different.[18] With these costs in mind, assume that selling the house in Figure 7.4 costs $6,000. Turning from real-estate sales to dispute resolution, differences in the organization of the bar from one country to another cause differences in legal fees.

---

[17] There are other smaller fees such as title insurance and, in some states, lawyer's fees.

[18] In Europe many functions of the real-estate agent and the title company are performed by a notary. European notaries are lawyers with specialized training. In contrast, notaries play an insignificant role in such transactions in the United States.

As a benchmark, consider that the lawyer for a plaintiff typically charges 30% of the damages as legal costs in the United States. With these costs in mind, assume that settling a legal dispute in Figure 7.4 costs $5,000.

Now we apply these costs ($6,000 to sell and $5,000 to resolve disputes) to the two remedies. The remedy of specific performance requires A to settle his dispute with B, which costs $5,000 in legal fees by assumption. A then sells the house to B, which costs $6,000 by assumption. Next, B sells the house to C, which also costs $6,000. Thus, the remedy of specific performance resolves disputes and moves the house from A to C at transaction costs totaling $17,000. Subtracting the transaction costs of $17,000 from the surplus of $36,000 created by transferring the house from A to C yields the net surplus of $19,000. The first row of Figure 7.5 summarizes these numbers.

Now consider the remedy of damages. This remedy allows A to sell the house to C and pay damages to B. A sells the house directly to C at a cost of $6,000. Next, A settles his dispute with B at a cost of $5,000. Thus, the remedy of damages resolves all disputes and moves the house from A to C at a total cost of $11,000. Subtracting transaction costs of $11,000 from the total surplus of $36,000 created by transferring the house from A to C yields a net surplus of $25,000. The second row of Figure 7.5 summarizes these numbers.

In the example illustrated in Figure 7.5, damages save $6,000 in transaction costs relative to specific performance. The savings come from eliminating the sale between B and C. When a contingency arises that makes breach more efficient than performance, the remedy of damages often results in fewer negotiations than the remedy of specific performance. Fewer negotiations result in lower transaction costs.

On the other hand, the negotiations may be simpler when the remedy is specific performance. To see why, consider the task faced by the court when computing damages for A's breach of contract with B. To determine compensatory damages, the court must estimate the value that B places on the house. The subjective valuation of the buyer is difficult for courts to estimate. The buyer's subjective valuation must exceed the sale price, but by how much? Lawyers could use up a lot of money arguing about whether B valued the house at $105,000, $110,000, or $125,000.[19] This uncertainty clouds negotiations by the parties to settle the dispute out of court.

Unlike damages, the remedy of specific performance does not present courts with a problem of valuation. When the court applies this remedy to the example in Figure 7.5, the court orders A to sell the house to B at the *contract price*. The court does not have to set a price. B subsequently decides the price at which she will sell the house to C. The remedy of specific performance leaves prices to markets, not to courts. Leaving prices to markets simplifies negotiations, which saves transaction costs. Some economists think that the problem of valuation by courts is so severe that contract law should adopt specific performance more widely as a remedy.[20]

---

[19] Determining the extent of damages in litigation is a specific form of what economist call the "problem of preference revelation." The general problem is to close the gap between objective prices and subjective values. Economists have had limited success trying to solve this problem.

[20] See Ulen, *The Efficiency of Specific Performance: Toward a Unified Theory of Contract Remedies*, 83 MICH. L. REV. 358 (1984).

Transaction between

	A and B	B and C	A and C	Total	Net surplus
Specific performance	$11,000 (settlement & sale)	$6,000 (sale)	$0	$17,000	$19,000
damages	$5,000 (settlement)	$0	$6,000 (sale)	$11,000	$25,000

FIGURE 7.5 Transaction costs.

QUESTION 7.9: Assume that A values his house at $90,000. B is willing to pay $110,000 for A's house in order to relocate closer to work. (Forget about person C for purposes of this question.) After signing a contract, B's employer announces that the company will move to another city. In view of this fact, the value of the house to B is reduced to $75,000. From an efficiency viewpoint, who should own the house, A or B? How will the parties achieve efficiency in allocating the house if the court enforces the contract?

QUESTION 7.10: Give examples of unfortunate and fortunate contingencies that could make breach of contract more efficient than performance. Give reasons why the parties might not insert explicit terms in the contract to deal with these contingencies, such as a term excusing breach when performance is very costly.

QUESTION 7.11: State the Coase theorem as applied to remedies for breach of contract.

QUESTION 7.12: Assume that a fortunate contingency makes breach efficient for a sales contract, and assume that the parties cannot renegotiate the contract. Explain why the remedy of damages can save transaction costs by reducing the number of sales required to move the good to the person who values it most. Explain why the remedy of specific performance enables the court to avoid the problem of subjective valuations of the good.

C. Investment in Performance and Reliance

In the preceding section, we compared the incentive effects of two different remedies (expectation damages and specific performance) on one kind of behavior (performance or breach). Now we expand the model by considering the incentives effects of several different remedies on two kinds of behavior (performance and reliance). We develop the model through a concrete example.

1. The Waffle Shop Yvonne owns a restaurant for economists that is called the Waffle Shop because of what it serves and whom it serves. Her business prospers so that she needs a larger facility. She enters into a contract with Xavier, a builder, who promises to construct the new restaurant for occupancy on September 1. Xavier knows that events could jeopardize completing the building on time, such as striking plumbers, recalcitrant city inspectors, or foul weather. He can reduce the probability of late completion by working overtime before the plumbers' contract expires, badgering the city inspectors, or accelerating work on the roof.

Figure 7.6 graphs the relationship between Xavier's expenditure on such precautions and the probability that he will perform as promised. The variable x denotes Xavier's expenditure on precaution; the variable p denotes the probability of performing; and $p = p(x)$ denotes the functional relationship between the variables. The probability of performing increases when Xavier spends more on precaution; thus, p is an increasing function of x.

Now we turn from Xavier to Yvonne. Yvonne anticipates a surge in business when she opens the new facility. To accommodate the surge in business, she needs to order more food than she can use in her old restaurant. She would like to order supplementary food for delivery on September 1 to assure continuous service, but she risks disposing of the supplementary food at a loss if the building is not completed on time.

Figure 7.5 graphs the relationship between the size of Yvonne's food order and her profits in September. By definition, profits in September equal total revenues minus total variable costs. Food orders are one cost that Yvonne can vary on short notice. To keep the example simple, we assume that she cannot vary any other costs in September. So the variable y, which denotes Yvonne's expenditure on food orders, also indicates her total variable costs for the month.

Total revenues equal Yvonne's income from selling meals in September. Her income from selling meals depends upon whether she occupies the new building or the old building. If Xavier performs, then Yvonne occupies the new building on September 1 and she enjoys high revenues, as indicated in Figure 7.7 by the curve labeled $R_p(y)$. If Xavier does not perform, then Yvonne remains in the old building on September 1 and she enjoys low revenues, as indicated in Figure 7.7 by the curve labeled $R_{np}(y)$.

Figure 7.7 depicts profits, which equal the difference between total revenues and total variable costs, as the vertical distance between the appropriate total-revenue curve

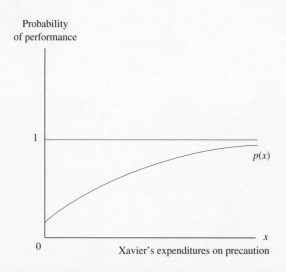

FIGURE 7.6 The direct relationship between levels of precaution and the probability of performance.

and the total-cost curve. The appropriate total-revenue curve depends upon the probability that Xavier finishes the building on time. If Xavier is certain to finish the building on time, then $R_p(y)$ is the appropriate total-revenue curve. Conversely, if Xavier is certain to finish the building late, then $R_{np}(y)$ is the appropriate total-revenue curve.

Yvonne maximizes profits by maximizing the vertical distance between the appropriate total-revenue curve and the total-cost curve. When $R_p(y)$ is the appropriate total-revenue curve, the high level of reliance denoted y_1 in Figure 7.7 maximizes Yvonne's profits. When $R_{np}(y)$ is the appropriate total revenue curve, the low level of reliance denoted y_0 in Figure 7.7 maximizes Yvonne's profits.

Increasing the food order above y_0 is risky. The farther y rises above y_0 (up to the maximum y_1), the more Yvonne's profits increase if Xavier performs, and the more Yvonne's profits decrease if Xavier breaches.

The concrete example of the Waffle Shop captures two general truths. First, the promisor can take costly precautions that increase the probability that he or she will perform as promised. Second, the more the promisee relies upon the promise, the greater the profits if the promise is kept, and the lower the profits if the promise is broken.

2. Efficiency Efficiency requires choosing precaution and reliance to maximize Yvonne's profits minus Xavier's costs. First consider precaution. More precaution by Xavier increases his costs and Yvonne's expected profits. Efficiency requires Xavier to balance his costs and her expected profits. Second, consider reliance. Yvonne's expenditures on reliance increase her profits if Xavier performs and decrease her profits if Xavier breaches. Efficiency requires Yvonne to balance the expected gains and losses of reliance.

We restate this verbal account of efficiency in notation. Efficiency requires choosing x and y to maximize Yvonne's expected profits minus Xavier's costs of precaution:

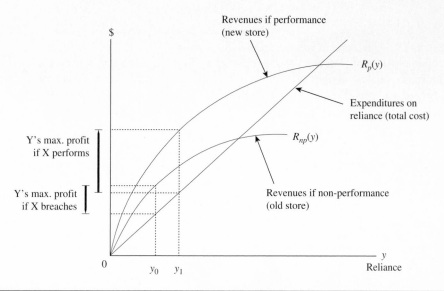

FIGURE 7.7 How a promisee's reliance depends on the probability of a promisor's performance.

maximize $\quad\quad p(x)R_p(y) + [1 - p(x)]R_{np}(y)$ $\quad - \quad y \quad - \quad x$
x,y

$\quad\quad\quad\quad\quad$ Y's expected revenues $\quad\quad\quad\quad\quad$ Y's food $\quad$ X's

$\quad\quad\quad\quad\quad\quad\quad\quad\quad\quad\quad\quad\quad\quad\quad\quad\quad\quad\quad\quad$ orders $\quad$ precaution

$\quad\quad\quad\quad\quad\quad\quad$ Y's expected profits $\quad\quad\quad\quad\quad\quad\quad\quad\quad\quad$ (7.1)

We will explain how to choose x and y to maximize the preceding function. First consider Xavier. He spends x on precaution, which increases the probability $p(x)$ that Yvonne enjoys high revenues equal to $R_p(y)$, rather than low revenues equal to $R_{np}(y)$. Efficiency requires the last dollar that Xavier spends on precaution to increase Yvonne's expected revenues by a dollar, which we write

$\quad\quad$ 1 $\quad\quad\quad\quad\quad\quad = \quad\quad\quad\quad p'(x)[R_p(y) - R_{np}(y)]$
$\quad\quad$ marginal expenditure $\quad\quad\quad\quad\quad\quad$ marginal expected
$\quad\quad$ on precaution $\quad\quad\quad\quad\quad\quad\quad\quad\quad\quad$ revenues $\quad\quad\quad\quad\quad\quad$ (7.2)

(If you know calculus, note that setting the partial derivative of equation 1 with respect to x equal to zero yields equation 7.2.)

Second, consider Yvonne. Increasing her expenditure y beyond y_0 increases her revenues $R_p(y)$ with probability p and decreases her revenues $R_{np}(y)$ with probability $1 - p$. Efficiency requires the last dollar that Yvonne spends in reliance to increase her expected revenues by a dollar, which we write

$\quad\quad$ 1 $\quad\quad\quad\quad = \quad\quad\quad pR_p{}'y \quad\quad\quad + \quad\quad (1 - p)R_{np}{}'y$
$\quad\quad$ marginal reliance $\quad\quad\quad\quad\quad$ expected increase $\quad\quad\quad$ expected decrease
$\quad\quad$ expenditure $\quad\quad\quad\quad\quad\quad\quad$ in revenues $\quad\quad\quad\quad\quad\quad$ in revenues $\quad\quad\quad$ (7.3)

(If you know calculus, note that setting the partial derivative of equation 7.1 with respect to y equal to zero yields equation 7.3.)

Equations 2 and 3 determine the values of x and y that maximize equation 7.1. These values, denoted x^* and y^*, are the efficient levels of precaution and reliance. The magnitude of y^* depends upon the probability p that Xavier will perform. If performance is unlikely, then little reliance is efficient, so the efficient value of y is close to y_0. If performance is likely, then heavy reliance is efficient, so the efficient value of y is close to y_1. If the probability of performance is greater than zero and less than 1, then y^* is in-between y_0 and y_1.

3. Damage Measures Consider several different damage measures. Expectation damages D_e put Yvonne in the same position as if Xavier performed. Thus, expectation damages equal the difference between Yvonne's profits if Xavier performs, $R_p(y) - y$, and her actual profits when he breaches, $R_{np}(y) - y$. Thus, we define expectation damages:

$\quad\quad$ D_e $\quad\quad\quad = \quad\quad\quad R_p(y) - R_{np}(y)$
$\quad\quad$ expectation damages $\quad\quad$ performance revenues minus actual revenues $\quad\quad$ (7.4)

Opportunity-cost damages D_o put Yvonne in the same position after breach as if she had signed the best alternative contract. Yvonne signed the actual contract because she found its terms at least as good as the best alternative contract. To keep the model simple, we will say nothing explicit about the best alternative contract.

Reliance damages D_r put Yvonne in the same position after breach as if she had not signed a construction contract with Xavier or anyone else. If she had not signed a construction contract, she would have spent y_o on food and sold it in the old restaurant, thus receiving profits equal to $R_{np}(y_o) - y_o$. She actually spent y on food, Xavier breached, and she received profits equal to $R_{np}(y) - y$. The difference in profits equals her reliance damages:

$$D_r \qquad = \qquad [R_{np}(y_o) - y_o] \qquad - \qquad [R_{np}(y) - y]$$

reliance damages $\qquad$ profits if no contract $\qquad$ actual profits $\qquad\qquad$ (7.5)

Now we compare the three damage measures. Performance on the contract that she actually signed is at least as good for Yvonne as performance on the best alternative contract. So expectation damages are at least as high as opportunity-cost damages: $D_e > D_o$. The best alternative contract is at least as good for Yvonne as no contract. So opportunity-cost damages are at least as high as reliance damages: $D_o > D_r$. In summary we have:

$$D_e > D_o > D_r \qquad\qquad (7.6)$$

4. Incentives for Efficient Precaution   We described efficient behavior in words and notation, and then we described alternative measures of damages. Now we consider which measure of damages creates incentives for the promisor and promisee to behave efficiently.

Xavier bears the full cost of his own precaution x. Xavier also bears liability for damages D with probability $1 - p(x)$. The sum, $x + [1 - p(x)D]$ equals Xavier's expected costs. Xavier chooses x to minimize his expected costs:

minimize $\qquad x \qquad + \qquad [1 - p(x)D]$

$x \qquad\qquad$ precaution $\qquad\qquad\qquad$ expected liability $\qquad$ (7.7)

Figure 7.8 depicts Xavier's problem. As the figure illustrates, Xavier's costs are high if he takes *no* precaution because his expected damages are large. His costs are also high if he takes *excessive* precaution, because it costs more than it saves in liability. Xavier minimizes* his costs by taking precaution at an intermediate level, denoted x^* in Figure 7.8, where the expected cost curve falls to its lowest point. Xavier's expected cost curve falls to its lowest point where an additional dollar spent on precaution reduces his expected liability by a dollar. In other words, his costs are minimized when the marginal cost of precaution equals the marginal reduction in expected liability:

$\qquad 1 \qquad\qquad\qquad = \qquad\qquad p'(x)D$

$\qquad$ marginal cost $\qquad\qquad\qquad$ marginal reduction

$\qquad$ of precaution $\qquad\qquad\qquad$ in expected liability $\qquad\qquad$ (7.8)

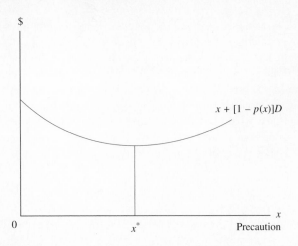

FIGURE 7.8 A promisor's expected costs of precaution and of breach.

(If you know calculus, note that setting the partial derivative of equation 7 with respect to y equal to zero yields equation 7.8.)

We can compare the incentive effects of alternative measures of damages by substituting their definition for D into equation 7.8. First consider expectation damages D_e as defined by equation 4. Substitute this definition of D_e for D in equation 8 to obtain

$$\underset{\substack{\text{marginal cost of}\\\text{precaution}}}{1} \qquad = \qquad \underset{\text{marginal expected revenues}}{p'(x)[R_p(y) - R_{np}(y)]} \qquad (7.9)$$

This equation is identical to the efficiency condition in equation 7.2, which proves that expectation damages cause Xavier to take socially efficient precaution in order to minimize his expected costs.

It is easy to see why expectation damages create incentives for efficient precaution by the promisor. Promisors bear the full cost of their precaution. Their incentives are efficient when they also enjoy the full benefit. The full benefit equals any benefit that they receive plus the benefit that the promisees expect to receive. The benefit that promisees expect to receive equals the promisor's liability under expectation damages. Therefore, *expectation damages cause promisors to internalize the benefits of their precaution against breach*, which creates incentives for efficient precaution.

Now consider opportunity-cost damages and reliance damages. According to equation 7.6, expectation damages are at least as high as opportunity-cost damages, and opportunity-cost damages are at least as high as reliance damages. If the three damages are equal, then each of them provides incentives for efficient precaution by the promisor. If expectation damages exceed an alternative measure, then the alternative provides incentives for deficient precaution by the promisor. "Incentives for deficient precaution" means that the promisor minimizes expected costs by taking precaution below the efficient level. We summarize our conclusions as follows.

Promisor's Incentives for Precaution Against Breach

expectation		*opportunity-cost*		*reliance*
D_e	$=$	D_o	$=$	D_r
efficient		efficient		efficient
D_e	$>$	D_o	$>$	D_r
efficient		deficient		deficient

Figure 7.9 depicts these facts. Increasing the expected damages D increases Xavier's incentive to take precaution against events that cause him to breach. As damages increase from D_r to D_o, and from D_o to D_e, Xavier's cost-minimizing level of precaution increases from x_r to x_o and from x_o to x_e.

It is not hard to understand why awarding less than expectation damages provides incentives for deficient precaution. As explained, expectation damages cause the promisor to internalize the expected benefits of precaution. Consequently, awarding less than expectation damages causes the promisor to externalize part of the expected benefits of precaution. For example, opportunity-cost damages externalize the part of the promisee's benefit from performance of the actual contract that the promisee could not obtain from the best alternative contract.

QUESTION 7.13: Explain why perfect expectation damages generally create incentives for efficient precaution by the promisor. Explain why perfect opportunity-cost or reliance damages do not generally create incentives for efficient precaution by the promisor.

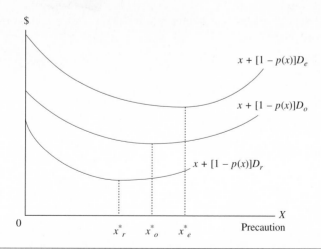

FIGURE 7.9 How precaution varies with the size of damages for breach of contract.

QUESTION 7.14: Assume that the remedy for breach is specific performance.

a. Use Figure 7.9 to find the amount of precaution that Xavier would take if specific performance costs the promisor the same as expectation damages.

b. Use Figure 7.9 to describe the amount of precaution that Xavier would take if specific performance costs the promisor more than expectation damages. (What are you implicitly assuming about renegotiation between the promisor and promisee?)

QUESTION 7.15: Assume that disgorgement damages are the remedy for breach, and assume that disgorgement damages exceed expectation damages. Use Figure 7.9 to describe the amount of precaution that Xavier would take.

5. Incentives for Efficient Reliance   We explained that the efficiency of the promisor's incentives for *precaution* depend upon the *level* of damages ("total damages"). Expectation damages provide incentives for efficient precaution by the promisor against breach, whereas opportunity-cost damages and reliance damages provide deficient incentives. Now we explain how the law creates incentives for efficient reliance by the promisee. We will show that the efficiency of the promisee's incentives for *reliance* depends upon *changes* in damages caused by reliance ("marginal damages").

Yvonne invests y in reliance; she receives revenues $R_p(y)$ with probability p; and she receives revenues $R_{np}(y)$ and damages D with probability $1 - p$. The probability-weighted sum equals her expected net profits. Yvonne chooses y to maximize her expected net profits:

$$\underset{y}{\text{maximize}} \quad \underset{\text{expected revenues and damages}}{pR_p(y) \; + \; (1 - p)(R_{np}(y) + D)} \quad - \quad \underset{\text{reliance}}{y} \quad (7.10)$$

Figure 7.10 depicts Yvonne's maximization problem. Yvonne's expected net profits are low if she does not rely ($y = 0$), because she does not order enough food in advance. Her expected net profits are also low if she relies excessively, because she orders too much food in advance. Yvonnes maximizes her expected net profits by relying at an intermediate level, denoted $y\~$ in Figure 7.10, where the expected-net-profits curve reaches to its highest point. Yvonne's expected-net-profits curve reaches its highest point where an additional dollar spent in reliance increases her expected revenues and damages by a dollar. In other words, her net profits are maximized when the marginal cost of reliance equals the marginal increase in expected revenues and damages:

$$\underset{\substack{\text{marginal cost} \\ \text{of reliance}}}{1} \quad = \quad \underset{\substack{\text{expected marginal} \\ \text{revenues}}}{pR_p(y) + (1 - p)(R_{np}(y)} \quad + \quad \underset{\substack{\text{expected marginal} \\ \text{damages}}}{(1 - p)D'} \quad (7.11)$$

(If you know calculus, note that setting the partial derivative of equation 7.10 with respect to y equal to zero yields equation 7.11.)

We can compare the incentive effects of alternative measures of damages by substituting their definition for D into equation 7.10. Recall that expectation damages restore the promisee to the position that he or she would have enjoyed if the promise had been kept. In the preceding chapter we defined *perfect* expectation damages as enough money to restore the promisee to the position that he or she would have enjoyed if the promise had been kept and if reliance had been *optimal*. Applied to the Waffle Shop, perfect expectation damages equal the difference between Yvonne's revenues when Xavier performs and her revenues when he breaches, *assuming optimal reliance* ($y = y^*$):

$$
\begin{array}{lcll}
D_e^* & = & R_p(y^*) & - & R_{np}(y^*) \\
\text{perfect expectation} & & \multicolumn{2}{l}{\text{expected revenues minus actual}} \\
\text{damages} & & \multicolumn{2}{l}{\text{revenues, given optimal reliance}} & (7.12)
\end{array}
$$

Notice that equation 7.11 does *not* contain Yvonne's actual reliance y. It contains her optimal reliance y^*. Consequently, Yvonne's expected recovery of damages does not vary with her actual reliance. An additional dollar of reliance y by Yvonne does not change the damages that she receives. "Marginal damages," denoted D', means the increase in damages when Yvonne spends another dollar in reliance. Thus, Yvonne's marginal damages equal zero: $D' = 0$. Substitute $D' = 0$ into equation 7.11 to obtain

$$
\begin{array}{lcll}
1 & = & pR_p y & + & (1 - p)R_{np} y \\
\text{marginal reliance} & & \text{expected increase} & & \text{expected decrease} \\
\text{expenditure} & & \text{in revenues} & & \text{in revenues} & (7.13)
\end{array}
$$

Equation 7.13 is identical to the efficiency condition in equation 7.3, which proves that perfect expectation damages cause Yvonne to rely at the socially efficient level.

It is easy to see why perfect expectation damages create incentives for efficient reliance by the promisee. Efficiency requires the person who increases risk to bear it. The promisee's reliance increases risk, specifically the risk that breach will destroy the value of the promisee's investment. Perfect expectation damages remain constant when the promisee relies more. Thus, the risk caused by more reliance remains with the promisee. In brief, perfect expectation damages cause the promisee to internalize the risk of more reliance.

To illustrate, we contrast perfect and imperfect expectation damages in Figure 7.11. The curve labeled "no damages" indicates Yvonne's expected net profits when $D = 0$. Shift this curve up by the amount of perfect expectation damages, $D = D_e^* = D(y^*)$, to obtain the curve labeled "perfect damages." Perfect damages remain constant as reliance increases, so $D' = 0$. The curve labeled "perfect damages" in Figure 7.11 achieves its high point when Yvonne relies optimally: $y = y^*$.

Finally, the curve labeled "imperfect damages" in Figure 7.11 indicates Yvonne's expected net profits when damages change as a function of reliance: $D = D(y)$.[21]

---

[21] Three facts explain the shape of the imperfect-damages curve as depicted in Figure 7.11. (1) Perfect damages exceed imperfect damages at deficient levels of reliance: $D_e^* > D(y)$ for $y < y^*$; (2) perfect damages equal imperfect damages at the efficient level of reliance: $D_e^* = D(y)$ for $y = y^*$; (3) imperfect damages exceed perfect damages for excessive levels of reliance: $D(y) > f D_e^*$ for $y > y^*$.

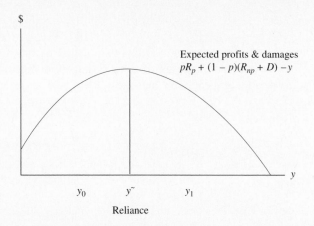

FIGURE 7.10 Promisee's expected net profits.

Notice that imperfect damages $D(y)$ increase as Yvonne's reliance y increases, so marginal damages exceed zero: $D' > 0$. This fact causes Yvonne's expected-net-profit curve to shift to the right for values of y above $y*$, as depicted in Figure 7.11. As a result of the shift to the right, Yvonne's expected-net-profit curve achieves its maximum at a level of reliance, denoted $y\tilde{}$, that exceeds the efficient reliance $y*$.[22] In brief, Figure 7.11 illustrates that positive marginal damages ($D' > 0$) cause over-reliance ($y > y*$).

QUESTION 7.16: Why does the "no-damages" curve achieve its maximum in Figure 7.11 for the same value of y as the "perfect-damages" curve? Explain why "no damages" provides efficient incentives for reliance by Yvonne and inefficient incentives for precaution by Xavier.

QUESTION 7.17: The "imperfect-damages" curve in Figure 7.11 lies below the "perfect-damages" curve for values of y smaller than $y*$. The opposite is true for values of y larger than $y*$. Consider a composite consisting of the imperfect-damages curve for values of y less than $y*$ and the perfect-damages curve for values of y greater than $y*$:

$$D = D(y) \text{ for } y < y*;$$

$$D = D(y*) \text{for } y > y*.$$

Assume that Yvonne's expected profits correspond to this composite curve. Thus, Yvonne receives compensation for actual damages up to a maximum value of $D(y*)$. Given this composite measure of damages, what level of reliance y maximizes Yvonne's expected profits?

---

[22] To prove that Yvonne's reliance increases when $D¢$ increases from zero to a positive number, notice that $D' > 0$ implies that the right side of equation 11 exceeds the efficiency condition given by equation 3 for given value of y.

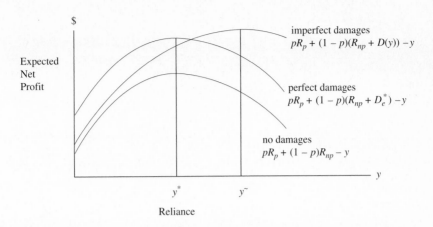

FIGURE 7.11 How reliance varies with marginal damages for breach of contract.

Question 7.18: Assume that the parties cannot renegotiate after breach. Also assume that the remedy for breach is specific performance. Specific performance guarantees that Xavier will perform. Will Yvonne set her reliance y equal to y_0, y^*, or y_1 in Figures 7.7 and 7.11? Explain your answer.

Question 7.19: Assume that disgorgement damages are the remedy for breach. Disgorgement damages depend upon the profits earned by the promisor as a result of breaching. Consequently, disgorgement damages do not vary with the promisee's reliance ($D\mathcal{C} = 0$). Use Figure 7.11 to explain the incentive effects of disgorgement damages upon Yvonne's reliance.

6. Overreliance in Law The victim of breach receives no compensation for overreliance. Consequently, the promisee has a strong incentive to avoid overrelying. Various legal doctrines define overreliance. An important doctrine in common law concerns foreseeability. Foreseeable reliance by the promisee equals the amount that the promisor could reasonably expect under the circumstances. Unforeseeable reliance by the promisee exceeds the amount that the promisor could reasonably expect under the circumstances.

The famous case of *Hadley v. Baxendale* established the principle that overreliance is unforeseeable and, consequently, noncompensable. To summarize the facts of this case, Hadley owned a grist mill, the main shaft of the mill broke, and Hadley hired a shipping firm where Baxendale worked to transport the shaft for repair. The shipper did not deliver the shaft expeditiously. The damaged shaft was the only one in Hadley's mill, which remained closed awaiting return of the repaired shaft. After the tardy return of the repaired shaft, Hadley sued for breach of contract and asked for damages equal to his profits lost while his mill remained closed awaiting the return of the shaft. The defendant claimed that the measure of damages (if there was a breach) should be much less. The shipper assumed that Hadley, like most millers, kept a spare shaft. The shipper contended that Hadley did not inform him of the special urgency in getting the shaft repaired.[23] The shipper prevailed in court on the damages issue, and the case subsequently stands for the principle that recovery for breach of contract is limited to the foreseeable damages.[24]

QUESTION 7.20: Explain the difference between foreseeable events and events actually foreseen.

QUESTION 7.21: Assume that you have taken some very valuable photographs. You want to give notice of this fact to the developer so that she will be liable for exceptional damages in the event that she damages the film. How could you succeed in giving notice for purposes of the law?

QUESTION 7.22: Restraining reliance before breach reduces the harm that it causes. "Mitigating" damages after breach also reduces the harm. In the Waffle Shop case, for example, Yvonne can mitigate harm by reselling the supplemental food order to another restaurant. The common law requires the promisee to mitigate damages. Specifically, the promisee must take *reasonable* actions to reduce losses from the promisor's breach. Describe the efficient amount of mitigation. How could the mitigation requirement create an incentive for efficient mitigation?

Conclusion to Part I

The first part of this chapter concerned the question, "What should be the remedy for breaking an enforceable promise?" We answered, "The remedy should provide efficient incentives." The efficiency of the promisor's incentives for *precaution* depends upon the *level* of damages ("total damages"). Expectation damages internalize the benefits of the promisor's precaution against breach, whereas opportunity-cost and reliance damages externalize some benefits. In contrast, the efficiency of the promisee's incentives for *reliance* depends upon *changes* in damages caused by reliance ("marginal damages"). Perfect expectation damages do not increase when reliance increases beyond the efficient level. Consequently, perfect expectation damages make the promisee internalize the risk of overreliance.

---

[23] Hadley contended that he *did* tell the shipper that repairs were urgent because this was his only shaft.

[24] The rule in *Hadley v. Baxendale* may be found in *Restatement (Second) of Contracts* § 351(1) (1979). For some economic writing on the foreseeability rule of *Hadley*, see, for example, Melvin A. Eisenberg, *The Principle of Hadley v. Baxendale*, 80 CAL. L. REV. 563 (1992); Ayres and Gertner, cited in the previous reading note; Jeffrey M. Perloff, *Breach of Contract and the Foreseeability Doctrine of Hadley v. Baxendale*, 10 J. LEGAL STUD. 39 (1981); Richard Epstein, *Beyond Foreseeability: Consequential Damages in the Law of Contract*, 18 J. LEGAL STUD. 105 (1989); and Lucien Bebchuk and Steven Shavell, *Information and the Scope of Liability for Breach of Contract: The Rule of Hadley v. Baxendale*, 7 J. L. ECON. & ORGANIZATION 286 (1991).

PARADOX OF COMPENSATION

Consider this paradox: (1) In order for the injurer to internalize costs, he or she must pay full compensation to the victim. (2) In order for the victim to internalize costs, he or she must receive no compensation for injuries. (3) In private law, compensation paid by the injurer equals compensation received by the victim. Therefore, private law cannot internalize costs for the injurer and the victim as required for efficiency.

In contract law, this paradox takes the following form: (1) In order for the promisor to internalize the benefits of precaution, he or she must pay full compensation to the promisee for breach. (2) In order for the promisee to internalize the costs of reliance, he or she must receive no compensation for breach. (3) In contract law, compensation paid by the promisor for breach equals compensation received by the promisee. Therefore, contract law cannot internalize costs for the promisor and promisee as required for efficiency.

The paradox has a solution. In fact, efficient incentives do not require internalization of total costs. Instead, efficient incentives require the internalization of marginal costs. Perfect expectation damages solve the paradox by setting damages so that the promisor bears the marginal benefits of precaution and the promisee bears the marginal costs of reliance. (Can you explain how perfect expectation damages accomplish this result?)

This paradox points out a problem that afflicts all areas of the law. You already met the paradox of compensation in Chapter 4 when we discussed compensation for the taking of property by the state, and you will meet the paradox again in the next chapter when we consider compensation for accidents.

Table 7.1

REGULATORY DOCTRINES OF CONTRACT LAW

Assumption	*If violated, contract doctrine*
A. INDIVIDUAL RATIONALITY	
1. stable, well-ordered preferences	1. incompetence
2. constrained choice	2. duress; necessity; impossibility
B. TRANSACTION COSTS	
1. spillovers	1. unenforceability of contracts derogating public policy or statutory duty
2. information	2. frustration of purpose; mutual mistake; fraud; failure to disclose;
3. monopoly	3. necessity; unconscionability.

II. FORMATION DEFENSES
AND PERFORMANCE EXCUSES

The second part of this chapter concerns the question, "What promises should be enforced?" Our answer develops the prescription from the preceding chapter, in which we divided contractual obligations into default rules and regulations. Default rules fill gaps in contracts in order to reduce transaction costs. Regulations prescribe terms for contracts in order to correct market failures. The remainder of this chapter analyzes some of the major doctrines that fill gaps and regulate contracts. We will analyze selected doctrines in the order in which they appear in Table 7.1, which categorizes contract regulations as forms of market failure. (Table 7.1 reproduces Table 6.5 in the preceding chapter.)

When defendants invoke these doctrines in contract disputes, they can make two different claims. First, defendants can claim that they have no legal obligation to the plaintiff because no contract exists between them. These claims rely upon "formation defenses." A formation defense asserts that the conditions for creating a contract were not satisfied. To illustrate, a man can argue that his promise to give a gift did not create a legal obligation.

Alternatively, defendants can concede that a contract exists, and then claim that they were excused from performing under the circumstances. These claims rely upon "performance excuses." A performance excuse admits the existence of a contract and denies liability for breach. Liability is typically denied because unusual contingencies prevented performance. To illustrate, a manufacturer may argue that she is excused from delivering the promised goods because her factory burned down. Imperfect procedures provide formation defenses, and unusual contingencies provide performance excuses.

A. Incompetence

A rational decision-maker can rank outcomes in order from least preferred to most preferred. In order to rank outcomes, the decision-maker must have stable preferences. If the decision-maker's preferences are unstable or disorderly, then he or she cannot make competent judgments about his or her own interests. Such a person is legally incompetent. For example, children, the insane, and some mentally retarded adults are legally incompetent.

In special circumstances, a competent person may suffer temporary incompetence. For example, ingesting a prescription drug can incapacitate. A temporarily incapacitated person may be unable to make legally enforceable promises. To illustrate, if a seller uses high-pressure tactics to confuse a consumer into signing an unfavorable contract, the consumer's lawyer may allege "transactional incapacity," which means an incapacity to make *this* transaction under *these* circumstances.

Most people look after their own interests better than anyone else would do for them. However, incompetent people cannot look after themselves, so others must look after them. Law assigns responsibility for protecting incompetent people from harmful contracts to the competent people with whom they deal. *Competent people must protect the interests of incompetent contractual partners or assume liability for failing to do so*. Thus, law interprets a contract between a competent person and an incompetent person so as to serve the best interests of the latter. For example, the law will excuse a legally incompetent promisor from performing a contract that he signed against his interests, whereas the law will require a legally competent person to perform a contract that serves the interests of an incompetent promisee.

Competent contractual partners are usually better situated than anyone else to protect incompetent people from harmful contracts. In other words, *competent contractual partners can usually protect incompetent contractual partners from harmful contracts at less cost than anyone else.* Thus, the law assigns liability for harm suffered by incompetent contractual partners to the competent people who can avoid the harm at least cost. In this matter, the law follows the general principle of tort law, according to which liability for accidents should fall upon the party who can avoid them at least cost. We develop this principle at length in the next chapter.

> **QUESTION 7.23:** A young girl found an attractive stone in the woods and sold it to a jeweler for $1. Later, her family discovered that the stone was a rough diamond worth $700. Her family asked the court to void the contract for incompetency. Who was situated to protect the young girl in this transaction at least cost?

> **QUESTION 7.24:** Suppose that excessive drinking causes temporary incompetence, and suppose that someone who has drunk too much alcohol seeks to enter into a contract with someone who is sober. Contrast the incentive effects of enforcing and not enforcing such contracts.

B. Dire Constraints and Remote Risks

We proceed down Table 7.1 from incompetence to constrained choice. Most bargains occur under conditions of moderate constraint, but sometimes one of the parties to a bargain faces a *dire* constraint. A dire constraint leaves the decision-maker with little or no choice. Contract law treats dire constraints differently from moderate constraints. A dire constraint can provide the promisor with a defense or an excuse for breaking a promise. We will discuss several relevant doctrines.

1. Duress   Law prohibits people from making threats such as, "Work for me if you want your sister to come home safely from school," or "I'll ruin your business unless you sell it to me for $3500." If a person extracts a promise by using such a threat, the promise is called a "contract made under duress." Contracts made under duress are unenforceable.

Unlike threats, law permits people to make demands such as "Pay me $10 per hour or I'll work for your competitor" or "My final offer for your car is $3500, take it or leave it." Demands occur routinely in bargaining. The fact that a person extracted a promise by making such a demand does not provide a defense or excuse for not keeping the promise.

A theory of duress must distinguish between forbidden threats and permitted demands. We will use bargaining theory to draw the distinction. First we review the fundamentals of bargaining as explained in Chapter 4. In a bargaining situation, the parties can produce more by cooperating ("surplus") than they can on their own. In order to cooperate, they must agree to divide the cooperative product. In dividing the cooperative product, both parties must receive at least as much as they can get on their own ("threat value"). Bargaining often involves exchanging demands and offers in an attempt to agree upon the price of cooperation.

It is easy to see why the law permits people to make demands when bargaining. People know more about their own interests than anyone else, and people protect their own interests more persistently than anyone else. Most people can decide for themselves which cooperative ventures to join far better than anyone else can decide for them. The state can help people to make their own decisions by enforcing private bargains. Conversely, the state can prevent people from making their own decisions by prohibiting private bargains. Efficiency requires the state to facilitate private bargains, not to prohibit them.

In so far as the law forbids private bargains, a third party must decide who should cooperate with whom. Third parties typically lack the information and motivation to make such decisions. For example, the most complete prohibition of private bargains occurred under central planning in communist countries. Many planning officials cared for personal power more than efficiency, and those who cared about efficiency lacked the information to make decisions for other people. Central planning collapsed under the weight of its own inefficiency.

Many modest attempts by the state to restrict private bargains have failed. For example, most wealthy nations have abandoned attempts by the state to set prices for consumer goods. As an alternative to state planning or price-setting, the law typically enforces promises given in response to demands.

Bargaining, which involves demands and offers, is opposite from coercion, which involves threats. A contract usually involves a bargain in which one party gives something to induce the other party to make a promise. The bargain facilitates cooperation which is productive. Both parties usually expect to gain from the bargain. Both parties usually want enforceability to secure a credible commitment to cooperate.

In contrast, a contract made under duress has the opposite traits. Duress usually involves extracting a promise by a threat. Enforcing the promise usually redistributes wealth from one person to the other. One party expects to gain from a coerced promise, and the other party expects to lose. One party wants enforceability of a coerced promise and the other party does not.

To illustrate, contrast voluntary and coerced exchange of goods. When exchange is voluntary, the parties agree to trade because they both perceive an advantage. Ownership usually passes from someone who values a good less to someone who values it more. Allocative efficiency requires moving a good from someone who values it less to someone who values it more. In contrast, when exchange is involuntary, one party may be coerced into selling a good for less than its worth to him or her. Consequently, ownership may pass from someone who values it more to someone who values it less. Moving a good from someone who values it more to someone who values it less causes allocative inefficiency. (We already encountered these facts about involuntary exchange in Chapter 5 when we discussed the state taking private property.)

We have explained that bargain contracts are usually productive, whereas coerced contracts are usually redistributive. Another important difference concerns the consequence of a failed attempt to form a contract. If bargaining fails, the parties do not cooperate or create a surplus. To illustrate, suppose I say, "Pay me $10 per hour or I'll work for your competitor." You offer $9 per hour, so I go to work for your competitor at $8 per hour. My best alternative bargain is apparently less productive than the proposed bargain.

In contrast, if coercion fails and the injurer acts on the threat, he or she destroys something valuable to the victim. To illustrate, suppose I say to you, "Work for me if you want your sister to come home safely from school." If you refuse to be coerced and if I act on my threat, a tragic crime ensues. In general, *failed bargains do not create, whereas failed coercion can destroy.*

Even unexecuted threats cause waste by inducing their victims to invest in defense. To illustrate, suppose that the local bully "buys" bicycles in exchange for $10 and the promise not to thrash the owner. The owners of bicycles will try to protect themselves from the bully. Protecting themselves against the bully uses resources. The state can often provide protection against threats more cheaply than anyone else. By providing protection against threats, the state channels resources from defense to production. [25]

We have explained that involuntary contracts usually redistribute wealth. The modern state suppresses private, involuntary redistributions of wealth, such as theft and fraud. The modern state reserves for itself the power to redistribute wealth involuntarily. The state redistributes wealth from rich to poor by progressive taxation and social-welfare expenditures. The state redistributes wealth from politically weak to politically favored groups by imposing regulations that restrict competition.

Economic analysis suggests the following rule for duress: *A promise extracted as the price to cooperate in creating value is enforceable, and a promise extracted by a threat to destroy value is unenforceable.* To illustrate the rule, consider this example. The captain of a boat in California contracts with the crew to make a fishing voyage to Alaska. After the boat reaches Alaska, the crew demands a bonus to finish the voyage. The captain cannot find replacements for the crew in Alaska, so he agrees. After the ship returns to California, the captain refuses to pay the bonus on grounds of duress.

This example illustrates the form of duress called the *holdup problem.* When negotiating the original contract, the crew faced competition from other crews. After the boat reached Alaska, the crew no longer faced competition from other crews. The captain's reliance on the contract caused him to forego the opportunity of contracting with another crew in California. Furthermore, the captain made investments in reliance upon the contract, such as purchasing fuel and supplies. The absence of competition and the captain's reliance upon the crew increased the crew's bargaining strength. So the crew tried to renegotiate the price.

Notice that this example fits our distinction between legal demands and illegal threats. If the parties failed to agree on the original contract, they would not cooperate together. By failing to cooperate, they would not create a surplus. Renegotiation is different. After making the contract, the captain relied by foregoing the opportunity to hire an alternative crew and outfitting the boat for the voyage to Alaska. In the renegotiations, the crew threatened to destroy the value of the captain's reliance. The destructive threat to breach a contract after reliance constitutes coercion in renegotiating the price. In general, courts do not enforce contract renegotiations motivated by

---

[25] We already made this point in Chapter 4 when we discussed a lawless world in which people divide their time between growing, protecting, and stealing corn. State security ideally diverts effort from protecting and stealing corn to producing it.

the increase in the promisor's bargaining strength that results from the promisee's reliance.

QUESTION 7.25: Suppose that person *A*, while aiming a gun at person *B*, invites *B* to write a check. Explain the efficiency argument for allowing *B* to cancel the check later.

QUESTION 7.26: Suppose that a baseball star signs a five-year contract for $1 million per year. In the third year of the contract, the player hits more home runs than anyone else in the league. Now he demands to renegotiate his salary. Does efficiency require the law to enforce the original contract or set it aside?

2. Necessity The following example illustrates the next doctrine, called "necessity." A surgeon runs out of gas on a lonely desert road. A passerby offers to sell the surgeon five liters of gas in exchange for a promise to pay $50,000. The surgeon makes the promise and uses the gas to escape from the desert, but later the surgeon refuses to pay $50,000. The surgeon asserts that "necessity" forced him to make the promise.

Like duress, necessity is a promise given under a dire constraint. As explained, *duress* concerns a dire constraint imposed on the promisor by the promisee. In contrast, necessity concerns a dire constraint imposed on the promisor by someone other than the promisee. The cause of the dire constraint could be the promisor, a third party, or bad luck. For example, the surgeon might run out of gas on a lonely desert road because he neglected to fill the tank, someone gave him false directions, or a rock punctured the fuel line.

In cases of duress and necessity, the promisee makes a destructive threat and the promisor responds by making a one-sided promise. The nature of the threat, however, differs for the two doctrines. With duress, the promisee threatens to destroy by *acting*. With necessity, the promisee threatens to destroy by *not* acting, specifically by not rescuing. For example, the passerby threatens to leave the surgeon stranded on a desert road unless he promises to pay $50,000 for five liters of gas.

In a Biblical parable, the "good Samaritan" saved the life of a man attacked by thieves and nursed him back to health, without expectation of reward. In the necessity cases, a "bad Samaritan" extracts the promise of an extravagant reward in exchange for a rescue. Rescue deserves an appropriate reward, not an extravagant reward. An appropriate award provides efficient incentives for rescue. Efficient incentives for rescue induce enough investment in rescue so that the cost equals the expected benefit. The expected benefit equals the probability of a rescue multiplied by its value.

To illustrate, return to the example of the surgeon who ran out of gas on a lonely desert road. The rescue cost the passerby at least five liters of gas, plus inconvenience and delay. In order to provide incentives for rescue, the rescuer should recover the cost of the rescue. In addition to costs, the rescuer should receive sufficient reward so that future rescuers will perform eagerly, not reluctantly.

We distinguish three kinds of rescues by their cost. First, a *fortuitous* rescue uses resources that were on hand by chance. For example, the passerby happens to have extra gas in her tank when she happens to encounter the stranded surgeon, so the passerby siphons five liters of gas from the tank of her car to the tank of the surgeon's car. Second, an *anticipated* rescue uses resources set aside in case they are needed for a rescue. For example, the passerby always carries a 5-liter can of gas in the trunk of her car just in case she happens to encounter someone stranded. Third, a *planned* rescue occurs when the rescuer searches for people who need rescuing. For example, a professional rescuer patrolling the desert comes upon the stranded surgeon.

The difference in costs affects the difference in rewards required to create incentives for the three kinds of rescue. Fortuitous rescue uses resources that just happen to be available. Incentives for fortuitous rescue require a modest reward to compensate for resources actually consumed in the rescue. Anticipated rescue uses resources set aside for emergencies. Incentives for anticipated rescue require sufficient reward to compensate for preparations against emergencies. Preparations use more than the resources consumed in an actual rescue. Planned rescue uses resources invested in searching for people in distress. Incentives for planned rescue require sufficient reward to compensate for search. Searching uses more than the resources consumed in preparing for emergencies or rescuing. In general, incentives for planned rescues require larger rewards than for anticipated rescues, and incentives for anticipated rescues require larger rewards than for fortuitous rescues.

The reward should be adjusted by law to induce investment in rescue at the efficient level. When jeopardy is rare and its consequences are slight, investment in fortuitous rescue may be sufficient. For example, if people seldom run out of gas in the desert and the consequences are temporary discomfort, then a trivial reward may be sufficient. As probability and seriousness increase, efficiency may require anticipated or planned rescue. If people occasionally run out of gas in the desert and the consequences are serious, then an extra reward should be given to rescuers for carrying extra gas. Finally, if people often run out of gas in the desert and the consequences are life-threatening, then an even larger reward should be given to planned rescuers in order to induce them to form a "desert patrol."[26]

QUESTION 7.27: Explain why professional rescuers should typically receive a larger reward than anticipated rescuers, and anticipated rescuers should typically receive a larger reward than fortuitous rescuers.

QUESTION 7.28: A house catches on fire. The fire is extinguished by the combined efforts of (1) professional firefighters, (2) volunteer firefighters who help the professionals, and (3) passersby who spontaneously help the professionals and volunteers. The owner of the house makes various promises to induce the help of the three groups. Use economics to explain why a court should not enforce the promises, but the court should require the homeowner to pay (1) more than (2), and to pay (2) more than (3).

QUESTION 7.29: In *Post v. Jones,* 60 U.S. (19 How.) 150 (1857), the whaling ship *Richmond* ran aground on a barren coast in the Arctic Ocean and began to sink with a full cargo of whale oil. A few days later three other whaling ships came upon the *Richmond*. The three captains, while agreeing to save the crew, threatened not to take any of the *Richmond*'s whale oil unless the captain of the *Richmond* agreed to an auction. One of the three captains bid $1 per barrel for as much as he could take; the other two took as much as they could hold at $0.75 per barrel. Both prices were well below the competitive price of whale oil. When

---

[26] Free entry in the market for rescuing, like open-access fishing, has an incentive problem due to congestion, but this is a technical detail.

the three vessels returned to port with the *Richmond*'s oil and crew, the owners of the *Richmond* sued, asking the court not to enforce the sale of the whale oil at the low auction prices. Did the captains who purchased the oil make destructive threats? Should the court set aside the auction on efficiency grounds? What compensation should the rescuers receive? (Note: sea captains have a legal duty to rescue ships and cargo in distress.)

3. Impossibility   With duress and necessity, the dire constraint *precedes* the promise. Sometimes a dire constraint *follows* the promise and prevents performance. For example, a surgeon may promise to operate and then break her hand before the scheduled operation. Although the surgeon cannot perform, she can pay damages. If the surgeon cannot physically perform, the law can either excuse her or require her to pay damages. In general, when a contingency makes performance impossible, should the promisor be excused or held liable? The "impossibility doctrine," which we analyze in this section, answers this question.

As discussed in the preceding chapter, perfect contracts contain terms that explicitly allocate all risks. Explicit allocation of risk requires costly negotiating. The cost of negotiating must be balanced against the benefit from explicit allocation of risk. On balance, the cost of negotiating over remote risks may exceed the benefit. Consequently, efficient contracts have gaps concerning remote risks.

Sometimes the explicit terms in the contract provide guidance to filling a gap. To illustrate, assume that a company promises to drill a well for a landowner, but the drill runs into impenetrable granite rock. If the contract remains silent about this contingency, the court must decide whether the driller owes damages to the landowner. If the price in the drilling contract exceeds competing offers, perhaps the driller implicitly guaranteed success to the landowner. If the driller gave an implicit guarantee, he should be held liable. Or perhaps the industry custom requires drillers to bear the cost of breach whenever the contract remains silent. If industry custom holds drillers liable, the court should apply the custom to the case.

In other instances, however, the terms of the contract and the custom of the industry provide no guidance to the allocation of risk. When the contract does not allocate the risk explicitly or implicitly to one of the parties, the law must do so. In contract law, the promisor is typically liable for breach, even though the breach was not his or her fault. In other words, contractual liability is *strict*. For example, a construction company is liable for late completion of a building, regardless of whether or not the construction company did its best to meet the deadline. Similarly, when the contract was silent about the contingency causing breach, the promisor is typically liable, even though the breach was not the promisor's fault. In the typical case, the promisor is liable for breach caused by a remote contingency that was not mentioned in the contract.

In some circumstances, however, physical impossibility of performance excuses nonperformance.[27] For example, the estate of a famous portrait painter is not liable if death prevents the artist from completing a contract to paint someone's picture.[28] Similarly, a

---

[27] *L.N. Jackson & Co. v. Royal Norwegian Govt.*, 177 F.2d 694 (2d Cir. 1949), *cert. den.*, 339 U.S. 914 (1950).

[28] Note that this exception, as in the example given, most typically involves the promise to provide personal services. The law, both common and statutory, has frequently been reluctant to compel performance of personal service contracts under any circumstances.

manufacturer may be excused from fulfilling its contracts to deliver goods because light-ning ignited a fire that destroyed her factory. [29] The burning of the factory is an "act of God" or *force majeur*. Also, breach is excused if performance became illegal before it could occur. For example, a shipping company is excused from its contract to carry civilian cargo in time of war if the government commandeers its ships to carry military cargo.

These examples concern physical impossibility. In other cases, performance is *phys-ically* possible and *economically* impossible. [30] For example, the driller may be excused for not completing the well as promised to the landowner because the drill could only penetrate granite at ruinous cost.

What underlies and unifies these cases? According to a traditional legal theory, a contingency destroyed a "basic assumption on which the contract was made" in each case.[31] For example, the contract with the portrait painter assumed that he would live, the contract with the factory assumed that it would not burn down, and the contract with the shipping company assumed that the government would not commandeer its ships. According to this theory, breach of a contract made in good faith is excused whenever events destroy one of its basic assumptions.

How do we decide whether an assumption is basic or dispensable? Economics can clarify this vague distinction or dispense with it. The impossibility doctrine concerns contingencies that make performance impossible. These contingencies represent a risk, much like the risk of pneumonia or an automobile accident. Economics has a theory of efficient risk-bearing. Efficiency requires allocating risk to the people who can bear it at least cost. If the impossibility doctrine in contract law were efficient, it would *assign liability to the party who can bear the risk that performance becomes impossible at least cost.*

Several factors determine who can bear risk at least cost. First, people can often take steps to decrease the probability that performance becomes impossible or to reduce the losses from breach. For example, an elderly and ailing painter might delay other work in order to complete a portrait as commissioned. The ship's owner might alert the customer to the need for alternative supplies in the event that war causes the government to commandeer ships. The factory owner might install a sprinkler system to reduce the damage caused by fire. These considerations suggest that a risk should be assigned to the party who can take *precautions* to reduce it at least cost.

Second, even if no one can take precautions to reduce risk, someone can usually *spread* it. For example, assume that an earthquake prevents a seller from delivering goods on time. No one can prevent earthquakes, but people can insure against them. Insurance companies specialize in spreading risk. Even without insurance, an individ-ual may be able to spread risk by other means. For example, the investors in a factory subject to an earthquake hazard can spread risk by purchasing stocks from companies in different locations ("portfolio diversification"). Risk is cheaper to bear when spread

---

[29] RESTATEMENT (SECOND) OF CONTRACTS § 263 (1979).

[30] Economic impossibility is called "impracticability" or "commercial impracticability." Sometimes the defense concerns the absolute cost of performance, and sometimes the defense concerns the cost of performance relative to the promisor's assets (e.g., performing bankrupts the promisor).

[31] See Chapter 11, RESTATEMENT (SECOND) OF CONTRACTS (1979).

than when concentrated. These considerations suggest that risk should be assigned to the party who can spread it at least cost, by insurance or other means.

A person's ability to reduce and spread risk determines his or her cost of bearing it. Efficiency requires allocating risk to the people who can bear it at least cost. Thus, efficiency requires interpreting the impossibility doctrine as follows: *If a contingency makes performance impossible, assign liability to the party who could reduce or spread the risk at least cost.*

The concept of "lowest-cost risk-bearer" provides a clear interpretation of the impossibility doctrine in many difficult cases. To illustrate, consider two versions of the example of the commandeered ship. In the first version, the shipping company has easier access to alternative transportation than the owner of civilian goods. Consequently, the shipping company can bear the risk of its ship's being commandeered at lower cost than the owner of civilian goods, so the shipping company should be held liable for breach of contract. In the second version, the owner of civilian goods has easier access to alternative transportation than the shipping company. Consequently, the owner of civilian goods can bear the risk of commandeering at lower cost than the shipping company, so the shipping company should be excused for breaching the contract. (To see the improvement made by economic analysis, try to distinguish these two versions of the case of the commandeered ship using the "basic assumption" theory.)

Similar analysis applies to the other examples. The portrait painter can bear the risk of breach at least cost if he can easily rearrange his schedule to paint commissioned pictures first, whereas the person who ordered the portrait can bear the risk of breach at least cost if he can easily obtain a portrait from another artist with equal talent. The factory owner can bear the risk of fire at least cost if she can easily purchase fire insurance whose coverage includes liability for not delivering goods, whereas the customer can bear the risk at least cost if he can easily obtain substitute goods from another factory.

Interpreting the impossibility doctrine to assign liability to the lowest-cost risk-bearer minimizes the cost of remote risks. Minimizing the cost of remote risks maximizes the surplus from the contract, which the parties can divide between them. Both parties stand to gain from the economic interpretation of the impossibility doctrine. We presume that, if the parties had explicitly allocated the risk, they would have assigned it to the party who can bear it at least cost. Thus, the economic principle can be defended as a rational reconstruction of the will of the parties.

QUESTION 7.30: Lightning is an "act of God." Describe some of its incentive effects upon people.

QUESTION 7.31: In the famous case of *Taylor v. Caldwell*, 3 B. & S. 826, 122 Eng. Rep. 309 (K.B. 1863), the plaintiff, Taylor, had leased the defendant's concert hall for four nights at 100 pounds sterling to be paid to Caldwell after each night's performance. Shortly after the first performance, the concert hall was destroyed by fire. Taylor sued Caldwell for breach of contract and asked the court to award him as damages the expenses he had incurred in preparation for the last three performances. The defendant sought to be excused from performing on the ground that it was literally impossible for him to perform the contract after the fire.

   a. What factors enable one party to prevent a risk better than another?

   b. What factors enable one party to insure against a risk better than another?

c. Do these factors tend to converge or diverge, or is their association merely coincidental?

d. How would you decide this case in light of economic analysis?

QUESTION 7.32: In the mid-1970s, the Westinghouse Corporation persuaded electric companies to purchase nuclear reactors, and Westinghouse agreed to supply purchasers with uranium at a fixed price of $8–10 per pound. By mid-1975 Westinghouse had commitments to supply 40,000 tons of uranium more than it held in inventory or forward contracts, at which time the market price of uranium had risen to more than $30 per pound. To cover its shortage, Westinghouse would have incurred losses of nearly $2 billion, which would have led to its bankruptcy. In September 1975, the company announced that it would not honor its contracts. It sought to be excused on the ground that performance was economically impossible ("commercial impracticability"). Most of the utilities sued Westinghouse. What considerations do you think should have been used by courts to determine whether Westinghouse was excused from supplying the uranium?[32]

4. Frustration of Purpose   Having discussed a contingency that prevents performing, we now consider a contingency that destroys its purpose. To illustrate, a coronation parade was planned for June 1902 in London. Many owners of property along the parade route leased rooms for the day to people wishing to observe the ceremony. When the king's illness caused the parade to be postponed, many people refused to pay the rent, and some of the property owners sued to enforce the contracts. The courts held that the contracts were unenforceable because their purpose was destroyed by postponing the ceremony.[33]

As explained, the impossibility doctrine provides a default rule to allocate losses caused by remote contingencies that make performance impossible. Similarly, the frustration doctrine provides a default rule to allocate losses caused by contingencies that make performance pointless. Pointless performance does not serve the purpose that induced the parties to make the contract. For example, the scheduled coronation parade induced the parties to make a contract for viewing it. Efficiency requires allocating risk to the party who can bear it at least cost. Thus, efficiency requires interpreting the doctrine of frustration of purpose as follows: *If a contingency makes performance pointless, assign liability to the party who could bear the risk at least cost.*

As explained, a person's ability to reduce and spread risk determines his or her cost of bearing it. Returning to our example, the property owners who rented rooms could completely eliminate their losses caused by postponement of the coronation parade by renting the rooms a second time for the rescheduled parade. Bearing the risk of postponement was probably costless to the owners. Alternatively, the people who rented the rooms to view the parade face the risk of having to pay the rent twice. Efficiency apparently requires allocating the risk of postponement to the property owners, not the renters of the rooms.

---

[32] See Paul Joskow, *Commercial Impossibility, the Uranium Market, and the "Westinghouse" Case*, 6 J. LEGAL STUD. 119 (1976). All of the lawsuits were settled out of court.

[33] See, for example, *Krell v. Henry*, 2 K.B. 740 (1903).

QUESTION 7.33: We divided the doctrines of contract law into default rules that fill gaps and regulations than restrict promises. Classify the following doctrines as default rules or regulations: incompetence, duress, necessity, impossibility, and frustration of purpose.

5. Mutual Mistake About Facts   We discussed a contingency that materializes and makes performance of a contract pointless. As explained, frustration of purpose occurs when the contingency materializes *after* the parties sign the contract. Another possibility is that the contingency materializes *before* the parties sign the contract, without them knowing it. To illustrate, assume that Buyer contracts to buy a tract of timber land from Seller. Both Seller and Buyer believe that the land has timber, but in fact a forest fire has destroyed it. The parties have made a mutual mistake about a fundamental fact concerning the object of sale.

In analyzing frustration of purpose, we proposed the following principle: *If a contingency makes performance pointless, assign liability to the party who could bear the risk at least cost.* The same principle applies to a mutual mistake concerning a fundamental fact about the object of sale. The law should assign liability in such cases to the party who can take precaution to prevent the contingency at least cost, or to the party who can insure against the contingency at least cost. To illustrate, if Seller can prevent forest fires or insure against them more cheaply than Buyer, then Seller should be *unable* to enforce the contract against Buyer. Conversely, if Buyer can prevent forest fires or insure against them more cheaply than Seller, then Seller should be *able* to enforce the contract against Buyer.

6. Mutual Mistake About Identity   Now we turn from mutual mistakes about facts to mutual mistakes about identity. A mutual mistake about identity occurs when the buyer and seller have different objects in mind, so their "minds do not meet." To illustrate a mutual mistake, recall the example of the rusty Chevy, in which the seller and buyer agreed to a price of $1000 for a car, but the seller intended to sell a rusty Chevy and the buyer intended to buy a shiny Cadillac. In the example, the buyer was mistaken about what the seller proposed to sell, and the seller was mistaken about what the buyer proposed to buy.

When the parties make a mutual mistake about identity, there is no true agreement to exchange. If the courts were to force an exchange, it would be involuntary. Involuntary exchange can destroy value rather than create it. Involuntary exchange destroys value by transferring ownership from someone who values the good more to someone who values it less. To illustrate, the buyer may value the shiny Cadillac at $2000, and the seller may value it at $2500. Forcing the Cadillac's transfer of ownership destroys $500 ("negative surplus"). By setting aside contracts based upon mutual mistake, courts preclude the destruction of value by involuntary exchange.

QUESTION 7.34: In *Raffles v. Wichelhaus*, 2 Hurl. & C. 906, 159 Eng. Rep. 375 (Ex. 1864), the plaintiff sold the defendants 125 bales of cotton to arrive "ex *Peerless* from Bombay," that is, by way of the ship *Peerless* sailing from Bombay, India. A ship by that name sailed from India in December, but when it arrived, the defendants refused to take delivery of the cotton on the ground that they had meant a second ship named the *Peerless* that had left Bombay in October. The Court of Exchequer gave judgment for the defendants on the argument that there had been no meeting of the minds. How would you analyze this case?

C. Information

We have been discussing contract doctrines that allocate risk. Now we consider contract doctrines that allocate information. Doctrines that allocate information are different from doctrines that allocate other economic goods. The difference in doctrines is caused by a difference in the goods themselves. Information is discovered and transmitted, whereas most other goods are made and consumed. Unlike the makers of goods, the discoverers of information have difficulty appropriating its value, which creates a need for patents. Unlike consuming commodities, using information does not diminish the amount that remains for others. Consequently, information can be transmitted to many people without diminution. These facts make information different from most other goods. (Recall the discussion of public goods in the section on information economics in Chapter 5.)

We will explain how contract doctrines contribute to the efficient discovery and transmission of information. Economists say that *public* information is known to both parties in a bargain, whereas *private* information is known to one party and unknown to the other. Private information often motivates exchange. To illustrate, assume that someone knows how to get more production from a resource than its owner. To increase production, knowledge must be united with control. To unite knowledge with control, the owner of the resource must acquire the information, or else the informed person must acquire ownership of the resource. In general, the transmission of information and the sale of goods unites knowledge and control over resources. *Efficiency requires uniting knowledge and control over resources at least cost, including the transaction costs of transmitting information and selling goods.*

The parties can usually solve the problem of private information through private bargaining. For example, the informed party may offer to buy the resource and pay more than the uninformed owner can earn from using it. Or the informed party may offer to share the information with the uninformed owner of the resource in exchange for a proportion of the resulting increase in profits. Private bargaining usually solves the problem of asymmetrical information much better than any alternative, such as having the state dictate a solution. Consequently, the law usually enforces contracts based upon asymmetrical information.

Instead of uniting knowledge and control, however, some contracts separate them. Separating knowledge and control reduces efficiency in the use of resources. Contracts that separate knowledge and control should be suppressed for the sake of efficiency. In subsequent sections, we will discuss three such doctrines: mistake, failure to disclose, and fraud.

1. Unilateral Mistake Each of the parties to a bargain usually knows something that the other does not know. Sometimes one of the parties knows that the other party has a mistaken belief. For example, the seller of a car may think that it is merely old, whereas the buyer may know that it is a classic. Although the seller was mistaken about the car's value, the buyer was not, so mistake is unilateral. When one party to a bargain knows the truth and other party does not, the exchange is based on a "unilateral mistake," according to the language of the law. Courts usually enforce contracts based upon unilateral mistakes. For example, if the owner promises to sell a classic car for less than its market value, the law will usually enforce the promise.

When the buyer acquires the classic car in this example, knowledge and control are united, which typically increases efficiency. For example, the buyer will probably take better care of the car because he or she knows its worth. The contract also increases efficiency in another way. Discovering information often requires investing time and resources, which requires a reward. In this example, the buyer may have searched long and hard to find a seller who does not know that he or she owns a classic car. The profit from buying the classic car at a low price rewards the buyer for the search.

We explained above that a mutual mistake about facts or identity is a valid formation defense in common law, whereas unilateral mistake is not. Consequently, a party who seeks performance of a contract may say that mistake was unilateral, and a party who seeks release from a contract may say that mistake was mutual. Economic efficiency provides a criterion for making this distinction. Mutual mistake converts a contract into an involuntary exchange, which can destroy value. In contrast, a contract based upon a unilateral mistake usually promotes efficiency by rewarding discovery and uniting knowledge with control. We propose the following principle to improve the legal distinction underlying the doctrines of unilateral and mutual mistake: *Withhold enforcement from contracts involving involuntary exchange, and enforce contracts that reward discovery and unite knowledge with control.*

We apply this principle to the famous case of *Laidlaw v. Organ*, 15 U.S. (2 Wheat.) 178 (1815). During the War of 1812 between Britain and the United States, the British blockaded New Orleans, which depressed the price of export goods like tobacco. Organ, a buyer of tobacco, received private information that the war had ended by treaty, so he called on a representative of the Laidlaw firm and offered to buy tobacco. The representative of the Laidlaw firm was ignorant about the peace treaty, so a contract was concluded between them at the depressed price. The next day public notice was given in New Orleans that peace was concluded and the price of tobacco soared. The mistake in this contract was obviously unilateral, not mutual—Organ knew about the treaty and Laidlaw did not. Even so, the contract was apparently set aside by the court after a trial.[34]

This outcome can be defended on economic grounds. According to the preceding principle, the contract should be enforced if doing so rewards discovery and unites knowledge with control. The evidence suggests that Organ discovered fortuitously that peace was concluded, rather than investing time and resources in making the discovery. Furthermore, the contract merely accelerated by one day the uniting of knowledge and control, which did not contribute to production of tobacco. So enforcing the contract would probably not increase efficiency.

To sharpen this analysis, distinguish between *productive* information and *redistributive* information. Productive information can be used to produce more wealth. To illustrate, the discovery of a vaccine for polio and the discovery of a water route from

---

[34] A verdict at trial for the buyer was appealed to the U.S. Supreme Court, which remanded it for retrial, but it is not entirely clear what happened upon retrial. See Anthony T. Kronman, *Mistake, Disclosure, Information and the Law of Contracts*, 7 J. LEGAL STUD. 1 (1978).

Europe to China were productive. Efficiency demands giving people strong incentives to discover productive facts. Transmitting information is so easy that the person who discovers productive information seldom captures its full value. Consequently, the state must take special measures to reward people who discover productive information. For example, the state must subsidize basic scientific research and provide patents to inventors.

In contrast, redistributive information creates a bargaining advantage that can be used to redistribute wealth in favor of the informed party. To illustrate, knowing before anyone else where the state will locate a new highway conveys a powerful advantage in real-estate markets. Investment in discovering redistributive information wastes resources. In addition, investment in redistributive information induces defensive expenditures by people trying not to lose their wealth to better-informed people. Defensive expenditures prevent redistribution, rather than produce something. Thus, investment in redistributive information wastes resources directly and indirectly.

The state should not create incentives to discover redistributive information. Instead, the state should discourage investment in discovering redistributive information. For example, the state should punish officials who leak information about the location of a new highway prior to the public announcement. Such leaks encourage real-estate dealers to devote resources to gaining privileged information from officials.

These considerations prompt another formulation of the economic principle for improving the legal distinction underlying the doctrines of unilateral and mutual mistake: *Contracts based upon one party's knowledge of productive information should be enforced, whereas contracts based upon one party's knowledge of purely redistributive information should not be enforced.* This principle rewards investment in discovering productive information and discourages investment in discovering redistributive information.[35]

In our discussion of information economics in Chapter 5, we explained that most information is both productive and redistributive. To illustrate, the invention of the cotton gin in 1792 by Eli Whitney increased cotton production and promoted speculation in land suitable for growing cotton. The example of the informed buyer who purchased a classic car from an uninformed seller also illustrates mixed information. The information was productive because the informed buyer knew that the car deserved special care. The information was redistributive because the informed buyer's gain from buying the car probably exceeded the increase in value from taking special care of it. We argued that private bargains usually succeed in rewarding discovery and uniting knowledge with control. Consequently, most bargains based upon differences in information affecting production and distribution should be enforced. In other words, most bargains based upon mixed information (productive and redistributive) should be enforced.

---

[35] In his article cited in the previous footnote, Professor Kronman asserts that the contract between Organ and Laidlaw should have been set aside because the facts known to Organ were acquired *fortuitously*, rather than through *deliberate* investment. This is an important distinction because it raises an additional level of analysis in mistake cases. Thus, the *deliberate* acquisition of *productive* information is clearly to be protected. And, just as clearly, the *deliberate* acquisition of *redistributive* information is to be discouraged. But the *fortuitous* acquisition of productive information is not so firmly to be protected; nor is the *fortuitous* acquisition of redistributive information so firmly to be discouraged.

We have arrived at three economic principles to govern the analysis of contract cases in which the formation defense of mistake is raised:

1. Enforce contracts based on differences in productive information;
2. enforce most contracts based on difference in mixed information (productive and redistributive); and
3. set aside contracts based on differences in purely redistributive information.

These normative principles clarify the principle underlying the legal doctrines of mutual and unilateral mistake.

QUESTION 7.35: Consider the case of *Laidlaw v. Organ*. List the ways in which Organ's information might be productive. Explain how Organ's information might be redistributive. What do you conclude about whether or not efficiency requires enforcing the contract?

QUESTION 7.36: A large number of cases involve a dispute about whether a mistake was mutual or unilateral concerning the *quality* of the object or its *value*. In a famous case, *Sherwood v. Walker*, 66 Mich. 568, 33 N.W. 919 (Mich. 1887), the seller (Walker) promised to deliver a cow to the buyer (Sherwood). The seller, who apparently believed that the cow was incapable of becoming pregnant, learned before the delivery was to take place that the cow was pregnant. A pregnant cow is far more valuable than a barren cow. The seller refused to deliver the cow to the buyer as promised. He contended that the contract was premised on the mutual mistake that the cow was barren. The buyer denied that he had made such a mistake.

a. The knowledge that a cow is fertile, rather than barren, is productive, rather than merely redistributive. Why?

b. Suppose the law imposed upon Sherwood (the plaintiff-buyer) the duty to disclose to Walker (the defendant-seller) any evidence that the cow is fertile. Would there be an objection to such a duty on efficiency grounds?

c. Should it matter in this case that Walker was a professional cattle rancher and that Sherwood was a banker?

2. The Duty to Disclose   In the preceding section, we discussed productive and redistributive information. Now we consider another kind of information. *Safety information* helps people to avoid harm. For example, the safety information on an electrical appliance helps consumers to avoid fires. Conversely, the absence of safety information increases the probability and magnitude of accidents.

The law treats safety information differently from productive and redistributive information. As explained, contracts are often motivated by a difference in information between the parties. The law does not generally require an informed person to disclose productive or redistributive information to uninformed people. However, the law typically requires informed people to disclose safety information to uninformed people. For example, manufacturers must provide safety information concerning their products or assume liability when accidents occur. Regulatory law imposes most duties to disclose safety information. In this section we discuss the duty to disclose imposed by contract law.

The case of *Obde v. Schlemeyer*, 56 Wash.2d 449, 353 P.2d 672 (1960), provides an example of the common law duty to disclose. In this case, the seller of a building knew that it was infested with termites. The seller deliberately withheld the information about the termites from the buyer. The seller did not lie to the buyer, who never inquired about termites. Not long after the sale, the buyer discovered the termite infestation and sued the seller.[36]

To minimize termite damages, the termites should have been exterminated as soon as they were discovered. By not disclosing the infestation, the seller gave the termites the opportunity to cause further destruction. The court in the *Obde* case departed from tradition and imposed a duty to disclose.[37] By enforcing a duty to disclose, the court avoided future harms caused by the failure to disclose safety information, and the court diminished the need for future buyers to be wary or to undertake defensive expenditures against this sort of concealment by sellers.

The seller knew about the termite infestation, and the buyer did not know about it. Thus, the sale of the termite-infested house *separates* knowledge from control. A contract separates knowledge from control when the seller fails to disclose information needed by the buyer to prevent the good's destruction. Earlier we explained that contract law seeks to *unite* knowledge and control. Thus, contracts based upon the failure to disclose safety information undermine one purpose of contract law. These considerations suggest a fourth economic principle for contract cases involving information: *When bargaining to a contract, the parties should divulge safety information.*

> **QUESTION 7.37:** Suppose that a seller has not bothered to investigate whether her house has termites, so she does not know. When asked by a buyer if it does, she says, "I guess not." On efficiency grounds, should this statement be enough to void the contract?

> **QUESTION 7.38:** Professor Schmidt, a geologist, has agreed to purchase McDonald's farm for a price of $2,000 per acre, which corresponds to the price of good quality farmland in the vicinity. However, Schmidt, on the basis of his own geological studies, is convinced that McDonald's farm contains valuable mineral deposits, which make the property worth $25,000 per acre. Schmidt's true motive is discovered by McDonald before Schmidt takes possession, and McDonald refuses to hand over the property. Schmidt sues for breach of contract. McDonald defends on the ground that Schmidt had a duty to disclose the results of his studies. According to our economic principles, who should win?

3. Fraud and Misrepresentation   The seller in *Obde v. Schlemeyer* failed to disclose safety information, but he did not claim that the property was free from termites. If the seller in *Obde* had actually claimed that the property was free from termites, the claim would have been fraudulent. Fraud at common law requires a lie—a false assertion

---

[36] In the case, the buyer asked not for invalidation of the contract but rather for damages for the costs that correcting the termite infestation imposed upon him.

[37] The common law tradition held that sellers had no duty to disclose. The old rule was *caveat emptor*, "Let the buyer beware!" Sellers did, however, have the duty not to lie. See the discussion of fraud in the next section. Note that regulations in many parts of the United States now require the seller of real estate to provide the buyer with a certificate from a licensed exterminator that the house is free of termite infestation.

made with the intention to deceive. Under the traditional common law doctrine, the victim of fraud is entitled to damages for harm caused by fraud.

Many misleading statements lie between fraud and nondisclosure, and these cases cause the most disputes. Courts and legislatures in the United States have recently broadened the circumstances in which a contract may be voided for nondisclosure. For example, lenders are now required by law to divulge the annual percentage rate of interest on all consumer loans. Used-car dealers are required in many states to reveal any major repairs done to their cars. Sellers of homes in most states are required to reveal latent defects, such as a cracked foundation. Producers of food are required to list ingredients. Manufacturers of some appliances must notify consumers about the appliance's energy use. Like the traditional common law rules on fraud, these regulations aim to improve the exchange of information in private contracts. Enforcing these regulations can be costly. Consequently, legislation directed at a real abuse can end up costing consumers more than the harm they suffer in the absence of regulation.

> **QUESTION 7.39:** Suppose that the seller is very attached to her home and wishes to sell only to someone who will maintain the property as a single-family dwelling. A prospective buyer says that he, too, wants to use the property as a single-family dwelling. The sale is completed, and the seller moves out. However, several days later, she learns that the buyer intended all along to demolish the house in order to open a commercial establishment. Does efficiency commend enforcing the contract or rescinding it?

D. Monopoly

We discussed dire constraints that leave the promisor with no choice. A less extreme situation occurs when a monopolist controls a product valued by many people. Strictly defined, a *monopolist* is the *only seller of a product for which no close substitutes exist.* A monopolist can dictate the price and nonprice terms of the contract offered to many buyers. The buyer must respond by accepting the monopolist's offer or doing without the good.

Monopoly contrasts with its polar opposite, *perfect competition*, in which *many buyers and sellers substitute perfectly for each other.* In perfect competition, no one can dictate the price or nonprice terms of contracts. No one has power over the contractual terms because each buyer or seller who dislikes a contractual partner can get an alternative contract from someone else. Perfect competition shades into monopoly as the availability of substitutes decreases.

Monopolists set prices too high, which distorts the economy. A price is too high when it exceeds the marginal cost of producing the good. When price exceeds marginal cost, some consumers, who would be willing to pay more for it than its cost of production, do not purchase the good. If producing a good costs less than people would be willing to pay for it, then *not* supplying the good is inefficient ("allocative inefficiency"). In addition to high prices, monopoly depletes the drive and dynamism of entrepreneurs ("dynamic inefficiency"). Consequently, economists condemn monopoly as inefficient.

Lawyers often condemn monopoly as unfair. In monopoly, the seller faces many potential buyers, whereas the buyers face only one potential seller. This asymmetry between seller and buyer constitutes the unfairness of monopoly. The law, consequently, looks on monopoly contracts with skepticism. Earlier we explained that a dire constraint can provide a defense or excuse for breaking a promise. Now we discuss whether monopoly provides a defense or excuse for breaking a promise.

Under the bargain theory, the courts enforce bargained promises and do not ask if the terms are fair. Consequently, the common law historically contains weak protection against monopolies. Most protections against monopolies come from statutes, not common law. Similarly, the "mercantilist" tradition in continental Europe favors monopolies protected by the state. The civil codes of Europe originally provided little protection against monopolies. To illustrate, companies often wish to keep prices high by promising not to compete with each other. Agreements not to compete enable cartels to extract monopoly prices from buyers. The courts in England and America were reluctant to enforce nineteenth century contracts to create cartels. However, the common law did nothing beyond not enforcing cartel contracts to undermine cartels. Cartels were finally outlawed by antitrust statutes, not common law.

Besides contracts to create cartels, two common law doctrines sometimes lead courts not to enforce monopoly contracts. We will explain and critique two doctrines that provide performance excuses for monopoly contracts. For these doctrines, the healthy skepticism of courts concerning monopoly combines with confusion about the underlying economics.

QUESTION 7.40: Explain the relationship between the availability of substitutes and the elasticity of demand for a good.

QUESTION 7.41: I want to build a garage in my backyard. My neighbor's driveway offers the only practical way to reach the proposed garage. I offer to purchase an easement from my neighbor, thus giving me the right to share her driveway. Economists describe the relationship between my neighbor and me as "bilateral monopoly." Explain why this phrase is appropriate.

1. Fill in a Form: Contracts of Adhesion Most written contracts use standard forms. Some terms in a standard-form contract are fixed; others may be variable. For example, the legal staff of an automobile manufacturer may provide its salespersons with form contracts that stipulate the warranty (fixed terms) and leave the price open for negotiation (variable term). Some standard forms do not allow the parties to vary *any* terms. In an extreme situation, one party makes a take-it-or-leave-it offer, meaning that the other party must sign the standard form or not make a contract.

Many fixed terms in standard-form contracts are uniform throughout an industry. For example, many automobile manufacturers promise to repair certain problems with their new cars within the first five years or 50,000 miles of the car's life. When terms are uniform, sellers do not compete over them. Narrowing the scope of competition can reduce its intensity.

To see why, consider cartels. The members of a cartel agree to keep prices up, which profits the members as a group. Each individual member, however, profits even more by undercutting the cartel's price and luring buyers away from other members. To prevent such "cheating," the cartel must punish members who undercut the cartel's price. Uniform, fixed terms in contracts prevent sellers from offering special concessions to buyers. Consequently, the cartel can focus on determining whether all members charge the cartel's price. Monitoring "cheating" in the cartel is much easier when all sellers use the same contract with fixed terms.

In an influential article, Friedrich Kessler called take-it-or-leave-it agreements "contracts of adhesion." (Friedrich Kessler, *Contracts of Adhesion: Some Thoughts About Freedom of Contract*, 43 COLUM. L. REV. 629 [1943].) This term suggests that standard-form contracts indicate the existence of a monopoly, which deprives buyers of bargaining power. Consequently, courts sometimes use "contract of adhesion" as a term of opprobrium to undermine the enforceability of a contract.

This court practice can be justified when sellers use standard-form contracts to reduce competition. However, this court practice is unjustified when sellers use standard-form contracts to increase the efficiency of exchange. Standard-form contracts narrow the scope of bargaining, which can promote efficiency in two ways. First, standard-form contracts can promote price competition by reducing product differentiation. To see why, consider an analogy. Toothpaste comes in different sizes, shapes, colors, textures, tastes, and smells. Manufacturers tinker with these differences in an attempt to attract customers by differentiating their product. Product differentiation complicates price comparisons. Price competition would be more intense if all toothpaste were the same. Similarly, uniformity reduces differences among contracts and intensifies the competition over price.

Second, standard-form contracts reduce transaction costs. The parties can bargain over variable terms, such as the price, and the parties cannot bargain over fixed terms. Thus, standard forms reduce the number of terms requiring drafting, bargaining, and agreement. One of the standard assumptions of a perfectly competitive market is that transaction costs are zero. Standard-form contracts can move a market closer to the perfectly competitive ideal by reducing transaction costs.

The availability of substitutes in perfectly competitive markets prevents anyone from bargaining over price. Similarly, the availability of substitutes in perfectly competitive markets prevents anyone from bargaining over nonprice terms in contracts. In general, substitutes turn everyone into "takers" of the price and nonprice terms of contracts, not bargainers. The fact that many firms use the same standard form may indicate a high level of competition among them. Take-it-or-leave-it contracts can indicate perfect competition rather than monopoly.

Because standard-form contracts can increase competition and efficiency in exchange, the phrase "contract of adhesion" should not be applied to standard-form contracts. Rather, the phrase should be reserved for monopoly contracts. The relevant question is whether a market is competitive or monopolistic. The fact that a contract was made on a standard form does not establish a presumption in either direction.

QUESTION 7.42: Explain how uniformity can reduce price competition by strengthening cartels or increase price competition by reducing product differentiation.

QUESTION 7.43: Competition drives prices down to costs, whereas monopolies price above cost. California banks have paid large damages for allegedly charging fees greater than the cost of certain services that they provide. Suppose a car manufacturer charges an additional $450 for an automatic transmission in a new car. What inefficiencies would result if the consumer could sue the manufacturer and make the company prove that $450 is not disproportionately above the actual cost of the automatic transmission?

QUESTION 7.44: Monopoly distorts contracts by making prices too high. Why would a monopolist ever want to distort the nonprice term by, say, limiting liability for harm caused by defective products?

QUESTION 7.45: Assume that two kinds of buyers purchase contracts from a monopolist who promises to deliver goods in the future. One kind of buyer values the good more highly than the other. The monopolist would like to charge a higher price to the buyers who value the good more highly, but he cannot identify who they are. To overcome this problem, he offers two different contracts. One contract charges a high price and offers to pay high damages in the event that the seller fails to deliver the goods. The other contract charges a low price and offers to pay low damages in the event that the seller fails to deliver the goods. Explain why the two kinds of buyers might prefer different contracts. Explain why the monopolist might gain from offering two kinds of contracts. (In economic jargon, the "menu" of contracts "separates" the "pool" of buyers and permits "price discrimination.")

2. Unconscionability   When a contract seems so one-sided that its enforcement would violate the conscience of the court, it may be set aside according to the common law doctrine of *unconscionability*. The civil law tradition contains a concept similar to unconscionability. "Lesion" refers to a contract that is too unequal to enforce in civil law. It is easy to see why judges do not want to use their power to enforce unconscionable contracts. It is difficult, however, to create legal doctrine about what shocks, or ought to shock, the conscience of a judge.[38] We will use economics to dispel some of the obscurity in the unconscionability doctrine.

Lacking generally accepted definitions, the analysis of unconscionability must proceed from cases. We briefly discuss the famous case of *Williams v. Walker-Thomas Furniture Co.*, 350 F.2d 445 (D.C. Cir. 1965), to show how economics can contradict common sense. *Williams* concerns the purchase of a durable good from a retailer on credit. When a retailer loans the money for a consumer to buy a good, the lender-retailer wants a guarantee of repayment. The borrower offers something valuable that he or she owns (collateral). The lender acquires a right to the valuable object (security interest). If the borrower defaults on the loan, the lender can take

---

[38]Both the *Uniform Commercial Code* and the *Restatement (Second) of Contracts* have attempted definitions of unconscionability, but neither is precise. Here is what they say:

UNIFORM COMMERCIAL CODE, §2–302 comment 1 (1977): "The basic test [of unconscionability] is whether . . . the clauses involved [in the contract] are so one-sided as to be unconscionable under the circumstances existing at the time of the making of the contract . . . The principle is one of the prevention of oppression and unfair surprise . . . "

RESTATEMENT (SECOND) OF CONTRACTS, §208 (1979): "c. Overall imbalance. Inadequacy of consideration does not of itself invalidate a bargain, but gross disparity in the values exchanged may be an important factor in a determination that a contract is unconscionable . . . Such a disparity may also corroborate indications of defects in the bargaining process. . . . gross inequality of bargaining power, together with terms unreasonably favorable to the stronger party, may confirm indications that the transaction involved elements of deception or compulsion, or may show that the weaker party had no meaningful choice, nor real alternative, and hence did not in fact assent or appear to assent to the unfair terms."

possession of the valuable object, sell it, and use the proceeds of the sale to discharge the debt.[39]

In theory, the borrower can offer anything valuable as a guarantee, but in practice the borrower usually offers the item that he or she is buying with the borrowed money, such as a refrigerator or an automobile. The lender-retailer obviously knows the market for that item and can easily resell it. However, consumer durables typically lose value faster than the purchase price is paid off. Consequently, the right to repossess the item being purchased will not fully protect the lender-retailer from loss due to default by the borrower. For example, assume that a car dealer lends $20,000 to a consumer to buy a new car. The instant the car leaves the dealership, it becomes a "used car" and falls in value to, say, $16,000. If the consumer-borrower defaults on the $20,000 loan, the most that the dealer can recover by repossessing the car and reselling it is $16,000.

We explained that the right to repossess the item being purchased does not fully protect the lender-retailer from loss due to default by the borrower. Consequently, consumer-borrowers need additional guarantees in order to borrow money to purchase consumer durables. The best alternative is a cash payment, called a "down payment," equal to the difference between the purchase price and the amount of the loan. But what about the consumer who does not have the cash to make a down payment? That problem can be solved by an "add-on clause," which specifies that any goods that the borrower has previously purchased on credit from the lender-retailer will serve as additional security for the current purchase.

To illustrate, assume that *A* bought a refrigerator from *B*'s store two years ago for $800. *A* borrowed $600 from *B* to make the purchase, and *A* promised to repay the loan at $10 per month for five years. *A* has made payments each month for the past two years and still owes $360 on the refrigerator. Now *A* decides to purchase a television set for $500. *A* does not have the cash for a down payment. Instead, *B* suggests an add-on clause, by which *A* offers the refrigerator and the television as a guarantee. Thus, if *A* should default on the payments for the television, *B* may repossess the television *and* the refrigerator to discharge *A*'s debt on the television.[40]

The *Williams* case involved such an add-on clause. Mrs. Williams was a single mother of seven children and had a limited education. The Walker-Thomas Furniture Company laid claim to most of the household goods she had purchased from it under 14 contracts over a five-year period. In such individual cases, the consumer's situation

---

[39] Most jurisdictions have statutes that limit the repossessor to recovering the debt and the cost of its collection. See Alan Schwartz, *The Enforceability of Security Interests in Consumer Goods*, 26 J. LAW & ECON. 117 (1983).

[40] Recall that *B* cannot realize a profit on this repossession. Of the proceeds from the resale of the repossessed items, *B* may only keep the amount of the loan to which the store is entitled. Anything more than that which comes from the resale must be turned over to *A*.

There is more to the add-on clause. It also provides, typically, that the lender may use discretion in applying each installment payment made with respect to *any* item purchased from the lender-retailer against whatever outstanding balance the lender-retailer chooses. This may allow the creditor to keep the security interest in the refrigerator alive after the five years for which the original loan was to run. By adroit accounting, the creditor can keep this security interest in all previously purchased goods until all the loans have been paid off.

is desperate, and the impulse to provide legal relief is powerful. The *Williams* court held the add-on clause to be unconscionable. To make this showing, we shall need to explain some economics of consumer-credit transactions.

Lawyers focus on individual cases, whereas economists focus upon statistics. Statistically, the paternalistic protection of Mrs. Williams by legal restrictions on the credit market imposes high costs on poor consumers as a class. [41] The add-on clause presumably represents the cheapest way for some poor consumers to obtain credit. Denying them this instrument for borrowing will either force them to borrow at higher costs, or prevent them from borrowing to purchase needed goods. The poor as a class will borrow at higher cost and purchase fewer consumer goods than they otherwise would. Those retailers who offered the add-on clause in an attempt to lower the costs of consumer credit may also be made worse off by the holding. Their sales may decline or their costs may rise; in either case their profits are likely to fall.

We have suggested that Mrs. Williams deserved protection as an individual, and that refusing to enforce add-on clauses harms poor consumers as a class. The courts need a finer analysis to distinguish between consumers who need paternalistic protection and those whom it harms. Some consumers do not understand the complexities of the add-on clause. Perhaps they think that if they fail to make their payments on the most recent purchase, the lender-retailer will repossess only their most recent purchase. Such people undertake an additional loan without fully appreciating the risks and consequences of default. In cases like *Williams*, the court might require proof that the buyer understood the add-on clause as a condition for enforcing it. The courts would require the contractual process to contain protections against ignorance about add-on clauses. The unconscionability doctrine might protect people from their own ignorance, but otherwise let them make their own decisions.

Courts frequently distinguish between *substantive* and *procedural* unconscionability. Substantive unconscionability usually refers to a price that is utterly disproportionate to market value. In contrast, procedural unconscionability consists of circumstances and procedures present at the formation of the bargain that violate widely accepted norms of fairness. Substantive and procedural unconscionability are often combined in actual cases because an unfair procedure frequently results in an unfair price.

QUESTION 7.46: A 21-year-old songwriter signed a contract in 1966 with a music publisher. The standard-form contract assigned the copyrights of all the plaintiff's output to the defendant company in return for the defendant's agreement to pay 50% of the net royalties to the plaintiff. The contract was to run for five years, with automatic renewal for another five years if the plaintiff's royalties during the first term exceeded 5000 pounds sterling. The defendant company could terminate the contract on one month's notice and could assign the contract and any copyrights held under it without the plaintiff's consent. For signing the contract, the plaintiff received 50 pounds as an advance against future royalties. The plaintiff became a successful songwriter and sought to be released from the contract on the ground that it was unconscionably one-sided in the music publisher's favor. *Macaulay v. Schroeder Publishing Co. Ltd.*, (1974) 1 W.L.R. 1308 (H.L.). Use economics to analyze this case.

---

[41] See Richard Epstein, *Unconscionability: A Critical Reappraisal*, 18 J. LAW & ECON. 293 (1975).

Conclusion to Part II

We summarize our analysis of excuses and defenses. The doctrine of incompetence is triggered when an incompetent person makes a promise. The law provides incentives to protect incompetent people at least cost by interpreting contracts in their best interests. The doctrine of duress gets triggered when the promisor threatens destruction in order to induce the promisee to make a one-sided promise. The law creates incentives to deter threats by not enforcing coerced promises. The doctrine of necessity gets triggered when the promisor threatens not to rescue the promisee in order to induce a one-sided promise. The law creates incentives for efficient rescue by requiring the beneficiary to pay the rescuer the cost of rescue plus a reward, and by refusing to enforce the one-sided promise. The doctrine of impossibility gets triggered when a contingency prevents performance. The law encourages efficient precaution and risk-spreading by allocating liability to the party who can bear the risk of the contingency at the least cost.

A contract can separate information and control when both of the parties make a mistake, or when the seller fails to disclose information needed by the buyer to prevent the good's destruction, or when the promisee supplies false information to the promisor.

Turning to monopoly, standard-form contracts can be used to promote collusion in a cartel. Such "contracts of adhesion" should not be enforced. More typically, standard-form contracts increase competition by reducing product differentiation and lowering transaction costs. Finally, "unconscionability" covers a confusing array of doctrines, including bargaining processes that leave consumers ignorant of important terms. If events trigger these terms, the consumers are "unfairly surprised." The remedy is to require process that communicate the information as a condition of enforceability. Table 7.2 encapsulates our analysis.

READING NOTE:

Game theory has become an important tool for analyzing contracts. Here are some articles using those techniques: Avery Katz, *The Strategic Structure of Offer and Acceptance: Game Theory and the Law of Contract Formation*, 89 MICH. L. REV. 215 (1990); Ian Ayres and Robert Gertner, *Filling Gaps in Incomplete Contracts: An Economic Theory of Default Rules*, 99 YALE L. J. 87 (1989); Richard Craswell, *Contract Law, Default Rules, and the Philosophy of Promising*, 88 MICH. L. REV. 489 (1989); Jason S. Johnston, *Strategic Bargaining and the Economic Theory of Contract Default Rules*, 100 YALE L. J. 615 (1990); and Charles Goetz and Robert Scott, *The Limits of Expanded Choice: An Analysis of the Interactions Between Express and Implied Contract Terms*, 75 CALIF. L. REV. 261 (1985).

Recent law and economics papers on the legal doctrines covered in this chapter include the following: Ian Ayres and Robert Gertner, *Strategic Contractual Inefficiency and the Optimal Choice of Legal Rules*, 101 YALE L. J. 729 (1992); Robert Birmingham, *A Rose by Any Other Word: Mutual Mistake in Sherwood v. Walker*, 21 U. CAL.-DAVIS L. REV. 197 (1987); Richard Craswell, *Precontractual Investigation as an Optimal Precaution Problem*, 17 J. LEGAL STUD. 401 (1989): Mark Gergen, *Liability*

Table 7.2

DEFENSES AND EXCUSES

legal doctrine	fact triggering legal doctrine	incentive problem	legal solution
incompetence	incompetent person makes promise	protect incompetents at least cost	interpret contract in incompetent's best interests
duress	promisee threatens to destroy	deter threats	no enforcement of coerced promises
necessity	promisee threatens not to rescue	reward rescue	beneficiary pays cost of rescue plus reward
impossibility	contingency prevents performance	encourage precaution and risk-spreading	liability for the least-cost risk-bearer
frustration of purpose	contingency destroys purpose of performance	encourage precaution and risk-spreading	liability for the least-cost risk-bearer
mutual mistake about facts	buyer and seller make same mistake about facts	encourage precaution and risk-spreading	liability for the least-cost risk-bearer
mutual mistake about identity	buyer and seller have different object in mind	prevent involuntary exchanges	unwind contract
unilateral mistake	buyer or seller mistaken about facts	unite knowledge and control; encourage discovery	enforce contract
duty to disclose	promisee harms by withholding information	induce supply of true information	liability for harm
fraud	promisee supplies false information knowingly	deter supply of false information	no enforcement of contract and liability for harm
adhesion contracts	cartel uses standard forms to promote collusion	destabilize cartels	deny enforcement to contracts of cartels
procedural unconsionability	consumer ignorant of critical terms in retailer's contract	create incentive to communicate meaning of contract terms	deny enforcement unless bargaining process communicates crucial information

for Mistake in Contract Formation, 64 SO. CAL. L. REV. 1 (1990); Andrew Kull, *Unilateral Mistake: The Baseball Card Case*, 70 WASHINGTON U. L. Q. 57 (1992); Eric Rasmusen and Ian Ayres, "Mutual and Unilateral Mistake," *Stanford Law and Economics Working Paper Series* (1992); and Janet and Richard Smith, *Contract Law, Mutual Mistake, and Incentives to Produce and Disclose Information*, 19 J. LEGAL STUD. 467 (1990); and Ayres and Rasmusen, *Mutual Versus Unilateral Mistake in Contracts*, 22 J. LEGAL STUD. 309–343 (1993).

8

AN ECONOMIC THEORY OF TORT LAW

"The early law asked simply, 'Did the defendant do the physical act which damaged the plaintiff?' The law of today, except in certain cases based upon public policy, asks the further question, 'Was the act blameworthy?'"

—

James Barr Adams, Law and Morals, 22 HARV. L. REV. 97, 99 (1908)

"Even if there is no negligence, public policy demands that responsibility be fixed wherever it will most effectively reduce the hazards to life and health inherent in defective products that reach the market."

—

Judge Roger Traynor, Escola v. Coca Cola Bottling Company, 150 P.2d 436
(1944)

People often harm each other by doing something wrong: motorists collide on the highway; a patron in a bar punches the person standing next to him; an intra-uterine birth control device causes infertility; a newspaper inaccurately reports the arrest of a businessman for soliciting a prostitute; a professor gives an unfair exam; and so forth. Some of these wrongs are accidental and some are intentional; some are serious and others are trivial; some are crimes and others are annoyances.

Suppose that the victim in each of these cases initiates a law suit. Under what body of law can the victim sue? Because the plaintiff and defendant are private persons (not the state), the suit belongs, by definition, to "private law." We have already studied two bodies of law that are mostly private—the law of property and law of contracts. The victim cannot sue under contract law because a broken promise did not cause the injury in any of these cases. The victim cannot sue under property law for damage to body, reputation, or scholastic record because these things are not *property.* (You cannot transfer your body, bequeath your reputation, or sell your scholastic record.) In contrast, an automobile is property, and the owner can sue under property law to protect it. However, the conventional remedy in property law would not succeed in the case of an automobile accident. The conventional remedy for interfering with a property right is a court order forbidding future interference, which cannot remedy past harms such as the damage from an automobile accident.

These facts demonstrate the need for a third major body of private law other than property and contracts. The third body of law concerns compensable wrongs that do not arise from breach of contract and cannot be remedied by an injunction against future interference. Here are some more detailed examples:

EXAMPLE 1: Joe Potatoes has been driven to distraction by the escapades of his wife, Joan Potatoes. At the end of a hard night's work at the loading dock, Joe is approached by Jim Bloggs. Suspecting that Jim has been romancing Joan, Joe insults and strikes him, breaking his nose. Bloggs subsequently sues for the injury to his reputation and his nose.

EXAMPLE 2: Three hunters go into the woods after pheasants. They are spread out in a straggling line about 25 yards apart, walking in the same direction, when the hunter in the center flushes a bird that flies up, its wings pounding. The hunters to his left and right turn toward the bird in the middle and fire. The bird escapes, but the hunter in the middle is blinded by birdshot. One of the two hunters certainly caused the harm, but there is no way to determine which one of them it was. The victim sues both of them.

EXAMPLE 3: A manufacturer produces automobile fuel additives that demand careful control over quality. If quality control is maintained at a high level, the chemical mixture in the product is correct, and it never causes damage to automobile engines. If, however, quality control is relaxed and allowed to fall to a low level, some batches of the chemical mixture will be flawed. A few of the cars using the flawed batch will be harmed; specifically, the engine will throw a rod and tear itself to pieces. After a rod is thrown, an alert mechanic can detect the cause of the harm by examining the car's fuel and other signs. The manufacturer determines that a high level of quality control costs more than the harm to some automobile engines caused by a low level of quality control, so the manufacturer adopts a low level of quality control.

In English-language countries, the name for the body of common law relevant for these cases is *tort* law. After the Normans conquered England in 1066, they soon lost the French language, but they retained a peculiar form of it for writing about law. *Tort* is "law-French," itself derived from the Latin word *tortus* (twisted). The common law of torts overlaps the law of "civil responsibility" in continental Europe. The continental Europeans use this phrase to refer to private suits over injuries, as opposed to criminal prosecutions. However, different legal traditions locate the boundaries of these broad areas of law somewhat differently and adopt somewhat different legal doctrines.

Example 1 illustrates an "intentional tort," so named because the injurer intentionally inflicted the harm on the victim. Many intentional torts are also crimes, such as assault, battery, false imprisonment, and intentional infliction of emotional duress. The person who commits such an act may be sued for damages under tort law by the victim and also prosecuted under criminal law by the state. Intentional torts are so much like crimes that we shall not discuss them here. Instead, we shall rely upon our analysis of crime in Chapter 11 to serve as an introduction to intentional torts.

Most of the wrongs that we shall consider in the two chapters on torts are *unintentional*, that is, inadvertent accidents. To illustrate, Example 2 describes a hunting accident. Example 3 is more complicated. The manufacturer's low level of quality control is deliberate, and the resulting harm to automobiles is statistically predictable, but the harm to particular cars is accidental. Example 3 also differs from the other two examples in that the injurer sold a product to the victim, so the two parties participated in a commercial transaction.

The law of accidents was one of the first bodies of private law successfully analyzed using formal economic models. We shall explain these models in this chapter. As with all our introductory chapters in this book, we focus first on theory. In the next chapter we apply economic theory to some specific areas of tort law, develop a more detailed analysis, and explore proposals to reform the tort-liability system.

I. DEFINING TORT LAW

We began this chapter by listing examples of harm for which the laws of contracts and property offer no remedy. The victim cannot use these laws to sue when there is no breach of contract, or no damage to property, or no continuing harm to enjoin. We explained that this gap creates the need for tort law. Now we want to demonstrate that this gap in the law of property and contracts *necessarily* exists and, by doing so, we shall describe the economic essence of tort law.

A. Economic Essence of Tort Law

As explained in Chapter 4, property law facilitates cooperation among people by defining rights clearly. As we explained in Chapter 6, contract law facilitates cooperation among people by enabling them to make credible commitments. Property and contract laws enable people to cooperate over many kinds of harm that one person imposes upon another. To illustrate, recall the examples that we discussed when explaining the Coase theorem, such as the rancher's cows and the farmer's crop, or the electrical company's smoke and the laundry's white clothes, or the sparks from the railroad and the farmer's wheat fields.

For some kinds of harm, however, the costs of bargaining are so high that the parties cannot cooperate together. For example, every driver cannot negotiate with every other driver and agree among themselves concerning how to allocate the cost of future accidents. Nor can every driver enter into a contract with every pedestrian who might get hit by a car. Motorists will not reach a private agreement to take socially efficient care.

For other kinds of negotiations, the absolute costs are low, but the relative costs are high. To illustrate, consider the three hunters in Example 2. Before hunting pheasants, they could negotiate an agreement to allocate the cost of an accident. However, the cost of negotiating (including the unpleasant atmosphere it creates) is large relative to the small probability of a hunting accident. As these examples illustrate, a gap necessarily exists in property and contract law when high transaction costs preclude bargaining.

In Example 1, Joe Potatoes was not in a frame of mind to negotiate when he broke the nose of Jim Bloggs. The obstacle to cooperation in Example 1 is emotions, not costs. In Example 3, where defective fuel additives destroy automobile engines, the manufacturer may think that most consumers will remain ignorant of the dangers caused by defective fuel additives. Consequently, the manufacturer of fuel additives may not want to alert consumers by mentioning the danger in the consumer contract or the product's warranty. The obstacle to cooperation in Example 3 is consumers' ignorance and the producer's strategic decision to keep information private.

Recall that the Coase theorem treats all obstacles to bargaining—including bargaining costs, emotions, private information, and strategy—as "transaction costs." We can use this idea to explain the boundary between the law of contracts and torts. Contract law concerns relationships among people for whom the transaction costs of private agreements are relatively low, whereas tort law concerns relationships among people for whom transaction costs of private agreements are relatively high. Economists describe harms that are outside private agreements as *externalities*. The economic purpose of tort liability is to induce injurers to *internalize* these costs. Tort law internalizes these costs by making the injurer compensate the victim. When potential wrongdoers internalize the costs of the harm that they cause, they have incentives to invest in safety at the efficient level. The economic essence of tort law is its use of liability to internalize externalities created by high transaction costs.

Tort liability is only one of several policy instruments available to internalize externalities created by high transaction costs. Alternative policy instruments include criminal statutes, safety regulations, and tax incentives. Each alternative has its advantages and disadvantages. This chapter will explain the strengths and weaknesses of tort liability as an instrument for internalizing externalities.

QUESTION 8.1: In Chapter 6, we distinguished between a default rule and a regulation. A default rule applies unless the parties explicitly agree to an alternative. A regulation applies regardless of what the parties agree to. In Chapter 6 we contrasted the circumstances under which default rules in contract law are more efficient than regulations, and the circumstances under which regulations are more efficient than default rules. Use economics to draw this same contrast between default rules and regulations in tort law.

B. The Traditional Theory of Tort Liability

We described the essence of tort law in terms of its economic function. Before analyzing these functions, we describe a traditional legal theory of torts. In the early twentieth century, a legal theory specified the essential elements of a tort. This traditional theory of tort law enjoyed substantial acceptance in America at the turn of the century, although it never achieved the same degree of consensus as did the classical theory of contracts. We discuss the traditional theory because the essential elements of a tort as stipulated by it serve as building blocks in the economic model of tort liability.

Three elements must be present for recovery by the plaintiff under the traditional theory of torts:

1. the plaintiff must have suffered *harm*;
2. the defendant's act or failure to act must *cause* the harm; and
3. the defendant's act or failure to act must constitute the *breach of a duty* owed to the plaintiff by the defendant.

We will explain each element in turn and develop an economic account of it.

1. Harm   The first element required for a plaintiff to sue in tort is that he or she must have suffered harm. Without harm, there can be no suit in tort, even if the act was dangerous. To illustrate, suppose that the manufacturer in Example 3 sold a batch of fuel additives that were harmless in cars with conventional carburetors and dangerous in cars with turbocharged carburetors. The owner of a car with a conventional carburetor might feel outrage when these facts become known, but outrage is not compensable. Similarly, liability law does not compensate for exposure to risk, as opposed to the realization of risk. To illustrate, suppose that a manufacturer accidentally exposes 100 of its workers to a chemical that, according to medical experts, will cause 15% of them to develop liver cancer 20 years from now. Under traditional tort doctrine, the victims cannot recover for exposure to the risk. Instead, the victims must wait until 20 years have passed and then the people who actually develop cancer can sue for damages. Some scholars advocate compensating victims for exposure to risk, but so far U.S. courts have not allowed it.

Harm has a simple economic interpretation: a downward shift in the victim's utility or profit function. To illustrate, Charlie's utility function in Figure 8.1 is defined over two goods—health (along the vertical axis) and wealth (along the horizontal axis). An indifference curve in Figure 8.1, such as u_0 or u_1, depicts all the combinations of health and wealth that give Charlie the same level of satisfaction. Higher indifference curves indicate more satisfaction. Thus, any combination of health and wealth that lies above u_0 is more desirable to Charlie than any combination that lies below u_0. The shape of Charlie's indifference curves indicates that he is willing to trade off one good to get more of the other. To illustrate, as Charlie moves down u_0, his wealth increases at a rate that exactly offsets his declining health. Similarly, as Charlie moves up u_1, his health improves at a rate that exactly offsets his declining wealth.

Suppose that Charlie initially has health in the amount H_0 and wealth in the amount W_0, which results in utility $u_0 = u(H_0, W_0)$. Now suppose that Amanda injures Charlie, causing his health to fall to H_1 and his wealth to fall to W_1. Charlie has been harmed in that he has been pushed from u_0 down to u_1 by Amanda. Perfect compensation requires Amanda to restore Charlie's satisfaction to level u_0. Money damages are the traditional means of doing this. Assume that costly medical treatment can restore Charlie's health. Typically, those damages would constitute a sum equal to $(W_0 - W_1)$ to compensate for the lost wealth and a sum equal to the cost of providing $(H_0 - H_1)$ units of health. This would restore Charlie to his original position before the wrong was done to him.

Suppose, however, that the accident did irreparable damage to Charlie's health, so that he is stuck at H_1 forever. Amanda could, nonetheless, restore his preaccident level

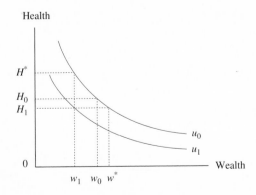

FIGURE 8.1 Showing harm as a displacement from a higher to a lower indifference curve and the measures of compensation.

of satisfaction by increasing his wealth, not to its preaccident level of W_0, but rather to level W^*. Because Charlie trades off wealth and health, Amanda can give him the monetary-equivalent of his irreparable decline in health. (Note that our account of compensatory money damages here is identical to the account of *Hawkins v. McGee* in Chapter 7.)

Figure 8.1 illustrates the ideal of perfect compensation. In reality, tort law limits the harms for which victims can receive compensation from their injurers. Traditionally, courts were willing to compensate for tangible losses that are easy to document, such as medical costs, lost income, the costs of replacing or repairing damaged property, and the like. By contrast, courts were traditionally reluctant to compensate for intangible losses or those that are difficult to measure, such as emotional harm, distress, loss of companionship, and "pain and suffering." Over the years, however, American courts have steadily expanded the list of compensable harms to include many intangibles. To illustrate by Example 1, Bloggs may receive compensation for the emotional distress of being reviled and struck by Potatoes. Other countries have also expanded the scope of compensable harms, but not so far as the United States.

Expanding the scope of compensable harm has advantages and disadvantages. On the one hand, this expansion allows compensation for real harms that would have gone unredressed, as illustrated by the following historical example. Suppose that a motorist accidentally kills one of the dependent children of a loving family. The death of the child entails no loss of income to the rest of the family; on the contrary, death saves the family the expense of raising the child. This fact once posed a difficult problem for courts: they wished to confine compensable damages to economic losses that are measurable, and yet no such losses follow from the death of dependent children. For the surviving members of the family to recover damages, courts had to allow compensation for emotional distress and loss of companionship.

Expanding the scope of compensable harms also creates a vexing problem: how is the court to assign a dollar value to intangible (but real) losses? As explained, *perfect compensation* means a sum of money sufficient to make the victim of an injury equally well off with the money and the injury as he or she would have been without the money or the injury. Perfect compensation is the right goal for courts trying to internalize costs, but implementing the goal is difficult for intangible harms. Implementation is difficult because the court cannot observe and measure the plaintiff's subjective valuation of the loss of companionship, emotional distress, or pain and suffering. Even worse, the very idea of perfect compensation sometimes fails in court. Compensation for a child's death is *not* an amount of money such that the parents would just as soon have the money as their child.

Is the benefit of expanding the scope of compensable harms greater or less than the cost of trying to measure intangible harms? Economic analysis suggests how to begin answering this difficult question, but this discussion will have to wait until the next chapter, when we consider how to set damages for intangible harms.

QUESTION 8.2: Suppose that a person who is burned in an accident suffers intense pain for one week and then fully recovers. What does "perfect compensation" mean in principle as applied to the burn? Why do you expect actual compensation to be imperfect?

QUESTION 8.3: Describe some difficulties in implementing perfect compensation for the destruction by fire of Blackacre, the estate of the Gascoyne-Stubbs family for 15 generations.

2. Cause   According to the traditional theory, the second element of a tort is "cause." In order for the plaintiff to sue, according to the traditional theory, the defendant must have *caused* the plaintiff's harm. To illustrate by modifying Example 1, suppose that just as Potatoes' fist was about to strike Bloggs' nose, the floor board broke under Bloggs and he fell down, breaking his nose when he struck the ground. The fall enabled Bloggs to avoid Potatoes' fist, but he broke his nose anyway. In this new example, there is a wrong (throwing a punch), and there is damage (a broken nose), but the former did not cause the latter. Without causation, the wrongdoer who threw the punch is not liable in tort law for the harm.

The element of causation sharply differentiates torts from morality. To illustrate, suppose that in Example 2, both of the hunters were equally reckless when they discharged their guns at the pheasant. It was a matter of mere chance that one of the hunters actually blinded the victim and the other hunter missed. Because they were equally reckless, they are on the same plane morally. They may be equally blameworthy, but they are not equally liable. Under traditional rules of tort liability, only the hunter who actually *caused* the harm is liable; the hunter who missed is not liable.

The idea of causation may seem simple—perhaps an image comes to mind of billiard balls colliding with each other—but this impression is misleading. Causation is a notoriously difficult philosophical topic, and that difficulty carries over into law. The law distinguishes two types of causes. The first and more comprehensive is "cause-in-fact." Lawyers often use a simple criterion, called the "but-for test," to decide whether action *A* was the cause-in-fact of event *B*: "But for *A*, would *B* have occurred?" If the answer to this question is "no," then *A* is the cause-in-fact of *B*. If the answer to this question is "yes," then *A* is *not* the cause-in-fact of *B*.

To illustrate, we apply the but-for test to Example 3. An automobile owner cannot recover unless the defective fuel additive was the cause-in-fact of her engine's having thrown a rod. But for the defective fuel additive, would the car have thrown a rod? If the answer is "no," then the defective fuel additive is the cause-in-fact; if the answer is "yes," then the defective fuel additive is not the cause-in-fact.

The but-for test can determine causation in many legal cases, but in some cases it is useless or misleading. It is often useless in cases involving multiple causes of harm. To illustrate by changing Example 1 again, suppose that Potatoes takes a swing at Bloggs, who dodges the punch and lands on some rotten floorboards that collapse under him, and the fall breaks Bloggs' nose. But for Potatoes' trying to strike Bloggs, would Bloggs have broken his nose? The answer depends upon whether or not Bloggs would have stepped on the rotten floorboards even if he did not have to dodge the punch from Potatoes. It is unclear whether or not Potatoes' punch was the cause-in-fact of the broken nose.

Another problem arises when applying the but-for test to a sequence of events that precede an injury: the but-for test allows distant causes to have the same weight as proximate causes.[1] To illustrate, return to the original Example 1, in which Potatoes'

---

[1] A famous illustration of how great events can be said to be caused by remote causes comes from *Mother Goose*:

> For want of a nail, the shoe was lost;
> For want of a shoe, the horse was lost;
> For want of a horse, the rider was lost;
> For want of a rider, the battle was lost;
> For want of the battle, the kingdom was lost;
> And all for the want of a horseshoe nail.

fist breaks Bloggs' nose. The fist is the cause-in-fact of Bloggs' broken nose, but so are many other things. For example, but for having been born, Potatoes would not have broken Bloggs' nose; but for Joe's parents conceiving him, he would have not been born; so Joe's parents are a cause-in-fact of Bloggs' broken nose. The but-for test does not discriminate between the proximate cause (Joe's fist) and the remote cause (Joe's conception).

The defendant's act must be the *proximate* cause of the plaintiff's harm to establish legal liability under the traditional theory. Proximity is a matter of degree, so the question arises, "How close must the connection be in order for a particular cause to be 'proximate' in law?" One of the most famous cases addressing this problem is *Palsgraf v. Long Island Railway Co.* (248 N.Y. 399, 162 N.E. 99 [1928]). The relevant facts, as determined by the court, were these:

> Plaintiff [Mrs. Palsgraf] was standing on a platform of defendant's railroad after buying a ticket to go to Rockaway Beach. A train stopped at the station, bound for another place. Two men ran forward to catch it. One of the men reached the platform of the car without mishap, though the train was already moving. The other man, carrying a package, jumped aboard the car, but seemed unsteady as if about to fall. A guard on the car, who had held the door open, reached forward to help him in, and another guard on the platform pushed him from behind. In this act, the package was dislodged, and fell upon the rails. It was a package of small size, about fifteen inches long, and was covered by a newspaper. In fact it contained fireworks, but there was nothing in its appearance to give notice of its contents. The fireworks when they fell exploded. The shock of the explosion threw down some scales at the other end of the platform many feet away. The scales struck the plaintiff, causing injuries for which she sues.

The New York court determined that the railroad was *not* liable for Mrs. Palsgraf's injuries because the railroad guard's actions in pushing the passenger were too remote in the chain of causes to be deemed the legal cause of the plaintiff's harm.[2] As this case illustrates, "proximity" in law is imprecise, although sometimes decisive, for liability.

The idea of cause in tort law connects to functions in economic models. In economic models, the consumer's preferences are described by a utility function, and the producer's technology is described by a production function. The values of the variables in the utility function determine the consumer's level of utility, and the values of the variables in the production function determine the level of output. The consumer chooses the values of variables that he or she controls in the utility function to maximize it, and the producer chooses the values of the variables that he or she controls in the production function to maximize profits. One person harms another when the variables that he or she controls lower the utility or production of someone else. For example, the Long Island Railway Company controlled variables affecting its production that also affected Mrs. Palsgraf's utility. The functional representation of cause in tort law is a variable controlled by one person that appears in the utility or production function of someone else.

---

[2] As is often true with famous cases, the facts are not as straightforward as generations of law students are led to believe. See John Noonan, PERSONS AND MASKS OF THE LAW 127(1976).

To illustrate, assume that Amanda enjoys smoking, which we indicate by the function $u_A = u_A(S, \ldots)$, where u_A denotes Amanda's utility, S denotes the amount that Amanda smokes, and " $\ldots$ " indicates all the other variables affecting Amanda's utility. Charlie's utility depends upon his health and wealth, which we write $u_C = u_C(H,W)$. Assume that Charlie's health is a decreasing function of Amanda's smoking: $H = H(S)$. Amanda's utility function, $u_A = u_A(S)$, and Charlie's utility function, $u_C = u_C(H(S),W)$, both contain the variable S. The variable S that Amanda controls directly affects Charlie's utility. (By further complicating the preceding functions, we could represent a probabilistic relationship between Amanda's smoking and Charlie's health.[3])

When the same variable appears in different people's utility or production functions, the functions are "interdependent." Interdependent utility or production functions constitute an externality when obstacles prevent the parties from bargaining together and reaching an agreement to set the interdependent variable at the efficient value. "Cause" in tort law typically involves an externality created by interdependent utility or production functions.

> **QUESTION 8.4:** Suppose that a car stalls on the railroad tracks because its carburetor is badly maintained. A train collides with the car because the train's brakes are badly maintained. What is the proximate cause of the accident? Who had the "last clear chance" to avoid the accident? Does the answer to the first question affect the answer to the second question?

3. Breach of a Duty In some circumstances, the first two elements that we have just identified—harm and proximate cause—are sufficient to establish liability in tort for the defendant. A rule of liability based upon harm and causation is called "strict liability." For example, a construction company that uses dynamite to clear rocks from the path of a road is liable in common law for any harm caused by the blasting. In general, the common law applies a rule of strict liability to "abnormally dangerous activities" like blasting with dynamite.[4]

In the usual case, however, the victim must demonstrate more than harm and cause in order to recover damages from the defendant. In addition to these two elements, the plaintiff must usually demonstrate that the defendant breached a duty that he or she owed to the plaintiff, and that the breach caused the plaintiff's harm. To illustrate, Joe Potatoes in Example 1 breached a duty not to strike Bloggs. When an injurer breaches a legal duty, he or she is said to be "at fault" or to have been "negligent." For example, one or both of the hunters in Example 2 was at fault in handling a gun.

A rule of liability requiring the plaintiff to prove harm, causation, and fault is a rule of "intentional tort" or a "negligence" rule. Rules of intentional tort concern inflicting harm on purpose, and negligence rules concern fault in taking precaution against accidents. Unlike a rule of strict liability, a negligence rule permits the defense that the accident occurred in spite of the fact that the injurer satisfied all of the applicable standards of care.

---

[3] To illustrate, let $H = 1$ indicate "no cancer," and $H = 0$ indicate "cancer." Let p indicate the probability of cancer, where $p = p(S)$ is an increasing function. Charlie's expected utility can be written $p(S)u_c(0,W) + (1 - p(S))u_c(1,W)$.

[4] RESTATEMENT (SECOND) OF TORTS §519(1) (1977).

We want to develop an economic representation of fault. Some fault is binary (either-or, yes-no, on-off). For example, either a passenger fastens her seat belt or she does not fasten it; either a swimming pool has a lifesaving ring or it does not have one. Sometimes, however, the legal standard of care applies to a continuous variable. For example, a car can change speed continuously, and the trustee can vary continuously the proportion of the trust's portfolio in government bonds (a very safe investment). Economists often prefer to develop theory using continuous variables. Consequently, we denote precaution by the continuous variable x, with larger values of x corresponding to higher levels of precaution. The plaintiff in a tort suit must usually demonstrate that the defendant breached a duty owed to the plaintiff. A duty of care is a legal standard prescribing the minimum acceptable level of precaution. In Figure 8.2, $\tilde{x}$ denotes the legal standard. Precaution below $\tilde{x}$ breaches the duty of care, and precaution equal to $\tilde{x}$ or exceeding it satisfies the duty of care. Precaution $\tilde{x}$ partitions the line in Figure 8.2 and creates two zones—a permitted zone and a forbidden zone. Thus, $x < \tilde{x}$ implies that the actor is at fault, whereas $x > \tilde{x}$ implies that the actor is not at fault, where x indicates the actual amount of precaution taken by the injurer. Under a negligence rule, decision-makers who take precaution as great or greater than the legal standard escape liability for another person's accidental harms. Those who take less precaution than the legal standard may have to pay compensatory damages for another person's accidental harms.

How is fault determined by law? In many nations, the government imposes precise safety regulations upon certain activities, such as speed limits on highways, whereas other legal duties are left vague, such as the legal definition of "reckless driving." For activities such as reckless driving, the law may draw upon unwritten social norms and community conventions, such as the "rule of the road." Legal traditions differ in their reliance upon broad principles of care and their preferred language for expressing these principles. The common law in the English-language countries stresses the duty of *reasonable* care. This standard compares the defendant's actual care and the care that a *reasonable person* would have taken under the circumstances. The civil codes of Europe are not anchored by the concept of "reasonableness." Continental lawyers often feel discomfort toward a rule of reasonable care, which seems to give too little guidance to people and too much discretion to judges. Consequently, the civil codes often strive for greater specificity in prescribing duties. Civilian lawyers sometimes invoke broad principles, such as "abuse of right" (*e.g.,* an owner exercises property rights in a way that harms others), or the "pater familias" (a person obligated to treat some other people much like the father treats his family), or "rationality" (choosing effective means to legal ends). As we shall see, economic analysis reveals similarities in behavior underlying these differences in legal language and traditions.

We have used Figure 8.2 to explain the meaning of "negligence." Under that liability rule, proof of negligence is a necessary condition for liability. In contrast, under a rule of strict liability, proof of causation is a necessary condition for liability, and proof of negligence is unnecessary. Some scholars detect a pattern of movement between these two rules over the history of liability law. Strict liability was the usual rule between clans in stateless tribes. Similarly, strict liability was the usual rule in much of Europe before the nineteenth century, but, according to these historians, negligence became the usual rule by the beginning of the twentieth century. Thus, the requirement of fault as a condition for liability triumphed recently, as suggested by the first quota-

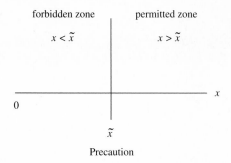

FIGURE 8.2 Legal standard of care for continuous precaution.

tion at the beginning of this chapter. The rule of strict liability, however, enjoyed a renaissance in the second half of the twentieth century, especially for the liability of manufacturers to American consumers. Manufacturers in America are now held liable for the harms caused by their defective products, regardless of whether or not the manufacturer was at fault, as suggested by the second quotation at the beginning of this chapter. To illustrate by Example 3, the manufacturer of a defective fuel additive is strictly liable for harm it causes to automobile engines.

> **QUESTION 8.5:** Adapt Figure 8.2 to represent the rule that motor vehicles must stay within a designated speed limit (say 90 kilometers per hour).

> **QUESTION 8.6:** Offer an economic explanation for why the owner of a dog is liable for the harm it causes due to his negligence, whereas the owner of a tiger is strictly liable for any harm that it causes.

Conclusion to Part I

The three elements of tort liability fit neatly into a coherent picture of social life. We impose risks upon each other in our daily lives. Society has developed norms that prescribe standards of behavior to limit these risks. People sometimes cause harm by violating these standards of behavior. The cost of the harm must fall upon someone. The courts trace cause of the harm back to the violation of the standard and assign liability either to the party at fault or simply to the party who caused the harm.

Most torts correspond to this picture, which makes it useful as an introduction to the subject. The actual practices of the courts, however, have departed from the traditional theory of torts. Modern courts sometimes find liability in cases where one of the three elements of a tort is missing. Later we describe some of these departures from the traditional theory, and, in doing so, we sketch the frontiers of liability law in the United States.

We have been discussing the definition of tort law. Philosophy concerns definitions, but science concerns causes. Rather than defining "tort" by identifying its essential elements, economic analysis models the effects of alternative liability rules. Models of tort rules can explain much more than definitions, as we will show.

LET US NOW PRAISE REASONABLE MEN

The following famous parody of the reasonable person standard is from an essay entitled "The Reasonable Man" by Lord A. P. Herbert:

"The Common Law of England has been laboriously built about a mythical figure—the figure of 'The Reasonable Man.' He is an ideal, a standard, the embodiment of all those qualities which we demand of the good citizen. . . . It is impossible to travel anywhere or to travel for long in that confusing forest of learned judgments which constitutes the Common Law of England without encountering the Reasonable Man. . . .

The Reasonable Man is always thinking of others; prudence is his guide, and 'Safety First' is his rule of life. He is one who invariably looks where he is going and is careful to examine the immediate foreground before he executes a leap or bound; who neither star-gazes nor is lost in meditation when approaching trap-doors or the margin of a dock; who records in every case upon the counterfoils of checks such ample details as are desirable, who never mounts a moving omnibus, and does not alight from any car while the train is in motion; who investigates exhaustively the *bona fides* of every mendicant before distributing alms, and will inform himself of the history and habits of a dog before administering a caress; who believes no gossip, nor repeats it, without firm basis for believing it to be true; who never drives his ball till those in front of him have definitely vacated the putting-green which is his own objective; who never from one year's end to another makes an excessive demand upon his wife, his neighbors, his servants, his ox, or his ass; who in the way of business looks only for that narrow margin of profit which twelve men such as himself would reckon to be 'fair,' and contemplates his fellow-merchants, their agents, and their goods, with that degree of suspicion and distrust which the law deems admirable; who never swears, gambles, or loses his temper; who uses nothing except in moderation, and even while he flogs his child is meditating only on the golden mean. [He] stands like a monument in our Courts of Justice, vainly appealing to his fellow-citizens to order their lives after his own example. . . . "

QUESTION 8.7: Describe the three elements of a tort in the following situations:

a. Motorists driving on crossing streets come to an intersection with a stop light and collide.

b. The owner of Al's Donut Shop spreads the false rumor that patrons of Betty's Donut Shop got ptomaine poisoning from the jelly in her donuts.

c. The escalator in a store rips a customer's pant leg to shreds.

II. AN ECONOMIC THEORY OF TORT LIABILITY

We have explained that, when high transaction costs preclude private agreements, tort liability can induce injurers to internalize the costs that they impose on other people. Now we develop the simplest model of cost internalization by tort law, using the economic interpretations of harm, cause, and fault.

A. Minimizing the Social Costs of Accidents

We begin with some notation and simple functions. The probability of an accident, which we denote p, decreases with increases in precaution, which we denote x. Thus $p = p(x)$ is a decreasing function of x. If an accident occurs, it causes harm such as lost income, damage to property, medical costs, and the like. Let A denote the monetary value of the harm from an accident. A multiplied by p equals the *expected* harm in dollars ("expected" because of the probabilistic element).

Like $p(x)$, the expected harm $p(x)A$ is a decreasing function of precaution x.[5] To depict this fact, the horizontal axis in Figure 8.3 indicates the quantity of the actor's precaution, x, and the vertical axis indicates dollar amounts, including the dollar amount of expected harm $p(x)A$. The curve labeled $p(x)A$ in Figure 8.3 slopes down, indicating that expected harm decreases as precaution increases.

Taking precaution often involves the loss of money, time, or convenience. We assume that precaution costs $\$w$ per unit. To keep the analysis simple, we assume that w is constant and does not change with the amount of precaution x. Consequently, wx equals the total amount spent on precaution. The graph of wx in Figure 8.3 is a straight line through the origin whose slope equals w.

Figure 8.3 depicts two kinds of costs of accidents: the cost of precaution and the cost of expected harm. In the simplest model, we assume that accidents have no other social costs.

Consequently, we may add the costs of precaution and expected harm to obtain the expected social costs of accidents, which we denote SC:

$$SC = wx + p(x)A. \tag{8.1}$$

The expected social cost curve in Figure 8.3 is thus obtained by adding vertically the line wx and the curve $p(x)A$ at every level of precaution x. The result is the U-shaped curve, which is labeled $SC = wx + p(x)A$.

Because the expected-social-cost curve is U-shaped, a value of x exists that corresponds to the bottom of the U. This value, denoted x^* in Figure 8.3, is the level of precaution that minimizes the expected social costs of the accident. Efficiency requires minimizing social costs, so x^* is the *socially efficient* level of precaution or, simply, the *efficient* level of precaution.

Let us characterize x^* mathematically. The cost of a little more precaution (marginal cost) equals the price per unit w. A little more precaution reduces the expected cost of harm (marginal benefit). This reduction in the expected cost of harm equals the reduction in the probability of an accident, which we denote $-p'(x)$ multiplied by the cost of harm A.[6] When precaution is efficient, the cost of a little more precaution (marginal cost) equals the resulting reduction in the expected cost of harm (marginal benefit). Thus, the efficient level of precaution x^* can be found by solving the following equation:

---

[5] To keep the graph simple, we assume that A is a constant. The analysis would not be changed by assuming that A is a decreasing function of x, so long as $p(x)A$ is a concave function.

[6] The prime ($'$) after p indicates the slope of the graph of the function $p(x)$ at x. The slope is negative in Figure 8.3, so that minus sign in front of the p makes the expression $-p'(x)$ positive.

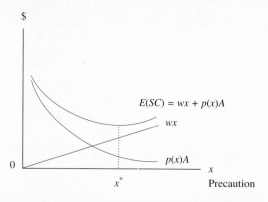

FIGURE 8.3 The expected social costs of accidents shown as the sum of precaution costs and the expected cost of harm.

$$w \qquad = \qquad -p'(x^*)A.$$

$$\text{marginal social cost} \qquad\qquad \text{marginal social benefit} \qquad (8.2)$$

(Those of you who are familiar with calculus can obtain equation 8.2 by setting the first derivative of equation 8.1 with respect to precaution equal to zero.)

If precaution is less than the efficient amount, then the marginal social cost of precaution is less than the marginal social benefit: $(x < x^*) \Rightarrow (w < -p'(x)A)$. When the marginal social cost of precaution is less than the marginal social benefit, efficiency requires taking more precaution. In these circumstances, we say that more precaution is *cost-justified*. Similarly, if precaution exceeds the efficient amount, then the marginal social cost of precaution exceeds the marginal social benefit: $(x > x^*) \Rightarrow (w > -p'(x)A)$. In these circumstances, efficiency requires taking less precaution.

Figure 8.3 describes the effects of precaution on social costs. We have not said whose precaution is depicted in Figure 8.3. Sometimes the potential injurer can take precaution and the potential victim cannot, as when a surgeon operates on an unconscious person. Sometimes both the injurer and the victim can take precaution, as when the manufacturer assures the purity of a drug and the consumer takes the recommended dosage. Figure 8.3 can be taken to represent the relationship between social costs and precaution by the victim or the injurer.

B. Incentives for Precaution Under Strict Liability and No Liability

Having characterized the efficient level of precaution, we now consider the incentives needed to obtain it. In general, incentives are efficient when the decision-maker internalizes the marginal costs and marginal benefits of his or her action. Incentives for precaution in the simple model depend upon who can take precaution against accidents, and how the law allocates the costs of harm. We shall contrast the incentive effects of several different legal rules for allocating the costs of harm.

First, we consider the case in which the victim chooses precaution, which we indicate by placing subscript v on x and w. The victim pays the cost w_v for x_v units of precaution. Now consider the cost of harm A, which is suffered by the victim. Assume that the law does not entitle the victim to receive compensation from the injurer for the accident. In other words, assume that the tort rule is *no liability*. Consequently, the victim bears the expected harm $p(x_v)A$. The total costs that the victim expects to bear equal the cost of precaution plus the expected cost of harm: $w_v x_v + p(x_v)A$. The victim has an incentive to minimize the costs that he or she bears. Consequently, the victim chooses x_v to minimize $w_v x_v + p(x_v)A$. The minimum occurs at the level of precaution, denoted x_v^*, where the victim's marginal cost of precaution equals the resulting reduction in the expected cost of harm:

$$w_v \qquad = \qquad -p'(x_v^*)A.$$

victim's marginal cost   victim's marginal benefit   (8.2$'$)

Equation 8.2$'$ corresponds to the efficiency condition given by Equation 8.2. Thus, we have shown that *the rule of no liability causes the victim to internalize the marginal costs and benefits of precaution, which gives the victim incentives for efficient precaution.*

Now we repeat the analysis with a different legal rule. Consider the victim's incentives for precaution when the injurer is *strictly liable,* and the victim receives *perfect compensation.* (Although unrealistic, the assumption of perfect compensation is very useful analytically.) As before, the victim bears the cost of precaution $w_v x_v$, and the victim also bears the expected cost of harm, $p(x_v)A$. In addition, the victim receives damages D when an accident occurs. By assumption, the damages are perfectly compensatory damages: $D = A$. Thus, total *net* costs that the victim expects to bear under the rule of strict liability with perfectly compensatory damages equal the cost of precaution:

$$w_v x_v + p(x_v)A - p(x_v)D = w_v x_v.$$

The victim has an incentive to minimize the costs that he or she bears. Consequently, the victim chooses x_v to minimize $w_v x_v$. Because x_v cannot fall below zero, the minimum occurs when precaution is zero: $x_v = 0$. Thus, we have shown that *the rule of strict liability with perfectly compensatory damages gives the victim no incentive to take precaution.*

This conclusion has a simple explanation. With a rule of strict liability and perfect compensation, the victim is indifferent between an accident with compensation, and no accident. The victim pays the cost of his or her own precaution and gains no advantage from reducing the probability of accidents. In other words, the victim internalizes the costs of precaution and externalizes the benefits. So, the victim has an incentive not to take any precaution.

We have analyzed the effects of the rule of no liability and the rule of strict liability on the victim's incentives for precaution. The first rule gives incentives for efficient precaution by the victim, and the second rule gives the victim no incentives for precaution. Now we consider the effect of these two rules on the *injurer's* incentives for precaution. Instead of assuming that precaution x is chosen by the victim, assume that it is chosen by the injurer, which we indicate by placing a subscript i on x. The injurer pays the cost w_i for x_i units of precaution. The harm A, however, is suffered by the victim. Unless the law re-allocates the cost of the harm, the injurer will externalize it.

Assume that the rule of law is strict liability with perfect compensation. Thus, whenever an accident occurs, the injurer must pay damages equal to the cost of the harm: $D = A$. The injurer's expected liability equals the probability of an accident multiplied by the harm caused by it: $p(x_i)A$. The total costs that the injurer expects to bear under the rule of strict liability with perfect compensation equal $w_i x_i + p(x_i)A$. The injurer has an incentive to minimize the costs that he or she bears. Consequently, the injurer chooses x_i to minimize $w_i x_i + p(x_i)A$. The minimum occurs at the level of precaution, denoted x_i^*, where the injurer's marginal cost of precaution equals the resulting reduction in the expected cost of harm:

$$w_i \qquad = \qquad -p'(x_i^*)A.$$
$$\text{(injurer's marginal cost)} \qquad \text{(injurer's marginal benefit)} \qquad (8.2'')$$

Equation 8.2″ corresponds to the efficiency condition given by Equation 8.2. Thus, we have shown that the *rule of strict liability with perfect compensation causes the injurer to internalize the marginal costs and benefits of precaution, which gives him or her incentives for efficient precaution.*

Finally, we consider the effect of the rule of no liability on the injurer's incentives for precaution. Assume that precaution x_i is chosen by the injurer, so the injurer bears the cost of precaution $w_i x_i$. The harm A, however, is suffered by the victim, and, under the rule of no liability, A remains where it falls on the victim, and the injurer pays no damages: $D = 0$. The total costs paid by the injurer thus equal $w_i x_i$. The injurer has an incentive to minimize the costs that he or she bears. Consequently, the injurer chooses x_i to minimize $w_i x_i$. Because x_i cannot fall below zero, the minimum occurs when precaution is zero: $x_i = 0$. Thus, we have shown that the *rule of no liability gives the injurer no incentive to take precaution.* This conclusion has a simple explanation: With no liability, the injurer is indifferent between an accident and no accident. Thus, the injurer internalizes the costs of precaution and externalizes the benefits.

We summarize these conclusions in the box in Table 8.1. Notice the symmetry in the box: The victim's incentives for precaution under either rule are the same as the

---

Table 8.1

EFFICIENCY OF INCENTIVES CREATED BY LIABILITY RULES

"yes" indicates efficient incentives

"no" indicates inefficient incentives

"zero" indicates no incentive

(assuming perfect compensation and legal standards equal to efficient precaution)

legal rule	PRECAUTION		ACTIVITY LEVEL	
	victim	injurer	victim	injurer
no liability	yes	zero	yes	no
strict liability	zero	yes	no	yes
simple negligence	yes	yes	yes	no
negligence + contributory negligence	yes	yes	yes	no
strict liability + contributory negligence	yes	yes	no	yes
comparative negligence	yes	yes	yes	no

injurer's incentives for precaution under the other rule. The box suggests how the law could create incentives for efficient precaution. If only the victim can take precaution, then a rule of no liability provides incentives for efficient precaution. If only the injurer can take precaution, then a rule of strict liability with perfect compensation provides incentives for efficient precaution.

C. Bilateral Precaution

In the preceding discussion, we assumed that only one party to an accident can take precaution against it, which we call the assumption of *unilateral precaution*. We concluded that, since no liability provides incentives for efficient precaution by the victim, a rule of no liability is preferable when only the victim can take precaution against accidents. Conversely, because strict liability provides incentives for efficient precaution by the injurer, a rule of strict liability is preferable when only the injurer can take precaution against accidents.

Now we consider the case in which *both* the victim and injurer *can* take precaution, and efficiency *requires* both of them to take it. We call this condition the assumption of *bilateral precaution*. Under this assumption, the social cost function has the form

$$SC = w_v x_v + w_i x_i + p(x_v, x_i)A,$$

and social costs are minimized at positive values of precaution for both parties: $x_v^* > 0$ and $x_i^* > 0$. We have already explained that a rule of no liability causes the victim to internalize the cost of harm and the injurer to externalize it. Consequently, the victim has efficient incentives, and the injurer has inefficient incentives. This is true whether precaution is unilateral or bilateral. Conversely, a rule of strict liability with perfect compensation causes the injurer to internalize the cost of harm and the victim to externalize it. Consequently, the injurer has efficient incentives, and the victim has inefficient incentives. This is also true whether precaution is unilateral or bilateral. We have arrived at a dilemma: *Neither the rule of strict liability nor the rule of no liability creates incentives for efficient precaution by both parties, as required for efficiency under the assumption of bilateral precaution.*

We cannot escape this dilemma by dividing the costs of harm between the victim and injurer. Dividing the costs of harm between them causes each of them to externalize part of it, so both of them have incentives for deficient precaution.[7] The solution to the dilemma lies in a negligence rule, which we explain in the next section.

QUESTION 8.8: Assume that you park your car in a legal parking space on a corner, and a driver who comes around the corner too fast rams the bumper of his truck into your car,

---

[7] To see why, assume that the rule is strict liability with *deficient* compensation, by which we mean that actual compensation falls short of the amount required for perfect compensation ($D < A$). Under strict liability with deficient compensation, the injurer *in*ternalizes the fraction of harm *ex*ternalized by the victim (specifically, D), and the injurer *ex*ternalizes the fraction of harm *in*ternalized by the victim (specifically, $A - D$). Consequently, the rule of strict liability with deficient compensation does not provide incentives for efficient precaution by the injurer. To repeat the argument in notation, efficiency requires the injurer to choose x_i to minimize $w_i x_i + p(x_v, x_i)A$, whereas a rule of strict liability with compensatory damages D causes the injurer to minimize $w_i x_i + p(x_v, x_i)D$. If $D = A$, then the injurer's incentives are efficient; if $D < A$, then the injurer's incentives are deficient.

This same argument can be repeated for the victim.

damaging your car but not his truck. A rule of no liability gives the driver of the truck the same incentives to avoid such accidents as the incentives given to you to park you car in a safe place under a rule of strict liability with perfect compensation. Explain why.

QUESTION 8.9: Explain why the incentive problem in the previous question cannot be solved by a rule of strict liability with imperfect compensation (say, actual compensation equal to 50% of perfect compensation).

D. Incentives for Precaution Under a Negligence Rule

We shall now prove that a negligence rule can give efficient incentives to the victim and the injurer. A negligence rule imposes a legal standard of care with which actors must comply in order to avoid liability. We assumed that courts apply a definite standard requiring a fixed amount of precaution, and this assumption permitted us to represent the legal standard, denoted $\tilde{x}$, as partitioning precaution into permitted and forbidden zones in Figure 8.2. Now we combine the representation of a negligence rule in Figure 8.2 and the economic analysis of incentives developed using Figure 8.3.

The legal standard in Figure 8.2 is denoted $\tilde{x}$, and x^* denotes the efficient level of precaution in Figure 8.3. To combine the figures, we must say how $\tilde{x}$ relates to x^*. The simplest assumption, which we justify later, is that the legal standard equals the efficient level of care: $\tilde{x} = x^*$. This assumption permits us to combine the figures as represented in Figure 8.4. The forbidden zone $(x < \tilde{x})$ in Figure 8.4 corresponds to deficient precaution relative to the efficient level $(x < x^*)$, and the permitted zone $(x > \tilde{x})$ corresponds to excessive precaution relative to the efficient level $(x > x^*)$. Precaution at the boundary between the two zones equals efficient precaution $(x = x^*)$.

Consider the injurer's costs as a function of his level of precaution. In the permitted zone, injurers are not liable, so they bear the cost of their own precaution $w_i x_i$, but they do not bear the cost of the victims' harm. Thus, the injurer's costs in the permitted zone $(x_i \geq \tilde{x})$ are indicated by the straight line $w_i x_i$ in Figure 8.4. In the forbidden zone, injurers are liable, so they bear the cost of their own precaution $w_i x_i$ and the expected harm to the victim $p(x_i)A$. Thus, the injurer's expected costs in the forbidden zone $(x_i < \tilde{x})$ are indicated by the curve $w_i x_i + p(x_i)A$ in Figure 8.4. Thus, the injurer's costs under a negligence rule are indicated in Figure 8.4 by a smooth curve that jumps down at $x = \tilde{x}$ and then becomes a straight line. The lowest point on this curve occurs

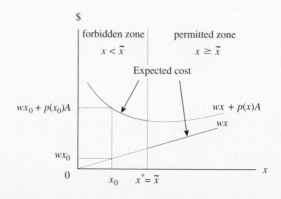

FIGURE 8.4 Expected costs with a discontinuity at x^*.

when the injurer's precaution equals the legal standard: $x = \tilde{x}$. The injurer has an incentive to set precaution at this level in order to minimize costs. We have shown that *a negligence rule with perfect compensation and the legal standard equal to the efficient level of care gives the injurer incentives for efficient precaution.*

To illustrate the incentive effects of a negligence rule, consider how the injurer would find his or her preferred level of care. Assume the injurer sets his precaution equal to x_0 in Figure 8.4, in which precaution costs him $\$wx_0$ and he expects to pay $\$p(x_0)A$ in liability for accidents. The cost to the injurer of taking one more unit of precaution beyond x_0 is less than the resulting savings in expected liability because of the lower probability of an accident. Consequently, the rational injurer will take more precaution. He or she will continue taking more precaution until he or she reaches x^*, where liability falls to zero. Having reached x^*, the injurer has no incentive to increase precaution. If injurers' precaution exceeds x^*, they pay only for their own precaution, which costs w_i per unit, but their liability remains zero, so they will not take additional precaution beyond x^*.[8]

Recall that we began this section with a dilemma: How can a liability rule provide incentives for efficient precaution by the injurer and the victim? We have explained how a negligence rule can provide incentives for efficient precaution by the injurer. Now it is simple to explain how a negligence rule can provide incentives for efficient precaution by the victim. As explained, a rational injurer takes precaution at the legal standard ($x_i \geq \tilde{x}$) in order to avoid liability for the harm caused by accidents. When the injurer is not liable, the victim of an accident receives no compensation for accidental harm. Consequently, the victim responds as if the rule of law were no liability. We have already proved that a rule of no liability causes the victim to internalize the marginal costs and benefits of precaution, which gives incentives for efficient precaution. In general, a negligence rule that induces the injurer to escape liability by satisfying the legal standard provides incentives for efficient precaution by the victim. Our conclusions about the incentives created by a negligence rule are summarized in the third line of Table 8.1.

QUESTION 8.10: A game is in equilibrium when no player can increase his or her payoff by changing strategy, so long as the other players do not change their strategies.[9] Prove that the simple liability game is in equilibrium when the injurer and the victim take efficient care.

E. Contributory Negligence And Comparative Negligence

The negligence rule has several different forms. We have been discussing its simplest form, which holds the injurer liable for accidents that he or she causes if, and only if, precaution is below the legal standard, regardless of the victim's level of precaution. Symbolically, we may describe simple negligence as follows:

---

[8] We can prove this more formally. Given a negligence rule with perfect compensation and the legal standard equal to the efficient level of care, the injurer faces the following cost function:

$$x < x^* \text{ (forbidden zone)} \qquad \Rightarrow \qquad \text{injurer's costs} = w_i x_i + p(x_i)A;$$
$$x \geq x^* \text{ (permitted zone)} \qquad \Rightarrow \qquad \text{injurer's costs} = w_i x_i.$$

In the forbidden zone, the injurer's costs approach a minimum as x approaches x^*. In the permitted zone, the injurer's cost are minimized when x equals x^*. Therefore, the injurer minimizes costs by setting x equal to x^*.

[9] This is the definition of a *Nash equilibrium*.

simple negligence:

injurer at fault, $x_i < x_i{}^*$	$\Rightarrow$	injurer liable;
injurer faultless, $x_i \geq x_i{}^*$	$\Rightarrow$	injurer not liable.

Now we consider the rule of *negligence with a defense of contributory negligence*. Under this rule of law, the negligent injurer can escape liability by proving that the victim's precaution fell short of the legal standard of care. You already encountered contributory negligence in Chapter 3 in the case of *Butterfield v. Forrester*. The defense of contributory negligence imposes a legal standard of care upon the victim. Symbolically, we may represent this form of the negligence rule as follows:

negligence with a defense of contributory negligence:

injurer at fault, $x_i < x_i{}^*$, and victim faultless, $x_v \geq x_v{}^* \Rightarrow$ injurer liable;

injurer faultless, $x_i \geq x_i{}^*$, or victim at fault, $x_v < x_v{}^* \Rightarrow$ injurer not liable.

The following example contrasts the two forms of the negligence rule. Someone dives into a swimming pool and strikes her head on the bottom. She sues the owner of the pool for failing to post signs warning that the pool was too shallow for diving. The pool owner admits that he posted no warnings, but he also asserts that the victim was negligent for diving without checking the depth of the water. If both parties are negligent, the pool owner is *liable* under a rule of *simple* negligence, and the pool owner is *not liable* under a rule of negligence with a defense of *contributory negligence*.

Under the rules of simple negligence or negligence with a defense of contributory negligence, one party is responsible for all the costs of accidental harm, even though both parties are at fault. Another form of the negligence rule, called "comparative negligence," divides the cost of harm between the parties in proportion to the contribution of their negligence to the accident. For example, if the victim's negligence is 20% responsible for her accidental harm, and the injurer's negligence is 80% responsible for her accidental harm, then the victim may recover 80% of her losses from the injurer.

Symbolically, we may represent the rule of comparative negligence as follows:

comparative negligence:

injurer at fault, $x_i < x_i{}^*$, and victim faultless, $x_v \geq x_v{}^* \Rightarrow$ injurer bears 100%;

injurer faultless, $x_i \geq x_i{}^*$, and victim at fault, $x_v < x_v{}^* \Rightarrow$ victim bears 100%;

injurer at fault, $x_i < x_i{}^*$, and victim at fault, $x_v < x_v{}^* \Rightarrow$ bear cost in proportion
to negligence.[10]

We have discussed the rules of simple negligence, negligence with a defense of contributory negligence, and comparative negligence. Other forms of the negligence rule exist. For example, the rule of *strict liability with a defense of contributory negligence*

---

[10]The extent of the injurer's negligence equals $\tilde{x}_i - x_i$. The extent of the victim's negligence equals $\tilde{x}_v - x_v$. The proportion of each party's negligence, which can be used to divide liability under a rule of comparative negligence, is given as follows:

$\tilde{x}_i - x_i / [(\tilde{x}_i - x_i) + (\tilde{x}_i - x_v)]$	$=$	negligent injurer's porportion of liability;
$\tilde{x}_v - x_v / [(\tilde{x}_v - x_i) + (\tilde{x}_v - x_v)]$	$=$	negligent victim's proportion of liability.

To illustrate, if a car going 40 kilometers per hour collides with a car going 35 kph on a street with a speed limit equal to 30 kph, then the two motorists divide liability in the proportions $2/3$ and $1/3$, respectively.

assigns the cost of accidental harm to the injurer, regardless of his or her level of precaution, unless the victim was at fault:

strict liability with a defense of contributory negligence:

victim at fault, $x_v < x_v^*$ $\Rightarrow$ injurer not liable;

victim faultless, $x_v \geq x_v^*$ $\Rightarrow$ injurer liable.

To illustrate, consumer products are sometimes subject to the rule of strict liability with a defense of contributory negligence. Under this rule, the manufacturer of a defective product is liable for the harm it causes to nonnegligent consumers and not liable for the harm it causes to negligent consumers.

The different forms of the negligence rule have an elegant mathematical symmetry, which we describe in the appendix to this chapter.

We have characterized four different forms of the negligence rule. The economic analysis of law proved a startling fact about the simple model of tort liability: *Assuming perfect compensation and each legal standard equal to the efficient level of care, every form of the negligence rule gives the injurer and victim incentives for efficient precaution.*

It is easy to explain why. Recall why the simple negligence rule provides incentives for efficient precaution by both parties: a rational injurer takes precaution equal to the legal standard in order to escape liability, and, knowing this, a rational victim internalizes the harm from accidents, which gives incentives for efficient precaution. We can generalize this proof to every form of the negligence rule. Assume perfect compensation and each legal standard equal to the efficient level of precaution. Under every form of the negligence rule, *one* of the parties can escape bearing the cost of harm by satisfying the legal standard. This party will take efficient precaution in order to avoid the cost of harm. The *other* party will, consequently, internalize the cost of the harm from accidents, which creates incentives for efficient precaution. Table 8.1 summarizes our conclusions about liability rules and incentives for precaution.

QUESTION 8.11: Suppose that B's faulty driving causes an accident that injurers driver A. A was not at fault in her driving, but she was not wearing her seat belt, and this fact aggravated her personal injury. Discuss liability under the rules of simple negligence, negligence with a defense of contributory negligence, and comparative negligence.

QUESTION 8.12: Would the efficiency of a rule of simple negligence increase by imposing a standard of care on victims? Explain your answer by reference to the simple model.

F. Activity Levels

In the simple model, the rules of no liability and strict liability provide incentives for efficient precaution by the victim or injurer, but not both, whereas the various forms of the negligence rule create incentives for efficient precaution by the injurer and victim. Thus, the simple model provides a policy reason to prefer a negligence rule whenever precaution is bilateral. The simple model does not, however, provide a reason for preferring one form of the negligence rule to another. A complication of the model will provide an efficiency argument for distinguishing different forms of the negligence rule.

In the simple model, the injurer and victim choose precaution. Now we complicate the model by allowing them to make an additional choice. The probability of an automobile accident depends upon the level of precaution when driving, and the *amount* that one drives. By driving 10,000 miles a year, the probability that you will injure someone in an accident is approximately 10 times higher than it would be if you drove only 1,000 miles per year. We shall compare the incentive effects of different liability rules on the amount of risky activities, such as driving, that people engage in.

First, we contrast the rules of simple negligence and strict liability. Under a negligence rule, a driver can escape liability by conforming to the legal standard of care, no matter how much he or she drives. So the driver can increase driving by tenfold, which increases the risk of harm to others by tenfold, without increasing his or her expected liability. Under a negligence rule the marginal risk of harm to others from more driving is externalized.

The incentive structure is quite different under a rule of strict liability. If a driver is strictly liable for the harm caused, then he or she internalizes the social costs of accidents from whatever source—whether from the activity level or a lack of precaution. Strict liability induces the potential injurer to set every variable affecting the probability of an accident at its efficient level. So, the rule of strict liability can induce both efficient precaution and an efficient activity level by drivers.[11]

We can generalize this conclusion to all activities and all liability rules. Some liability rules induce some actors to avoid liability by satisfying the legal standard of care. In the end, however, someone must bear the cost of accidental harm. We call that person the *residual* bearer. To illustrate by the simple model, the victim is the residual bearer of harm under the simple negligence rule, whereas the injurer is the residual bearer of harm under the rule of strict liability with a defense of contributory negligence. In general, *the residual bearer of harm internalizes the benefits of any of his or her actions that reduce the probability or severity of accidents, including more precaution and less activity*.

We can use this generalization to expand Table 8.1. The last two columns show the effect of alternative liability rules on the incentives for the activity levels of the victim and injurer. Under each rule, the residual bearer of harm has incentives for an efficient activity level, whereas the party who escapes bearing the cost of accidental harm has incentives for an inefficient activity level.

Table 8.1 provides a useful guide for lawmakers to choose among liability rules. First, consider the problem of efficient incentives for precaution. If efficiency requires only one party to take precaution, then "no liability" and "strict liability" are just as efficient as a negligence rule. If efficiency requires bilateral precaution, then a negligence rule provides more efficient incentives for precaution than "no liability" and "strict liability." Second, consider the problem of efficient incentives for the activity level. Usually one party's activity level affects accidents more than the other party's activity level. Efficiency requires choosing a liability rule so that the party whose activity level most affects accidents bears the residual costs of accidental harm.

Besides providing a useful guide, Table 8.1 shows some limits of liability law in creating efficient incentives. To illustrate, the different liability rules can provide incentives for an efficient activity level by either one of the parties, but not both of them. In other words, *bilateral activity levels* create a dilemma for lawmakers. In general, policy-makers have difficulty hitting two targets with one policy variable. To hit two policy targets, two controls are usually required, just as two stones are usually

---

[11] The original statement of this result is found in Steven Shavell, *Strict Liability versus Negligence*, 9 J. LEGAL STUD. 1 (1980).

needed to hit two birds. Thus, an additional control variable from outside liability law may be needed to control activity levels. For example, the number of miles driven by motorists can be influenced by a gasoline tax or an insurance policy whose premiums increase with the number of miles driven.

QUESTION 8.13: Who is the residual bearer of the costs of harm under a rule of comparative negligence? Explain your answer.

QUESTION 8.14: In Table 8.1, *no liability* and *strict liability* have the opposite incentive effects upon activity levels. Why?

QUESTION 8.15: For purposes of the theory of accidents, how would you define the *activity level* of a railroad? An airline? For some activities, the *level* relevant to the probability of an accident is difficult to define. Can you define an activity level relevant to a homeowner's maintenance of her front steps? A pharmaceutical company's sale of a drug with dangerous side effects?

G. Setting Legal Standards: The Hand Rule

Our discussion of negligence rules assumes that the legal standard equals the efficient level of precaution ($\tilde{x} = x^*$). Now we want to explain how lawmakers can identify the efficient level of precaution when setting the legal standard. An American judge developed a famous rule to solve this problem in the case called *United States v. Carroll Towing Co.*[12] We describe the facts of the case and excerpt the part of the judge's decision in which he formulates his rule.

The case concerned the loss of a barge and its cargo in New York Harbor. A number of barges were secured by a single mooring line to several piers. The defendant's tug was hired to take one of the barges out of the harbor. In order to release the barge, the crew of the defendant's tug, finding no one aboard any of the barges, readjusted the mooring lines. The adjustment was not done properly, with the result that one of the barges later broke loose, collided with another ship, and sank with its cargo. The owner of the sunken barge sued the owner of the tug, claiming that the tug owner's employees were negligent in readjusting the mooring lines. The tug owner replied that the barge owner was also negligent because his agent, called a "bargee," was not on the barge when the tug's crew sought to adjust the mooring lines. The bargee could have assured that the mooring lines were adjusted correctly. In deciding the case, Judge Learned Hand formulated his famous rule as follows:

L. HAND, J. . . . It appears from the foregoing review that there is no general rule to determine when the absence of a bargee or other attendant will make the owner of a barge liable for injuries to other vessels if she breaks away from her moorings. . . . Since there are occasions when every vessel will break away from her moorings, and since, if she does, she becomes a menace to those about her; the owner's duty, as in other similar situations, to provide against resulting injuries is a function of three variables: (1) the probability that she will break away; (2) the gravity of the resulting injury, if she does; (3) the burden of adequate precautions. Possibly it serves to bring this notion into relief to

---

[12] 159 F.2d 169 (2d Cir. 1947).

state it in algebraic terms: if the probability be called P; the injury, L; and the burden, B; liability depends upon whether B is less than L multiplied by P, *i.e.*, whether $B < PL$ ... [Judge Hand subsequently applied the formula to the facts of the case and concluded that, because $B < PL$ in this case, the barge owner was negligent for not having a bargee aboard during the working hours of daylight.]

Judge Hand's statement of his rule is unclear as to whether the variables refer to marginal values or total values. If we assume that he was a good economist who had marginal values in mind, then we can translate his notation into our notation as used in the simple model of precaution:

Hand's name	Our name	Hand's notation	Our notation
burden	marginal cost of precaution	B	w_i
liability	cost of accidental harm	L	A
probability	marginal probability	P	p'

Substituting our notation into Hand's formula, we obtain the following rule:

marginal Hand rule: $w_i < -p'A$ $\Rightarrow$ injurer is negligent.

The marginal Hand rule states that the injurer is negligent if the marginal cost of his or her precaution is less than the resulting marginal benefit. Thus, the injurer is liable under the Hand rule when further precaution is cost-justified. Further precaution is cost-justified when precaution falls short of the efficient level ($x < x^*$).

To escape liability under Hand's rule, the injurer must increase precaution until the inequality becomes an equality:

$$w \qquad = \qquad -p'(x^*)A.$$

$$\underset{\text{marginal social cost}}{} \qquad \underset{\text{marginal social benefit}}{} \qquad (8.3)$$

If the injurer's precaution is efficient ($x = x^*$), then the marginal social cost equals the marginal social benefit ($w_i = -p'A$). At this point, further precaution is not cost-justified.

American courts frequently use the Hand rule to decide questions of negligence.[13] Repeated application of the Hand rule enables adjudicators to discover the efficient level of care. In a series of cases, the adjudicators ask whether further precaution was cost-justified. If the answer is "yes," then the injurer has not satisfied the legal standard and the injurer is liable. Injurers will presumably respond to this decision by increasing their level of precaution. Eventually a case will reach the adjudicators in which further precaution is not cost-justified. Just as a climber can reach the peak of a smooth mountain in a fog by always going up, so the court can discover the efficient level of care by

---

[13] The Hand rule is enshrined in the definition of negligence offered by the American Law Instistute in the RESTATEMENT (SECOND) OF TORTS.

holding defendants liable for failing to take cost-justified precautions. In fact, the Hand rule follows the same search pattern used by some computer programs to maximize a function.[14]

Case-by-case application of the Hand rule is one way to find an efficient legal standard. Another approach is to draft regulations or statutes specifying a legal standard that equals the efficient level of precaution. For example, highway officials may compute the efficient speed for motorists on a particular road, taking into account the value of the time of motorists and the reduction in accidents from driving more slowly. The officials can then declare the efficient speed to be the legal speed limit. Politicians and bureaucrats sometimes behave in this way, but their decisions more often reflect their own interests.

To apply the Hand rule, the decision-maker must know whether a little more precaution costs more or less than the resulting reduction in expected accident costs. Calculating the expected accident costs $p(x)A$ can be difficult. For example, if you increase your driving speed from, say, 40 miles per hour to 50, will the average loss resulting from an accident increase by $1,000,000, or by $10, or something in between? Cost-benefit analysis demands a lot of information from anyone who uses it, whether an injurer, a court, a legislature, or an administrator. Liability law should take into account who is in the best position to obtain information about accidents. If courts can obtain accurate information about accidents at moderate cost, this fact favors case-by-case adjudication. Alternatively, if a legislature or regulator can obtain accurate information about accidents at moderate cost, this fact favors a system of public law for accidents, like workers' compensation for on-the-job injuries.

Another approach is for the law to enforce social customs or the best practices in an industry. In this approach, the lawmakers do not try to balance marginal costs and benefits. Rather, the lawmakers rely upon the community of people who created the norm, or the industry that engages in the practice, to balance costs and benefits. For example, a residential community has norms concerning the maintenance of steps leading to houses, and the accounting industry has practices concerning careful auditing. When enforcing these "community standards," the courts need much less information than when they compute the marginal costs and benefits of precaution. Before enforcing the community standard, however, the lawmakers should ascertain whether the community actually balances costs and benefits. In Chapter 10 we will return to this topic when we consider the evolution of social norms towards efficiency.

QUESTION 8.16: Suppose that the sunken barge in *United States v. Carroll Towing Co.* and its cargo are worth $100,000. Assume that the probability that the barge would break loose if the bargee is not present equals 0.001. If the bargee is present, then the probability of the barge's breaking loose is reduced by half, to 0.0005. Paying the bargee to stay on the barge will cost the barge owner $25. If the barge owner does not incur this $25 expense, is his behavior negligent under the Hand rule?

---

[14] The maximum of a continuous, concave function can be found by going in the direction where the derivative is largest, just as a mountain climber in a fog might go in the direction where the grounds slopes up the steepest.

H. Errors

In tort disputes, mistakes are often made concerning the extent of harm, the cause of the accident, and the actor's fault. Such mistakes are unavoidable by courts and law-makers because they must rely upon information provided to them by interested par-ties, such as the plaintiff and defendant. Such mistakes are also common among injur-ers and victims of accidents because they lack expert information about risks and precaution. In this section we explain how such mistakes affect incentives, and how lawmakers and courts should take account of their own fallibility.

First consider how a mistake by the court in estimating harm affects precaution. The effects are different under a rule of strict liability and a rule of no liability. The injurer's incentives for precaution are efficient under a rule of strict liability with perfect com-pensation. But suppose the court estimates harm inaccurately and fails to set damages equal to perfect compensation. If the damages actually awarded by the court fall short of perfect compensation, then the injurer will externalize part of the cost of accidental harm, so he or she will have incentives to take deficient precaution. Conversely, if the damages actually awarded by the court exceed perfect compensation, then the injurer will have incentives to take excessive precaution. In general, *court errors in setting damages under a rule of strict liability cause the injurer's precaution to respond in the same direction as the error.*

Second, consider mistakes in determining who caused an accident under a rule of strict liability. Specifically, assume that the court sometimes fails to hold someone liable who caused an accident. This kind of error lowers the expected liability of the injurer, just like awarding deficient damages. The effect of lowering the probability of liability is the same as the effect of lowering the amount of damages: the injurer takes less precaution. In general, *court errors in determining who caused accidents under a rule of strict liability cause the injurer's precaution to respond in the same direction as the error.*

The situation is different under a negligence rule. Under a negligence rule, the injurer's expected costs jump at the legal standard $\tilde{x}$, as depicted in Figure 8.4. To the left of this discontinuity, the injurer's expected costs are $\$[wx + p(x)A]$; to the right of this discontinuity, the potential injurer's expected costs are $\$wx$. The injurer's expected costs are minimized when precaution exactly equals the legal standard ($x = \tilde{x}$) and he or she escapes liability. In general, *injurer's precaution does not respond to modest court errors in setting damages under a negligence rule.*[15]

This fact is illustrated in Figure 8.5, where lines A through D indicate different lev-els of expected accident costs. When the court awards perfectly compensatory dam-ages, the injurer's expected liability costs in Figure 8.5 are given by curve B. Above curve B, the courts award excessive damages, which results in an expected-cost curve such as A. Below curve B, the courts award deficient damages, which results in an

---

[15] Here is a more precise, and more technical, statement of the contrast: Many injurers respond a little to changes in damages under a rule of strict liability (response on the intensive margin), whereas a few injurers respond a lot to change in the legal standard under a negligence rule (response on the extensive margin, with nonconvexity in expected-cost function).

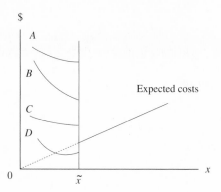

FIGURE 8.5 A single legal standard and different expected accident costs.

expected-cost curve such as *C*. Regardless of these court errors, the injurer's expected costs jump down to $w_i x$ when the injurer satisfies the legal standard, so the injurer still minimizes expected costs by setting his or her precaution equal to the legal standard, $x = \tilde{x}$. To change the injurer's cost-minimizing precaution, the error made by the court in awarding damages must be *very* large, as illustrated by the curve labeled *D*.

We discussed errors by the court in awarding damages under a rule of strict liability. Rather than interpreting Figure 8.5 as depicting errors by courts, we can interpret the figure as depicting errors by injurers. For example, think of curves *A, B, C,* and *D* as depicting the expected-costs of four different injurers. Curve *B* depicts the injurer who predicts court behavior accurately, curve *A* depicts the injurer who errs by overestimating court damages, and curve *C* depicts the injurer who errs by underestimating court damages. Regardless of these errors, the injurer's expected costs jump down to $w_i x$ when he or she satisfies the legal standard. So, each injurer still minimizes expected costs by setting precaution equal to the legal standard, $x = \tilde{x}$. To change the injurer's cost-minimizing precaution, the error in predicting damages must be *very* large, as illustrated by the curve labeled *D*. In general, *injurer's precaution does not respond to injurer's modest errors in predicting damages under a negligence rule*.

We interpreted the different expected-cost curves in Figure 8.5 as indicating an error by the court or the injurer in computing damages. Alternatively, the different expected-cost curves could be interpreted as indicating an error in determining who caused the accident. In general, *injurer's precaution does not respond to court's modest errors in determining who caused an accident under a negligence rule*.

Having discussed errors in computing damages and determining causes, we turn to errors in setting the legal standard. By "errors," we mean situations in which lawmakers set the legal standard different from the efficient level of precaution. Most injurers minimize their costs by conforming exactly to the legal standard, regardless of whether it exceeds or falls short of efficient precaution. Consequently, an excessive legal standard causes excessive precaution, and a deficient legal standard causes deficient precaution. In general, *injurer's precaution responds exactly to court errors in setting the legal standard under a negligence rule*.

To illustrate, Figure 8.6 depicts the injurer's expected costs under a negligence rule when the legal standard is less than the efficient level of precaution: $\tilde{x} < x^*$. The darkened curves in Figure 8.6 indicate the injurer's costs as a function of the level of precaution. The injurer minimizes costs by setting precaution equal to the legal standard: $x = \tilde{x}$. His or her precaution is less than the efficient level: $x < x^*$. Consequently, too many accidents occur.

QUESTION 8.17: Use a graph to explain the efficiency consequences of a legal standard that exceeds the efficient level of care: $\tilde{x} > x^*$.

QUESTION 8.18: "In general, the injurer's precaution responds to court errors in setting the legal standard under a negligence rule." Is this statement true for all forms of the negligence rule, or only for the simple negligence rule?

I. Vague Standards and Uncertainty

We have analyzed precise rules—both precisely efficient rules and precisely inefficient rules—that are called "bright-line rules" because their meaning is as clear as a bright line. In reality, however, legal rules are often vague and unpredictable. Vague and unpredictable tort rules leave people uncertain about the legal consequences of their acts. We shall discuss how people adjust their precaution in response to legal uncertainty.

Assume that the court makes purely random errors, or, what amounts to the same thing, assume that the injurer makes purely random errors in predicting what courts will do. By "purely random," we mean that excess is just as probable as deficiency, so that the average error is zero. (Technically, we assume that errors follow a random distribution with zero mean.) We shall consider purely random errors in damages and standards.

First, consider purely random errors by the court in computing damages or by the injurer in predicting damages. A purely random error in damages does not change the expected liability of the injurer. Expected liability remains unchanged because errors of excess offset errors of deficiency on average. Because expected liability remains unchanged, an injurer who minimizes expected costs does not change his or her precaution in response to purely random errors in damages.[16] This is true for every liability rule. In general, *the injurer who minimizes expected costs does not change his or her precaution in response to random errors in computing or predicting damages under any liability rule.*

The situation is different, however, for random errors concerning the legal standard in a negligence rule. To keep the analysis simple, consider the injurer's legal standard of care, $\tilde{x}_i$, under a rule of simple negligence. Assume that the court makes random errors in setting the legal standard $\tilde{x}$, or the court makes random errors in comparing the injurer's precaution x to the legal standard $\tilde{x}$, or the injurer makes random errors in predicting the legal standard $\tilde{x}$. Given any of these possibilities, injurers are uncertain about whether a particular level of precaution on their part will result in the court's

---

[16] In technical terms, the solution to Equation 8.2 does not change if we replace A with $E(A + \mu)$, where E is an expectation and μ is a random variable with zero mean.

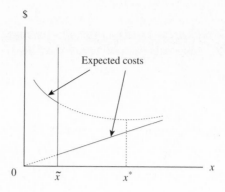

FIGURE 8.6 Expected costs when the legal standard is less than the social optimum.

finding them liable or not liable for accidents. If the court finds that their precaution exceeded the legal standard, then they will have taken unnecessary precaution. Unnecessary precautions cost them a little. Alternatively, if the court finds that their precaution fell short of the legal standard, then they will be liable. Liability costs them a lot. This asymmetry gives injurers an incentive to take more precaution in order to create a margin of error within which they will not be liable. In general, *small random errors in the legal standard imposed by a negligence rule causes the injurer to increase precaution*. In the next chapter, we shall prove this proposition.

Table 8.2, which summarizes our conclusions about precise errors and vague standards, suggests some prescriptions for lawmakers and courts. First, with a rule of strict liability, errors by the court in computing damages distort precaution, so the court

Table 8.2

CONSEQUENCES OF ERRORS OF EXCESS

liability rule	court's error	injurer's error	effect on injurer
strict liability	excessive damages	overestimates damages	excessive precaution
negligence	excessive damages	overestimates damages	none
negligence	excessive legal standard	overestimates legal standard	excessive precaution
strict liability	random error in damages	random error in damages	none
negligence	random error in legal standard	random error in legal standard	excessive precaution

should avoid these errors. Second, with a rule of negligence, errors by the court in setting standards distort precaution more than errors in computing damages, so the court should concentrate on avoiding errors in setting the standard of care. Given these two prescriptions, a court that assesses damages more accurately than standards for a given class of cases should favor a rule of strict liability, whereas a court that assess standards more accurately than damages for a given class of cases should favor a rule of negligence. Third, with a rule of negligence, vague standards cause excessive precaution, so the court should apply vague standards leniently in order to avoid aggravating the problem of excessive precaution.

QUESTION 8.19: "Excessive damages increase expected liability under a negligence rule, which results in excess precaution." Explain the mistake in this proposition.

QUESTION 8.20: "If the legal standard of care in a negligence rule is necessarily vague, the court should set it below the level of efficient precaution." Explain the economic argument in favor of this proposition.

J. Administrative Costs and Tailored Rules

In the simple model, the economic goal of the tort-liability system is to minimize the sum of the costs of precaution and the harm caused by accidents. A more complex model includes another important element of costs: administration. Administrative costs are incurred to allocate the costs of accidental harm. For example, a system of private law incurs the costs of lawyers, judges, and other officials involved in resolving legal disputes. Similarly, a public system to compensate workers injured on the job must collect taxes, decide claims, and pay benefits. In general, accidents impose three basic kinds of costs on society: precautionary costs, the costs of accidental harm, and the administrative costs of determining who should bear the costs of accidental harm. We may describe the economic goal of the tort-liability system as follows: *The rules of tort liability should be structured so as to minimize the social costs of accidents, where the social costs of accidents are defined to be the sum of precaution, accidental harm, and administrative costs.*[17]

We begin by analyzing administrative costs in isolation from the costs of precaution and accidental harm. We compare the administrative costs of three rules: no liability, strict liability, and negligence. The rule of no liability leaves the costs of accidental harm where they fall, without attempting to reallocate them. Consequently, a rule of no liability eliminates the administrative costs of reallocating the costs of accidental harm. In contrast, the rule of strict liability and the rule of negligence reallocate the costs of accidental harm under certain conditions. Thus, a rule of no liability saves administrative costs relative to a rule of strict liability or a rule of negligence liability.

This fact has lead reformers to advocate adopting the rule of no liability for most motor vehicle accidents. Under a so-called "no fault" rule, each of the parties to an automobile accident bears his or her own costs of accidental harm. In practice, this

---

[17] This goal was first proposed by Guido Calabresi in THE COSTS OF ACCIDENTS: A LEGAL AND ECONOMIC ANALYSIS 26–31(1970).

means that each accident victim recovers from his or her own insurance company, rather than recovering from the insurance company of the injurer. The rule of no liability has the disadvantage that injurers have no incentive to take precaution. For example, the owners of trucks with steel cattle guards welded to the front of the vehicle may respond to a rule of no liability by driving aggressively. Thus, the no-fault systems presumably save administration costs and erode incentives for precaution.

Now we compare the administrative costs of a rule of strict liability and a rule of negligence. Recall that a rule of strict liability requires the plaintiff to prove harm and cause, whereas a rule of negligence requires the plaintiff to prove harm, cause, and fault. The additional element of proof requires an additional decision, which increases administrative costs. Thus, *a rule of strict liability lowers administrative costs relative to a rule of negligence by simplifying the adjudicator's task.*

This advantage of strict liability may be offset by a disadvantage. A rule of strict liability gives more victims the right to recover damages than a rule of negligence. Specifically, a rule of strict liability gives every victim who suffers harm caused by the injurer's activity the right to recover, whereas a rule of negligence gives every victim who suffers harm caused by the injurer's fault the right to recover. Thus, *a rule of negligence lowers the administrative costs relative to a rule of strict liability by reallocating the cost of harm in fewer cases.* In summary, a rule of strict liability results in more claims that are simpler to settle, whereas a rule of negligence results in fewer claims that are more complicated to settle.

We have contrasted the administrative costs of strict liability and negligence. Besides the form of the liability rule, administrative costs also depend upon the simplicity and breadth of the rules. Simple rules are based upon easily-proven facts, and broad rules lump together many different cases. Conversely, complicated rules are based upon facts that are difficult to prove, and narrow rules apply to a few cases. We may characterize the extremes of simplicity and breadth as *wholesale* rules, and we may characterize the extremes of complicated and narrow as *case-by-case* adjudication. Wholesale rules are cheaper to make, enforce, and understand. However, wholesale rules distort incentives by treating people alike who have different utility and cost functions. An ideal legal standard would be tailored to fit individuals, so that injurers with different technologies and costs of precaution faced different standards. In general, *wholesale rules save administrative costs and distort the relationship between the marginal cost of precaution and the marginal reduction in harm, whereas case-by-case adjudication has the opposite effects.*

Besides allocating the cost of accidental harm, the law also allocates the costs of administration. Different countries allocate administrative costs differently. To illustrate, an accident victim who successfully sues in the United States recovers damages for the harm suffered, but does not usually recover costs of litigating. In contrast, many European countries require the winner of a lawsuit to pay the litigation costs of the loser. The allocation of administrative costs decisively affects the incentives of the victim to sue and the incentives of the parties to settle out of court. We shall analyze these incentives in Chapter 10.

QUESTION 8.21: Doctors are liable when their negligence injures patients. Suppose the rule were changed from negligence to strict liability. How would administrative costs change?

QUESTION 8.22: The rungs of ladders must be constructed to support the weight of the people who climb them. Compare the relative efficiency of a precise government standard for all ladders concerning the weight that the rungs must support, as opposed to the rule that the strength of the rungs should be determined as suits arise on a case-by-case basis using the Hand rule.

K. Insurance

Our discussion of administrative costs focused upon courts and other adjudicators. In reality, insurance companies bear much of the administrative costs of accidents. Insurance companies have to set premiums, process claims, and monitor the behavior of policy-holders. We could describe insurance as a private system of liability law, which allocates the cost of accidents according to contracts. When insurance markets are competitive, the premiums collected from policy-holders equal the sum of the claims paid to policy-holders and the costs of administration. When insurance markets are complete, everyone can purchase all of the insurance that he wants against any contingency. When everyone insures completely, the victims have insurance coverage against every kind of accident.

We formulated the goal as minimizing the sum of the costs of precaution, accidental harm, and administrative costs. Our analysis of insurance suggests a reformulation. Complete insurance covers the cost of accidental harm and administration. Consequently, we could reformulate the goal of tort law as follows: *In a system of complete, competitive insurance markets, the rules of tort liability should be structured so as to minimize the sum of the costs of precaution and insurance.*

To illustrate this approach, we contrast no liability and strict liability. A rule of no liability causes victims to insure themselves. Under no liability and perfect insurance markets, the social costs of accidents equal the sum of *victims'* insurance premiums and the cost of precaution by both parties. In contrast, a rule of strict liability causes the injurers to insure victims. Under strict liability and perfect insurance markets, the social costs of accidents equal the sum of *injurers'* insurance premiums and the cost of precaution by both parties. The more efficient rule is the one that costs less. Thus, critics have argued for limiting strict product liability on the ground that consumers can insure more cheaply than manufacturers against certain kinds of harm. We shall discuss this and additional issues of insurance and tort law in the next chapter.

L. Consumer Product Injuries: Between Torts and Contracts

At the beginning of this chapter we explained that tort law uses liability to internalize externalities created by high transaction costs. The model of torts applies when transaction costs prevent the injurer and victim from dealing with each other prior to the accident, as with most automobile accidents. When the parties have a market relationship, however, the analysis must change, as we now show with an example of consumer product injuries.

---

[18] A. Mitchell Polinsky, AN INTRODUCTION TO LAW AND ECONOMICS (2nd ed. 1989), Table 11, p. 98.

Table 8.3 reproduces the numbers from a hypothethical example developed by Polinsky.[18] Consumers face a choice between buying soda in bottles or cans. Bottles are cheaper to produce than cans, as indicated by column 1, but bottles are twice as likely to cause an accident to the consumer, as indicated by column 2, and the accidents involving bottles are more severe, as indicated by column 3. The expected loss in column 4 equals the probability of an accident in column 2 multiplied by the loss in column 3. The full cost per unit, indicated by column 5, equals the sum of the cost of production in column 1 and the expected accident loss in column 4.

Notice that the full cost of bottles (50 cents) in this hypothetical example exceeds the full cost of cans (45 cents). Thus, efficiency requires the use of cans, not bottles. Let us consider whether consumers will actually use cans instead of bottles. The behavior of consumers depends upon the information that they possess, liability law, and the market for sodas. We assume that the market is perfectly competitive. Competition drives the price of a good down to its cost, as explained in Chapter 2. The cost of supplying soda depends upon production and liability. We assume that the price of a unit of soda equals the production cost plus the cost of manufacturer's liability. Under a rule of no liability, the price of a unit of soda thus equals the production cost as shown in column 1: 40 cents per bottle and 43 cents per can. Under a rule of strict liability, the price of a unit of soda equals its full cost as shown in column 5: 50 cents per bottle and 45 cents per can.

First, consider the behavior of *perfectly-informed* consumers under a rule of *no liability*. Being perfectly informed, the consumers know the expected accident costs and the fact that they must bear these costs. Consequently, consumers will prefer the soda whose full cost to them is lower, specifically, soda in cans. *Thus, perfectly-informed consumers will choose the most efficient product under a rule of no liability.*

Second, consider the behavior of *imperfectly-informed* consumers under a rule of *no liability*. Being imperfectly informed, the consumers do not know the expected accident costs. If consumers overestimate the greater danger associated with bottles, they will buy cans. If consumers underestimate the greater danger associated with bottles, or if they disregard the danger, they may buy bottles to obtain the (perceived) lower price of 40 cents per bottle, as opposed to the higher price of 43 cents per can. *Thus, imperfectly-informed consumers will not necessarily choose the most efficient product under a rule of no liability.*

Table 8.3

COST OF SODA

Behavior of firm	Firm's cost of production per unit	Probability of accident to consumer	Loss if accident	Expected accident loss	Full cost per unit
	(1)	(2)	(3)	(4)	(5)
Use bottle	40 cents	1/100,000	$10,000	10 cents	50 cents
Use can	43 cents	1/200,000	$4,000	2 cents	45 cents

Third, consider the behavior of *imperfectly-informed* consumers under a rule of *strict liability*. Strict liability and perfect competition cause the price of soda to equal its full cost, which is 50 cents per bottle and 45 cents per can. Consumers will prefer cans rather than bottles, regardless of whether they overestimate, underestimate, or disregard the greater danger associated with bottles. *Thus, imperfectly-informed consumers will choose the most efficient product under a rule of strict liability.*

This example provides the basic rationale for holding manufacturers strictly liable for the harm that defective products cause consumers: the cost of liability will be captured in the price, thus directing consumers towards efficiency in spite of having imperfect information. This analysis, however, ignores many shortcomings of a system of strict liability for consumer product injuries, such as administrative costs, the lack of incentives for precaution by victims, and overinsurance of consumers by producers. We will discuss these shortcomings in detail in the next chapter.

QUESTION 8.23: In effect, a rule of strict liability requires the seller to provide the consumer with a joint product: soda and insurance. What inefficiencies arise from such a compulsory purchase?

CONCLUSION

In communist countries like the former Soviet Union, planners could not get the information that they needed to manage an increasingly complex economy, which caused central planning to deteriorate. An increasingly complex economy must rely increasingly upon markets, which decentralize information. Making law is much like making commodities. As the economy grows in complexity, central officials cannot get the information that they need to make precise regulations. Instead of centralized lawmaking, the modern economy needs decentralized lawmaking analogous to markets.

Tort law uses liability to internalize externalities created by high transaction costs. Tort liability removes many decisions about accidents from bureaucrats and politicians and allows judges to make laws, plaintiffs to decide when to prosecute violators, and courts to determine how much the violators must pay. Thus, the liability system decentralizes much of the task of internalizing externalities. Everywhere in the world, however, tort liability suffers from serious deficiencies. In this chapter we developed the fundamental theory required to understand tort law. In the next chapter, we refine the economic theory in order to address the problems that beset tort law.

SUGGESTED READINGS

Brown, John P., *Toward an Economic Theory of Liability*, 2 J. LEGAL STUD. 323 (1973).

Grady, Mark, *A New Positive Economic Theory of Negligence*, 92 YALE L. J. 799 (1983).

Keeton, William; Dan Dobbs; Robert Keeton; David Owen & William Prosser, PROSSER AND KEETON ON TORTS (5th ed. 1984).

Landes, William, and Richard A. Posner, THE ECONOMIC STRUCTURE OF TORT LAW (1987).

Rabin, Robert, ed., PERSPECTIVES ON TORT LAW (3rd ed. 1993).

Shavell, Steven, *An Analysis of Causation and the Scope of Liability in the Law of Torts*, 9 J. LEGAL STUD. 463 (1987).

Shavell, Steven, AN ECONOMIC ANALYSIS OF ACCIDENT LAW (1987).

APPENDIX

Liability and Symmetry

A negligence rule imposes a standard of care upon the injurer, which we depicted as partitioning the injurer's precaution into permitted and forbidden zones. The defense of contributory negligence imposes a legal standard of care upon the victim, which can be represented by partitioning the victim's precaution into permitted and forbidden zones.

Figure 8.7 shows the injurer's precaution on the horizontal axis and the victim's precaution on the vertical axis. The two legal standards partition Figure 8.7 into four quadrants. The following table summarizes the relationship between the four quadrants and the fault of the parties:

Quadrant	Injurer	Victim
I	fault	no fault
II	no fault	no fault
III	no fault	fault
IV	fault	fault

For example, in quadrant I, the injurer is at fault because $x_i < \tilde{x}_i$, and the victim is not at fault because $x_v > \tilde{x}_v$.

The following table summarizes the way different liability rules allocate the costs of accidental harm between the parties, depending upon their precaution by quadrant:

Liability rule	Injurer bears cost of harm	Victim bears cost of harm
simple negligence	I, IV	II, III
negligence with defense of contributory negligence	I	II, III, IV
strict liability with defense of contributory negligence	I, II	III, IV
strict liability with defense of dual contributory negligence	I, II, IV	III

If we switch the labels of the axes in Figure 8.7 so that the injurer's precaution is on the vertical axis and the victim's precaution is on the horizontal axis, then compare how the liability rules allocate the burden of harm, we shall find some interesting relationships. "Simple negligence" is the mirror image of "strict liability with a defense of contributory negligence," and "negligence with defense of contributory negligence" is the mirror image of "strict liability with defense of dual contributory negligence."

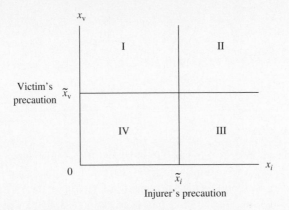

FIGURE 8.7 Legal standards for injurer and victim.

QUESTION 8.24: Explain why the victim bears the costs of accidents under a rule of strict liability with a defense of contributory negligence in quadrant IV.

QUESTION 8.25: Explain why the injurer bears the costs of accidents under a rule of strict liability with a defense of contributory negligence in quadrant II.

9

TOPICS IN THE ECONOMICS
OF TORT LIABILITY

The preceding chapter introduced the fundamental concepts of tort law and developed an economic analysis of tort liability. In this chapter we wish to advance the understanding of the economic analysis of the tort-liability system in two ways. First, we relax some simplifying assumptions in order to bring the model closer to reality.

Second, we shall examine some arguments that the tort-liability system does not work well and needs thorough reform, especially in the areas of products liability and medical malpractice. In the course of this examination, we shall look at some recent evidence on how well the tort system minimizes the social costs of accidents.

I. EXTENDING THE ECONOMIC MODEL

The model that we introduced in the last chapter made some simplifying assumptions. The grand tradition in economics would have us assert our intention to relax these simplifications but then forget to do so. We turn immediately to the task of exploring the conclusions of our simple model when we relax our simplifying assumptions.

A. Relaxing the Core Assumptions

In the previous chapter we implicitly made five simplifying assumptions before we developed our economic analysis of tort law:

1. Decision-makers are rationally self-interested.

2. The transaction costs of internalizing the external costs that potential injurers may impose on potential victims are so high that contractual solutions are impossible.

3. There is no insurance.

4. There are no other social policies designed to reduce external costs.

5. Litigation costs are zero.

The purpose of this section is to relax these assumptions—particularly assumptions one and three through five—to see what effect, if any, such relaxation might have on the conclusions from the economic theory of tort liability.

1. Rationality One of the central assumptions in economic theory is that decision-makers are rationally self-interested. As a technical matter, this means (as we saw in Chapter 6) that decision-makers have stable, well-ordered preferences,[1] which implies something about the decision-maker's cognitive and reasoning abilities. Specifically, it suggests that decision-makers can calculate the costs and benefits of the alternatives available to them and that they choose to follow the alternative that offers the greatest net benefit.

There is a vital connection between the assumption of rationality and the economic model of tort liability in Chapter 8. We saw that the rules for assigning tort liability are, economically speaking, designed to send signals to potential victims and potential injurers about how they ought to behave. For the tort liability system to have this effect, it must be the case that those whose behavior the law is seeking to affect are rational: they must be able to perceive that they can minimize their liability by taking precautionary actions of a particular kind and amount.

But do people really make decisions about potential liability in this way? Some people do, and others do not. Recent academic literature suggests that many decision-makers make errors in making calculations of the sort that tort liability encourages them to make. For instance, Kahneman and Tversky report two disturbing conclusions.[2] First, they find that *most* people simply cannot accurately estimate low-probability events; they seem to deal with them by assuming that "low probability" means that the event will never happen—that the probability of the event's happening is zero. Second, they find that, for some well-publicized, potentially catastrophic outcomes—such as accidents from nuclear power plants—*most* people systematically exaggerate the probability of an accident's occurring, regardless of objective information to the contrary.

These findings have implications for the economic model of tort liability. If many people do not accurately estimate risks, then they cannot make the appropriate calculations of net benefits and costs that the economic theory assumes that they make. Using the symbols of the previous chapters, some people may inaccurately set $p(x)$ equal to 0 and, therefore, take no precaution, when, in fact, that probability is positive and they *should* take precaution. The inability of these decision-makers to make accurate calculations may lead to too many or too severe accidents. In other cases, decision-makers may *over*estimate $p(x)$—that is, they may think that an accident is far more likely than it, in fact, is—and may, therefore, take far too much precaution. As a result of these inabilities to calculate correctly, the tort-liability system may not induce people to take actions that minimize the social costs of accidents.

---

[1] Recall that such preferences are stable in the sense that they do not change too rapidly or quixotically and that they are well-ordered in the sense that they are transitive, which means that if A is preferred to B and B is preferred to C, then A must be preferred to C.

[2] See generally Daniel Kahneman and Amos Tversky, eds., JUDGMENT UNDER UNCERTAINTY: BIASES AND HEURISTICS (1981). See also Ulen, *Rational Choice and the Economic Analysis of Law*, LAW AND SOCIAL INQUIRY (Spring, 1994).

The economic theory of tort liability not only draws our attention to the importance of the rationality assumption in analyzing tort law, but it also suggests a corrective measure when that assumption is violated. Consider accidents involving power tools. One might suppose that precaution in such cases is bilateral: there is something that both the consumer and the producer can do to reduce the probability and severity of an accident. As a result, the economic theory would suggest that some form of the negligence rule should be used to induce efficient precaution by both consumers and producers. However, suppose that there was strong evidence that consumers could not accurately assess the risks associated with the use of power tools. They might presume that the tools are so safe that they need not take any particular care in how they are used. In short, consumers might mistakenly assume that the probability of an accident is zero and take very little precaution. That fact would make this a situation of *unilateral, rather than bilateral*, precaution: only manufacturers could realistically be expected to take steps to reduce the probability and severity of an accident.[3]

These thoughts raise concerns about whether or not tort liability induces the appropriate precautionary action by potential injurers and victims. We shall tentatively maintain the rationality assumption but shall be ready to amend our conclusions about efficient tort rules when there is sound evidence that the appropriate decision-makers are not behaving rationally.

QUESTION 9.1: Wearing seat belts and shoulder harnesses is an efficient means of minimizing the costs of automobile accidents. Assuming that the benefits of these passive restraints exceed their costs, why is it that only about 50% of drivers and passengers routinely wear them? Is this an example of irrationality? If so, how might the rules of tort liability be changed so as to induce a greater number of people to wear seat belts and shoulder harnesses?

2. Insurance   In Chapter 8 we briefly discussed the effect of insurance on precautionary behavior. Here we elaborate.

a. First-party Insurance If potential victims have first-party insurance, then the efficiency of the tort-liability system might suffer in one or all of the following three ways. First, in the event of an accident, victims might receive compensation for their losses from their insurers and, therefore, not seek compensation from the injurer. Second, this being so, the injurer will not bear the full costs of wrong-doing and has, therefore, a diminished incentive to take care. Third, in circumstances in which victims might take precaution and in which they are insured against loss, potential victims might not take as much care as they ought to reduce the likelihood and severity of accidents—a reaction that creates a "moral hazard." The cumulative result of these three effects might be that first-party insurance leads to more accidents and to more severe accidents than would be socially optimal.

However, there are reasons for believing that the presence of first-party insurance does *not* change the incentives of either the victims or the injurers in inefficient ways.

---

[3] Note, further, that if the rationality assumption fails, then there is not a great deal to be said for a policy of better informing the parties about the objective values of the risks. They either discount that information or they ignore it.

First, insurance companies are well aware of this effect and seek to minimize it by means of co-insurance and deductibles.[4] As to the incentive to bring an action against an injurer (and thereby to preserve the incentive for the injurer to take care), the victim's insurance company can keep those incentives alive by means of what is called a *subrogation clause* in the insurance contract. That clause assigns to the insurance company any cause of action that the insured party may have against the injurer. When an insurance contract has such a clause, an accident results in the insurance company's paying its policyholder's losses and then seeking reimbursement for those payments from the injurer. The subrogation clause preserves the incentive to seek legal relief for wrongful injury and increases the likelihood that the potential injurer will bear the consequences of the wrong, thus preserving the deterrent effect of tort liability.

b. Third-party (Liability) Insurance We also assumed that potential injurers did not have liability insurance. The reason for that assumption was to make sure that, through exposure to liability, potential injurers would bear the full cost of their carelessness. If injurers have liability insurance, then they need not be so careful if their insurers will pay for the consequences of their failure to take due care. But this is not news to insurance companies. They are aware of this moral hazard problem and attempt to preserve potential injurers' incentive to take adequate care by imposing deductibles and co-insurance. They may also hold out the possibility that insurance premiums will rise (or the policy be canceled) if there is consistent evidence of the insured's failure to take care. Presumably, potential injurers will seek to avoid this increase in premiums (or policy cancellation) by taking care not to have accidents.

3. Other Social Policies   Another assumption of the basic model of Chapter 8 was that there were no other social policies besides the tort-liability system that seek to minimize the social costs of accidents. But there *are* other social policies that seek to achieve the same result. For example, there are administrative agency regulations of product safety—for example, regulations requiring warnings or specifying production standards or safety features—that seek to achieve the same deterrence results as does the tort-liability system. How, if at all, might our conclusions of the previous chapter be altered by the presence of these alternative safety regulations?

Our discussion of negligence considered the effect of a statutorily designated level of care for potential injurers (and contrasted the economics of that definition of negligence with a case-by-case analysis). We saw that if the statutory safety standard is set equal to the social-cost-minimizing level of care, then the socially optimal amount of precaution will be taken. However, if the safety regulation is different from the social optimum, potential injurers are likely to comply with the safety regulation rather than to search for the social optimum. In that case, there will be an inefficient number and kind of accidents. We concluded that the key to achieving efficiency is to set the safety regulation equal to the socially optimal amount of precaution.

A further problem arises when there is a safety regulation in place but courts seek to determine liability not by whether or not the injurer complied with that regulation but

---

[4] Remember from Chapter 2 that under a deductible the insured pays a fixed *dollar amount* of the insured loss. Under co-insurance the insured pays a fixed *percentage* of the insured loss. Either device preserves the incentive of the insured to take care to reduce the likelihood or severity of a loss.

on a case-by-case basis. For example, a potential injurer may believe that he has complied with all relevant safety regulations and that he has no further legal obligations to potential victims. Imagine his surprise if the victim sues him, he presents his defense (that he complied with relevant safety regulations), and yet the jury finds him liable for the victim's injuries for not having taken enough precaution.

Does a situation of this sort alter any of our conclusions from Chapter 8? Not necessarily. There is, nonetheless, an interesting efficiency question raised by the coexistence of tort liability and safety regulations: how should the (perhaps differing) requirements of these two means of minimizing the social costs of accidents be coordinated?

4. Litigation Costs The final core assumption of the economic theory of tort liability was that litigation is costless. Of course, nothing could be further from the truth: litigation is expensive and sometimes ruinously so. A more complete analysis of the efficiency of the various liability rules we have discussed should introduce these costs explicitly.[5]

Costly litigation will have different effects on potential victims and potential injurers. Moreover, these different effects will have very different implications for the efficiency analysis of Chapter 8.

Consider, first, the impact of costly litigation on potential victims. If victims must incur a cost to assert their claims for compensation, then they may assert fewer claims. Consider an extreme case in which litigation costs exceed the expected compensatory damages. Victims will not bring suit, and so the potential injurers will not receive the signal from the tort-liability system that what they are doing is unacceptable. They may, as a result, take less precaution than they should, with the consequence that there may be more accidents (and more severe accidents) than there should be.

However, costly litigation may have a contrary effect on the decisions of potential injurers. If it is expensive for an injurer to litigate, then it may make sense to take more precaution than would be the case if litigation were costless. By taking more precaution, the potential injurer makes an accident less likely or less severe; if the cost of this additional precaution is less than the cost of litigation, then we should expect potential injurers to take *additional* precaution when litigation is costly. As a result, there should be fewer and less severe accidents.

Because the effects of costly litigation on potential victims and on potential injurers pull in different directions (one suggests less precaution; the other suggests more precaution), we cannot be sure of the net effect of relaxing the assumption of costless litigation.

QUESTION 9.2: Use the economic theory of bargaining to characterize the torts in which the transaction costs of settling disputes are likely to be large. (*Hint*: recall the distinction between public bads and private bads.)

QUESTION 9.3: For which liability standard would you expect the litigation costs to be greater—negligence or strict liability? Why? Is that an additional efficiency argument for preferring one standard to the other?

---

[5] See Janusz Ordover, *Costly Litigation in the Model of Single Activity Accidents*, 7 J. LEGAL STUD. 243 (1978); and A. Mitchell Polinsky and Daniel Rubinfeld, *The Welfare Implications of Costly Litigation in the Theory of Liability*, 17 J. LEGAL STUD. 151 (1988).

5. Conclusion Taken altogether, what is the ultimate result of relaxing the core assumptions for the conclusions of the previous chapter? Perhaps somewhat surprisingly, the conclusions of the economic model survive almost intact. We have seen that relaxing the rationality assumption may not be warranted, but that where it is relaxed, the economic theory helps us to see how tort law ought to take into account the cognitive imperfections of those whose behavior it seeks to affect. We also saw that relaxing the assumption that there is no first- or third-party insurance does not change the results of the economic theory of tort liability: when there is insurance, co-insurance, deductibles, subrogation clauses and the implied threat of higher premiums or of policy cancellations preserve the incentives of potential injurers to take optimal care and of potential victims (through their insurers) to bring actions in order to induce potential injurers to internalize the social costs of their carelessness. Nor does the presence of other social policies, such as safety regulation, necessitate our changing any of the economic conclusions. These alternative social policies do require some account of how best to coordinate tort liability and safety regulation, and that coordination is likely to require an understanding of the economic trade-offs involved. Finally, the fact that litigation is costly does not necessitate a change in our economic model. Rather, we have seen that costly litigation points in different directions: on the one hand, it may induce potential victims not to file actions (thus allowing potential injurers not to bear the full costs of their carelessness and inviting them to take less care in the future), but, on the other hand, it may induce potential injurers to take more care (if taking additional care makes accidents less likely or less severe and is cheaper than the costs of litigating).

B. Extending the Basic Model

The economic model that we have been exploring in this and the previous chapter explains not just the broad questions of tort liability's purposes and the differences between negligence and strict liability, but it also helps us to understand some of the more special doctrines of tort liability. In this section we shall show how the economic theory applies to certain special cases—for example, the liability of employers for the torts of their employees—and to some issues at the frontiers of tort liability.

1. Vicarious Liability There are circumstances in which one person may be held responsible for the torts committed by another. Where this happens, the third party is said to be *vicariously liable* for the tortfeasor's acts. Vicarious liability may extend from an agent to his or her principal or from a dependent child to a parent, but by far the most common instance of vicarious liability is that of employers' responsibility for the tortious wrongs of their employees under the doctrine of *respondeat superior* ("let the master answer"). The bare bones of this doctrine are that an employer will be held to answer for the unintentional torts of an employee if the employee was "acting within the scope of [his or her] employment."

Does *respondeat superior* induce efficient behavior by employers and employees? The rule creates an incentive for the employer to take care in selecting employees, in assigning them various tasks, and in deciding with which tools to equip them. This is efficient if it is the case—as it generally would seem to be—that employers are better placed than are employees to make these decisions.[6]

> **QUESTION 9.4:** What if an accident has occurred because an employee was performing a job for which he was not qualified after the employee had falsely told the employer that he *was* qualified? Should the employer still be liable for the victim's losses under *respondeat superior*?

> **QUESTION 9.5:** The common law did not hold parents liable for their children's unintentional torts unless the parents' negligent supervision led directly to the tort. But the common law did hold husbands vicariously liable for their wives' torts (a rule since abrogated by statute). Can you provide an efficiency explanation for these common law rules?

> **QUESTION 9.6:** In many states, a bartender (under so-called "dram shop" laws), friend, party host, or other person who serves liquor to an already intoxicated person is held vicariously liable for any damages that person subsequently inflicts on other people or their property. Does this form of vicarious liability make economic sense?

2. Joint and Several Liability With and Without Contribution   One of the examples from the beginning of the previous chapter concerns a hunter who is injured when both of his companions unintentionally fired birdshot toward him. In the example we imagined that one of the companions, and perhaps both, caused the hunter's injuries. This sort of situation has been treated in the common law as one of *joint and several liability*. Defendants are said to be "jointly and severally liable" if each of them is liable for all the victim's losses, not just a portion of them. The plaintiff may proceed jointly against all the injurers or may elect to recover all damages from only some of them or only one of them. (Typically, the plaintiffs proceed against the defendants who have "deep pockets," that is, the resources to compensate the plaintiff.)

The common law recognized two circumstances in which joint and several liability would hold:

1. if the defendants acted together to cause the victim's harm, or
2. if the fault for victim's harm was indivisible between multiple tortfeasors.

An example of the first is where two cars driven by *A* and *B* are racing down a street and one of them hits *C*, a pedestrian. An example of the second circumstance is our case of the pheasant hunters. In both examples the defendants are jointly and severally liable.

Suppose that the plaintiff chooses to recover from only one of several injurers. May that defendant then force the other injurers to contribute to paying the damages? At common law for unintentional torts, the defendant did not generally have a right to *contribution*, as this is called, from other joint tortfeasors. This was true even if the plaintiff's selection of which tortfeasor to sue was malicious or totally capricious. This

---

[6] For a full discussion of the economics of this issue, see Alan Sykes, *The Economics of Vicarious Liability*, 93 YALE L. J. 1231 (1984).

harsh rule against contribution has been abrogated, usually by statute but sometimes by judicial decision, in almost all the states.[7]

There are several economic reasons for joint and several liability. One is that it relieves the victim of the potentially extraordinary costs of proving who caused the harm. The doctrine allows the victim to assert that one of these people and perhaps many of them caused the injuries without incurring the special costs of showing which one or more of them was, or were, responsible. In essence, the doctrine shifts to the defendants the costs of establishing exactly what happened. Imagine a situation in which a patient is anesthetized and taken into surgery. During the operation someone injures the patient. Later she sues all those who were in the operating room, but for obvious reasons she cannot tell who caused her injury.

Another economic reason for joint and several liability is that it makes the victim's recovery more certain by allowing him or her to get to what is called a "deep pocket." Suppose that an uninsured motorist is going at high speed, strikes a pothole in the road, loses control of his car, and hits another car, seriously injuring its driver. Assume for the sake of argument that 90% of the fault is attributable to the speeding driver, and 10% of the fault is attributable to the city government for not filling the pothole. The victim will have difficulty recovering anything from the speeding driver because he lacks insurance. However, if the law allows the victim to hold the motorist and the city jointly and severally liable and if the victim can prove that the city was negligent in maintaining the road, then the victim can recover 100% of his losses from the city, even though the pothole only contributed 10% to the accident.

A third economic issue in joint and several liability is whether a rule of contribution or a rule of no contribution is more efficient. Just as was the case in distinguishing between negligence rules and strict liability, here the crucial distinction is between situations in which the optimal precaution is unilateral by one of the defendants and those in which optimal precaution is joint among all of them. When the optimal precaution involves joint action by multiple defendants, the no-contribution rule, by imposing residual liability on each defendant, creates the optimal incentive for each of them to take precaution. Thus, in the example in which A and B are racing their cars, and C, a pedestrian, is struck and injured by one of them, optimal precaution requires both parties, not just one, to take care. If there is no contribution, each of them is liable for the plaintiff's entire losses. The rule of no contribution increases the expected accident costs that each must use in computing the amount of precaution to take. Note that the efficiency argument for the no-contribution rule among joint or multiple tortfeasors is precisely analogous to our efficiency argument for the imposition of some form of the negligence rule in situations of bilateral precaution. Recall that when there is the possibility for bilateral (or joint) precaution by injurer and victim, a form of the negligence rule induces optimal precaution by both parties through the creation of residual liability; if victims fail to satisfy the legal standard of care, they are responsible for all their losses; if injurers fail to satisfy the legal standard of care, they are responsible for

---

[7] This is true only for unintentional torts; for intentional torts, such as a violation of the antitrust statutes, there is still no right of contribution among joint tortfeasors.

all the victim's losses. This is precisely the result reached by a rule of no contribution that induces precaution among joint tortfeasors.[8]

3. Evidentiary Uncertainty and Comparative Negligence[9]

In the previous chapter we discussed the several forms of the negligence rule: simple negligence, negligence with contributory negligence, and comparative negligence. For most of the last 200 years, negligence with contributory negligence has been not only the dominant form of the negligence rule but the dominant tort-liability rule in the common law countries. However, within the last 20 years all this has changed. Today, all but a handful of the states in this country have altered their law of accidents so that the prevailing liability standard is one of comparative negligence for non-product-related torts. The change has been effected principally by statute, with a minority of states adopting the rule by judicial decision. In this section we shall explain briefly how the comparative-negligence rule works and how it differs from the rule of negligence with contributory negligence. Then we shall show how something called "evidentiary uncertainty" can give rise to an efficiency argument for comparative negligence.

The simple reason for the rise of comparative negligence is an increasing dissatisfaction with the rule of contributory negligence. Recall that a contributorily negligent plaintiff could not recover anything from the defendant, even from a negligent defendant. This rule struck most people as exceedingly harsh. To see why, imagine that an automobile accident has occurred; both the plaintiff and the defendant were driving. Suppose that violation of the speed limit constitutes negligence and that the evidence shows that the plaintiff was going 35 miles per hour in the 30 mile-per-hour zone and that the defendant was going 65 miles per hour in that same zone. Under the rule that bars recovery for a contributorily negligent plaintiff, the plaintiff will not be able to recover. This seems harsh in that the plaintiff's negligence was trivial in comparison to the defendant's.

To avoid this sort of harsh result, most jurisdictions found a means of limiting the scope of the rule of contributory negligence—for example, by means of the last-clear-chance doctrine we discussed in Chapter 3.[10] But eventually these limitations on the application of the rule of contributory negligence gave way to comparative negligence.

The principal difference between comparative negligence and the rule of negligence with contributory negligence is that under comparative negligence the plaintiff's contributory fault is a partial but not a complete bar to recovery from a negligent defendant. Thus, under comparative negligence the negligent injurer usually owes something, but not full compensation, to the negligent victim.[11]

---

[8] See Landes and Posner, *Multiple Tortfeasors: An Economic Analysis*, 9 J. LEGAL STUD. 517 (1980); and Polinsky and Shavell, *Contribution and Claim Reduction Among Antitrust Defendants: An Economic Analysis*, 33 STAN. L. REV. 447 (1981).

[9] The material in this section draws on Cooter and Ulen, An *Economic Case for Comparative Negligence*, 61 N.Y.U. L. REV. 1067 (1986).

[10] Each of these limitations allowed an otherwise contributorily negligent plaintiff to recover *all* losses. Note how this differs from the result under comparative negligence described below.

[11] There are three different forms of comparative negligence: pure, modified, and slight-gross. These are extremely interesting but are not central to our economic analysis.

The equitable argument is the principal justification for the switch to comparative negligence. However, there are economic efficiency arguments that can be made on behalf of comparative negligence. To make these arguments requires relaxing at least one of the core assumptions that we made in the previous chapter. Recall that the basic economic theory of tort liability of Chapter 8 showed that *all* forms of the negligence rule (simple, contributory, and comparative negligence) were equally efficient. The only way we can draw efficiency distinctions among them is to relax one of the core assumptions. Suppose that, in a negligence case, we assume that litigation is costly in the sense that it is not certain how the court will evaluate the evidence developed at trial. Thus, neither the plaintiff nor the defendant can be certain whether or not the court will determine that their precautionary behavior was sufficient to absolve one of them of fault. It is possible, for example, that the court will determine that the precaution of one of the parties was insufficient, even though that party thought that he or she had complied with the relevant duty to take due care. Or the court may find one of the parties nonnegligent when in fact the party was violating the legal standard of care. We may call this condition "evidentiary uncertainty."

We show the effects of evidentiary uncertainty on the precautionary decisions of a potential injurer in Figures 9.1 and 9.2. The first figure shows how the potential injurer's probability of being held not liable varies with the amount of precaution. We assume, as seems realistic, that the probability that potential injurers will be found not liable increases as their precaution increases. This is indicated by the bell-shaped curve centered on x^*, which we assume to be the potential injurer's best guess as to the exonerating level of care. The mass under the curve, as one moves from left to right, represents the probability of *not* being held liable. If the injurer takes no precaution, then the likelihood of being held liable is the entire mass under the curve—that is, one. But for a level of precaution such as x^{**}, the probability of being held not liable is the area under the curve from 0 to x^{**}. (There is still a positive probability of being held liable if the injurer takes x^{**} precaution: the area to the right of x^{**} under the bell curve.)

We show the impact of these considerations about evidentiary uncertainty in Figure 9.2. The effect of that uncertainty is to smooth the discontinuity in expected liability at the (presumed) legal standard that we developed in Chapter 8. Smoothing occurs

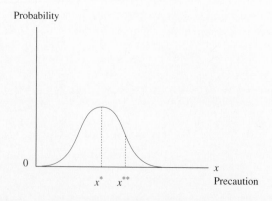

FIGURE 9.1 The effect of evidentiary uncertainty on the precautionary decision of a potential injurer.

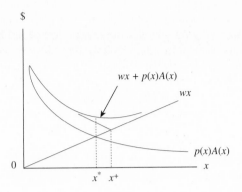

FIGURE 9.2 Evidentiary uncertainty smoothes the discontinuity at the legal standard of care and induces extra precaution by the potential injurer.

because injurers' expected costs are a weighted average of their costs when liable and their costs when not liable, with the weights given by the probability that they will be found liable. The effect is indicated in Figure 9.2 by the sloping curve that connects the expected-cost curve and precautionary-cost line. Uncertainty about the court's assessment of a party's precautionary level with regard to the legal standard of care induces most injurers to take more precaution than is prescribed by the legal standard of care. In effect, they give themselves a margin of error to be sure that they avoid liability. This behavior is represented in Figure 9.2, which illustrates the fact that an injurer's costs are minimized on the smoothed curve at x^+, which is a higher level of precaution than the legal standard x^*.

Evidentiary uncertainty causes potential injurers to go beyond the level of precaution that might just barely exonerate them.[12] That is, evidentiary uncertainty will cause overprecaution relative to the efficient level of precaution.

This result is true under *any* form of the negligence rule. What efficiency advantage, if any, does comparative negligence provide when there is evidentiary uncertainty? The overprecaution caused by evidentiary uncertainty is less under comparative negligence than it is under any other form of the negligence rule. The simple reason is that under comparative negligence, if either party makes a mistake in choosing the level of precaution that is necessary to satisfy the legal standard of care, the consequence of that mistake is not visited entirely on the person who made it, as it would be under any other form of the negligence rule, because, under comparative negligence, the losses are shared between the two parties rather than being concentrated on one party.

One frequent criticism that is made of comparative negligence is that its administrative costs are too high. The rules to be used in apportioning fault are vague, it is said, even when the parties are engaged in the same activity: no one is quite sure how to apportion fault when *A* was going 45 in a 30 miles-per-hour zone and *B* was going 60.

---

[12] This is an instance of the point we made earlier in this chapter—namely, that the prospect of costly litigation will induce potential injurers to take more precaution than they would otherwise. A little extra precaution makes an accident (and thus, a lawsuit) less likely.

But things are even worse when the parties are engaged in different activities. How, for instance, would you have apportioned fault in *Butterfield v. Forrester*, the case in Chapter 3 involving an obstruction in the road left by Forrester and a negligent horseman, Butterfield, who crashed into the obstruction? Given this difficulty, it is alleged that litigants and juries will spend inordinately large amounts of effort trying to establish exact percentages of fault when such exactitude is impossible to achieve.

There may be some truth in the contention that comparative negligence has high administrative costs. If so, there is a balance to be struck between the efficiency gains of comparative negligence and these administrative costs. Until we can examine careful empirical studies, we cannot say whether or not there is a net efficiency gain from moving to this new liability standard.[13]

II. COMPUTING DAMAGES

In the previous chapter we noted that the ability of liability rules to induce efficient precaution depends in part on the ability of the court to award truly compensatory damages to the victims of a tort. These damages accomplish two things at once: first, they put the victim back onto the utility level or indifference curve occupied before the tortious act, and second, they are the "price" that the injurer must pay for having harmed the victim. In this section we elaborate the ways in which microeconomics can help to determine the appropriate amount of damages. Additionally, we use microeconomics to discuss the efficiency aspects of punitive damages in tort awards.

A. Risk-equivalence

Compensatory damages are intended to "make the victim whole." In some circumstances, this is impossible. For example, when a child is killed in a tortious accident, damages cannot be computed on the formula, "Find a sum of money such that the parents are indifferent between having the money and a dead child, and not having the money and having their child alive." The same difficulty arises in a more attenuated form for irreparable physical injuries, such as those resulting from a crippling accident.

There are, in fact, two distinct concepts of compensatory damages in tort law. One concept is the standard economic concept of indifference: compensation is perfect when the victim is indifferent between having the injury and the damages, and having neither. Compensatory damages are thus perfect when the potential victim is indifferent about whether there is no accident or an accident with compensation. This concept is relevant for injuries in which a substitute for the lost good is available in the market. When a substitute is available, the market price of the substitute measures the value of the good to the plaintiff. This concept is also relevant for goods that are bought and sold from time to time but for which there is no regular, organized market. For exam-

---

[13] See David Haddock and Christopher Curran, *An Economic Theory of Comparative Negligence,* 14 J. LEGAL STUD. 49 (1985); Michelle White, *An Empirical Test of the Comparative and Contributory Negligence Rules in Accident Law,* 20 RAND J. ECON. 308 (1989); Daniel Orr, *Another Vote for Comparative Negligence,* 20 J. LEGAL STUD. 119 (1990); and Aaron Edlin, *Efficient Standards of Due Care: Should Courts Find More Parties Negligent Under Comparative Negligence?,* 14 INTERNATIONAL REV. LAW & ECON. 21 (1994).

ple, a handwritten letter by James Joyce and a 1957 Chevy convertible are sold from time to time, but these items are so rare that a regular market for them does not exist. The owners of these rare goods usually have prices at which they are prepared to sell them, and these prices measure perfectly compensatory damages.[14]

This concept of perfect compensation, based on indifference, is fundamental to an economic account of incentives. If potential injurers are liable for perfectly compensatory damages, then they will internalize the external harm caused by accidents. And this creates incentives for the potential injurers to take efficient precaution. Compensation of this kind is most easily computed for those losses for which there is a ready market substitute.

But for some tortious injuries there is no ready market substitute. For example, there is no price at which a good parent would sell a child. The idea that a person could be "indifferent" between a sum of money and a child is repugnant. And, for some people, there may be no price at which they would sell an arm or a leg.[15] So, for injuries involving the loss of a child or a limb, compensation simply cannot be perfect. Juries must, nevertheless, award damages for the wrongful death of a child or for grievous personal injuries. Our task, then, is to provide a more satisfactory understanding of their computation.

A necessary part of living is being exposed to the risk of death or serious injury. For example, flying on an airplane or driving down the expressway involves such a risk. These risks can often be reduced, but doing so is costly. To illustrate, we may note that airplanes must be inspected and repaired at regular intervals, which is costly, but the shorter the intervals, the fewer the accidents. Similarly, heavy cars with special safety features provide extra safety to passengers. But these cars are more expensive to produce and, therefore, more costly to consumers. When a parent decides what features of a car to buy or a commercial air carrier decides how frequently to inspect planes for safety, a decision is being made that balances the cost of additional precaution against reductions in the probability of injury.

A rational decision about these risks involves balancing the costs and benefits of precaution. By reasoning in this way, it is possible to impute a value to the loss of life. To illustrate, we may suppose that the probability of a fatal automobile accident falls by 1/10,000 when an additional $100 is spent on automotive safety. If expenditures on automotive safety are rational, then the reduction in the probability of a fatal accident, multiplied by the implicit value assigned to a life, equals the marginal cost of care:

$$(1/10,000)(\text{implicit value of life}) = \$100,$$

or

$$(\text{implicit value of life}) = 100/(1/10,000),$$

which suggests that the implicit value of a life is $1,000,000.

---

[14] Economists use the term "reservation price" to refer to the minimum price at which the owner of a good is willing to sell it. Determining the owner's reservation price for a unique good is a difficult practical problem, but it is not a problem conceptually.

[15] For some people, there may be an amount of money at which selling an arm is an attractive bargain, but their concept of morality would not permit them to do it.

This method of computing the value of life, which is sometimes referred to as the *risk-equivalent* method, takes actual market purchases as a guide to how much the purchaser values safety. For example, suppose that a consumer may purchase a safety device, such as an air bag, by paying extra to the retailer. If we know how much the safety device costs the consumer and by how much that device reduces the likelihood of death, then we may infer the consumer's valuation of safety, which implies an implicit value of life. Using the figures from the previous paragraph, we may assume that the device costs $100 and that it reduces the likelihood of death by 1/10,000. (Remember that this implies a $1,000,000 value on being alive.) If consumers purchase the device, then they must value safety at a level that implies that the value of a life equals at least $1 million.

To apply the risk-equivalent method in a legal dispute, the court should consider those situations in which risk is "reasonable" and well-known. In those circumstances, there will be some value p for the probability of a fatal accident, and some value B for the burden of precaution. Efficiency requires taking additional precaution until the burden equals the change in probability p multiplied by the loss L, or $B = pL$. (Notice that this is the Hand rule.) Thus, the court would compute the risk-equivalent value of a life by solving the equation for L, yielding $L = B/p$.

We have described two distinct methods for computing compensatory damages: the *indifference* method and the *risk-equivalent* method. The first method is appropriate for market goods—that is, for losses for which there is a market substitute; the second method is appropriate when there are legal and moral barriers to such markets. Only when the indifference method is appropriate can damages be perfectly compensatory. However, both methods, when applied without error, provide incentives for an efficient level of precaution by potential injurers.

QUESTION 9.7: Is this pattern of damages an anomaly? Does it create incentives that are inefficient or even perverse?

B. Measuring Compensation

If utility functions could be observed, computing perfect compensation would be easy. After an injury, the utility curves of the victim would be sketched as in Figure 8.1 and damages would be read off the graph. Utility curves, however, are not observed directly. Instead, economists impute a preference ordering to a decision-maker on the basis of the choices the person makes. It is the choices, not the ordering, that are directly observed. So, part of the problem of computing damages is to infer the preference ordering from the decision-maker's choices.[16]

Unlike utility, demand and supply are observable. We may link the utility theory of compensation to demand and supply. In general, demand for a good by an individual, or by an aggregate of individuals, is a function of many variables, including price, income, and tastes. The demand curve picks out one of these variables, specifically price, and depicts its relationship to the quantity of the good demanded. The other vari-

---

[16] The technical name for the theory of such imputations is "revealed preference theory."

"FORTUNATELY FOR MY CLIENT, THE VICTIM DIED."

Would you rather be dead or crippled? In most tortious accidents, victims and their families prefer the person alive and crippled rather than dead. It is, consequently, worse to cause someone's death in a tortious accident than to cause him or her to be crippled. Yet, the death of the victim can be fortunate for the injurer, because the damages awarded by courts are often greater when the victim of a tortious accident is crippled than they are when he or she dies. Someone who is injured severely but has a relatively long life still ahead will require extraordinary compensation. The income that the victim can no longer enjoy must be replaced, and the fact that he or she may require constant, expensive medical attention every day must be taken account in the assessment of damages.

By contrast, if the victim is killed, the family (or other dependents) will receive only what they would have received from the victim if he or she had been alive. Thus, if the decedent would have made $100,000 per year for the next 20 years and would have given his or her dependents two-thirds of that income each year, then the dependents are entitled to receive the two-thirds of $100,000 for 20 years, discounted to present value.

ables affecting demand, which are not represented explicitly in the demand curve, are implicitly held constant while the price varies. The variables held constant are the prices of other goods, the income of the buyers, and the tastes of the buyers.

When the price falls, and all the other variables in the preceding list are held constant, consumers move down the demand curve. The fact that consumers can obtain the good at a lower price implies that their utility has increased. Thus, moving down the demand curve corresponds to an increase in utility caused by a fall in price. For conceptual purposes, it is possible to imagine that just enough income is taken away from buyers as they move down the demand curve to offset the effect of the fall in price. In other words, the fall in the price of the good, which makes them better off, could be offset by taking some income away from the buyers, which makes them worse off, so that the net effect is to make them no better off and no worse off. Of course, offsetting the lower price by a fall in income is a conceptual exercise, not a real event.

In welfare economics, a special type of demand curve—called a *constant-utility demand curve*—is frequently used for conceptual purposes, and it has just this characteristic: as consumers move down the demand curve, the fall in price is exactly offset by a fall in income, so that their utility remains constant. Every point on this special demand curve represents the same level of utility. The constant-utility demand curve is fundamental to the theory of compensation and, more generally, to applied welfare economics. To see why, think of the constant-utility demand curve as the relationship between the maximum amount that people can pay for a good without affecting their utility. That is, the constant-utility demand curve describes decision-makers' willingness to pay for the good. When applied in law, the willingness to pay for a good equals the amount of compensation that must be paid to the victim for depriving him of the good. In other words, perfect compensation for harm resulting from a decrease in the quantity of a good equals the corresponding area under the constant-utility demand curve.

To illustrate, we can assume that the demand curve in Figure 9.3 is drawn by holding utility constant as the quantity x_2 and letting the willingness to pay, p_2, vary. Let the initial quantity be denoted x_{02}, and let harm reduce the quantity to x_{12}. The shaded area in the figure, which lies under the demand curve and inside the interval between x_{02} and x_{12}, indicates the amount the person could pay for receiving the quantity of the good $(x_{02} - x_{12})$ without any change in utility. Consequently, the shaded area also indicates the amount that must be paid in compensation to the victim for taking away the quantity of the good $(x_{02} - x_{12})$ in order to restore him or her to the initial level of utility. Thus, perfectly compensatory damages for depriving someone of a quantity of a good equal the victim's willingness to pay for it, which in turn equals the shaded area under the constant-utility demand curve.

From a formal standpoint, goods and bads are the same but for the positive or negative sign. Thus, the preceding argument about compensation for depriving someone of a good also applies to imposing a bad upon someone. Specifically, the harm caused by imposing the bad equals the victim's willingness to pay to be free from it. The willingness to pay to be free from a bad can be represented as a constant-utility demand curve, and the area under the appropriate segment will indicate the perfectly compensatory damages for imposing a bad upon the victim.

Instead of depriving someone of a good or imposing a bad, sometimes injurers wrongfully prevent victims from buying a good at a particular price. The preceding analysis can easily be extended to such cases. The difference between a person's willingness to pay for a good and what is actually paid is called the "consumer surplus" that the person enjoys from the transaction. Perfectly compensatory damages for wrongfully preventing someone from buying at a particular price equal the loss in consumer surplus caused by the wrongful act.

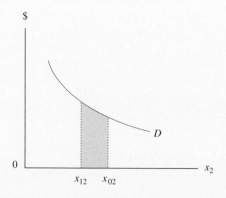

FIGURE 9.3 A constant-utility demand curve shows how to use willingness-to-pay as a measure of lost utility.

To illustrate, suppose that someone is wrongfully prevented from buying good x_i at price p_{oi}, as a result of which the person has to purchase the good at the higher price p_{li} (see Figure 9.4). At the low price p_{oi}, the person would buy x_{oi} units of x_i; at the higher price p_{li} the person only buys x_{li}. A rough approximation of compensatory damages is the additional cost of the purchase, which could be computed to equal the overcharge on the good purchased, $x_{li}(p_{li} - p_{oi})$, or could be computed to equal the overcharge on the goods that would have been purchased at the lower price, $x_{oi}(p_{li} - p_{oi})$. These measures, which are not exact, are usually good enough for practical purposes. (An exact determination is represented by the shaded areas in Figure 9.4 and explained in a footnote.[17])

Perfect compensation, as measured by the area under the constant-utility demand curve in Figure 9.4, exactly equals perfect compensation as measured graphically in Figure 8.1, where we used indifference curves. The purpose of changing from the utility representation of Figure 8.1 to the demand representation of Figure 9.4 is to move from unobservable variables to observable variables. The reader's impression may be that this task has not been accomplished because, like indifference curves, the constant-utility demand curve is not readily observable. Specifically, the demand curves that are actually estimated for markets are not constant-utility demand curves. Fortunately, in measuring welfare changes caused by small changes in quantities and prices, the constant-utility demand curve is the same, or nearly the same, as the ordinary demand curve. Thus, in practice, the ordinary demand curve can be estimated, and welfare changes can be measured by proceeding as if the demand curve were a constant-utility demand curve.

C. Punitive Damages

Punitive damages are, by definition, damages given to the plaintiff as a way of punishing the defendant. We must begin our economic analysis of punitive damages by answering two questions:

1. Under what conditions are punitive damages awarded?
2. How is the amount of punitive damages computed?

In most states there is a statute describing the conditions under which punitive damages may be awarded. These are usually attempts to state the common law practices actually followed by the courts. According to the usual formulation, punitive damages

---

[17] Relative to perfect compensation, the first of these measures undercompensates and the second measure overcompensates. Perfect compensation can be computed by considering the constant-utility demand curve. The willingness to pay for the additional good is the area under the constant-utility demand curve between x_{oi} and x_{li} in Figure 9.4. The price that would have been paid, but for the wrongdoing, is p_{oi}. Thus, the surplus enjoyed by the consumer on this incremental quantity of the good is the difference between the area under the constant-utility demand curve and the total price that would have been paid, $p_{oi}(x_{oi} - x_{li})$, as indicated by the heavily shaded area in the figure. The overcharge on the goods actually purchased is $x_{li}(p_{li} - p_{oi})$, as indicated by the lightly shaded area. Thus, the perfectly compensatory damages equal the loss in the consumer's surplus on the goods that would have been purchased at the lower price and were not purchased at the higher price, as indicated by the heavily shaded area, plus the overcharge on the goods that were actually purchased, as indicated by the lightly shaded area.

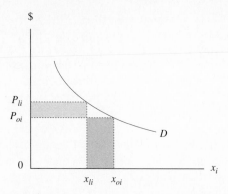

FIGURE 9.4 Compensation for wrongfully being denied the ability to purchase a good or service.

can be awarded when the defendant's behavior is malicious, oppressive, gross, willful and wanton, or fraudulent.[18] These statutes merely provide guidelines for awarding punitive damages. Because the guidelines have not been formulated into exact rules, there is much uncertainty about when punitive damages can be awarded.

There is even more uncertainty concerning how to compute punitive damages. Statutes typically contain no specific instructions for computing punitive damages. Punitive damages are supposed to bear a reasonable relationship to compensatory damages and to the ability of the defendant to pay, but the courts have not specified what "reasonable" or "ability to pay" mean in this context. It is uncertain, for example, whether punitive damages may be only double the amount of compensatory damages or up to 10 times compensatory damages. Judges apparently have an idea of how much is enough, and jury awards have often been reduced by judges, but there are no rules regarding the computation of punitive damages. There is a compelling need in torts for a more coherent account of punitive damages, and economic analysis can provide guidelines for the development of this account.

To begin the economic analysis of punitive damages, let us supply some numbers to the situation described in Example 3 of the preceding chapter.

FACTS: A manufacturer of a fuel additive for automobile engines is keeping a careful eye on costs. He can set quality control at a high or a low level. High-level quality control costs $9,000 per year and guarantees that the fuel additive is pure and never causes damage to automobile engines. Low-level quality control is costless (thus saving $9,000)

---

[18] The following is the section on "Exemplary Damages" (which is another name for punitive damages) from the CALIFORNIA CIVIL CODE, §3294:

"For Oppression, Fraud or Malice.

(a) In an action for the breach of an obligation not arising from contract, where the defendant has been guilty of oppression, fraud, or malice, the plaintiff, in addition to the actual damages, may recover damages for the sake of the example and by way of punishing the defendant."

That is not much detail to govern actions upon which millions of dollars turn. Notice that nothing is said about how to compute punitive damages.

ORGANIZATIONS AS VICTIMS

Economists routinely impute utility functions to individual consumers and workers. But what if the victim seeking compensation is an organization, such as a partnership, a corporation, a government, or a club? Like individuals, organizations can be regarded as decision-makers, and their choices can be regarded as revealing organizational preferences. Like those of an individual, the preferences of a rational organization can usually be represented by a well-ordered utility function. So the question arises, "Can the utility analysis of the idea of compensation be extended to organizations?"

In applied welfare economics, benefits or harms to institutions are traced to individuals, at least in principle. For example, the loss in profits suffered by a business is traced back to a loss in income to the business's owners. A common practice is to assume a one-to-one relationship between the loss in profits to the organization and the loss in income to individual owners, and to assume that the owners are interested in the business only for the sake of profits. Under these assumptions, the company's profits "stand in" for the utility of affected persons. Because the changes in profits to the business equal changes in income to its owners, compensating the organization is equivalent to compensating its owners.

In the case of business firms, the conventional assumption in economics is that they maximize profits. Thus, when a utility function is imputed to a business, it has a simple form: profits are the only thing that the business cares about. For a business, the fall from a higher indifference curve to a lower indifference curve corresponds to a fall in profits that can be compensated for, when the fall results from another's wrongdoing, through an award of damages to the business equal to the lost profits.

In general, when there is a one-to-one relationship between the loss as measured by the institution's preferences and the losses to individuals, the institutional preferences can be used as a surrogate for the welfare of affected individuals. However, the extension of the utility analysis of compensation to organizations that are not profit-seeking, such as governments, clubs, and non-profit corporations, is problematic because there is less agreement about the behavioral theories used in describing them. In the absence of an accepted behavioral theory, there cannot be agreement about how to trace the consequences of harm suffered by these organizations back to its effects upon the welfare of individuals.

but results in some batches of the fuel additive's being flawed. A few of the cars using the flawed batch will be harmed; specifically, the expected damage to cars is $10,000 per year ($1000 in expected damages to each of 10 cars).

From an economic viewpoint, efficiency requires the manufacturer to make the quality-control expenditures because the company can expect to save consumers $10,000 per year by spending $9,000 per year on quality control.

Will making the manufacturer strictly liable for compensatory damages produce this result? The answer is "yes" if the tort-liability system is perfect, but "no" if it is imperfect. Suppose that the tort liability system is perfect in the sense that disputes between the manufacturer and consumers can be resolved costlessly and without error, and damages are perfectly compensatory. With a perfect tort-liability system and a rule of strict liability, every car owner harmed by the product will recover from the manufacturer without having to spend anything to resolve the dispute. The manufacturer thus faces $10,000 in expected liability if he does not take precautions costing $9,000. A rational manufacturer maximizes profits net of expected tort liability; so, our manufacturer will set quality control at the high level.

But suppose we make the more realistic assumption that the tort-liability system works imperfectly. Specifically, let us suppose that for every two consumers whose cars suffer damage, only one actually brings suit and recovers. Call the ratio of compensated victims to total victims, which is ½ in this example, the "enforcement error."[19] Given an enforcement error of ½ and assuming the successful plaintiff only receives compensatory damages, the manufacturer's expected liability will be $5,000 if he adopts the low level of quality control. He can, however, save $9,000 by reducing his quality control from high to low. So, enforcement error in this example creates a situation in which a profit-maximizing manufacturer, whose expected liability is limited to compensatory damages, will choose low-level quality control, which is inefficient.

The efficiency loss due to enforcement error can be offset by augmenting compensatory damages with punitive damages. Suppose, as above, that the actual damages are $1000 per car but that the court doubles this compensatory amount so that total damages are $2000 per car. If we call the amount in excess of compensation "punitive damages," then the punitive damages are $1000 per car. We might also refer to the multiplicative factor by which we adjusted the compensatory damages in order to offset the enforcement error as the "punitive multiple." In our example, a punitive multiple of two exactly offsets the enforcement error of ½ and restores the manufacturer's liability to the level that would have prevailed under perfect enforcement.[20]

We can state this method of computing punitive damages more formally. Define the relevant variables as follows:

x = precaution, whose cost is w per unit;

p = the probability of an accident as a function of x, with $p' < 0$ and $p'' > 0$ (*i.e.*, the probability of an accident declines as precaution increases, but declines at a decreasing rate);

A = the harm caused by an accident;

L = the injurer's liability conditional on an accident's actually occurring;

---

[19] Later in this chapter we shall see that enforcement error is a characteristic of harms arising in the delivery of medical care.

[20] Implicit in this argument is the assumption that the rate at which consumers successfully bring suit against the manufacturer does not change when punitive damages are added to compensatory damages. This is a strong and unrealistic assumption. When damage awards are high, victims and their attorneys have stronger incentives to bring action against those who have injured them. This then causes a second-round effect, in that, as the number of actions increases, the enforcement error falls, and therefore the punitive multiple should fall. It is an open question whether the existence of a punitive multiple can increase the number of actions just enough to correct for the inefficiency caused by enforcement error or whether it leads to overenforcement.

m = the punitive multiple; and

e = the enforcement error.

Assume that precaution, x, whose unit cost is \$$w$, is continuous and that taking precaution reduces the probability, p, of an accident. Socially responsible decision-makers take precaution to minimize the sum of the costs and the expected cost of harm:

$$\min [wx + p(x)A].$$

By contrast, purely selfish actors are not concerned with the harm, A, suffered by others, but only with their own expected liability, L. Purely selfish actors thus take precaution to minimize the sum of their costs and their liability times the probability of an accident:

$$\min [wx + p(x)L].$$

Consider, first, the consequences of an enforcement error e when there are no punitive damages. By assumption, then, decision-makers' liability is limited to compensatory damages, A, which are imposed with enforcement error e in the event of an accident. Thus,

$$L = Ae.$$

Because $e < 1$, the expected liability is a fraction of the actual harm done by an injurer. Substituting this into the preceding relation yields

$$\min [wx + p(x)Ae].$$

This equation differs from the one for socially responsible decision-makers by the term e; the enforcement error represents an externalization of social costs that causes decision-makers to take too little precaution.

To make selfish actors internalize social costs, compensatory damages must be augmented by punitive damages. When punitive damages are allowed, liability equals the punitive multiple times the compensatory damages net of the enforcement error:

$$L = Aem.$$

The minimization equation for purely selfish actors then becomes

$$\min [wx + p(x)Aem].$$

If the punitive multiple equals the inverse of the enforcement error—that is, if $m = 1/e$—then the last two terms in this equation cancel, and the equation becomes identical to the one for socially responsible decision-makers. Thus, we conclude that a punitive multiple equal to the inverse of the enforcement error will restore efficient incentives.

The law might adopt as a rule that, when punitive damages are awarded, the punitive multiple should equal the inverse of the enforcement error. If such a rule were written into the law, either by statute or by judges, juries would have some guidance in setting the punitive multiple. For example, if there were proof that an injurer had failed to take the appropriate amount of care, because she suspected that only a fraction of those injured would bring an action against her, the court could impose punitive damages in an amount determined by application of a punitive multiple equal to the inverse of the enforcement error.

Institutionalizing this rule poses difficulties. One of them is the difficulty of observing the enforcement error. This problem, however, is not insurmountable, as we explain in the box titled "Observability and the Punitive Multiple."

III. APPLYING THE ECONOMIC THEORY OF TORT LIABILITY: TORT LAW REFORM

In the United States there is a strong political movement to reform the tort-liability system. The evidence favoring reform is largely anecdotal but arresting. For example, a woman in New Mexico recently received a jury award of $200,000 in compensatory damages and $2.7 million in punitive damages against McDonald's for injuries she received when a hot cup of coffee spilled on her as she drove away from the restaurant. Many municipalities have removed play structures and swing sets from their public parks and diving boards from their public swimming pools because of the fear of liability. In this section, we shall examine the more systematic evidence for reform of the tort-liability system by focusing on products liability and medical malpractice—the two areas of most concern. Before we look at those specialized areas, we first look at some general information about the United States' tort-liability system.

A. Some General Facts About the American Tort-Liability System

To this point we have been speaking of the tort-liability system in theoretical terms or with regard to particular facts in particular cases. Now we turn briefly to some general facts about the United States' tort-liability system. Here we see what the broad sweep of statistics can tell us about the number and kinds of accidents in the United States and how the legal system deals with them.

The U.S. Department of Justice, Bureau of Justice Statistics, recently studied tort filings in state courts in the year between July 1, 1991, and June 30, 1992. (98% of all cases, not just torts, are filed in state courts.) Plaintiffs filed approximately 750,000 tort actions during that period. More than three-fourths of those claims involved automobile accidents or property liability claims. Medical malpractice, product liability, and toxic substances together accounted for about 10% of all the cases filed. The study (and others) found that the total number of tort filings in the state courts was constant between 1986 and 1993. The average award for personal-injury cases was $48,000.[21]

Critics of the tort-liability system in the United States contend that juries award punitive damages too often and too liberally. However, punitive damages are extremely rare. In all product-liability cases between 1965 and 1990 there were only 353 punitive awards, and those averaged $625,000. Appellate panels reduced many

---

[21] Steven K. Smith, Carol J. DeFrances, Patrick A. Langan, and John Goerdt, *Tort Cases in Large Counties*, (NCJ-153177), Department of Justice, Bureau of Justice Statistics (1995). The study also looked at all civil cases filed in 29 states during 1993. It found that there were nearly 6 million civil cases filed in those state courts. "Domestic relations" accounted for 41% of the total; "small claims," for 12%; contracts for 11%; and torts for 10%.

OBSERVABILITY AND THE PUNITIVE MULTIPLE

We have shown that efficient incentives to take precaution can be restored by setting the punitive multiple equal to the inverse of the enforcement error. The enforcement error, however, may be unobservable or observable only with error. When the enforcement error is difficult to observe, the decision-maker's subjective beliefs about its magnitude may depart from objective reality. Under these conditions, achieving efficient incentives depends upon setting the punitive multiple according to the decision-maker's subjective beliefs about the enforcement error. Here we describe how that can be accomplished.

We explained in the text that purely selfish actors minimize the sum of the costs of precaution and expected liability: min $[wx + p(x)L]$. Furthermore, if decision-makers expect to escape punitive damages, their expected liability equals the harm times the enforcement error: $L = Ae$. Substituting into the preceding relationship yields this minimization equation for purely selfish actors: min $[wx + p(x)Ae]$.

The cost-minimizing level of precaution occurs when the marginal cost of precaution, w, equals the marginal reduction in the probability of an accident, p' times the liability Ae:

$$0 = w + p'(x)Ae.$$

(Here we are assuming that A and e do not vary with x; that assumption can easily be relaxed, but the conclusions do not change.) Rearranging the terms in this equation yields

$$e = w / [-p'(x)A].$$

According to this equation, the enforcement error as perceived by the decision-maker equals the unit cost of precaution divided by the reduction in compensatory damages from additional precaution. Furthermore, the optimal punitive multiple equals the inverse of the enforcement error: $m = 1/e$. Hence,

$$m = (A / w)[-p'(x)A].$$

We have thus proved the following proposition: if we assume that precaution is continuous, that taking it reduces the probability of an accident, and that the marginal injurer thinks he or she will escape punitive damages, then to cause the internalization of social costs for such a class of actors, we should make the punitive damages multiple equal to the ratio of compensatory damages to the cost of precaution, multiplied by the marginal probability of averting an accident.

of these punitive awards so that, after appeal, the average fell to $135,000. More than 25% of those 353 awards involved asbestos. Over the entire period there was an average of 11 punitive-damages awards per year in product-liability cases. A careful study of punitive damages in product-liability cases found that at the trial level the ratio of punitive to compensatory damages was 1.2 to 1; in more than one-third of the cases in which punitives were awarded, compensatory damages were larger than the punitives.[22] More than half the states prohibit or cap punitive damages or raise the evidence standard that must be met before they can be awarded.[23] Recall that the usual standard in civil actions is "preponderance of the evidence," which is generally taken to mean 51% believability. The "clear and convincing" evidence standard is more demanding, but not as demanding as the criminal law's standard of "beyond a reasonable doubt."

The theme of much of the empirical literature is that the tort-liability system (perhaps in conjunction with the administrative agency regulatory system) works reasonably well at deterring accidents. In most situations in which accidents might happen, the recent trend in the United States has been toward fewer and less severe accidents. For instance, the number of motor vehicle deaths and injuries peaked around 1970 and has declined ever since. The death and injury *rate* per capita has shown a dramatic drop.[24]

B. Products Liability

Thirty years ago products liability was a minor part of tort law, but recently it has become a large and important specialty and the focus of much of the public dissatisfaction with the entire tort-liability system. In some cases, insurers have decided that the products liability area is so uncertain that they have withdrawn from the market entirely. Some of the manufacturers and others who have been left without insurance coverage have decided to stop making their products. A recent survey of chief executive officers by the Conference Board (a business interest group) found that liability concerns caused 47% of those surveyed to drop one or more product lines, 25% to stop some research and development, and 39% to cancel plans for a new product. For example, the G.D. Searle Company, a manufacturer of pharmaceuticals and medical supplies, became so frightened by the bankruptcy of the A.H. Robins Company (a bankruptcy attributable to liability actions involving Robins' intrauterine birth-control device called the Dalkon shield) that it announced that it would no longer produce intrauterine birth-control devices, even though Searle's product was generally regarded as safe and effective.

---

[22] Michael Rustad, *Demystifying Punitive Damages in Products Liability Cases: A Survey of a Quarter Century of Verdicts*, The Roscoe Pound Foundation (1991).

[23] Twelve states require a "clear and convincing" evidence standard for punitive damages. Another twelve states cap the amount of damages and require the "clear and convincing evidence" standard. Seven states require a portion of the punitive award to be paid to the state. Five states prohibit punitive-damages awards.

[24] For an excellent survey of the empirical literature on accidents and the U.S. tort-liability system, see Michael J. Saks, *Do We Really Know Anything About the Behavior of the Tort Litigation System—And Why Not?*, 140 U. PA. L. REV. 1147 (1992).

1. The Efficient Liability Standard for Product-related Accidents   The liability standard in product-related accidents is called "strict products liability."[25] For a defendant-manufacturer to be held liable under this standard, the product must be determined to be defective. A defect can take three forms:

1. **a defect in design**, as was alleged against the Ford Motor Company's design of the Pinto gas tank;

2. **a defect in manufacture**, as would be the case if a bolt were left out of a lawnmower during its assembly, causing a piece of the mower to fly off and injure a user; and

3. **a defect in warning**, as when the manufacturer fails to warn consumers of dangers in the use of the product.

What liability standard would economic theory recommend for product-related accidents? Recall that our discussion of negligence and strict liability focused on whether precaution for reducing the likelihood and severity of the accident is unilateral or bilateral. If it is bilateral (*i.e.*, if both parties can take precautionary action to reduce the probability and severity of an accident), then a form of the negligence rule is the appropriate standard. If precaution is unilateral (*i.e.*, if only the injurer can be looked to for actions to reduce the probability and severity of an accident), then strict liability is the appropriate liability standard. Using this economic analysis, which standard would modern products-liability law apply?

The more efficient standard would seem to be strict liability because in most instances of product-related harms precaution lies unilaterally with the manufacturers. It is they who are in control of the design of the products and of the manufacturing process and who are most likely to be aware of any special dangers that their products present and, therefore, can most efficiently convey information about those dangers through warnings.

However, on further reflection, one finds elements of *bilateral* precaution in the product-accident situation. *Users* can also take precautions to reduce the probability and severity of accidents. For example, they can pay heed to the warnings and use the products only for their intended uses. There are stories about some consumers picking up their gasoline- or electric-powered lawnmowers and turning them sideways in order to trim their hedges. No manufacturer intends a lawnmower to be used in that fashion.

Products-liability law can steer a middle course between the view that precaution is unilateral (and, therefore, that strict liability is the appropriate standard) and the view that precaution is bilateral (and, therefore, that negligence is the appropriate standard). It can do so by holding defendant-manufacturers strictly liable for defective design, manufacture, or warning but allowing them to escape liability if the victim voluntarily assumed the risk of injury or misused the product. These defenses encourage the efficient allocation of risk of loss from product-related injuries between the consumer and manufacturer.

---

[25] RESTATEMENT (SECOND) OF TORTS (1965), §402A, published by the American Law Institute, lays out this standard.

TWO THEORIES OF THE EVOLUTION OF PRODUCTS-LIABILITY LAW

Products-liability law first evolved in the United States from contract principles to tort; and then from negligence to strict liability. Some scholars believe that it recently evolved to "enterprise liability," which means that manufacturers are absolutely liable for all accidents arising from use of their products. Has the evolution been an improvement or a mistake?

Two recent articles provide insights into these questions. Professor George Priest of the Yale Law School contends that the evolution of enterprise liability resulted from promotion of a mistaken theory of products liability by a few prominent legal scholars. (George L. Priest, *The Invention of Enterprise Liability: A Critical History of the Intellectual Foundations of Modern Tort Law*, 14 J. LEGAL STUD. 461 [1985].) Beginning in the 1940s these scholars convinced the profession that strict products liability was preferable to any alternative method of dealing with product-related injuries for three reasons:

1. manufacturers possess market power, which allows them to dictate unfair terms in warranties and underinvestment in product-safety technology;

2. manufacturers are better placed than are consumers to spread the losses from product-related injuries; and

3. manufacturers are better placed than are consumers to minimize the losses from product accidents by taking precaution and improving technology.

Professor Priest believes that the first two of these premises are mistaken, a conclusion supported by our examination of the economics of products-liability law above.

continued . . .

If the lawnmower manufacturer could not exclude liability for consumer misuse or for voluntarily assumed risk, it would be forced to insure each of its consumers. To cover the cost of this insurance policy, the manufacturer would have to raise the product price. The difficulty with this result is that *all* consumers must pay the higher price, not just those who are careless. Consumers who are careful would prefer to pay a lower price for the product and to purchase insurance against loss elsewhere.

The conclusion we draw is that strict liability with the defenses of assumption of the risk and product misuse is an efficient standard for minimizing the social costs of product-related injuries. The absence of these defenses compels manufacturers to offer insurance with their product, probably an inefficient outcome.

QUESTION 9.8: Some scholars discern a trend in modern products-liability law toward absolute liability or what is sometimes called "enterprise liability." Under that theory manufacturers would be held liable for almost every injury resulting from the use of their outputs. Give an economic analysis of that liability standard for product-related harms.

2. Reforming Products Liability   Since the early 1980s in the United States there has been a powerful political interest in reforming products-liability law both at the federal and state level. But until very recently no reform occurred.

Two Theories of the Evolution of Products-Liability Law Continued . . .

A completely different view of the evolution of products-liability law is that of Professor William Landes of the University of Chicago Law School and Judge Richard A. Posner of the United States Court of Appeals for the Seventh Circuit. (William M. Landes and Richard A. Posner, *A Positive Economic Analysis of Products Liability*, 14 J. LEGAL STUD. 529 [1985].) They contend that the evolution from contract to negligence to strict liability is, in general, efficient. (They do *not* suggest that the movement toward absolute or enterprise liability is efficient.)

Landes and Posner stress that the broad trends in products-liability law over the last century are economically sound. The change in the doctrinal basis of the law of product-related injuries may be explained, they contend, by changing underlying economic variables. For example, the increasing mechanization and complexity of products raised the costs to consumers of informing themselves about the risks associated with product use. Consequently, the costs of insuring or taking precaution against losses from product failure became relatively smaller for the manufacturer than for the consumer. Similarly, the increasing urbanization of American society physically separated manufacturers from consumers, making the bargaining costs of a contractual solution (through warranties) prohibitively high. Landes and Posner hypothesized that the year in which a state's courts moved from contract to tort principles for determining liability in product-related harms was a function of the rate of urbanizaton in the state, the per capita income of its citizens, the stock of automobiles, and other social, economic, and demographic factors that are taken to be related to product complexity. Landes and Posner gathered and analyzed data to test this hypothesis and found that only the degree of urbanization was a significant determinant of the date at which state courts moved from contract to tort principles.

Manufacturers have long argued for reform at the federal level for two reasons. First, they contend that a uniform federal products-liability law that would standardize the law among the states, would save costs, with consequent savings to consumers. Secondly, many manufacturers believe that the products-liability law that has become the norm in the states is seriously flawed. Specifically, they believe that plaintiffs win too easily, and that juries are overly generous to successful plaintiffs (as evidenced by the example of the award against McDonald's for a hot coffee spill).

The argument that the manufacturers make is that these inefficiencies could be corrected by Congress' enacting a sensible uniform federal products-liability law. After many years of no success at the federal level, manufacturers may have finally succeeded in 1995 in persuading Congress to reform products liability. The terms of the final bill are not yet clear.[26]

At the state level, there was a spate of reforms in the mid-1980s and a second round in the mid-1990s. State reform has typically been limited to putting a cap or upper limit on the amount that victims can recover. Sometimes the states place this

---

[26] In the spring of 1995, the House of Representatives passed a sweeping tort-reform bill (called the "Common Sense Legal Reform Act") that applies to *all* civil cases. The Senate bill applies only to products liability. According to the rules of the U.S. Congress, a conference committee of representatives from each chamber must draft a compromise measure for passage by each chamber.

VACCINES AND PRODUCTS LIABILITY

Many recent products-liability cases have involved the duty that pharmaceutical manufacturers and doctors have to warn those taking drugs of the potential risks involved. These cases teach an important lesson about the consequences of extending products-liability law too far.

One such case involved two polio vaccines. The first vaccine against this crippling disease was the Salk vaccine or IPV, which is a so-called "killed-virus" vaccine. The virtue of a killed-virus vaccine is that it prevents polio in the person who receives it without presenting the risk that the recipient will contract polio. The second vaccine was the Sabin vaccine or OPV, a "live-virus" vaccine. The Sabin vaccine has several advantages over the Salk vaccine. First, it is administered orally. Secondly, the recipient retains the live virus in his or her system and can pass it to others. Because the virus is very weak, those who receive it through contact with someone who has taken OPV are themselves immunized against polio. Thus, the OPV has an external benefit: it immunizes some of the people with whom the initial recipient comes in contact. This benefit is so considerable that public-health authorities strongly recommended that young children take the Sabin vaccine instead of the older Salk vaccine. When only the Salk vaccine was available, there were 2500 cases of polio a year. After the development of the live-virus vaccine, polio virtually disappeared. However, the live-virus presents a risk.[28] Approximately one of every 4 million people who take the vaccine or come in close contact with those who have taken OPV contracts polio and is either permanently crippled or dies.

Can products-liability law deal with the risks presented by OPV without sacrificing its benefits? Certainly. The law should require the vaccine manufacturers to warn recipients of the risk from the live-virus vaccine and offer them the killed-virus vaccine if they do not want to accept that risk. That is precisely what the U.S. Court of Appeals for the Fifth Circuit held in *Reyes v. Wyeth Laboratories*, 498F.2d 1264 (1974). After *Reyes* it became standard practice for vaccine manufacturers to include package inserts warning recipients of the risks of the OPV vaccine.

continued . . .

cap only on what is perceived to be the offending element in damage awards, such as pain-and-suffering or punitive damages. For example, Illinois' 1995 Civil Justice Reform Act put a cap on noneconomic damages of $500,000 and limited punitive damages to three times compensatory damages. Some states have limited the *total* amount that can be recovered for certain torts. For example, New Mexico limits to $50,000 the amount that can be recovered from a tavernowner for serving alcohol to drivers who subsequently cause accidents. South Dakota limits the total amount that can be recovered in a medical-malpractice action to $1 million.

These reforms may sometimes have perverse results. In the mid-1980s, Indiana capped medical-malpractice awards at a maximum of $500,000 for all damages and instituted a professionally-administered patient-compensation fund to decide all losses above $100,000. The unexpected result was that malpractice awards in Indiana became one-third higher than those in Michigan and Ohio, which had kept the traditional

Vaccines and Products Liability Continued . . .

However, that resolution was only temporary. The more general trend, noted above, toward absolute or enterprise liability for product-related harms has been felt in this market, too. In several recent cases, children, whose parents had been properly warned in accordance with *Reyes* but who, nonetheless, took the live-virus vaccine and developed polio, sued the manufacturers and received large awards. Juries may have had the very best motives for making these awards. Nonetheless, these awards are likely to lead to inefficiencies. By making the vaccine manufacturer liable, despite the warning, these awards preclude a balancing of the social costs and benefits of these superior vaccines. Instead, the social costs are given much greater weight. Without the defense of assumption of the risk after an adequate warning, there is no way for the manufacturer to avoid liability. Therefore, the company must build this higher expected-liability cost into the costs of production. These costs may become so high that it is not profitable for the manufacturer to continue to produce the pharmaceuticals.

This is not mere speculation. There is evidence that pharmaceutical manufacturers are so fearful of products-liability awards that they have become reluctant to manufacture and distribute beneficial drugs. In 1976, after an outbreak of swine flu, a very dangerous illness, manufacturers of a vaccine against that disease refused to market it because private insurers, fearful of the products liability consequences of 100 million or more injections, would not issue liability insurance. The companies offered the inoculations only after the federal government agreed to be the exclusive defendant in any actions for harms arising from the swine flu vaccine.[29] The DPT vaccine against whooping cough is in short supply in this country because the largest manufacturer, Eli Lilly & Company, has stopped producing the drug because of its fear of adverse products-liability judgments. Only one manufacturer of that vaccine is willing to gamble that it will not be held liable for those side effects of the vaccine. Currently in the United States the following vaccines that were once manufactured by a number of firms are now produced by a single firm: measles, mumps, Sabin polio, Salk polio, and rabies. Worse still, the threat of products-liability suits may reduce the incentive of pharmaceutical companies to invest in research and development of potentially beneficial new drugs.[30]

[28] See Edmund Kitch, *Vaccines and Product Liability: A Case of Contagious Litigation*, REGULATION (May/June 1985).

[29] The vaccine's manufacturers proved particularly astute in this matter. The vaccine seems to have caused a potentially paralyzing or fatal disease called Guillain-Barre syndrome in a small fraction of those who were inoculated. Numerous plaintiffs brought actions against the federal government, as the sole defendant, on a theory of inadequate warning. The federal government relatively quickly stopped the program of inoculation for swine flu.

[30] See Peter Huber, *Safety and the Second Best: The Hazards of Public Risk Management in the Courts*, 85 COLUM. L. REV. 277 (1985).

method of compensation. Perhaps the reason for the Indiana result was that the professional administrators were better able than lay jurors to calculate damages and, therefore, came closer to the "true," higher losses of the victims.

CONTRACTUAL SOLUTIONS TO THE TORT LIABILITY CRISIS[31]

Victims do not have a cause of action against their injurers until they are harmed in an accident. It is not currently possible for *potential* victims to sell their right to compensation in the event of a future accident. We might call an entitlement to recover at some time in the future on behalf of a victim an "unmatured tort claim" (UTC). Current law and practice prohibit a market in UTCs. But is that the right stance? Would the efficiency of the tort-liability system be helped or hindered by allowing a market in unmatured tort claims?

Imagine a market for UTCs. Potential tort victims could sell their right to recover and could include in the sale whichever of their tort rights they chose to sell and retain others for their own use. For example, a victim might sell the right to recover her nonpecuniary losses in an automobile accident but retain her right to recover her major pecuniary losses. Or she might sell the right to recover in the event of medical malpractice but keep the right to recover in the event of a product-related injury. If someone had sold her tort claims to a third party and was later injured, she would either receive payment from her insurer for her losses or bear those losses herself.

When would the potential victim sell her unmatured tort claims to a third party? In either of the following situations—(1) if the victim already had first-party insurance for the loss in a particular tort, or (2) if the victim believed that insurance was *not* appropriate for that loss.

A market for UTCs could be extremely flexible. Consider, for example, how a regime of no-fault automobile insurance could result from a market in UTCs. Suppose that drivers sell some of their rights to recover for tortious injuries in automobile accidents to their own insurance companies. Their own insurers might then waive these rights in exchange for payment from the insurance companies of other drivers. (Be sure that you can show how this might be done.)

If it were legal to sell and buy UTCs, potential victims would probably substitute first-party insurance for the current method of compensation through the tort-liability system. This first-party insurance would probably be a cheaper means of compensating victims than is the tort-liability system. But what about the deterrence

continued . . .

QUESTION 9.9: Analyze caps and limitations on litigation awards using the analysis of rent control in Chapter 2.

QUESTION 9.10: Use the graphical analysis of liability of the previous chapter to show the effect on the precautionary decisions of a potential injurer when the amount of compensatory damages that a victim may receive is capped.

QUESTION 9.11: Suppose that any punitive damages awarded to the plaintiff were to be paid, not to the plaintiff, but rather to, say, a charity designated by the plaintiff. How might plaintiffs' incentives to seek punitive damages be affected by such a scheme? How might the jury's disposition to award punitive damages be affected?

Contractual Solutions to the Tort Liability Crisis Continued . . .

function of tort law? How will the creation of a market for UTCs induce potential victims and injurers to take care? Interestingly, there might be no significant difference in deterrence from the current system, and there might be an improvement. There will, after all, be *someone* proceeding against the injurer for recovery in the event of an accident; it just might not be the victim. Indeed, the deterrence effect under UTCs may be better than under the current system: third parties who have purchased UTCs may have a strong incentive to monitor the behavior of potential victims and injurers for optimal precaution.

One possibility to consider is this: what if potential injurers purchase UTCs from potential victims? Might that not induce those potential injurers to act strategically and not take as much care? Presumably, the UTCs would become assets in the portfolios of the potential injurers. They would decide whether to hold or sell those assets depending on their market price and expected return. It should be the case that the price for UTCs would reflect the probability and degree of injury. When accidents are more frequent, the price of UTCs would be relatively high. But as precaution increases, and the frequency and severity of accidents falls, then the price of UTCs should fall. To minimize total accident-related costs, potential tortfeasors would invest in precaution to the point where an additional $1 spent on precaution reduces the price of UTCs by $1. This calculation should not, in principle, be any different from the sort of calculation that rational potential injurers make under the current system. And it is not inconceivable that the decision to take precaution might be more immediately in the interest of potential injurers when they hold UTCs than is the case under the current tort-liability system.

There are several objections that might be made to a market in UTCs. First, potential victims may lack sufficient information or bargaining power to demand a price that reflects the true worth of UTCs. Third parties, including potential injurers, might take advantage of them. We can protect potential victims by enforcing only those UTCs that pass muster under the criteria for a bargain that we examined in Chapter 7. Second, the compensation goal of tort law might suffer if imprudent potential victims sold their UTCs but did not purchase substitute first-party insurance. We could deal with this undesirable outcome by making it a condition of enforceability that the seller of a UTC must have purchased first-party insurance.

---

[31] The material in this box is based on Robert D. Cooter, *Towards a Market in Unmatured Tort Claims*, 75 VA. L. REV. 383 (1989). See also Paul Rubin, TORT REFORM BY CONTRACT (1993).

Notwithstanding specific problems, there are other indications that the system is working reasonably well. Product-liability actions in the United States increased in the mid- and late 1980s, but the vast majority of those cases involved asbestos. If we

---

[27] See James A. Henderson and Theodore Eisenberg, *The Quiet Revolution in Products Liability: An Empirical Study of Legal Change*, 37 UCLA L. REV. 479 (1990). The figures cited in this study are for actions filed in federal courts. Most tort actions are filed in state courts, but the authors feel that the federal statistics also reflect trends in state courts.

exclude asbestos claims, the number of products-liability cases in the federal courts between 1985 and 1991 *decreased* by 40%. Another interesting recent change regards plaintiff success rates. Between 1981 and 1987 the defendant won 51% of the verdicts in product-liability cases. Between 1988 and 1994 defendants won 64% of the cases. Finally, products-liability insurance costs amount to one-quarter of one cent for each dollar of product purchase price—an insignificantly small amount.[27]

> **READING NOTE:** Some of the classic works on the economics of products liability are these: Michael Spence, *Consumer Misperceptions, Product Failure, and Producer Liability*, 44 REV. ECON. STUD. 561 (1977); A. Mitchell Polinsky and William P. Rogerson, *Products Liability, Consumer Misperceptions, and Market Power*, 14 BELL J. ECON. 581 (1983); and Richard A. Posner, *A Positive Economic Analysis of Products Liability*, 14 J. LEGAL STUD. 535 (1985). More recent work includes the American Law Institute Reports' Study, ENTERPRISE RESPONSIBILITY FOR PERSONAL INJURY (1991); and W. Kip Viscusi, REFORMING PRODUCTS LIABILITY (1992).

> **QUESTION 9.12:** Explain how a potential victim's waiving a future claim (*e.g.*, an employee's agreeing not to seek compensation from his employer if he is injured on the job) is like a transaction in a UTC.

> **QUESTION 9.13:** Imagine a system of contractual or elective no-fault with respect to product-related injuries. Manufacturers would offer with their products schedules of benefits that they would pay if consumers should be injured while using the products. In the event of an injury, there would be no inquiry into the product's defect or the user's fault; benefits would simply be paid to the injured consumer according to the contractual schedule. Pain and suffering would not be compensable; collateral benefits would be deducted; and a few other restrictions would apply. Those manufacturers who chose not to offer elective no-fault would still be strictly liable for product-related injuries under the current system. Explore the efficiency of this elective no-fault system. (See J. O'Connell, ENDING INSULT TO INJURY [1975].)

C. Medical Malpractice[32]

The argument that the medical-malpractice system in the United States is not performing well rests on three related pieces of evidence: (1) the increase in the frequency and size of malpractice claims brought against physicians; (2) the resultant increase in the value of medical-malpractice insurance premiums paid by physicians; and (3) the increase in health-care costs attributable to these first two facts. Let's look at these in turn.

The evidence on the frequency of malpractice claims is startling. In the late 1950s malpractice claims were filed at a rate of one claim per 100 doctors per year. By the mid-1970s these claims had risen to an annual rate of one per 35 doctors, and by the

---

[32] Some of the information in this section comes from Paul Weiler, MEDICAL MALPRACTICE ON TRIAL (1992) and Patricia Danzon, MEDICAL MALPRACTICE: THEORY, EVIDENCE, AND PUBLIC POLICY (1985). See also Edward Snyder and James Hughes, *The English Rule for Allocating Legal Costs: Evidence Confronts Theory*, 6 J. LAW, ECON. & ORG. 345 (1990), and Snyder and Hughes, *Litigation Under the English and American Rules: Theory and Evidence*, 38 J. LAW & ECON. 225 (1995). These last two articles are about Florida's adoption between 1980 and 1986 of the "loser-pays-all" rule for attorney compensation for medical-malpractice cases. In 1986 the Florida legislature reversed itself and returned to the rule of "each-pays-his-own" legal fees. See the discussion in Chapter 10.

early 1990s the rate was approximately one in 10 doctors. Put succinctly, physicians are ten times more likely to be sued for malpractice today than they were in 1960.

What about the dollar amounts that successful malpractice claimants receive? The amounts paid on successful claims against physicians rose sharply from the 1960s to the 1980s. The RAND Institute on Civil Justice studied jury verdicts in malpractice actions in Chicago and San Francisco over that time period. They reported that, measured in real dollars (*i.e.*, net of inflation), the average malpractice award in Chicago was $50,000 in the 1960s; $600,000 in the early 1970s; and $1.2 million in the early 1980s. In San Francisco, the average award was $125,000 in the early 1960s; $450,000 in the early 1970s; and $1.2 million in the early 1980s. Other studies have found similar results in other jurisdictions.

These rapid increases in the frequency and size of malpractice claims have caused a dramatic rise in the amount spent by physicians on liability insurance. In 1960 the total amount spent by physicians in the United States on medical-liability insurance premiums was about $60 million. Today the figure is $9 billion, a 150-fold increase in thirty years.[33] For the individual physician, malpractice insurance premiums in 1988 averaged $16,000 per year, or about 6% of the average physician's gross revenues. This figure itself was up from $8,000 in 1984.[34]

Finally, the conventional argument points out that the rapid increase in the frequency and size of awards in medical-malpractice cases, and the consequent increase in the amount of liability insurance purchased by physicians, have contributed significantly to the increase in the costs of health care. These contributions are both direct and indirect. An example of increased direct costs is the practice of "defensive medicine"—for example, the redundant tests that a physician might order so as to avoid later allegations of improper or insufficient care. A recent Hudson Institute study of Indiana hospitals found that these and other direct costs of malpractice liability added $450 to the cost of each patient admitted. This raised the total medical costs of the hospitals by 5.3%.[35]

Why did this explosion in medical malpractice occur? Most commentators, including a 1987 Department of Health and Human Services task force on medical liability and malpractice, attribute the explosion to a general increase in litigiousness, a lower tolerance for the risks of life among citizens, increasingly greedy lawyers who bring more and more outrageous claims, and jurors who make unpredictable and indefensible awards in a field about which they know very little. According to this view, the principal thing that is wrong with medical malpractice is that there are too many claims being asserted and that juries are awarding plaintiffs too much money. Reform, therefore,

---

[33] Let us put this figure in context. The total annual U.S. expenditures on all forms of tort-liability insurance are $130 billion. If we add in the cost of the workers' compensation system ($60 billion), which we describe in a box later in this chapter, then the total annual liability insurance bill in the United States is $190 billion. Of this total, $90 billion is for motor-vehicle accident insurance alone. Thus, medical malpractice insurance (at $9 billion) is slightly less than 5% of the total annual liability insurance bill. The $190 billion constitutes approximately 3.5% of the U.S. gross domestic product. Total liability costs in other wealthy countries account for about half that percentage of their GDPs.

[34] The burden imposed by rising malpractice premiums varied according to a physician's specialty and region of the country. For example, a general practitioner in Arkansas or an allergist in Indiana paid less than $2,000 per year in malpractice insurance premiums. But a neurosurgeon in Miami or an obstetrician in Long Island paid almost $200,000 per year in malpractice premiums.

[35] Defensive medicine is the most important cause, accounting for $327 of the $450 or 3.9% of the 5.3% cost increase. The authors of the Hudson Institute study attribute the remaining 1.4% (or $123 per patient) to direct costs of insurance, payments to patients, attorneys' fees, and litigation costs.

should seek to make malpractice claims more difficult to assert (so as to screen out the frivolous claims) and to limit the discretion of juries (by, for example, limiting their ability to award pain-and-suffering and punitive damages).

More recent empirical evidence on medical malpractice suggests that there may *not* be a crisis at all or, rather, that the crisis is *not* one of too many lawsuits and overly generous juries. For example, the Harvard Study (conducted jointly by the Harvard School of Public Health, Medical School, and Law School) looked at over 30,000 hospital files in 52 New York hospitals in one year in the mid-1980s. There were two principal findings. First, only 1% of all those admitted to hospitals were injured by physician or hospital negligence. Second, a very small percentage (about 12%) of those who were injured ever filed a lawsuit. Of those with very serious iatrogenic injuries, fewer than one-third filed suit. This is such a small percentage that it fuels speculation that the problem with medical malpractice may not be that there are too *many* malpractice actions, as the conventional view has it, but rather that there are too *few*.

Other recent work has led to additional surprising and unconventional discoveries about the medical-malpractice system. First, several studies have shown that plaintiffs in malpractice actions are much less likely to win than not and much less likely to win than are plaintiffs in products-liability and auto-accident cases.[36] Another study found that the rate of error in malpractice litigation is very low: doctors rarely lose a case they should win, and they win a significantly high proportion of cases their insurers think they should lose (apparently because juries bend over backwards to make sure that doctors are not unfairly stigmatized by a malpractice verdict). Second, the conventional evidence on the rising size of malpractice awards is more complicated than previously thought. The relatively few plaintiffs who win are awarded a great deal more, on average, than are similarly injured and successful plaintiffs in products-liability and automobile-accident actions.[37] Moreover, there is a great deal of variance in the amounts that juries award successful plaintiffs in medical-malpractice cases. The principal reason appears to be a variance in nonpecuniary damages (*i.e.*, in damages for pain and suffering). For those states that still follow common law rules of tort damages, 40-50% of the compensation paid is for pain and suffering. Another of these surprising recent discoveries about the medical-malpractice system is that the widespread belief that only a few physicians are responsible for the vast bulk of malpractice incidents may be mistaken. Repeat offenders appear to be responsible for only a small fraction of malpractice. A more accurate picture shows that many doctors commit errors that are avoidable and a few of those errors lead to significant harm.

More recent evidence also suggests that since 1989 medical-malpractice liability insurance premiums have fallen. Additionally, there is doubt about the contention that the malpractice crisis has contributed significantly to the rise in health-care costs. Medical-malpractice insurance premiums account for only about 1% of the nation's health care

---

[36] Malpractice plaintiffs win between 15-30% of the cases that go to trial. See Weiler, MEDICAL MALPRACTICE ON TRIAL (1993).

[37] The Harvard Study reports, "The average malpractice verdict is three times the size of motor vehicle verdicts, and twice the size of products and governmental liability verdicts, after adjusting for the age of the victim and the severity of injury."

[38] Even in 1960, malpractice insurance premiums accounted for only 0.5% of the nation's total health-care bill.

bill.[38] When one adds in indirect costs (such as those associated with defensive medicine), malpractice accounts for no more than 5% of that bill. This means that curing the medical-malpractice crisis would not lead to a significant lowering of health-care costs.

Finally, it is important to note that the rise in malpractice liability has also occurred in some other developed countries. In Canada, for example, the annual frequency of claims per 100 physicians tripled between 1971 and 1990, and the average malpractice claim payment increased fivefold in real terms between 1971 and 1990. This suggests that the ills of our malpractice system are not unique to the United States. Rather, they may be due to very broad social trends affecting all of the developed economies. For instance, the frequency of medical-malpractice claims may be rising because medical technology has so greatly extended the scope of treatment that there are simply more opportunities for slipups to occur.

1. Reforming Medical Malpractice   How one feels about reform of the medical-malpractice system depends on how one assesses the evidence presented in the previous section. If one finds the conventional evidence on the frequency and size of malpractice claims persuasive, then one is in favor of reforms that seek to limit the number and severity of malpractice claims. President Clinton's comprehensive health-care reform proposal contained an eight-point plan for reforming the medical-malpractice system that was premised on the conventional evidence of the previous section. Many state-based reforms have sought to limit pain-and-suffering damages and to require certification of the merits of a malpractice claim by a nonjudicial panel before the matter could proceed to trial.

However, the alternative evidence of the previous section argues for a very different reform. According to this evidence what is wrong with the medical-malpractice system is that it is not doing a very good job either at compensating deserving victims or at deterring physicians and hospitals from negligent acts. The vast majority of deserving victims do not file malpractice actions. For those who do, the malpractice system is inefficient: it takes on average three years for all claims and five years for more serious claims to be resolved; and almost 60 cents of every malpractice-award dollar go toward administrative costs, not victim compensation.

The Harvard Study suggested a far more radical malpractice reform—namely, replacement of the fault-based tort-liability system with a no-fault system. Under the latter system a patient who had been seriously injured as the result of medical treatment would receive compensation, regardless of whether or not the treatment was negligent. This compensation would commence with an application by the patient and would require a minimal factual showing by the patient to a competent review panel. Compensation would be relatively swift and certain but would not necessarily be as complete as under litigation. In exchange for being relieved of the burden of demonstrating fault, injured patients would receive a sum that would pay for all medical expenses not covered by other insurance, replace 80% of all lost earnings, and pay modest additional amounts for severely injured patients to help them adjust to the loss of the enjoyment of life's pleasures. Fees for patients' attorneys would become an explicit element of damages. There would be no awards for pain and suffering, and compensation payments would be periodic (rather than in a lump sum, as is the current practice). Liability in the reformed system would attach to hospitals or to health-care organizations rather than to individual physicians.

WORKERS' COMPENSATION

The most prominent form of no-fault liability in the United States is the system for dealing with employee accidents that occur on the job. These accidents are very common. In any given year approximately 10% of all industrial workers will be injured while on the job. However, only one-third of these accidents results in lost work time. This risk of on-the-job accidents is slightly higher than the risk of accidents off the job—for example, in the home—and about half the risk of injury in an automobile accident.

Through the late nineteenth century the common law of job-related accidents made it extremely difficult for plaintiff-employees who had been injured on the job to recover from their employers or from anyone else.[39] Early in the twentieth century, most industrialized countries, including the United States, adopted an alternative to tort liability for dealing with on-the-job accidents—namely, a system of compulsory compensation of injured employees without regard to fault, financed by a levy on employers, and administered by the government. Almost every state in the United States enacted some form of no-fault compensation for injured employees between 1911 and 1920. At first, these workers' compensation systems, as they were known, were elective and confined only to very dangerous occupations. But by 1950 workers' compensation systems in this country had spread so that today all but three states have a compulsory system for nearly all workers. The result is that 90% of the United States labor force is covered by workers' compensation systems. Workers' compensation systems differ slightly from state to state. Some states still have elective coverage; others have size-of-firm restrictions that exempt small firms from joining the system; and most states exclude farm workers from coverage. The federal government's only role is to offer special workers' compensation for employees who are excluded under state laws, for example, coal miners and railroad employees.

continued . . .

How might this no-fault system perform the compensation and deterrence functions of tort liability better than does the traditional, fault-based system? Compensation, while less complete, would be more certain and less costly to obtain. Thus, the no-fault system would mitigate the problem (noted in the previous section) of relatively few injured patients' bringing actions for compensation. Moreover, it would accomplish this at a significantly lower administrative cost than does the current system. The Harvard Study estimated that no-fault would cut the administrative costs of the medical-liability system in half—from 60% of total liability expenditures to about 30%. The authors of that study claim that a no-fault proposal like the one they favor would have cost $900 million in New York State in the year they studied, slightly less than the $1 billion that the state's health-care providers actually spent on malpractice insurance in that year.

As to deterrence, the imposition of liability on hospitals (where more than 80% of all medical-treatment injuries occur) rather than on individual physicians would have two benefits. First, it would create a clear financial incentive for the enterprise to take steps to reduce the risk of medical-treatment injuries in the future; for example, hospitals perhaps

Workers' Compensation Continued . . .

The purpose of this no-fault system is to guarantee injured employees relatively swift and certain compensation for their job-related harms. The system relieves employees and their employers of the costs of demonstrating and challenging fault, respectively, and guarantees injured employees swift *partial* (not complete) compensation for their losses.

The systems typically work in the following way. Employers contribute sums to the state workers' compensation system based on the dollar amount of their payroll. When an employee is injured, he files a claim with the state governmental agency that administers the system. If the agency determines that the harm is job-related, then it awards the employee compensation according to a statutory schedule of benefits. For some injuries the benefits are a fixed sum, regardless of the actual losses or the employee's actual job. For example, the compensation for a lost arm may be $5,000. For other injuries, the benefits are variable, according to the injured employee's actual losses. For example, the victim may be awarded two-thirds of the lost wages and full compensation without restriction on his or her actual medical and rehabilitation expenses. In the event of a dispute between the employee and the workers' compensation commission, a process of appeal and adjudication is available. Every system excludes those harms that are attributable to willful misconduct, aggressive assault, and drunkenness.

One of the most important differences among the states has to do with the relationship between the workers' compensation and the tort-liability systems. In some states workers may collect workers' compensation benefits and then sue their employers for recovery on a negligence theory. In other states, employees must choose an exclusive remedy; they must proceed through workers' compensation or the tort-liability system.

---

[39] There were three defenses available to the employer: (1) common employment (also known as the "fellow servant rule"), under which the employer could escape liability by claiming that the proximate cause of the plaintiff's harm was the negligence of another employee; (2) assumption of the risk, under which the employer could argue that the employee willingly assumed the risk of a job-related injury (on the economics of job-related risks, see Kip Viscusi, RISK BY CHOICE [1983]); and (3) contributory negligence, under which the employer could escape liability by showing that the employee's own negligence had contributed to the harm.

---

would become more scrupulous in granting privileges to physicians who were particularly risky. Second, it would remove the emotional, risk-averse decisions in medical treatment from the shoulders of individual doctors, thus, presumably, making their professional lives more pleasant. Third, doctors would probably order fewer defensive medical procedures, doing so only if the costs of those tests were justified by the reduction in the enterprise's liability. (Of course, these same incentives exist under the current tort-liability system. The contention must be that they would be more effective under the no-fault alternative.)

There are potential problems with no-fault malpractice. First, the difficulty of differentiating between injuries caused by medical treatment and injuries caused by the patient's underlying illness may be more acute in the no-fault system than in the fault-based system. If this is a serious problem, then there may be no administrative-cost savings under the no-fault system. Second, there is a problem in defining the scope of iatrogenic injuries to be covered by the no-fault system. It might be prohibitively expensive to cover all injuries. Rather, the system might be limited to serious medical injuries. This line-drawing exercise is fraught with problems, too. Only solid empirical work (and carefully crafted legislation) can address these issues. We currently do not have such empirical evidence, but we may in the near future. Two states (Virginia and Florida) have recently adopted narrow versions of a no-fault medical-malpractice system; in each of those two states the new system deals only with brain-damaged newborns. Three countries (Sweden, Finland, and New Zealand) have adopted broad no-fault compensation systems (covering *all* torts, not just medical malpractice), and Canada and Great Britain are considering adopting no-fault for medical injuries.

Political considerations (as well as the practical problems noted above) probably argue against moving to a full-blown no-fault malpractice system in the near future. However, there is an intermediate step: the adoption of no-fault medical insurance on a voluntary, contractual basis. The terms of the Harvard proposal could become part of the contractual relationships between patients and their health-care providers. That is, in exchange for waiving their common-law tort-liability rights, patients would receive a guarantee of compensation in the event of an injury arising in the course of medical treatment, according to the terms outlined above. Although this has not happened to any appreciable degree yet, voluntary no-fault insurance is an attractive, efficient reform of the current malpractice system.

CONCLUSION

In this chapter we have extended the economic theory of tort liability of the previous chapter. We have relaxed some of the simplifying assumptions of the previous chapter, discussed several actual tort cases from an economic point of view, and used the economic theory of tort liability to examine such issues as vicarious liability and joint and several liability. In the final section of the chapter we applied economics to the issue of tort reform. We saw how a knowledge of the empirical evidence regarding the tort liability system was vital to one's evaluation of the assertions that products liability and medical malpractice need to be reformed.

Despite the length of this chapter, we stress the point that it is truly only an introduction. There is much more to be done in the economic analysis of tort liability. For instance, we have not discussed the economics of dignitary wrongs, such as defamation (libel and slander), the invasion of privacy, and misrepresentation. If you learn the central legal issues in those further areas, perhaps you will be able to discern the important efficiency aspects of different legal rules in those areas by applying the economic theory of this and the previous chapter.

SUGGESTED READINGS

Calabresi, Guido, *First Party, Third Party, and Product Liability Systems: Can Economic Analysis of Law Tell Us Anything About Them?,* 69 IOWA L. REV. 833 (1984).

Craswell, Richard, and John Calfee, *Some Effects of Uncertainty on Compliance with Legal Standards,* 70 VA. L. REV. 965 (1984).

Landes, William, and Richard A. Posner, THE ECONOMIC STRUCTURE OF TORT LAW (1987).

Rabin, Robert, ed., PERSPECTIVES ON TORT LAW (3d ed. 1993).

Schwartz, Gary T., *The Beginning and the Possible End of the Rise of Modern American Tort Law,* 26 GA. L. REV. 601 (1992).

Shavell, Steven, AN ECONOMIC ANALYSIS OF ACCIDENT LAW (1987).

Symposium: *Alternative Compensation Schemes and Tort Theory,* 73 CAL. L. REV. 548 (1985).

Symposium: *Critical Issues in Tort Law Reform: A Search for Principles,* 14 J. LEGAL STUD. 459 (1985).

10

AN ECONOMIC THEORY OF THE
LEGAL PROCESS

"The first thing we do—let's kill all the lawyers."

—

William Shakespeare, HENRY VI, Part II

Act IV, Scene ii

The preceding chapters applied economics to the *substantive* law of property, torts, and contracts. The substantive law allocates the costs of the injuries that trigger legal disputes. This chapter applies economics to the *procedural* aspects of civil disputes. The procedural aspects concern the process from the filing of a complaint to the resolution of the dispute.

Although different countries follow different legal procedures, broad similarities exist. To illustrate the common core, consider some stages in the following legal dispute as it would develop in almost any country. Joe Potatoes suspects that Jim Bloggs has been romancing his wife, Joan Potatoes, and insults Bloggs and breaks his nose. Bloggs consults a lawyer, who files a legal complaint against Potatoes. Potatoes also consults a lawyer, who contacts Bloggs's lawyer, and the two lawyers try to settle the dispute. If the attempted settlement fails, the dispute proceeds through a series of legal steps leading up to a trial, including the reply by Potatoes's lawyer to the complaint, a pretrial hearing with a judge, and the exchange of information about the case between the lawyers. If further negotiations fail to settle the dispute, a trial occurs and, after the trial, either party may decide to appeal the decision to a higher court.

As this example illustrates, a full-blown legal dispute has the stages depicted in Figure 10.1, regardless of the substantive issues. Each stage in Figure 10.1 presents problems for predicting behavior and analyzing legal rules. Here are some examples of problems that we will analyze.

EXAMPLE 1: In response to a magazine advertisement for "a sure means to kill grasshoppers," a farmer mails $25 and receives by return post two wooden blocks with the instructions, "Place grasshopper on Block A and smash with Block B." Filing a legal complaint will cost the farmer far more than the $25 that he lost. The farmer consults a lawyer to determine whether he has a legal remedy that is economically viable.

EXAMPLE 2: Some consumers file suit alleging that the engines in their cars were destroyed by a defective fuel additive. The manufacturer of the fuel additive would like to settle the dispute before it goes to trial and newspapers learn about it. In order to decide how much money to offer as a settlement, the manufacturer's lawyer asks the judge to require the consumers' lawyer to disclose all available evidence concerning the cause and extent of damage to the cars.

EXAMPLE 3: Joan Potatoes wants to divorce her husband, Joe. They disagree over how to divide the value of their house. After bargaining between their lawyers fails, the judge considers whether to require them to consult a professional mediator before proceeding to trial.

EXAMPLE 4: A Los Angeles manufacturer faces large liabilities for dumping hazardous waste in 1965. The manufacturer files a claim with the London insurer that supplied its policy in 1965. The insurer denies that the insurance policy covers the loss. The manufacturer has the option of suing the insurer in Los Angeles or London. In Los Angeles, each side pays its own legal costs, whereas in London the loser pays the legal costs of the winner. The manufacturer asks its counsel how the allocation of legal costs should influence its choice of the place to file suit.

EXAMPLE 5: Someone dives into a swimming pool and strikes her head on the bottom. She sues the owner of the pool for failing to post signs warning that the pool was too shallow for diving, and the pool owner replies that the victim should have checked the depth of the water before diving. At trial, the court applies the rule of negligence with a defense of contributory negligence, and the pool owner escapes liability. The plaintiff wonders whether to appeal the case and ask the court to depart from past precedent and apply the rule of comparative negligence.[1]

We explain briefly the procedural issue in each of these examples. In order to bring suit, the plaintiff must have a "cause of action," which usually consists of harm caused by the defendant for which the law provides a remedy. In Example 1, the injury is the loss of $25, plus any additional losses from relying upon the false advertisement. Not every plaintiff with a cause of action can sue profitably. Example 1 raises the question, "When does it pay to file a suit?" We will answer this question by computing the plaintiff's expected value from asserting a legal claim. The rules of procedure decisively affect this value.

Most legal systems require the parties to disclose some of their *private information* (facts known by one party to the dispute and unknown by the other) prior to trial. In the American legal system, the parties exchange extensive information before trial. Example 2 suggests that compulsory disclosure of private information promotes settlements. We will use game theory to test this proposition.

Critics often complain that the formality of trials increases the cost of resolving disputes. Example 3 raises the question of whether informal processes, like compulsory mediation, could improve upon formal legal procedures. In order to answer this question, we will use game theory to explain why bargaining sometimes succeeds and sometimes fails. The public often perceives legal procedures as opaque and arcane,

---

[1] Comparative negligence would require the pool owner to pay damages in proportion to the harm caused by the negligence.

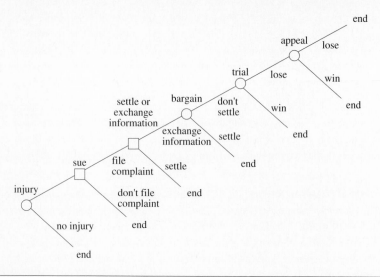

FIGURE 10.1 Stages in a legal dispute.

which inspires the sentiment quoted above: "let's kill all the lawyers." Game theory suggests more complicated improvements to the legal process.

Different legal systems allocate the costs of trials differently, the polar opposite rules being "each-pays-his-own" legal costs and "loser-pays-all" legal costs. Example 4 asks whether one of these rules especially favors defendants. To answer this question, we will consider the incentives created by alternative allocations of legal costs.

Finally, Example 5 raises the question of whether the state should subsidize court proceedings that give judges the opportunity to make law. This question relates closely to the dispute about whether the common law evolves toward economically efficient rules.

Minimizing Social Costs

Is the legal process unnecessarily complicated and expensive? Evaluating different procedural rules and practices requires a measure of social costs. In Chapter 8, we found that a simple measure of the social cost of accidents provided a useful guide to the analysis of tort law. Similarly, a simple measure of the social costs of the legal process provides a useful guide to the analysis of procedural rules and practices. To develop a simple measure, think of procedural rules as instruments for applying substantive law. Using the instruments cost something, which, following Chapter 8, we call "administrative costs." In addition, using these instruments sometimes causes errors in applying substantive law. For example, the wrong party may be held liable, or the right party may be held liable for the wrong amount. Errors distort incentives and impose a variety of costs on society. Our simplest measure of social costs, denoted SC, combines administrative costs, denoted c_a, and costs of errors, denoted $c(e)$. *We assume that the economic objective of procedural law is to minimize the sum of administrative costs and error costs:*

$$\min SC = c_a + c(e) \tag{10.1}$$

To illustrate, assume that the parties settle on the same terms as the judgment that the courts would have reached if the case had been tried. Because the results of settlement or trial are the same by assumption, the error costs (*if* there is an error) of settlement equal the error costs of trial. The administrative costs of the settlement, however, are much lower than a trial. Consequently, the settlement saves social costs. In general, settlements that replicate the results of trials reduce the social costs of resolving disputes.

To sharpen the objective of cost minimization, we explain its elements. Administration is the sum of the costs to everyone involved in passing through the stages of a legal dispute, such as the costs of filing a legal claim, exchanging information with the other party, bargaining in an attempt to settle, litigating, and appealing. In comparison to administrative costs, error costs are more difficult to understand and measure, because measuring an error requires a standard of perfection.

To obtain a standard of perfection, consider the information possessed by courts. In reality, courts have imperfect information, which causes them to make mistakes when applying substantive law. As information improves, however, courts make fewer mistakes. As a thought experiment, imagine an independent court that possesses *perfect* information about the facts and the law for every case it decides. Such a court never makes mistakes; it gives ideal decisions relative to existing law. We will call such a decision the *perfect-information judgment,* which we denote j^*.

The difference between the perfect-information judgment, j^*, and the actual judgment, j, equals the *extent of the court's error: $e = j^* - j$.* To illustrate by Example 2, the perfect information judgment j^* might award the owner of an automobile the exact cost of replacing the engine destroyed by a defective fuel additive, which equals, say, $2500. If the actual judgment j equals $2000, then the extent of the error equals $j^* - j = \$500$.

The *extent* of the error, however, does not necessarily equal its *social cost,* denoted $c(e)$ in equation 1. The social cost of an error depends upon the distortions in incentives caused by it. To illustrate, if perfect compensation equals $2500 and actual compensation equals $2000, the error of $500 may cause the manufacturer of fuel additives to lower quality control. Lowering quality control saves the manufacturer, say, $1000 and causes, say, an additional $10,000 in losses to the owners of automobiles. In this example, the social cost of the error equals the *net* loss of $9000 from lower quality control: $c(\$500) = \$9000$.

In the rest of this chapter, we will model each stage in the legal process, show the incentive effects of different procedural rules and practices, and evaluate the alternatives in terms of social costs. In general, the social costs of errors are difficult to measure. Consequently, we will avoid conclusions that rely upon precise measurements of error. The differences in legal procedure across countries present us with a formidable challenge in constructing general models. Fortunately, these differences also supply us with variation for comparing the efficiency of different processes.

QUESTION 10.1: Assume that the following legal rule applies to Example 1 (the "grasshopper killer"): "Breach of contract arising from false advertising results in liability equal to two times the consumer's out-of-pocket expenditures in reliance on the promise." Given this rule, what is the perfect-information judgment?

QUESTION 10.2: Why is a trial economically inferior to a settlement on the same terms as the expected trial judgment?

I. WHY SUE?

Most private disputes remain outside the courts. The courts typically get involved when the injured party asks them for a remedy. The filing of a suit marks the beginning of this formal process. These facts raise the question, "Why sue?" We will explain game theory's answer to this question.

A. Computing the Value of a Legal Claim

To file a complaint, the plaintiff must usually hire a lawyer and pay filing fees to the court. Filing a complaint creates a legal claim. To decide whether to initiate a suit, a rational plaintiff compares the cost of the complaint and the expected value of the legal claim. The expected value of the legal claim (*EVC*) depends upon what the plaintiff thinks will occur after filing a complaint. Figure 10.1 depicts the possible events. To decide whether to file a complaint, the rational plaintiff must attach probabilities and payoffs to these events. Let us assume that the plaintiff, with the help of a lawyer, attaches the probabilities and payoffs to these events as depicted in Figure 10.2. (We scale down the numbers in Figure 10.2 below realistic levels to simplify the arithmetic.) We will explain how to compute the expected value of the legal claim depicted in Figure 10.2.

Before making the computations, we must explain our assumptions about who pays for legal costs. In America, each side usually pays its own legal costs. In Europe, the loser usually pays most of the winner's legal costs. The European rule is more complicated analytically, because it makes the distribution of costs contingent on who wins. Consequently, we will first develop our example assuming that each side pays its own legal costs and consider later the consequences of the loser paying the legal costs for both sides.

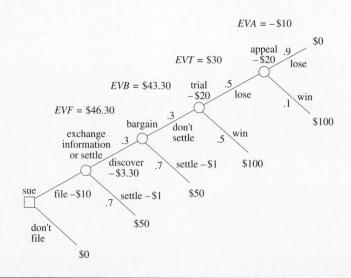

FIGURE 10.2 Expected value of a legal claim.

In order to compute expected values in a sequence of events, one begins with the last possible event, which is "appeal" in Figure 10.2, and works towards the first event, which is the decision to file a complaint in Figure 10.2. We will take this approach to computing the expected value of the legal claim at each step in the legal process. According to Figure 10.2, the plaintiff who has lost at trial must pay $20 to appeal the case. On appeal, the plaintiff stands to win $100 with probability .1 and to lose with probability .9. Thus, the expected value of the appeal (*EVA*) equals $-$10$:

$$EVA = .1(\$100) + .9(\$0) - \$20 = -\$10.$$

Because the expected value of appeal is negative, the plaintiff who loses at trial will not appeal the case.

Having computed the expected value of appeal (second trial), we can now compute the expected value of the first trial. According to Figure 10.2, the plaintiff who failed to settle out of court by bargaining must pay $20 to go to trial. At trial, the plaintiff stands to win $100 with probability .5 and to lose with probability .5. If the plaintiff loses, he or she will not appeal the case and so will receive a payoff equal to $0. We combine these numbers to obtain the expected value of the first trial (*EVT*):

$$EVT = .5(\$100) + .5(\$0) - \$20 = \$30.$$

Having computed the expected value of the trial, we can now compute the expected value of bargaining to settle before beginning the trial. According to Figure 10.2, the plaintiff who completed the process of exchanging information with the defendant can bargain to settle out of court with probability of success equal to .7. If bargaining succeeds, the plaintiff settles for $50 and pays settlement costs of $1. Bargaining fails to reach a settlement with probability .3, in which case the plaintiff proceeds to trial, whose expected value equals $30. We combine these numbers to obtain the expected value of the bargain (*EVB*):

$$EVB = .7(\$50 - 1) + .3(\$30) = \$43.30.$$

Because the expected value of the bargain is positive, the plaintiff who reaches this stage will bargain.

Having computed the expected value of the bargain, we can now compute the expected value of the legal claim when the complaint is filed. After the complaint is filed, the parties may settle. According to Figure 10.2, the plaintiff who files a suit settles immediately with probability .7, in which case he or she receives $50 and pays $1 in settlement costs. Alternatively, the plaintiff fails to settle immediately with probability .3 and proceeds to exchange information with the defendant, which costs $3.30. After exchanging information, the parties continue to bargain. We already computed the expected value of the bargain, which equals $43.30. We combine these numbers to obtain the expected value of the legal claim when the plaintiff initiates the suit by filing the complaint (*EVF*):

$$EVF = .7(\$50 - 1) + .3(\$43.30 - \$3.30) = \$46.30.$$

The filing costs (*FC*) include the costs of hiring a lawyer, drafting the complaint, and paying the filing fee assessed by the court. According to Figure 10.2, the filing costs equal $10. After filing, the plaintiff expects to receive the value of the claim at the time of filing (*EVF*), which equals $46.30. Therefore, the expected net payoff from filing equals $46.30 − $10 = $36.30. The rational plaintiff files a complaint if its expected net payoff is positive:

$$EVF \geq FC => \text{file legal complaint};$$

$$EVF < FC => \text{do not file legal complaint}. \qquad (10.2)$$

Thus, the rational plaintiff in Figure 10.2 files a legal complaint.

Having discussed the plaintiff, we briefly discuss the defendant. When the plaintiff files a complaint, the defendant must respond to it. To compute the best response, a rational defendant must solve a decision problem similar to the plaintiff's problem depicted in Figure 10.2. The defendant's decision problem is to minimize the expected cost of his or her legal liability. Because the decision problem of the defendant parallels the decision problem of the plaintiff, we will not explicitly analyze the former.

QUESTION 10.3: Working from the last possible event to the first possible event is called solving a problem "recursively." The following tree is identical to Figure 10.2, except that a trial costs the plaintiff $40 instead of $20. Solve recursively for the expected values of the legal claim by filling in the blanks at each stage in the following tree. What is the plaintiff's expected net profit from filing a legal complaint?

Problem: Compute expected value
of the legal claim at each step

$EVA = \$\_\_\_\_$

$EVT = \$\_\_\_\_$

appeal .9 $0
−$20   lose

$EVB = \$\_\_\_\_$

trial   .5
−$40   lose   win
.1

$EVF = \$\_\_\_\_$

.3 $100

bargain   don't   win
settle   .5

exchange
information   .3 $100
or settle

discover   settle −$1
−$3.30   .7

sue

file −$10   settle −$1 $51
.7

don't $51
file

$0

QUESTION 10.4: In Europe, the party who loses at trial pays the litigation costs of the winner. Assume that the plaintiff in the preceding figure pays litigation costs of $40 if she loses at trial, and the plaintiff pays litigation costs of $0 if she wins. Recompute the expected values of the legal claim under this assumption.

B. Damages Determining Suits

Our model identifies three immediate causes of the filing of legal complaints:

1. injuries that trigger disputes,
2. the cost of filing a complaint, and

3. the expected value of the claim.

Filing of legal complaints should increase with increases in underlying events that cause them, such as accidents, broken promises, invasion of property, and so forth. Filing of legal complaints should also increase with decreases in the cost of filing a complaint, including the cost of hiring a lawyer. Finally, filing of legal complaints should increase with increases in the expected value of the claim.

To see these causes at work, consider how an increase in the money damages awarded at trial to successful plaintiffs would affect the filing of legal complaints. An increase in money damages awarded at trial increases the expected value of a trial (*EVT*), which increases the expected value of the legal claim and leads to more claims being filed. To illustrate, assume that an accident victim must pay $501 to go to trial, where he expects to lose with probability .5 and to win $1000 with probability .5. Thus the expected value of trial equals $-$501 + .5($0) + .5($1000) = -1. The plaintiff is unlikely to file a complaint in this case. If, however, the damages awarded to a successful plaintiff increase to $2000, then the expected value of the trial equals $499, and the plaintiff is likely to file a complaint.

We have explained that an increase in damages awarded to successful plaintiffs tends to increase the filing of legal complaints by increasing the expected value of trial. An increase in damages awarded to successful plaintiffs also has an effect in the opposite direction. Potential defendants can often avoid disputes by avoiding the injuries that cause them. If the damages awarded to successful plaintiffs increase, potential defendants will take more precaution and thus give potential plaintiffs less opportunity to file legal complaints. For example, a manufacturer may increase quality control to avoid defects that would expose the company to liability claims by injured consumers.

These considerations suggest a prediction about the connection between the magnitude of damages awarded to successful plaintiffs and the number of legal complaints filed. If damages equal zero, then the expected value of trial is so low that potential plaintiffs seldom file complaints. As damages increase, more potential plaintiffs file complaints. As damages increase further, however, potential defendants respond by giving fewer potential plaintiffs cause for legal action. Eventually a point is reached where the number of complaints begins to decrease as damages increase. Figure 10.3 depicts these facts. The number of suits, which is read off the vertical axis, is largest when the expected judgment, which is read off the horizontal axis, equals a value

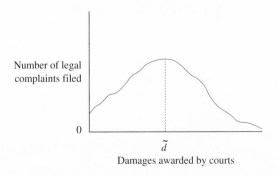

FIGURE 10.3 Suits as a function of damages.

denoted $\tilde{d}$. The effect of a small increase in damages upon the filing of complaints depends upon whether the starting point is below or above $\tilde{d}$. Below $\tilde{d}$, a small increase in damages increases the number of lawsuits filed. Above $\tilde{d}$, a small increase in damages decreases the number of lawsuits filed.

QUESTION 10.5: In America, the average monetary value of judgments awarded to plaintiffs in recent years has increased, although scholars disagree about the extent of the increase.[2] Under what assumption would this increase lead to more suits?

C. Filing Costs as a Filter

Now we consider how filing costs affect suits. The horizontal axis in Figure 10.4 indicates the expected value of the legal claim at the time of filing (*EVF*), and the vertical axis indicates the corresponding number of potential plaintiffs. Some potential plaintiffs have valuable legal claims and others have worthless legal claims. The line indicating filing costs (*FC*) partitions the distribution of potential plaintiffs into two groups. For those plaintiffs to the left of *FC*, the filing cost exceeds the expected value of the legal claim, so these plaintiffs do not sue. For those plaintiffs to the right of *FC*, the expected value of the legal claim exceeds the filing cost, so these plaintiffs sue. Thus, filing costs act as a filter for disputes. High-value disputes pass through the filter and result in lawsuits, whereas low-value disputes are caught by the filter and do not result in suits.

By changing filing costs, officials move the partition in Figure 10.4 and change the value of suits. By raising the fees charged by the court for filing a legal complaint, the authorities shift the boundary in Figure 10.4 to the right and cause the filing of fewer complaints. Thus, the state can increase the minimum value of suits. Alternatively, by lowering the fees, the authorities shift the boundary in Figure 10.4 to the left and cause the filing of more complaints, thus decreasing the minimum value of suits.

Now we relate the filing of complaints to social efficiency. The authorities should set the fees charged by the court for filing a legal complaint to minimize the sum of administrative costs and error costs: min $c_a + c(e)$. The filing of a complaint imposes the administrative costs of resolving it upon the plaintiff and defendant. As for error costs, consider the perfect remedy for an injury from the viewpoint of existing law. From this viewpoint, the perfect remedy is a resolution on terms equal to the judgment that a court would reach with perfect information about the facts of the case and the law (the perfect-information judgment). The resolution of the dispute on any other terms creates error costs, $c(e)$. *The court imposes optimal fees for filing a complaint when the administrative costs equal the error costs of providing no remedy for the injury in the marginal case.*

The authorities can make calculations to determine whether they should raise or lower the fees for filing a complaint. When making these calculations, the authorities should focus on the marginal case, which is on the boundary between "don't

---

[2] Recall the data in the previous chapter on average and median awards in medical malpractice actions. While the mean award has been relatively constant for several decades, the median award has increased.

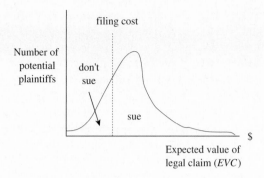

FIGURE 10.4 Number of suits filed.

sue" and "sue" in Figure 10.4. For the marginal case, the filing costs equal the expected value of the legal claim, $FC = EVC$. A small increase in the fees charged by courts for filing a legal complaint will cause the marginal plaintiff to drop the suit. Thus, the marginal plaintiff will receive 0 instead of receiving EVC. The authorities must compare the resulting savings in administrative costs and the cost of the resulting error.

The social value of reducing errors depends upon whether the errors affect production or merely distribution. Errors affect production when they have strong incentive effects upon behavior that causes injury, such as trespassing on property, breaching contracts, or driving carelessly. If errors have large incentive effects upon precaution, then filing fees should be kept low. Conversely, errors affect redistribution when they do not cause changes in the behavior that causes injuries. If errors affect redistribution but not incentives, then economic efficiency requires keeping filing fees high.

QUESTION 10.6: Assume that breach of business contracts strongly influences production, whereas property disputes in divorces affect distribution (but not production). Explain the consequences of these assumptions for setting filing fees at the efficient level in disputes involving business contracts and property disputes in divorces.

D. Supply of Legal Services

Next, consider how an increase in the number of lawyers affects the filing of legal claims. (In fact, the number of lawyers in the United States has increased rapidly in recent years.) The effect of an increase in the number of lawyers depends upon the organization of the market for legal services, which the bar regulates in all countries. As a benchmark, first consider the effects of an increase in the number of lawyers in a country with relatively lax regulation of the market for legal services. By "lax regulation" we mean that lawyers enjoy much freedom in creating contracts with their clients, as in the U.S. In a free market, where supply and demand determine prices, an increase in the number of lawyers shifts the supply curve out, as depicted in Figure 10.5. The shift in the supply curve from S to S' causes the price of lawyers' services to fall from p_1 to p_2. Thus, the increase in the supply of lawyers lowers the cost of filing suits. A fall in the price of lawyers' services from p_1 to p_2 causes the demand for the services of lawyers to increase from q_1 to q_2. We conclude that an increase in the number of lawyers causes more suits to be filed.

To illustrate, the plaintiff's lawyer in a typical tort case in the United States receives compensation in the form of a "contingency fee," which means that lawyers get a share of the judgments if their clients win and nothing if their clients lose.[3] Suppose that the plaintiff expects to win $1000 with probability 0.5, and the contingency fee equals 0.3. Then the expected value of the case to the plaintiff's lawyer equals $1000(0.5)(0.3) = $150. If the case takes two hours to prepare and try, then the lawyer's expected remuneration equals $75 per hour. Thus, a profit-maximizing lawyer will take the case so long as he or she does not have an alternative that pays more than $75 per hour. As the number of lawyers increases, the opportunities available to the average lawyer decrease. When the number of lawyers increases, some cases that no lawyer would previously have taken will be brought on a contingency-fee basis.[4]

Like other professional associations, the bar in every country attempts to control the portals of the profession in order to keep the supply of legal services low and the price high. The bar exercises this power primarily by setting high professional qualifications for the right to argue in court or supply other legal services. We predict that success by the bar in limiting the number of lawyers will increase their fees and thus reduce the number of suits.

The proposition that an increase in lawyers causes more suits amounts to the proposition that the bar is not immune from the law of supply and demand. The bar in many countries, however, has insulated itself as far as possible from the market for legal services. For example, many countries, such as Germany, rigidly prescribe the price of legal services by law. When the law prescribes a schedule of fees for legal services, and the fee schedule is enforced effectively, an increase in the supply of lawyers cannot change the fees for legal services. Instead, an increase in lawyers causes more unemployment among them.

To demonstrate this fact, assume that the price of legal services is set at p_1 in Figure 10.5 by law. If the supply curve for lawyers is given by S, then the *legal* price p_1 has no effect, because it merely confirms the *market* price. Suppose, however, that the supply curve for lawyers shifts from S to S', while the price of legal services remains equal to p_1. The demand for lawyers at this price equals q_1, but after the shift in supply from S to S', the supply of lawyers at price p_1 equals q_3. The expression $q_3 - q_1$ measures the amount by which supply exceeds demand ("excess supply"), which correlates closely with the number of lawyers who want to work at the price p_1 and cannot find employment.

In fact, young German lawyers sometimes complain of unemployment or underemployment, and the law forbids them to attract clients by charging lower fees. To circumvent the prohibition, young German lawyers may try to attract business by spend-

---

[3] Most plaintiffs' lawyers use a sliding scale for contingency fees. A common practice is for the lawyer to take one-third of the plaintiff's award if the case is settled without trial; 40% if the plaintiff wins at trial; and 50% if a judgment for the plaintiff is affirmed on appeal. The fee scheme may vary from place to place and over time.

[4] Outside of the United States most legal systems do not allow lawyers to take cases on a contingency-fee basis.

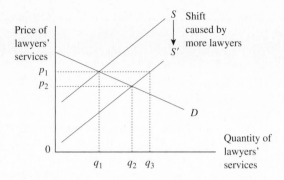

FIGURE 10.5 The effects of more lawyers on the market for lawyers' services.

ing more hours on the same legal task that a senior German lawyer would complete quickly, or by supplying extra services for "free." In general, the prohibition of price competition promotes quality competition and secret discounting.

For another example of how procedural rules influence the rate of litigation, see the box below titled "Class Actions."

QUESTION 10.7: Price regulation prevents some people from buying a good who value it more than it costs to supply. Apply this proposition to Figure 10.5, assuming that the state sets the price at p_1 and S' gives the supply.

QUESTION 10.8: If most litigation is a costly form of redistribution, then public policy should discourage it for the sake of economic efficiency. Compare the efficiency of the following restrictions on the market for legal services: (a) low damages awarded as compensation for injuries; (b) high fees charged by the court for the filing of a legal complaint; (c) lawyers' fees set by the state at a high level.

QUESTION 10.9: Litigation insurance shifts the legal costs of plaintiffs or defendants to insurers. How do you think this insurance would affect the number of suits filed?

E. Agency Problem

Recall that we built the theory of contracts in Chapter 6 upon the "agency game." In this game, the principal decides whether or not to put a valuable asset under the control of the agent, and the agent decides whether to cooperate or appropriate. In a legal dispute, the plaintiff puts a legal claim under a lawyer's control. The lawyer can serve the client or exploit the client. Consequently, the market for legal services is an agency game. The lawyer provides his or her client with advice and the lawyer provides effort to win the case. We will consider the lawyers' incentives for providing information and effort to their clients.

First consider the lawyer's incentives to work on a case. As explained in Chapter 6, the agency relationship is efficient from the viewpoint of the principal and agent when the parties maximize their joint payoffs. To maximize the joint payoffs, the lawyer should work on the case until the marginal cost equals the marginal benefit for both parties. The marginal cost of the lawyer's time spent on a suit equals its value in the

CLASS ACTIONS

Did you ever write a check for more money than was in your account? Such a check usually "bounces," and your bank charges you a fee called an "NSF charge" (not-sufficient-funds charge). In California in 1975, Mr. Perdue was charged $6 by Crocker Bank for writing an NSF check. He sued the bank in a case that eventually went to the California Supreme Court. It costs a lot more than $6 to pursue a case that far. Mr. Perdue and his lawyers pursued this case because the stakes far exceeded $6. In fact, Mr. Perdue brought this action not merely on his own behalf but also on behalf of *all* those account holders at Crocker Bank who paid NSF charges. If successful, Mr. Perdue would recover his $6 and all the other alleged overcharges made by Crocker Bank against its customers.

When a plaintiff attempts to bring an action on behalf of a class of plaintiffs, the court must decide whether to "certify" a "class action" and permit someone like Mr. Perdue to sue on behalf of himself and everyone else in the alleged class. This is a delicate problem because a successful suit by Mr. Perdue will extinguish everyone else's claims. Once a class action succeeds, the members of the class, most of whom were not even consulted about the case, will have lost their right to sue.

When should a class be certified? Economics suggests that class actions are appropriate when the stakes are large in aggregate and small for any individual plaintiff. In our example, the sum of NSF charges to all account holders at Crocker Bank roughly measured the stakes in dispute, and the stakes for each individual accountholder roughly equaled $6. So the certification of a class seems appropriate.

Once a class is certified, if the plaintiff who represents the class agrees to a settlement, or if that plaintiff succeeds at trial, damages will be paid by the defendant. These damages must be distributed in such a way that the whole class of plaintiffs benefits, rather than merely the active plaintiff and his or her lawyers, who are naturally inclined to grab a large share for themselves. The courts must decide whether a proposed distribution in a class action is fair. For example, should the active plaintiff's lawyers, who are often responsible for organizing and initiating the suit, be compensated at their standard billing rate? Or should they receive more than their usual fee in order to compensate them for taking the high risk of losing the suit? Distributing small sums of money to everyone in the class is usually prohibitively expensive. Sometimes the court approves a distribution to some members of the class and the donation of the remaining recovery to a charity that benefits people similar to the members of the class.

In technical terms, class actions ideally consolidate litigation to achieve economies of scale and provide a legal remedy for small injuries that are large in aggregate.

QUESTION 10.10: Explain the effects of class actions on the number of suits, using our distinction of causes into (1) injuries, (2) filing costs, and (3) expected value of the legal claim.

best alternative use ("opportunity cost"). The marginal benefit to the client equals the resulting increase in the expected value of the client's legal claim (or decrease in the expected value of the client's legal liability).

Devising a contract to achieve this ideal is notoriously difficult. Contracts with lawyers usually focus upon three variables: (1) time spent working, (2) services performed, and (3) outcome of the dispute. In many cases, the lawyers bill by the hour (or rather the minute[5]). Hourly billing causes lawyers to externalize the cost of working on a case, which gives them an incentive to devote too much time to it. Lawyers also bill by the service performed (so many dollars for filing a complaint, so many dollars for arguing the case in court, so many dollars for an appeal, and so forth). Fee-for-service contracts cause lawyers to internalize the cost of additional time spent on the service and to externalize the benefit, which gives lawyers an incentive to devote little time to performing many services. With contingency fees, the plaintiff's lawyer receives a share of the outcome, such as one-third of the settlement or judgment.[6] When working for a contingency fee of one-third, the lawyer internalizes the cost of additional time spent on the service and internalizes one-third of the resulting benefit.

We have considered the lawyer's incentives to provide effort. Second, consider the lawyer's incentive to provide information. Imagine that a plaintiff consults a lawyer to find out whether or not the cost of filing a complaint exceeds the expected value of the resulting legal claim, as depicted in Figure 10.4. A truthful answer may not maximize the lawyer's expected payoff. A lawyer who is paid by the hour, or a lawyer who is paid for services performed, may exaggerate the expected value of the legal claim in order to induce the client to pay for filing a complaint.

Alternatively, a lawyer who is paid a contingency fee has an incentive to mislead in the opposite direction. Imagine that a plaintiff consults a lawyer to find out whether or not he will take the case on a one-third contingency. Under this contract, the lawyer internalizes all the cost of filing the complaint, and the lawyer internalizes one-third of the expected value of the claim. Therefore, the lawyer may refuse to take the case, even though the expected value of the claim exceeds the filing costs.

Notice that this incentive problem would be solved if the lawyer took the case on a "100% contingency." With a 100% contingency, the lawyer internalizes the cost of working on the case and the lawyer also internalizes 100% of the payoff from a settlement or judgment. A "100% contingency" means that the lawyer keeps the full value of a settlement or judgment; in effect, the client sells the claim to the lawyer. A competitive

---

[5] Joke: A businessman receives a bill from his lawyer which reads: "Crossed street to see client. Thought it was you. $50."

Joke: A sociologist studying longevity found that the average lawyer lives twice as long as the average doctor and three times as long as the average school teacher. Life span for lawyers was computed using billing hours.

[6] If the *defendant's* lawyer took the case on a one-third contingency, the defendant would pay his lawyer a flat fee at the beginning of the suit and the defendant's lawyer would agree to pay a proportion of trial judgment or settlement. For example, the defendant might pay a flat fee of $5,000 and the defendant might agree to pay two-thirds of the judgment. (The defendant's lawyer would agree to pay the remaining one-third.) Thus, if the case ended in a judgment of $10,000, the defendant's net costs would equal $5,000 + $6,667, and the net gain of the defendant's lawyer would equal $5,000 − $3,333. Where allowed by law, contingency fees are common for the plaintiff's lawyer, but not for the defendant's lawyer. We know of no cases where the defendant's lawyer actually had a contingency contract.

market for the sale of legal claims would solve the incentive problem for lawyers, but the law prohibits such transactions everywhere.[7]

In markets with lax regulation like the United States, lawyers and their clients have scope to design their own contracts. Thus the plaintiff's lawyer might charge by the hour for some activities, charge fixed fees for other services, and also take a contingency. In tightly regulated markets like Germany, the state may prescribe the fees for services performed, limit additional fees for time spent on the case, and prohibit contingency fees. In addition, some countries like Britain have a "split bar", which means that the client deals with one lawyer (the "solicitor"), and the client's lawyer chooses another lawyer (the "barrister") to argue the case in court. The wide variation in solutions to the agency problem by different countries reflects its difficulty, as well as reflecting the political power of an ancient profession.

In general, the agency problem between lawyer and client has two causes: asymmetrical information and randomness. The lawyer knows much more about the law than the client, and the client usually knows more about the facts of the case than the lawyer. Furthermore, the case's outcome depends on random events such as the assignment of a judge and the availability of a witness. Randomness prevents the client from inferring the lawyer's performance from the cases' outcomes.

To overcome these problems, people often choose lawyers based upon reputation and long-run relationships, which inspire trust. (Recall the demonstration in Chapter 6 that long-run relationships solve agency problems.) Reputation explains why established law firms command a premium for their services. The growing importance of reputation may also explain the steady increase in the size of law firms in many countries. Large firms are the "brand names" that stand for quality in legal services. However, many countries create obstacles to retard the growth of "brand names" in law. For example, some countries prohibit law firms from naming themselves after anyone not currently working in the firm, so the firm's name has to change with the retirement of senior partners. Furthermore, most countries restrict or prohibit advertising by lawyers, so lawyers cannot build a reputation by broadcasting their accomplishments.

We have explained how the agency problem inhibits the client and lawyer from maximizing their joint expected payoffs from a suit. This discussion views suits from the perspective of client and lawyer. A broader perspective focuses on social efficiency and tries to minimize the sum of the costs of administration and errors. From this perspective, the law should deter costly injuries by encouraging suits, whereas the law should discourage disputes over distribution. By imposing rules that aggravate the agency problem, officials of the state can raise administrative costs and thus discourage suits. However, officials should choose the most efficient means to discourage disputes. Aggravating the agency problem distorts the efforts of lawyers in representing their clients; so, aggravating the agency problem is an inefficient way to discourage disputes. A more efficient way is to raise the cost of filing a legal complaint.

QUESTION 10.11: From an economic viewpoint, restrictions on advertising by lawyers look like a device used by the bar to limit competition. (Such advertising restrictions

---

[7]The common law prohibition is called "champerty." If the lawyer buys the legal claim, a new incentive problem arises: the plaintiff has no incentive to cooperate or testify. (We discussed a market for unmatured tort claims in a box in Chapter 9.)

broke down in America, not because they violated antitrust laws, but because the courts found them to violate the constitutional right of free speech.) From an economic viewpoint, is advertising by lawyers any different from advertising by other professionals, such as accountants or insurers?

QUESTION 10.12: Contingency fees:

    a. If the plaintiff is more averse to risk than his or her lawyer, would this fact incline the client to prefer a contingency fee or an hourly fee?

    b. Under a contingency fee, the plaintiff bears none of the lawyer's costs of a trial. Consequently, the plaintiff can take a hard position in bargaining over a settlement. Explain why the plaintiff's lawyer might also benefit from this commitment to hard bargaining.

    c. Contingency fees are common for the plaintiff's lawyer in America, but not for the defendant's lawyer. Under a contingency fee contract, the defendant would pay a fixed amount to a lawyer at the beginning of the legal process and the lawyer would pay a fraction of the trial judgment. (See n. 6 in this chapter.) Are the incentive effects of contingency fees the same for the plaintiff's lawyer and the defendant's lawyer?

II. EXCHANGE OF INFORMATION

Having analyzed the filing of a complaint, we consider the next stage in a legal dispute, as depicted in Figure 10.1.

A. Bad News Is Good for Settlements

After the plaintiff complains and the defendant responds, the two parties try to resolve their dispute before it leads to a trial. Why do some complaints end up being tried rather than settled? It might seem on first impression that trials, being so costly, would not occur unless someone behaves irrationally. Like many first impressions, this one is wrong. Game theory explains why rational bargainers sometimes fail to settle their disputes and end up in trial. Although there are several strands of argument, the simplest explanation is that trials occur because the plaintiff expects a large judgment at trial and the defendant expects a small judgment at trial. In these circumstances, the parties are *relatively optimistic*. Given relative optimism, the plaintiff demands a large settlement and the defendant offers a small settlement, so the parties cannot agree on the terms for settling out of court.

    To illustrate this fact concretely, assume that a bus collides with a pedestrian. The bus company admits fault, but the parties disagree over damages. The bus company, which believes that the pedestrian suffered minor injuries, predicts that a trial will cost it $1000 and result in a judgment of $1500, thus costing a total of $2500. The pedestrian, who actually suffered a serious injury requiring surgery, predicts that a trial will cost $1000 and result in a judgment of $15,000, thus resulting in a net gain of $14,000. The bus company's false optimism about trial will cause it to reject any settlement on terms acceptable to the pedestrian.

We will explain more abstractly how divergent expectations of the parties affect their ability to settle out of court. When the two parties try to settle out of court, the plaintiff's demand reflects the expected value of the legal claim as computed in Figure 10.2. The plaintiff usually rejects an offer by the defendant that falls short of the expected value of the legal claim. To illustrate by the preceding example, the plaintiff will reject an offer to settle for less than $14,000.

Turning from the plaintiff to the defendant, the defendant's offer reflects the expected value of his or her legal liability. The defendant usually rejects a demand by the plaintiff that exceeds the expected value of the legal liability. To illustrate by the preceding example, the defendant will reject a demand to settle for more than $2500. *If the plaintiff's expected value of the claim exceeds the defendant's expected cost of the liability, we say that the parties are relatively optimistic.*

Relative optimism about trial makes settlement out of court difficult. (A strict proof comes later.) Conversely, settling out of court is easy when plaintiffs believe they can win far less at trial than defendants believe they will lose. To illustrate this fact concretely, we revise the numbers in the bus-pedestrian example to reflect relative pessimism, not relative optimism. Assume as before that a bus collides with a pedestrian, the bus company admits fault, and the estimates of damages by the two parties diverge to reflect pessimism about trial. The bus company, which knows that the pedestrian had surgery, believes that a trial will cost it $1000 and result in a judgment of $15,000, thus costing a total of $16,000. The pedestrian knows that the surgery corrected a preexisting condition, not an injury caused by the accident. Therefore, the pedestrian predicts that a trial will cost $1000 and result in a judgment of $1500, thus resulting in a net gain of $500. The bus company's false pessimism about a trial will cause it to accept a settlement offer of, say, $10,000, which far exceeds what the pedestrian believes can be had at trial. As long as the bus company remains ignorant of the facts, the case should settle out of court.

In many suits, the defendant knows less than the plaintiff about the extent of the injury, and the plaintiff knows less than the defendant about the extent of the defendant's precautions against the accident. If the defendant overestimates the plaintiff's injury, and the plaintiff overestimates the defendant's precaution, then both parties are relatively pessimistic, so settlement is easy. Conversely, if the defendant underestimates the plaintiff's injury, and the plaintiff underestimates the defendant's precaution, then both parties are relatively optimistic, so settlement is difficult.

The expected value of the legal claim diverges for the parties because of *private information,* which means information possessed by one party and not possessed by the other. When relative optimism initially prevents the parties from settling out of court, they may be able to correct the relative optimism before trial and then settle. In other words, transmitting bad news is good for settlements. Next we will analyze the exchange of information and its affect upon settlements.

B. Bad News Is Free

The parties to a legal dispute exchange some private information voluntarily, without the law requiring it. Voluntary pooling of information occurs informally through discussions between the parties, and it also occurs formally, as when the judge holds a pretrial conference in which the parties, are asked to discuss their predictions about what will happen at trial. In addition to the voluntary exchange of information, some pooling of information is compulsory. For example, the law may require the party making a complaint to tell the other side what it will prove in court in the event a trial occurs. In the United States the law compels each side to answer questions about the case asked by the other side. This practice is called *discovery,* because one party has the right to discover certain facts known to the other party.

We will ask two questions about the relationship between voluntary and involuntary pooling of information. First, "Does the voluntary pooling of information promote settlements out of court?" Second, "Does involuntary pooling of information promote more settlements beyond the number achieved by voluntary pooling?"

In general, *the parties tend to disclose information voluntarily before trial to correct the other side's relative optimism, thereby promoting settlements.* In other words, bad news is free. To see why, return to the bus example, in which a bus collides with a pedestrian, the bus company admits fault, and the bus company mistakenly believes that the pedestrian suffered a minor injury. The bus company predicts inaccurately that a trial will cost it $1000 and result in a judgment of $1500, and the pedestrian predicts accurately that a trial will cost $1000 and result in a judgment of $15,000. A settlement could save each party $1000 in trial costs. However, the bus company's false optimism about a trial will cause it to reject any settlement on terms acceptable to the pedestrian. Knowing these facts, the pedestrian has an incentive to correct the bus company's false optimism by revealing the extent of the injuries. By doing so, the pedestrian can probably enable the parties to settle and save the costs of a trial, which will benefit both of them.

We will state the conclusion of this example more abstractly. As explained, trials occur when the parties are relatively optimistic about their outcome, so that each side prefers a trial rather than settlement on terms acceptable to the other side. When the parties are relatively optimistic, at least one of them is uninformed. Pooling of information before trial that reduces relative optimism promotes settlements. Furthermore, by revealing private information to correct the other side's false optimism, the party making the disclosure increases the probability of settling on more favorable terms. Thus, efficiency (save costs of trial) and redistribution (strengthen your bargaining position) provide incentives to voluntarily disclose facts correcting the other side's false optimism.

Similarly, *the parties tend to withhold information that would correct the other side's relative pessimism, thereby promoting settlements.* To see why, return to the preceding example, but assume that the bus company's mistaken belief is pessimistic: the bus company, which knows that the pedestrian had surgery and mistakenly attributes its cause to the bus accident, believes that a trial will cost it $1000 and result in a judgment of $15,000, whereas the pedestrian, who knows that the surgery corrected a preexisting condition, predicts that a trial will cost $1000 and result in a judgment of $1500. The bus company's false pessimism about a trial will cause it to accept a settlement offer that far exceeds what the pedestrian would win at trial. As long as the bus company remains ignorant of the facts, the case should settle out of court. Knowing these facts, the pedestrian has \an incentive to withhold information about the true extent of the injury.

We will state the conclusion of this example more abstractly. As explained, settlements occur when the parties are relatively pessimistic about the outcome of a trial, so that each side prefers a settlement rather than risking a trial. When the parties are relatively pessimistic, at least one of them is uninformed. By revealing private information to correct the other side's false pessimism, the disclosing party makes worse the terms that the other party would accept to settle out of court. These facts provide a strong incentive to withhold information that would correct the other side's false optimism.

We have explained that voluntary pooling of information tends to correct false optimism and leave false pessimism uncorrected, which promotes settlements out of court. This conclusion relates to our discussion of asymmetrical information in contracts in Chapter 7. We argued that people often value goods differently because they possess different information. Even so, they usually capture all the potential gains from trade through free exchange. Similarly, parties to a suit usually exchange information voluntarily and thus avoid the waste of litigation costs.

So far we have discussed voluntary disclosure. Now we turn to involuntary disclosure, which occurs when one party discovers information withheld by the other party. As explained, the information withheld is the mirror image of the information voluntarily disclosed: parties withhold information that would correct the other side's false pessimism. As used in the United States, "discovery" refers to the pretrial process that forces the disclosure of private information. We used the word "discovery" to refer to the involuntary disclosure of private information. Discovery tends to uncover the information that was withheld, thus correcting false pessimism. Correcting false pessimism decreases the likelihood that someone will make unnecessary concessions when bargaining. In general, *the parties tend to discover information that corrects their relative pessimism, thereby causing them to demand better terms to settle out of court.*

To illustrate, return to the example of the bus company that believes incorrectly that a trial will result in a large judgment, whereas the pedestrian knows that a trial will result in a small judgment. The bus company's false pessimism about a trial will cause it to accept a settlement offer that far exceeds what the pedestrian would get at trial. If the bus company discovers the truth, it will save itself a lot of money by demanding better terms to settle out of court.

When parties discover information withheld by the other party, the pooling of information reduces uncertainty and suspicion, which makes settling out of court more likely. However, discovering information that causes someone to demand better terms makes settling out of court less likely. Given these contradictory tendencies, it is uncertain whether discovery increases or decreases settlements beyond the number achieved by voluntary disclosure.

C. United States vs. Europe

Different countries and jurisdictions have different rules about discovery. The most extensive and elaborate discovery occurs in the United States. Long before a trial begins in America, each side must reveal the basic arguments that it plans to use in trial, the evidence supporting these arguments, the names of witnesses, and the general nature of the testimony that witnesses will supply. The failure to disclose arguments or evidence may cause the judge to prevent their use in a trial. Further, the American rules of procedure entitle each side to discover any evidence possessed by the other side that has material relevance to the case, such as inspecting physical objects, reading documents, and deposing witnesses. The discovery of new facts can radically alter the course of the legal dispute.

Unlike the United States, most European countries have little or no discovery. Several practical reasons account for this difference in procedures. In America, a party to a suit has a constitutional right to request a trial by jury. Serving on a jury takes its members away from their jobs and other activities. The court tries to minimize the disruption of jurors' lives by making the parties prepare extensively before the trial, and then proceeding from beginning to end of the trial without interruption. In contrast, European countries seldom use juries to decide civil cases. Delays and interruptions in proceedings inconvenience judges less than juries, so European trials often pause and resume several times before reaching an end. American trials are like performing a play from the first act to the final act, whereas European trials are like filming a movie in segments with pauses in between.

Another difference concerns the role of the judge. In the civil tradition of Europe, the judge takes an active role in developing arguments and exploring evidence ("inquisitorial procedure"). Indeed, the judge may not allow the lawyers to examine witnesses or scrutinize certain evidence before the trial. Unprepared witnesses are more candid and reveal many facts inadvertently. In the common law tradition, however, the judge takes a more passive role. Instead of directing the case, the common law judge referees a contest between opposing attorneys ("adversarial procedure"). In America, the judge expects the lawyers to develop the arguments and explore the evidence *before* the case comes to trial. Preparation improves the quality of the argument, and a prepared witness goes directly to the point of his or her testimony.

D. Minimizing Social Costs

Now we relate our contrast between voluntary and involuntary pooling of information to the objective of minimizing the sum of administrative costs and error costs. The voluntary pooling of information avoids trials, and avoiding trials saves administrative costs. Furthermore, the voluntary exchange of information corrects some miscalculations that cause the terms of a settlement to diverge from the expected trial judgment. Narrowing the gap between the terms of the settlement and the expected trial judgment usually reduces error costs. (More on this later.) Therefore, *the voluntary pooling of information usually reduces both components of social costs: administrative costs and error costs.*

The effects of *compulsory* pooling of information on social costs are more ambiguous. First consider the effect of discovery on administrative costs. As explained above, game theory does not generally predict whether discovery encourages or discourages settlements. In the event of a trial, discovery prior to trial often simplifies the arguments and proofs made during trial. However, it is uncertain whether or not discovery reduces the cost of trials by an amount commensurate with the cost of discovery itself.[8] Current research does not permit us to conclude whether or not discovery reduces administrative costs.

Now we turn to error costs. As explained, discovery corrects some miscalculations that cause the terms of a settlement to diverge from the expected trial judgment. Since discovery narrows the gap between the terms of settlement and the expected trial judgment, we conclude that *discovery usually reduces error.* In summary, the involuntary pooling of information reduces one component of social costs (error costs), but may not reduce the other (administrative costs).

---

[8] Discovery is a cheaper process than litigation. Consequently, discovering facts prior to trial is cheaper than finding the same facts in trial. However, discovery is more certain to occur than trials. Consequently, postponing the compulsory disclosure of facts until trial implies the possibility that a settlement will completely avoid this cost.

DISCOVERY ABUSE: THE PROCESS IS THE PUNISHMENT

Suppose that you had the legal power to require someone to bear the expense of supplying you with enough documents to fill a railroad boxcar. In complex legal disputes in America, the legal right to discovery sometimes gives such powers to one of the parties. One party can require the other to deliver a boxcar of documents, provided that they are materially relevant to the suit and compliance is not unduly burdensome [FEDERAL RULES OF PROCEDURE, Rule 26(b)(1)].

Unlike current federal law, economics provides a clear account of discovery abuse and its remedy. From an economic perspective, abuse occurs when the cost of making and complying with a discovery request exceeds the expected value of the information to the requesting party. The cost of making and complying with a request for documents equals the cost of formulating the request, finding the documents, examining all of them, and reproducing and delivering some of them. The expected value of the information to the requesting party equals the expected increase in the value of the legal claim caused by the evidence obtained from the documents.

Under current U.S. law, the plaintiff pays most of the cost of *making* an additional discovery request, and the defendant pays much of the cost of *complying* with it. Externalizing compliance costs provides an incentive for discovery abuse. To illustrate, assume that the plaintiff spends $500 to make a discovery request, and the defendant spends $2000 to comply. The total cost of the request to both parties equals $2500. Assume that the plaintiff expects the request to produce evidence increasing the value of the legal claim by less than $1500. Because the plaintiff pays $500 to obtain an expected payoff of $1500, the plaintiff has a strong incentive to make the request. Because the cost ($2500) exceeds the expected benefit ($1500), the request is abusive. Thus, current U.S. law gives strong incentives for discovery abuse.

Notice that the incentive for abuse would disappear if the plaintiff had to pay the defendant's cost of compliance, thus internalizing the full cost of the discovery request. Discovery illustrates a general proposition: *People can use legal procedures to abuse others whenever one party has the right to request a procedure and the other party must bear part of the cost of complying with the request. Furthermore, shifting the cost of compliance to the party making the request eliminates the incentive for abuse.*

QUESTION 10.13: Example 4 concerns whether a judge should order a divorcing couple to attempt mediation before beginning a trial. Assume that false optimism causes trials and predict whether compulsory mediation would cause more disputes to be settled without trial.

QUESTION 10.14: Assume that discovery increases the optimism of plaintiffs and thus increases the value of their legal claims. Explain the consequences for the number of claims filed.

QUESTION 10.15: Trial procedures are formal and involve a lot of people, whereas discovery procedures are relatively informal and involve relatively few people.

Consequently, discovering a fact before trial is cheaper than finding it during trial. Most trials, however, are averted through an out-of-court settlement. As a result, if the parties postpone finding a fact until trial, they may avoid the cost completely. To appreciate this trade-off between cost and certainty, consider a numerical problem. Let x denote the ratio of the cost of finding a fact during the trial and the cost of discovering the fact before trial. Assume that the probability of a settlement out of court equals .9. How large must x be in order for the expected cost of finding the fact at trial to exceed the cost of discovering it before trial?

QUESTION 10.16: Discovery increases deliberation, which improves the quality of argument. However, discovery reduces spontaneity, and spontaneous answers by witnesses are sometimes more revealing than considered answers. ("When desperate, tell the truth.") A complete economic theory of discovery would thus model the tradeoff between deliberation and spontaneity in revealing the truth. Describe some considerations that you think would go into modeling this trade-off.

III. SETTLEMENT BARGAINING

Having analyzed the exchange of information, we move to the next stage in Figure 10.1, which concerns bargaining to attempt to settle out of court. Unlike the other stages, procedural law does not prescribe a time for bargaining to settle disputes. Rather, bargaining can occur at any time in the legal process. We place bargaining at the stage just before trial in Figure 10.1 because bargaining often intensifies before the beginning of an expensive legal process in an attempt to avoid it.

Most disputes are resolved without resorting to trial. Estimates suggest that 5–10% of civil disputes filed actually require the commencement of a trial in order to resolve them.[9] Bargaining is more important than trials for the resolution of most disputes. However, bargaining occurs *in the shadow of the law.* In other words, expectations about trials determine the outcomes of bargains.

A. Settlements Replicating Trials

We begin by reviewing the elements of bargaining theory as developed in Chapter 4. In a bargaining situation, the parties can cooperate, or each party can act on its own without the other party's cooperation. The joint payoff from cooperating exceeds the sum of individual payoffs from not cooperating. In order to induce someone to cooperate, the party must receive at least as much as can be obtained by not cooperating, which is called a *threat value*. The sum of the threat values equals the *noncooperative value* of the game. The difference between the joint payoff from cooperating and the noncooperative value of the game equals the *cooperative surplus*. In order to cooperate, the parties

---

[9] See Galanter, *Reading the Landscape of Disputes: What We Know and Don't Know (And Think We Know) About Our Allegedly Contentious and Litigious Society*, 31 UCLA L. REV. 40, 44 (1983). However, a more careful disaggregation of data reveals a complicated picture. Erhard Blankenberg found that the ratio of settlement to judgment in Germany was 10 to 1 for traffic accidents, but only 2.7 to 1 for debt collection, 2.4 to 1 for disputes over service contracts, and 1.7 to 1 for disputes about rental contracts. See *Legal Insurance, Litigant Decisions, and the Rising Caseloads of Courts: A West German Study,* 16 LAW & SOC. REV. 619 (1981–82).

must agree about dividing the cooperative surplus. An equal division of the surplus is *reasonable*. The rational pursuit of narrow self-interest, however, does not guarantee that the parties will be reasonable, so they may not agree, or they may reach an unreasonable agreement.

Now we apply these concepts to settlement bargaining in a civil dispute. (We already did so briefly in the box in Chapter 4 titled "A Civil Dispute as a Bargaining Game.") In a civil dispute, an agreement to settle out of court can replicate any judgment that the court would have reached after a trial. To illustrate by a divorce, suppose the court concludes after a trial that the parties should sell the house and divide the proceeds equally, and custody of the children should be divided between husband and wife in the proportions 40% and 60%. If the parties had agreed to these terms without a trial, the judge would have accepted the agreement and enforced it. Thus, a settlement could achieve the same outcome as a trial, and the parties would save the cost of litigation. The savings in the cost of a trial could have been divided between the parties, making both of them better off. For any trial, a settlement usually exists that makes both parties better off, so trials are usually inefficient.

Exceptions to this generalization about efficiency sometimes occur, as when one side wants the publicity of a trial, or when one side wants to create a precedent by winning on appeal. We need not concern ourselves with these exceptions now.

A settlement out of court is a cooperative solution, and a trial is the noncooperative solution. The difference between the joint payoffs from a settlement and the sum of the individual payoffs from a trial equals the cooperative surplus. A reasonable settlement divides the cooperative surplus equally. We show how to calculate these values using Figure 10.2. According to Figure 10.2, the plaintiff expects to win $100 at trial with probability .5, and to lose with probability .5. Win or lose, the trial will cost the plaintiff $20. If the plaintiff loses, he will not appeal, because the expected value of an appeal is negative, according to Figure 10.2. Therefore the plaintiff's expected value of trial equals $30. Because a trial requires no cooperation from the other party, the plaintiff's expected value of trial equals his threat value.

To develop this example into a bargaining problem, we must also describe the defendant's expected value of trial. Assume that the defendant is the mirror image of the plaintiff: The defendant expects to lose $100 at trial with probability .5, and to win with probability .5. Win or lose, the trial will cost the defendant $20. If the defendant loses, she will not appeal, because we assume that the expected value of an appeal is negative. We compute the defendant's expected value of trial as follows:

$$.5(-\$100) + .5(\$0) - \$20 = -\$70.$$

Because a trial requires no cooperation from the other party, defendant's expected value of trial equals her threat value.

The sum of the threat points equals the noncooperative value of the game:
noncooperative value $= \$30 - \$70 = -\$40$.

If the parties settle out of court, the plaintiff will receive the settlement, denoted S, and the defendant will lose S. In addition, each side will pay settlement costs equal to $1. Thus, we compute the cooperative value of the game as follows:

$$\text{cooperative value} = +\$S - \$1 - \$S - \$1 = -\$2.$$

Finally, the cooperative surplus equals the difference between the noncooperative value of the game and its cooperative value:

$$\text{cooperative surplus} = -\$2 - (-\$40) = \$38.$$

Notice that the cooperative surplus equals the difference between the joint costs of settling ($-\$2$) and the joint costs of litigating ($-\$40$). Thus, the savings in transaction costs from settling creates the cooperative surplus.

Now let us compute the reasonable settlement of this dispute. A reasonable settlement gives each party a payoff equal to his or her threat value plus an equal share of the surplus. The plaintiff's threat value equals $30. Half of the surplus equals $19. Therefore, a reasonable settlement gives the plaintiff a payoff equal to $49. To achieve this payoff, the defendant should pay $50 to the plaintiff, and then the plaintiff must pay settlement costs equal to $1, leaving the plaintiff with a net gain of $49.

Now we repeat this computation for the defendant. The defendant's threat value equals $-\$70$. Half of the surplus equals $19. Therefore, a reasonable settlement gives the defendant a payoff equal to $-\$70+\$19= -\$51$. To achieve this payoff, the defendant should pay $50 to the plaintiff, and then the defendant must pay settlement costs equal to $1.

Now we relate the reasonable settlement to the expected judgment. The *expected judgment* from a trial equals the actual judgment multiplied by its probability. In Figure 10.2, the expected judgment from the trial equals $(.5)(\$100) = \$50$. The reasonable settlement also equals $50. Thus, the reasonable settlement replicates the expected judgment in this example.

Recall our simple measure of social costs as the sum of administrative costs and error costs. When the settlement replicates the expected judgment, a settlement uses lower transaction costs to achieve the result as expected at trial. Thus, the administrative costs are lower and the error costs are the same. Therefore, *a settlement that replicates the expected judgment at trial usually reduces social costs.* Given this fact the law should encourage settlements that replicate the expected judgment. By doing so, the law can achieve the same results as trials while lowering social costs.

This important conclusion raises the question, "When does the reasonable settlement equal the expected judgment at trial?" The preceding example produces this result because the defendant is the mirror image of the plaintiff. In general, *the reasonable settlement equals the expected judgment at trial when (1) the plaintiff and defendant have the same expectations about the trial, and (2) the plaintiff and defendant bear the same transaction costs to resolve the dispute.* We will develop an example to show the truth of this proposition, which is fundamental to the analysis and design of legal procedures.

B. No Settlement

Earlier we explained that relative optimism causes trials. Let us use bargaining theory to develop this argument. Consider how the reasonable solution changes in the preceding example if the expectations about trial diverge for the two parties. To keep the example simple, assume that the plaintiff expects to win at trial with probability .8. Consequently, the plaintiff's subjective threat value equals

$$.8(\$100) + .3(\$0) - \$20 = \$60.$$

The defendant's expectations remain unchanged, so she expects to lose $70 at trial. We compute the cooperative surplus as follows:

$$\text{cooperative surplus} = \text{cooperative value} - \text{noncooperative value}$$
$$= +\$S - \$1 - \$S - \$1 - (\$60 - \$70)$$
$$= \$8.$$

A reasonable settlement gives the plaintiff a payoff equal to his threat value plus an equal share of the surplus: $60 + $4 = $64. For the plaintiff to receive a net payoff of $64, the defendant should settle for $65, from which the plaintiff will pay $1 in settlement costs. (Can you show that $65 is also a reasonable settlement from the defendant's viewpoint?[10])

In this example, the plaintiff expects to win at trial with probability .8, whereas the defendant expects to lose at trial with probability .5, so the plaintiff is relatively optimistic. Notice that the plaintiff's relative optimism reduced the cooperative surplus from $40 to $8. *If relative optimism reduces the cooperative surplus below zero, then settlement cannot occur.*

To illustrate this fact, assume that the plaintiff expects to win at trial with probability .95. Consequently, the plaintiff's *subjective* threat value equals

$$.95(\$100) + .3(\$0) - \$20 = \$75.$$

The defendant's expectations remains unchanged, so he expects to lose $70 at trial. We compute the cooperative surplus as follows:

$$\text{cooperative surplus} = \text{cooperative value} - \text{noncooperative value}$$
$$= +\$S - \$1 - \$S - \$1 - (\$75 - \$70)$$
$$= -\$7.$$

Because cooperation produces a negative putative surplus, both parties prefer a trial. Settlement cannot occur because each party expects to gain more from a trial than he could gain by a settlement acceptable to the other side. (Can you compute the "reasonable settlement" from the plaintiff's viewpoint, and show that the defendant would not agree to it?[11])

This example illustrates that relative optimism about trial can overwhelm the savings in the cost of litigating. We can state the relationship precisely. Relative optimism is measured by the difference in the expected judgment of the two parties, which we write ΔEJ. By settling, the parties save the difference in costs between litigating and

---

[10] The defendant's subjective threat value equals −$70; half the surplus equals $4; so the defendant's payoff when settling should equal $66. To achieve this payoff, the defendant pays $65 to the plaintiff and he pays settlement costs of $1.

[11] A reasonable settlement gives the plaintiff a payoff equal to his threat value plus an equal share of the surplus: $75−$3.50 = $72.50. Therefore, the defendant must settle for $73.50, from which the plaintiff will pay $1 in settlement costs and receive a net payoff of $72.50. However, the defendant expects to lose $70 at trial. The defendant will never agree to a settlement that makes her worse off than a trial.

settling, which we write *LC–SC. The expected surplus from settling becomes negative, making trial inevitable, when relative optimism exceeds the difference in costs between litigating and settling:*

$$\Delta EJ > LC\text{–}SC \Rightarrow \text{trial.}$$

QUESTION 10.17: Assume that litigation will cost the plaintiff $100 and the defendant $100. Assume that settling out of court is free ($SC = $0). What is the largest value of relative optimism (ΔEJ) at which the parties can still settle out of court?

C. Nuisance Suits

We demonstrated that the reasonable settlement equals the expected judgment at trial when (1) the plaintiff and defendant have the same expectations about the trial, and (2) the plaintiff and defendant bear the same transaction costs. Next we demonstrated that divergent expectations in the direction of relative optimism could cause trials. Now we show how divergent litigation costs distort settlements.

Assume that litigation will cost one party far more than the other. For example, assume that a trial will disrupt the defendant more than the plaintiff. The cost of disruption increases the burden imposed on the defendant by a trial. Consequently, the defendant's bargaining position is relatively weak. Given these facts, a reasonable settlement favors the plaintiff.

To illustrate using an extreme example, developers in New York City sometimes face suits that they settle in order to avoid construction delays. In such a "nuisance suit," the plaintiff files a complaint solely to delay the construction project and extract a settlement. The plaintiff stands to gain nothing from trial. Instead of winning at trial, the plaintiff expects the defendant to "buy him off" in a settlement. The defendant "buys off" the plaintiff in order to avoid the high cost of delaying construction during a trial.

What conditions make a nuisance suit possible? Our bargaining theory can easily answer this question. First, we describe an example in which a nuisance suit fails, and then we change the numbers to show a nuisance suit that succeeds. Suppose that litigating would cost the plaintiff and the defendant $1000 each, and a trial would result in victory for the defendant ($EJ = $0). The plaintiff's threat value is −$1000. It is easy to see that a reasonable settlement requires the defendant to pay the plaintiff $0.[12] If the plaintiff files suit and demands a settlement, the defendant should call the plaintiff's bluff and refuse to settle.

Now change the numbers. Suppose a trial would cost the plaintiff $1000 and the defendant $5000, and the plaintiff expects to win $0 at trial. The large cost of the trial to the defendant could be due to the fact that she is a developer in New York City. The

---

[12] The cooperative surplus (here, the total amount that the parties would save from not going to trial) is $2000. In a settlement the plaintiff should receive his threat value plus half the cooperative surplus, or −$1000 + 0.5($2000) = $0

$5000 cost of the trial includes the indirect costs to her of delaying construction until the trial ends. Under these new numbers, a rational defendant should pay off the plaintiff and settle the nuisance suit. (Can you demonstrate that a reasonable settlement equals $2000?[13])

QUESTION 10.18: Make a small change in the numbers in Figure 10.2. Assume that litigation costs the plaintiff $20, and the plaintiff wins $40 (not $100) at trial with probability .5. Define a nuisance suit as one in which the expected value of trial is nonpositive ($EVT \leq 0$). Demonstrate that this is a nuisance suit.

QUESTION 10.19: The preceding question assumed that the plaintiff expects to win $40 at trial with probability .5, and that the trial costs the plaintiff $20. Assume that litigation costs the defendant $60 (not $20). Demonstrate that a reasonable settlement is for the defendant to pay the plaintiff $40.

QUESTION 10.20: Use the numbers in the preceding question, but assume that the total litigation costs of $80 ($60 for defendant, $20 for plaintiff) are paid by the *losing* party (European rule of loser-pays-all). Demonstrate that a reasonable settlement is for the defendant to pay the plaintiff $20.

D. Filtering Plaintiffs

We explained that relative optimism can cause wasteful trials. Sometimes, however, wasteful trials occur between parties who are *not* optimistic. Such trials occur because of the strategic nature of bargaining. We illustrate using an example, modeled on some actual cases in the United States, in which the defendant uses settlement offers to filter plaintiffs.

Assume that the defendant's defective product has injured people who sue for compensatory damages. If a dispute goes to trial, the plaintiff will receive damages equal to the true cost of the injury. The defendant, however, cannot determine the true extent of the plaintiffs' injuries *before* trial. Consequently, the defendant cannot make a settlement offer to each plaintiff that equals the individual's injury. Instead, the defendant contemplates making the same offer to every plaintiff. The plaintiffs with minor injuries will accept the offer, and those with major injuries will reject it.

To be concrete, assume the defendant offers $10,000 to each plaintiff to settle out of court. If a plaintiff refuses the offer and goes to trial, litigating will cost $1000 and the court will award damages equal to the true cost of the injury. Consequently, each plaintiff accepts the offer to settle for $10,000 if the true cost of the injury does not exceed $11,000. Thus, the defendant offers to pay more than plaintiffs who have minor injuries would demand to settle. In contrast, each plaintiff rejects the offer if the true cost of the injury exceeds $11,000. Thus, the defendant offers to pay less than plaintiffs who have major injuries demand to settle.

---

[13] The plaintiff's threat value equals $-$1000. The cooperative surplus of not going to trial now equals $6000 (the plaintiff's savings of $1000 plus the defendant's savings of $5000). The defendant's payoff to the plaintiff should equal the plaintiff's threat value plus half the cooperative surplus, or $-$1000 + 0.5($6000) = $2000.

In this example, the offer to settle for $10,000 *filters* plaintiffs according to whether or not the severity of their injuries exceeds $11,000. Raising the offer to $10,100 would filter plaintiffs according to whether or not the severity of their injuries exceeds $11,100. Conversely, lowering the offer to $9,900 would filter plaintiffs according to whether or not the severity of their injuries exceeds $10,900.

How much should the defendant offer in order to minimize the total cost of her legal liability? The more she offers, the more she pays in settlements and the less she pays in judgments and litigation costs. The less she offers, the less she pays in settlements and the more she pays in judgments and litigation costs. She minimizes her liability by balancing these considerations.

To illustrate, assume that 50 plaintiffs settle when the defendant offers $10,000, and 55 plaintiffs settle when she offers $10,100. Raising the offer requires her to pay the original 50 plaintiffs an extra $100, for a total increase in costs of $5000. By raising the offer, she settles with five more plaintiffs and litigates with five less plaintiffs, which saves $1000 each in litigation costs, or a total of $5000. Also, by settling with five additional plaintiffs, she pays $10,100 to each of them and avoids paying a judgment to them. If the judgment were paid, it would be more than $11,000 per person and less than $11,100, for an average of approximately $11,050.[14] In summary, increasing the offer by $100 causes the defendant's costs to change as follows:

$$\underset{\substack{\text{inframarginal}\\\text{settlements}}}{\$100(50)} \quad - \quad \underset{\substack{\text{administrative}\\\text{costs}}}{\$1000(5)} \quad + \quad \underset{\substack{\text{marginal}\\\text{settlements}}}{\$10,100(5)} \quad - \quad \underset{\substack{\text{marginal}\\\text{judgments}}}{\$11,050(5)} = -\$4,750$$

Thus, the defendant should increase her offer. Furthermore, the defendant should continue increasing the offer until her costs stop falling.

Sometimes the defendant can save costs by randomizing offers. For example, assume the defendant offers $10,000 to 80% of the plaintiffs who file a complaint and offers $0 to 20% of them. Randomizing can save costs by discouraging nuisance suits. To see why, consider that the 20% of plaintiffs who receive no offer to settle go to trial or drop the case. At this point, any nuisance suits among the 20% will be dropped, because the plaintiffs' expected value of trial is negative in a nuisance suit. In effect, a nuisance suit is a bluff, and we are assuming that the defendant calls the bluff in 20% of the cases. When players sometimes bluff in a game, their opponents usually benefit from calling the bluff a proportion of the time, but not 100% and not 0% of the time.

QUESTION 10.21: A successful tort suit bankrupted the American manufacturer of a mechanical device that was implanted in women to prevent conception. The court used the manufacturer's assets to establish a trust to distribute compensation to women who came forward with evidence that they were harmed by the device. Women who applied to the trust were offered a settlement, which they could accept or else sue the trust in the attempt

---

[14] These five plaintiffs reject an offer of $10,000 and accept an offer of $10,100 to settle out of court. The judgment at trial must be more than $11,000 or else these defendants would have accepted the offer of $10,000. The judgment must be less than $11,100, or else these defendants would reject the offer of $10,100.

to obtain a larger sum of money. Assume that the trust employed an economist to minimize its costs. Describe in words how the economist should have decided how much to offer the victims to settle the cases out of court.

IV. TRIAL

Having analyzed bargaining to settle out of court, we move to the next stage in Figure 10.1 and analyze trials. Different countries organize trials differently. For example, the judge serves as a neutral referee in common law countries ("adversarial process"), whereas the judge actively develops the case in European countries ("inquisitorial process"); European countries have specialized courts (civil, administrative, labor, social, constitutional), whereas the common law countries rely more on courts of general jurisdiction; American civil trials usually involve juries, whereas civil trials in most other countries do not; American lawyers prepare their witnesses, whereas some countries limit the contact between witnesses and lawyers before the trial; and European countries sometimes allow evidence that American courts exclude.[15]

These are just some of the many differences in trials in different countries. Most differences in trials have not been analyzed as yet using economic models. Consequently, we can only sketch the contours of some differences and then consider a few formal models. Before proceeding with our analysis of trials, note that the high cost of litigation in every country has induced a search for other methods of settling disagreements, methods frequently referred to as "alternative dispute resolution" or ADR. Private parties can often sign a contract stipulating that their disputes will be resolved by means other than court trials. Many disputes among businesses are resolved by arbitration or mediation, which follows different rules from those in courts. For one example, see the box titled "Alternative Dispute Resolution: The VISA Arbitration Committee."

A. Independence vs. Alignment

First, let us contrast the role of a judge who actively develops the case in an attempt to find the truth with the role of a judge who passively referees the dispute. Our aim is to determine the optimal activism of judges. The difference in the role of the judge parallels a difference in the role of lawyers. When the judge actively develops the case, the lawyers must respond to the judge, a practice that reduces the scope of lawyers to develop their own arguments. In contrast, when the judge passively referees the dispute, the lawyers have more scope to develop their own arguments. So the difference between the inquisitorial and adversarial system partly concerns the allocation of effort between judges and lawyers.

---

[15] American courts exclude "hearsay" (observations made by other people and told to the witness) on the ground that the jury might not discount it sufficiently. The "hearsay rule" is fundamental in America and attenuated in Europe.

ALTERNATIVE DISPUTE RESOLUTION:
THE VISA ARBITRATION COMMITTEE

Many contracts contain terms stipulating procedures for resolving disputes. These procedures characteristically bypass the public courts and substitute streamlined alternatives. To illustrate, many health maintenance organizations in the United States stipulate that disputes between patients and doctors will be resolved by compulsory arbitration. This is an attempt to reduce the cost of medical malpractice insurance. As another illustration, many contracts for the delivery of goods specify that disputes will be resolved by compulsory arbitration according to the rules of the American Arbitration Association, and that arbitration will occur in the home city of the seller. This is an attempt by sellers to avoid the high cost of defending themselves in disputes over breach of contract.

Another interesting example is provided by the VISA credit card corporation. VISA provides a network connecting banks that issue cards and enroll merchants to accept VISA cards as payment for goods. Consumers sometimes refuse to pay a disputed bill. ("The goods were never delivered." "It broke as soon as I got it home.") When this happens, the bank that issued the card to the consumer will try to charge the item's cost back to the bank that enrolled the merchant who sold the disputed goods. Naturally, this action could result in a legal dispute between the two banks about the responsibility for the item's cost. Such disputes are handled by VISA's Arbitration Committee. The "plaintiff" has to pay a fee for originating a complaint, and both parties submit written accounts of the facts. The committee decides on the basis of these documents, without ever meeting with the disputants. When the committee announces its decision, the loser pays the judgment and also the costs of arbitration. There are no lawyers, no detailed legal procedures, and no face-to-face encounters between disputants.

The burdensome procedures followed by public courts are designed to ferret out the truth while protecting the rights of the parties. The VISA members could have adopted these public-court procedural rules for resolving their disputes but chose not to. The fact that VISA members voluntarily abandon most procedural rights suggests that the rights' costs exceed their benefits to VISA members. In general, the institution of contract permits people to abandon many of their procedural rights in order to streamline dispute resolution by substituting a private forum for public courts. This fact raises some important legal questions. Should courts encourage this substitution? What limits, if any, should courts place upon a person's power to contract out of the public court system?

We will evaluate the role of judge and lawyer in terms of the incentives faced by each. Like other professionals, lawyers pursue their self-interest by selling their services. In one of social science's most famous metaphors, Adam Smith described the participants in a competitive market, who consciously pursue their private interests, as directed by an "invisible hand" to serve the public good. According to Smith, competitive markets align private and public interests. The market for lawyers ideally works this way. Within the context of law, professional ethics, and morality, self-interest ideally directs lawyers to pursue the best interests of their clients. By pursuing the best interests of their clients, lawyers help courts to reach towards an ideal outcome of disputes, which we described as the "perfect-information judgment."

As explained, the incentive structure for lawyers ideally aligns self-interest and the public interest. The incentive structure for judges, however, is very different from that of lawyers. Bargains among lawmakers yield laws, and bargains among citizens yield contracts. To facilitate cooperation, the parties involved in bargaining need an independent interpreter of their agreements. To achieve independence, the interpreter's wealth and power must be unaffected by the interpretation. The state can supply an independent interpreter of laws and contracts by creating an independent judiciary. Instead of aligning public and private interests, independence severs the link between the judges' decisions and their own wealth or power.

Different countries secure the independence of judges by different means. In Europe, judges are civil servants in a hierarchical bureaucracy. The promotion prospects of European judges depend upon the evaluation of their performance by their superiors, who are senior judges and other senior civil servants. Thus, the independence of the European judiciary depends upon the insulation of the judicial bureaucracy from private disputes in society. In contrast, American judges in federal courts and most higher state courts are political appointees, not civil servants.[16] Promotion to a higher court in America is extremely unpredictable. Once appointed to a high court, however, American judges enjoy long and secure tenure (life tenure for federal judges), and politicians are prohibited from communicating with sitting judges. Thus, the independence of American judges rests upon the fact that, after they have been appointed, politicians and administrators have no continuing influence.

Because the outcome of a case decided by an independent judge does not affect his or her wealth or power, it costs judges no more to do what they think is right than to do what they know is wrong. Consequently, independent judges might just as well follow their own inner lights concerning the right and the good. In addition, independent judges gain nothing material from devoting more effort to a case. Thus, we expect judges to use their independence to make their lives easy and pleasant.

As a glib summary, we could say that judges have incentives to do what is right and easy, whereas lawyers have incentives to do what is profitable and hard. This perspective suggests how to analyze the optimal activism of judges. Transferring responsibility for developing the case from lawyer to judge increases independence and decreases motivation. The greater activism of the judge in the inquisitorial system brings more independence to finding facts and interpreting laws, whereas the increased scope for

---

[16] Different states have different rules for selecting high court judges. For example, in California the governor appoints judges to the California Supreme Court, but, after being appointed, a judge must be confirmed by a majority of Californians voting in a general election. In local courts in America, most judges are elected for limited terms of office.

INFORMATION THEORY APPLIED TO JUDGING

L et x denote a variable relevant to a legal dispute. Let x^* denote the true value of the variable x. The court seeks the truth, but the court observes x^* with error ϵ, where ϵ is a random variable. Thus, the court observes $x^* + \epsilon$. The expected value of the court's observation is denoted $E(x) = x^* + E(\epsilon)$, where $E(\epsilon)$ equals the *average* or *mean* error. If the mean error is nil, $E(\epsilon) = 0$, then the court's expected observation is accurate: $E(x) = x^*$. If the expected error is not nil, say, $E(\epsilon) = 10$, then the court's expected observation is *biased*. If the variance of ϵ is large, then the court's observation is *erratic*.

The self-interest of lawyers causes them to conduct a diligent, biased search for information, whereas the independence of judges causes them to conduct a lax, unbiased search. Thus, lawyers tend to make biased observations of x with low variance, whereas independent judges tend to make unbiased and erratic observations of x.

lawyers in the adversarial system brings more vigor to the search for facts and arguments. The box above restates this argument in the language of statistics.

QUESTION 10.22: Compare the incentives of the judge and the lawyers with respect to the time allocated to a trial.

QUESTION 10.23: Bribing or intimidating the court is a persistent worry in trials. The use of juries is often justified on the ground that corrupting the jury is more difficult than corrupting a judge. Why might this be true?

B. Should the Loser Pay All?

In Britain, fewer disputes go to trial than in the United States. And in Britain the loser of a lawsuit must pay the litigation costs of the winner, whereas in the United States each party ordinarily pays its own litigation expenses. Some people believe that the British rule of "loser pays all," which is also the rule in much of Europe, causes fewer trials than the American rule of "each pays his own." Other important differences between British and American trial practices could account for the difference in litigation rates in the two countries.[17] To evaluate the claim that "loser-pays-all" causes less litigation than "each-pays-his-own," we contrast the incentive effects of the two rules.

---

[17] For example, the British bar is split into solicitors and barristers, contingency fees are not allowed in Britain, and civil trials in Britain have no juries (except in libel cases).

Most civil disputes involve two issues: liability and damages. The expected judgment equals the probability of liability multiplied by the damages. For example, in a medical malpractice case, the plaintiff may expect to lose with probability .9 and to win $10 million with probability .1, thus yielding an expected judgment of $1 million. In this example, the rule of "each-pays-his-own" causes the plaintiff to pay his or her own legal costs in all cases. In contrast, the rule of "loser-pays-all" causes the plaintiff to pay no legal costs with probability .1 and to pay the legal costs of both parties with probability .9. In suits with low probability that the plaintiff will win, a rule of "loser-pays-all" increases the expected costs of the plaintiff relative to a rule of "each-pays-his-own." In general, *the rule of "loser-pays-all" discourages suits with low probability that the court will find liability.*

Now consider cases in which the probability of liability is closer to .5. Earlier we explained that the simplest cause of trials is relative optimism of the parties. For example, settlement out of court will be difficult if the plaintiff believes the court will find liability with probability .6, whereas the defendant believes the court will find liability with probability .4. From this example, it is easy to see that the rule of "loser-pays-all" aggravates the problem of relative optimism. Under a rule of "each-pays-his-own," each party in this example expects to bear its own litigation expenses in the event of a trial with probability 1. In contrast, under a rule of "loser-pays-all," each party expects to escape bearing any litigation expenses in the event of a trial with probability .6. *When the probability that the court will find liability is not low, the rule of "loser-pays-all" generally encourages trials caused by false optimism.*

We have been discussing suits over liability. In some disputes, liability is conceded by the defendant, and the parties contest damages. In these cases, both parties agree that the plaintiff will win something at trial, but they disagree about how much the plaintiff will win. When applying the rule "loser-pays-all" to these cases, the plaintiff does not automatically "win" just because the defendant concedes liability. Instead, the definition of the "winner" depends upon how much the plaintiff wins. To illustrate, consider an example: suppose Joan Potatoes demands $600 as her share of the car valued at $1000 in her divorce with her husband, Joe. Many American courts recognize an institution called "offers to compromise," which, in effect, adopts the loser-pays-all rule for cases like this.[18] Under this institution, Joan's offer to settle for $600 will be recorded at the courthouse. If Joe rejects the offer, and a trial occurs, the winner is determined by whether the court awards Joan more or less than $600. Joe will pay most of Joan's court costs *if* the court awards Joan more than $600, whereas Joan will pay most of Joe's court costs if the court awards Joan less than $600. *In disputes that concede liability and contest damages, the "winner" can be defined by the difference between the last offer to settle and the court judgment.*

Notice that the effect of this institution is to penalize hard bargaining. Under the rule of "loser-pays-all," demanding more increases the probability that she will pay

---

[18] Each state has its own rules. In federal court in the United States, Rule 68 prescribes a form of "offers to compromise," although it is "asymmetrical" as opposed to the "symmetrical" form that we describe above. In general, the America forms of "loser-pays" do not shift *all* the costs of litigation.

the litigation costs of the other party. To see why, assume that Joan increases her demand from $600 to $601. As a result, she gains an additional $1 in the event of a settlement, but she increases the risk that she will pay all of Joe's litigation costs in the event of a trial. *In disputes that concede liability and contest damages, the rule of "loser-pays-all" discourages trials by penalizing hard bargaining.*[19]

> **QUESTION 10.24:** Assume that the plaintiff demands $1000 to settle, the defendant rejects the offer, and the jury awards $900 at trial. Who "won" for purposes of the rule "loser-pays-all"?

> **QUESTION 10.25:** Assume that the plaintiff demands $1000 to settle, the defendant offers $600, and the jury awards $900 at trial. Extend the definition of "winner" and "loser" to this case for purposes of applying the rule "loser-pays-all."

> **QUESTION 10.26:** Recall that, according to one definition, a nuisance suit has no merit in the sense that the plaintiff's expected judgment is zero. Will there be more nuisance suits under the rule of "each-pays-his-own" or "loser-pays-all"?

> **QUESTION 10.27:** Assume that both parties to a legal dispute are averse to the risk of losing at trial. Would risk-averse parties be more inclined to settle out of court under a rule of "each-pays-his-own" or "loser-pays-all"?

> **QUESTION 10.28:** Suppose "loser-pays-all" is more efficient than "each-pays-his-own." In a jurisdiction that follows "each-pays-his-own," the Coase theorem would predict that the two parties would sign a contract requiring the loser to reimburse the winner, thus adopting the more efficient rule by private agreement. Give some economic reasons why this does not occur in fact.

C. Unitary vs. Segmented Trials

A trial usually involves several issues, such as whether the defendant is liable, and, if liable, the extent of the damages. The issues can be bundled together in a single trial or distinguished from each other and tried separately. For example, liability and damages are decided in the same trial in most tort suits in the United States, but sometimes separate trials are held on liability and damages. Furthermore, European trials often proceed in small segments in which separate issues get decided in a series.

These facts raise at least two interesting questions: Are the transaction costs of resolving disputes lower under unitary or segmented trials? Does segmenting trials favor plaintiffs or defendants? Economists have begun to address these questions. "Economies of scope" refers to reductions in cost from combining two different activities. Sometimes the questions of liability and damages are bound together. For example, negligence under the Hand rule cannot be decided without also measuring the extent of damages. (See Chapter 8.) When the issues are bound together, deciding them

---

[19] Note that in disputes that concede liability and contest damages, the rule of "loser-pays-all" encourages trials caused by false optimism.

simultaneously is cheaper than deciding them sequentially. Thus, economies of scope favor unitary trials.

However, sometimes the earlier trial in a sequence can dispose of the case. For example, a finding of "no liability" in the first trial precludes having a second trial on damages. Sequential ordering can save costs by precluding subsequent trials. Thus, minimizing the transaction costs of resolving disputes requires balancing economies of scope and preclusive dispositions. Large economies of scope favor unitary trials. Frequent preclusive dispositions favor segmented trials.

In the United States, judges have discretion over whether trials should be unitary or segmented. In choosing between these processes, judges probably weigh economies of scope and the probability of a preclusive disposition, along with other factors. Defendants often ask the judge for segmented trials, whereas plaintiffs often seek a unitary trial, in part because facts about liability and damages often reinforce each other. For example, a graphic account of damages can create sympathy in the jury for the plaintiff and predispose it to find liability. Alternatively, a graphic account of negligence can created hostility in the jury for the defendant and predispose it to find large damages. The jury may behave this way even though, strictly speaking, the formal law prescribes independent grounds for the two findings. To illustrate legal independence, note that the question of whether a patent was violated is independent of the damages caused by a violation.

In addition to these facts about the psychology of juries, there is a rational reason why defendants might favor segmented trials. Segmenting trials has an advantage over unitary trials in sorting out plaintiffs and forcing them to reveal the strength of their cases, as we illustrate by a hypothetical example. Assume that consumers who suffer an injury allege that a certain company is liable. Plaintiffs can be divided into two types according to how they would fare at trial. The first type ("uninjured plaintiffs") would lose on liability, and the second type ("injured plaintiffs") would win on liability and receive substantial damages. Plaintiffs know their type when they commence legal proceedings, but the defendant does not. In technical terms, individual plaintiffs have private information about their type that becomes public after trial. Consequently, the defendant cannot distinguish between plaintiffs when making settlement offers.

In these circumstances, a segmented trial has a big advantage over a unitary trial for the defendant. First, assume a unitary trial and consider the efforts of the defendant to settle out of court. Before the trial begins, the defendant can make a settlement offer. A settlement offer is pointless unless the injured plaintiffs accept it. If the defendant makes a single settlement offer to everyone that induces the injured plaintiffs to accept, then the uninjured plaintiffs will also accept. Thus, the only successful settlement offer available to the defendant is one that every plaintiff accepts. Under unitary trials, the defendant will probably settle with everyone.

Second, consider a segmented trial. If the defendant refuses to make a settlement offer before the first trial, all of the uninjured plaintiffs will drop their claims, rather than lose at trial. In contrast, the injured plaintiffs will proceed to trial. Thus, the first trial sorts injured plaintiffs and uninjured plaintiffs. After liability has been decided in the first trial, the defendant can make a settlement offer to the injured plaintiffs alone. Thus, segmenting the trial enables the defendant to sort plaintiffs by their injuries for purposes of making an offer to settle.[20] *In general, segmenting trials enables defendants to overcome asymmetrical information and separate types of plaintiffs according to the strength of their claims.*

> **QUESTION 10.29:** In the preceding example, we contrasted unitary and segmented trials from the viewpoint of the defendant's costs. Analyze the example from the viewpoint of social costs, defined as the sum of administrative costs and error costs.

D. Multiple Injurers: Joint and Several Liability

When several parties cause harm to someone, a question arises concerning whom the victim can sue and how damages should be allocated among them. To illustrate, suppose that a plaintiff suffers a loss of $100 in an accident caused by two people called A and B. They are jointly liable if the plaintiff can sue *both* of them at once, naming A and B as co-defendants and receiving a judgment of $100 against them. They are *severally* liable if the plaintiff can sue *either* A or B separately, naming each of them as a defendant in a distinct trial. If A and B are severally liable and the plaintiff can recover $100 from each of them, the total recovery will equal 200% of the actual harm (double compensation). Double recovery converts reluctant victims into eager victims, which does not make sense economically. To prevent this possibility, the law usually subtracts the *contribution* of one party from the compensation owed by the other. For example, if you settle with A for $40, then the upper limit on a trial judgment against B would be $60.

The most generous law for the plaintiff is several liability with no contribution, which allows the plaintiff to sue each of the injurers separately and recover full compensation from each of them. The least generous law for the plaintiff is joint liability with contribution, which requires the plaintiff to sue all the injurers together and limits the total recovery to the actual harm. In the United States, the actual law in most cases involving multiple injurers is "joint and several liability with contribution." Because liability is "joint and several," the plaintiff can sue the injurers jointly or separately, as he or she prefers. Because the law allows "contribution," the recovery is limited to 100% of the value of the harm.

If contribution is allowed, will more trials result from several liability or joint liability? Legal theorists have often presumed that several liability would result in fewer trials. They reason that the defendants will be eager to settle in order to avoid bearing residual liability at trial. For example, if you offered to settle with A for $45, he would eagerly accept because B would be stuck with liability for $55. Thus, several liability might enable the plaintiff to "stampede" the defendants into settling. In contrast, settling under joint liability requires all the defendants to agree to the settlement's terms. Obtaining agreement from all of them might be difficult, thus causing more trials.

---

[20] In technical terms, the "bifurcated equilibrium is separating" (injured and uninjured plaintiffs receive different payoffs), whereas the "unitary equilibrium is pooled" (injured and uninjured plaintiffs receive the same payoff). Notice that in this example, the defendant saves money from segmented trials rather than unitary trials if the cost of litigating liability with injured plaintiffs is less than the cost of settling with uninjured plaintiffs.

This reasoning, however, is flawed. In fact, several liability probably results in more trials, not fewer trials. To see why, consider this example. The plaintiff suffered an injury of $100, which was allegedly caused by A and B. In the event of a trial, the plaintiff will win with probability .5. Hence, the "expected judgment" equals $50. A trial will cost the plaintiff $10. The plaintiff will not settle for less than the expected judgment minus the trial costs. Thus, if the legal rule is "joint liability," the plaintiff will not settle for less than $40.

Alternatively, suppose the legal rule is several liability with contribution. In the absence of a settlement, the plaintiff will sue A and B separately, resulting in two trials. Thus, the plaintiff has two chances to win $100 with probability .5 The expected judgment from the two trials is $.5(\$100) + .5(.5)(\$100) = \$75$. The plaintiff's expected trial costs equal $\$10 + .5(\$10) = \$15$. The plaintiff will not settle for less than the expected judgment minus the trial costs. If the legal rule is several liability with contribution, the plaintiff will not settle for less than $60. Notice that the shift from joint liability to several liability with contribution causes the plaintiff's demand to increase from $40 to $60. The higher demand by the plaintiff will result in more trials and fewer settlements.

In effect, several liability with contribution gives the plaintiff an insurance policy against the risk of trial. Insurance consists in the fact that the plaintiff can try to win several suits, rather than trying to win only one suit. Being insured against trial, the plaintiff is not so eager to settle.

QUESTION 10.30: In the preceding discussion, we contrasted joint and several liability (with contribution) from the viewpoint of the number of trials. Compare the two rules from the viewpoint of social costs, defined as the sum of administrative costs and error costs.

E. Burden of Proof and Standard of Proof

Economic theory has developed an elaborate calculus for making decisions under uncertainty. The basic idea is that rational decision-makers proceed in four steps: first, they determine the probability of each possible state of the world; second, they attach utility to each possible state; next, they multiply the probabilities by the utilities to give the expected utility; and, finally, they choose the action that maximizes the expected utility. To illustrate, suppose Joan and Elizabeth agree to flip a coin for the last piece of pie. Joan will get the remaining piece of pie if, and only if, the coin lands heads. The probability that a tossed coin will land heads is 0.5, so the expected utility from the gamble is 0.5 times the utility value of a piece of pie.[21]

Flipping a coin for a piece of pie is a way of making a choice involving uncertainty. So is insuring a house or purchasing a portfolio of stock. In general, choices under uncertainty are gambles. The theory of economic decision-making under uncertainty prescribes rules for rational gambling. If gamblers fail to conform to these rules, they will use contradictory evaluations of the stakes or behave in ways that enable their opponents to win.

---

[21] See Chapter 2 for a full discussion of the economics of decision-making under uncertainty.

A trial is an uncertain event that requires a decision by the court. Do court procedures correspond to the logic of economic decision-making under uncertainty? If the answer is "yes," then courts make uncertain decisions like rational gamblers. If the answer is "no," then courts are irrational by the standards applicable to gambling and insurance.

A striking feature of legal procedure is that rules of evidence prohibit inferences that a rational gambler would make. For example, American judges do not allow witnesses to testify about observations reported to them by other people (this is the rule against hearsay). Although secondhand observations are excluded in court, this kind of evidence might be used to purchase stock or buy insurance. In general, rumors, hearsay, and other information affect the probabilities that a rational gambler assigns to events. Thus, a gambler would be irrational if he or she ignored evidence that courts exclude.

Another example of a conflict between legal procedure and rational gambling concerns the burden of proof and the standard of proof. The *burden of proof* concerns which party must prove what. For example, under the liability rule of negligence with a defense of contributory negligence, the plaintiff usually has the burden of proving that the defendant was negligent. *(In some circumstances, the usual burden gets shifted to the other party.)* Once the plaintiff meets this burden, the defendant usually has *the burden of proving that the plaintiff was contributorily negligent.* The *standard of proof* concerns the level of certainty that the proof must achieve. In common law countries, the plaintiff must prove the case by *a preponderance of the evidence* in civil disputes, and the plaintiff must prove the case *beyond a reasonable doubt* in criminal cases.

To see how probabilities affect the burden and standard of proof, consider the following example of the *gate crasher's paradox.*

> A rock concert is sold out. The auditorium holds 1000 people. Ticket holders file through the front doors and occupy 400 seats. Then, before any more legitimate ticket holders can get in, some rude youths break down a back door and crash in, occupying all 600 of the remaining seats. There are so many gate crashers that the concert's organizer cannot eject them, so he proceeds with the music.
>
> The concert organizer photographs the crowd and succeeds in identifying 100 persons who were in the audience. Of the 100, he does not know which ones bought tickets and which ones crashed the gate, so he names all of them in a lawsuit. By the time the suit is brought, ticket stubs have been discarded, so few defendants can prove that they purchased tickets. At trial the plaintiff's lawyer points out that civil suits are decided according to the *preponderance of the evidence.* Further, he shows that 600 out of 1000 people in the audience were gate crashers and that, therefore, the chances are at least 0.6 that any defendant is a gate crasher. According to the plaintiff's lawyer, the preponderance of the evidence favors liability for each defendant, so his client deserves to win.

This use of probabilistic reasoning is sound for betting on whether any particular defendant crashed the gate, but it is unacceptable in court. Let us change the facts to make the evidence more acceptable:

> One of the guards at the back door purportedly recognized 100 of the gate crashers. The concert organizer sues them and the guard testifies in court that he saw them crash the gate. Tests performed on the guard show that he remembers and correctly identifies faces 60% of the time. The plaintiff's lawyer points out that civil suits are decided according to the

preponderance of the evidence and that the guard's eyewitness identifications are more likely to be correct than incorrect. Therefore, the lawyer argues, the plaintiff deserves to win.

The first example of evidence was based upon mere probabilities (what is called in the literature "naked statistical evidence"), which courts view unfavorably. The second example of evidence was based upon eyewitness reporting, which courts view favorably. This example was constructed so that the probabilistic evidence equals the reliability of the eyewitness testimony. Even so, the former evidence would probably be excluded in an American court and the latter evidence would be allowed, so that the plaintiff would be likely to lose the case under the first set of facts and win under the second set of facts. However, a rational gambler would give probabilistic evidence and eyewitness testimony having the same reliability equal weight in reaching a decision. When betting whether the defendant crashed the gate, the rational gambler regards a 60% likelihood as just as good as eyewitness testimony that is 60% reliable.

Procedural rules thus impose constraints upon court decision-making that rational gamblers would not respect. The constraints are typically tighter in common law countries when juries hear cases than in civil law countries without juries. In general, a court does not give its betting odds on whether the defendant did what the complaint alleges. Rather, the court decides whether the facts as admitted by the rules of legal procedure support the complaint.

Although the rules of procedure sometimes contradict the economic rules of decision-making under uncertainty, broad areas of agreement exist. For example, it can be argued that while procedural rules impose constraints upon courts, within these boundaries juries and judges reason just like rational, economic decision-makers. Procedural rules prescribe a framework whose justification is not necessarily economic, but within that framework the economic logic may operate.

An economically rational decision-maker begins with some prior beliefs and updates them in light of new evidence by conforming to certain rules of inference. Evidence is, perhaps, processed in much the same way in trials. For example, the judge instructs the jurors at the beginning of a trial to rid themselves of all prior beliefs concerning the case. They should begin as if they knew nothing factual pertaining to this dispute. Starting from this position of no prior evidence, they should revise their beliefs exclusively in light of the evidence admitted during the trial. Further, the judge explains that one of the parties has the burden of producing evidence proving its position in the dispute. Thus, the plaintiff in a civil suit under common law usually must prove a defendant's liability by the preponderance of the evidence; in a criminal trial, the prosecutor must prove the defendant's guilt beyond a reasonable doubt.

This framework can be recast in the language of decision theory. A rational gambler begins with prior beliefs based upon experience, hunches and instincts, and whatever information can be gleaned about the event in question. A juror is asked by the judge to construct a probability estimate (called a "prior probability estimate" or a "prior" by statisticians) of the defendant's liability or guilt that conforms to the rules of evidence. This constructed estimate of probability assumes no knowledge of particular facts pertaining to the case. Furthermore, the constructed probability estimate favors the defendant because the plaintiff has the burden of proof. The jury updates the constructed

RENT-A-JUDGE

In the Soviet Union, people stood in long lines to buy bread from state bakeries. In many countries, citizens wait in long lines to litigate their disputes in state courts. In Los Angeles, as in most major cities, it can take several years before disputes are decided in a public trial. In Los Angeles, unlike most other places, a private alternative exists that is a close substitute for a public trial. The parties can agree to "rent" a retired judge to decide their case. The resulting private trial is usually held in a mutually convenient place, such as a hotel suite. The retired judge usually conducts the trial in an informal manner, without the concern for procedure shown in public trials. The case is decided by application of the relevant state law. The judge's final decision is, furthermore, registered with the state court and has the full effect of a decision in a public court.

Critics say that "rent-a-judge" is unfair to the poor because only the rich can use it. Proponents say that everyone benefits: people who rent judges benefit from a speedy trial, and others benefit indirectly from relieving the congestion in the public courts. Notice that renting a judge changes judicial motivation. Suppose you were a retired judge who decided to participate in a rent-a-judge program. In your former role as a public judge, you were supposed to be "independent." That is, the income that you enjoyed as a public judge was unrelated to how you decided cases. Now that has changed. Your income is directly determined by how often you are "rented." To be rented, you must be chosen by both parties to a potential dispute.

QUESTION 10.31: In what ways do you think a "rent-a-judge" who sought to maximize income would decide cases differently from an independent public judge?

---

probability estimate in light of the evidence allowed to enter the trial. At the trial's end, the decision-maker, whether juror or judge, will have a posterior probability estimate of the defendant's liability (*i.e.*, a probability formed after hearing the evidence presented and admitted at the trial). If the posterior probability exceeds 50%, the plaintiff has proved the case by the preponderance of the evidence and deserves to win; otherwise, the plaintiff deserves to lose. Reasoning in the courtroom may thus be described as constrained rational choice under uncertainty, where the constraints are formed by rules of evidence that confine betting behavior within legal limits.

QUESTION 10.32: Should the law give more weight to eyewitness testimony than to equally reliable statistical inference?

QUESTION 10.33: The probability of flipping a coin two times and getting all heads is $.5^2$ = .25. Suppose that liability in a tort case requires the plaintiff to prove that the defendant caused the injury and that the defendant's behavior was negligent. The plaintiff presents evidence proving each proposition with probability .7. Thus, the probability that both propositions are true equals $.7^2 = .49$. Apparently, the preponderance of the evidence supports each proposition separately but not jointly. How should the court decide the case?

V. APPEALS

Many court systems consist of a hierarchy of courts in which a discontented litigant can appeal the decision of a lower court and request a new trial by a higher court. Sometimes the higher court *must* accept the appeal and hear the case, and sometimes the higher court can *choose* whether to accept the appeal or reject it. For example, U.S. federal courts consist of three levels in which the highest court (the U.S. Supreme Court) can decide whether to accept or reject most appeals from the intermediate court (a circuit court of appeals), and the intermediate court must accept appeals from the lowest court (a district court). Sometimes the appeals court can hear the entire case from the beginning ("trial de nouveau"). For example, appeals courts in continental Europe often hear cases from the beginning, considering matters of fact and law. Sometimes, however, the appeals court considers some issues but not others. For example, the appeals courts in common law countries usually limit consideration to matters of law, accepting without review all the facts found by lower courts.

Appeals courts have two distinct functions. First, they correct mistakes in decisions made by lower courts. Second, they make law, either directly as in common law or indirectly through the interpretation of statutes. We will consider each function of appeals courts in turn.

A. Correcting Mistakes

Hierarchical court systems enable the highest judges to monitor the performance of lower judges and correct their mistakes at low cost. The system of appeals keeps monitoring costs low because litigants typically appeal when the lower court makes a mistake. Thus, a system of appeals enables the highest judges to draw upon the private information of litigants about whether a mistake was made by a lower court. By using this information, a system of appeals can reduce the sum of administrative costs and error costs in deciding disputes.

To illustrate, consider a numerical comparison of a system without appeal and a system with appeal. Assume that a trial costs the plaintiff and defendant $500, for a total of $1000 in administrative costs. Assume the probability of an error by the trial court in deciding the case equals .2 and the social costs of an error equal $25,000. Thus, the social cost of deciding the dispute in the trial court is

$$\text{Social cost} \quad = \quad \underset{\substack{\text{administrative} \\ \text{costs}}}{\$1000} \quad + \quad \underset{\substack{\text{expected error} \\ \text{costs}}}{.2(\$25,000)} \quad = \quad \$6000.$$

Now consider how the creation of an appeals court affects social costs. Assume for now that the case is appealed if, and only if, the trial court made an error. Assume that an appeal costs each party $1000, for a total of $2000 in administrative costs. The appeals court is likely to reverse the trial court when the latter made an error. Specifically, let .9 equal the probability of reversal conditional on an error by the trial court, which implies that the probability of the appeals court sustaining an error made by the trial court equals .1. The social cost of deciding the dispute in a court system with the possibility of appeal is

Social cost =	$1000	+	.2		[$2000	+	.1($25,000)]
	administrative		probability		admin. cost		expected
	cost of first trial		of appeal		of 2nd trial		error cost
= $1900.							

In this example, the existence of an appeals court causes social costs to fall from $6000 to $1900.

A rational litigant does not appeal a case unless the expected value of appealing exceeds its cost. The expected value of appealing is high when the appeals court is likely to reverse the decision of the trial court. The appeals court is likely to reverse when the lower court makes an error. Thus, appeals courts are most likely to lower social costs when (1) the appeals court is more likely to reverse an error by the lower court than to reverse a correct decision, and (2) when this behavior by the appeals court causes litigants to appeal errors with higher probability than correct decisions by the lower court.

QUESTION 10.34: By setting fees for appealing, the state can discourage appeals with low probability of success. Construct a numerical example to illustrate this fact.

QUESTION 10.35: Appeals are often subsidized in the sense that the state bears part of the litigation costs. Use the preceding theory to construct a justification of state subsidies for appeals.

QUESTION 10.36: Assume that delay is more costly to the plaintiff than the defendant. How does the possibility of appealing an adverse court decision, which delays resolution of the case, affect bargaining between the parties to settle the dispute out of court?

B. Efficiency of the Litigation Market

Now we turn from the function of deciding cases to making law. Some social goals can be achieved without government's pursuing them. For example, Adam Smith argued that competitive markets cause people who consciously pursue their private interests to serve the public good. A competitive market is a kind of social machine whose laws of operation allocate resources efficiently without anyone's consciously striving for that goal. Litigation has some elements of a competitive market; specifically, plaintiffs and defendants compete with each other to advance their own ends. Are courts like competitive markets in the sense that judge-made law tends toward efficiency without anyone's consciously striving for this goal?

The economic analysis of law has investigated the inspiring possibility that litigation can make the law more efficient without the conscious help of judges. This might occur through *selective litigation.* Assume that inefficient laws are litigated more than efficient laws. (In a moment we shall explain why that might occur.) By assumption, inefficient laws are repeatedly challenged in court, whereas efficient laws are challenged less frequently. If efficient laws are not favored or disfavored by judges, the probability of a law's surviving a court test is independent of whether it is efficient or inefficient. But we are assuming that inefficient laws are challenged in court more often than efficient laws. These two assumptions—that efficiency is negatively correlated to the probability of a court test and that efficiency is not negatively correlated to the probability of a law's surviving such a test—are sufficient to cause the law to evolve towards efficiency.

Under these assumptions, selective litigation works like a strainer that catches inefficient laws while allowing efficient laws to slip past. The law, being repeatedly sieved, becomes more efficient with the passage of time. The process of filtering out inefficient laws could operate without judges' consciously favoring efficiency; indeed, it is sufficient for judges not to disfavor efficiency. In order for selective litigation to cause the law to evolve toward efficiency, selection must be biased against inefficient laws.

We have shown that selective litigation, by which we mean a process causing the litigation of inefficient laws with higher probability than of efficient laws, can cause the law to evolve toward efficiency. Is there any reason to think that inefficient laws will be challenged in court more often than efficient laws? The answer is "yes," but this is not a strong yes—more like a "probably." To see why, consider that inefficient laws allocate entitlement to the wrong parties. To illustrate, return to Example 3, which concerned the division of property in a divorce. Suppose that Joan Potatoes and Joe Potatoes place different valuations upon their house: Joan values it at $150,000 and Joe values it at $100,000. Efficiency requires the allocation of legal entitlements to the parties who value them the most; so, efficiency requires Joan to get the house. If Joan gets the house, the value to Joe of overturning that allocation equals $100,000. In contrast, if Joe gets the house, the value to Joan of overturning that allocation equals $150,000. Because Joan has more at stake than Joe, Joan would be more likely than Joe to challenge an unfavorable legal allocation. In general, the party who values a legal entitlement the most will spend more on a suit to obtain it than anyone else. So, an inefficient allocation of the entitlement will provoke more expenditure on litigation than will an efficient allocation.

We have explained why more money will be spent challenging inefficient laws than challenging efficient laws. More will be spent extensively and intensively: more extensive litigation means more frequent challenges in court; more intensive litigation means that the plaintiffs hire more expensive lawyers and spend more on preparing the case. Insofar as expenditures improve the quality of the argument in court and insofar as courts are influenced by arguments of higher quality, litigation against inefficient laws will tend to be more successful than litigation against efficient laws.

We have argued that litigation selects against inefficient laws, resulting in more frequent court challenges and better preparation of plaintiffs' cases. Thus, a mechanism in the common law works similarly to the "invisible hand" in markets. Unfortunately, the invisible hand guides courts weakly compared to its guidance on markets. To understand why, consider an analogy between legal precedents and scientific discoveries. Some scientific advances, including the discovery of basic principles, are unpatentable. Insofar as scientific advances are unpatentable, investors in research cannot capture its full value to society. Part of the value spills over, which constitutes an externality. Markets for basic scientific discoveries may fail because value spills over, unlike, say, the market for bananas, where the grower captures the product's full value.

Trials have more in common with basic scientific research than with the market for bananas. A law is, by its nature, general in the scope of its application; so, challenging a law affects everyone who is subject to it. The effects of a new, more efficient precedent spill far beyond the litigants in the case in which the precedent is set. Consequently, most plaintiffs appropriate no more than a fraction of the value that a new precedent creates and redistributes. Other beneficiaries free-ride on this plaintiff's success. Consequently, litigation selects against rules whose costs are internalized by a single plaintiff.Free-riding is more powerful than inefficiency in channeling litigation pressure.

QUESTION 10.37: The plaintiff who brings a suit to establish a more efficient precedent enjoys only a fraction of its social value. Does this fact show that the government should subsidize lawsuits by paying part of the cost of litigation?

QUESTION 10.38: What features of the inquisitorial system might attenuate the pressure of selective litigation as compared to the adversarial system?

C. Enacting Social Norms

We have asked whether competition in the litigation market drives judge-made law toward efficiency. Apparently, competitive pressures towards efficiency are present but weak in the litigation market. Economic analysis of law has demonstrated more consistency between the common law and efficiency than anyone anticipated when the intellectual enterprise first began in the 1960s. The degree of consistency far exceeds what could be expected from competitive pressure in the litigation market. Besides litigation pressure, another possible cause of efficiency is competition among "social norms," by which we mean norms that arise outside of the legal system. Norms arise in communities where people interact repeatedly. Social norms compete for peoples' allegiance, and, under certain conditions, the more efficient norms win the competition. Judges sometimes enforce social norms. If judge-made law evolves in the same direction as social norms, then competition in the "market for norms" will drive judge-made law toward efficiency.

The traditional account of the "law merchant" provides an example. Medieval merchants engaged in a variety of commercial practices, such as paying each other with bills of exchange. These practices competed against each other and the more efficient ones prevailed. A practice that prevailed was raised to the level of an obligation among merchants. These obligations constituted the social norms of the community of medieval merchants. The merchants in the medieval trade fairs of England developed their own courts to regulate trade. As the English legal system became stronger and more unified, English judges increasingly assumed jurisdiction over disputes among merchants. The English judges often did not know enough about these specialized businesses to evaluate alternative rules. Instead of making rules, the English judges then tried to find out what rules already existed among the merchants and selectively enforced them. Thus, the judges dictated conformity to merchant practices, not the practices to which merchants should conform. The law of notes and bills of exchange in the eighteenth century especially exemplifies this pattern.[22]

The model of the law merchant once enjoyed a special place in the philosophy of law. According to an old theory of jurisprudence, courts should *find* the common law, not *make* it. Judges find the common law by identifying social norms and selectively raising them to the level of law. When judges follow this pattern, the common law has the authority of custom behind it. This philosophy is not limited to common law. The makers of legal codes often follow this philosophy. For example, the scholar who directed the creation of America's most successful code, The Uniform Commercial Code, explicitly identified the best business practices and wrote them into the code. Similarly, the creators of the great European codes often tried to identify and enact the best business practices of the day.

We now live in an age of a new law merchant. The modern economy creates many specialized business communities and norms arise in them to coordinate the interaction of people. The formality of the norms varies from one business to another. Self-regulating professions, like law and accounting, and formal networks like VISA promulgate their own rules. Voluntary associations, like the Association of Home Appliance Manufacturers, may issue guidelines. Informal networks, such as the computer software manufacturers, may have inchoate ethical standards. All of these social norms provide a rich source for decentralized law-making by judges. As the economy develops and becomes more complex, social norms should become more important as a source of law.

We stated that social norms compete for people's allegiance, and, under certain conditions, the more efficient norms win the competition. Economists have begun to study social norms in an attempt to understand when they evolve toward efficiency. A short answer is that social norms evolve toward efficiency when they coordinate the behavior of people in long-run relationships and when the effects of the norms do not spill over to other people. We cannot develop this body of theory any further here.

> **QUESTION 10.39:** Central planning was the method used in the communist system for making commodities. It failed because the planners lacked the information and motivation to direct an increasingly complicated economy. Instead of being inevitable, socialism proved to be impossible. Making laws is not so different from making commodities. Contrast centralized and decentralized ways of making laws.

D. Efficiency as a Judicial Motive

We have asked whether judge-made law tends toward efficiency without anyone's consciously striving for it. We found a weak pressure toward efficiency in the litigation market and a stronger pressure in the market for norms. What about more conscious forces? Do judges consciously adopt efficiency as a goal? Philosophers disagree about

---

[22] The extent to which the medieval law merchant was substantive, rather than procedural, is disputed, and its relationship with common law and admiralty law is difficult to reconstruct. The process of assimilating bills of exchange and negotiable instruments into the common law, which occurred in the eighteenth century, is well documented. The traditional theory is developed by Holden in EARLY HISTORY OF NEGOTIABLE INSTRUMENTS (19). Holden is criticized by John Baker in *The Law Merchant and the Common Law Before 1700,* 38 CAMBRIDGE LAW J. 295 (1979).

whether a judge can properly decide a case on the ground of efficiency. It can be argued, for example, that judges should allocate legal entitlements fairly and that the fair allocation has no systematic connection to an efficient allocation. In spite of such arguments, judges often prefer more efficient rules, but their own descriptions employ terms other than "efficiency." The law embeds efficiency principles under other names.

We cannot develop this theory systematically, but we can provide some suggestive examples. We have argued repeatedly that efficient incentives require the internalization of costs and benefits by the private decision-maker. That is, private decision-makers face efficient incentives when they bear social costs. The law often prescribes the internalization of costs. To illustrate, recall our analysis of tort law in Chapter 8. An injurer can avoid harming someone else by taking precaution against accidents. Internalization requires injurers to proceed as if the harm were their own (*i.e.*, as if the harm were part of their expected costs). When injurers internalize the cost of the harm, they will balance it against the cost of precaution, as required for economic efficiency. Thus, tort law requires injurers to take precaution as if accidental harm to others were their own. Judges may call this "a requirement that injurers show equal concern for the harms suffered by others as for themselves." But this is simply cost-internalization under another name.

Here is another example of courts using alternative terminology when they decide cases on efficiency grounds: Each dollar the plaintiff receives in a lawsuit must be paid by the defendant, so the immediate effect of the judgment is pure redistribution. Self-interested litigants may have diametrically opposite preferences concerning the distribution of the stakes. But suppose they look beyond the immediate division of the stakes and consider the future effects of the legal rule that applies to their dispute. Even though they disagree about this case, they may agree over the rule that they would like to use to resolve new disputes that arise in the future.

Consider an example. Negligence rules as they used to operate in the common law countries (when contributory negligence was a complete bar to recovery) were all-or-nothing: either the plaintiff was entitled to full compensation for the injury, or the defendant was not liable. In recent years many jurisdictions have abandoned all-or-nothing rules in favor of comparative negligence. Under the rule of comparative negligence, each party is responsible for accident costs in proportion to the harm she caused. Thus, if the defendant was twice as negligent as the plaintiff, the defendant is liable for two-thirds of the harm.

Suppose that everyone who lives in a jurisdiction governed by an all-or-nothing rule favors changing to comparative negligence. Further, suppose that someone is injured under circumstances in which the current rule puts all the costs on the other party, whereas comparative negligence would split the costs between them. The accident victim will want this dispute resolved by using the current law, even though he, and everyone else, favors resolving future disputes by the new rule of comparative negligence.

In a common law system, a court may take such a case as the occasion to change the law from the old all-or-nothing rule to the new rule of comparative negligence. Good arguments can be made that judges have the power to abandon a rule in favor of an alternative that makes everyone better off in the future. Certainly a court that made such a change would justify it by pointing to the future benefits that everyone will enjoy. The retrospective application of the new rule can be defended on the ground that everyone prefers its prospective application.

An important normative standard in economics is Pareto efficiency. An improvement by this standard makes someone better off without making anyone worse off. When an appeals court adopts a new precedent, one party to the dispute wins and the other loses. A change in which there are some losers is not an improvement by the Pareto standard. So, the Pareto standard in its simplest interpretation does not provide a guide to adjudicating disputes. We have explained, however, that people who disagree about the best rule for resolving their current dispute may yet agree about the best rule for resolving future disputes. If the prospective application of a new rule makes some people better off and no one worse off, we will say that the new rule is an improvement by the *ex ante* Pareto standard.

This modified concept of Pareto efficiency is very valuable in the economic analysis of law. When an appeals court adopts a new rule whose prospective application is better for everyone, the court may be arguing in different language that the new precedent is *ex ante* Pareto efficient.

QUESTION 10.40: In Chapter 8 we explained the Hand rule for determining whether or not an injurer was negligent. Does the Hand rule require that "injurers show equal concern for the harms suffered by others as for themselves"?

CONCLUSION: SOCIAL COSTS OF THE LEGAL PROCESS

Social costs of the legal process vary from one country to another, with the United States at one extreme. There are 20 times as many lawyers per capita in America as there are in Japan, five times as many as there are in West Germany, and almost 45 times as many as there are in England. In 1992, U.S. trial courts disposed of about 17.5 million civil cases, nearly 12 million criminal cases, and about 1.5 million juvenile cases. This means that there were about 8.4 dispositions by courts per 100 U.S. citizens. Total dispositions (criminal and civil) nearly tripled between 1981 and 1992. For the civil cases, historical data reveal an upward trend for filings as a percentage of the population in many American jurisdictions over the course of the twentieth century. As for the composition of civil disputes in America, the data suggest that contract disputes produce about ten times as many trials as tort disputes, with property disputes somewhere in between.[23]

No one knows how much legal disputes cost society. In the United States, combined federal, state, and local spending on civil and criminal justice was estimated at $39.7 bil-

---

[23] Administrative Office of the United States Courts, MANAGEMENT STATISTICS FOR THE UNITED STATES COURTS (1981), pp. 13 and 129, as reported in Table 3 of Marc Galanter, *supra* n. 9 at *52*. National Center for State Courts, STATE COURT CASELOAD STATISTICS: ANNUAL REPORT 1981 (Court Statistics and Information Management Project, April, 1985), Table 20, pp. 84–86. National Center for State Courts, STATE COURT CASELOAD STATISTICS: ANNUAL REPORT, (1992), Table 7, p. 98 (1994). For the period 1985–1992, the aggregated total of real-property cases tended to rise; contract cases were relatively the same but with a great deal of variation over the period; and tort filings were almost constant. These numbers should be treated with caution because of wide variance among states and because of errors in the variables.

lion in 1983, or $170 per capita, or about 3% of all government spending for the fiscal year. Of this per capita total, police protection accounted for $88; correctional services (*e.g.*, prisons and jails) for $44; and judicial services for $37. Expenditures on police protection mostly concern deterring crime; expenditures on correctional services mostly concern punishing criminals; and expenditures on judicial services mostly concern resolving disputes. It is the latter number of $37 per capita that concerns us in this chapter.

Direct government expenditures on judicial services, as represented by the $37 per-capita figure quoted above, represent only a small fraction of the true cost of resolving disputes by the courts. Most of the costs are borne by private parties, not the state. For example, the $37 per-capita figure does not include the costs of hiring lawyers by the plaintiff and defendant in a civil dispute, paying expert witnesses, taking depositions, and so forth. Exact data on the full cost are unavailable, but a back-of-the-envelope estimate of the labor costs of a full-blown trial in the United States is $400 per hour.[24] This rough estimate shows that the total social costs of litigation far exceed the costs attributed to all judicial services in government statistics ($37 per capita). Lawsuits are as American as apple pie and a lot more expensive.

Various theories have been advanced to explain the high rates of litigation in contemporary America. A cyclical view is that American law (especially procedural law) has been created by lawyers to benefit lawyers. Countless jokes about lawyers,[25] including the quote from Shakespeare at the beginning of this chapter, suggest that other people besides Americans view the social contribution of lawyers with cynicism. In contrast, the cheerful view favored by the plaintiffs' bar (those lawyers who specialize in representing plaintiffs), is that some Americans, who previously suffered indignities in silence, are finally asserting their legal rights. According to this view, litigation now protects rights that were formerly invaded with impunity. If so, increasing litigation rates indicate increasing social justice, and more litigation in the United States than in other countries indicates that the United States legal system protects those who have been wronged better than do the systems of other countries.

In this chapter we developed the theory required to analyze the efficiency of the legal process. We defined a simple measure of social costs; we distinguished the legal process into stages; and we modeled the incentive effects of different rules at each stage. Theory, alone, does not answer the question of whether the legal process is unnecessarily cumbersome and expensive in some countries. However, the theory developed in this chapter provides the basis for future empirical studies to provide a critique of the legal process.

---

[24] A full-blown trial typically involves a judge, a 12-person jury, the plaintiff and the plaintiff's lawyer (or prosecutor in a criminal case), the defendant and the defendant's lawyer, a court stenographer, and a court guard. In addition, someone is usually presenting testimony, possibly an expert witness. That adds up to 20 people. The labor of these participants is valued at widely different rates. Lawyers working for large firms may bill at around $400 per hour, whereas the jurors are usually reimbursed by the state at around $10 per day (which is far less than the opportunity cost of a juror's time). The value of most people's time lies between these extremes. If we estimate the average value of the labor of all twenty participants in the trial at, say, $20 per hour, then the labor value of a full trial would be around $400 per hour.

[25] Two examples of jokes about the legal process: "Litigation is like wrestling with a pig: you both get dirty, and the pig enjoys it." And, "When I was the only lawyer in Shinbone, I almost starved, but now that another lawyer has come to town, I eat steak, and I'm building a new house."

SUGGESTED READINGS

Cooter, Robert, and Daniel Rubinfeld, *Economic Analysis of Legal Disputes and Their Resolution,* 27 JOURNAL OF ECONOMIC LITERATURE 1067 (1989).

Cooter, Robert. *Structural Adjudication and the New Law Merchant: A Model of Decentralized Law,* 14 INTERNATIONAL REVIEW OF LAW AND ECONOMICS 215–231 (1994).

Donohue, John, *Opting for the British Rule, or If Posner and Shavell Can't Remember the Coase Theorem, Who Will?* 104 HARV. L. REV. 1093 (1991).

Hadfield, Gillian K., *Bias in the Evolution of Legal Rules,* 80 GEO. L. J. 583 (1992).

James, Jr., Fleming, and Geoffrey C. Hazard, Jr., CIVIL PROCEDURE (3d ed. 1985).

Kornhauser, L. A., and R. L. Revesz, *Multi-Defendant Settlements: The Impact of Joint and Several Liability,* 23 J. LEGAL STUD. 41 (1994).

Landes, William, *An Economic Analysis of the Courts,* 14 J. LAW & ECON. 61 (1971).

Landes, W. M. *Sequential Versus Unitary Trials: An Economic Analysis* 22 J. LEGAL STUD. 99 (1993).

Posner, Richard A., THE FEDERAL COURTS: CRISIS AND REFORM (1985).

Priest, George, and Benjamin Klein, *The Selection of Disputes for Litigation,* 13 J. LEGAL STUD. 1 (1984).

Shavell, Steven, *Suit, Settlement, and Trial: A Theoretical Analysis Under Alternative Methods for the Allocation of Legal Costs,* 11 J. LEGAL STUD. 55 (1982).

Shavell, S., *The Appeals Process As a Means of Error Correction,* 24 J. LEGAL STUD. 379 (1995).

Spier, K. E., *Pretrial Bargaining and the Design of Fee-Shifting Rules,* 25 RAND JOURNAL OF ECONOMICS 197 (1994).

11

AN ECONOMIC THEORY OF CRIME
AND PUNISHMENT

"The true measure of crimes is the harm done to society."

—

Cesare Beccaria, ON CRIMES AND PUNISHMENT 64 (1764)

In countries where crime once seemed rare in the typical person's life, it now seems endemic. For example, in the United States crime directly affects nearly one in three households each year. As a result, passionate arguments are made on behalf of radical reform to make punishment more certain, swift, and severe. And equally passionate arguments are made that such reform would interfere disastrously with personal freedom. Crime and punishment are among the most important public-policy issues of the day.

In the next two chapters we shall define crimes and distinguish them from civil offenses, explore the broad statistics on the crime wave, examine economic models of behavior by criminals and law enforcement agencies, and survey such important issues as capital punishment, handgun control, illegal drugs, and the deterrent effect of criminal sanctions.

Consider these examples of issues in criminal law:

EXAMPLE 1: Jim Bloggs is convicted of assault for striking and breaking the nose of Joe Potatoes. As punishment, the judge has discretion to choose a stiff fine or a short jail sentence. If the judge believes that each punishment would deter future crime equally, which punishment should the judge use?

EXAMPLE 2: Bloggs is sentenced to jail, but the jail is full and the jailer cannot legally add any more inmates. The state could build another jail or release some current inmates to make room for Bloggs. Which response will lead to the right amount of deterrence of criminals and minimize the social costs of crime?

EXAMPLE 3: A thief shatters a car window costing $100 and steals a radio worth $75. Is the social cost of the crime $175 (the victim's loss), $100 (the victim's loss minus the injurer's gain), or some other number?

EXAMPLE 4: Yvonne wishes to increase the security of her home against burglars. She considers three alternatives: (1) install bars on her windows; (2) install a loud burglar alarm; or (3) buy a gun. How will each alternative affect burglaries of her house and of *neighboring* houses? For example, will bars on Yvonne's windows reduce crime in the neighborhood or merely redirect it to other houses? Will an alarm alert neighbors? Will burglars know that she has a gun? Which alternative should the state encourage Yvonne to adopt?

In this chapter we shall examine the answers that the traditional theory of criminal law gives to these questions. Then we shall propose an economic theory of crime and punishment that, we think, surmounts the limitations of the traditional legal theory.

I. THE TRADITIONAL THEORY OF CRIMINAL LAW

In England much of the criminal law was originally part of the common law, but over many decades criminal statutes replaced the common law of crimes. Modern criminal law is now codified in statutes in common law and civil law countries. This body of law embodies what we might call a traditional theory of crimes, according to which criminal law differs from civil law by the following characteristics:

1. The criminal *intended* to do wrong, whereas some civil wrongs are accidental.
2. The harm done by the criminal was public as well as private.
3. The plaintiff is the state, not a private individual.
4. The plaintiff has a higher standard of proof in a criminal trial than in a civil suit.
5. If the defendant is guilty, then he or she will be punished.

As an introduction to criminal law, we shall briefly elaborate on these characteristics.

A. Criminal Intent

A careful driver is not at fault and imposes moderate risk on others, whereas a careless driver is negligent and imposes excessive risk on others. Negligent drivers must compensate those they have harmed. Even careless drivers, however, do not disregard the safety of others and intentionally impose excessive risk on them. A driver who intentionally imposes excessive risk on others is reckless. As we saw in Chapter 9, recklessness can oblige the injurer in some countries to pay punitive damages in addition to compensatory damages.

Even a driver who disregards the safety of others does not intentionally run into someone. Beyond recklessness lies intentional harm. According to an old adage, "Even a dog knows the difference between being stumbled over and kicked." So does the law. The law makes much over the distinction between accidental and intentional harm. Tort law concerns accidental harm, and criminal law concerns intentional harm.

---

[1] For an economic account of *mens rea*, see Jeffrey S. Parker, *The Economics of Mens Rea,* 79 VA. L. REV. 741 (1993).

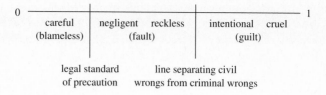

FIGURE 11.1 Culpability scale.

Mens rea (Latin for "a guilty mind") is the legal term for criminal intent.[1] To develop this idea of *mens rea,* we must draw the boundary between accidental and intentional harm. Consider the ranking of acts along a continuum in Figure 11.1.

Starting at the left side of the scale, the injurer is careful and blameless. Moving to the right, the injurer's behavior becomes negligent, then reckless, and then criminal. Careful behavior is less culpable than negligent behavior; negligent behavior is less culpable than intentional harm. According to this continuum, the line separating fault from *mens rea* lies between recklessness and intentional harm. As actors cross this boundary line, they pass from fault to guilt.

Further gradations in criminal intent are sometimes relevant to determining punishment. To illustrate, harming someone intentionally to gain a personal advantage is not as bad as harming someone cruelly and taking pleasure in the victim's pain. There is, thus, a continuous gradation in the moral evaluation of the actor from blameless on the good end to cruel on the bad end.[2]

> **QUESTION 11.1:** We defined crime as "intentional harm to persons or property." In the communist countries, "crime" was often defined as "socially dangerous." Relate the difference in definitions to the continuum depicted above.

B. Public Harm and Public Prosecution

Proceeding down our list, the second distinguishing feature of a crime is the nature of the harm. In the areas of the law we have examined to this point—property, contract, and torts—most of the harm has been private. In criminal law much of the harm is public. Consider that a murder threatens the peace and security of society at large and thus puts others besides the victim in fear for their lives. The great eighteenth-century commentator on the laws of England, William Blackstone, said that "in these gross and atrocious injuries [which we call crimes] the private wrong is swallowed up in the public: we seldom hear any mention made of satisfaction to the individual; the satisfaction to the community being so great."[3]

The idea that crimes harm the public has several implications. First, it justifies the difference between the plaintiffs in civil and criminal suits. In a civil suit the plaintiff is a private individual (the victim). In a criminal prosecution the plaintiff is society as represented by the public prosecutor or attorney general.

---

[2] We could, of course, extend the line and fill in the gaps with fine distinctions found in criminal law. To illustrate, off the scale to the left lie meritorious acts, and off the scale to the right lie sadistic acts.

[3] William Blackstone, COMMENTARIES ON THE LAWS OF ENGLAND, v. IV. p. 6 (1776, reptd. 1977).

Second, the idea that crimes harm the public implies the possibility of "victimless" crimes, such as gambling, prostitution, and the sale of illegal drugs. The parties to these crimes often engage in voluntary sales for mutual advantage. However, the traditional theory of criminal law holds that these transactions have victims—namely society, whose peace and security is threatened.

Third, the traditional theory of public harm justifies punishing *attempts* to cause harm, even when they fail. When potentially harmful behavior causes no actual harm, the victim's injury is nil, so the victim usually has no cause for a civil suit. However, failed attempts at crime cause fear and other harm to the public. The traditional theory of criminal law holds that a person who tries to injure another and fails should be punished.

QUESTION 11.2: Explain why counterfeiting money is a crime. Who is the victim?

QUESTION 11.3: Distinguish between (1) imposing risk on others by driving carelessly without an accident actually occurring, and (2) inspiring fear in others by attempting to commit a crime and failing.

C. Standard of Proof

The fourth characteristic of a crime is the high standard of proof imposed upon the plaintiff. The prosecutor in a criminal case must satisfy a higher standard of proof than the plaintiff in a civil case. In a civil case in common law countries, the plaintiff must prove the case by a preponderance of the evidence, that is, the case must be more believable than the defendant's. In a criminal action in common law countries, the plaintiff must prove the case *beyond a reasonable doubt.*

The traditional theory gives two reasons for imposing this high standard on the prosecution. First, convicting an innocent person seems worse than failing to convict a guilty person. Criminal law strikes the balance between these two errors (which statisticians call Type II and Type I errors, respectively) in favor of the defendant. Second, the prosecution can bring the full resources of the state to bear on winning. Imposing a heavy burden of proof on the prosecution diminishes this advantage.

Unlike the common law countries, civil law countries sometimes take a different approach. In the alternative approach, the accused are guilty in principle unless they prove their innocence. The rationale for the presumption of guilt is that the state would not bring charges unless it were certain of the defendant's guilt. In this approach, the prosecutor helps strike the balance between convicting the innocent and failing to convict the guilty. The court acknowledges its confidence in the prosecutor by proceeding under a presumption that the prosecutor was right unless the defendant proves otherwise.

QUESTION 11.4: Explain how the confidence of the public in the prosecutor influences the standard of proof in criminal trials.

QUESTION 11.5: Most jurisdictions have two possible verdicts in criminal trials: guilty or not guilty. Scottish criminal trials have three possible verdicts: guilty, not proven, or not guilty. Explain the difference between binary and trinary verdicts, with reference to the standard of proof.

D. Punishment

People who commit crimes expose themselves to the risk of punishment. Punishment can take several forms: criminals' freedom may be curtailed through imprisonment, their movements restricted by probation, or fines may be imposed. In some jurisdictions, the defendant faces the possibility of being beaten, mutilated, or executed by the state.

Punishment in criminal law is different from compensation in civil law. Compensation in civil law aims to restore the victim's welfare at the expense of the injurer. Punishment in criminal law makes the injurer worse off without directly benefiting the victim. Because the motivation is different, the issues of compensation and punishment are often independent of each other in a given instance. Thus, punishment may be imposed on top of compensation, as when criminal prosecution follows recovery in tort. Alternatively, punishment may be imposed in lieu of compensation, as when the state imprisons a pauper for assault and the victim does not sue in tort because the injurer could not pay compensation.

In cases involving money, a strict definition illuminates the difference between compensation and punishment. *Perfect compensation* is a sum of money that leaves the *victim indifferent* between the injury with compensation or no injury. In Chapter 9, we defined the parallel concept of perfect disgorgement: *perfect disgorgement* is a sum of money that leaves the *injurer indifferent* between the injury with disgorgement or no injury. By definition, punishment goes beyond disgorgement. *Monetary punishment* is a sum of money that makes the *injurer prefer no injury* rather than the injury with payment of the money. To illustrate by Example 3, if a thief shatters a car window costing $100 and steals a radio worth $75, then perfect compensation equals $175, perfect disgorgement equals $75, and punishment is a sum of money exceeding $75. Thus, the criminal might be required to pay $175 as compensation to the victim and also to pay the state a fine of $100.

QUESTION 11.6: For burglary, the victim's loss usually exceeds the injurer's gain, but the opposite is true for breach of contract. Why? What are the implications for relative dollar values of compensation and punishment?

II. AN ECONOMIC THEORY OF CRIME
AND PUNISHMENT

The traditional theory of criminal law offers reasons for the characteristics of a crime and distinguishes criminal prosecutions from civil disputes, but it does not offer a predictive model of criminal behavior or propose a clear goal for criminal law. The economic theory of crime, which we develop in this chapter, does all of this and more. We shall begin by distinguishing criminal prosecutions from civil disputes and offering reasons for the characteristics of a crime. Next we develop a predictive model of criminal behavior based upon a theory of the rational choice to commit a crime. Finally, we propose a clear goal for criminal law and policy: it should minimize the social cost of crimes. Using this standard, we show how to compute optimal policies.

A. Inadequacy of Tort Law, Necessity of Criminal Law

In Chapters 8 and 9, we discussed how tort law achieves efficient incentives by making injurers internalize the cost of accidents. Most crimes are also torts, which means that most criminals are vulnerable to civil suits. If civil suits made the injurer internalize the cost of crimes, then criminal law would be unnecessary from an economic viewpoint. For several reasons, however, civil suits cannot minimize the cost of crimes. We will explain these reasons in order to justify the existence of criminal law.

The first reason concerns some inherent limitations on compensation. In Chapter 8, we said that compensation is perfect when potential victims are indifferent about accidents in the sense that they would just as soon have the injury and the damages as have no injury and no damages. Perfect compensation internalizes the harm caused by injurers. In Chapter 9 we argued, however, that perfect compensation is impossible for most people who lose a leg or a child. In those cases, courts award damages to deter unreasonable risks, not to compensate for actual harm.

Similarly, criminal punishment aims to deter intentional harms, not to compensate for them. Consider a thought experiment regarding a crime. How much money would you require in order to agree to allow someone to assault you with a hammer? This question does not make much sense. The concept of indifference is difficult to apply to crimes like assault. Consequently, the relevant law cannot take as its goal the perfect compensation of victims and the internalization of costs by injurers. Rather than pricing crime, the goal of punishment is to deter it. The state prohibits people from intentionally harming others and backs this prohibition by punishment. Thus, criminal law is a necessary supplement to tort law when perfect compensation is impossible.

Even if perfect compensation is possible in principle, it may be impossible in fact. Let us suppose, for example, that a level of compensation exists that makes Jonny indifferent about whether Frankie lops off Jonny's arm. It would be impossible to prove this level in court. The obstacle to proof is that arms are not bought and sold in a market; there is no objective way to know how much the loss is worth to Jonny. If the court asks Jonny what amount he feels would compensate for the loss, he may not know the answer, or he may answer by exaggerating. When there is no market to induce people to reveal their subjective valuations, economists say that there is a "problem of preference revelation." When perfect compensation is possible in principle, it may be impossible in fact because of the problem of preference revelation.

We have justified criminal law where compensation is imperfect. But suppose that perfect compensation is possible. Can private law accomplish efficiency without the need for criminal law? The answer is no. To see why, we must consider another argument. In the first chapter on property, we distinguished between protecting an interest and protecting a right. Recall that if the law allows trespass on the condition that the trespasser compensates the owner for any harm caused, the law protects the interest of the owner in the property. But the law does not protect the owner's right to use the property as he or she chooses without interference from others. Similarly, if the victims of car accidents were perfectly compensated, their interests in their persons and property would be protected, but their right to go about their business without interference from others would be infringed. Protecting interests secures wealth, but allowing the infringement of rights diminishes liberty.

There are good economic arguments for protecting rights rather than interests. In earlier chapters we saw that society is, in general, better off when goods are acquired through voluntary exchange, because such exchange guarantees that goods move to those who value them the most. Goods that change hands without the consent of both parties—as by theft—do not carry this same guarantee. The stolen good may be more valuable to its owner than to the thief, but the theft occurs because the thief need not pay the owner's asking price. This is an argument for the proposition that remedies in criminal law should, in part, be set so as to protect and encourage voluntary exchange through markets.

We have argued that two obstacles prevent substituting compensation for punishment: first, perfect compensation may be impossible, and, second, even if perfect compensation were possible, the law may seek to protect the rights of potential victims rather than their interests.

There is a third reason to supplement liability with punishment in some circumstances: punishment is often necessary for deterrence. To illustrate, assume that a thief is considering whether to steal a $1000 television set. Assume that the probability of the thief's being apprehended and convicted equals .5. Assume that the thief is liable in property law, but not punishable in criminal law. The expected cost of the theft to the criminal equals the expected liability: .5($1000) = $500. The benefit to the thief equals $1000. Thus, the *net* expected benefit to the thief equals $1000 − $500 = $500. In this example, civil liability without punishment makes theft profitable.

In general, thieves cannot be deterred by the requirement that they return what they have stolen whenever they happen to get caught. In order to deter thieves, the law must impose enough punishment so that the expected net benefit of crime to the criminal is negative. In the preceding example, deterring the thief requires a fine of at least $1000, as well as the return of the television set.

QUESTION 11.7: We gave three reasons for having criminal punishments instead of tort liability. Give a concrete example illustrating each reason.

B. Rational Crime

We have offered some economic reasons why criminal law is needed to supplement tort law. Now we develop a predictive theory of criminal behavior, first by explaining how a rational, amoral person might decide whether or not to commit a crime. By a "rational, amoral person," we mean someone who carefully determines the means to achieve illegal ends, without restraint by guilt or internalized morality. Crimes can be ranked by seriousness, and punishments can be ranked by severity. The more severe punishments typically are attached to the more serious crimes. We represent these facts in Figure 11.2.

We measure the seriousness of the crime along the horizontal axis and the severity of the punishment along the vertical axis. The curved line labeled "punishment" shows the severity of the punishment prescribed in the criminal code as a function of the seriousness of the offense. The punishment curve slopes up to indicate that the punishment becomes more severe as the crime becomes more serious.

To give this graph more concrete meaning, consider the crime of embezzlement and the graph in Figure 11.3. The seriousness of embezzlement is sometimes measured by

CRIMINAL CORPORATIONS?

Corporations regularly commit torts. For example, much of the law of consumer-product liability concerns torts by corporations. When a corporation commits a tort, liability is imposed upon the organization, not upon its individual members. But what about crimes? Can a corporation commit a crime? There is a legal obstacle to convicting corporations of crimes: *mens rea*. An individual can have a guilty mind, but it is not clear that organizations can. *Mens rea* requires the intention to do wrong and cause harm. Presumably, organizations lack minds, so they also lack intentions (except metaphorically).

So long as it was thought that organizations could not have criminal intent, the crimes that corporations could commit were limited to so-called *strict-liability crimes*. Strict criminal liability does not require intending to do anything wrong. Examples of strict liability crimes are selling uncertified drugs or transporting explosives by forbidden routes. Other crimes, like manslaughter, fraud, or assault, could be committed by the members of the corporation, but not by the corporation itself.

There is now an effort to overcome this obstacle and prosecute corporations for acts requiring criminal intent. For example, the Ford Motor Company has been prosecuted, so far unsuccessfully, for manslaughter in connection with manufacturing the Pinto with a gas tank that allegedly explodes when struck from the rear.

QUESTION 11.8: What does it mean to say that a corporation *intends* to do something? Can corporations be punished beyond the value of their assets?

---

the amount stolen. Under this assumption, the metric for the horizontal axis in Figure 11.3 is dollars. Similarly, assume that the punishment at issue is a fine, so that a more severe punishment corresponds to a higher fine. Under this assumption, the metric for the vertical axis in Figure 11.3 is also dollars. Because both metrics are dollars, the

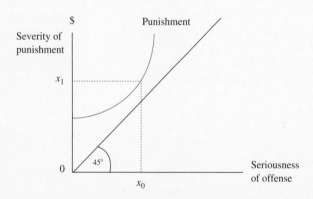

FIGURE 11.2 Severity of the punishment as a function of the severity of the offense.

offense and the punishment are easy to compare. The benefit of embezzlement to the criminal equals the dollar amount stolen. We indicate this by the benefit line (or payoff curve), which is identical to the 45° line in Figure 11.3. Thus, if the criminal embezzles $1000, the "benefit" of the crime (measured on the vertical axis) also equals $1000.

If a criminal statute imposes penalties on embezzlers, then the dollar value of the punishment should exceed the dollar value of the amount embezzled. Suppose that the punishment for embezzlement is given by the higher punishment curve in Figure 11.2, so that the punishment for the crime of embezzling x_0 is x_1. Thus, if the criminal embezzles $1000, so that $x_0 = 1000, the fine equals $2000, so that $x_1 = 2000. This fine, if certain, deters the rational criminal from embezzling because the cost of committing the crime exceeds its benefit. (These facts also are represented in Figure 11.3.)

The punishment of criminals is probabilistic. The offender may escape detection or apprehension, or be apprehended but not convicted. A rational decision-maker takes the probability of punishment into account when contemplating the commission of any crime, including embezzlement. We may say that the rational embezzler calculates an expected value for the crime by discounting the amount he or she hopes to gain by the uncertainty of the punishment.

To illustrate, if the fine for embezzling $1000 equals $2000, and the probability that an offender will be caught and convicted equals .75, then the expected punishment equals .75($2000) = $1500. To reflect this element of uncertainty, we have drawn a second punishment curve in Figure 11.3 (labeled the expected-punishment curve) below the first one. The lower punishment curve in the figure equals the higher punishment curve minus a discount for the uncertainty of punishment.

How would a rational criminal respond to the expected-punishment schedule? As before, a rational, amoral decision-maker will embezzle money so long as the benefit exceeds the expected punishment.[4] Even though punishment is uncertain by assumption, the expected punishment still exceeds the benefit in the figure, so embezzlement will not occur. Presumably, crime does not usually pay, even for rationally self-interested people without moral qualms. Consequently, Figure 11.3 represents the situation in which most people actually find themselves.

The situation is different in Figure 11.4. In this case, the expected punishment dips below the payoff curve for embezzlement at least as serious as x_1 and no more serious than x_2. Under these circumstances, a rational decision-maker would embezzle some money. We can read off the graph exactly how serious the most profitable offense is. The expected profit from the offense equals the difference between the payoff and the expected punishment, which is represented on the graph by the vertical distance between the payoff curve and the expected-punishment curve. The vertical distance is maximized when the seriousness of the offense equals x^*. We may conclude that the rational decision-maker will embezzle the amount x^*.

QUESTION 11.9: What is the significance of the fact that the severity-of-punishment curve in Figure 11.2 intersects the vertical axis asymptotically at a positive value?

---

[4] We implicitly assume risk neutrality. A risk-averse person is more deterred by a severe punishment applied with low probability than by a mild punishment applied with high probability, holding expected punishment constant.

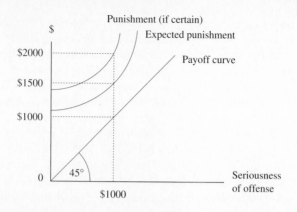

FIGURE 11.3 The effect of uncertainty in punishment.

QUESTION 11.10: How do Figures 11.3 and 11.4 change if the police become more efficient and catch a larger proportion of criminals? What does the change in the figures indicate about a change in criminal behavior?

C. Mathematics of Rational Crime

The rational criminal's behavior can be explained by using mathematical notation corresponding to the graphical analysis of Figure 11.3. Let the variable x indicate the seriousness of the crime (in dollar amounts). Let the variable y indicate the criminal's payoff from the crime (in dollar amounts). We assume that the payoff is an increasing function of the seriousness of the crime: $y = y(x)$. [Note that in Figures 11.2, 11.3, and 11.4, $y(x)$ has the simple form $y = x$, so the 45°-line depicts the function $y(x)$.]

Let the punishment f, assumed to be a fine, for committing a crime of seriousness x be given by the function $f = f(x)$. Furthermore, let the probability of being punished for com-

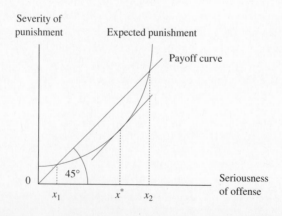

FIGURE 11.4 Expected punishment and the decision to commit a crime.

mitting a crime of seriousness x be given by the function $p = p(x)$. Thus, the expected punishment equals the product of the amount of punishment and its probability: $p(x)f(x)$.

The rational, amoral criminal chooses the seriousness of crime x to maximize his or her net payoff, which equals the payoff $y(x)$ minus the expected punishment:

$$\max y(x) - p(x)f(x), \text{ where } y = y(x).$$

The marginal values of the functions $p(x)$ and $f(x)$, which we denote p' and f', give the changes in the probability of punishment and its severity when the seriousness of the crime, x, changes slightly. Similarly, the marginal value of y, which we denote y', gives the change in the payoff as the seriousness of the crime changes slightly. The criminal maximizes the net benefits of the crime by embezzling an amount of money up to the point at which the marginal benefit of an additional amount embezzled equals the marginal expected punishment:

$$y' \qquad = \qquad p'f + pf'$$

criminal's   criminal's marginal
marginal benefit   expected cost of punishment

The marginal expected punishment for embezzling an additional dollar has two components: the change in the probability of punishment, p', multiplied by the level of the fine; and the change in the severity of punishment, f', multiplied by the level of probability of punishment. We can attach signs to these two components. More serious crimes attract greater enforcement effort by the authorities, so the probability of punishment usually increases with the seriousness of the crime. Thus, p' is usually a positive number. Furthermore, the severity of the punishment almost always increases with the seriousness of the crime, so f' is a positive number. Since p' and f' are usually positive, the expected-punishment curve in Figures 11.2, 11.3, and 11.4 slopes up.

We can use this equation to predict the response of criminals to changes in marginal costs and benefits. An investment of more effort in enforcing criminal law can increase the marginal probability p' of punishing the criminal. Similarly, an investment of more effort in punishing criminals, such as improving the system of collecting fines, can increase the marginal severity f'. According to the preceding equation, an increase in p' or f' will decrease the *seriousness* of the offense committed by the rational criminal.

We explained that more certain and severe punishment reduces the seriousness of crime. Now consider a change in the opportunity to commit crimes like embezzlement. The marginal benefit of crime falls when the opportunities to commit lucrative crimes diminish. According to the preceding equation, a decrease in the marginal benefit of crime y' will decrease the *seriousness* of the offense committed by the rational criminal.

The proposition that the seriousness and frequency of crime decreases when the expected punishment increases correspond to the proposition that the consumer's demand curve for goods slopes downward. Economists have a lot of confidence in this prediction, just as they have a lot of confidence in the prediction that the demand curve slopes downward. The downward slope in the demand curve may mean that a lower price causes each consumer to buy a little more of the good, as with gasoline, or the downward slope may mean that some consumers buy the good who would not otherwise have bought it, as with houses. With a slight adjustment, our model can be made to yield the conclusion that an increase in p' or f', or a decrease in y', will decrease the number, rather than the seriousness of, offenses committed by rational criminals. The same reasoning applies to the seriousness and the number of crimes.

Our model of rational crime simplifies reality in various ways. The simplifying assumptions do not usually affect predictions *qualitatively,* by which we mean that introducing more complexity into the model does not affect the *direction* of most predictions. To illustrate, even in a more complicated model, the amount of crime usually falls when the expected punishment increases. However, the simplifying assumptions usually affect the predictions *quantitatively,* by which we mean that more complexity in the model affects the predicted magnitude of most changes. Empirical research on crime, consequently, requires more complexity than our simple model.

We cannot develop more complex models here, but we will briefly discuss our simplifying assumptions. We assume an informed criminal, who knows the costs, benefits, and probabilities associated with the crime; we assume a risk-neutral criminal; and we assume that all the criminal's costs and benefits are monetary. Most criminals are imperfectly informed about the benefits of crime and the probabilities and magnitudes of punishment. Criminals are unlikely to be neutral towards risk. Most people are risk-averse, although criminals may be unusually risk-loving. (Later we discuss more about risk.) Many crimes have nonmonetary punishments and rewards, such as disapproval in the larger society and prestige within the society of criminals. These remarks indicate some corrections in the simple model required for empirical research.

QUESTION 11.11: Assume that the punishment function $f(x)$ increases by a constant k, so that $f(x)$ becomes $f(x) + k$. What is the effect on the criminal's behavior?

QUESTION 11.12: Assume that the payoff function $y(x)$ increases by a constant k, so that $y(x)$ becomes $y(x) + k$. What is the effect on the criminal's behavior?

D. Criminal Behavior and Criminal Intent

Economists usually describe the economic model of decision-making as an account of behavior, not as an account of subjective reasoning processes. Thus, consumers are said to act *as if* they were computing marginal utilities. Similarly, criminals are said to act *as if* they were comparing marginal benefits of crime and expected punishments. The commission of most crimes, however, requires criminal intent. To commit crimes, it is not enough for people to act *as if* they had criminal intent. They must actually have it. So criminal law concerns reasons, not just behavior.

Notwithstanding its focus on behavior rather than reasons, the economic model of rational choice remains useful as an account of the criminal mind. Criminal intent is often distinguished according to the level of deliberation. To illustrate, a crime may be committed spontaneously in the sense that the criminal did not make any plans in advance. Spontaneous criminals do not search out opportunities to commit crimes, but, when opportunities come their way, they avail themselves of them. At the opposite extreme, crimes may be carefully planned out in advance and all the possibilities weighed. Thus, a premeditated crime shows a greater degree of deliberation than a spontaneous crime.

The economic model may be understood as an account of the deliberations of a rational, amoral person when deciding in advance whether to commit a crime. In the case of premeditated crimes, the economic model may correspond to the actual reasoning process of the criminal. In the case of spontaneous crimes, where there is no deliberation, the economic model may nevertheless be understood as an account of the criminal's behavior. For spontaneous crimes, criminals may not actually reason as in the economic model, but they may act as if they had. By saying that criminals act "as if" they had deliberated, we mean that, when presented with the opportunity to commit crimes, they respond immediately to benefits and risks as if they had weighed them. If they respond in this way, their behavior can be explained by the economic model, even though their reasoning processes are only a fragment of it.

Even when interpreted as a behavioral model, the model of rational choice is valuable in the study of criminal law. To see why, consider another difference between the application of the rational choice model to markets and to criminal prosecution. When economists study markets, they are concerned with aggregate behavior. Eccentric and erratic behavior washes out by aggregation with the mass of ordinary people. In contrast, criminal prosecutions focus upon individuals, and individual criminals are often statistical outliers. Seen in this perspective, the economic model of rational choice does not seem applicable to the criminal law.

But this focus on individuals is not the only perspective on criminal law. Criminal law involves more than the prosecution of individuals. General policies toward crime must be set by legislators and officials in the criminal-justice system. General policies must be formulated with an eye to their aggregate effects, such as their ability to minimize the social costs of crime. At this level of inquiry, the economic model is very valuable.

We have asserted that the economic model of choice describes the deliberation of rational criminals when their crimes are premeditated, and we have asserted that rational criminals behave as if guided by the economic model when they commit spontaneous crimes. If this assertion is true, empirical investigations should demonstrate that crime rates are responsive to the considerations identified in our model, specifically, that crimes rates respond in the predicted manner to punishments and payoffs. This is an empirical question to be answered by facts, not logic. Fortunately, there is a great deal of evidence on this matter, and we shall present a summary of the literature on deterrence in the next chapter. Now we turn to computing the optimal punishment in light of the economic theory of how criminals decide to commit crimes. The first step is to explain the goal of minimizing the social costs of crime.

QUESTION 11.13: Why should the law punish a person more severely for committing the same crime deliberately rather than spontaneously?

QUESTION 11.14: Laboratory experiments demonstrate that rats respond in an economically rational way to punishment, yet rats cannot legally commit crimes. Why not?

E. The Economic Goal of Criminal Law

Crime imposes various costs on society, which we reduce to two basic kinds. First, the criminals gain something and the victims suffer harm to their persons or property. The resulting social harm, according to the standard view among economists, equals the net loss in value. To illustrate by Example 3, if a thief shatters a car window costing $100 and steals a radio worth $75, then the criminal gains $75 and the victim loses $175, for a net social loss of $100. The net loss equals value destroyed, not value redistributed. Second, the state and the potential victims of crime expend resources to protect against it. For example, homeowners install bars on their windows and the city employs police officers to patrol the streets.

We described two basic kinds of social costs: the net harm caused by crime and the resources spent on preventing it. The optimal amount of crime, or efficient deterrence, balances these costs. We propose the following simple goal for analyzing criminal law: *Criminal law should minimize the social cost of crime, which equals the sum of the harm it causes and the cost of preventing it.*

These two basic kinds of social costs often suffice for purposes of analysis. When analysis requires more complexity, we can refine and expand the types of social costs. To illustrate, criminal activities divert the efforts of criminals from legal to illegal activities, which imposes an opportunity cost. For example, an accountant who devotes herself to embezzling funds has less time for legitimate bookkeeping. Furthermore, while in prison, an accountant cannot audit books for clients. The opportunity cost of crime among accountants may be large enough to affect the optimal deterrence of embezzlement. From time to time, we will expand the definition of social costs to include such losses as the criminal's opportunity cost, as required by our analysis.

Another complexity concerns the criminal's perceived benefit from crime. According to the standard view among economists, as mentioned, the criminal's benefit partly offsets the victim's cost. Moralists, however, might say that the criminal's illicit gain should not count as a social benefit. Ordinarily people reach different conclusions on different examples. To illustrate, most people agree that the benefit enjoyed by a person who steals food from an unoccupied cabin to save his life when lost in the wilderness should count as a social gain, and most people agree that the pleasure felt by a rapist (if there is such a pleasure) should not count as a social gain commensurate with the victim's pain.

Unfortunately, many important examples that confront policy-makers do not provoke a consensus, even among economists, about the social value of the criminal's gain. To illustrate, some government regulations on industry promote efficiency by correcting market failures, such as prohibitions against dumping toxic chemicals in rivers, whereas other regulations profit politically favored groups by making competition a crime, such as restrictions on agricultural production. A dramatic example of disagreement over regulations concerns the United States' most creative and profitable financier in the 1970s, Michael Milken, who used high-risk bonds ("junk bonds") to finance leveraged buyouts and hostile takeovers of corporations. He was sentenced to prison for violating technical regulations in security laws. Some economists believe that he did more than any other person to help modernize American industry, and other economists believe that he undermined the stock market by engaging in fraud.

When policy-makers disagree about the social benefits of crime, a good strategy for economists is to clarify the issues without necessarily resolving the dispute. Similarly, we will avoid arguments whose conclusions require taking sides in such debates.

LAPSES

The economic theory of behavior begins with superrationality, but it need not end there. Many crimes and torts occur under conditions of diminished rationality, which economists have begun to model. For example, many crimes result from *lapses*, which are temporary aberrations in behavior. Thus, young men often commit crimes when they temporarily lose control of their emotions and act impulsively.

Economics can model lapses. Lapses occur because the actor temporarily discounts the future consequences of his or her behavior at a much higher level than ordinarily would be the case. A high discount rate prevents the actor from giving as much weight to future punishment and remorse as he or she would give with a lower discount rate. To formalize this idea, imagine that a person draws his discount rate for future costs and benefits from a probability distribution. Most of the time, the person draws a moderate discount rate from the center of the distribution, so he acts prudently and does not commit crimes. From time to time, however, he draws a very high discount rate from the tail of the distribution. In this situation, the person may lapse and commit a crime. Young men commit more crimes than other people because their emotions spread the probability distribution, thus increasing the probability that they will draw a high discount rate.

Question 11.15: What difference would it make to deterrence if crime usually results from lapses?

QUESTION 11.16: What are some ways to measure the social cost of the harm caused by murder? (Recall our discussion in Chapter 9 of how to assign value to a life lost in an accident.)

QUESTION 11.17: Compare the simple economic goals of criminal law and tort law.

F. Optimal Deterrence and Efficient Punishment

Figure 11.5 depicts how to strike the balance between the net cost of the harm caused by crime and the cost of preventing it. In the figure, the horizontal axis measures reductions in the amount of criminal activity, ranging from no reduction at the origin up to a complete absence of crime at the amount 100%. Dollar amounts are measured along the vertical axis. The curve MSC_D represents the marginal social costs of achieving a given level of crime reduction. MSC_D slopes upward because officials undertake easy deterrence before resorting to harder deterrence. Consequently, achieving additional reductions in crime becomes increasingly costly. For example, reducing crime by an additional 1% is easier when crime has already been reduced 5% than when crime has already been reduced 95%.

The curve labeled *MSB* measures the marginal social benefit of achieving various levels of crime reduction or deterrence. *MSB* slopes downward because the benefit to

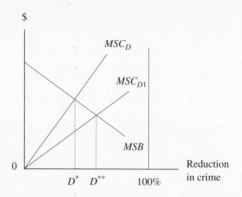

FIGURE 11.5 The efficient level of deterrence.

society of a small reduction in the amount of crime declines as the total amount of crime declines. Thus, the reduction from, say, 5% to 7% benefits society more than the reduction from 95% to 97%.

Socially optimal deterrence occurs at the point where the marginal social cost of reducing crime further equals the marginal social benefit. In Figure 11.5 the social optimum occurs at the level of deterrence marked D^*. Notice that for any level of reduction in crime less than D^*, the marginal social benefit of a further reduction exceeds the marginal social cost, so society should reduce crime further. Similarly, for any level of reduction in crime more than D^*, the marginal social costs of a further reduction exceed the marginal social benefit, so society should allow more crime to go undeterred.

Notice that changes in MSC_D and MSB can change the optimal level of deterrence. For example, suppose that the opportunity cost of resources devoted to deterring crime falls, and the marginal social benefit of deterrence remains the same; MSC_D would fall to MSC_{D1} and the optimal level of deterrence would increase to D^{**}.

In the next chapter, we describe efforts to determine whether marginal deterrence costs more or less than the resulting savings in the cost of crime in the United States; in other words, these studies try to determine whether the value of D for the United States is above, below, or equal to the optimal value of D^*.

QUESTION 11.18: Assume the acquisition of computers by the police increases the force's efficiency. How would Figure 11.5 change?

QUESTION 11.19: Assume the acquisition of computers by criminals increases their elusiveness. How would Figure 11.5 change?

G. Mathematics of Optimal Deterrence

In this section we use simple mathematics to derive the intuitive results of the previous section on the optimal amount of deterrence. A crime directly harms the victim, such as the $175 lost by the car owner in the preceding example. Denote the direct harm by d. In addition, a crime has an indirect cost i suffered by society, which includes, say, the cost of the fear of future thefts of car radios among potential victims and the additional resources that they devote to preventing theft. Harm caused by a crime is, therefore, the sum of the direct cost and the indirect cost: $(d + i)$.

As explained, the criminal often benefits from the crime, and the standard economic view subtracts the criminal's benefit from the cost of the harm. According to this approach, the net harm of crime is the sum of the direct and indirect harm less the benefit: $d + i - b$.

Crime occurs with probability p, where p depends upon the level of deterrence. Let z represent expenditures on police, courts, prosecutors, probation officers, prisons, and so forth. For now we assume that expenditures are efficiently allocated among the various factors contributing to deterrence. (The following section explains how to make such an efficient allocation.) The frequency of crime, p, is a decreasing function of expenditures on deterrence: $p = p(z)$ with the marginal probability negative, $p' < 0$.

The probability of crime multiplied by its net harm equals the expected net harm: $(d + i - b)p(z)$. Finally, the expected net social cost of crime equals the sum of expected harm and expenditures on deterrence:

$$\underset{\substack{\text{expected net} \\ \text{social cost}}}{} = \underset{\substack{\text{expected net harm}}}{(d + i - b)p(z)} + \underset{\substack{\text{deterrence}}}{z.}$$

Efficiency requires choosing expenditures on deterrence z to minimize expected net social costs. The marginal cost of spending an additional dollar on deterrence equals a dollar. The resulting marginal benefit equals the reduction in expected net harm resulting from the marginal decrease in crime caused by spending an additional dollar on deterrence, which we already denoted p'. Thus, optimal deterrence requires choosing z so that

$$\underset{\substack{\text{marginal} \\ \text{cost of} \\ \text{deterrence}}}{1} = \underset{\substack{\text{expected} \\ \text{net cost} \\ \text{of crime}}}{(d + i - b)} \underset{\substack{\text{marginal decrease} \\ \text{in probability} \\ \text{of crime}}}{(-p').}$$

Consider two implications of this equation. First, so long as deterrence is costly, optimal deterrence is unlikely to be perfect deterrence. In other words, costly deterrence precludes a rational society from eliminating crime by deterring it perfectly. Second, if the cost of deterrence rises, the optimal amount of it falls. Third, if the net harm from crime rises, optimal deterrence increases.

Note that this mathematical model simplifies the computation of optimal deterrence in several ways. One important simplification concerns the fact that we have not modeled the construction of an optimal *schedule* of punishments. Rather than standing alone, criminal penalties form part of an integrated schedule that influences their optimal values. Using powerful deterrents on less serious crimes often precludes using them on more serious crimes.

To illustrate, assume that life imprisonment is the maximum punishment available in a society, and the law prescribes life imprisonment for embezzling. Now assume that a police officer runs after an embezzler who has a gun. If the officer apprehends the embezzler, he will be imprisoned for life as required by the harsh law. So, the embezzler might as well try to shoot the officer. If he succeeds in killing the officer, he will escape. If he fails, there will be no additional punishment because the punishment for embezzling is already the maximum. In this example, harsh penalties for less serious crimes undermine the deterrence of more serious crimes. Unfortunately, taking such facts into account when determining punishments requires mathematics beyond the scope of this book.

Where efficient, harsh penalties may violate the moral and constitutional rights of criminals. For example, consider a law imposing the death sentence for embezzling petty cash. This law would create a large disparity between the severity of the punishment and the seriousness of the offense. Most people would regard the law as immoral, and American judges would probably declare it unconstitutional. Such noneconomic considerations can operate as constraints upon the computation of optimal deterrents.

QUESTION 11.20: Explain how a shift in $p(z)$ that increases p' changes the optimal level of deterrence.

QUESTION 11.21: Assume that the state forbids competition in a naturally competitive market, so that producers who break the law ("black marketers") contribute to efficiency. In the measure of the social costs of crime, is the amount $(d + i - b)$ positive or negative?

H. Mathematics of Optimal Means of Deterrence

Having shown how to determine the optimum amount of deterrence, we next turn to an analysis of the optimal *means* of deterring crime. There are many allocation decisions to be made, such as the choice between foot patrols and car patrols by police, the choice between more police and more prosecutors, and the choice between more use of fines and more use of jails. We shall examine several of these choices to bring out some underlying principles.

First, consider a choice between allocating resources to make punishment more certain or more severe. For example, allocating more resources to police makes punishment more certain, and allocating more resources to prisons permits longer sentences. We depict the choice between certainty and severity in Figure 11.6. The vertical axis measures the probability of the criminal's being punished; the horizontal axis measures the severity of punishment.

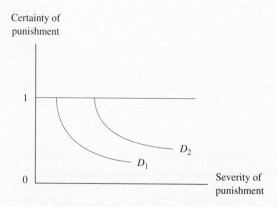

FIGURE 11.6 Deterrence isoquants.

When the probability of punishment is multiplied by its severity, the result is the expected punishment. The downward-sloping lines in Figure 11.6 represent combinations of certainty and severity of punishment that generate the same expected punishment. The expected punishment is the same along any one line because, when moving along the line, changes in the probability of punishment exactly offset changes in its severity. However, moving from any point on one line, say, D_1, to a higher line, say, D_2, represents an increase in the expected punishment.

To keep the analysis simple, assume that the amount of crime is constant when the expected punishment is constant, and that the amount of crime decreases when the expected punishment increases. Consequently, the lines D_1 and D_2 in Figure 11.6 can each be interpreted as lines of constant deterrence. Thus, along each line the amount of crime is constant. In technical language, these lines are *deterrence isoquants.* Moving to a higher isoquant corresponds to a lower crime rate. Thus, the total amount of crime deterred by the combinations of certainty and severity along D_1 is less than that deterred along D_2.

The isoquants in Figure 11.6 hold *deterrence* constant, which, in this model, implies holding constant the amount of crime. Now consider holding constant the total *expenditure* on deterring crime. For example, the curve labeled "high expenditure" in Figure 11.7 indicates the combinations of certainty and severity that a locality can achieve by spending a high amount on deterrence, say, $10 million. Similarly, the curve labeled "low expenditure" indicates the combinations that the locality can achieve by spending a low amount on deterrence, say, $5 million. Expenditures on deterrence remain constant when moving along any line of constant expenditure, whereas expenditures increase when moving from a lower line to a higher line.

Having depicted deterrence and expenditures in Figure 11.7, we can describe the optimal combinations of severity and certainty. If the legal system can achieve a higher level of deterrence at its current level of expenditure, then the current situation cannot be efficient. For example, compare the points (x_1, y_1) and (x^*, y^*) in Figure 11.7. The two points are on the same expenditure line, but the second point lies on a higher deterrence line than the first point. Therefore, the first point cannot be optimal.

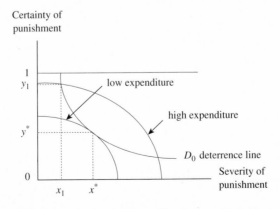

FIGURE 11.7 The efficient combination of certainty and severity of punishment.

Efficiency requires decision-makers to maximize deterrence for a given level of expenditures. To illustrate finding the optimum, start at either end of the "low expenditure" line and move toward the center. As you move toward the center, you cross higher deterrence lines, which indicate an increase in deterrence. Deterrence continues to increase until you reach the point (x^*, y^*). If you continue moving past (x^*, y^*), deterrence decreases. Therefore, the optimum occurs at (x^*, y^*).

Notice the following fact about point (x^*, y^*) in Figure 11.7: At this point, the expenditure curve is tangent to the deterrence isoquant. In general, the efficient combination of severity and certainty occurs at the point where the expenditure curve is tangent to the deterrence isoquant. This conclusion corresponds to a familiar result in consumer theory. Lines of constant deterrence in the analysis of crimes correspond to lines of constant utility in consumer theory. A line of constant expenditures in the analysis of crimes corresponds to the budget line in consumer theory. The optimum in consumer theory occurs where the budget line is tangent to the utility curve, which corresponds to a point in Figure 11.7 where the expenditure line is tangent to the deterrence isoquant.

To make this abstract exercise more concrete, consider some real examples. Suppose that the certainty of the punishment depends upon expenditures for police and prosecutors and that the punishment for the relevant crime is a fine. Police and prosecutors are costly, whereas fines are so cheap to administer that they yield a profit to the state, at least so long as the fine is not too large relative to the offender's income. Thus, certainty of punishment is costly for the state to achieve relative to severity of punishment by a fine.

Figure 11.8 represents this fact through an expenditure curve that is almost horizontal for modest fines. When certainty is costly and severity is cheap, efficient deterrence requires severe punishment (large fines) administered with low probability of apprehension and conviction. This fact is represented in Figure 11.8 by the point (x^*, y^*); the probability of punishment y^* is small relative to the fine x^*. Thus, in this instance the efficient means of achieving deterrence D is to spend relatively little on police and prosecutors and to impose a heavy fine on criminals.

Instead of assuming that the punishment is a fine, assume that it is imprisonment. Unlike fines, imprisonment is very expensive. Assume that longer prison sentences,

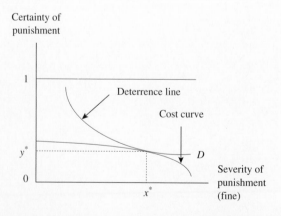

FIGURE 11.8 Allocating resources to deterrence when certainty of punishment is relatively more expensive than severity of punishment.

which increase the severity of punishment, cost the state more than additional police and prosecutors, which increase the certainty of punishment. Under these assumptions, efficient deterrence may require modest punishment with high probability. This possibility is illustrated in Figure 11.9, where the optimal point (z^*, y^*) corresponds to a certain, but short, jail sentence.

There is another immediate consequence of this argument concerning combinations of fines and jail sentences. The previous figures depicted the trade-off between certainty and severity of punishment. In contrast, Figures 11.10 and 11.11 depict the trade-off between fines and imprisonment. In those figures we represent the severity of imprisonment on the horizontal axis and the severity of the fine on the vertical axis. The deterrence isoquant, labeled D_0 in the figures, connects combinations of fines and imprisonment that deter equal amounts of crime. In other words, D_0 indicates the amount by which fines must increase to offset a decrease in imprisonment in order to hold constant the amount of crime.

It seems safe to assume that imprisonment is far more costly to the state than collecting fines. The relative cost of imprisonment and collecting fines is represented in Fig. 11.10 by the line of constant expenditure. Total expenditures on punishment are the same everywhere along the expenditure line. At what point on the expenditure line is deterrence greatest? Deterrence is greatest where the expenditure line touches the highest deterrence line, which occurs at point y^* in Figure 11.10. Furthermore, point y^* is on the vertical axis. This means that the state achieves the greatest deterrence at given cost by relying exclusively on fines and not using imprisonment.

There is another line in the figure that we have not discussed, the line S_a. S_a represents the offender's financial solvency constraint: The offender is not capable of paying a fine greater than S_a. Fortunately, the optimal fine of y^* lies below S_a in Figure 11.10, which indicates that the offender can pay the fine.

Now assume that the offender *cannot* pay the full fine. In Figure 11.11 the curves are the same as in Figure 11.10, but note that this offender's solvency constraint, S_b, is considerably below that of the offender depicted in Figure 11.10. As a result, deterrence

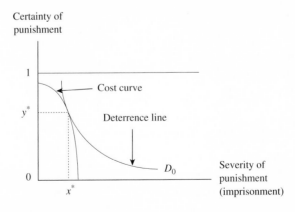

FIGURE 11.9 Allocating resources to deterrence when severity of punishment is relatively more expensive than certainty of punishment.

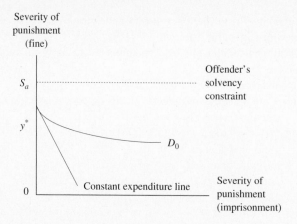

FIGURE 11.10 The trade-off between fines and imprisonment when the optimal severity is less than the offender's solvency constraint.

D_0 cannot be achieved without combining a fine and imprisonment—specifically, through a fine of S_b and a jail sentence equal to x^*.

Notice two important facts about the optimum in Figure 11.11. First, the optimal punishment includes the maximum fine that the criminal can pay. In general, efficiency requires exhausting the ability to punish criminals cheaply with fines before resorting to the costly punishment of imprisonment. Second, the state must spend much more to deter people who cannot pay fines than to deter people who can pay fines. This fact prompts policy-makers to look for ways to increase the capacity of criminals to pay fines. In the next chapter, we describe a system developed in northern Europe, called the "day-fine", which attempts to overcome the criminal's solvency constraint.

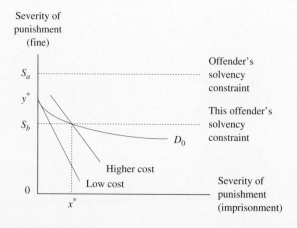

FIGURE 11.11 The trade-off between fines and imprisonment when the offender's solvency constraint restricts the use of fines as a deterrent.

INSURANCE FOR CRIMINALS?

We explained that the state should deter crimes through fines rather than imprisonment whenever possible. The inability of the criminal to pay a fine limits its use. The criminal's bankruptcy forces the justice system to resort to imprisonment. Insurance can overcome the bankruptcy constraint. For example, a $100,000 insurance policy against criminal fines would enable a person with only $10,000 in wealth to pay a $50,000 fine.

It might seem, then, that the state would encourage insurance against criminal fines. In fact, the law in the United States and elsewhere typically forbids writing insurance policies to cover criminal fines. Apparently, officials fear that insurance will cause criminals to commit more crimes because the punishment will fall upon the criminals' insurers. According to this argument, insurance blunts deterrence. If insurance against criminal fines were allowed, however, the insurance companies would want to monitor policy holders to make sure that they do not commit crimes. Thus, private enforcement by insurance companies would supplement public enforcement by the police. Private enforcement by insurance companies might be effective in deterring crime. This body of law needs rethinking.

QUESTION 11.22: Explain in words when efficiency requires severe punishments with low probability, and when efficiency requires mild punishments with high probability.

QUESTION 11.23: How does full employment reduce the cost of deterring crime?

I. Private Deterrence

Example 3 concerns whether Yvonne should protect herself by (1) installing bars on her windows; (2) installing a loud burglar alarm; or (3) buying a gun. Much deterrence of crime is by private individuals, not public officials. The example raises the question of whether or not private citizens have incentives to invest optimally in deterring crime. In general, the answer is "no." Private citizens are mostly concerned with private costs and benefits, which do not necessarily align with public costs and benefits.

To illustrate, suppose that Yvonne installs a brand X double-bolt lock on her front door. Installing the lock has private value for her if it prevents the burglary of her house. Call this effect *private deterrence* because it benefits the private investor in precaution. Installing the lock has public value for Yvonne's neighbors if burglars tend to avoid neighborhoods in which some houses have brand X double-bolt locks. Call this effect *public deterrence* because it benefits the public. Installing the lock has little social value if it prevents the burglary of Yvonne's house by causing a burglar to rob the house next door. Call this effect *redistributing crime*. Redistributing crime has no net social benefit.

Private investment in preventing crime usually has these three effects (and other effects that need not concern us here.) The state should encourage private investments that contribute to public deterrence, but the state need not encourage private investments that contribute to private deterrence or redistribute crime.

MODERN BOUNTY HUNTERS?

People complain about increasing crime. Would privatizing enforcement help? Consider this privatization plan: whoever apprehends a criminal receives the fine the criminal owed to the state. Instead of relying on police, society would rely upon bounty hunters to apprehend criminals whose crimes are punishable by fines. To keep the bounty hunters under control, they would be bonded and held liable for any harm that they cause by apprehending the wrong person.

This system has a defect much like open-access fishing, which results in overfishing the sea. Giving the full fine to a private bounty hunter might attract too many bounty hunters. To eliminate the defect and prevent excessive bounty-hunting, the state could retain part of the fine and pay the remainder to the bounty hunter. By continually adjusting this "tax," the state could induce optimal private-enforcement effort. This system could work well, for example, in apprehending people who flout parking and motor vehicle laws.

A simple condition determines whether the redistributive effect is small or large. Before committing a crime, the criminal can observe some private precautions. For burglary, examples of *ex ante observable precautions* include lights on walkways, bars on exterior windows, and exterior alarms. *Ex ante* observable precautions tend to redistribute crime. Criminals cannot observe other private precautions until they begin committing the crime. For burglary, examples of *ex post observable precautions* include locks on interior doors, interior alarms, and guns owned by residents. *Ex post* observable precautions promote public deterrence by reducing the average profitability of crime. These facts lead to a definite prescription about private investment in preventing crime: *The state should encourage ex post observable precautions; the state need not encourage ex ante observable precautions.*

QUESTION 11.24: Classify the following precautions against crime into *ex ante* observable and *ex ante* unobservable, and explain your answer: private guards in stores, auto alarms, "quick-dial" emergency phone systems (911 numbers in the United States), hidden cameras, and plain-clothes detectives.

QUESTION 11.25: Assume that burglars correctly believe that many people in your neighborhood keep guns. How might this fact increase your security? How might this fact endanger you?

CONCLUSION

We began this chapter with a discussion of the traditional characteristics of a crime. We then recast the theory of crime in terms of an economic theory of criminal behavior. That theory holds that rational criminals compare the benefits of crime with the expected punishment imposed by the criminal justice system. We used this behavioral theory to develop an economic theory of optimal punishment, based upon the goal of minimizing the sum of the social harm caused by crime and the cost of deterring it. We showed how to determine the optimal level of deterrence and how to allocate society's resources optimally among alternative ways to deter crime. Our task in the next chapter is to show how to use these models in formulating policy in the area of criminal law.

SUGGESTED READINGS

Becker, Gary S., *Crime and Punishment: An Economic Approach,* 76 J. POL. ECON. 169 (1968).

Hart, H. L. A., PUNISHMENT AND RESPONSIBILITY (1968).

Jevons, Marshall, MURDER AT THE MARGIN (1979) and THE FATAL EQUILIBRIUM (1984).
[These are murder mysteries solved by the application of microeconomic theory.]

Katz, Leo, BAD ACTS AND GUILTY MINDS: CONUNDRUMS OF THE CRIMINAL LAW (1987).

12

TOPICS IN THE ECONOMICS OF CRIME
AND PUNISHMENT

"We have strict statutes and most biting laws,
The needful bits and curbs to headstrong weeds,
Which for this nineteen years we have let slip;
. . . so . . . liberty plucks justice by the nose;
The baby beats the nurse, and quite athwart
Goes all decorum."

—

Shakespeare, MEASURE FOR MEASURE, Act I, Scene 2.

In this chapter we apply the theoretical insights of the previous chapter to public-policy issues in criminal law, especially those current in the United States. We shall review the evidence on whether or not people respond to punishment as predicted by the economic theory of crime, summarize the economic literature on the death penalty, examine the connection between crime and drug addiction, and discuss the economics of handgun control.

I. CRIME IN THE UNITED STATES

We begin with a brief overview of crime in the United States. As in the preceding quote from Shakespeare, American voters apparently think that the criminal justice authorities have "let slip" the "needful bits and curbs to headstrong weeds." Legislators have responded to the cry of voters for harsher treatment of criminals in recent years by enacting "strict statutes and most biting laws." The total number of prisoners, which has risen sharply in the United States in recent years, is approximately 1 million today and may rise to 2.26 million by 2004. The United States today has 450 people per 100,000 population in prison, the highest proportion in the world. By contrast, the figure in France is 81 per 100,000.[1]

This legislation responds to the public's perception that too much crime imposed too high costs on society. To test the accuracy of this perception, this section briefly explores statistics on the amount of crime in the United States and its social costs.

---

[1] James Q. Wilson, *What To Do About Crime?* COMMENTARY (September, 1994).

A. Crime Rates

In 1993 there were 14 million serious crimes and about 2 million violent crimes reported to the police in the United States. The total number of persons arrested in the United States for all crimes in 1993 was also about 14 million. In 1992, an estimated 400,000 prisoners were being incarcerated for violent crimes. In order to appreciate these statistics, we will compare the present with the past, and then we will compare the United States with other countries.

Trends in the rate of crime (the amount of crime divided by population) in recent decades in the United States were as follows:

1. from a peak in the mid-1930s, the rate of most crimes (both violent and nonviolent) decreased to a low point in the early 1960s;

2. between the early 1960s and the mid- to late 1970s, a rapid and unprecedented increase in the rate of crime occurred;

3. between the early 1980s and the mid-1990s, the rate of most nonviolent crime among adults decreased markedly; the rate of violent crime decreased slightly among adults and increased among youth.[2]

How do these rates compare with other countries? With respect to nonviolent crimes, the recent rates in the United States are roughly the same as those in other developed nations. More accurately, the recent trends in nonviolent-crime rates in other countries have been upward, while those in the United States have been constant or declining, with the result that nonviolent-crime rates in the United States are now roughly equivalent to those in other developed countries. Consider, for example, that in the early 1980s the burglary rate in Great Britain was significantly lower than the U.S. rate, but that by the mid-1990s the Great Britain burglary rate was higher than the U.S. rate. Similarly, the auto-mobile-theft rate in France in the early 1980s was lower than that in the United States; by the mid-1990s the rate in France was greater than that in the United States. Finally, as early as 1984 the burglary rate in the Netherlands was almost twice that in the United States.

While the United States resembles Europe in rates of nonviolent crime, they differ in rates of violent crimes. The United States has been the leader of the industrialized world in homicide rates (murders divided by population) as long as records have been kept. For well over 100 years, large U.S. cities have had significantly higher homicide rates than similarly sized European cities. Nonetheless, the surge in U.S. homicides and other violent crimes beginning in the 1960s is unlike anything that has occurred in Europe.

The differences in rates of violent crime prompt a search in the statistics for possible causes. First, most large cities have violent-crime rates that are two to seven times higher than those in their suburbs. While this fact suggests that urbanization contributes to crime, changes in urbanization cannot account for the trends described above.

Second, a disproportionate amount of criminals are young males. Arrest statistics suggest that two-thirds of all street crime in the United States is committed by persons under age 25. Changes in crime rates often follow changes in the distribution of people by age. An

---

[2] The principal sources for statistical information on crime are the U.S. Federal Bureau of Investigation's UNIFORM CRIME REPORTS (annual) and the U.S. Department of Justice, Bureau of Justice Statistics, SOURCEBOOK ON CRIMINAL JUSTICE STATISTICS (annual).

increase in the proportion of adolescents will increase the rate of crime. The discernible jump in all crimes in the early 1960s coincided with the maturing into adolescence (roughly ages 14 to 24) of the "baby boom" generation that had been born just after World War II, and the decline in crime in the 1980s coincided with the aging of the population.[3] The increase in the amount of crime since the 1960s, however, was so large that we can explain only a fraction of it by the increase in the number of 14- to 24-year-olds. For example, one study found that the rise in the murder rate during the 1960s was more than 10 times greater than what one could have predicted from the changing age distribution of the population.[4]

Third, violent criminals and their victims in the United States are disproportionately African-Americans. To illustrate, homicides are committed against the U.S. non-black population at about the same rate as the nonminority populations in European countries and, in fact, at *lower* rates than some European countries. Black homicide victims elevate U.S. murder rates to the highest among developed countries. One of the most vitriolic policy debates in the U.S. concerns the cause of the connection between violence and race. One side blames discrimination as the cause, and the other side locates the problem in black society. (See the box, "African-Americans and Crime.")

Fourth, a small number of people commit a large proportion of violent crimes. Approximately 6% of the young males of a given age commit 50% or more of all the serious crimes committed by all young males of that age. The characteristics of this 6% of young males are remarkably consistent across different cultures. They tend to come from dysfunctional families, have close relatives (including parents) who are criminals, have low verbal-intelligence quotients, do poorly in school, are alcohol- and drug-abusers, live in poor and chaotic neighborhoods, and begin their misbehavior at a very young age.[5]

This sociological sketch suggests a connection between crime and poverty, which further suggests a connection between crime and the economy's performance. For example, an increase in unemployment rates might cause an increase in crime rates. In fact, this connection is weak. During the prosperous 1960s, the U.S. economy grew and the distribution of income became slightly more equal, yet the United States experienced a rapid increase in the amount of crime.

We have been discussing the social statistics of crime, whereas the previous chapter analyzed the use of punishment to deter crime. Another explanation for increased crime, one that is in keeping with the economic theory of the previous chapter, is that the expected punishment in the United States for committing a *serious* crime (violent or not) has fallen precipitously over the last four decades. In the 1950s it was 22 days. Today it is just 11 days. For juveniles the expected punishment is particularly low.[6]

---

[3] In 1950 there were 24 million people ages 14 to 24, and by 1960 that figure had increased only marginally to 27 million. However, within the next decade the number increased by 13 million, or by 1.3 million per year. In 1990 there were 1.5 million fewer boys ages 15 to 19 than there had been in 1980. This group accounted for 9.3% of the U.S. population in 1980 but for only 7.2% of the population in 1990.

[4] A detailed discussion of these figures and of alternative explanations for the crime wave of the 1960s may be found in James Q. Wilson, THINKING ABOUT CRIME (rev. ed. 1983), pp. 13–25 (Ch. 1, "Crime Amidst Plenty: the Paradox of the Sixties") and pp. 223–49 (Ch. 12, "Crime and American Culture"). It is also important to note that this secular increase in the amount of crime has been observed in *all* of the developed economies, not just in the United States.

[5] For a discussion of the policy implications of these connections, see Wilson, *supra* n. 1.

[6] Id.

AFRICAN-AMERICANS AND CRIME[7]

B lacks and whites had, in 1992, identical victimization rates for personal theft. However, for more serious theft (burglary, larceny, and automobile theft) the rate of black victimization was 33% higher than the rate for whites. More dramatically, in 1988 blacks accounted for 20% of the population in the 75 most populous urban counties in the United States but accounted for 54% of all murder victims in those counties.[8] Why are black Americans disproportionately victims of violent crime? Professor DiIulio of Princeton University concludes that affluent Americans move to safer communities, choose safer jobs, and enjoy relatively safe forms of recreation, whereas poverty prevents many black Americans from distancing themselves from criminals. (Note that most violent crime in the United States is *intra*racial: black criminals tend to have black victims, and white criminals tend to have white victims.[9]

A similar racial disparity exists among criminals. In the 75 most populous counties in the country, blacks account for 20% of the population but for 62% of all defendants in murder cases. In 1991 the arrest rate for violent crime for young black males was five times higher than for young white males (1456 per 100,000 for black youth and 283 per 100,000 for white youth).

Disproportionate arrest rates resulted in a disproportionately African-American prison population. In 1990, 48.9% of all state prisoners and 31.4% of all federal prisoners were black. (The proportions were almost the same in 1980.)[10] Why are black Americans disproportionate perpetrators of violent crime? Professor DiIulio points to the tragic fact that a disproportionate share of African-American youth grow up in dysfunctional families and in neighborhoods in which delinquent and deviant behavior is common. Conversely, low crime rates among Chinese immigrants to the United States are often attributed to family and cultural characteristics.[11]

---

[7] The material in this box comes from John J. DiIulio Jr., *The Question of Black Crime,* THE PUBLIC INTEREST (Fall, 1994). See also the commentaries on that article by Glenn C. Loury, James Q. Wilson, Paul H. Robinson, Patrick A. Langan, and Richard T. Gill.

[8] For violent crimes of all types, the victimization rate in 1992 was 113 per 1000 for teenage black males, 94 per 1000 for teenage black females, 90 for teenage white males, and 55 for teenage white females. For slightly older black males (ages 20-34) the rate was 80; for white males of the same age the rate was 52. Finally, for adult black males between the ages of 35 and 64 the rate was 35; for adult white males, it was 18.

[9] Approximately 84% of the single-offender violent crimes committed by blacks are committed against other blacks, and about 73% of violent crimes committed by whites are committed against other whites.

[10] Some contend that the arrest, conviction, and imprisonment records reflect a racist criminal justice system. There is much evidence against this view. A recent National Academy of Sciences study said, "[F]ew criminologists would argue that the current gap between black and white levels of imprisonment is mainly due to discrimination in sentencing or in any of the other decision-making processes in the criminal justice system." Similarly, a 1991 RAND Corporation study of adult robbery and burglary defendants in 14 large urban areas found no evidence of racial or ethnic discrimination in conviction rates, disposition times, or other important indicators of outcomes.

[11] "During the 1960s, one neighborhood in San Francisco had the lowest income, the highest unemployment rate, the highest proportion of families with incomes under $4000 per year, the least educational attainment, the highest tuberculosis rate, and the highest proportion of substandard housing. . . . That neighborhood was called Chinatown. Yet in 1965, there were only five persons of Chinese ancestry committed to prison in the entire state of California." Wilson and Herrnstein, CRIME AND HUMAN NATURE (1985).

B. Social Cost of Crime

Now we turn from the quantity of crime to its costs. We may divide the social cost of crime into the property and personal losses of victims and the public and private costs of preventing crime. We can make a rough estimate of each of these elements in order to compute the social costs of crime in the United States in a recent year.

The easiest costs to document are state expenditures on preventing crime and punishing criminals. Spending on the criminal-justice system in 1992 constituted 7.5% of all governmental spending at the local, state, and federal levels. The total amount spent annually by all levels of government in the United States on the criminal-justice system is $90 billion. Of that total, approximately $35 billion is spent on police protection. Federal and state prison systems cost about $21 billion per year. Prosecutors, public defenders, probation officers, courts, record-keeping, and so on account for the remaining $34 billion.

Expenditures by individuals and private organizations to prevent crime are more difficult to estimate than state expenditures. This money is spent on alarms, private guards, security systems, and the like. In 1993 private expenditures to prevent crime in the United States amounted to approximately $65 billion.

The value of lost property and the losses to individual victims of crime are the most difficult elements of the social costs of crime to estimate. The value of all stolen goods in 1992 was estimated to be $45 billion. We have only rough estimates of personal losses to victims: for example, the medical costs of attending to those injured in crimes was $5 billion in 1992, ignoring the many indirect costs of crime to the victims such as trauma, anxiety, and shattered lives.

If we add these elements, we conclude that expenditures on preventing crime equal approximately $155 billion, and the direct costs of crime to victims equal at least $50 billion. Thus, the total cost equals $205 billion, or approximately 5% of the U.S. gross domestic product.[12]

QUESTION 12.1: Do statistics support the perception that the United States has been swept by a wave of crime?

QUESTION 12.2: If expenditures on preventing crime equal $155 billion and the costs of crime to victims equal at least $50 billion, could the United States save $105 billion by abandoning all efforts to prevent crime?

QUESTION 12.3: How would economics try to answer the question, "Does crime increase or decrease as a society becomes more wealthy?"

QUESTION 12.4: When statutes prescribe the exact punishment for each crime, the judge's discretionary power decreases and the prosecutor's increases. Predict how this change might affect the charges made against arrested persons.

---

[12] See John Donohue III and Peter Siegelman, *Does the United States Have the Optimal Amount of Crime?* (Northwestern University School of Law Working Paper, 1994).

II. DOES PUNISHMENT DETER CRIME?

In the previous chapter we outlined an economic theory of the decision to commit a crime. According to that theory, an increase in expected punishment causes a decrease in crime, holding other variables constant. How much of a decrease? The *deterrence hypothesis* holds that an increase in expected punishment causes a *significant* decrease in crime. In technical terms, the deterrence hypothesis holds that the supply of crime is elastic with respect to punishment. If so, then increasing the resources that society devotes to the arrest, conviction, and punishment of criminals should reduce the social costs of the harm caused by crime.

An alternative hypothesis holds that variations in the certainty and severity of punishment do *not* significantly deter criminals. Rather, crime is the result of a complex set of socioeconomic factors or possibly biological factors. The appropriate way to minimize the social costs of crime is to attack these root causes of crime—for example, devote resources to job-creation, income maintenance, family counseling, mental health, and other programs designed to alleviate the social, economic, and biological causes of crime.

Although public debate frames these two hypotheses as mutually exclusive, they might both be correct in the sense that many variables cause crime, including the absence of certain punishment. If both hypotheses are true, the optimal public policy for reducing crime is a mix of criminal justice and socioeconomic programs. We shall examine the relevant literature for each of the two hypotheses and then, at the end of this section, draw a tentative conclusion on their merits.

A. Deterrence

The usual statistical study of deterrence seeks to explain a certain kind of crime as a function of three types of variables. These explanatory variables include, first, proxies for the expected punishment, such as the probabilities of being arrested and convicted and the average prison sentence for that crime. Second, certain labor market conditions used to measure the opportunity cost of crime, such as the unemployment rate and the income level of the jurisdiction. And third, certain socioeconomic variables, such as the age, race, and urbanization of the jurisdiction's population. The statistics may be from a single jurisdiction over time, or from different jurisdictions at the same point in time, or both.

Numerous empirical studies have this form. Here we discuss three especially noteworthy examples. First, a famous study by the economist Isaac Ehrlich used data on robbery for the entire United States in 1940, 1950, and 1960 to estimate the deterrence hypothesis and concluded that, holding all other variables constant, the higher the probability of conviction for robbery, the lower the robbery rate.[13] Second, Alfred Blumstein and Daniel Nagin studied the relationship between draft evasion and penal-

---

[13] Isaac Ehrlich, *Participation in Illegitimate Activities: A Theoretical and Empirical Investigation,* 81 J. POL. ECON. 521 (1973). Ehrlich also found that there was no deterrent effect attributable to the severity of punishment, as measured by the average length of a prison sentence for robbery in the years 1940 and 1960, but that there was such a deterrent effect in 1950.

ties for it in the 1960s and 1970s. They concluded that a higher probability of conviction and a higher level of penalty caused a lower rate of draft evasion.[14] Third, a study by Kenneth Wolpin used time-series data from England and Wales over the lengthy period 1894–1967 to test for a deterrent effect in those countries. Wolpin found that crime rates in the United Kingdom were an inverse function of the probability and severity of punishment.[15]

These studies found a significant deterrence effect. The National Research Council of the U.S. National Academy of Sciences established the Panel on Research on Deterrent and Incapacitative Effects in 1978 to evaluate the many academic studies of deterrence. The panel concluded that "the evidence certainly favors a proposition supporting deterrence more than it favors one asserting that deterrence is absent."[16]

These studies seek to explain the "crime rate," which is a highly aggregated statistic. Rather than studying crime rates, another approach to deterrence studies the behavior of small groups of people. We know that a relatively small proportion of the population commits a large proportion of the crime. Economists have had some success in predicting who will become violent criminals. (See box titled "Guilty of Future Crimes.") We describe two studies on deterring offenses by such people.

First, Professor Ann Witte followed the post-release behavior of 641 convicted criminals for three years. She gathered information on whether the men were arrested again during that period (about 80% were), on their previous convictions and imprisonments, on their labor-market experience after release, and on whether they were addicted to alcohol or drugs. Professor Witte tested the hypothesis that conviction and imprisonment induced these high-risk offenders to engage in fewer crimes in the future. She concluded that the higher the probability of conviction and imprisonment, the lower the number of subsequent arrests per month out of prison.[17]

Second, Charles Murray and Louis Cox Jr. tracked the records of 317 Chicago males, with an average age of 16, who had been imprisoned for the first time by the Illinois Department of Corrections. Notwithstanding their youth, this was a hardened group of young men: before receiving their first prison sentence, they averaged 13 prior arrests per person; as a group, they had been charged with 14 homicides, 23 rapes, more than

---

[14] Alfred Blumstein and Daniel Nagin, *The Deterrent Effect of Legal Sanctions on Draft Evasion,* 28 STAN. L. REV. 241 (1977).

[15] Kenneth Wolpin, *An Economic Analysis of Crime and Punishment in England and Wales 1894–1967,* 86 J. POL. ECON. 815 (1978). The data were better than any comparable data from the United States and, because of the length of the time period covered, allowed for considerable flexibility in the hypotheses tested.

[16] Blumstein, Cohen, and Nagin, eds., DETERRENCE AND INCAPACITATION: ESTIMATING THE EFFECTS OF CRIMINAL SANCTIONS ON CRIME RATES (1978). A critique of that report may be found in Ehrlich and Mark, *Fear of Deterrence,* 6 J. LEGAL STUD. 293 (1977).

[17] Ann Witte, *Estimating the Economic Model of Crime with Individual Data,* 94 Q. J. ECON. 57 (1980). Additionally, she discovered that the strength of the deterrent effect varied between different classes of potential offenders. For those who engaged in serious, including violent, crimes, severity of punishment had a stronger deterrent effect than certainty of punishment. For those whose engaged in property crimes, certainty of arrest and conviction had a stronger deterrent effect than severity of punishment. The deterrent effect was weakest for drug addicts. Lastly and somewhat surprisingly, the ease of subsequent employment had no significant effect on future criminal offenses.

GUILTY OF FUTURE CRIMES

Social scientists have modestly increasing abilities to predict crime. For example, Peter Greenwood's study for RAND titled SELECTIVE INCAPACITATION (1982) found that high-rate criminal offenders could be predicted as having seven characteristics: (1) conviction of a crime while a juvenile; (2) use of illegal drugs as a juvenile; (3) use of illegal drugs during the last two years; (4) employment less than 50% of the time in the previous two years; (5) incarceration in a juvenile facility; (6) imprisonment during more than 50% of the last two years; and (7) a previous conviction for the current offense.

A controversial conclusion that some people reach is that criminals with these characteristics should be incapacitated in prison for a longer period than other criminals. For example, M. Moore, S. Estrich, D. McGillis, and W. Sperlman give "qualified endorsement" to a policy of "selective incapacitation" in DANGEROUS OFFENDERS: THE ELUSIVE TARGET OF JUSTICE (1985). Of course, decisions about whether to grant bail, about the severity of punishment, and about parole are all currently made on the basis of predictions about the criminal disposition of the offender. In *Barefoot v. Estelle,* 463 U.S. 880 (1983), *reh. den.* 464 U.S. 874 (1983), the U.S. Supreme Court allowed psychiatric testimony on an individual's likely future dangerousness to be put before a jury that was deciding whether the defendant should be given the death penalty.

QUESTION 12.5: Does efficiency require the adjustment of punishment according to predictions about future crime? Is doing so unfair?

---

300 assaults, over 300 auto thefts, almost 200 armed robberies, and more than 700 burglaries. The average sentence for their offenses was 10 months. Murray and Cox followed these young offenders for about 18 months after their release and found that during that period the group's arrest record fell by two-thirds. The authors concluded that imprisonment served as a deterrent to future crime for this high-risk group.[18]

B. Economic Conditions and Crime Rates

A rational criminal responds to the opportunity cost of crime, so an increase in the opportunities for earning income legally should cause a decrease in criminality. If opportunity cost has a powerful effect, then the best policies for reducing the amount of crime are those that ameliorate economic and social conditions. We review briefly

---

[18] C. A. Murray and L. A. Cox Jr., BEYOND PROBATION: JUVENILE CORRECTIONS AND THE CHRONIC DELINQUENT (1979). Note that Murray and Cox found that re-arrest rates were higher for comparable juveniles who had *not* been imprisoned, but instead were put on probation.

some empirical studies of the extent to which employment and income-enhancing policies reduce the amount of crime. (We do not discuss the statistical studies of the influence of early family life, heredity, and other noneconomic factors on crime rates.[19])

Perhaps unemployed workers commit crimes to gain income or to deal with their
idle time and frustration, so that worsening employment conditions lead to an increase
in the amount of property crimes. Is there a discernible relationship between cyclical
fluctuations in economic conditions and crime rates? Plausible though it may be, statistical support for this hypothesis is weak. In a 1981 survey of the literature on this point,
Thomas Orsagh and Ann Witte found little evidence of a significant relationship.[20]
More recently, Cook and Zarkin found a small increase in the number of burglaries and
robberies during recent recessions, no correlation between the business cycle and homicides, and a countercyclical relationship between economic conditions and auto theft.
Finally, Cook and Zarkin found that long-term trends in crime rates were independent
of the business cycle.[21]

These negative results do not contradict the economic theory of deterrence. In the
economic theory of deterrence, the business cycle influences the opportunity cost of
crime and also the opportunities for crime. These two influences work in opposite
directions. As the economy worsens, criminals have fewer opportunities for legitimate
earnings, and also fewer opportunities for crime. For example, unemployment creates a
motive to sell cocaine and also reduces the number of potential customers.[22]

We may summarize this brief survey of the literature on deterrence as follows:
increases in the probability of arrest, conviction, and punishment, and increases in
the severity of punishment, have a significant deterrent effect on the population at
large, as well as on that small portion of the population that is most likely to commit
crime; general improvements in the economy have no significant impact on the
crime rates.

Before concluding, we mention two general problems with all statistical studies of
deterrence. First, the accuracy of the data on the number of crimes differs significantly
among jurisdictions at any point in time, and within a jurisdiction at different points in
time. These inaccuracies create spurious statistical relationships. Second, estimated models omit some important but difficult-to-measure variables, such as whether adults were
abused as children. If omitted variables correlate with included variables, the estimated

---

[19] See, for example, James Q. Wilson and Richard Herrnstein, CRIME AND HUMAN NATURE (1985).

[20] Orsagh and Witte, *Economic Status and Crime: Implications for Offender Rehabilitation,* 72 J. CRIM. L. &
CRIMINOLOGY 1055 (1981). This study follows up a literature survey by Robert Gillespie, ECONOMIC
FACTORS IN CRIME AND DELINQUENCY (1978). Gillespie found three studies that discovered a significant
relationship between unemployment and crime and seven that did not.

[21] Philip J. Cook and Gary A. Zarkin, *Crime and the Business Cycle,* 14 J. LEGAL STUD. 115 (1985). This is,
perhaps, surprising given the correlation between the business cycle and less serious property crimes and
the usual belief that there is a correlation between those property crimes and homicides. See also Richard
Freeman, *Crime and Unemployment,* in CRIME AND PUBLIC POLICY (James Q. Wilson, ed., 1983), and
James Q. Wilson and Philip J. Cook, *Unemployment and Crime—What Is the Connection?* 79 PUBLIC
INTEREST 3 (1985).

[22] An excellent discussion of the literature on deterring crime through increasing the benefits of legal
alternatives may be found in Wilson, THINKING ABOUT CRIME (rev. ed. 1983), pp. 137–42.

relationship will be biased. Over time, improvements in measuring variables and better statistical techniques tend to overcome these two weaknesses in deterrence studies.

C. Does Crime Pay?

Most people never commit crime, but some people make a career of it. These career criminals apparently believe that the benefits of crime exceed the expected punishments. Why do career criminals reach a different conclusion from the rest of us? Is crime very profitable for them, or is legitimate work unprofitable for them, or do they have special attitudes toward risk and special valuations of time?

To address these questions, James Q. Wilson and Allan Abrahamse (in *Does Crime Pay?* 9 CRIMINAL JUSTICE QUARTERLY 359 [1992]) compared the gains from crime and from legitimate work for a group of career criminals in state prisons in three states. Wilson and Abrahamse divided prisoners into two groups: mid-rate offenders and high-rate offenders. Using data from the National Crime Survey's report of the average losses by victims in different sorts of crimes, the authors estimated the annual income for criminals.[23] They then compared these estimates of the income from crime with the prisoners' estimates of their income from legitimate sources. Two-thirds of the prisoners had reasonably stable jobs when they were not in prison and, on average, the prisoners believed that they made $5.78 per hour at those legitimate jobs.

As Table 12.1 indicates, Wilson and Abrahamse found that, for mid-rate criminals, working pays more than crime for every type of crime except auto theft. For high-rate offenders, however, crime paid more than legitimate work for *all* crimes except burglary. These figures concern the income from crime, but not the major cost of crime to these criminals: time in prison. When the authors included those costs, the net income from crime fell below the income from legitimate work for both mid-rate and high-rate offenders.

Why, then, do career criminals commit crime? Wilson and Abrahamse consider and reject two explanations. First, the prisoners may have felt they had to commit crime because they had no meaningful opportunity for legitimate work. The authors doubt this view: two-thirds of the prisoners were employed for some length of time during the period examined. Second, the prisoners may have had such serious problems with alcohol and drugs that they could not hold legitimate jobs. The authors argue that although two-thirds of the offenders had drinking or drug problems, the evidence from other studies indicates that these problems do not normally preclude legitimate employment. Wilson and Abrahamse conclude that career criminals are "temperamentally disposed to overvalue the benefits of crime and to undervalue its costs" because they are "inordinately impulsive or present-oriented." In economic terms, these people discount punishments for uncertainty and futurity more highly than other people.

---

[23] For example, they estimated that the value of a stolen car was 20% of its market value. And following a study of drug dealing in Washington, D.C., they estimated that the net income of the average drug dealer was $2000 per month.

Table 12.1

CRIMINAL AND LEGITIMATE EARNINGS PER YEAR (1988 DOLLARS)

Crime type	HIGH-RATE		MID-RATE	
	Crime	*Work*	*Crime*	*Work*
Burglary/theft	$5,711	$5,540	$2,368	$7,931
Robbery	6,541	3,766	2,814	5,816
Swindling	14,801	6,245	6,816	8,113
Auto theft	26,043	2,308	15,008	5,457
Mixed	6,915	5,086	5,626	6,956

SOURCE: WILSON AND ABRAHAMSE, *DOES CRIME PAY?* 9 CRIMINAL JUSTICE QUARTERLY 359, 367 (1992).

QUESTION 12.6: How could the collection of uniform crime statistics contribute to studies of deterrence?

QUESTION 12.7: Describe how statisticians might ideally separate the effect of the business cycle on the opportunity cost of crime and its profitability.

QUESTION 12.8: Assume that criminals discount risk and futurity more than other people. What policies might reduce crime by changing this fact?

III. EFFICIENT PUNISHMENT

What forms of punishment do we actually use in the United States and how efficient are they? In this section we shall first examine the social benefits and costs of imprisonment and then look at the benefits and costs of monetary fines as a deterrent to crime. We argue that the U.S. criminal justice system relies too much on incarceration and too little on fines.

A. Imprisonment

1. The social benefits of imprisonment In principle, incarceration has at least four social benefits: (1) deterrence, (2) retribution, (3) rehabilitation, and (4) incapacitation. We have already discussed empirical evidence on deterrence. We will consider the three remaining benefits in turn.

First, "retributivism" holds that justice requires punishing criminals in proportion to their crimes. In principle, varying the length of the sentence allows the state to adjust the shame and personal cost of imprisonment until it is proportional to the seriousness of the crime. You may think that economics concerns efficiency and has nothing to say about

RETRIBUTION AND ECONOMICS

According to the principle of retribution, justice requires absolving the innocent and punishing the guilty in proportion to their crimes. Conversely, injustice results from punishing the innocent, absolving the guilty, or punishing the guilty out of proportion to the seriousness of their crimes. To avoid these injustices, officials who arrest and prosecute people must have good information about who did what. Given the cost of information, officials make mistakes. Punishing the innocent is called a "false positive" by statisticians, or a "Type I error." Not punishing the guilty is called a "false negative" or a "Type II error."

As officials increase the efficiency of the criminal-justice system, a point is reached where one type of error cannot be reduced without increasing errors of the other type. To illustrate, assume that the prosecutor ranks cases from weak to strong according to the probability of obtaining a conviction. A cutoff point is selected, above which all cases are prosecuted and below which cases are not prosecuted. Raising the cutoff, so that cases are only prosecuted with a high probability of obtaining a conviction, decreases false positives (punishing the innocent) and increases false negatives (not punishing the guilty). Lowering the cutoff has the opposite effect.

One way to choose the cutoff is by finding the point where the expected social cost of false positives equals the expected social cost of false negatives. If punishing an innocent person has more social cost than not punishing a guilty person, then the cutoff will be chosen at a point favoring the accused. Justice, as represented by the principle of retribution, and efficiency, as represented by minimizing the social costs of crime, come together when balancing false positives and false negatives. The two come together because the social cost of false imprisonment or mistaken release from prison depend upon beliefs about justice.

---

this problem of justice. In reality, economics has something to say about any explicit policy goal, including fairness. See the box titled "Retribution and Economics."

The next benefit allegedly derived from imprisonment is "rehabilitation," which means that prison changes criminals so that, after their release, they do not commit future crimes. For example, prison might teach the criminal a marketable job skill or provide religious instruction. The ideal of rehabilitation, which once enjoyed favor in the United States, has fallen out of favor, partly because rehabilitative programs show poor results.[23] Expenditures in U.S. prisons on counseling, job training, and general education have declined in recent years.

The final social benefit, "incapacitation," refers to the fact that, while confined, an offender cannot commit crimes against people outside prison. Even if prison fails to deter or rehabilitate, imprisonment may reduce crime by incapacitating criminals. Most

---

[23] See Francis Allen, THE DECLINE OF THE REHABILITATIVE IDEAL (1981).

recent studies indicate that about two-thirds of all inmates had criminal records before their current stay in prison. Additionally, between 25% and 50% of all offenders are arrested within a very short time—six months to one year—of their release from prison. According to a Brookings Institution study, violent criminals who pass in and out of prison commit 12 serious crimes per year on average while out of prison (excluding drug crimes).[24]

From facts such as these, people conclude that incapacitation significantly lowers crime rates. These facts, however, require scrutiny. Two conditions must be met in order for incarceration to reduce crime rates. First, criminals incapacitated by imprisonment must not be replaced immediately by new criminals. For example, if imprisoning one drug dealer immediately results in his replacement by someone else, then incapacitation does not reduce total sales of drugs. In technical terms, *incapacitation is most effective at reducing crime when the supply of criminals is inelastic.* In general, inelastic supply results from a fixed factor of production. For example, an important drug dealer may have superior knowledge of illegal markets, so that after his arrest, no one else can quickly take his place.

Second, in order for incarceration to reduce crime, imprisonment must reduce the total number of crimes committed by repeat offenders over their criminal careers. For some criminals, incarceration affects the timing, but not the number, of their crimes. To see why, consider that punishment grows more severe with each criminal conviction of a repeat offender. Suppose that after, say, the third conviction, the prospect of a very severe punishment for a fourth conviction causes this person to stop committing crimes. In this example, the fact that the person could not commit crimes while in jail after each of the first three convictions might not influence the total number of crimes the person committed. Rather, the time spent in jail just delayed the arrival of the day the criminal received the third conviction. The punishment for a fourth conviction could be so severe as to deter any further crime. In general, if a person commits crimes until the expected punishment exceeds the benefit, the deterrent effect of imprisonment determines how many crimes the person commits, and incapacitation has no effect.

Now consider the opposite kind of criminal. For this person, the urge to commit crime is irresistible in youth and fades with age. If the state keeps such a person in prison during her youth, and releases her later in life, she will commit fewer crimes over her criminal career. Thus, incapacitation reduces the rate of crimes caused by youthfulness.

The fact that repeat offenders commit fewer crimes as they get older could be due to biological and sociological factors associated with aging, or it could be due to the higher expected penalties faced as their criminal records lengthen. The effect of incapacitation on crime rates has never been measured because existing studies do not take into account the elasticity of the supply of crime and the effects of imprisonment on the timing of crimes.

2. The social costs of imprisonment   Now we turn from the social benefits of imprisonment to the social costs. The social costs of imprisonment include the direct costs of

---

[24]John D. Iullio, *The Costs of Crime*, BROOKINGS REVIEW (Fall, 1994).

building, maintaining, and staffing prisons, and the opportunity cost of losing the productivity of imprisoned people. As to direct costs, recent estimates are that it costs between $20,000 and $30,000 per year to keep one prisoner in a maximum security prison in the United States.

Turning to opportunity costs, inmates in U.S. prisons devote the bulk of their time to making highway signs, doing one another's laundry, preparing meals, and the like. More productive uses of their time surely could be found. One proposal, which former Chief Justice Warren Burger has called "factories with fences," is to invite private industry to hire prisoners to produce marketable goods. At Attica State Prison in New York a metal shop that manufactures file cabinets showed a profit of approximately $1.3 million in 1984. In Minnesota, Stillwater Data Processing Inc.—a private, nonprofit corporation—employs inmates of a maximum-security prison as computer programmers. Legal obstacles confine these developments, such as a federal law that makes transport of prison-made goods in interstate commerce illegal, and the "state use" statutes that forbid the sale of prison-made goods to the governments of most states. Several states, eager to take advantage of the "factories with fences" idea, have repealed their state-use statutes, despite predictable opposition from labor unions.

Is there a cheaper method of deterring criminals than incarceration? One candidate that we shall look at shortly is the use of fines. Another is the use of high-technology monitoring equipment to enforce restrictions on criminals who are not in prison. For example, the terms of probation may prohibit a criminal from leaving a certain city, and the criminal may be required to report to his probation officer each week. In 1994, 40,000 criminals in the United States were wearing ankle bracelets that cannot be removed by them and that emit a signal enabling the police to locate them. The daily cost to the authorities of the ankle bracelet is $5, a fraction of the daily cost of imprisonment.

3. Sentencing Reform Two reforms in the sentencing of prisoners caused the sharp increase in the number of prisoners in the United States that we mentioned earlier. In 1980, most states followed a system called "indeterminate sentencing." Under indeterminate sentencing, the criminal statute prescribed an indefinite term for committing a particular offense, such as imprisonment "for not less than five years, nor more than ten years." The judge had discretion in determining the sentence within these broad boundaries. After the judge pronounced the sentence, the actual time served would be determined by the prison authorities and the parole board, depending on the prisoner's behavior and rehabilitative progress.[25]

In the early 1980s state and federal authorities replaced this system of judicial discretion with a system of determinate or mandatory sentencing. Under this system, the criminal statute prescribes a specific sentence for a particular crime, say 15 years in prison for committing crime X. The offender becomes eligible for parole only after having served some fixed amount of time prescribed in the statute. Sometimes the judge reads the mandatory sentence from a grid. The vertical side of the grid lists crimes by their seriousness, ranging from a lesser felony to first-degree murder. Along the top of the grid, the history of the offender is scaled from 0 (a first-time offender) to

---

[25] The average violent offender in a state prison today spends only 40% of the sentence in prison.

PRISONS FOR PROFIT AND FACTORIES WITH FENCES

The U.S. government buys fighter planes, banking services, and hospital care from private companies. Why not pay private companies to confine prisoners? The profit motive spurs cost-cutting, quality control, and technological innovation, which make private businesses more efficient than the state. To illustrate, the Corrections Corporation of America Inc., constructed the detention center of the U.S. Immigration and Naturalization Service in Houston for one-half the cost, and in one-third the time, required for the construction by the government of a comparable facility. CCA contends that its costs are generally about 6% below those of similar facilities operated by governmental bodies. Recently, CCA made an offer to lease and operate the entire Tennessee state prison system for a fee based on the number of prisoners.

Another private company, Behavioral Systems Southwest, incarcerates 600 to 700 prisoners per day in leased hotels and large houses for a state prison system. The company deals only with low-risk prisoners and manages to detain them in its leased facilities for about $25 per day, compared with the $75 to $100 per-day cost of detention in a conventional facility.

Only a handful of privately operated prisons exist today in the United States, but penologists believe that the trend will broaden. The John Howard Association, a private, nonprofit group that lobbies for prisoners' rights, has not decided whether to support or oppose private prisons. The American Correctional Association is also adopting a wait-and-see attitude. However, the National Sheriffs Association and the American Federation of State, County and Municipal Employees, which represents 40,000 corrections employees, oppose privatization vigorously. (Can you see why?)

9 (a violent career criminal). Entries in the table increase in severity as one reads down or across. Judges have very little discretion to alter the sentence.[26]

We mentioned that the total number of prisoners in the United States rose to 1 million in the mid-1990s, and may rise to 2.26 million by 2004. The principal reason for this increase is the mandatory sentencing of drug offenders. Today, 60% of all inmates in federal prisons and 20% of all those in state prisons are there on drug charges. (Later we analyze drug crimes.)

In complying with the requirements of mandatory sentencing, states are running out of prison space and money. For example, Texas today has 415,000 offenders in prison, at an annual cost of $3 billion. Ten years ago there were 188,000, at an annual cost of

---

[26] For a critique of mandatory sentencing and an argument by a former state court trial judge in Pennsylvania that the prior system of judicial discretion worked well, see Lois G. Forer, A RAGE TO PUNISH: THE UNINTENDED CONSEQUENCES OF MANDATORY SENTENCING (1994).

$600 million. Federal law prevents the states from packing more prisoners into the same prisons.[27] Congress has tried to help the states by providing them with prison space under certain conditions.[28]

Another new law to increase imprisonment is known as "three strikes, you're out." Under this law, an offender convicted of a third violent crime must be sentenced to natural life in prison without possibility of parole. Four states have currently adopted such laws, and the 1994 anti-crime bill passed by Congress contained a "three strikes, you're out" provision. The economic wisdom of "three strikes, you're out" is dubious. Imprisoning a 25-year-old for life would cost a total of $600,000 to $1,000,000. Keeping older inmates in prison is very costly and does not provide much social benefit. A California study found that the annual medical costs for prison inmates 55 and older are $60,000 to $80,000. Moreover, only 2% of inmates over 55 who are released are ever re-arrested.

B. Fines

Imprisoning more people for longer periods may not be the most efficient way to reduce crime. A leading alternative to imprisonment is fines. In the previous chapter we examined the theory of fines, so our focus here is on the benefits and problems of implementing a system of fines for deterring crime.

Table 12.2 compares the use of fines and incarceration in several Western nations. Note the much greater reliance in Western Europe on fines, and the greater reliance in the United States on incarceration. What explains this difference? One possible explanation is that the United States' criminal population differs in significant ways from the European criminal population. For instance, Americans may use a gun or other dangerous weapon more frequently, thus deserving a stronger punishment. A second possibility is that a higher percentage of the United States' criminal population consists of repeat offenders, for whom imprisonment may be the preferred sanction, while European criminals may tend to be first-time offenders, for whom fines may be the preferred sanction. A third possibility is that European criminals are more responsive to the threat of punishment than are criminals in the United States. Thus, authorities in this country must use more severe penalties to achieve the same level of deterrence that less severe sanctions generate in Europe. Finally, the difference may be due to different

---

[27] In North Carolina, inmates sued the state, contending that crowded state prisons violate the Eighth Amendment of the U.S. Constitution, which forbids cruel and unusual punishment. The 1988 agreement settling the suit stipulated that North Carolina would provide 50 square feet of space for each prisoner. With its current facilities, North Carolina can only house 21,400 prisoners and still satisfy this agreement. To keep the total state prison population at 21,400, the average time served by prisoners in North Carolina over the past seven years has fallen from 40% of the original sentence to 18.5%.

[28] In its 1994 anti-crime act, Congress appropriated money for the federal government to build ten "regional prisons," designed to add 50,000 to 100,000 new prison spaces within the next five years. Congress invited the states to place their prisoners in these new facilities (thus saving the states the politically painful cost of building their own new prisons), but only if the states would reform their criminal codes in several ways—most importantly by assuring the federal government that violent offenders would spend 85% of their sentence in prison.

Table 12.2

COMPARATIVE PUNISHMENT FOR SELECTED TRADITIONAL CRIMES, 1977

Country/Jurisdiction	Total of selected defendants	Percent of all defendants	Incarceration	Fine only	All other
England, Wales	293,580	69%	14%	56%	30%
Germany	191,329	77%	10%	77%	13%
Sweden	29,121	67%	13%	43%	44%
U.S. Federal District Courts	16,057	56%	39%	5%	56%
Washington, D.C., Superior Court, 1974	1,847	38%	32%	4%	64%

*THE TABLE AND ACCOMPANYING TEXTUAL INFORMATION ARE FROM ROBERT GILLESPIE, *SANCTIONING TRADITIONAL CRIMES WITH FINES: A COMPARATIVE ANALYSIS,* 5 INTERNATIONAL J. OF COMPARATIVE AND APPLIED CRIM. JUSTICE 197 (1981).

philosophical and cultural traditions. Europeans exhibit a distrust of imprisonment[29] as a deterrent while Americans exhibit a distrust of fines.[30]

The typical fine in the United States is a fixed fine per offense, independent of the offender's wealth, with statutorily defined absolute maximums. By contrast, many European countries combine the use of the fixed-fine-per-offense system with an additional fine (called the "day-fine" system) scaled according to the offender's income. Under this scheme, the prosecutor determines the defendant's recent daily income and recommends that the defendant be punished, if guilty, by being responsible for paying that daily income times a certain number of days. For a trivial crime, such as a traffic offense, the figure may be 5 or 10 days. For a serious crime, the number of days may rise to a maximum of 120.[31] Instead of paying the day-fine all at once, the convicted person is allowed to spread the payments over a period of time. Spreading the payment overcomes the problem that fines can be large relative to income or wealth.

---

[29] G. Mansell, *Comparative Correctional Systems: United States and Sweden,* 8 CRIM. L. BULL. 748 (1972).

[30] American Bar Association Project on Standards for Criminal Justice, STANDARDS RELATING TO SENTENCING ALTERNATIVES AND PROCEDURES (1971), and National Advisory Commission on Criminal Justice Standards and Goals, PROCEEDINGS OF THE NATIONAL CONFERENCE ON CRIMINAL JUSTICE (1973).

[31] For details on how the system works, see H. Thornstedt, *The Day-Fine System in Sweden,* 1975 CRIM. L. REV. 307. The reason that we may perceive criminal fines to be independent of the criminal's income and wealth is that we ignore the implicit economic effect of conviction on subsequent employment opportunities. John Lott Jr. (in *Do We Punish High Income Criminals Too Heavily?* 30 ECON. INQ. 583 [1992]) shows that high-income criminals suffer a much larger loss in subsequent earnings due to a criminal conviction than do low- and medium-income criminals. Lott calculates that adding in this element of loss makes the total monetary penalty for crime (criminal fine plus the loss in subsequent earnings) steeply progressive.

QUESTION 12.9: Competition among sellers improves the quality of goods for consumers. Could this mechanism work for the private supply of prisons?

QUESTION 12.10: How do full employment and high wages contribute to the power of fines as a deterrent?

IV. THE DEATH PENALTY

The ultimate punishment is death. In recent years, many countries have abandoned this sanction, and executions virtually ceased in the United States during the 1960s. In 1972, the Supreme Court found the death penalty to be unconstitutional when applied "capriciously and discriminatorily."[32] This court decision provoked hostility among voters in some states, and many legislators responded by introducing legislation to revive capital punishment. After 1972, state legislatures amended their death statutes to comply with the Supreme Court's decision and to allow executions for the most serious crimes. In 1976 the Supreme Court upheld three revised state capital-punishment statutes as constitutional.[33] Currently, 37 states and the U.S. government have capital punishment statutes; 13 states and the District of Columbia do not. Between 1976 and 1994, there were 227 executions of criminals in the United States. As of January 1994, there were 2,802 inmates in state and federal prisons awaiting execution in the United States.

The literature on the economics of capital punishment focuses on the empirical question of whether or not executions deter murders. The debate has centered on statistical issues, such as the specification of the model to be estimated or the adequacy of the data. In this section we shall review this literature and draw some tentative conclusions about the deterrent effect of capital punishment.

A. The Deterrent Effect of Capital Punishment

The sociologist Thorsten Sellin made the first major study of the deterrent effect of the death penalty.[34] Sellin used four tests to detect a deterrent effect. First, he compared the homicide rates for adjacent states that did and did not have the death penalty. He discerned no difference in homicide rates among these adjacent states and, therefore,

---

[32] *Furman v. Georgia,* 408 U.S. 238 (1972). Justices Thurgood Marshall and William Brennan felt that the death penalty was cruel and unusual punishment (and, therefore, violated the Eighth Amendment to the Constitution) under any circumstances and, thus, would always be unconstitutional. (Justice Harry Blackmun announced in 1994, shortly before his retirement, that he, too, had come to believe that capital punishment was unconstitutional under any circumstances.) The other three justices of the majority were not prepared to go so far, holding instead that capital punishment was unconstitutional only when the state applied it capriciously and discriminatorily.

[33] *Profitt v. Florida,* 428 U.S. 242 (1976); *Jurek v. Texas,* 428 U.S. 252 (1976); and *Gregg v. Georgia,* 428 U.S. 153 (1976).

[34] Thorsten Sellin, CAPITAL PUNISHMENT (1967), pp. 135–160. See also T. Sellin, THE PENALTY OF DEATH (1980).

PROBABILISTIC PUNISHMENTS: GOOD ECONOMICS, BAD LAW

Most people dislike taking chances with very large stakes, such as their lives. The classical Chinese legal system took advantage of this fact to deter criminals cheaply and effectively.[35] A large number of crimes were punishable by death in imperial China, in principle. In reality, few criminals from noble families were executed, but many were threatened with execution. Criminals convicted of capital offenses had to pass through a series of rituals that resulted in random executions. In the last ritual, the names of everyone convicted of a capital offense were written on a scroll that was presented to the Emperor annually. The emperor took a red brush and stroked it across the scroll. Anyone whose name was touched by red ink, which was a fraction of the names on the scroll, was executed. Anyone passing safely through this ritual several times was set free. The main advantage of this system was that many people could be deterred from committing serious crimes without actually executing very many people, and without significant cost to the state. Risk is cheap, effective punishment.

Public opinion, however, has turned decisively against random punishments, as dramatically illustrated by an infamous New York case. After a criminal was convicted of a felony, the judge explained that he would flip a coin to determine whether the young man would be set free or sentenced to prison. These facts found their way into the newspapers, producing an uproar, and the judge was eventually removed from the bench for misconduct and barred from serving as a New York judge again.[36]

QUESTION 12.11: What are the main sources of randomness in the contemporary criminal justice system?

QUESTION 12.12: Do you think that this randomness discourages or encourages crime?

---

[35] Martin Shapiro, COURTS: A COMPARATIVE AND POLITICAL ANALYSIS, pp. 157–93 (1981).

[36] W. G. Blair, (Feb. 2, 1982). *Flip of Coin Decides Jail Term in a Manhattan Criminal Case,* NEW YORK TIMES. K.R. Shipp (April 7, 1983). *Ex-Jurist Who Made Coin-Toss Decision Is Barred From Being New York Judge Again,* NEW YORK TIMES.

---

inferred that the death penalty had no deterrent effect. Second, Sellin compared homicide rates within the same state before and after the abolition or restoration of the death penalty. He found no significant difference in those rates depending on the legal status of the death penalty. Third, Sellin looked at homicide rates within cities where executions had taken place and had been well publicized. There was no difference in the rates just before and just after executions. Lastly, he examined death rates for police officers in states that did and did not have the death penalty for murdering a police officer. The rate at which officers were killed was the same, regardless of whether that state executed the murderers of police officers.[37] Sellin's overall conclusion from these four tests was that the death penalty does not deter homicides.

Critics found three fatal flaws in Sellin's study. First, he did not adequately hold "all other things equal." For example, we know that there are more murders in urban areas; thus, Sellin should have taken account of differences in the degree of urbanization in the states he compared. Additionally, young males commit far more homicides than any other group in society; thus, he should also have taken account of differences in the age distribution among states. Second, there is an ambiguity in Sellin's definition of homicide. The data that Sellin used—and that most investigators have used, for that matter— did not distinguish between those homicides, like first-degree or premeditated murder, for which capital punishment was a sanction, and other homicides, like second-degree murder or nonnegligent manslaughter, for which it was not an available sanction. Thus, the greater the extent to which the proportion of these two broad classes of homicides differed among states or over time within the same state, the less reliable are Sellin's conclusions. Third, Sellin did not adequately control for the consistency with which the jurisdiction actually executed criminals. He correlated the number of homicides with the presence of a capital punishment statute in the jurisdiction. Many states held out the possibility of capital punishment but, in fact, never used it. For example, Massachusetts had a death penalty statute into the late 1960s, but no criminal had been executed in that state since 1947. In 1965, the year in which Sellin's study appeared, there were only seven executions in *all* jurisdictions, even though almost all states still had capital punishment statutes.

Given these serious flaws in Sellin's research, the connection between the death penalty and homicide required further and more careful consideration.[38] The most famous study of the deterrent effect of capital punishment was by Isaac Ehrlich, an economist.[39] Ehrlich assumed that the potential murderer balances the expected punishment against the expected benefit. Ehrlich allowed certain economic and social variables to measure the benefit of homicide to the killer. He included data on the unemployment rate, the labor-force participation rate, the level of wealth, the age composition of the population, and the racial composition of the population.[40]

---

[37] Some people assert that in the absence of the death penalty, hardened criminals have nothing to lose from killing prison guards or other inmates, and, therefore, will commit more of those murders.

[38] In a study similar to Sellin's in methodology, Professor Hans Zeisel sought to determine the effects of the moratorium on executions that occurred between 1968 and 1976. His prediction was that, if there was a deterrent effect of capital punishment, there should have been a larger increase in homicides in those states that had most recently abolished the death penalty than in those states, like Massachusetts, that had had no executions for a much longer time. He found no perceptible increase and concluded that the death penalty did not deter murder. Hans Zeisel, *The Deterrent Effect of Capital Punishment: Facts v. Faith,* 1967 THE SUPREME COURT REVIEW 317. The same criticisms that were made of Sellin's work can be made of Zeisel's study. For example, it is not at all clear that 1968 really represents an important breaking point. As noted above, executions had fallen to a very low level as early as 1960.

[39] Isaac Ehrlich, *The Deterrent Effect of Capital Punishment: A Question of Life and Death,* 65 AM. ECON. REV. 397 (1975). See also Ehrlich, *Capital Punishment and Deterrence: Some Further Thoughts and Additional Evidence,* 85 J. POL. ECON. 741 (1977).

[40] He justified inclusion of the race variable on the ground that legitimate employment opportunities for blacks, especially for young male blacks, are limited. Thus, there may be a greater tendency for blacks to commit property crimes and, because of the correlation between those crimes and homicide, to commit murder.

Ehrlich took the criminal's expected costs of homicide to depend on three variables: the probability of being arrested for the crime (measured by the total number of arrests for homicide divided by the total number of reported homicides); the probability of being convicted of homicide (measured by the total number of convictions for homicide divided by the total number of arrests for homicide); and the probability of execution if convicted (measured by the total number of executions divided by the total number of convictions for homicide). Ehrlich predicted an inverse relationship between each of these three probabilities and homicide rates.

Using time-series data for the United States for the period 1933–1969, Ehrlich concluded that the homicide rate was negatively and significantly correlated with each of the three deterrence measures. Ehrlich's model also predicted that the strongest deterrent effect on homicides would arise from an increase in the probability of arrest; the next strongest, from an increase in the probability of conviction; and the next strongest, from an increase in the probability of execution. The data confirmed his predictions about the relative strength of each of these variables. The most dramatic of his conclusions was that one additional execution per year resulted in seven or eight fewer homicides per year.[41]

Critics found two statistical shortcomings in the Ehrlich study. First, in Ehrlich's model of behavior, homicide rates could be a linear function of the independent variables, a multiplicative function, a logarithmic function, or some other form. Ehrlich offered no persuasive reason for the particular functional form in which he estimated his regression; yet, changing the functional form changed his results.[42]

Second, Ehrlich's results are much too sensitive to the time period over which the estimations were made. Recall that Ehrlich's original study covered the period 1933–1969. In the last seven years of that period, the number of executions dropped precipitously, from 47 in 1962 to 2 in 1967 and to 0 in 1968 and 1969. During those same seven years, crime rates escalated sharply. These facts commend excluding the period 1962–1969 from the data used in the regression. John Taylor and Peter Passell redid Ehrlich's study, excluding the period 1962–1969, and found that the statistical significance of the deterrent relationship between the number of executions and the number of homicides disappeared.[43]

---

[41] The Department of Justice cited this particular result in its argument before the Supreme Court in *Gregg v. Georgia* in favor of the death penalty. Kenneth Wolpin did a study similar to Ehrlich's for England and Wales for the period 1929–1968 and concluded that an additional execution would have led to four fewer homicides. Wolpin, *Capital Punishment and Homicide: The English Experience,* 68 AM. ECON. REV. 422 (1978). An additional finding of the Ehrlich study—a finding frequently overlooked in the debate on the deterrent effect of capital punishment—is that the deterrent effect of an improvement in labor-market conditions is stronger than that of any of the criminal-justice-system variables.

[42] John Taylor, *Econometric Models of Criminal Behavior,* in ECONOMIC MODELS OF CRIMINAL BEHAVIOR (J. M. Heineke, ed. 1978).

[43] Passell and Taylor, *The Deterrent Effect of Capital Punishment: Another View,* 57 AM. ECON. REV. 445 (1977). In response to these criticisms, Ehrlich did a cross-sectional study of the deterrent effect of capital punishment on homicide for various states between 1940 and 1960. Ehrlich, *Capital Punishment and Deterrence: Some Further Thoughts and Additional Evidence,* 85 J. POL. ECON. 741 (1977). Again Ehrlich found a deterrent effect on homicide from increases in the probability of execution. This later study is not subject to the same criticisms that were made of the earlier work, but other objections have been raised to Ehrlich's use of cross-sectional data.

In addition to these statistical problems, the critics identified a subtle theoretical problem. Ehrlich found that the number of homicides was an inverse function of the probability of being convicted for murder, which implies that the greater the conviction rate for homicide, the lower the number of murders. Suppose that juries know that if they convict a defendant of homicide, the chances of execution are extremely high. They may be reluctant to convict for first-degree murder. If so, then the following paradoxical behavior may result: greater use of execution as the punishment for certain homicides might lead to *fewer* convictions. This would reduce the deterrent effect of both capital punishment and of convictions on subsequent murderers.

There is evidence that precisely this sort of relationship occurred in Great Britain. Before the abolition of the death penalty in 1965, British judges had less discretion to avoid sentencing defendants guilty of first-degree homicide to execution than did juries and judges in the United States. Offenders who were found insane could not be executed. The percentage of murderers in Great Britain who were found to be insane was much larger than it was in the United States before 1965. Not surprisingly, the number of murderers in Great Britain found to be insane fell dramatically after 1965 when the death penalty was abolished. There was no sudden and dramatic improvement in the mental health of the British criminal class. Rather, British judges before 1965 were reluctant to sentence convicted murderers to death.

Professor Richard Lempert, using this insight into the connection between conviction and the reluctant to execute, reestimated Ehrlich's model and found that an increase in the use of the death penalty would have lowered the probability of a murderer's being convicted by 17%.[44]

B. The Social Costs of Capital Punishment

While the deterrent effect of capital punishment—the social benefit of the death penalty—remains an open question, the high administrative *costs* of capital punishment are not in doubt. Jury selection is more painstaking, because state statutes usually allow both the prosecution and the defense to challenge more jurors. A recent study of California capital cases found that jury selection in capital cases averaged thirteen days, while jury selection in noncapital cases averaged three days.

Once the jury is selected, the trial itself is much more expensive in a capital case than in a noncapital case. Both the prosecution and the defense put on more complicated and thorough cases. Moreover, the capital trial is typically divided into two trials: one to determine guilt, the other to assess the penalty. The safeguards that have been put in place in the penalty phase of the trial are so elaborate that it is not unusual for that phase to be nearly as long as the trial on the determination of guilt.

Finally, the post-conviction legal proceedings in death cases have become elaborate and expensive. Most states require automatic review of all capital cases by the state's highest court. Not only is this review directly expensive to the prosecution and the

---

[44] Richard Lempert, *Desert and Deterrence: An Assessment of the Moral Bases of the Case for Capital Punishment,* 79 MICH. L. REV. 1177 (1981). Wolpin's work, mentioned above, also noted that, in order for his conclusions about the deterrent effect of the death penalty in England to hold, a change in the probability of execution of convicted murderers must not cause a change in the probability of conviction for murder.

defense, it also diverts the scarce judicial resources of the state court of last resort from other pressing business.

Even excluding the appeals process, the costs of the death penalty to the state are high. Imprisonment on death row is twice as expensive as imprisonment among the normal prison population. Death-row inmates require more elaborate security and supervision. They cannot be employed in the usual prison enterprises, and consequently, they make little contribution to the revenues of the prison. Because of extreme stress, the inmates' medical and psychiatric costs are high on death row.

C. Conclusion on Deterrence and Capital Punishment

The statistical evidence does not support the firm conviction that executions deter homicides. Perhaps we will not ever obtain compelling statistical conclusions.[45] Separating the effect of executions from other variables requires good data on a large number of cases.[46] States restrict executions to such a small group of killers that statisticians have little data to analyze.

> **QUESTION 12.13:** Opponents and proponents of capital punishment deny that their beliefs depend on the presence or absence of deterrence effects;[47] yet Ehrlich's study provoked intense debate and outrage. What do these facts say about the contribution of econometrics to criminal law?

> **QUESTION 12.14:** In the eighteenth century, prisoners were not only executed, they were also whipped, branded, and mutilated. Can you think of any economic reasons why many modern states have eliminated these punishments, retaining only fines, imprisonment, and probation?

V. THE ECONOMICS OF ADDICTIVE DRUGS AND CRIME

One of the popular explanations for increased crime is increased drug abuse. The use of such addictive drugs as heroin, crack cocaine, and PCP contributes to crime in three ways. First, some drug addicts are incapable of maintaining legitimate jobs. Their habit is so debilitating that they must turn to illegal activities to generate income. Second, those under the influence of drugs, like those under the influence of alcohol, may be emboldened to commit crimes. About 70% of those arrested in all large U.S. cities for robbery, weapons offenses, and larceny test positive for heroin, cocaine, or PCP. Third, drug dealing can be a lucrative business, and, therefore, a business worth protecting

---

[45] See Edward Leamer, *Let's Take the 'Con' Out of Econometrics,* 73 AM. ECON. REV. 31 (1983). Professor Leamer uses an econometric study of the deterrent effect of capital punishment to demonstrate the impact of the investigator's prior beliefs on his conclusions. *Id.* pp. 40-43.

[46] This point is forcefully made in Wilson, *supra* note 4, p. 188. See also Barnett, *The Deterrent Effect of Capital Punishment: A Test of Some Recent Studies,* 29 OPER. RES. 356 (1981). Barnett uses some of the recent studies to retrodict (*i.e.,* to "predict" backwards) the number of homicides in given past years and finds the predictions to be wildly inaccurate.

[47] For example, 90% of those in favor say that they are in favor of that sanction even if it could be shown to them conclusively that there is no deterrent effect. Vidmar and Ellsworth, *Public Opinion and the Death Penalty,* 26 STANFORD L. REV. 1245 (1974).

RACIAL DISCRIMINATION AND THE DEATH PENALTY

Does the defendant's race significantly influence the probability of capital punishment? A study by Wolfgang and Amsterdam of 3000 rape convictions in 11 southern states between 1945 and 1965 showed that the execution of African-Americans convicted of rape was unusual (13%). However, the study found that blacks were seven times more likely to be executed than whites convicted of the same crime, and a black man who had raped a white woman was 18 times more likely to be executed than when the victim and injurer were any other combination of race. These facts are consistent with the traditional hostility of some southern whites to sexual relations between black men and white women. A similar comparison of black and white executions for the same crimes in the North yielded much less evidence of race differences.

A different conclusion was reached for murder. For the period 1930–1967, the murder of a black person by another black person was slightly less likely to result in the murderer's execution than the murder of a white person by another white person. For the period 1967–1978, the statistics showed clearly that blacks were less likely to be sentenced to death for murder than were whites.

Behind such statistics lies a simple fact: The over representation of blacks among criminals who commit capital crimes guarantees that capital punishment will result in the execution of blacks in greater proportion than their numbers in the general population. This fact alone will open capital punishment to the charge of racism in future political debates.[48]

---

[48] See Stanley Rothman and Stephen Powers, *Execution by Quota?* 116 PUB. INTEREST 3 (1994).

---

against competition. Drug dealers commit violent crimes against those who try to enter their markets.

Drug use is a significant contributor to the amount of crime, and, therefore, an important means of minimizing the social costs of crime is to minimize the use of illegal addictive drugs.

A. Punishing Drug Sales

Current policy in the United States seeks to break the connection between the use of addictive drugs and crime by curtailing the supply of drugs and by reducing the demand for them. One means of reducing the supply and use of illegal drugs is to increase the expected punishment for selling or using them. Some suppliers will leave the business of supplying drugs in favor of legitimate, less-risky activities. At the same time, the higher market price caused by the restriction in supply may cause consumers to purchase fewer drugs.

Some economists have argued that this policy is incorrect because its factual premises are incorrect. Critics argue that addicts' demand for drugs is inelastic. Therefore, a restriction in supply and the resulting increase in the market price of the illegal drug will not cause addicts to reduce their consumption significantly. Instead, it

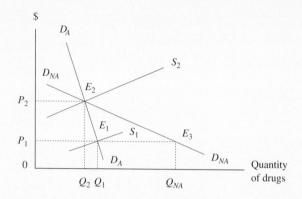

FIGURE 12.1 The economics of drug addiction and crime.

will cause them to increase the amount of crime they engage in to produce the greater revenue required to support their habits.

Figure 12.1 depicts this argument. The demand curve D_A (the demand for an illegal drug by those already addicted) is inelastic. Suppose that the supply curve is initially S_1. The equilibrium price and quantity are then P_1 and Q_1. The total amount spent by addicts for the drug is the rectangle $0Q_1E_1P_1$. If we make the simplifying assumption that drug addicts pay for all their drugs by committing crimes, then the total expenditure by addicts comes from committing crimes in the amount $0Q_1E_1P_1$.

Now suppose that the government raises the expected punishment for using or selling addictive drugs. Suppose that the result of this policy is to reduce the supply of the drug, causing the supply curve to shift to S_2. The new equilibrium price and quantity are P_2 and Q_2. Because of the inelasticity of demand, the reduction in the quantity of the illegal drug demanded is small.

When demand is inelastic, an increase in price causes an increase in consumers' total expenditures on the commodity. In Figure 12.1, when the price of the addictive drug rises to P_2, the total expenditures of addicts increase to the amount $P_2 Q_2$, or the rectangle $0Q_2E_2P_2$. Clearly, this amount is greater than that spent before the authorities raised the expected punishment. Our example illustrates the possibility that the harsher punishment of the sellers of drugs, which raises the price of drugs, causes buyers of drugs to commit more crimes.[49]

If this analysis is correct, then current policy, far from reducing the amount of crime attributable to drug addiction, may in fact *increase* it. A very different policy may be in order. To describe such an alternative policy, we begin with the supply curve S_2, where the initial equilibrium price and quantity are P_2 and Q_2. Now suppose that the government *lowers* the expected punishment for selling drugs. The result is that the supply curve shifts downward to S_1, with the effect that the illegal drug becomes *cheaper* (at P_1), and the quantity demanded increases slightly to Q_1. Through our previous analysis of inelasticity, the total amount spent by addicts at this new equilibrium price and quantity is less than before. If those revenues come from crime, then the reduction in the

---

[49] Note that the interests of organized crime and of public policy are in accord in wishing to drive up the price of addictive drugs. Organized crime wishes to establish a monopoly; public policy seeks to discourage consumption and supply by raising the price.

price of the illegal drug causes a reduction in the amount of crime. Taken to the extreme, the illegal drug could be made available at no cost to certain users, thus completely severing the connection between addiction and crime.[50]

The inelastic demand curve shown in Figure 12.1 represents the demand of addicts. Nonaddicts may have an *elastic* demand curve for the illegal drug, like D_{NA} in the figure. Nonaddicts respond to changes in the price of illegal drugs very differently than addicts do. The same increase in price that induces addicts to engage in more crime dissuades nonaddicts from consuming the drug. If nonaddicts are initially consuming Q_{NA} when the price is P_1, the increase in price to P_2 causes nonaddicts to reduce their demand to Q_2. Thus, the policy of lowering the expected punishment for selling illegal drugs to addicts also lowers the price for nonaddicts. Because this latter group has an elastic demand, this lower price could induce more experimentation with the drug, possibly leading to more addiction. If this were to happen, then the policy of reducing the price of illegal drugs might reduce the social costs of crime by addicts, but it might also increase the social costs of drug use by nonaddicts.[51]

The social costs of experimentation by nonaddicts can be avoided if the authorities can maintain a policy of price discrimination for the addictive drugs. Addicts would pay a low price, and nonaddicts would pay a higher price. (Thus, in the figure, addicts might pay P_1 or even zero, while nonaddicts might pay P_2.) This, in effect, was the solution attempted for heroin addiction in Great Britain. British addicts registered and obtained heroin from pharmacies at modest prices. Nonaddicts (or unregistered addicts) could not legally purchase heroin from pharmacies; instead, they had to purchase it illegally on the black market at a higher price.

B. Suppressing and Interdicting

In the preceding section, we criticized policies attempting to increase the expected punishment of the sellers of illegal drugs. Now we consider the failure of policies aimed at suppressing drug production and interdicting the importation of drugs.

First, consider attempts to limit the production of illegal drugs abroad. In the 1970s the U.S. government tried to eradicate opium production in Turkey, then the source of most of the raw opium that ultimately became heroin for the U.S. market. The program was moderately successful in Turkey, but Mexico began to grow opium and quickly became the supplier of 80% of the U.S. market. The U.S. government next began an eradication program in Mexico, but production simply moved elsewhere. The odds against the success of these programs are overwhelming. U.S. citizens demand approximately six tons of heroin per year. To make that much heroin requires about 60 tons of opium, which equals 2-3% of the total illicit production of opium in the world each year. The world market for opium and heroin is too large, and production is too flexible, for the United States to suppress heroin.

---

[50] For such a proposal, see Michael Adams, *Drug Enforcement in Germany and Abroad—A New Way to Destroy the Market for Drugs,* 17 INT. REV. L. & ECON. 203 (1993).

[51] For a forceful argument in favor of maintaining criminal sanctions on the sale, distribution, and consumption of most addictive drugs, see James Q. Wilson, *Against the Legalization of Drugs,* COMMENTARY (February, 1990), pp. 21-28.

Similarly, the attempt to restrict the import of illegal drugs has failed.[52] Small amounts of illegal drugs are so valuable that tens of thousands of dollars worth can be easily concealed in personal luggage on commercial airlines. The authorities cannot effectively monitor the millions of individuals who arrive in this country on commercial airlines. When one route is blocked, suppliers easily shift to alternative routes. Drug suppliers also smuggle by boat into remote harbors or by airplane into private rural airstrips.

C. Legalization

These dubious policies against drugs are very expensive. During the 1980s federal expenditures on drug enforcement tripled from about $1 billion per year to more than $3 billion per year and then rose in the early 1990s to $6.7 billion per year. State governmental expenditures are even greater. The best available estimate is that by the mid-1990s all levels of government in the United States were spending more than $15 billion per year to eradicate illegal drugs. In addition, recall that criminals convicted of drug offenses are clogging courts and prisons.

While there is a strong economic case for the legalization of drugs, there is a wide spectrum of legalization policies from which to choose. At one end is legalization with almost no governmental control. At the other end is total government control over the production and sale of drugs. In between are many possibilities—such as licensing of production and consumption, prohibition of sale to minors, regulations on the time-manner-and-place of consumption and sale, more extensive programs to help addicts, and increasing education on the dangers of drug abuse.[53]

A comparison of drugs and alcohol suggests an alternative to the current failed policies. In the United States alcohol is the direct cause of 80,000 to 100,000 deaths per year and a contributing factor in another 100,000 deaths. More than one-third of all serious crimes resulting in state prison sentences involve the abuse of alcohol. There are in the United States an estimated 20 million alcoholics or alcohol abusers. The annual social cost of alcohol abuse to the United States is estimated to be over $100 billion. Tobacco has similar social costs. Approximately 320,000 people die each year from consuming tobacco. By comparison, in 1985 only 3,562 people died from the use of all illegal drugs. All of the social costs of illegal drugs are only a fraction of the social costs imposed by alcohol and tobacco.

In spite of the harm caused by alcohol, the American experiment with criminalizing its use in the 1920s failed. To illustrate, during the era of "prohibition" the murder rate soared to levels comparable to today. Then the murder rate plummeted when alcohol was decriminalized and regulated by the state, largely because the "alcohol wars" ceased. While alcohol causes crime, it seems that its prohibition caused even more crime.

Perhaps the same is true of drugs today. The murder rate would probably plummet today if drugs were decriminalized and regulated by the state, bringing an end to the "drug wars." Repealing many of the current laws might lead to a moderate increase in

---

[52] See Peter Reuter, *Can the Borders Be Sealed?* 82 PUB. INTEREST 36 (1988).

[53] For an illuminating discussion of the many varieties of legalization, see Mark Kleiman and Aaron Sager, *Drug Legalization: The Importance of Asking the Right Question,* 18 HOFSTRA L. REV. 527 (1990).

drug abuse, but moderately more abuse in an environment of drug regulation is probably preferable to the current level of abuse in a criminal environment.[54]

> QUESTION 12.15: During the "war on drugs" in the United States, the street price of most
> illegal drugs has remained stable or falling. What does this fact indicate about who is
> winning the "war"?

> QUESTION 12.16: Use economics to compare three ways to reduce the *demand* for
> heroin: (1) the substitution of another less dangerous and less debilitating drug, such as
> methadone for heroin, to registered addicts; (2) the free availability of the illegal substance
> to registered addicts; and (3) a legal proscription on use, which is the current policy.

> QUESTION 12.17: If violent criminals were tested immediately after arrest, do you think
> that more of them would test positive for the recent consumption of drugs or a hamburger?
> What, then, is the significance of the high rate of drug use among criminals?

VI. THE ECONOMICS OF HANDGUN CONTROL

The United States has higher rates of violent crime than western European nations. The
United States also has higher rates of gun ownership, especially handguns, than most
European nations. In this section we explore whether widespread gun ownership causes
crime, or whether crime causes widespread gun ownership. Criminals obtain guns to
make crime easier and apprehension more difficult, so guns tend to create crime. The
potential victims of crime obtain guns to make their victimization harder and more
risky for criminals, so guns tend to reduce crime. We shall consider evidence on the relative strength of these two effects.

A. U.S. Gun Data

The correlation between the number of guns and the amount of crime is high. There are
an estimated 200 million firearms in private possession in the United States, of which
approximately 67 million are handguns. Approximately one-half of U.S. households
contain guns; the average number of guns per household is 4.5. One hundred thousand
schoolchildren take handguns to school each day.[55]

Gun ownership and crime have increased at roughly the same time in the United
States. During the 1960s and the 1970s the robbery rate in the United States increased
sixfold, and the murder rate doubled. The rate of handgun ownership almost doubled,
too. There are approximately 640,000 crimes committed with handguns every year in
the United States. There were about 12,000 murders committed in the United States in
1992 with handguns. (In the same year there were 87 murders by handgun in Japan, 22
in Great Britain, and 10 in Australia.) Since 1989, homicides committed by handgun

---

[54] For an argument that decriminalization would not lead to increased drug addiction, see Ethan Nadelman,
The Case for Legalization, 82 PUB. INTEREST 3 (1988).

[55] See James Q. Wilson, *supra* n. 1.

have increased by 59% in the United States, while homicides by all other means have fallen by 10%.

B. Gun Control

The effort to break the connection between handguns and crime has focused on two general methods of regulation: first, restrictions on the production and possession of handguns; and second, more severe punishment for those who use handguns in the commission of crimes.[56] In economic terms, these regulations seek to increase the relative price of handguns, either directly or by raising the expected punishment for failure to comply with ownership restrictions.

Since late in the nineteenth century, when governments passed the first laws regulating guns (specifically, concealed weapons), the first method of regulation has been the one most used by federal, state, and local governments. For example, in the 1930s Congress prohibited the use of the U.S. mail system for the sale of handguns across state lines; required the registration of machine guns, sawed-off shotguns, and silencers (weapons and equipment favored, at that time, by criminals), and the photographing and fingerprinting of registered owners of these weapons; and instituted a $200 tax to be paid whenever the ownership of these registered weapons was transferred.

The latest federal attempt at limiting the possession of handguns is the Brady Act (passed by Congress in late 1993 and named after James Brady, President Reagan's press secretary, who was shot in 1981). The act requires gun buyers to wait five business days and undergo a background check before taking possession of the guns they have purchased. Because good record-keeping is vital to this act's success and because most states do not have good records, the act authorizes the federal government to spend up to $200 million per year to help states improve their record-keeping. The goal is to replace the five-day waiting period with instant background checks within five years.[57]

Regulations like the Brady Act may prevent those people most likely to commit a crime from obtaining handguns legally. More than 20 states, containing half the population of the United States, already have similar waiting periods. The experience in those states is that 1-2% of prospective gun buyers are disqualified by the background check. For instance, California's background-check law has prevented about 12,000 people with a criminal record or a history of mental illness or drug abuse from buying handguns in the last two years. A similar law in Illinois has prevented 2000 from buying handguns there in the last two years.[58] We have no evidence on how many of these people subsequently purchased handguns illegally.

---

[56] About 80% of U.S. citizens (including about 60% of the membership of the National Rifle Association, typically thought to be the principal lobby against handgun regulations) favor more restrictions on the possession of firearms, especially handguns. Only 30% support a complete ban.

[57] The purpose of these checks is to keep handguns out of the hands of convicted felons, fugitives, minors, current and former drug addicts, and those who have been involuntarily committed for mental illness.

[58] In the future there may be additional federal regulations. Senator John Chafee has already proposed that the manufacture, sale, and home-possession of handguns be made illegal in the United States and that all such weapons in private hands be surrendered.

At the local level, regulations have taken a different tack. It has been illegal to sell handguns in Chicago since April 1982.[59] Recently, some local governments have offered to purchase guns from their residents, no questions asked. In 1992, St. Louis offered to pay $25 for each handgun turned in. The city collected 7465 guns in the course of one month and melted them. Many public schools in large cities have metal detectors; the Clinton administration has proposed random sweeps of housing projects to search for guns; and some localities have instituted random roadblocks to check cars for guns.

Besides these restrictions on production and possession, the punishment for violating handgun-possession regulations or for committing a crime with a handgun has increased. Several states have passed legislation that requires more severe and more certain punishment for those who carry a handgun without a permit. For example, the Massachusetts Bartley-Fox law in 1974 imposed a mandatory penalty of one year in prison without the possibility of probation, parole, or other diminution of sentence for failure to license a private handgun. Several studies have been conducted to measure the impact of Bartley-Fox, and the reported evidence suggests that the result of the law was, first, a reduction in the casual carrying of handguns, and, second, a decline in the proportion of assaults, robberies, and homicides committed with handguns.[60]

Notwithstanding this evidence, the two types of regulation noted do not appear to have had a large effect on crime rates. There are reasons for doubting the major premise of those regulations—namely, that more handguns inevitably lead to more violent crime. If criminals know that honest citizens are less likely to have guns, they will perceive smaller risk from committing crime and will, therefore, commit more of it. But if criminals know that many private citizens have guns, they might be increasingly wary of committing crime. This observation muddies the direction of causation between handguns and crime. The standard argument is that more handguns cause more crime. But perhaps more handguns lead to *less* crime. If so, then reducing the number of handguns may lead to an *increase* in the amount of crime.[61]

Both casual and some detailed evidence[62] suggest that increases in handgun ownership have no simple causal connection to violent crime. The casual evidence notes that during the 1980s the stock of privately owned handguns in the United States increased by more than a million units each year and that most crime rates fell. Additionally, Switzerland, New Zealand, and Israel have the same number of firearms per civilian household as does the United States, but do not have as much crime. Conversely, Mexico and South Africa have very strict handgun-control laws, and these countries have murder

---

[59] Rifles, shotguns, and ammunition are available to those who have an Illinois Firearm Owner's Identification card. This FOID takes up to one month to get, and even if a potential gun buyer has one, he or she must go through a waiting period before receiving the gun. Notwithstanding these efforts, there are hundreds of thousands of illegal handguns in Chicago. The reason is that it is extremely difficult for Chicago to seal its borders. Handguns come from the suburbs, where they are not as tightly regulated, or from the neighboring states of Indiana or Wisconsin. This experience suggests that local regulation is likely to be ineffective.

[60] See Wilson, THINKING ABOUT CRIME, pp. 135–36 (rev. ed 1983). This reduction in homicides associated with other felonies occurred even though the total number of these offenses was going up in Boston and in other large cities.

[61] Daniel Polsby, *The False Promise of Gun Control,* THE ATLANTIC MONTHLY (March, 1994), p. 57.

[62] Arthur Kellerman, et al., NEW ENGLAND JOURNAL OF MEDICINE, October 7, 1993.

rates more than twice as high as those in the United States. Florida's murder rate has been falling since the state made it easier for citizens to carry concealed weapons.

Yet another fascinating piece of evidence on this matter is the correlation between private handgun ownership and "hot" burglaries. (A "hot" burglary is one in which there are people at home when the burglary occurs.) If homeowners can legally own handguns, then potential burglars will be less likely, all other things equal, to invade houses in which someone is at home. However, if homeowners cannot legally own handguns, then burglars will not be as reluctant to invade when someone is at home. Thus, one ought to observe fewer "hot" burglaries in jurisdictions that allow homeowners to keep handguns. And, indeed, that is what one finds. The United States, Canada, and Great Britain have roughly equal burglary rates. However, the "hot" burglary rate in the U.S. (where private handgun ownership is generally allowed) is about 10%, and that in Canada and Great Britain (where private handgun ownership generally is not allowed) is about 50%.[63]

This issue, like many of the other issues we have studied in the economics of crime and punishment, is complex. Better empirical work is needed before we can reach firm conclusions on the relationship between handguns and crime that could point to definite policy recommendations. The issue is not so much a free market in guns versus banning their possession. Rather, the problem is to find specific regulations that actually succeed in reducing violent crime.

> **QUESTION 12.18:** Use economics to predict the ranking by crime rates of the following situations:
> a. no private person has a gun (effective prohibition).
> b. only criminals have guns (ineffective prohibition on criminals).
> c. everyone has easy access to guns.
> d. only honest citizens have access to guns.

> **QUESTION 12.19:** Is it possible to design and enforce a law so that only honest citizens have access to guns?

> **QUESTION 12.20:** Gun control is politically unpopular in neighborhoods with the highest crime rates in the United States. Use economics to explain why.

> **QUESTION 12.21:** About 38,000 Americans die of gunshot wounds each year. Fewer than half these deaths are homicides. Accidents and suicides account for 54% of firearms deaths. Assume that guns in honest households deter crimes and cause accidental deaths. How would you compare the costs of each?

CONCLUSION

In this chapter we have used the economic theory of crime and punishment to examine some pressing policy issues in criminal justice. Economic theory is valuable in framing the problems and the possible solutions, and empirical research is necessary to weigh the policy options designed to minimize the social costs of crime.

---

[63] Our thanks to John Lott Jr. for this evidence.

SUGGESTED READINGS

Luksetich, William, and Michael White, CRIME AND PUBLIC POLICY: AN ECONOMIC APPROACH (1982).

Reiss, Albert J., Jr., and Jeffrey A. Roth, eds., UNDERSTANDING AND PREVENTING VIOLENCE (National Research Council of the National Academy of Sciences, 1994).

Reuter, Peter, DISORGANIZED CRIME: ILLEGAL MARKETS AND THE MAFIA (1983).

SUGGESTED ANSWERS

The following answers are meant to be suggestions rather than complete answers. In some of the following questions, there is only one correct answer. But in many questions, there is no single correct answer. We hope that both types of questions will spark your interest to delve more deeply into the issues raised. If you have ideas about correct answers to some of the questions, please share them with us. (We owe special thanks to Tomas Nonnenmacher for his help with this section of the book.)

CHAPTER 2

2A. Remember that the slope of the line is the coefficient of x. When that coefficient is positive, there is a direct relationship between x and y. The second equation says that there is an inverse relationship between x and y: when x increases in value, y decreases in value.

2B. Think about transitivity over time. Is it necessarily true that a hot dog at lunch is the same good as a hot dog at dinner? Why would this not be the case?

2C. Increases and decreases in income will shift the curve, while a change in the price will cause the line to rotate.

2D. Compare the marginal costs with the marginal benefits. If the initial level is greater than the optimum, then marginal costs are higher than marginal benefits. That is, the cost of the final unit exceeds the benefit received from it. The decision-maker will continue to decrease the amount being maximized until marginal benefit equals marginal cost.

2E. Another way to ask this question is, "At what point does society stop receiving benefits from additional units of pollution reduction?"

2F. Refer to you answer to question 2D. In Figure 2.7 show the area that constitutes the net benefits.

2G. Parts 1 and 2 will cause shifts in one of the two curves. Under what circumstances might the intersection be to the right of the "100%" line?

2H. Given the technology used by this firm, external costs will always exist under any positive level of production. Think of an extreme case: Would society be better or worse off if the firm did not produce at all?

2I. Think about the convexity of the curve in Figure 2.19. How does the risk-seeking individual view the sure thing $EMV(A_1)$ *versus* the riskier $EMV(A_2)$?

End-of-chapter questions

2.1. Economists generally assume that economic decision-makers are attempting to maximize something subject to constraints. Thus, consumers are assumed to maximize utility subject to an income constraint, and firms are assumed to maximize profits subject to a production function constraint. Maximization helps to posit the goal or end that the economic decision-maker seeks. Equilibrium is a state of rest, the condition from which no further endogenous change will occur. The notion of equilibrium helps to specify the point (*e.g.*, the quantity of output produced, the amount of bananas consumed) toward which the maximizing behavior of economic decision-makers tends.

2.2.   Efficiency describes a point of equilibrium with particular characteristics. A productively efficient equilibrium describes the condition of a firm or firms in which it is impossible to produce a given level of output at lower cost or, alternatively, to use a given combination of inputs to produce a greater level of output. An allocatively efficient equilibrium describes an equilibrium distribution of goods and services among consumers. A particular distribution of goods among consumers is allocatively efficient if it is not possible to redistribute the goods so as to make at least one consumer better off without making another consumer worse off. (That, of course, is the Pareto criterion.)

2.3.   In microeconomic theory consumers are assumed to maximize utility subject to an income constraint. The income constraint or budget line is described by the consumer's income and the relative prices of goods and services. The consumer's utility is maximized when she achieves the highest attainable indifference curve. This occurs at the point at which the highest attainable indifference curve is tangent to the budget line. At that point the benefit (*i.e.*, the utility) from spending an additional dollar on any given good is equal for all commodities. That is, at the consumer's constrained maximum the marginal benefit (in terms of the increase in utility) of an additional dollar spent on any good is exactly equal to the marginal cost (*i.e.*, the dollar) of any good.

2.4.   The partner who has the children is assumed to have a utility function of $u = cv$, where c equals the weekly child support payment from the other partner, and v equals the number of days per week that the children spend with this partner. Initially, $c = 100$ and $v = 4$ days, so that $u = 400$. If the partner paying child support payments wishes to reduce the weekly support payment to $80, then the number of days that the children spend with the other partner must increase to 5 in order for utility to be maintained unchanged at 400.

2.5.   Price elasticity of demand measures the responsiveness of consumer's quantity-demanded to changes in relative price. Mathematically, price elasticity is defined as the percentage change in the quantity-demanded of a commodity divided by the percentage change in the commodity's price. Because quantity-demanded and price move in opposite directions (when price declines, quantity-demanded increases; when price increases, quantity-demanded decreases), the sign of price elasticity will be negative. To avoid having to remember whether -5 is greater or less than -4, economists drop the sign from price elasticity and talk about it as if it were simply a positive number. The ranges of value of price elasticity of demand are inelastic (price elasticity has a value less than 1), unitary elasticity (price elasticity equal to 1), and elastic (price elasticity has a value greater than 1). When price elasticity is greater than 1, the percentage change in quantity-demanded is greater than the percentage change in price—*e.g.*, a 10% drop in price gives rise to a 23% increase in quantity demanded.

There is an interesting relationship between a commodity's price elasticity of demand and total consumer expenditures (price times quantity-demanded) on that commodity. When price elasticity of demand is less than one, an increase (decrease) in price will lead to an increase (decrease) in the total amount that consumers spend on the commodity. When price elasticity of demand is unitary, consumers will spend the same total amount on the commodity regardless of the price. When price elasticity of demand is greater than one, an increase (decrease) in price will lead to a decrease (increase) in the total amount that consumers spend on the commodity.

We shall use this last relationship between price elasticity and consumer expenditures in Chapter 12 to explain the relationship between drug addiction and crime.

2.6. The expression "There is no such thing as a free lunch" is one of the most famous quotes in all of economics. Its origins are interesting. In order to encourage customers to drink, taverns used to post a sign saying "Free Lunch." The implication was that those who had purchased drink were entitled to eat from the bar's buffet at no extra charge. Clearly the bar expended real resources providing the luncheon buffet, and the explicit and opportunity costs of these resources figure in the bar's determination of the costs of doing business and, therefore, in its calculation of its profits. But what about the bar's customers? Was the lunch really free to them if they purchased a drink? No. The bar included a charge for the costs it incurred in putting on the buffet in the prices it charged its customers for drink. The fact that the charge for the buffet is hidden in the price of drink does not make the lunch free.

On many domestic and international airplane flights, passengers are offered meals, music, and movies at no apparent price. Are these entertainments really "free"?

2.7. Use your answer from 2.6 to think about this issue.

2.8. Firms are assumed to maximize profits, which are defined as the difference between total costs (including opportunity costs) and total revenues. A firm maximizes profits by choosing that output level for which the marginal cost (the addition to total cost of the last unit of output produced) equals the marginal revenue (the addition to total revenue of the last unit of output produced). (Note that if we call marginal revenue "marginal benefit," then the rule to maximize profits by choosing the output level for which marginal cost equals marginal revenue is exactly equivalent to our general maximization rule of equating marginal cost and marginal benefit.) If the firm finds itself producing an output level for which it is the case that marginal revenue exceeds marginal cost, then by producing more output it can add more to total revenue than to total cost and thereby increase its profits. Alternatively, if marginal cost exceeds marginal revenue, the firm should cut back on production: the revenue lost from lower output will be less than the cost savings.

2.9. In a perfectly competitive industry there are a large number of buyers and sellers, so large that no single buyer or seller can influence the market price by his or her individual decisions. Entry and exit of resources into and out of the industry is free. These are the core characteristics of perfect competition about which there is general agreement among economists. There are several other conditions about which there is less widespread agreement, *e.g.*, that all buyers and sellers have perfect and complete information and that products are homogeneous. It is often said that the stock market and the market for agricultural commodities (such as wheat) are examples of perfectly competitive industries.

Monopoly occurs when there is only one seller. (For more on monopoly see the suggested answer to the following question.) By comparison to a perfectly competitive industry, a monopolist produces too little and charges too much.

Oligopoly holds where there are only a few sellers, so few that they recognize the interdependence of their decisions. That is, what is optimal for firm *A* to produce or to charge for its output depends not just on market price, marginal revenue, and the firm's own costs but on what firms *B* and *C* produce and charge. This interdependence gives rise to strategic considerations that are best analyzed through the use of game theory and such notions as a Nash equilibrium. The television programming market may be an example of an oligopolistic market.

An imperfectly competitive industry shares some of the aspects of perfectly competitive and monopolized industries. As in perfect competition, there are a large number of sellers, although the number is not as large as in perfect competition. Entry and exit are free. As in monopoly, each seller has some limited market control over the consumers of his output. Sellers distinguish their product by brand name, quality, and other characteristics. The market for breakfast cereals is probably imperfectly competitive.

2.10.   A monopoly occurs when there is only one seller. There are technological conditions, known as "natural monopoly," that can give rise to monopoly. There are also social welfare conditions that may make a case for the government's granting a monopoly—as with the patent, copyright, and trademark systems. (See the discussion of intellectual property in Chapter 5).

A monopoly can be sustained only if other resources are prevented from flowing into the industry to set up competitive firms. This might happen when a monopolist gains control of the only input that can be used to produce a particular output. Far more common are cases in which the government permits the monopoly to endure by forbidding lawful entry into the industry. Where entry is not so restricted, it will eventually occur, leading to the demise of the monopoly.

A special kind of monopoly is a cartel, which is collusion among otherwise competitive firms that seek to operate as a joint profit-maximizing monopoly. An example is the Organization of Petroleum Exporting Countries (OPEC). OPEC illustrates very well the difficulties that monopolies have in forestalling entry. The more successful the monopoly initially is in raising the price above the competitive level, the greater the incentive to others to enter the industry. After OPEC's success in raising the price of oil to nearly $33 per barrel (from $3 per barrel) in the early 1970s, the entry into the petroleum-extracting industry by other countries was substantial, so much so that the OPEC countries now account for less than half of world petroleum output. (Later, the high price of oil induced a substantial amount of cheating by OPEC member countries, too.)

2.11.   We discussed the adverse effects of a price ceiling with respect to rent control. The price ceiling is set below the equilibrium price so that there is an excess demand for the price-controlled product. Suppliers can make more money supplying unregulated goods and services and so transfer their efforts and resources elsewhere. Those suppliers that remain attempt to keep their profit rates at normal levels by letting the quality of their product (and therefore its costs of production) decline and by insisting on secret payments from consumers over and above the controlled price. Consumers of the controlled product may also alter their behavior in inefficient ways: they may, for example, inefficiently substitute other goods and services for those whose price is controlled.

2.12.   Refer to your answer to 2.11. Instead of placing a ceiling above which prices cannot rise, the government sets a floor below which they cannot fall. The effect of a price floor is that too much is produced and not enough demanded. The simplified outcome in the labor market is that minimum wage constraints cause unemployment (*i.e.*, an excess labor supply).

2.13. The interaction between a minimum wage law and a law forbidding firing would play out at many subtle levels. Among the many issues to consider are: the decision to hire new workers, the use of overtime, and the decision to declare bankruptcy.

2.14. All other things equal, the implicit price of divorce would fall under a no-fault divorce law, thus leading to more divorce. (Exactly how much depends, of course, on the price elasticity of demand for divorce.) This fall in price might also influence the decision to marry. Perhaps there would be less hesitation to marry, knowing that the decision to marry was easily reversed.

2.15. The effort associated with acquiring information concerning interest rates effectively raises the price of obtaining a loan. With lower costs faced by consumers, all else equal, one would expect more lending activity. The profits to the lenders depend on the cost of supplying the information to consumers and the market power they exhibited before the Act was passed. The more competition in the lending industry, the closer the interest rate should reflect the true risks and costs to the lender.

2.16. General equilibrium is the condition in which all markets are in simultaneous equilibrium. The conditions under which this will happen are that all markets are perfectly competitive and that there are no sources of market failure. (See the answer to the next question.) Given the resources available to the economy, it is not possible for the economy to be productively or allocatively more efficient than it is in general equilibrium. (As we argue in the text, distribution is another matter.)

2.17. Market failure can arise from four sources. The first is non-competitive market structures, such as monopoly (the condition of one seller) and monopsony (the condition of one buyer). We have already examined the reasons why monopoly leads to sub-optimal results. In general, policies of regulation (in the case of natural monopoly) and of antitrust enforcement (in the case of collusion and artificially sustained monopoly) will help to correct for the social costs of monopoly. The second is external effects, costs and benefits involuntarily imposed on others. In the case of external costs, such as water pollution that results from a firm's discharge of waste chemicals into a nearby stream, the externality-generator does not take into account the costs he has involuntarily imposed on others. As a result, his output costs him less to produce than it should in terms of the social resources his production really uses. So, someone who is generating external costs produces too much. To correct for these social costs, he must be induced to "internalize" these external costs, in which case he will reduce his output to the socially optimal level. Policies of taxation and subsidization, of exposure to legal liability, and of prior regulation can help to minimize the social costs of externalities. (In Chapters 4 and 5 we discuss how property law can help in this internalization, and in Chapters 8 and 9 we show how tort law helps to internalize risks of injury.)

The third source of market failure is the presence of public goods. These are goods for which the cost of excluding non-paying consumers are so high that no private profit-maximizing firm can earn enough to justify producing the socially-optimal amount of the public good. The market fails in respect to public goods in that it produces too little of them. A policy of subsidization of private producers or of public provision of the public good can correct for this failure.

The fourth source of market failure is extreme informational asymmetries. Because of the special characteristics of information, where access to information is highly skewed or where the ability to process information is highly unequal, questions arise about the optimality of otherwise voluntary transactions. (In Chapters 6 and 7 we discuss how contract law, and in Chapters 8 and 9 we discuss how tort law, can help to correct for problems arising because of informational asymmetries.)

2.18.a. A swimming pool large enough to accommodate hundreds of people does *not* seem to have either of the characteristics of a public good non-rivalrous consumption or costliness of excluding non-paying consumers. A fence and charging an entrance fee through a central entrance dispose of the costliness issue. Only when the pool is congested does the amount of the pool that one person can consume depend on the amount that others consume. The swimming pool does not seem to be a public good, and it therefore follows that a private profit-maximizing firm could provide the optimal pool.

b. A fireworks display is clearly a public good. Consumption is non-rivalrous in the sense that one person's enjoyment does not diminish the amount available for another to enjoy. And it is costly to exclude non-paying consumers; they may, after all, simply stand on a hill away from the display and enjoy it without charge. For those reasons it is not surprising that it is municipalities, not private firms, that provide fireworks displays on the 4th of July and that they are generally financed from general tax revenues, not from a user fee.

c. A heart transplant is clearly a private good. Nonetheless, many will shy away from the conclusion that this particular private good should be allocated according to the usual rules prevailing in the market for private goods—presumably because transplants are extremely costly. For an interesting discussion of this issue and of other issues where high cost is an important component of choice, see Guido Calabresi and Philip Bobbitt, TRAGIC CHOICES (1978).

d. Vaccination against a highly contagious disease is a private good but one that has such strong external benefits that the market will provide sub-optimal amounts of it—*i.e.*, in deciding whether or not to receive inoculation, people are likely to take into account only their own well-being and that of their immediate friends and neighbors and not the public health benefits that their inoculation will confer on others. Thus, either public provision of vaccination or public subsidization of private provision is called for.

e. A wilderness area could conceivably be a private good. But today wilderness areas and national parks are federally owned and operated, presumably on the theory that these areas should be held in trust for future generations and that private owners would not do that. But there are a few examples of private ownership of natural resources that do work. A private organization called the Nature Conservancy attempts to preserve bird sanctuaries, wilderness areas, and other significant natural resources by using the contributions of its members to purchase and hold these areas.

f. (Also, **g** and **h**.) All three examples of education given here are largely private goods with trace elements of public goods—*e.g.*, in the sense that they contribute to societal well-being by giving those trained a sense of worth and a set of skills. There is general agreement that elementary education has such strong external benefits (in that all citizens are better off when their fellow citizens can read and write and reckon) that it should be subsidized or publicly-provided.

2.19. Pareto efficiency (or Pareto optimality) describes a situation of equilibrium from which it is impossible, given the economy's resources, to produce more of one commodity without producing less of another or to make one person better off without making another worse off. Although Pareto efficiency is to be desired, we saw that it does not define a unique distribution of resources among the members of society. The set of Pareto efficient distributions that results from voluntary exchange depends crucially on the initial distribution of resources among the members of the society. Different initial distributions lead to different Pareto optimal outcomes.

2.20.   Although votes cannot be bought and sold in the marketplace, a market for votes does exist in the form of campaign contributions and logrolling (legislators trading votes). What benefits would follow from allowing and legal and open market for votes rather than the current "hidden" market? More troubling, how would allowing an open market change the balance of power between the have's (who can supply money and votes) and the have-not's (who can only supply votes)? Would allowing this market to exist fundamentally change our concept of government?

2.21.   A Pareto improvement is a change in which at least one individual is made better off, while no one is made worse off. The Kaldor-Hicks requirement recognizes that some changes will be very beneficial to one subset of society, while harming another subset. As long as the benefits outweigh the costs, Kaldor-Hicks views the change as a superior outcome. A Pareto improvement requires those who benefit to compensate (or to purchase the consent) of those who lose. A Kaldor-Hicks improvement does not require explicit consent by the losers, only that someone objectively verify that the benefits of the change exceed the costs.

2.22.   A dominant strategy is a strategy that is optimal regardless of what the other player does. If both players have a dominant strategy, then there is a Nash equilibrium. A Nash equilibrium is a strategy where an individual player cannot do better, so long as the other players do not change their strategies. Some games have multiple Nash equilibria, and many games (the most common of which are the prisoner's dilemma games) have a Nash equilibrium that is not the Pareto efficient outcome.

CHAPTER 3

3.1.   Butterfield, the plaintiff, asked to be compensated for injuries he incurred when he rode his horse into a pole put across the street by Forrester, the defendant. Butterfield claimed that Forrester was negligent in leaving the pole across the street. The judge stated the law and the jury determined the facts. The law was that a person who exercised reasonable care could collect damages caused by the negligent behavior of others. The jury determined that the *plaintiff* did not exhibit reasonable care and found in favor of the defendant.

3.2.   The plaintiff appealed the case and lost. The judge ruled that any negligence on the part of the plaintiff (contributory negligence) was a complete bar to recovery.

3.3.   The defendant, Mann, appealed the judgment on the ground that the judge had misinterpreted the common law. He lost the case again. The court ruled that the defendant could have avoided the donkey had he been driving his wagon in a less reckless manner. The defendant acted last and could have avoided the outcome had he been acting responsibly.

CHAPTER 4

4.1.   After receiving the bid from Clair, Adam values the car at $3200, which is the opportunity cost of selling it to Blair. (Recall that opportunity cost is defined as the value of the next best use, which is, in this case, selling the car to Clair.) Adam's threat value vis-à-vis Blair is now $3200. The surplus from cooperating with Blair falls to

$800. A reasonable solution is for Blair to buy the car for $3,600, leaving Adam with $3,600 and no car and Blair with a car worth $4,000 to her and $1,400 in cash.

4.2.a.   Arthur's threat value is his expected net gain from trial. Because the value of the kettle is $300, because he has a 50% probability of winning, and because the trial will cost him $50, the expected net value of a trial is $300(0.5) − $50 = $100.

b.   Betty's threat value is her expected loss from trial. Because the value of the kettle is $300, because she has a 50% probability of losing, and because the trial will cost her $50, the value to her of a trial is −$300(0.5) − $50 = −$150 − $50 = −$200.

c.   The cost to Arthur and Betty of cooperatively resolving their dispute without trial is $0 because the transaction costs of settling are, by assumption, zero.

d.   The surplus from cooperating (*i.e.*, from settling the dispute rather than litigating) is $100, which is the sum of the two parties' costs of litigating.

e.   A reasonable settlement would be for Betty to pay Arthur $150. Thus, Arthur gets his threat value ($100) plus half the surplus ($50). And so does Betty: −$200 (her threat value) + $50 (the saving in litigation costs) = −$150.

f.1.   Assuming that the cost of litigating is still $50, Arthur's net expected gain from litigating is $300(2/3)−$50 = $150.

2.   Betty believes that the probability of her losing the case and having to pay for the kettle is 1/3. Her probability of winning the case and not having to pay for the kettle is 2/3. Thus, Betty's threat value is (−$300)1/3 − $50 = −$150.

3.   Now the actual cooperative surplus from settling rather than litigating is still $100. But because of their optimism, the parties both anticipate doing better from litigating than from cooperating. If the actual cooperative surplus is $100 and each party anticipates a reasonable split of that surplus, then Arthur anticipates receiving $200 from cooperating with Betty in settling the dispute: $150 (his threat value) + $50 (his share of the cooperative surplus) = $200. Betty expects to lose $150 from going to trial; with her share of the cooperative surplus, she would be willing to offer Arthur $100 to settle: −$150 (her threat value) plus $50 (her share of the cooperative surplus) = −$100. What Arthur expects from cooperation ($200) is much greater than what Betty is prepared to offer for cooperating ($100). Thus, neither party prefers cooperating to litigation. The putative cooperative surplus is 0.

4.   Neither party anticipates a surplus from cooperating because each party is optimistic about winning the trial.

4.3.   You will recall at the beginning of our section on suggested answers that we said that there are some questions in the book to which we don't know the answers. This is one of them. There is no correct answer to this question, but a great deal can be learned from discussing and comparing your ideas with those of your colleagues about just distribution and threats versus the marginal productivity theory as a method of distributing income and wealth.

4.4.   If transaction costs are zero, then the initial distribution of property rights over land will not bar the efficient outcome. The efficient solution will be reached whether the law protects the farmer or allows the railroad to emit sparks. However, if the costs of bargaining are high, then the efficient solution may not necessarily be reached. One scenario under which high bargaining costs may exist is when there are a multitude of actors on either side of the conflict.

4.5. Think about how short-run contracting differs from long-run contracting. Do the higher costs in the long-run involve anything other than higher transaction costs? That is, if the costs of searching, bargaining, and enforcing contracts was zero in the long-run, then the Coase theorem should still hold.

4.6. The invariance principle is a strong version of the Coase theorem and states that not only does any initial endowment lead to an efficient outcome, but that the same outcome will be reached no matter what the initial endowment. The income effect is the change in the quantity demanded for a good whose price has fallen attributable to a rise in real income due to the price change. The price effect is the increase in quantity demanded directly attributable to the fall in price.

4.7. One way to approach this problem is to consider the increase in wealth associated with an increase in the initial endowment. For instance, suppose the farmers were granted the right to be free from cattle and all the ranchers' land. The farmers may decide to build a house on the rancher's land rather than allowing cattle to graze. While this is the efficient outcome, it is a very different result from a situation where land is split evenly.

4.8. The formal, legal rules of society are most effective when they are compatible with the informal social norms of everyday life. Informal norms often arise in situations where high transaction costs of contracting exist. Instead of relying on government to lay the ground-rules of economic interaction, people in long-term stable relationships form "rules of the game" that are specific to their situation. The loss of reputation of actors that cheat in a game with repeated play is often a sufficient enforcement mechanism in long term contracts.

4.9.a. bargaining.
   b. enforcement.
   c. search.
   d. search.
   e. search.
   f. search.

Arguments can be made, however, for many of these to be considered in a different category.

4.10. In terms of the transaction costs of search, bargaining and enforcement, buying an artichoke would seem to be the easiest, and perhaps getting married the most difficult. But the level of transaction costs involved in the other situations would vary greatly depending on the situation. For instance, selling a Burger King franchise may have very low costs if standard forms and a clear legal framework exist. However, if a unique contract is written for each franchise and if there is uncertainty in the legal system as to how franchising law operates, then the transaction costs could be very high.

4.11. Place each contract along the spectrum of transaction costs. In which situations are the costs of contracting a market-based solution "too high"?

4.12.a. The 45° line indicates the threshold where transaction costs are higher than the gains from trade. Trade will not occur to the right of the 45° line.
   b. The area to the right of the 45° line is where government intervention is needed to either reduce transaction costs or to assign property rights.
   c. If the transaction costs of reaching a collective bargaining agreement are very high, then the government may feel justified in assigning property rights in order to

reduce inefficiencies in the market. This assumes that government knows who values the rights more.

d. The normative Hobbes theorem is based on the assumption that it is human nature for people to disagree. Therefore, the government is justified in intervening and dictating some transactions.

4.13. If parties act cooperatively, then the efficient solution will be reached no matter what the legal rule. Therefore, if E is enjoined from polluting, the parties will contract cooperatively so that L installs filters while E does not install scrubbers. The total cooperative surplus is $400 more in this scenario. The monetary transfer from E to L in this case will be somewhere between $200 (the difference between L's profits with and without scrubbers) and $500 (the difference between E's profits with and without scrubbers). So the cost of the injunction will be at least as large as the cost of paying damages.

4.14. When transaction costs are low, injunctive relief is preferred, while legal relief is preferred when high transaction costs are high. Think about the transaction costs (particularly those involved in a collective agreement with large numbers) in each situation.

4.15. When a case is litigated, the judge determines the law, while the jury determines the facts. Are transaction costs the same before and after these issues are determined by the court?

4.16. If everyone has free access to a beach, there is a real danger that there will be very little discretion in the use of this resource. The result may be that there are too many people, too many cars, and too many conflicting activities (such as fishing and swimming or free access and the building of beach homes). A rationing device is called for to minimize these and other problems. One such rationing device is assigning private property rights to the beach; another is governmental ownership of the beach but establishing rules of use of the beach and charging a user fee to those who make use of the beach.

CHAPTER 5

5.1 and **5.2.** Post, the plaintiff, has sued Pierson, the defendant, for interfering with his property. Post had been chasing a fox, apparently as part of the sport of fox-hunting (or "riding to hounds") when Pierson intervened and killed and carried off the fox. The lower court found for Post, and Pierson appealed. The highest court in New York State reversed that judgment. The issue is how to establish a property right to a wild animal: must the pursuer have actual possession—"manucaption"—of the animal (the majority's view), or is it enough simply to exhibit the intent to catch or kill the animal by chasing it (Justice Livingston's (minority) view)? One way to resolve the issue is to ask if some legitimate social goal is more efficiently advanced by one rule rather than another. There are really two closely-related legitimate social goals suggested. The first is to minimize the considerable damage done to crops and barnyards by foxes by increasing the incentives of hunters to pursue foxes. The second is to maximize the enjoyment of those who are riding to hounds. (Today, depredations to farms by foxes and the sport of fox hunting are not closely related, but in 1805 they were.)

One side (the minority) argues that the rule of giving the ownership claim to those originally pursuing a fox will create a heightened incentive for the killing of foxes. Under the majority's alternative rule of manucaption, a pursuer of these "wild and noxious beasts" could pursue a fox all day only to see another person rightfully take the fox and that that result could lessen the incentive to hunt foxes.

But this distinction between the rules isn't entirely correct. The majority's rule might lessen the fun of riding to hounds, but it does not necessarily lessen the incentive to kill foxes in less sporting ways. In fact, the rules seem equally efficient at contributing to the objective of killing foxes in order to reduce the damage they do to farms. The choice between the rules must be made on other grounds. What may be said in favor of the majority view is that the actual possession rule is clearer, less subject to misinterpretation, and easier to enforce than the intent rule.

5.3. The continuing conflicts over fishing rights between countries and the increasing value of resources to be found in the open ocean have led to ever-broadening claims to territorial waters. But this broadening of claimed national rights conflicts with the open-access problem surrounding the sea. That is, it is costly to enforce these broader claims of national right.

5.4. In order to answer this question, one must consider why the rule concerning water took the shape that it did in each historical setting. Why might riparians have been allowed to use only a small amount of the water flow in eighteenth century England? Why is the legal rule different in different parts of the United States? Is this a story about political power or is it about economic efficiency? What role do you think that resource endowments might play in these legal differences? That is, will the quantity of rivers in an area affect water law? How and why?

5.5. We assume that the invention allows the inventor to accurately predict the weather during the growing season. He determines that the weather will be beautiful and concludes that there will be a bountiful crop at harvest time. He further knows that a large crop means a large supply, that is, that the supply curve of the crop shifts to the right. This will cause the market price of the crop to fall after the harvest. Knowing this, the inventor may enter into contracts to sell quantities of the crop at a price slightly below that expected by others. (His invention is what gives him alone accurate information about the post-harvest price.) When delivery time comes, the inventor will be able to purchase the crop on the spot market at the depressed price and deliver it to his customers for the higher price agreed upon earlier. The difference between what the inventor paid for the crop in the spot market and the price he receives from his promises to sell at the higher price contribute to his profit on the invention.

5.6. There is an extensive law-and-economics literature on this topic. See, *e.g.*, the symposium issue of the *Columbia Law Review* (November, 1989) on corporate law issues and the chapter on insider trading in Frank Easterbrook and Daniel Fischel, THE ECONOMIC STRUCTURE OF CORPORATION LAW (1989).

5.7. The government-granted monopoly to the maker and inventor of Librium ended when the patent expired. Prior to the patent expiration, the drug-maker earned monopoly profits to reward them for their development of the drug. But after the patent's expiration competition (or the threat of competition) caused the price to fall. (Why shouldn't a rational patent-holder charge less than the full monopoly price during the life of the patent so as to discourage competitive entrants when the patent expires?)

5.8 and **5.9.** If transaction costs are zero, one would predict that the two companies would contract around the problem surrounding a narrow patent. If Firm A never made the initial discovery, Firm B would not be able to invest in its subsequent developments. Some cooperative solution should be reached where Firm B pays Firm A for its research efforts. This is not necessarily the case where transaction costs are high. Why not? If dominant and subservient patents are issued, then the gains from invention may depend on the timing of the contract. Will the solution be closer to that reached under a broad or under a narrow patent law?

5.10. The net social benefit is the area between the two curves. If the patent life is extended to (t^* + 1 years) then the marginal social cost of the extra year of patent life will exceed the marginal social benefit. That is, society is hurt more than it is helped from an extension of the patent life.

5.11. Consider how private benefits are related to social benefits. Social benefits are higher than the private benefits, leading to a situation where inventors may produce too few inventions if the renewal fee is set equal to the marginal social cost curve. One solution may be to set a renewal fee lower than the marginal social cost.

5.12. If the courts interfere with the patent process by ordering compulsory licensing, firms that were previously following a profit-maximizing strategy in marketing the invention would experience a decline in profits. How does this influence the decision of other firms to engage in inventive activities in the future?

5.13. At the margin, an additional year of copyright protection would have very little influence on the production of copyrighted materials. This is because the present discounted value of that benefit (*i.e.*, the value today of a benefit conferred many years in the future) is likely to be very small.

5.14. A high-cost oil-cracking process or a poorly written drama could not be infringed upon: but who would want to infringe? It would be very difficult to copyright enough musical dramas to gain monopoly status, and alternative oil-cracking processes are available. Only in conditions where no alternatives exist will a patent or copyright grant complete monopoly status.

5.15. One facet of "fair use" is that it does not detract from the economic value of the copyrighted material. How might courts decide on what is fair or unfair?

5.16. Consider the problems that might arise if copyrights carried an indefinite duration. Would it be possible to keep track of all the copyrights ever issued?

5.17. Consider the effect on the value of a trademark. If Coca-Cola licensed its name to an inferior Cola producer, the value of the Coca-Cola trademark would fall. It may be the case that the value of the Pepsi-Cola trademark also falls. Why? What about the value of trademarks generally to consumers under this alternative?

5.18. The "electromagnetic spectrum" is a term used to describe the entire range of light radiation, from gamma rays to radio waves. When the spectrum first began to be used commercially in the early 1920s, there was no system for allocating rights. In the 1930s Congress rejected a market-based method of allocating rights to the spectrum in favor of allocating the frequencies through application to the Federal Communications Commission (FCC). Applicants must demonstrate that their receiving the right to use a portion of the spectrum serves the "public convenience and necessity."

Over the years, new technologies have made additional frequencies of the spectrum commercially useful. How should these new frequencies be allocated: by the rule of adverse possession, by a mandate from the FCC, or through the market? When would it matter for efficiency reasons? Because of the advent of new technologies such as cellular phones and personal communications services, there is a great deal of interest in this topic today. The FCC has used game theory to devise interesting new methods of auctioning off portions of the spectrum for these new uses.

5.19.   Because the representatives of the white settlers made the legal rules and because the Indians had little representation in the formation of those rules, the rules favored settler-acquisition of Indian land. Additionally, the high costs to the Indians of monitoring white settler behavior and a court system that favored the settlers hastened the transfer of land to the whites.

5.20.   One consequence of this rule is that the original owner would have to spend more time monitoring her property under the gradual depreciation rule than under the sudden-dispossession-10-years rule.

5.21.   Compare the costs of searching for the owner and bargaining with her with the value of the lost object. Will the efficient lower bound be the same in all circumstances?

5.22.   There are various social goals at issue with regard to property lost or abandoned at sea. The rightful owners have an interest in recovering their property; society has interests in keeping the chain of title unbroken, in keeping shipping lanes clear, and in minimizing debris that floats onto beaches. Salvors are typically awarded their expenses plus a fraction of the value of property they recover. This is true whether the salvor explicitly contracted with the rightful owner or came across it by chance. A rule of granting complete ownership to a salvor without requiring an effort to identify the rightful owner would create the sort of moral hazard problems and title controversies that the text said the law of lost property seeks to avoid. (Notice that these problems may not arise if the rule is that the abandoned property belongs to the state.) The rule of granting the salvor an award of his expenses plus a fraction of the value of the recovered property creates an incentive for chance salvors, as well as professional salvors, to search for lost property at sea and to return it to its rightful owners. (See the discussion of whether and how to enforce a contract between a rescuer and the person rescued in Chapter 7.)

5.23.   Would reducing the time period fail to skip a generation? Would extending it skip more than one generation?

5.24.   Circumvention costs are the costs that the owner of the property incurs in attempting to work around the law. Depletion costs are the losses due to the inefficient use of the property.

5.25.   Generally, even if, as part of a bequest, the testator set aside enough money to deal with any future legal controversies that might arise in complying with the bequest, that would not fully deal with the social inefficiency of a bequest's stretching too far into the future. This is because the testator's concern would only be with the *private* costs of compliance, not with the *social* costs. See if you can show this graphically—namely, that the marginal social cost of complying with a bequest exceeds the marginal private cost.

5.26.   Analyze the decision of the ship's captain. One would suspect that he possessed the best information concerning the expected damages to his ship had he left the dock and the expected damages to the dock from staying moored. In light of this information, does it make sense for him to be absolved from paying for damages to the dock?

5.27.   Consider the types of people society wants in juries and the types of people who offer their services as jurors. Do these necessarily coincide?

5.28.   Consider the number of people involved in each situation in order to determine whether the externality is private or public. A market can exist in many of these situations. For instance, an apple grower may allow free access to his apple groves in order to encourage people to raise bees. Ships using a certain port may have to pay a fee to maintain the lighthouse.

5.29.   Since the third good is consumed by all persons in the economy, the utility of person j is: $u^j = u^j(x_1^j, x_2^j, x_3^1, x_3^2, x_3^3 \dots, x_3^n)$.

5.30 and **5.31.**   There are a large number of actors involved on the plaintiffs' side. This can create high transaction costs.

5.32.   If the cement company tried to bargain with its neighbors, one possible problem might be a hold-out problem. One neighbor or a group of neighbors may try to extract a large payment in order to get their approval.

5.33.   The court granted the plaintiffs a "once and for all" settlement by awarding permanent damages. This is accompanied by a *servitude on the land*, which transfers the court's decision onto all subsequent owners of the property.

5.34.   Yes. Notice that temporary damages create no efficiency problem: if money damages are compensation for a fixed amount of harm inflicted in a past time period, then if, in the future, the amount of harm increases, then so will the subsequent amount of damages. Are permanent damages amenable to this adjustment? Certainly. They may be considered as the present discounted value of the amount necessary to compensate the neighbors for a *given level of harm for a specified number of future time periods*. If the level of harm rises or if the number of future periods during which harm is inflicted rises, the permanent damages previously awarded become under-compensatory. The neighbors should have a new cause of action to have the level of permanent damages increased.

5.35.   If all property rights (rights to air, water, etc.) were explicitly assigned and the transaction costs of bargaining were zero, then an efficient outcome would ensue. For instance, if the cement company owned the right to pollute, then the plaintiffs could approach them with a contract to reduce emissions. However, because all rights are not assigned, and transaction costs are high, considerable effort is spent on litigating these decisions.

5.36.   A flat price line indicates that the market is perfectly competitive. An infinite amount of the good will be provided at price P_0.

5.37.   A new health hazard would raise the marginal social cost of cement production and decrease the efficient level of production.

5.38.   Supply an answer from your personal experiences.

5.39.   The question has been phrased so that there is no doubt of the legitimacy of the government's taking: it is truly for a public purpose—the provision of a public good. What is at issue here is the computation of "just compensation." The situation in which a monopolist (one seller) faces a monopsonist (one buyer) is known as a "bilateral monopoly." In the absence of governmental intervention, the price and quantity at which an exchange takes place in a bilateral monopoly are indeterminate. In our example of the governmental purchase of a parcel of land for use as a satellite tracking station, there is no controversy about the quantity of land to be purchased. The dispute is about the price. The monopolist landowner hopes to maximize his profits by charging a price that is consistent with marginal cost being equal to marginal revenue. The monopsonist (the government) wishes to pay as little for this parcel as possible. If there were bargaining between the government and the parcel owner, the price would be somewhere between the monopoly and monopsony price depending on the relative bargaining skills of the parties. If there were no constraint on the government, then it is likely that the price paid for the parcel would be close to the monopsony price. But the existence of the just compensation requirement for compulsory sales to the government should compel the government to take the parcel at a price closer to the perfectly competitive price.

5.40. There may be an economic rationale for the actions of the City of Detroit if they were providing a public good. A public good is a commodity or service that has two closely related characteristics: consumption of the good by one person does not diminish the amount available for consumption by others, and the cost to private providers of excluding non-paying beneficiaries of the good or service is high. The jobs to be provided by the expansion of the General Motors plant do not fit either of these criteria. Employment is a private good. If the residents derive a large subjective value from being part of the neighborhood, then it is very likely that the market value of the homes in the neighborhood is much less than the subjective value to the residents. Therefore the taking of land in Poletown can be viewed as an inefficient solution. Argue the other side of the case.

5.41.a. How might this influence the behavior of people who have information as to where the government will seize land?

b. Consider the frequency with which government seizes private property. Would the current level lead to under or overvaluation of property by owners?

CHAPTER 6

6.1. When the nephew gives the uncle the peppercorn, he seeks to make the promise enforceable by the presence of consideration. If consideration is the only necessary requirement, then the bargain should be enforceable. If however the court views the bargain as being extremely unfair, then the court should refuse to enforce it.

6.2. The promise to give a gift is not enforceable under bargain theory because there is no consideration for the promise. But Roman law might have enforced a gift promise because there was offer and acceptance. Later we explain the circumstances under which a gift promise is now enforceable in the common law countries.

6.3. When the offers were made and accepted, the parties to the contract wanted enforceability. In the case of the Chevrolet, the buyer and the seller would have both had a lower expected utility if the contract was not enforceable.

6.4. If the second player performs the contract, the first player can expect to receive a profit of .5. Therefore the second player must compensate the first player for the value of the investment and the services she would have provided.

6.5. Consider again the car dealer promising to hold the new Chevrolet for a period of time. At the time the bargain was made, the car dealer calculated the probability of selling the car to the current party and the probability of somebody else walking in and offering to buy the car. Given this information, he chooses to hold the car. If someone else in fact does show an interest in buying the car, the dealer may regret promising to hold it. If no penalties were incurred, it would be better for the dealer to breach. But recall that part of the purpose of making promises enforceable is to allow the first player to *rely* upon the commitment made by the second player. Part of this commitment is the willingness to forego alternatives that may arise between the time that the contract is formed and it is performed.

6.6. This is like being in law school. Consideration is something of value that the promisee gives to the promisor. What did the second player give to the first player in exchange for his promise to invest?

6.7.

6.8. If the expectation damages are perfectly compensatory, then the promisee is indifferent between performance and breach.

6.9. In Figure 6.4, performing is efficient when performance is costless. If the promisor still decides to breach, total payoffs fall from 1 to 0.

6.10. There are many facets to the answer. Consider one: if the breachee receives compensation for excessive reliance, then breachees have an incentive to over-rely, which is inefficient. From the point of view of the breacher, the liability for excessive reliance by the breachee may induce performance when breach is more efficient.

6.11. Once a party has "given notice" of special losses that will occur in the event of breach, then the parties are free to bargain about whether or not that makes any difference to the terms of the contract. For example, it is possible that if the telegraph company is made aware of special losses to the stockbroker from non-performance, they may decide not to enter the contract or only to enter it if the stockbroker pays a premium price for the telegraph company to assume this risk.

6.12. That is, the more efficient a default rule is, the greater the savings in transaction costs. By supplying routine contract terms, default rules allow parties to save on the costs of crafting their own contract terms. See the Ayres and Gertner piece mentioned in n. 16 for an additional benefit of default rules.

6.13. Among other considerations, shouldn't the court seek to determine how the parties would have allocated the risk of delay from inclement weather if they had bargained over that risk? And how do you think they would have resolved that issue?

6.14. Who has the private information in this example? How would this private information have influenced the decisions of the other party? What penalty should the court impose?

6.15. Consider a situation where the cost of allocating risk is less than the cost of allocating a loss times probability of loss. This is usually a situation where risk instead of loss is assigned. In what situations would parties wish to shape behavior using the high costs of allocating loss? What about marriage? Wouldn't anyone about to enter a long-term relationship be reluctant to discuss terms for dissolution? See the section on long-term contracts near the end of Chapter 6.

6.16. For a thorough answer to each of these objections, see the article by Professor Kull mentioned in n. 22.

6.17. Consider items that may be valuable to a corporation, but of little value to the party they contract with. What about the location of the corporation's headquarters or a manufacturing plant?

CHAPTER 7

7.1. Expectation damages would compensate B fully for the amount of B's expected profits. What was B's expected profit from this series of transactions? Reliance damages would compensate B to the point where he was just as well off as he was prior to making the contract. What costs did B incur that would be compensated under reliance damages? Opportunity-cost damages would pay B the profits from his next best alternative. How much would *B* have earned had he contracted with the other dealer for a price of $10,500?

7.2.   For the first question, consider situations where the payoff from a certain action is unknown, but the payoff from next best alternative is known. For the second question, consider situations where the amount invested in reliance of a contract is easily observed, but the opportunity cost is difficult to measure.

7.3.   If the opportunity cost is the same as the expected payoff, then the expectation damages should equal the opportunity-cost damages.

7.4.   One simple way to think about this issue is to imagine yourself canceling an airline ticket versus canceling a purchase of a hearing aid. Who is hurt more by your decisions? Has the seller lost a profitable sale in one case and not lost a profitable sale in the other? Which is which?

7.5.   Think about the ease of finding substitute performance in each situation.

7.6.   Restitution is very easy to measure.

7.7.   As long as there is a positive probability of not getting caught, the swindler's profits are positive. That is, the probability of getting caught must be 1.

7.8.   Specific performance may simply be impossible: the travel agency promised you no rain on your trip to Cancun, but there *was* rain. She cannot specifically perform something that has already been performed. Under what legal rule would specific performance be "unfair" in the example given in the hint? Would paying the third party her cost of the manuscript compensate her for her loss?

7.9.   After the employer announces the move, the house is more valuable to *A* than to *B*. It therefore should never be the case that *B* moves into the house. What bargain might the two parties strike to make them both better off?

7.10.   One situation might be a contract to ship goods overseas. What fortunate or unfortunate contingencies might appear? Think of some other contracting situations. Would parties insert clauses to cover these contingencies if to do so would reveal a special subjective value on performance?

7.11.   The Coase theorem states that given zero transaction costs, private bargaining always succeeds in allocating resources efficiently, no matter what the initial endowments. In the contract setting, when transaction costs are zero, the parties will always bargain to an efficient agreement, including efficient performance and efficient breach.

7.12.   For the first question, consider the example given in the text. For the second question, think about the court's problem of measuring subjective valuation. If the court awards specific performance, who or what process determines the subjective value that the breachee attaches to performance?

7.13.   This is an important exercise. Spend some time trying to get this right.

7.14.   Which curve depicts the cost of expectation damages? For part b think about how you would redraw this curve if specific performance was higher than expectation damages. This should lead to a higher level of precaution.

7.15.   Again, think about the shape and location of the disgorgement curve.

7.16.   Consider who bears the risk both when there are perfect damages and when there are no damages.

7.17.   At what level of *y* are Yvonne's expected profits maximized when the composite curve is used?

7.18. Think about how Yvonne would act if she knew absolutely that performance was forthcoming. Would she take the efficient amount of reliance or would she over-rely? Why?

7.19. Disgorgement damages can be thought of as a transfer of unknown size to Yvonne in case of breach. Will Yvonne's optimal reliance curve still be concave? Consider the factors that give shape to the "no damages" curve.

7.20. The plaintiff in *Hadley v. Baxendale* might have claimed that all future events are foreseeable when enough effort is made. To take a trite example, it is foreseeable that you and I will die, but is the date of our date an event that is actually foreseen?

7.21. In many instances, such as dropping off the film at the local supermarket, giving notice is difficult. How might your desire to "give notice" influence your choice of developer? Could you develop them yourself? In the event that giving notice of spe-cial value was not possible, what else might you do to protect yourself from loss? Could you take duplicate photos? Could you make duplicates of the negatives?

7.22. Compare the costs of mitigating with its benefits. What (transaction) costs are involved in contracting with a new party? Suppose that we rent an apartment from you for a two-year term at $500 per month but that after six months we announce that we intend to breach. You sue us for breach of contract and ask for 18 months of rent. Is that efficient? Should the court award you this "expectancy"? What if you attempt to mitigate and rent the apartment for the balance of the term we owe you to your cousin for $1 per month? Have you satisfied your legal duty to mitigate?

7.23. In this case, we cannot presume competency on the part of the young girl. The law assigns responsibility for protecting the incompetent to the competent people with whom they deal.

7.24. One issue to think about is how different legal rules might influence the deci-sion of a competent (sober) person to make herself incompetent (drink heavily). What about the behavior of those who deal with the temporarily-incompetent person? Do they have any special duties?

7.25. This is a fundamental question that has different but mutually reinforcing answers. *A*'s threat to harm *B* unless she engages in a transaction destroys *B*'s security in her person. This destruction can be faulted on both moral and efficiency grounds. For example, one might argue that everyone is entitled by reason of morality to liberty over his or her person. That freedom may be surrendered only voluntarily. (And only perhaps temporarily; an argument may be made that no one should be allowed even voluntarily to become a slave.) Threatening someone's freedom over her person is, therefore, immoral. Not allowing a destructive threat to *B*'s person also promotes effi-ciency. If such threats were allowed, people would incur costs to avoid being so threatened; they might carry weapons, avoid being alone, or surround themselves with hired toughs. These costs of avoiding being coerced would be reduced (but not elimi-nated) by adopting a legal rule of not enforcing promises elicited by coercive, destruc-tive threats.

7.26. Is the baseball star demanding renegotiation under the condition of coercion? Think about the issue in these terms: is the baseball player "creating value" or "threat-ening to destroy"? If the club refuses to negotiate, what incentives does that create for the player in the remaining years of his contract? Would it have an effect on other play-ers? Incidentally, the labor agreement between the owners of the Major League

Baseball teams and the Players Association forbid contract bonuses to players for individual performances, such as leading the league in home runs. Why?

7.27.   What costs do each of these types of rescuers incur in performing the rescue?

7.28.   Apply your answer from the previous question.

7.29.   Sea captains have a legal duty to rescue ships and cargo in distress. The captains in this case threatened not to do their legal duty, which would have resulted in the destruction of valuable cargo. Thus, their threat involved destruction of value, not merely the refusal to participate in its creation. And as we have seen, promises extracted under threats to destroy existing values should not be enforced on both moral and efficiency grounds.

7.30.   Think about how the threat of being struck by lightning might affect the terms of a contract. What might be some situations in which this threat would have a substantial impact on the contract?

7.31.   The relevant question is whether Taylor (the performer) or Caldwell (the concert hall owner) could have prevented or insured against the unavailability of the hall due to this contingency at a lower cost. The fact that it is physically impossible to perform in the hall is really beside the point. Caldwell probably has better information about the fireworthiness of the hall and its risks of being destroyed by fire. Moreover, being an impresario, he was better able to arrange an alternative venue for the concert than was the performer. In short, Caldwell breached the contract and should be responsible to Taylor for damages. Such a holding, made on those grounds, is likely to induce more efficient risk-allocation among future contracting parties.

7.32.   There are many issues to consider in determining the validity of the contract. Did the rise in the price of uranium make fulfillment economically impossible? How would your answer differ if the trade was merely a futures transaction on a commodity exchange? Was the rise in uranium prices foreseeable? Did the actions of Westinghouse in any way *cause* the increase in the price? See the marvelous discussion of these issues in Professor Joskow's piece cited in n. 32.

7.33.   We leave this to you.

7.34.   The opinion that this contract is void because there was "no true meeting of the minds" is not particularly helpful. An economic analysis can provide clearer guidelines. The problem that has arisen to frustrate the performance of the contract is the unforeseen contingency that there were two ships named *Peerless*. If this contingency could have been foreseen by one of the contractual parties at a reasonable cost, then responsibility for nonperformance in the event of the contingency could have been and should have been assigned in the contract. Presumably, the parties would have assigned responsibility for nonperformance in the event of that contingency to the party who could have more cheaply taken steps to prevent or insure against this contingency. For example, if either of the parties had had extensive business dealings in the England-India cotton trade, he could or should have known that there were two ships named *Peerless*. Notice, however, that if neither party could have foreseen this contingency, then the issue is no longer so much one of creating a rule to induce efficient risk allocation as it is one of apportioning unavoidable losses between two innocent parties. If there is a content to the expression "no true meeting of the minds," it is precisely to cover those circumstances in which a contingency that was not foreseeable at reasonable cost has arisen to frustrate contract performance. In those circumstances the task of the court becomes one of equitably dividing the unavoidable loss.

7.35. In *Laidlaw v. Organ*, the court ruled the contract void because Organ had discovered fortuitously that peace was concluded. The important issue is whether the information was solely redistributive in nature or whether it had productive use. Which do you think this is?

7.36.a. If the information is productive, it will change the economic incentives facing the owner and may, therefore, cause him to change his behavior. (If the information is merely redistributive, then it is not likely to change incentives and thereby behavior; redistributive information merely changes the identity of the economic agent, the person who receives the economic reward.) Here, if the owner knows the cow is fertile, he will breed her rather than butcher her.

b. Sherwood would have no incentive to invest time and effort in discovering such facts if the payoff from such information goes to Walker.

c. Professionals assume the risk of mistaking the fertility of a cow as part of their job.

7.37. No. The buyer should be suspicious of a conditional statement and should push the seller farther. Notice that there is a difference between the circumstance here and an intentional falsehood.

7.38. The informational asymmetry in this case concerns productive facts, not destructive facts, so the economic analysis suggests that the contract should be enforced. Enforcing the contract will reward people like Schmidt for the cost of discovering minerals. If the buyer had acquired the information casually and fortuitously, as did Organ in *Laidlaw v. Organ*, rather than by an investment, the economic case for compensating him is weakened.

7.39. This is a destructive fact by the buyer, an affirmative and intentional misrepresentation that may have caused the seller to sell to him when, if she had known the truth, she would have sold to someone else. The court should rescind the contract.

7.40. The elasticity of demand measures the change in the quantity demanded in response to a change in price. Consider the demand curve faced by a particular firm. If the firm has many competitors, how will demand for its product react to an increase in its price?

7.41. What substitutes are available to the agent wishing to build the garage or to the neighbor contemplating the easement?

7.42. Try answering this question in terms of a specific example, such as housing or apartment rental. How do standard forms reduce or increase competition in this market?

7.43. What options are open to the consumer if she believes the transmission is not worth $450?

7.44. Suppose that there is a regulation that specifies a maximum price that is well below the monopoly price.

7.45. When a firm discriminates between consumers, it either offers the same good at different prices to different consumers, or it offers different quality goods at different prices to different consumers. This helps the firm capture as much of the surplus as possible. If the firm offers the three choices to each consumer (standard monopoly price or the two differentiated products) we can assume that the consumer will choose the option which maximizes her expected benefits.

7.46. It could be that the terms are efficient in the sense that there are lots of music publishing companies with whom the young songwriter might have signed and that the terms efficiently allocate the risk that this songwriter, like most young songwriters, will not be successful. Why do you think the plaintiff brought this action? The most likely reason is that he has, contrary to the odds, been successful and finds the constraints imposed on him when he originally signed with the publisher to be confining. The House of Lords voided the contract as being unconscionable. Assume that it is, in fact, not unconscionable, but rather, an efficient allocation of risk. What effect might the decision have on the fortunes of other young songwriters who do not yet have contracts and on those who do have the standard form here held void? Music publishers and untried songwriters must find some alternative method of allocating between them the risks that are inherent in the business. If the terms that were here held to be unconscionable were the most efficient method of doing that, then this decision will impose unnecessary costs on future contracting panties.

See Michael Trebilcock, *The Doctrine of Inequality of Bargaining Power: Post-Benthamite Economics in the House of Lords*, 26 U. TORONTO L. J. 359 (1976).

CHAPTER 8

8.1. Regulations typically correct for market failures, while efficient default rules reduce the transaction costs of bargaining. How do the concepts of "transaction cost reduction" and "market failure" apply to tort law?

8.2. The court would need to decide what amount of money would perfectly compensate the burn victim for her one week of pain. This is extremely difficult to calculate, thus illustrating the problem.

8.3. The uniqueness of the estate and the subjective valuation by the family makes perfect compensation difficult.

8.4. Causation is a notoriously difficult issue in the law. Here, is the contributory negligence of the car driver in not maintaining her car properly or the negligence of the train in not maintaining its brakes the proximate cause? Once the car had stalled, who *should* have had the last clear chance to avoid the accident?

8.5. At what speed does the driver enter the forbidden zone?

8.6. Part of the answer has to do with the commonness of dogs as pets and the unusualness of keeping a pet tiger. An old legal adage says that every dog is allowed one bite. What does that mean? Would you say that every tiger is allowed one bite?

8.7. The three elements of tort are: harm, cause and breach of a duty of care. Describe the elements in each case.

8.8. The rule of *strict liability with perfectly compensatory damages* gives the victim no incentive to avoid the harm. On the other hand, the rule of *no damages* gives the injurer no incentive to avoid the harm.

8.9. What will be the level of precaution taken by both parties if the actual compensation equals 50% of perfect compensation?

8.10. Once each party is taking efficient care, is there any incentive for either party to change the amount of care he is taking? No.

8.11. Focus, particularly, on the incentive under the different forms of the negligence rule that driver *A* has to use her seat belt. There will be no difference in that incentive under any of the forms of negligence. Why?

8.12. No. Under a rule of simple negligence, what should the potential victim presume about the level of precaution that will be taken by potential injurers? And what amount, then, of precaution should the potential victim take?

8.13. Good luck. See Table 8.1.

8.14.   Which party is the residual bearer of the costs of harm under *no liability* versus *strict liability*?

8.15.   The level of activity of airlines and railroads can be objectively measured in several ways. However, some activities are difficult to measure. For instance, the front step of a home could be perfectly maintained even though the homeowner has not engaged in any maintenance activities.

8.16.   To determine whether to incur the $25 expense of keeping the bargee present, we must compare the marginal cost of precaution ($25) with the marginal benefit (the reduction in the expected accident costs from taking the precaution). The rule for determining $x^{\sim}$ is $w = p'(x)A$. If $w < p'(x)A$, then $x < x^{\sim}$ and the injurer is negligent. If $w < p'(x)A$, then $x < x^{\sim}$ and the injurer is not liable. Here $w = \$25$, $A = \$100,000$, and $p'(x) = 0.001 - 0.0005 = 0.0005$. Thus, $p'(x)A = 0.0005(\$100,000) = \$50$. Because $w < p'(x)A$, the barge owner would be negligent if he did not pay the bargee to be present.

8.17.   Apply the logic of Figure 8.6 to this question. Will "too few" or "too many" accidents occur?

8.18.   Under what forms of negligence does the court (or the state) have to impose legal standards in order to attain the efficient levels of precaution? Will an error in setting this legal standard always result in an inefficient level of precaution?

8.19.   Excessive damages awarded by the court will increase the expected liability of the injurer, but will not influence her level of precaution. Why not? At what level will the injurer set precaution in either case?

8.20.   This is related to the fact that small random errors in the legal standard will cause the injurer to increase precaution. Why?

8.21.   Strict liability excuses the plaintiff from proving fault by the injurer. This lowers her cost of suing the doctor. But that might lead to more malpractice actions so that even though the administrative costs of each action was less, there might be more total actions.

8.22.   Compare the benefits and costs of wholesale rules with those of case-by-case adjudication. Which rule do you think is more efficient?

8.23.   One inefficiency might result if the seller is an inefficient producer of one of the joint products. Or the purchaser might be able to produce or to buy one of the tied products more cheaply elsewhere.

8.24 and **8.25.**   Remember that under strict liability with contributory negligence the injurer is assigned the cost of the accidental harm, regardless of the level of precaution, unless the victim was negligent. Then the victim is assigned the cost of the accidental harm.

CHAPTER 9

9.1.   Three hypotheses might explain the limited use of seat belts. First, the decision to wear belt is a utility-maximizing decisions made by fully informed, rationally self-interested economic actors. A second hypothesis is that people fail to wear belts because they have made an inaccurate estimate of the benefits of doing so. A third hypothesis holds that people mis-estimate the benefits from wearing seat belts because of an inability to make the relevant calculations, not because a lack of information. How do public policy recommendations differ under each of these hypotheses?

9.2.   Recall our discussion in Chapter 4 of the distinction between a private bad (an external cost imposed only on one person or a very few people) and a public bad (an external cost imposed on many parties). We argued there that the appropriate remedy for a private bad was an injunction because that remedy clearly delineates rights and induces the parties to solve their disagreement through negotiation. For a public bad the costs of achieving a bargaining solution are too high so that the court must undertake a hypothetical market transaction and determine, through the levying of compensatory damages, the appropriate price to impose on the wrongdoer. The same factors apply to the issue of settling disputes when litigation is costly. If only a few parties are involved, bargaining costs are low and a settlement is likely. If many parties are involved, bargaining costs are high. It is possible that if the bargaining costs exceed litigation costs, a trial will result. We will return to the important issue of litigation versus settlement in the next chapter.

9.3.   The plaintiff needs to prove harm, cause, and breach of a duty of care under the negligence standard. Under strict liability she need only show harm and cause.

9.4.   Another way to ask this question is whether an employer can accept information from employees as true without verification. Consider a bus company that asks potential employees if they know how to drive a bus. Should the company be penalized if the employee answers in the affirmative but then causes an accident due to lack of training?

9.5.   The justification for the distinction was apparently that although parents could not at reasonable cost control their children's actions, husbands could at reasonable cost control their adult wives.

9.6.   We saw in Chapter 7 that contract law treats a person who is drunk as incapacitated, so that a promise that a drunk makes is unenforceable. Similarly, tort law recognizes that a drunk is no longer capable of making reasonable decisions about precaution although his condition creates a high probability of causing harm. One way to reduce this probability or to make accidents involving drunks less severe is to make sober people responsible for the drunk's actions. As between the drunk and the bartender or social host, there is now a situation of what we have called unilateral precaution: only the sober bartender can guide the drunk into taking adequate precaution. It is worth thinking about whether the bartender or social host should bear complete or only partial liability for the drunk's action. Are social hosts more likely to help if liability is shared with the drunk? Will helpers avoid drunks if they realize they become fully responsible for the drunks' actions? If so, can this effect be reduced by applying comparative fault principles to the helper?

9.7.   It does seem strange that, in general, recoveries are larger for unintentionally inflicting a crippling injury than for unintentionally killing someone. But there may be a simple economic explanation for this. When someone is unintentionally crippled, they should be compensated for their lost opportunities for the remainder of their lives in a lump-sum payment. The present discounted value of these lost opportunities can be extremely large, especially so the younger the victim and the greater the value of the lost opportunities. However, when the victim dies, so do those lost opportunities and, therefore, the ability to recover for them; the only recovery that can be had is by the decedent's family and dependents and only for well-defined losses attributable to the decedent's absence. Tragic though the loss may be, these losses to the survivors tend to be less than the decedent's lost opportunities.

The potential inefficiency of this anomalous situation is that it might induce injurers who have unintentionally inflicted harm to minimize their losses by killing the victim. For example, if a driver has struck a pedestrian and severely injured her, he might reduce his liability by backing up and running over the victim again until she is dead. Most people are prevented from behaving in this hideous manner by moral constraints. But if those constraints are not enough, the act of returning to kill is not an unintentional harm, as was the initial injury. Instead, it is an intentional harm, for which there are severe criminal sanctions.

9.8.   Reconsider Figure 8.7 in the Appendix of Chapter 8. Enterprise liability is a situation where the victim bears the liability only in quadrant III, but the level of precaution legally required of the injured party is exceedingly low. Similarly, the precaution legally required of the defendant is exceedingly high. How will this influence the incentives of potential injurers and injurees?

9.9.   Remember that in the rent control example in Chapter 2, a cap was placed on the amount of rent that landlords could charge. This led to a shortage of housing. More people wanted apartments at the capped price than was being supplied by the market. This created a housing shortage and problems such as fewer improvements in existing structures and black markets for apartments. Would a cap on damages in tort have analogous inefficiencies? To whom?

9.10.   Your answer will differ if the legal standard is negligence or strict liability. Why?

9.11.   Plaintiffs' incentive to ask for punitives would be greatly diminished by the proposed scheme. If the plaintiff can recover none of the punitives, then he has no incentive to ask for them. Thus, punitives may not be asked for or awarded in circumstances in which they are, in fact, warranted. This is the opposite extreme from the current case in which plaintiffs have a strong (and probably inefficient) incentive to ask for punitives in a wide range of torts, even where punitive damages are unwarranted. Neither extreme is efficient. Some compromise is necessary: perhaps the appropriate public policy is to allow successful plaintiffs to receive a fraction of the punitive award with the bulk going to the State or to an umbrella charitable organization. The jury might be *more* willing to award punitives if they knew that the award would not necessarily enrich the plaintiff.

9.12.   If an employee waives the right to seek compensation if he is injured on the job, he transfers the liability from himself to the firm. Why would he agree to such an action? That is, how is the employee reimbursed for losing the right to future compensation?

9.13.   One way to consider this problem is to go back and review the arguments that you made for and against standard forms in Chapter 7. The elective no-fault proposal, like the UTC, imports contract principles into tort law where (contrary to our general assumption about tortious situations) the costs of bargaining between injurer and victim are low.

CHAPTER 10

10.1.   The court would award the farmer two times his expenditures in reliance on the promise.

10.2.   Consider the administrative costs associated with a trial and with out-of-court settlement.

10.3. Work your way backwards as in the example in the text. The only difference is that the expected value of the trial (*EVT*) is now $10 instead of $30.

10.4. This will change the *EVT*. Instead of subtracting the trial costs as a lump sum, you must include them in the probability. That is $EVT = .5(\$100) + .5(-\$40) = \$30$.

10.5. At least two other things must remain constant. What are they?

10.6. These assumptions may result in the policy prescription that the courts should set lower administrative fees for business decisions than for divorces. Why?

10.7. In economic jargon, this is called a "price floor." This is the opposite of the rent control example of Chapter 2, which was a "price ceiling.". The quantity demanded is q_1 while the quantity supplied is q_3. How does this influence the market for lawyers?

10.8. Consider the question in the framework of Figures 10.1 and 10.2. Do each of these three propositions influence incentives in the same way?

10.9. Figures 10.1 and 10.2 assume that the plaintiff is risk neutral. What if she is risk averse? That is what if she preferred a certain payoff of $50 rather than a 50% chance of earning $100? How might insurance then influence the number of suits? In thinking about this, remember our discussion at the beginning of Chapter 9 about the influence of insurance on precautionary decisions.

10.10. Will the total number of suits rise or fall? Does the option of class action resolve problems centering around (1) injuries, (2) filing costs, or (3) the expected value of the legal claim?

10.11. A general argument against advertising by lawyers is that, to the extent that they are successful in attracting business through advertising, they are fostering litigation (or settlement) and that this is socially costly. When an accountant advertises, he only proposes to help the purchaser of his services; his actions do not impose a cost on other parties.

10.12. Does a contingency fee increase or decrease the variance of the expected payoff?

Think about this in terms of the lawyer's ability to bear risk. If the lawyer can bear a lot of risk, might she push for a riskier strategy with a higher expected payoff?

This depends on how the contract for each type of lawyer is structured. Under what type of contract would the payoff to the defendant's lawyer be similar to that of the plaintiff's?

10.13. This depends on whether you think that compulsory mediation will reduce the information asymmetry and thereby reduce the false optimism to a point where the parties are willing to settle out of court.

10.14. Again, think about Figures 10.1 and 10.2. If the plaintiff knows *ex ante* that he will discover information that will increase the expected value of the payoff, how will this influence his decision to sue?

10.15. Consider the question in this way. There is only a 10% probability that the dispute will go to trial. Therefore, if the actual cost of obtaining the information is $100, the expected cost is only $10. In general, how much smaller must the cost of discovering the information before trial be in order for parties to seek pretrial information?

10.16. Think about the costs and benefits of both deliberation and spontaneity.

10.17.   Use the equation immediately preceding the question. $SC = \$0$, and LC of the two parties combine to equal \$200. Therefore, how large can the value of the relative optimism be where the parties still settle out of court?

10.18.   Calculate the expected value of the trial. Is it positive or negative?

10.19.   What is half of the cooperative surplus?

10.20.   Include the litigation costs as part of the value multiplied by the probability of winning. For instance, the plaintiff will win \$40 with probability .5, and will lose \$80 with probability .5.

10.21.   The economist would advise a level that would minimize the total cost of the legal liability to the firm. What factors that we have discussed in this chapter would the economist consider?

10.22.   Why did we claim in the text that judges have the incentive to do what is easy and lawyers have the incentive to do what is hard?

10.23.   Is it easier to bribe one person (a judge) or many people (a majority of the jury or, in some instances, all of the jury)?

10.24.   If the court follows Rule 68 of the FEDERAL RULES OF CIVIL PROCEDURE (the "offer to compromise" rule), then the plaintiff will pay most of the defendant's legal fees.

10.25.   Both parties made offers that the court ruled between. Who should pay the legal fees?

10.26.   The British rule will cause fewer nuisance suits because the threat position of an undeserving plaintiff is weakened by facing the prospect of paying the defendant's trial costs.

10.27.   Under which rule is the variance of the payoffs higher?

10.28.   Think about the transaction costs that might inhibit this deal from occurring.

10.29 and **10.30.**   Remember that the administrative costs are the costs of passing through the stages of a legal dispute. These include the costs of filing a claim, exchanging information, bargaining, litigating and appealing. The social costs of an error depend on the distortions in incentives caused by it.

10.31.   Think of this example in a zero transaction cost world. If everybody knew that a "rent-a-judge" was bribable or arbitrary, would she be used? How does this change when the costs of obtaining information about a judge rise asymmetrically to the litigants?

10.32.   The law clearly gives eyewitness testimony greater weight than statistical inference. Why do you think that is the case? Should it be?

10.33.   Most courts do not take into account the joint probability of the two events. They rule on each issue separately to determine whether there is a preponderance of the evidence. In this sense, trials in the United States are segmented. Is this the right way of deciding on the evidence when the plaintiff must prove "simultaneously" that the defendant caused the injury and was negligent?

10.34.   Many examples are possible where appeals with high probability of success are pursued, but appeals with low probability of success are not. You can build on the above example.

10.35.   Think about the error cost of a mis-ruled lower court decision. Who bears this cost? Clearly the party pursuing the appeal is unhappy, but errors in lower court rulings also cause other inefficiencies in society. What are they?

10.36.   We have already considered the situation where there are differential costs to litigating. This question asks whether the decision to pursue and appeal is affected when the cost of litigating is much higher to the plaintiff than to the defendant. The answer is yes. Why?

10.37.   Refer to your answer to 10.35.

10.38.   The inquisitorial system is common to most civil law countries. The judge directs much of the questioning and determines the course of events in the courtroom. In the adversarial system the lawyers of the litigants direct questions and present evidence. How might this affect selective litigation?

10.39.   The central planners in a communist society need to know the preferences of all people in society. How might the wholesale creation of laws by a central authority differ from a decentralized way of making law? Think about both the preferences of the central planner (is she a benevolent dictator?) and the transaction costs of obtaining information.

10.40.   Remember that under the Hand Rule, the injurer is negligent when the marginal cost of her precaution is less than the marginal benefit resulting from her precaution.

CHAPTER 11

11.1.   This would shift the line separating civil from criminal wrongs to the left. How far?

11.2.   We have suggested that the term "victimless crime" implies that society or the social fabric, rather than a single individual, is the victim. Counterfeiting is a crime in two senses: it imposes extraordinary costs on individuals and on society. For example, counterfeiting causes losses to the individuals who accept the counterfeit currency. But by threatening the value and acceptability of the currency, it also raises the cost to everyone of engaging in mutually beneficial exchange. Other aspects of counterfeiting that are important in explaining why it is a crime are that it is an intentional wrong and that it is frequently difficult to apprehend and convict counterfeiters. Why these are elements of a crime will become evident shortly.

11.3.   One might argue that speeding or running a stop light or stop sign when no one was around or no one was injured are examples of inchoate crimes. But why can one not alternatively argue that they are examples of "negligence in the air," faulty actions that result in no harm? The reason for punishing speeding and running a stop sign as inchoate crimes is twofold. First, the probability of harm from those actions is very high; society does not want its members to be subjected to such large risks. Second, there may be a large detrimental spillover effect from the failure to punish inchoate crimes. Those who get away with such actions as speeding or running a stop sign may deduce that it is acceptable to scoff at other laws as well, thus imposing even more risks on other members of society.

11.4.   In the United States, if the public has great confidence in the prosecutor, then the jury, which is a random sample of the public (is it?), may be predisposed to believe the prosecution's case. They may resolve controversial evidence in favor of the state, thus making conviction easier.

11.5.   Send us your answers.

11.6.   Two things to think about are the efficiency of breach of contract *versus* criminal activity, and the type of compensation chosen in each case. Would a breach ever be efficient? Would a crime? For example, perfect disgorgement is an inappropriate means of compensating the victim of a crime. Why?

11.7.   The three reasons for having criminal instead of tort punishments are: limitations on compensation, protecting rights rather than interests, and deterrence. Give an example of each.

11.8.   Bankruptcy may present problems if the value of the firm's assets is less than the amount of compensation plus punishment. In a few rare instances the law allows a "piercing of the corporate veil," that is, reaching out to the corporation's owners and going after their personal assets to satisfy a claim against the corporation. This could happen if the corporation committed an intentional tort for which its assets were inadequate, and it could therefore be appropriate if the corporation is guilty of a crime.

11.9.   The intersection at a positive value along the vertical axis indicates that even when there is no crime, there may be a punishment. This may be taken to mean several things—*e.g.*, that inchoate crimes are punished or that innocent people are sometimes punished.

11.10.   This will shift the expected punishment curve closer to the certain punishment curve. How does this affect criminal behavior?

11.11 and **11.12.**   Adding a constant k to either equation will shift the curve up or down. What is the effect on behavior?

11.13.   We defined a lapse as an episode where an actor temporarily discounts the future consequences of her actions at a very high level. This leads the actor to care less than she normally would about the penalties associated with her crime. Therefore, deterrence is much more difficult when the actor experiences a lapse. Lapses are difficult for the potential offender to anticipate. By contrast, a deliberate crime was not spontaneous or the result of a momentary lapse. All of us sense that deliberately doing wrong is far worse than doing so spontaneously.

11.14.   Can a rat have *mens rea*?

11.15.   See the answer to 11.13.

11.16.   Remember that the social cost of a crime is the sum of the cost of crime prevention and the harm it causes. Your answer should include both of these aspects.

11.17.   The economic goal of criminal law is to minimize the social cost of crime. The economic goal of tort law is to use liability to reduce transaction costs and induce injurers to internalize the externalities involved in private agreements.

11.18 and **11.19.**   When police acquire computers, the cost of deterrence decreases. When criminals acquire computers, the cost of deterrence increases. How will this affect Figure 11.5?

11.20.   Remember that $p(z)$ is the probability of crime when deterrence level is set at z. p' is the marginal probability of crime.

11.21.   Negative. Why?

11.22.   Go back and consider Figures 11.7, 11.8, and 11.9. Your answer should include how criminals respond to different combinations of severity and certainty. It should also include the costs to society of providing different levels of severity and certainty.

11.23.   Think about this question in the context of Figures 11.10 and 11.11. The state pays much more to deter crime through imprisonment than through fines. Therefore, it is much more costly to deter crimes when people cannot pay the fines.

11.24. Unobservable: phone systems, hidden cameras, plain-clothes detectives, auto alarms. Observable: private guards, auto alarms.

11.25. Think of this question in terms of public *versus* private deterrence. If one neighbor owns a gun, does this reduce the total amount of crime, or is crime merely redistributed?

CHAPTER 12

12.1. Some factors to consider are: violent versus non-violent crime and how crime is distributed by age, race and geographical location. In general, however, there is little support for the widespread perception that the U.S. is being swept by a crime wave.

12.2. The question tries to evoke the incorrect counterfactual. When we spend $155 billion on crime prevention, crime costs victims $50 billion. Would the costs to victims remain at $50 billion if crime prevention dropped to zero?

12.3. Think about the opportunity cost of committing crime. If everyone in society is richer, then the opportunity cost of crime increases and crime becomes less lucrative relative to working. Is this true however if both the average wealth and the variance of wealth increases? Also, if everyone is richer, how does this affect the payoff from crime?

12.4. Think about how prosecutors may anticipate the preferences of a judge when choosing what charges to pursue. For instance, if the judge is staunchly against the death penalty, and conviction of first degree murder requires the death penalty, is it likely the prosecutor will pursue a first degree murder charge? Moreover, if prosecutors have greater discretion, they might charge more criminals with more serious crimes. That, in combination with the more limited discretion of judges, may induce more plea bargaining by criminals.

12.5. In criminal cases, the prosecutor attempts to prove with a very high level of certainty that the defendant committed the crime. What if the prosecutor could "prove" with the same level of certainty that a defendant will commit crimes in the future? Is this consistent with further incarceration or penalties?

12.6. Without a clear idea of the level of crime, it is impossible to hypothesize or test hypotheses concerning the effects of deterrence measures on the level of crime.

12.7. Sorting out two offsetting effects that are highly correlated is very difficult. Employment levels are highly correlated with the overall wealth of society. Think about a situation where it might be that the opportunity cost (lost wages from a regular job) is not correlated with the profitability of crime.

12.8. One way to change the discount rate of prospective criminals is to educate them thoroughly as to the effect a crime would have on their future standard of living. What else might be done? How do the findings of Wilson and Abrahamse bear on this question?

12.9. The incentive to earn profit in a competitive environment spurs cost-cutting, technological innovation, and a superior quality output. Unregulated competition however is probably not the best way to provide prison services. Critics are concerned that cost-cutting may lead to a sacrifice in the quality of prisoner care such as low quality food, shelter and other material conditions for the prison population. We might try to control those forms of competition by regulating the minimum terms and conditions that private prisons must maintain. But will there be adequate monitoring and enforcement of those regulations? Perhaps not, but even so, will it not be the case that low-quality conditions within prisons will further deter prisoners from committing crimes on release?

12.10.   Think again about the opportunity cost of committing crime. When society is fully employed at high wage jobs, the opportunity cost of switching to crime is the loss of the income from time spent perpetrating the crime, and the expected time of incarceration.

12.11.   Take a look again at Figures 10.1 and 10.2. Can you provide a similar analysis for the criminal law? This may help you sort your thoughts out on where randomness enters the process.

12.12.   Think about whether criminals are risk-averse or risk-loving in the context of the above example. Would a criminal prefer a five year sentence or a 50% probability of a ten year sentence?

12.13.   Statistical analysis is a very powerful tool as it often appears to provide hard answers to difficult questions. Hypothesis tests however are rarely if ever perfectly formulated. Questions will always arise concerning the choice of variables, the construction of the test, and what the chosen variables actually measure. Still, econometric analysis is a useful tool for analyzing criminal behavior.

12.14.   One obvious reason is that "cruel and unusual" punishment is unconstitutional and therefore the administrative costs of enacting such punishments would be very high. Think about the effect of corporal punishment on criminal behavior.

12.15.   Remember that the equilibrium price is determined by the intersection of the supply and demand schedules. If the price of drugs is falling, then the supply must be increasing faster than the demand is decreasing. Why should that happen?

12.16.   Sophisticated answers using the elasticity of supply and demand and the deterrent effect of obvious and open heroine use could argue an increase or decrease in demand in each scenario. Attempt to argue each case both ways.

12.17.   Probably for a hamburger. (Does it follow that eating hamburgers induces crime?) But it is probably true that a greater percentage of criminals test positive for drugs than in does the non-criminal population. What does that tell us?

12.18.   Each case has an effect on both the cost of committing and the cost of preventing crimes. Explore these costs in each example.

12.19.   A simple law may state, "No one with any criminal record may purchase a gun." Would this have any effect on criminal's access to guns? Think of ways in which the law might be circumvented, and the additional statutes needed to plug these loopholes.

12.20.   Again, guns affect both the cost of committing and the cost of preventing crime. How does this affect demand for guns?

12.21.   Owning a gun reduces a household's cost of crime prevention. However, the risk associated with possessing a gun must be factored in when calculating the total benefit or cost to society of gun ownership.

CASE INDEX

NAME INDEX

SUBJECT INDEX